LAW, ETHICS, AND THE VISUAL ARTS

John Henry Merryman

Sweitzer Professor of Law, Stanford University

Albert E. Elsen

Walter A. Haas Professor of Art History,
Stanford University

second edition

VOLUME ONE

LAW, ETHICS, *and the* VISUAL ARTS

UNIVERSITY OF PENNSYLVANIA PRESS
Philadelphia 1987

upp

Jacket illustrations: Entablatures XA (vol. 1), X (vol. 2) by
Roy Lichtenstein. Printed and published by Tyler Graphics
Ltd. Copyright © 1976 by Roy Lichtenstein/Tyler Graphics
Ltd. Used by permission.

Library of Congress Cataloging-in-Publication Data

Merryman, John Henry.
  Law, ethics, and the visual arts.

  Includes index.
   1. Law and art—Cases.   2. Artists—Legal status, laws,
etc.—United States—Cases.   3. Cultural property,
Protection of—Law and legislation—United States—
Cases.   4. Artists—Legal status, laws, etc.—Cases.
5. Cultural property, Protection of—Law and legislation
—Cases.   I. Elsen, Albert Edward, 1927–   .   II. Title.
KF4288.A7M47   1987   344.73′097   86-30835
ISBN 0-8122-8052-0 (set)   347.30497

Design by Adrianne Onderdonk Dudden

To the artists Lazarus (see pp. 244–45) and Christo (see pp. 328–45),
and to Gil Edelson and Milton Esterow

Contents

VOLUME ONE

List of Illustrations   xi

Introduction   xiii

Acknowledgments   xvii

Table of Readings   xix

Table of Cases   xxiii

CHAPTER 1   PLUNDER, DESTRUCTION, AND REPARATIONS

Art and Society   3

Plunder of the Arts   4

The Elgin Marbles   4

Looting and the International Law of War   13

Napoleon and the Louvre   15

The Einsatzsab Rosenberg   20

The Act of State Doctrine and Related Matters   25

Destruction of Works of Art   28

The 1954 Hague Convention   28

Bomb the Church?   34

Cultural Reparations   39

World War I   40

World War II   40

CHAPTER 2   THE ILLICIT INTERNATIONAL TRADE IN ART: WHO OWNS THE PAST?

Two Overviews of the Problem   46

National Retention Policies   53

The Afo-A-Kom Case   56

Retention vs. Protection   59

The Effects of Legal Controls   62

The Tombaroli in Italy   65

The Demand Side   70

Should the United States Limit Art Export?   75

The Law   76

Multilateral Approaches   91

Simple Theft   107

National Theft   114

Repatriation of Cultural Property   124

Concluding Note on the Retention and Repatriation of Cultural Property   138

CHAPTER 3   THE ARTIST'S RIGHTS IN THE WORK OF ART

The Moral Right   143

Introduction   143

Illustrative Treaty and Statute Provisions   145

Some Cases   147

Moral Right in the United States   157

Protecting the Public Interest and the Artist's Reputation   161

Legislative Approaches   162

Applying the Law   171

Copyright   175
   Copyright Protection in the United States   *175*
   What Can be Copyrighted   *177*
   Formalities of Copyright   *186*
   Copyright Infringement   *196*
   Copyright and the Art Consumer   *208*
The Resale Proceeds Right   213
   *Selected European Statutes and
      Conventions*   *213*

   *Arguments for and Against the Resale
      Proceeds Right*   *217*
   The Contractual Proceeds Right   *230*
   The California Statute   *231*

CHAPTER 4   **ARTISTIC FREEDOM AND ITS LIMITATION**

Introduction   240
Some Historical Examples   244
   The Iconoclasts   *244*
   The Inquisition   *248*
   France   *251*
   The Academies of Art   *252*
   Christian Art   *253*
   The Soviet Union   *254*
   The Nazis   *259*
   The McCarthy Era   *268*
Artistic Speech and the First
   Amendment   276
   Moral Censorship: Libel   *278*
   Moral Censorship: Obscenity   *281*

   Political and Social Censorship of Art   *293*
   Censorship and Art Museums   *303*
Controversial Public Art   323
Government Patronage and the Limits of
   Artistic Freedom in Public Art   335
   The Act of 1965   *338*
   *Government Commission of Works of Art: The
      Commission of Fine Arts*   *345*
   The General Services Administration   *353*

Contents

VOLUME   TWO

CHAPTER 5   **THE ARTIST AND THE REAL WORLD**

The Artist and the Art Dealer   379
  *The Dealer-Artist Relationship
    and the Law   381*
  Contracts   382
  Artist-Dealer Relations Legislation   391
The Artist and the Museum   397
  *Areas of Potential Misunderstanding
    and Conflict   398*
  Museum Policy Toward Living Artists   400
Commissioned Works of Art   401
  Private Commissions   402
  Government Commissions   402
  Corporate Commissions   404
  *Things to Think About in the Commission
    Contract   404*

The Artist's Live/Work Space   414
Art as a Matter of Life and Death:
    Toxic Hazards   421
Taxes   429
  Income Taxes   429
  Charitable Contributions   438
  Transfer Taxes   444
The Death of the Artist   445
  The Mark Rothko Case   454
  Untangling the Picasso Estate   468
  The Lipchitz Case   472
Legal Services for Artists   475

CHAPTER 6   **THE COLLECTOR**

The Acquisition of Art: The Art
    Market   478
  Collecting Art for Pleasure and Profit   479
  Dealing with Dealers   483
  Title Problems   498
  The Collector and the Artist   502
  Dealing with Auction Houses   504
Consumer Protection and the Fine
    Arts   525
  The Print Market   525
  The Sculpture Reproduction Market   543
  Proposed Standards for Reproductions   547
  Counterfeit Art   551
  Experts   569
  The Disposal of Fake Art   578

Owning Art   582
  Theft and Artnapping   582
  Taxes, Gifts to Charity, and Appraisers   586
  The Collectors Divorce   612
The Collector Dies   616
  The Art of Donating Art   616
The New Medici   621

The Museum: Its History and
  Purpose   640
The Legal Character and Obligations
  of Museums   650
  *Public Access: The Barnes Foundation
    Case   650*
  Museums and Income Taxes   658
  Minding the Museum Store   664
  Museums as Real Estate Developers   670
Trustees, Directors, and Staff   672
  *Museum Structure and Organization: An
    Overview   672*
  Museum Trustees   675
  Museum Directors and Staff   696

Deaccession: Trading and Selling Works
  of Art from Permanent
  Collections   718
  The Metropolitan Museum Case   720
  The Norton Simon Museum Case   725
Insurance   730
  *Art and Artifacts Indemnity Act of
    1975   734*
Final Considerations   740
  The Museum Emigrates   740
  *The Death (and Reincarnation) of the
    Museum   740*

Index   747

Illustrations

1. The Parthenon   5
2. The so-called "Boston Raphael"   79
3. Metope: struggle between a Lapith and a Centaur   133
4. Metope: horse and rider   133
5. Alfred D. Crimi: Rutgers Presbyterian Church   150
6. Isamu Noguchi: *Shinto*   159
7. Paolo Veronese: *Christ in the House of Levi*   249
8. Hans Haacke: Excerpt from "Manet Projekt '74"   265
9. Paul Georges: *The Mugging of the Muse*   280
10. Hans Haacke: Excerpt from "Shapolsky et al. Manhattan Real Estate Holdings . . ."   307
11. Constantin Brancusi: *Bird in Flight*   319
12. Robert Arneson: *Portrait of George*   327
13. Red Grooms: *Shoot-Out (Wagon Piece)*   329
14. Christo: *The Gates*   330
15. George Sugarman: *People's Sculpture*   355
16. Richard Serra: *Tilted Arc*   359
17. Roy Lichtenstein: *Brushstrokes in Flight*   365

Introduction

This book describes how law and ethics apply to the people and institutions in the Art world—principally artists, collectors, dealers and auctioneers, and museums, with a large supporting cast that includes art historians, critics, bronze founders, the suppliers of artists' materials, local planning commissions, corporate sponsors and commissioners, governmental patrons from the National Endowments for the Arts and the Humanities and the General Services Administration to state and local art commissions, the Internal Revenue Service, insurers, artnappers, forgers and counterfeiters, and many others.

In an anthology of cases, laws, articles, excerpts, and clippings, connected by our comments and questions, we involve the reader in complex issues, many of which have long histories and all of which are alive today. Who owns the past; the present possessors of antiquities, their countries of origin or, in the words of the 1954 Hague Convention, "all mankind"? Should "military necessity" justify bombing a great architectural monument? Should the Elgin Marbles be returned to Greece? Are ugly or obscene artworks protected against suppression by the First Amendment? Who should commission and select public art? Should the owner of a work of art be free to change or destroy it? Are artists just like other people, or do they call for special legal treatment? Why should we care if a beautiful painting is a fake? What really goes on in art auctions? How do taxes effect artists and collectors? Is it right for a museum to violate a donor's wishes? What should be done about conflict of interests, insider advantage and self-dealing by museum trustees and staff?

Since the first edition of this book* was published the Art World and the applicable law and ethics have grown. Problems that seemed important then have been resolved or have diminished in perspective. New problems have emerged, and new information is needed by those who use this book. Much of this book is new, but those who are familiar with the first edition will recognize its structure and style.

Our first two chapters focus on works of art: their plunder and destruction in times of war, occupation and internal strife, and the international movement of stolen and smuggled works. At issue are such questions as who should own great works of art from the distant past? If international law has repudiated the view that "to the victor belong the spoils," is the attitude that "to the wealthiest belong the art treasures of the world" more defensible? Just what is the "national interest" in art?

Chapter 3 takes up the artist's rights in the work of art. Until its recent passage in a few states, American law lacked the moral right, which is available to artists in Civil Law countries and protects works of art against mistreatment after they pass out of the artist's hands. The moral right is fundamentally different from copyright, which treats the work of art as property and gives the artist limited but important (although generally neglected) rights to control reproduction. Some copyright and customs cases show the way judges have come to grips with the problem of defining art. The background of and arguments for and against artists' retaining a portion of the future sales of their work are examined in the section on the Resale Proceeds Right, where the reader should gain some insight into the economics of being an artist or a collector.

*John Henry Merryman and Albert E. Elsen, *Law, Ethics and the Visual Arts* (New York: Matthew Bender, 1979).

More than the literature of any country and more than science itself, art remains the only truly universal language. Andre Malraux once commented that there are two kinds of art: that which belongs to the country of its origin and that which belongs to mankind. Only as recently as the 1954 Hague Convention did an international body formulate claims for art that dissolve these distinctions: "Damage to cultural property belonging to any people whatsoever means damage to the cultural heritage of all mankind, since each people makes its contribution to the culture of the world." Such a declaration by an international body is historically unthinkable in any previous century, and perhaps even before World War II, because of strong cultural prejudices against the art of entire continents. Such prejudices have been known since antiquity. Tribal art, folk art, and even American art of the eighteenth and nineteenth centuries have only achieved international acceptance in the past few decades. In destroying these prejudices, scholars, collectors, statesmen and jurists were led by artists. This book is a partial record of how such an enlightened attitude came about.

WHY WE CARE ABOUT LAW AND ETHICS

It is easy to suppose that art and law are incompatible. In art we value the creative act—the gesture that transcends boundaries, defies conventions, breaks the rules. Law and ethics are a system of boundaries, conventions and rules, maintained by an established order. How can they coexist? Is there an inexorable equation: the more law the less the art, and vice versa?

Clearly not. Law establishes the conditions of social peace and stability that liberate the artist to make art, and it protects the artist against repression or censorship on political, religious or moral grounds. Law protects works of art against theft and destruction and against adulteration and misrepresentation through fakes and forgeries. Through copyright and property law the artist has enforcible rights in the work of art. Law makes possible the assembly and display of art collections and exhibitions, the formation and operation of public and private museums. It regulates the traffic in art, providing an orderly process for the distribution (and redistribution) of works of art. It defines and protects the interests of the parties in transactions between artists, dealers, auction houses, collectors and museums. It ensures the freedom of historians, experts and critics to study art and to express their views. Without a legal system, and the body of nascent law we call ethics, there could be nothing comparable to the sophistication, diversity and prosperity that art and artists presently enjoy.

There is a deeper sense in which law and art are sympathetically comparable. Professor Freund has written: ". . . all law resembles art, for the mission of each is to impose a measure of order on the disorder of experience without stifling the underlying diversity, spontaneity, and disarray. New vistas open in art as in law. In neither discipline will the craftsman succeed unless he sees that proportion and balance are essential, that order and disorder are both virtues when held in proper tension. . . . There are no absolutes in law or art except intelligence"* and ". . . the basic dilemmas of art and law are, in the end, not dissimilar, and in their resolution—the resolution of passion and pattern, of frenzy and form, of convention and revolt, of order and spontaneity—lies the clue to creativity that will endure."**

*Paul A. Freund, "New Vistas in Constitutional Law," *University of Pennsylvania Law Review,* vol. 112 (1964), p. 631.
**Paul A. Freund, "Constitutional Dilemmas," *Boston University Law Review,* vol. 45 (1965), p. 13. This and the preceding essay are reproduced in Paul A. Freund, *On Law and Justice* (Cambridge: Oxford, 1968), vol. 3, pp. 23ff.

This book was written and revised with the authors having in mind a broad, rather than specialized, readership. There are abundant desk or reference books on art law that tell you conveniently how to do or not do it. We are concerned with more than statutes and model contracts. This is a book that raises questions as well as answering them, and we hope it also elevates ethical consciousness with regard to art and artists. *Law, Ethics, and the Visual Arts* is intended not just for lawyers, artists, collectors, and dealers, but for historians of art and culture, and for the thinking lay person who is interested in the art world.

We have taught from this book almost every year since 1971. Our graduate students have come from law, business, and art history. Guests in our course at the Stanford University Law School have been artists, dealers, lawyers, curators, directors, trustees, and critics, all of whom exposed our students to the real world and caused rethinking of this book. Our own experiences in the art world have included working for and against art legislation, one of us being sued and both giving expert testimony, counseling museums and governments, advising artists and Attorneys General, appearing in public debates and international symposia. The revisions in the second edition come as much from our own experience of what is interesting and what is dull, what is important and what is trivial, as from what is new.

In Chapter 4 we take up the problems of artistic freedom and its limitation. The First Amendment to the U.S. Constitution was a landmark in the history of the artist's profession, and we see through a series of judicial decisions how this amendment has been interpreted to protect the visual arts. We also see that in addition to the Church and State as threats to artistic freedom, artists have been in many cases their own worst enemies when it comes to censorship. We also examine the troubling question of "censorship" by museums and the right of the museum to protect itself against the artist. Where is the line between censorship and selection or criticism? New to this edition is a section on controversial public art, a subject that in the 1970s did not receive the national attention it has in recent years.

"The Artist and the Real World" (chapter 5) surveys some of the practical sides of the art world: the relationship of artists to dealers, museums, and commissioners of public art. New to this edition are sections on the legal problems encountered by artists in living where they work, and the toxic hazards encountered in art materials. We discuss the important subject of the artist and taxes and the inescapable matter of the artist's death and estate problems.

Chapter 6 treats collectors and such subjects as their relationship with dealers and the tax collectors. Much of this chapter is devoted to consumer protection and the problems associated with counterfeit art. The perils of the print market and the auction system are discussed, as are those resulting from the lending of works from a private collection to exhibitions.

Art museums are the subject of the final chapter, introduced by something of their history and purposes, their legal status and character. The fiduciary responsibilities of trustees and questions about their supervision, along with ethical abuses by trustees, directors and staff, form the basis of several horror stories. The museums' business is everybody's business. At stake is nothing less than the proper preservation of the country's artistic heritage.

WHY WE CARE ABOUT ART

A good portion of this book is about what happens when we don't care about art. Daily the news media remind us of art in danger. Victims of the wrecker and bulldozer range from American Indian burial sites to Russian avant garde paintings in Moscow. The threats to Venice as its buildings sink into its its lagoon, the damage to medieval English cathedrals caused by sonic booms, and the disintegration of the Parthenon in Athens are of world as well as national concern. The kidnapping of great paintings and their ransom for the release of political prisoners induces international outrage. The theft of thousands of works of art from its churches and museums is Italy's shame. The attempted destruction of Michelangelo's *Pieta* and Rembrandt's *Night Watch* touched us all. Though smaller than nature, the world of culture is in equal peril.

We care about art because from its beginnings on the rude walls of caves, and for the millenia that passed before and after they were called art, painting, sculpture and architecture were the carriers of humanity's hopes and fears for our well being. Art has given tangible and esthetic form to the most cherished values of innumerable civilizations and has often provided their only surviving record. Art is basic to cultural history, which we recognize as being as important as biological history. Preserving the art of the past is essential to knowledge and wisdom. For scientists and scholars, even a minor work from the past embodies religious, political, social, economic and technological systems.

Paradoxically, our consciousness of the unique, irreplaceable character of art comes at a time when our society is committed to the mass-produced object that is calculated to become obsolescent. A work of art can be a simple but potent reminder of the creativity for good (and not destruction) so prized by civilization. For connoisseurs it can be an ageless testimony to beauty. It can exist outside of time for artists and inspire new works of art, thereby nourishing the health and growth of culture. Recent development of a consciousness by the American government about the "quality of life" of its citizens coincides with greatly expanded programs of support for the arts. For many nations art embodies the national spirit or "genius," and its protection is in the national interest. As we see in China and Israel, an artistic heritage is a country's identity card for the present and passport for the future. As if in answer to John Steinbeck's question in *The Grapes of Wrath*, "How will we know it's us without our past?", art tells us much about who we are and where we came from. These legacies of art are important justification for museums and their proper management.

For historians it would be valuable to have a counterpart of this book from the Renaissance, or a view of the art world such as ours, written a century ago, when the art world as we know it took form. Our readership is also in the future, among those who will cherish art and the past, and who are interested in knowing how they are abused and protected in our era.

Near the end of the Introduction to the first edition, we expressed optimism with regard to the response of law and ethics to social change and the direction of legal development in connection with the visual arts. We foresaw wider awareness and a more general interest in the dilemmas and vistas of law, ethics and the visual arts. Our optimism was not misplaced. We may have underestimated the way in which lessons were not learned, or laws and codes of ethics ignored and circumvented. Still to be developed, for example, is a greater awareness of the harm of counterfeit art and the need for more severe penalties for convicted counterfeitors. But artists are winning more rights, trustees are taking their responsibilities more seriously, governments are talking about returning and exchanging works of art to one another, and, perhaps best of all, more art is being protected from destruction.

Acknowledgments

A collection of cases and materials is necessarily made up largely of the work of others. Without their industry and wisdom this book could not exist. Our primary debt, which we gratefully acknowledge, is to the authors whose works we here cite and reproduce.

While none of the following people bears any responsibility for this book's defects, all of them have contributed substantially to its merits: Harold and Margaret Anderson, Kenneth Arrow, Roger Barr, Paul Bator, Bruce Beasley, Keith Boyle, Kristina Branch, Joan Brown Christo, Clemency Coggins, Gilbert Edelson, Evelyn Ehrlich, Lorenz Eitner, Patricia Elsen, Andre Emmerich, Milton Esterow, Charles Feingarten, Sidney Felsen, Marc Franklin, Diana Fuller, Dorothy Goldeen, Paul Goldstein, Gerald Gunther, Frank Hamilton, Gustave Harrow, Ashton Hawkins, Anne Healy, Tom Holland, Henry Hopkins, Erika Kaltenbach, Paula Kirkeby, Peider Könz, Roy Lichtenstein, J. Keith Mann, John Marion, Gordon Marsh, Jody Maxmin, Mike McCone, Chris Merillat, Nancy Merryman, Howard Nemerovsky, George Neubert, James E. O'Brien, Nathan Oliveira, Anthony and Isabelle Raubitschek, Tom Seligmann, Leon E. Seltzer, Byron Sher, Alan Sieroty, Jeremy Stone, Judy Teichman, Steve Tennis, Joann Thompson, Gene Trefethen, Kenneth Tyler, Alan D. Ullberg, Kirk Varnadoe, Palmer Wald, Stephen Weil, Ian White, Nicolas Wilder, Howard Williams, Steven Wirtz and Mitchell Zuckerman.

From the inception of the pioneer Art and the Law course at Stanford in 1971 we have had a succession of extraordinary research assistants. Sarah Cameron, Christine Cuddy, Jeffrey Yablon, Stephen Berke, Terry Schimek, and John MacCarthy, in particular, have contributed in substantial ways to the enterprise. The following students made major contributions to the materials in class projects conducted in 1974 and 1984:

Chapter 1: Nancy Goodman, Mary Jo McNamara, Ralph Maltes, Alma Robinson, Douglas Schwartz

Chapter 2: Jennifer Adams, Maria Dante Brown, Amy Halpern, Pat Maveety, Alex Nicholson, Mike Ostrach, Mark Rosenberg, Bob Ryan, Gail Sonnenschein

Chapter 3: Steven Buffone, Gary Gilden, Jude Kearney, Stephen McGough, Andrew S. Rotter, William Skrzyniarz, Anne Stanton, Risa Wolf

Chapter 4: Victor Chan, Marilyn Epstein, Helene Fromm, Paul Perret, Joe Pitts III

Chapter 5: Carlyn Clause, Lisa Cetlin, George Farias, Luzann Fernandez, Michael Fremuth, Marcia Goldstein, Greg Rael, Adrian Roscher, Margaret Spencer, John Wetenhall

Chapter 6: Margaret Caldwell, Susan Dennis, Grady Gamage, Julie Garrie, Barbara Heins, Elizabeth Malone, Sozeen Mondlin, Edward Schorr, Andrew Taper

Chapter 7: Jeffrey Babbin, Linda Bray, Sanjay Jain, Jerold E. Pearson, Penny Pritzker, Cynthia Saltzman, Minda Rae Schechter, R. Carlton Seaver

We also express appreciation to Deans Thomas Ehrlich, Charles J. Meyers and John Hart Ely of the Stanford Law School and to Professor Lorenz Eitner, Chairman of the Department of Art at Stanford University, for their encouragement and support; to Law Librarian J. Myron Jacobstein and Art Librarian Alex Ross and their staffs for invaluable library assistance; to Betty Dolan, whose devotion and industry were crucially important to the completion of this book; and to Patricia Regon for the uncountable ways in which an excellent secretary can make a difference.

Table of Readings

Agreement Relating to the Return of the Teotihuacán Murals (1979) 132–34

Akston and Messer, "Editorials on the Haacke Case" 308–10

ALI-ABA Course of Study on Legal Problems of Museum Administration 731–34

American Association of Museums, "Museum Ethics—A Report" 713–16

American Council for the Arts, The Visual Artist and the Law 398–400

"The Arrest of Jean Toche" 323

Art and Artifacts Indemnity Act 737–39

Artists Equity Association, Northern California, "Artists' Live/Work Space: Changing Public Policy" 415–21

Association of Art Museum Directors, "A Code of Ethics for Art Museum Directors" 706–07

Association of Art Museum Directors, Professional Practices Committee, "The Structure and Organization of Art Museums" 673–74

Baldwin, "Haacke: Refusé in Cologne" 264–68

Baldwin, "Art and Money: The Artist's Royalty Problem" 217–19

Barnes Foundation Indenture 651–52

Bator, "An Essay on the International Trade in Art" 50–52

Berne Convention for the Protection of Literary and Artistic Works 145, 216

Boswell, "Art as Reparations" 42–43

Brooks, "The Case of the Disenchanted Donor" 619–21

Brown, "Keeping an Eye on Each Other: The IRS and the Museum Store" 664–68

Browning, "The Case for the Return of the Parthenon Marbles" 135–36

California Art and Craft Materials Labeling Act 424–27

California Art Preservation Act 163–65

California Consignment of Fine Art Law 393

California Cultural and Artistic Creations Preservation Act 165–66

California Fine Print Act 534–39

California Resale Proceeds Right Law 232–33

Carey, "Bringing Museum Ethics into Focus" 703–05, 717

Carter, "The End of a Multimillion-Dollar Art Fraud" 491–92

Carter, "The Lipchitz Imbroglio" 473–75

Christie's: Contemporary Art Auction Catalog 515–18

Christo, "Proposal for 'THE GATES: PROJECT FOR CENTRAL PARK'" 331–32

Clapp, Art Censorship: A Chronology of Proscribed and Prescribed Art 251–52

"Colin-Merryman Correspondence" 682–84

Colin, "Tax and Economic Problems of Artists" 441–43

"Collage" 316

College Art Association, Code of Ethics for Art Historians and Guidelines for the Professional Practice of Art History 569–70

College Art Association, Resolution Concerning the Sale and Exchange of Works of Art by Museums 724–25

College Art Association, Standards for Sculptural Reproduction and Preventive Measures Against Unethical Casting 549–51

"Comment: Tax Treatment of Artists' Charitable Contributions" 443–44

"A Conflict of Interest . . . or a Conflict of Interpretation?" 697–98

Convention on Cultural Property Implementation Act 97–106

Convention on the Means of Prohibiting and Preventing the Illicit Import, Export, and Transfer of Ownership of Cultural Property 92–95

Convention for the Protection of Cultural Property in the Event of Armed Conflict 28–32

Cort, "The Artist's Right to Control Public Display" 207–08

Council of Europe Parliamentary Assembly, Resolution on Return of Works of Art 129

"Courting the Artist with Copyright: The 1976 Copyright Act" 195–96

Cunningham, "Letter to the Editor" 617–18

Curtis, "Museums on the Move: Creative Alternatives in Real Estate" 670–72

Davis, Report and Determination in the Matter of Christo: "The Gates" 332–34

Dean, "A Case History of Art Fraud" 489–91

de Varine, "The Rape and Plunder of Cultures" 46–50

Devree, "Is This Statuary Worth More Than a Million of Your Money?" 346–48

"Disposition Procedures Agreed to by the Metropolitan Museum"   722

Dufy, *Art Law: Representing Artists, Dealers, and Collectors*   391–92

"Editorial: Artists vs. Museums"   309–15

Eisenberg, "One Artist's Experience"   206–07

Elsen and Merryman, "The Harm of Exact Reproductions of Art"   547–48

Elsen with Merryman, "Legal and Illegal Counterfeiting of Art in America"   543–46, 557–60

Emmerich, "Letter to the Washington Post"   72–74

"Federal Tax Policies on Art Donations Under Scrutiny"   610–11

Feld, "Artists, Art Collectors, and Income Tax"   609–10

Fox, "Bank Allowed to Seize Art in Loan Default"   395–96

France, *Law of March 11, 1957 No. 296*   145–46, 213–14

Freedberg, "The Structure of Byzantine and European Iconoclasm"   245–47

General Services Administration, Public Buildings Service Contract for Fine Arts Services   411–13

Germany, *Law of September 16, 1965, No. 51*   214

Germany, *Law of September 9, 1965*   146

Getty, "The Case of the Boston Raphael"   78–82

Gilbert, "Tax Exempt Status and Unrelated Income"   661–64

Glueck, "Power and Esthetics: The Trustee"   675–76

Gould, *Trophy of Conquest*   15–16

Graff, "Art in Jail: The Sprayer of Zurich"   302–03

Haacke and the Guggenheim Museum, correspondence   305–08

"Handbill," Ad Hoc Artists' Movement for Freedom   321

Hansard Parliamentary Debates   10–12

"Harvard Statement on Acquisition of Works of Art and Antiquities"   71

Hauptman, "Suppression of Art in the McCarthy Decade"   268–75

Hart, "Statement on His Veterans' Vietnam Memorial Design"   350–51

Heath, "Bootleg Archaeology in Costa Rica"   64–66

Hendon, *Analyzing An Art Museum*   640–42

Hepp, "Royalties from Works of the Fine Arts: The Origin of Droit de Suite in Copyright Law"   219–20

Holt, *Literary Sources of Art History*   248–51

Hoover, "Resources for the Investigation of Title to Art Works"   501–03

House Committee on Education and Labor, "Art and Artifacts Indemnity Act: Report"   735–37

House Committee on Education and Labor, "Report 618, 89th Congress"   340–42

International Council of Museums, "Study on the Principles, Conditions, and Means for the Restitution or Return of Cultural Property in View of Reconstituting Dispersed Heritages"   128

Italy, *Law of April 22, 1941, No. 633*   146, 215–16

Kramer, "Questions Raised by Art Alterations"   172–73

Krauss, "Changing the Work of David Smith"   171–72

Lee, *Past, Present, East and West*   643–44

Lehmann-Haupt, *Art Under a Dictatorship*   254–58, 259–61

"Lifetime Agency Contract between O'Keeffe and Representative"   390–91

Lin, "Statement on Her Winning Design for the Vietnam Veterans Memorial in Washington, D.C."   349

Luna, "The Protection of the Cultural Heritage: An Italian Perspective"   67–69

Mango, "The Art of the Byzantine Empire"   244–45

Massachusetts Fine Art Protection Act   167–68

M'Bow, "A Plea for the Return of an Irreplaceable Cultural Heritage to Those Who Created It"   126–27

McAlee, "The McClain Case, Customs and Congress"   96–97, 122–23

McGill, "Sweeping Reassessment in the Auction Trade"   508–12

Merryman, "Are Museum Trustees and the Law Out of Step?"   677–81

Merryman, "Contracts and Understandings"   383–84

Merryman, "Expanding Standing: Stone Walls and the Friendly Dog"   691–93

Merryman, "The Refrigerator of Bernard Buffet"   143–44, 161–62

Merryman and Elsen, "A Draft Set of Principles and Code of Curatorial Conduct"   707–13

Merryman with Elsen, "Hot Art: A Reexamination of the Illegal International Trade in Cultural Objects"   53–56, 62–65

Metropolitan Museum of Art, *Report on Art Transactions 1971–1973*   618–19

Meyer, *The Plundered Past* 720—21

Millinger, "Copyright and the Fine Artist" 190—91

Morris, "When Artists Use Photographs" 200—03

Museum of Modern Art, "Critique of Disposition Procedures Agreed to by the Metropolitan Museum" 722—23

Museum Store Association Code of Ethics 668—69

Nafziger, "The New International Framework for the Return, Restitution, or Forfeiture of Cultural Property" 127—28

National Foundation on the Arts and Humanities Act 338—40

Nelson, "Public Art and Politics: The GSA Art in Architecture Program and Baltimore Federal" 354—57

New York Arts and Cultural Affairs Law: Artist-Dealer Relationships 394—95

New York Arts and Cultural Affairs Law: Warranties 563—64

New York *Arts and Cultural Affairs Law: Artists' Authorship Rights Act* 166—67

New York City Administrative Code: Auctioneers 513

Nicolson, "Marginal Comment" 37—39

Nochlin, "Museums and Radicals: A History of Emergencies" 646—49

Nordland, *Controversial Public Art* 324—25, 326—27, 343—45

Paul, "The Picasso Estate: Untangling the 'Inheritance of the Century'" 468—72

Pearson, "Title Disputes at Auction Houses" 521—22

"Peru Wages Campaign to Halt Trade in Stolen Art Treasures" 59—60

Pevsner, *Academies of Art: Past and Present* 252—53

Quynn, "Art Confiscations of the Napoleonic Wars" 17—19

Regulation of Importation of Pre-Columbian Monumental or Architectural Sculpture or Murals 89—90

Reif, "How to Bid at an Auction" 505—07

Rhodes, "The Medium of Payment: An Option in Estate Tax Reform" 633—37

Rigby, "Cultural Reparations and a New Western Tradition" 41—42

Rosenbaum, "Appraising the Appraisers" 596—602

Roth, "Copyright Remedies and the Fine Artist" 204—05

Rubin, "Art and Taxes" 621—23

Schecter, "The Inside Story: Dealing with Trustee Self-Dealing" 693—95

Schilit, "A Look at Copyright Revision Act Through the Eyes of the Art Collector" 211—12

Schlemmer, *The Letters and Diaries of Oscar Schlemmer* 264—65

Schumacher, "Peru's Rich Antiquities Crumbling in Museums" 60—62

Scigliano, "Tacoma Repeals One-Percent Law" 366—68

Society of London Art Dealers," Statement 227—29

Sotheby Parke Bernet: *Contemporary Art Auction Catalog* 518—20

Speiller, "The Favored Tax Treatment for Purchasers of Art" 592—95

Stalker and Glymour, "The Malignant Object: Thoughts on Public Sculpture" 368—73

St. Clair, *Lord Elgin and the Marbles* 4—10

Stewart, "Two Cheers for the Tombaroli" 66—67

"Stolen Art Sold at Auction" 522—24

Temko, "Environmental Design: 57,939 Names on Polished Black Granite" 350—51

Tietze, *Genuine and False* 552—56

Tolstoy, "What is Art?" 253—54

"$2 Million Art Swindle Stuns New York Trade" 492—93

Treaty of Cooperation between the United States of America and the United Mexican State Providing for the Recovery and Return of Stolen Archaeological, Historical and Cultural Properties 116—17

Treaty of Versailles 40

Trevor-Roper, *The Plunder of the Arts in the Seventeenth Century* 3—4

Trial of the Major War Criminals Before the International Military Tribunal 20—23

Ullberg, *Museum Trusteeship* 682, 690—91

"Under Stalin You Could Have Been Shot" 258

Uniform Commercial Code: Sale by Auction 512—13

Uniform Commercial Code: Warranties 562—63

Visual Artists Rights Society, "Statement" 220—21

Wallach, "The Trouble with Prints" 527—34

Ward, "Copyright in Museum Collections" 208—10

Weil, *Beauty and the Beasts* 689—90, 705—06

Weil, "Resale Royalties: Nobody Benefits" 221—27

Williams and Pappas, "Purchase of Paintings Questioned: Atheneum Officials' Ethics at Issue" 698—99

Table of Cases

Asterisks indicate principal cases

*Adams v. Commissioner   431–33
Alberts v. California   286
Alva Studios v. Winniger   196
American Tobacco Co. v. Werckmeister   191
Asia Society v. Tax Commission of the City of New York (1983)
*Attorney General of New Zealand v. Ortiz and Others (1983)   114–15

*Batlin & Son, Inc. v. Snyder   183–85
Bernard-Rousseau v. Société des Galéries Lafayette   155
Bleistein v. Donaldson Lithographing   175, 318
Brancusi v. U.S.   318–19
Brandenburg v. Ohio   278

Calder v. C.I.R.   453
Estate of Chandor v. C.I.R.   429
Chaplinsky v. New Hampshire   277, 278
*Churchman v. Commissioner   436–37
Close v. Lederle   277, 292
Cohen v. California   277
Coventry Ware, Inc. v. Reliance Picture Frame Co.   194
*Crimi v. Rutgers Presbyterian Church   149–53
Curtis Publishing Co. v. Butts   277

*Dawson v. G. Malina, Inc.   564–68
Drucker v. C.I.R.   431

*Ente autonomo "La Biennale" de Venezia c. De Chirico   156–57
Epoux Bernard c. Bellier et Ligue de la défense de l'art   217
Esquire, Inc. v. Ringer   180

*Factor v. Stella   502–03
F.C.C. v. Pacifica Foundation (1978)   277
Felseneiland mit Sirenen   156
*Franklin Mint v. National Wildlife Art Exchange, Inc.   180–82
*Matter of Friedman   384–90
*Furstenberg v. United States   602–08

Gertz v. Robert Welch, Inc.   281
Gilliam v. American Broadcasting Co.   162
*Goldsboro Art League, Inc. v. Commissioner   659–61
*Goldsmith v. Max   197–99
Goldstein v. California   175
*Grogan-Beall v. Ferdinand Roten Galleries, Inc.   540–42
Guatemala v. Hollinshead   115–16

*Hahn v. Duveen   574–77
Hajed v. ADAC   156
Hamling v. U.S.   290
Harris v. Attorney General   31
*Estate of Hermann   742–44
Hollinshead, U.S. v.   115–16, 118
*Hollis v. United States   588–90
Hollywood Jewel Mfg. Co. v. Dushkin   196
Hotel Dorset Co. v. Trust for Cultural Resources   46

Jacobellis v. Ohio   286, 378
*Janis v. De Kooning   381–82
*Jeanneret v. Vichey   83–88
Jenkins v. Georgia   290

*Kieselstein-Cord v. Accessories by Pearl   177–79
*King of Italy v. De Medici   77–78
*Estate of Kline   447–48
Knowles v. State   282
*Kraut v. Morgan   583–85
*Kunstsammlungen zu Weimar v. Elicofon   107–12

Lacasse et Welcome c. Abbe Quenard   156
Leger v. Reunion des theatres lyriques Nationaux   156
Lehman v. Shaker Heights   278
*Letter Edged in Black Press, Inc. v. Public Building Commission of Chicago   186–91
Levine, U.S. v.   291

Marks Music Corp. v. Continental Record Co. 205

Mazer v. Stein   180

*Meliodon v. Philadelphia School District   154–55

*McClain, U.S. v.   118–20

*Mellon v. Commissioner   624–28

Memoirs v. Massachusetts   287

Menzel v. List   26

Miller v. California   287–89

Millet   155

*Morseburg v. Balyon   234–37

Newmann v. Delmar Realty Co.   169

New York Times v. Sullivan   276, 278, 281, 282

*O'Keeffe v. Snyder   498–500

Olivotti, U.S. v.   318

113 Prints, U.S. v.   282–84

Pagano v. Chas. Beseler Co.   196

*Pennsylvania v. Barnes   654–58

People v.——— See name of defendant

Perry, U.S. v.   318

Piarowsky v. Illinois Community College   293

*Louis H. Porter   433–36

Porter v. Wertz   485–89

Pushman v. New York Graphic Society   176

*Radich, People v.   294–97

*Radich, U.S. ex rel. v. Criminal Court of New York   299–301

*Rebay v. Commissioner   438–40

Redrup v. New York   287

Roerich v. C.I.R.   429

Roth v. U.S.   281, 286

*Estate of Rothko   454–67

*Rowan v. Pasadena Art Museum   727–29

Schenck v. U.S.   277

*Scherr v. Universal Match Corp.   193–94

*Scott, People ex rel., v. Silverstein   685–88

*Scull v. Scull   612–15

*Security First National Bank of Los Angeles v. Commissioner   628–32

*Silberman v. Georges   279–81

*Shostakovich v. Twentieth-Century Fox   153–54

*Silvette v. Art Commission of Commonwealth of Virginia   351–52

*Estate of Smith, v. Commissioner   449–53

Société Le Chant de Monde c. Société Fox Europe et Fox Américaine Twentieth Century   154

*State v. Wright Hepburn Wesbster Gallery Ltd.   578–81

*Stroganoff-Scherbatoff v. Weldon   26–27

Stromberg v. California   276

Sudre c. Commune de Daixas   156

Symphony Space, Inc. v. Tishelman

Mark Tobey v. C.I.R.   429

*Taborsky v. Maroney   493–98

Thirty-One Photographs, U.S. v.   284

*Travis v. Sotheby Parke Bernet, Inc.   571–73

U.S. v.——— See name of defendant

*Vargas v. Esquire   147–49

Veazie v. Williams   514

Virginia Pharmacy Board v. Virginia Consumer Council   277

Weisz v. Parke-Bernet Galleries   520

Whistler v. Ruskin   578

Whitney v. California   276

*Weigand v. Barnes Foundation   652–53

Winkworth v. Christie Manson and Woods   113

*Wrightsman v. United States   586–88

Young v. American Mini-Theatres   277

*Zacchini v. Scripps-Howard Newspapers   203

PLUNDER, DESTRUCTION, AND REPARATIONS

WE begin by examining an ancient practice: the appropriation or destruction of the cultural treasures of one nation by the representatives of another, a practice common in antiquity and continuing into the twentieth century. Plunder and destruction have usually taken place in time of war and occupation. We examine the evolution of the attitude of public international law toward these practices and, in that context, introduce some of the questions that will occupy us throughout the book.

Notice that plunder and destruction are characterized as problems in *public international law*. What does that mean? The answer is best given in terms of the "subjects" of international law—that is, of the persons or entities who bear rights and duties under public international law.

Public international law deals with nation-states and their official representatives—the rights and obligations of the Soviet Union, Italy, Costa Rica, Canada, and so forth (as well as the status and rights and duties of persons who represent them in the international arena, such as ambassadors). In general, however, the rights and duties of individuals as individuals are of no concern to public international law. (This generalization can be debated among international lawyers, particularly since the Nuremberg Trials, but is close enough for purposes of the present discussion.) If we want to discuss the law applicable to individuals, we must look to private international law and to national law.

National law is the kind of law with which we are most familiar. To those of us in the United States it is the law of the United States and of the state in which we live—the rules, institutions and processes that regulate our societies. Individuals (and "legal persons," like corporations and foundations) are typical subjects of national law. In most of this book we will be talking about national law as it affects the world of art.

Private international law also applies primarily to individuals, but it is concerned with those problems that arise where all the relevant facts are not restricted to one nation. For example, if you rent an automobile in France and drive to Italy, where you have an automobile accident, and subsequently return to your home in the United States, and then are sued in a Canadian court by a German who was injured in the accident, some problems of private international law exist. Does the Canadian court have jurisdiction to hear the action brought by the German against you? According to what law should the nature of your liability, if any, be determined? And so on. We deal with some questions of private international law in Chapter 2, where we talk about the illegal export of artistic and cultural treasures.

Systematic plunder of the arts as a right of conquest dates at least to the fourth century B.C., when the Roman Empire came into being. What better way to dramatize for the citizens of Rome that their armies ruled the world than for the emperors to assemble in the Roman Forum what in effect was the earliest museum of international art. By their personal example, Roman emperors, and their generals and consuls, instructed society and ultimately their conquerors in the benefits of plunder. Roman patricians developed a passion for collecting and learning and built great personal art collections and libraries that were to be emulated by European royalty from the Middle Ages to the seventeenth century. Without plunder, the great museums of the world as we know them today would not be the same. American art museums were built on purchases, but the art thus acquired often had a long history of displacement from its original owner as a result of violence. Not one work of art entered American art museums after either of the two world wars as the direct result of military victories, yet, as the reader will find in the first two chapters, many acquisitions did result from plunder of a different sort.

Ask a class of college students under what circumstances they could conceive of (not approve) the acquiring or protecting of art as justifying the loss of human life. Chances are there will be silence, followed by a consensus that none could exist. In the past wars were fought in which art was not only a compensation but the cause itself. In 1648, for example, Queen Christina of Sweden ordered her army to subjugate Prague in order to obtain the magnificent art collection and library of the emperor Rudolph. Those who died defending Prague, and earlier Heidelberg, against an art-robbing army acting for the Vatican knew full well what was at stake. It was only after the terrible Thirty Years' War in the seventeenth century that rulers desisted from pillaging each other's picture galleries and libraries. Conversely, ask the same students if they could conceive of how at any time art could save human life, and the response would probably be the same as before. Like today's urbanites, in the past whole cities were threatened by robber armies who in effect told them, "Your art or your life!" On several occasions compliance saved the citizens of ancient Rome and Constantinople. In the seventeenth century Nuremberg was spared because earlier it had allowed its conqueror to buy some of its artistic treasures painted by Dürer.

For information on the subject of art plunder and art politics, see Wilhelm Treue, *Art Plunder: The Fate of Works of Art in War and Unrest* (New York: John Day, 1961); Hugh Trevor-Roper, *The Plunder of the Arts in the Seventeenth Century* (London: Thames & Hudson, 1970); and Karl Meyer, *The Plundered Past* (New York: Atheneum, 1973). The following excerpt from Trevor-Roper's book succinctly explains art's historical importance for society.

ART AND SOCIETY

HUGH TREVOR-ROPER *The Function of Art in Society**

Art has many functions, social as well as individual. It has one function for the artist, another for the patron. To the artist and the aesthete it expresses a Platonic conception of beauty or a personal conviction; to the patron, it may represent this, but it also represents other things: propaganda, pride, prestige. To the city state of ancient Greece or medieval Italy it illustrated the independence of the republic, the *virtù* of its citizens; to the Renaissance monarchy it illustrated the continuity and strength of the dynasty, the personal magnificence of the prince; and age after age, the Church, the greatest of all patrons, made it yet another instrument to capture, elevate, even hypnotize the devout mind. These are truisms which there is no need to emphasize. Without these "second causes" of art, art itself would be

very different—and there would be much less of it.

Every weapon of propaganda inevitably provokes opposition. If art, at times, is an instrument to enslave men's minds, heretics who wish to set them free will find themselves also enemies of art—or at least of that art. Like the Iconoclasts of eighth-century Byzantium, or the Puritans of Reformation Europe, they will seek to destroy this aesthetic arm of the enemy; or at least, like modern Communists in Russia or China, they will try to neutralize, to sterilize it, by separating it from its living context. Equally, if art gives an aura of prestige to a city or a dynasty, rival cities or dynasties, which set out to conquer and humble them, will seek also to destroy their "myth" by depriving them of this aura and appropriating it

*From Hugh Trevor-Roper, *The Plunder of the Arts in the Seventeenth Century* (London: Thames & Hudson, 1970), pp. 7–8. Reprinted by permission of Thames & Hudson, Ltd., London.

to themselves, like cannibals who, by devouring parts of their enemies, think thereby to acquire their *mana*, the intangible source of their strength. At least they will do this in certain periods of history: in times, particularly, of ideological struggle, when wars are fought not for limited objectives, between temporary enemies respectful of each other's basic rights and independent authority, but totally, to destroy altogether hated systems of government, to break and subject independent powers, to create a New Order.

PLUNDER OF THE ARTS

We turn now to three particularly interesting cases of art plunder and appropriations: the Elgin Marbles, the Napoleonic campaigns, and the Nazi art appropriations.

THE ELGIN MARBLES

Scotsman Thomas Bruce, 7th Earl of Elgin (1766–1841), was a member of the British House of Lords and a career diplomat. One of his assignments was as ambassador to Turkey. At the time, England was at war with Napoleon, who had recently invaded Egypt. Lord Elgin's official duty was to participate in the British effort to expel France from Egypt and to keep the Ottoman Empire on friendly terms with Great Britain. But Elgin also had a personal mission: to restore the position of fine arts in Great Britain by introducing British artists to the art of Athens. (Greece then was a part of the Ottoman Empire.) Before he left England for Constantinople, Elgin planned to return with a full set of casts and drawings of ancient Greek artworks, particularly those on the Acropolis of Athens, and he proposed that the British government fund the project. When the government refused, Elgin decided to proceed at his own expense. He interviewed a number of British artists, including Turner, then twenty-one years old, to work for him, but without success. While in Italy en route to Constantinople, Elgin engaged the Italian Giovanni Battista Lusieri as his chief artist, plus another painter, two architectural draftsmen, and two molders.

ACQUISITION OF THE MARBLES

WILLIAM ST. CLAIR *Lord Elgin and the Marbles**

In August 1800 Lord Elgin's artists at last arrived in Athens to begin the work that was to improve the arts in Great Britain. They paid their respects (with the usual presents) to the Turkish authorities and established themselves in the town. The British Consul Logotheti took them under his protection.

Athens was then a shabby, miserable little town. It was inhabited by a motley population from all parts of the Ottoman Empire who all lived on the north and east slopes of the Acropo-lis. About half were Greeks, a quarter Turks, and the rest Albanians, Jews, Negroes, and others. There were probably no more than thirteen hundred houses in all. Round the town was a wall only ten feet high that had been built twenty years before to keep out roving bands of bandits and to make the taxation of the enclosed inhabitants easier to collect. The Acropolis was nominally a military fortress but its few guns were dismounted and purely for show. The garrison lived with their families in huts on the Acropolis

*From William St. Clair, *Lord Elgin and the Marbles* (Oxford: Oxford Univ. Press, 1983), pp. 50–51, 88–89, 95, 96, 99–101, 102, 103, 109–110, 112–113, 119. Copyright © 1967, 1983 by Oxford University Press. Reprinted by permission. Footnotes omitted.

The Parthenon, Athens, fifth century B.C. *(Before recent removal of remaining sculptures.)*

so badly built that they crumbled whenever there was heavy rain. Athens was the forty-third city of European Turkey.

Among the mean houses of Athens there stood out, in violent contrast, the remains of its magnificent ancient buildings and these—as now—were its only claim to distinction. There were not many of them. On the Acropolis were the ruins of three buildings of the greatest age of Greece, the Parthenon, the Erechtheum and the Propylaea, and, in the lower town, another of the same period, the Theseum. Besides these four were the remains of several smaller and less interesting monuments of later centuries, the Tower of the Winds, the Monument of Lysicrates, and the Monument of Philopappos, and some pillars of a gigantic temple to Olympian Zeus. There were other signs of the greater days, but, for the most part, they were well hidden.

As the ancient buildings were the only substantial structures in the whole of Athens, every one that had any roof left was still in use. The Erechtheum was a gunpowder magazine, the Theseum was a church, the Tower of the Winds was the headquarters of the Whirling Dervishes, and the Monument of Lysicrates was a storeroom for a French Capuchin Convent. The Turks living on the Acropolis built their houses, vegetable gardens, and fortifications round about the ruins or made use of them as it suited their purpose. Inside the Parthenon was a small mosque, and the spaces between the pillars of the Propylaea were half bricked up to provide a kind of castellation for the guns. Everywhere it was obvious that for years the ruins had been a main source of building materials. Slabs of crisp-cut marble were built into the rude modern walls, and, here and there, pieces of sculpture could be seen among the fortifications. Many of the houses in the town had an ancient fragment set above their door as a charm. . . .

On 17 June General Hutchinson received the surrender of Cairo and the success of the Egyptian expedition was finally assured. On 6 July, Elgin obtained the firman he had asked for. These two events were intimately connected; indeed, allowing for the time news took to travel and the ceremoniousness of all Turkish business, one followed at once after the other. Elgin himself acknowledged that he was making little progress in the negotiations for a firman until suddenly the Turks began to shower all kinds of favours on their British allies. The granting of the firman was just another gift to be compared with the

aigrettes, pelisses, horses, snuff boxes, medals, and other favours lavished on the British.

The firman was a letter addressed to the Voivode and Cadi of Athens signed by the Caimacan Pasha who was still acting Grand Vizier. . . . It is in two parts, the first stating the request of Lord Elgin, the second granting it point by point. . . . Like most official documents it is drafted so as to be understandable by a half-wit and is so repetitious that only the most indefatigable reader is likely to read it to the end. But despite its appearance of being exact and comprehensive, it becomes ambiguous at the most crucial point. The text is as follows, translated from the Italian version given to Hunt. [The Rev. Philip Hunt was Elgin's chaplain and enthusiastic aide in acquiring the marbles.]

It is hereby signified to you, that our sincere Friend, his Excellency Lord Elgin Ambassador Extraordinary from the Court of England to the Porte of Happiness, has represented to us, that it is well known that the greater part of the Frank Courts are anxious to read and investigate the books, pictures and other works of science of the ancient Greek philosophers: and that in particular, the ministers, philosophers, primates and other individuals of England have a taste for the pictures remaining ever since the time of the said Greeks and which are to be seen on the shores of the Archipelago and in other climes; and have in consequence from time to time sent men to explore and examine the ancient buildings, and pictures. And that some Diletanti [*sic*] of the Court of England being desirous to see the ancient buildings and the curious pictures in the City of Athens, and the old walls remaining since the time of the Greeks, which now subsist in the interior part of the said place; he [the Ambassador] has therefore engaged five English painters now dwelling at Athens, to examine and view, and also to copy the pictures remaining there, "ab antiquo": And he has also at this time expressly asked us that it may be written and ordered that as long as the said painters shall be employed in going in and out of the citadel of the said city, which is Temple of the Idols there; and in modelling the said ornaments and the place of observation and in fixing scaffolding round the ancient visible figures, in plaster or gypsum; and in measuring the remains of other ruined buildings there; and in excavating when they find it necessary the foundations in order to discover inscriptions which may have been covered in the rubbish; that no interruption may be given them, nor any obstacle thrown in their way by the Disdar or any other person: that no one may meddle with the scaffolding or implements they may require in their works; and that when they wish to take away any pieces of stone with old inscriptions or sculptures thereon, that no opposition be made thereto.

We therefore have written this letter to you and expedited it by N.N., in order that as soon as you shall have understood its meaning, namely, that it is the explicit desire and engagement of this Sublime Emperor endowed with all eminent qualities to favour such requests as the above mentioned, in conformity with what is due to friendship, sincerity, alliance, and good will subsisting "ab antiquo" between the Sublime and ever durable Ottoman Court and that of England and which is on the side of both those Courts manifestly increasing; particularly as there is no harm in the said pictures, and buildings being thus viewed, contemplated, and drawn. Therefore after having fulfilled the duties of hospitality, and given a proper reception to the aforesaid Artists in compliance with the urgent request of the said Ambassador to that effect, and because it is incumbent on us to provide that they meet no opposition in walking viewing or contemplating the pictures and buildings they may wish to design or copy; and in any of their works of fixing scaffolding, or using their various instruments; it is our desire that on the arrival of this letter you use your diligence to act conformably to the instances of the said Ambassador as long as the said five artists dwelling in that place shall be employed in going in and out of the citadel of Athens which is the place of observation; or in fixing scaffolding around the ancient Temple of the Idols, or in modelling with chalk or gypsum the said ornaments and visible figures; or in measuring the fragments and vestiges of other ruined buildings; or in excavating when they find it necessary the foundations in search of inscriptions among the rubbish; that they be not molested by the said Disdar nor by any other persons; nor even by you to whom this letter is addressed; and that no one meddle with their scaffolding or implements nor hinder them from taking away any pieces of stone with inscriptions and figures. In the aforesaid manner see that you behave and comport yourselves.

(Signed with a signet)
Seged Abdullah Kaimmacam

The ambiguity in the firman is even more pronounced than in Hunt's memorandum. There is a great difference, as many were later to say, between permission to excavate and remove and permission to remove and excavate. The first implies that one can take away anything of interest that is dug up: the second lets one take away anything of interest from whatever place one likes. The interesting thing about the firman, if one

reads the last part closely, is its clear indication that the Turks, if they considered the point at all, only intended to grant permission to excavate and remove. After all the tedious detail about things which the artists are to be permitted to do the permission to remove is very much an afterthought.

Certainly at the time the Elgin family themselves put that interpretation on it. "I am happy to tell you," Lady Elgin wrote on 9 July to her parents:

Pisani has succeeded *à merveille* in his *firman* from the Porte, Hunt is in raptures for the *firman* is perfection and P. says he will answer with his whiskers that it is exact. It allows all our artists to go into the citadel to copy and model everything in it, to erect scaffolds all round the Temple, to dig and discover all the ancient foundations, and to bring away any marbles that may be deemed curious by their having inscriptions on them, and that they are not to be disturbed by the soldiers etc. under any pretence whatever. Don't you think this will do? I am in the greatest glee for it would have been a great pity to have failed in the principal part after having been at such an expense.

The "principal part" was of course Elgin's scheme that he had pressed ever since before he left England of drawing, modelling, and removing selected pieces from the debris scattered around the Acropolis.

Lord Elgin himself wrote to Lusieri to tell him that the firman had been obtained and to exhort him to seize the moment to do all he could. It is evident that he too was still thinking entirely of obtaining drawings and representations to improve British artistic taste.

Besides the general work (by which I mean that which had been begun at the departure of Mr. Hunt) it would be very essential that the *Formatori* should be able to take away exact models of the little ornaments *or detached pieces if any are found* which would be interesting for the Arts. The very great variety in our manufactures, in objects either of elegance or luxury, offers a thousand applications for such details. A chair, a footstool, designs or shapes for porcelain, ornaments for cornices, nothing is indifferent, and whether it be in painting or a model, exact representations of such things would be much to be desired. Besides you have now the permission to dig, and there a great field is opened for medals, and for the remains both of sculpture and architecture.

There is no suggestion that Elgin thought he had obtained permission to remove from the buildings.

Some of Hunt's answers to questions from the Select Committee when the legality of Elgin's actions was being investigated fifteen years later, make it clear that both he and the Voivode realized the terms of the firman were being exceeded. They hint at much more.

"Do you imagine," Hunt was asked, "that the firman gave a direct permission to remove figures and pieces of sculpture from the walls of temples, or that that must have been a matter of private arrangement with the local authorities of Athens?" "That was the interpretation," Hunt answered, "which the Vaivode of Athens was induced to allow it to bear."

"In consequence of what was the Vaivode induced to give it this interpretation?"

"With respect to the first metope, it was to gratify what he conceived to be the favourable wishes of the Turkish Government towards Lord Elgin, and which induced him rather to extend than contract the precise permissions of the firmaun."

Earlier in his interview before the Select Committee Hunt was asked: "Was there any difficulty in persuading the Vaivode to give this interpretation to the firmaun?" He replied "Not a great deal of difficulty."

And so, with not a great deal of difficulty, the vital twist to the firman was given. On 31 July the ship's carpenter with five of the crew mounted the walls of the Parthenon and with the aid of windlasses, cordage, and twenty Greeks succeeded in detaching and lowering down without the slightest accident the best of the surviving metopes. . . .

Thus it was that Elgin obtained his firman and thus did his agent put it into execution. The legality of Hunt's actions and of the later removals made under the authority of the firman was debatable, to say the least, but once the first fateful breach had been made the way was open for the removal of anything he liked. . . .

The first set of excavations on the Acropolis produced a rich harvest. The home of one of the Turkish soldiers at the west end of the Parthenon was bought and pulled down. Underneath the excavators found some colossal fragments of the west pediment that had been thrown down by the explosion of 1687—the Torso of Poseidon, the Amphitrite, the Hermes, and some other pieces. These are among the finest statues in the round that survive from classical Greece. Excavations were then begun on the south side and a number of other fragments and parts of the frieze were uncovered. Saws were sent for from Constantinople to cut off the back parts of the heavy marble blocks on which the sculptures were carved, and thus lightened the artists were able to transport them down to the Consul's yard. . . .

Turks and Greeks vied with one another in gratifying the wishes of Elgin's agents and, according to Hunt, no one made any objection or even expressed regret. More statues and fragments were dug up and an increasing number of vases, coins and other antiquities. The British Consul Logotheti, forgetting his scruples, made Elgin a present of some antiquities that had been lying in his yard for many years and the people of Athens were delighted to sell any fragments that they found. The labour force employed by Lord Elgin grew and grew. The greatest number of acquisitions, however, came from the buildings themselves. Scaffolds were erected, masons established on the Acropolis and a large number of porters engaged. Elgin's ambition had now gone far beyond drawings and moulds. "I should wish to have," he wrote to Lusieri, "examples in the actual object, of each thing, and architectural ornament—of each cornice, each frieze, each capital—of the decorated ceilings, of the fluted columns—specimens of the different architectural orders and of the variant forms of the orders,—of metopes and the like, as much as possible. Finally everything in the way of sculpture, medals, and curious marbles that can be discovered by means of assiduous and indefatigable excavation. This excavation ought to be pushed on as much as possible, be its success what it may." Despite all this activity, the original objects of the expedition were not forgotten. Elgin's moulders, architects, and artists were kept busy on all the monuments of Athens, making moulds and compiling an accurate record of their architecture and sculpture. When the moulders had difficulty in making moulds with the earth to be found near Athens, Elgin chartered a vessel to bring a more suitable type from Melos. It was hardly the scientific archaeology we know today but it was far superior to the simple treasure-hunting indulged in by all previous collectors in Greece or Italy.

When the Caryatid porch of the Erechtheum was first cleared of modern accretions Hunt suggested that the whole building could be removed and rebuilt in England. "If your Lordship," he wrote, "would come here in a large Man of War that beautiful little model of ancient art might be transported wholly to England." Elgin, who of course had not even been to Athens, seized on the idea and wrote to Lord Keith to ask for a ship to call there.

I have been at a monstrous expense at Athens where I at this moment possess advantages beyond belief. . . . Now if you would allow a ship of war of size to convoy the Commissary's ship and stop a couple of days at Athens to get away a most valuable piece of architecture at my disposal there you could confer upon me the greatest obligation I could receive and do a very essential service to the Arts in England. Bonaparte has not got such a thing from all his thefts in Italy. Pray kindly attend to this my Lord."

But for the time being no ship could be spared and, for the time being, the Caryatid porch survived. The artists had to content themselves with sawing off choice pieces selected to illustrate the various details. . . .

. . . Some of the removals were not very skilful. The blocks on which the metopes and frieze were carved were an integral part of the structure of the building and could not easily be separated from it. In some cases, the buildings were damaged as the artists attempted to get at the sculptures.

The traveller Edward Dodwell was a witness of these attempts. He had benefited from Hunt's firman and spent his days sketching on the Acropolis. He was now on the best of terms with the new Disdar, to whom he gave a bottle of wine (forbidden to Moslems) whenever his dinner was sent up. He wrote:

During my first tour to Greece I had the inexpressible mortification of being present when the Parthenon was despoiled of its finest sculpture, and when some of its architectural members were thrown to the ground. I saw several metopae at the south east extremity of the temple taken down. They were fixed in between the triglyphs as in a groove; and in order to lift them up, it was necessary to throw to the ground the magnificent cornice by which they were covered. The south east angle of the pediment shared the same fate; and instead of the picturesque beauty and high preservation in which I first saw it, it is now comparatively reduced to a state of shattered desolation. . . .

There can be no doubt that the Parthenon suffered severely as a result of Lusieri's efforts. Virtually the whole of the surviving cornice on the south side was thrown to the ground to allow the metopes to be extracted. A drawing made by William Gell in 1801 during the first removals show the cornice at both ends of the colonnade almost complete and the metopes well preserved underneath: a water-colour by Hobhouse painted in 1810 looks very sad by comparison—the cornice and metopes have entirely disappeared. All that was then left of the best cornice of the Parthenon was a series of jagged blocks sticking up like broken teeth.

Elgin urged his agents on, telling them to dig and buy and take away. No effort or money was to be spared to get what was wanted from the Acropolis and that work was to have priority over everything else. Lady Elgin instructed Lusieri to put about a story that she had a new set of powerful firmans which settled any lingering doubts about the legality of the removals. Individual Greeks who were unwilling to sell their antiquities at a reasonable price were brought before the Voivode and compulsory purchase orders were issued. By 2 June Lady Elgin was able to announce, "We yesterday got down to the last thing we want from Acropolis so now we may boldly bid defiance to our enemies." In the ten months since Hunt first arrived with the firman more than half of the Parthenon sculptures in the Elgin collection had been taken from the Acropolis. They included at least seven metopes, about twenty slabs of the frieze, and almost all the surviving figures from the pediments.

At Athens throughout the summer and autumn of 1802 more removals and excavations took place. Six continuous slabs of the Parthenon frieze were taken from the building and two more metopes. Another slab of the frieze was discovered in excavations. Four slabs of the frieze of the Temple of Athena Nike were discovered built into the fortifications of the Acropolis and successfully removed. Examples of all the architectural details were taken—capitals, bases, cornices, and pieces of pillar from the Parthenon, the Propylaea, the Erechtheum, and the Temple of Nike: the piece of the Parthenon capital had to be sawn in two before it could be moved.

The haste with which everything had to be done caused a few more casualties. On 16 September Lusieri reported "I have, my Lord, the pleasure of announcing to you the possession of the 8th metope that one where there is the Centaur carrying off the woman. This piece has caused much trouble in all respects and I have even been obliged to be a little barbarous." The barbarity was no doubt the destruction of part of the building as had been necessary several months before with other metopes in the presence of Dodwell and Clarke. Another slab of the frieze— the great central slab on the east side—was taken from the Acropolis wall to which it had been built many years before. On its way down to the Piraeus it broke into two pieces in a straight line down the middle: fortunately it broke at a place where there was no carving.

So the Elgin collection continued to grow. A seemingly inexhaustible amount of money was poured into Athens, and horses, telescopes, and shawls were heaped on the Voivode and Disdar until even they must have had enough. Perhaps most important of all, Elgin obtained from the Porte written documents saying that the Turkish Government approved of all that the Voivode and Disdar had done on his behalf. These documents were intended to reassure the Voivode and Disdar that they would be protected if policy changed in favour of France. Lusieri handed over the documents as one of the bribes. It is a pity no copy has survived: they would seem to prove Elgin's contention that the Turkish Government condoned everything he did. . . .

In the eighteen months between the obtaining of the firman and his departure for home Lord Elgin had done all that he had set out to do and far more. The indifference of the Turks, the jealousy of travellers, and the intrigues of the French had all been overcome. The buildings of Athens had been drawn, measured and moulded in detail never before attempted and the greatest part of the best surviving sculpture had been moved into his storehouses. Much of it was already on its way home and there was good hope of recovering the rest. It was a stupendous achievement.

PURCHASE BY PARLIAMENT

The following excerpts are from the debate in the House of Commons on June 7, 1816, when the government brought in a bill to purchase the Elgin Marbles from Lord Elgin for £25,000.

HOUSE OF COMMONS *June 7, 1816, Debate**

Mr. *Hammersley* said, he should oppose the resolution on the ground of the dishonesty of the transaction by which the collection was obtained. As to the value of the statues, he was inclined to go as far as the hon. mover, but he was not so enamoured of those headless ladies as to forget another lady, which was justice. If a restitution of these marbles was demanded from this country, was it supposed that our title to them could be supported on the vague words of the firmaun, which only gave authority to remove some small pieces of stone? It was well known that the empress Catharine had entertained the idea of establishing the Archduke Constantine in Greece. If the project of that extraordinary woman should ever be accomplished, and Greece ranked among independent nations with what feelings, would she contemplate the people who had stripped her most celebrated temple of its noblest ornaments? . . .

But whether the Turks set any value on them or no, the question would not be altered, as his objection was founded on the unbecoming manner in which they had been obtained. It was in the evidence of the noble earl himself, that at the time when he had demanded permission to remove these statues, the Turkish government was in a situation to grant anything which this country might ask on account of the efforts which we had made against the French in Egypt. It thus appeared that a British ambassador had taken advantage of our success over the French to plunder the city of Athens. The Earl of Aberdeen had stated that no private traveller would have been able to have obtained leave to remove them. But the most material evidence respecting the manner in which these statues had been obtained, was that of Dr. Hunt, who stated, that when the firmaun was delivered to the waywode, presents were also given him. It thus appeared that bribery had been employed, and he lamented that the clergyman alluded to should have made himself an agent in the transaction. It was his opinion that we should restore what we had taken away. . . .

It was to be regretted that the government had not restrained this act of spoliation; but, as it had been committed, we should exert ourselves to wipe off the stain, and not place in our museum a monument of our disgrace, but at once return the bribe which our ambassador had received, to his own dishonour and that of the country. He should

* *Hansard Parliamentary Debates,* 1st ser. (1816), pp. 1031–1033, 1035–1037.

propose as an amendment, a resolution, which stated—"That this committee having taken into its consideration the manner in which the Earl of Elgin became possessed of certain ancient sculptured marbles from Athens, laments that this ambassador did not keep in remembrance that the high and dignified station of representing his sovereign should have made him forbear from availing himself of that character in order to obtain valuable posessions belonging to the government to which he was accredited; and that such forbearance was peculiarly necessary at a moment when that government was expressing high obligations to Great Britain. This committee, however, imputes to the noble earl no venal motive whatever of pecuniary advantage to himself, but on the contrary, believes that he was actuated by a desire to benefit his country, by acquiring for it, at great risk and labour to himself, some of the most valuable specimens in existence of ancient sculpture. This committee, therefore, feels justified, under the particular circumstances of the case, in recommending that £25,000 be offered to the Earl of Elgin for the collection in order to recover and keep it together for that government from which it has been improperly taken, and to which this committee is of opinion that a communication should be immediately made, stating, that Great Britain holds these marbles only in trust till they are demanded by the present, or any future, possessors of the city of Athens, and upon such demand, engages, without question or negotiation, to restore them, as far as can be effected, to the places from whence they were taken, and that they shall be in the mean time carefully preserved in the British Museum."

[IN SUPPORT OF THE RESOLUTION . . .]

With regard to the spoliation, the sacrilegious rapacity, on which the last speaker had descanted so freely, he would say a few words in favour of the noble lord, in which he would be borne out by the evidence in the report. The noble lord had shown no principle of rapacity. He laid his hand on nothing that could have been preserved in any state of repair: he touched nothing that was not previously in ruins. He went into Greece with no design to commit ravages on her works of art, to carry off her ornaments, to despoil her temples. His first intention was to take drawings of her celebrated architectural monuments, or models of her works of sculpture. This part of his design he had to a certain extent executed, and many

drawings and models were found in his collection. Nothing else entered into his contemplation, till he saw that many of the pieces of which his predecessors in this pursuit had taken drawings had entirely disappeared, that some of them were buried in ruins, and others converted into the materials of building. No less than 18 pieces of statuary from the western pediment had been entirely destroyed since the time when M. de Nointel, the French ambassador, had procured his interesting drawings to be made; and when his lordship purchased a house in the ruins of which he expected to find some of them, and had proceeded to dig under its foundation with such a hope, the malicious Turk to whom he had given the purchase-money observed, "The statues you are digging for are pounded into mortar, and I could have told you so before you began your fruitless labour." [Hear, hear!]—Ought not the hon. gentleman who had spoken so much about spoliation to have mentioned this fact? Ought he not to have stated that it was then, and not till then, that Lord Elgin resolved to endeavour to save what still remained from such wanton barbarity? Had he read the report, and did he know the circumstances without allowing any apology for the noble earl? Did he not know that many of the articles taken from the Parthenon, were found among its ruins? More than one-third of that noble building was rubbish before he touched it. The hon. member (Mr. Hammersley) had referred to the evidence of the member of Northallerton (Mr. Morrit); but while he quoted one part of it, he had forgotten another, by which that quotation would have been explained and qualified. He had visited Athens in 1796; and when he returned five years afterwards, he found the greatest dilapidations. In his first visit he stated, that there were 8 or ten fragments on the pediment, with a car and horses not entire, but distinguishable: but when he returned, neither car nor horses were to be seen, and all the figures were destroyed but two. If the hon. member, whose statement he was combating, had read the evidence carefully, he would have seen that Lord Elgin interfered with nothing that was not already in ruins, or that was threatened with immediate destruction. The temple of Theseus was in a state of great preservation, and therefore, proceeding on this principle, he had left it as he found it, and only enriched this country with models and drawings taken from it. Much had been said of the manner in which Lord Elgin had prostituted his ambassadorial character to obtain possession of the monuments in question. There was no ground for such an imputation. Not a piece had been removed from Athens till Lord Elgin had returned, and of course till his official influence ceased. Signor Lucieri was even now employed there under his lordship's orders; and was he still prostituting the ambassadorial character? When his lordship was a prisoner in France, the work was still going on; and was he then prostituting the ambassadorial character? His lordship had remained after his return at his seat in Scotland; and was the character of ambassador injured in his person during his retirement? He (Mr. Croker) might have shown some warmth in defending the opinion of the committee, and removing the imputation thrown upon the noble person whose character had been attacked by the hon. member: but he hoped he would be excused, when the nature of the charges which had excited him were considered.—He could not sit in his place, and hear such terms as dishonesty, plunder, spoliation, bribery, and others of the same kind, applied to the conduct of a British nobleman, who was so far from deserving them that he merited the greatest praise, and to the nature of transactions by which so great a benefit was conferred upon the country, without any ground for a charge of rapacity or spoliation. But if the charges of improper conduct on Lord Elgin's part were groundless, the idea of sending them back to the Turks was chimerical and ridiculous. This would be awarding those admirable works the doom of destruction. The work of plunder and dilapidation was proceeding with rapid strides, and we were required again to subject the monuments that we had rescued to its influence. Of 20 statues that decorated the western pediments of the Parthenon, only seven miserable fragments were preserved: yet this part of the building was almost perfect at the beginning of last century; now only a few worthless pieces of marble were preserved—he called them worthless, not as compared with the productions of art in other countries, but in comparison with what had been lost. They would, however, remain to animate the genius and improve the arts of this country, and to constitute in after times a sufficient answer to the speech of the hon. member, or of any one else who should use his arguments, if indeed such arguments could be supposed to be repeated, or to be heard beyond the bottle hour in which they were made. . . .

The House divided: For the original Motion, 82; Against it, 30.

COMMENTS

1. Lord Elgin and his marbles stirred passions outside the halls of Parliament as well. The poet Byron attacked Lord Elgin in *The Curse of Minerva* as a "spoiler" worse than ravaging "Turk or Goth." He pursued this theme in *Childe Harolde*:

> But most the modern Pict's ignoble boast,
> To rive what Goth, and Turk, and Time hath spared:
> Cold as the crags upon his native coast,
> His mind as barren as his heart is hard,
> Is he whose head conceived, whose hand prepared,
> Aught to displace Athena's poor remains:
> Her sons too weak the sacred shrine to guard,
> Yet felt some portion of their mother's pains,
> And never knew, till then, the weight of despot's chains.

> What! shall it e'er be said by British tongue,
> Albion was happy in Athena's tears?
> Though in thy name the slaves her bosom wrung,
> Tell not the deed to blushing Europe's ears;
> The ocean queen, the free Britannia, bears,
> The last poor plunder from a bleeding land:
> Yes, she, whose generous aid her name endears,
> Tore down those remnants with a harpy's hand,
> Which envious Eld forbore, and tyrants left to stand.

A "Pict" is a Scotsman. Byron is careful to dissociate England from any responsibility for the plunder, but he is quick to condemn Scotland, "a land of meanness, sophistry, and mist."

Childe Harolde's Pilgrimage was an immediate best-seller in several languages. Byron was a romantic figure in the Romantic period and became a martyr in the Greek struggle for independence from four centuries of Ottoman rule. (He was also a noted graffitist, as any visitor to the temple at Sounion will have observed.) Byron's characterization of Elgin and of the removal of the Marbles had a powerful and lasting effect on public attitudes, which are by now built into Western culture in a variety of ways. An example is the term *Elginisme,* coined by the French to refer to a "*forme de vandalisme*" of cultural objects (*Grande Larousse de la langue française,* vol. 2 [Paris: Larousse, 1972]). In the 1980s Melina Mercouri, a Greek minister of culture, led a campaign for return of the Marbles to Athens, basing the Greek claim in part on the prevailing assumption that the taking was illegal or immoral or both. The Greek government formally requested their return in 1983. The British government formally rejected the request in 1984.

2. Was the taking illegal? In considering this question, recall that Athens had been a part of the Ottoman Empire for four centuries. The Acropolis of Athens was public property, and its sovereign resided in Constantinople. That sovereign and his local representatives appear to have authorized, tolerated, and/or ratified Elgin's action. If the appropriate state authority disposes of state property, whether by gift or otherwise, the transaction would appear to be legal, and the property belongs to the transferee. (But what of the use of bribery in dealing with Ottoman officials? What of Elgin's dual status as British minister to the Ottoman court and private acquirer of the Marbles?)

3. Was the taking, even if legal, morally wrong? Here a variety of factors seem relevant. What would have happened to the Marbles if Elgin had not taken them? Would the French or the Bavarians, who were avidly pursuing antiquities, have gotten them? If the Marbles had been left in place, would they have been further depleted by souvenir-hunters or destroyed by Ottoman misuse or negligence? (Recall that the Ottomans used the Parthenon as a powder magazine and that it was badly damaged by an explosion during an attack by Venetian forces in 1687.) If they had not otherwise been depleted or destroyed, would they have been eroded by the smog of Athens (which has had a disastrous effect on the remaining works in the Acropolis, to the point that they have had to be taken indoors to protect them)? The Elgin Marbles, by contrast, have been safe and—except for a period of overzealous cleaning that removed traces of the original paint and damaged the original surfaces—well-maintained in London. To have saved such great works from damage or destruction is certainly admirable, but what of the damage to the fabric of the Parthenon itself? (Recall Lusieri's admission that he had to be "a little barbarous.")

4. What of Elgin's motivation? Elgin wanted to show Europe that classical Greek art was superior to the then-prevailing Roman ideal, typified by the Apollo Belvedere in the Vatican Museum. He wanted to elevate the arts in Great Britain and to educate British taste. These objectives, and an evaluation of the actual impact of the Marbles on taste and the arts in Europe and England, are discussed in Jacob Rothenberg, "*Descensus ad Terram*": *The Acquisition and Reception of the Elgin Marbles* (New York: Garland, 1977).

5. What was in it for Elgin? It is clear that he never hoped to make a profit from the venture, though he probably hoped to recover expenses. But in fact the Marbles ruined him. The £35,000 paid by the Crown were far less than he had spent, and the entire sum went to his creditors. Elgin died in poverty, an expatriate recluse in France. Should we think of Elgin as one who saved a great cultural treasure at great personal cost? Or should we see his end as divine retribution, the Curse of Athena (the Parthenon was a temple to Pallas Athena)?

6. It is possible to argue, as Minister Mercouri has done ("The British say that they have saved the Marbles. Well, thank you *very* much. Now give them back."), that the Marbles should be returned to Greece even if they were taken legally and morally. We will examine that argument in the discussion of repatriation in the next chapter.

7. For further reading on the Elgin Marbles, see John Henry Merryman, "Thinking About the Elgin Marbles," *Mich. L. Rev.,* vol. 83 (1985), p. 1880.

LOOTING AND THE INTERNATIONAL LAW OF WAR

Although one sees occasional statements to the effect that traditional international law permitted the victor to loot, pillage, and plunder the loser (see, e.g., Gentile, *De iure belli* [1538], 3.3–7), it is better to consider such statements fabrications by treatise writers seeking to construct complete systems of international law. In fact, international law has grown up by bits and pieces and is still growing. Until late in the nineteenth century there was no developed body of international law specifically referable to looting. International law neither condoned nor condemned the practice; the area was only one of a number of lacunae in the field.

However, history provides many expressions about the desirability of the practice of looting. Predictably, it has been condemned by losers (or prospective losers) and justified by winners (or prospective winners, like imperial powers). More to the point, however, have been the comments of third persons not identified with either side. Almost without exception they have opposed or tried to limit the practice, from Polybius of Athens forward. This ethical attitude began to crystallize into something resembling law in the eighteenth century. We will see, for example, that Napoleon took the trouble to "legalize" his plunder of Italian art by expressly providing for it in the treaties imposed on the capitulating Italians. Concern about the legality of looting gained great momentum in the nineteenth century, when attitudes about war and about the inviolability of national sovereignty began to undergo drastic change away from the extremes of state-worship and justification of war found in sixteenth- to eighteenth-century political thought. That evolution, which is still going on, has had as one component a series of attempts to prevent and limit war and to control the actions of the belligerents and protect neutrals when war does occur. One of the first attempts by nations to set out an agreed coherent statement of the laws of war was the "Declaration of Brussels" of 1874. This declaration, which was never adopted as a multilateral convention because of the resistance of Great Britain and hence never became binding on the parties, was the product of an international conference of fifteen states called on the initiative of the Russian government. Article VIII (of the total of fifty-six articles) reads:

> The Property of parishes (communes), or establishments devoted to religion, charity, education, arts and sciences, although belonging to the State, shall be treated as private property.
>
> Every seizure, destruction of, or wilful damage to, such establishments, historical monuments, or works of art or of science, should be prosecuted by the competent authorities.

In the United States, Professor Francis Lieber of Columbia College prepared a field manual on the laws and customs of war for use by Union military commanders in the Civil War. It was adopted by the Union army, was widely admired and copied in Europe, and was the precedent for the Declaration of Brussels and for "Manual of the Laws and Customs of War" adopted by the Institute of International Law (a prestigious organization of scholars of international law) in 1880. Article 53 (of 86) of that manual reads:

> The property of municipalities, and that of institutions devoted to religion, charity, education, art and science, cannot be seized.
>
> All destruction or wilful damage to institutions of this character, historic monuments, archives, works of art, or science, is formally forbidden, save when urgently demanded by military necessity.

In 1899, again at the initiative of the Russian government, a conference of twenty-six nations was convened at the Hague. This important conference produced a Convention on Pacific Settlement of International Disputes (Hague I, 1899) and a Convention on Laws and Customs of War on Land (Hague II, 1899). Annexed to the latter convention was a set of "Regulations Respecting the Laws and Customs of War on Land" (Hague II Regulations) in sixty articles, of which Article 56 reads:

> The property of the communes, that of religious, charitable, and educational institutions, and those of art and science, even when State property, shall be treated as private property.
>
> All seizure of, and destruction, or international damage done to such institutions, to

historical monuments, works of art or science, is prohibited, and should be made the subject of proceedings.

In 1907, at the initiative of the United States (President Theodore Roosevelt) and again of Russia, another conference was convened at the Hague, this time attended by forty-four nations. The "Convention on Laws and Customs of War on Land" (Hague IV, 1907) adopted at the conference has a set of annexed "Regulations Respecting the Laws and Customs of War on Land." This contains fifty-six articles, of which Article 56 reads:

> The property of municipalities, that of institutions dedicated to religion, charity and education, the arts and sciences even when State property, shall be treated as private property.
>
> All seizure of, destruction or wilful damage done to institutions of this character, historic monuments, works of art and science is forbidden, and should be made the subject of legal proceedings.*

The United States is a party to Hague IV, 1907. Later developments are described in the following materials.

NAPOLEON AND THE LOUVRE

CECIL GOULD *Trophies of Conquest*†

The Musée Napoléon was born of three parents, republicanism, anticlericalism and successful aggressive war. Since the beginning of the Christian era the greatest works of art in France as in most European countries had been executed either for the Church or for secular princes and nobility. When the French Revolution attempted to suppress the first and temporarily abolished the second a vast hoard of pictures and sculpture became available in the neighbourhood of Paris alone. In 1793 the Louvre was first opened as a public institution, the exhibits being drawn from elements of the royal collection, together with a quantity of works from the local churches. When, during the succeeding twenty years, most of the countries of Europe were successively overrun by the conquering French armies works of art were brought back to Paris as trophies of conquest to augment the splendours of the museum. . . .

Little more than a year after the Louvre was first opened as a museum the first convoy of confiscated works of art reached it from Belgium. The dates in themselves are close enough to suggest a connection, and this train of thought becomes more insistent when it is borne in mind

that in the earlier Netherlandish campaign, in 1792, though there had been a great deal of looting there had been virtually no question of official confiscations. In this respect the Belgian campaign of 1794 became the prototype for all the later Napoleonic wars. . . .

The procedure was now established. The Louvre, the Bibliothèque Nationale, the Jardin des Plantes and various other institutions both in Paris and the provinces were henceforth, it was assumed, to be offered the spoils of each country as it was overrun. This was to be carried out by teams of specialists sent out from Paris or recruited on the spot. It was taken for granted that Italy would sooner or later fall a victim and that her richest treasures would then be brought to Paris. Grégoire said as much in his speech of the 31st August 1794 when announcing the arrival of the Flemish pictures: "Certainly, if our victorious armies penetrate into Italy the removal of the Apollo Belvedere and of the Farnese Hercules would be the most brilliant conquest."

As early as the 16th October 1794 the *Commission Temporaire des Arts* had appointed a subcommittee of four members to compile full infor-

---

*The passage from the "Manual of the Laws and Customs of War" is found in James Brown Scott, ed., *Resolutions of the Institute of International Law*, ed. (New York: Oxford University Press, 1916), pp. 36–37. All other passages quoted above are from Leon Friedman (comp.), *The Law of War; a Documentary History* (New York: Random House, 1972), pp. 195, 234, 323.

†From Cecil Gould, *Trophy of Conquest* (London: Curtis Brown, Ltd., 1965), pp. 13, 30, 41, 43–48. Copyright 1965 by Curtis Brown, Ltd. Reprinted by permission.

mation concerning works of art and science to be found in countries which the republican armies were expected to invade. A fortnight later (31st October) Le Brun, evidently in this connection, produced details of works of art (mainly pictures) in public and private collections in Holland and the Rhineland. Later, on the 8th February, 1795, he submitted another catalogue, this time of pictures remaining in Belgium. . . .

Thoughts of art as the trophy of conquest were in Bonaparte's mind from an early stage of the Italian campaign. Less than two months after his appointment to the command (3rd March 1796) he signed an armistice with the king of Sardinia at Cherasco (28th April). He later confided to one of the Piedmontese plenipotentiaries (Costa) that he had wanted on this occasion to specify an oil painting by Gerard Dou in the king's collection—evidently the *Dropsical Woman* now in the Louvre which was inordinately celebrated at the time—as part of the indemnity which was to be paid to France. Though he had refrained, thinking it might be considered a "nouveauté bizarre," he evidently regretted it at once and determined it should not happen again. Three days later (1st May) he wrote from his headquarters at Acqui to his friend Faypoult, the minister of Genoa, "above all, send me a note of the pictures, statues and other collections to be found at Milan, Parma, Piacenza, Modena and Bologna." Five days afterwards (6th May) he wrote in the same sense from Tortona to the Directoire asking them to send him three or four artists. Before he could have received their reply he included in the armistice signed with the Duke of Parma at Piacenza on the 9th May a clause demanding the surrender of twenty pictures at the choice of the Commander-in-Chief. It was on the same day that he announced in letters to Paris that Correggio's *Madonna with S. Jerome* would be coming. . . .

Delacroix said that the clause concerning the twenty pictures inserted by Bonaparte into the Parma armistice was a "nouveau trait qui vous distingue" (in his memoirs Napoleon claimed that the stipulation of works of art on this occasion for the benefit of the Louvre was an act unprecedented in modern history). . . .

The conqueror's path led roughly from west to east across the north of Italy. Following in some cases only a day or two behind Bonaparte himself the *commissaires,* during May and June 1796, visited and despoiled in succession Parma, Modena, Milan, Bologna and Cento. From each of the first two Bonaparte had demanded twenty pictures in the armistice terms. In the case of the last three

he seems to have been unspecific. While at Bologna, however, he signed an armistice agreement with the Pope's representative (23rd June) which gave him liberty to select a hundred pictures, busts, vases or statutes from Rome, together with five hundred manuscripts, as soon as he or the *commissaires* should get there. It was specified even at this stage that the bronze bust of Junius Brutus and the marble bust of Marcus Brutus should be included. Leaving the campaign to continue in the north the *commissaires* now headed for Rome, from which, on August 14, they listed eighty-three sculptures and seventeen paintings. The latter included three—a Perugino and two Raphaels—from the papal city of Perugia.

In September 1796 a further twenty-nine pictures were levied from Modena (much later still, in 1802, twenty-seven more pictures were levied from Parma on its incorporation into the Cisalpine Republic) and during the spring of 1797 some attention was paid to cities north of Rome which had hitherto been spared. In some cases the confiscations were imposed with punitive intent, notably at Verona, following a sanguinary revolt in April 1797, and in Rome, in 1798, as a result of the murder of General Duphot. At Perugia, in February, the *commissaire* Tinet, for reasons which are not entirely clear, so far exceeded the figure of three pictures specified in the preceding year as to take virtually everything that seemed to him worth taking—some thirty paintings, including the famous Raphael altarpiece from Foligno nearby (another Raphael removed soon afterwards, the so-called *Madonna of Loreto,* proved on arrival at Paris to be merely a copy: the fate of the original is still the subject of speculation). Conversely, Mantua, when it fell in February 1797 after a siege of many months, was treated lightly and got off with the loss of only four paintings. Venice, with whom Bonaparte had deliberately and cold-bloodedly picked a quarrel in May 1797, was called on to surrender twenty pictures and six hundred manuscripts. Tinet, the *commissaire* who had behaved so ruthlessly at Perugia, was careful, as one of the two active in Venice, to stick to the letter of the law; and though he managed to obtain approval for substituting two minor sculptures for two of the paintings he refrained from touching the celebrated bronze horses. Nevertheless they eventually reached Paris, together with the Lion of S. Mark. But they were not removed until after the *commissaires* had left Venice. Precisely what machinations had led to this is still not clear. . . .

DOROTHY MACKAY QUYNN *Art Confiscations of the Napoleonic Wars**

The French sense of the dramatic has resulted in many magnificent and impressive victory celebrations in Paris, but none has ever eclipsed that of the ninth and tenth Thermidor of the Year VI of the first French Republic (July 27 and 28, 1798).

The occasion was the arrival in Paris of the first convoy of art treasures confiscated by Napoleon during his Italian campaign. . . .

In these crates there traveled to Paris such treasures as the Apollo Belvedere, the Medici Venus, the Discobolus, the Dying Gladiator, the Laocoön, and sixty or more other pieces of sculpture from the Vatican and Capitoline museums and other collections. Nine paintings by Raphael, two famous Correggios, mineral and natural history collections, the bears of Bern, animals from zoos, and valuable manuscripts including those from the Vatican dated prior to A.D. 900. The popular interests were catered to by the inclusion of the animals and of such famous religious relics as the miracle-working wooden Virgin of Loreto, attributed to Luke; but the main purpose of Napoleon was to bring to Paris as many of the art treasures of Europe as he could. People justified this not only by the doctrine that the spoils of war belong to the victors but by more obscure theories. A petition had been sent to the Directory in October, 1796, signed by almost all of the great French artists of the day, in which it was argued that

The more our climate seems unfavorable to the arts, the more do we require models here in order to overcome the obstacles to the progress thereof. . . . The Romans, once an uncultivated people, became civilized by transplanting to Rome the works of conquered Greece. . . . Thus . . . the French people . . . naturally endowed with exquisite sensitivity, will . . . by seeing the models from antiquity, train its feeling and its critical sense. . . . The French Republic, by its strength and superiority of its enlightenment and its artists, is the only country in the world which can give a safe home to these masterpieces. All other Nations must come to borrow from our art, as they once imitated our frivolity.

And a lieutenant of Hussars who had escorted a collection from Belgium some years earlier made a speech to the Convention in which he said that works of art had been "soiled too long by slavery"

and that "These immortal works are no longer on foreign soil. They are brought to the homeland of arts and genius, to the homeland of liberty and sacred equality, the French Republic." Napoleon himself wrote from Milan in 1796, "all men of genius, all those who have attained distinction in the republic of letters, are French no matter in what country they may have been born." And a French general whose book appeared in English translation in 1799, wrote as follows:

. . . statues which the French have taken from the degenerate Roman Catholic to adorn the museum of Paris, and to distinguish by the most noble of trophies, the triumph of liberty over tyranny, and philosophy over superstition. Real conquests are those made in behalf of the arts, the sciences and taste, and they are the only ones capable of consoling for the misfortune of being compelled to undertake them from other motives.

The "Muséum français," where the works of art were to be installed, was already in existence in the Louvre. The treasures from Italy and the Low Countries were the beginning of a long procession of "conquests" which continued until the return of the Bourbons. At the time of the first abdication of Napoleon, wagonloads of pictures confiscated in Spain had just crossed the border and halted at Bayonne. . . .

When the tide finally turned in their favor, the owners of the collections plundered by Napoleon lost no time in trying to get their property back. Napoleon abdicated at Fontainebleau on April 6, 1814.

The pope, on April 19, negotiated successfully for the return of his archives, and on April 27, Daunou, director of the archives in Paris, was ordered to restore the documents emanating from the Papal States, as well as a number of articles used in papal ceremonies.

After the return from Elba and the defeat of Napoleon at Waterloo, the powers were less reticent in their behavior towards the French and their king. The French, aware of this, tried to get a clause inserted in the Convention of Paris of July 3, 1815, to "guarantee the integrity of museums and libraries." The Allies refused flatly to accept such a provision. For one thing, the French did not recognize the gesture of the previous year as a

*From Dorothy Mackay Quynn, "The Art Confiscations of the Napoleonic Wars," *American Historical Review*, vol. 50, no. 3 (April 1945), pp. 437–460. Reprinted by permission.

generous act. They merely accepted it as a deserved tribute to their importance.

To the great annoyance of the French, emissaries of the Dutch consul arrived at noon on September 18 to reclaim the posessions of the newly created state of the Netherlands. Some of the finest paintings had come from Antwerp, The Hague, Amsterdam, and religious establishments in Holland and Belgium. Denon wrote to Metternich and others in protest, and in his letter to Talleyrand, September 16, he said,

If we yield to the claims of Holland and Belgium, we deprive the Museum of one of its greatest assets, that of having a series of excellent colorists. . . . Russia is not hostile, Austria has had everything returned, Prussia has a restoration more complete. . . . There remains only England, who has in truth nothing to claim, but who, since she had just bought the bas-relief of which Lord Elgin plundered the Temple at Athens, now thinks she can become a rival of the Museum [Louvre], and wants to deplete this Museum in order to collect the remains [for herself]. . . .

On August 5, Metternich had asked for the return of the Austrian and Venetian treasures. On September 20, in Vienna, Austria, England, and Prussia agreed that all art objects should be returned to their original owners. The tsar was not a party to this agreement. Castlereagh said that the tsar wanted a compromise between Louis XVIII and the claimants. It has now been found, however, that the tsar had secretly purchased from Napoleon's relatives a number of valuable paintings for the Hermitage. He had received, by gift or purchase from Josephine, the valuable Vatican cameo of Ptolemy and Arsinoë. He would not wish for a restoration under these circumstances. . . .

How successful were the restorations? It is difficult to say. Many articles were damaged and even lost. Others, sent to the provinces or otherwise disposed of, were difficult or impossible to reclaim. . . .

The winged lion from St. Mark's in Venice had been placed on a fountain in the Esplanade des Invalides. When the workmen attempted to remove it, it was dropped, and broke in a thousand pieces, much to the delight of the jeering mob. Some Italian primitives were seriously damaged during the journey to Paris. The enormous canvas of Paul Veronese, the "Marriage at Cana," had been torn in two during the journey from Venice to Paris, and it had been restored in such a way as to make it even more difficult to move. In fact,

Napoleon had ordered it moved on the occasion of his marriage to Marie Louise and was so much annoyed at the difficulty that he had angrily ordered it burned—the orders were of course ignored. But it could not be returned to Venice, at least the Austrians were convinced that this was the case, and a painting by Lebrun was accepted as a substitute.

Several pieces of sculpture were considered too cumbersome and expensive to move. Canova agreed to give up the Tiber, the Melpomene and some others for this reason. . . .

One large group, the Quadriga, brought from the Brandenburg gate in Berlin to adorn Napoleon's projected "Temple of Victory," was successfully recovered and taken back to Berlin.

Some paintings were completely lost. The Prussians claimed that two valuable canvases, Rubens' "Diogenes," and Jordaens' "The King Drinks," were taken by the French, who claim to know nothing about them. They have never been found. One of the many risks encountered in the course of the restorations is suggested by the report of the Belgian commissioners to a museum official that an unidentified foreigner had offered them ten thousand francs to steal a certain painting, the money to be paid as soon as the painting was out of the building. . . .

The French were very bitter about the restoration of the treasures. They echoed the attitude expressed by Stendhal in connection with the return of one group to Italy. He said, "The Allies have *taken* eleven hundred fifty pictures. I hope I may be permitted to observe that we acquired them *by a treaty, that of Tolentino.* . . . On the other hand, the Allies have taken our pictures, *without treaty.*" In other words, the French acquisitions were legalized by treaties; the allied seizures were confiscations.

Nothing could be done about articles which had been sold, and in some cases important items were involved. One case, that of the collection of Empress Josephine, illustrates all too well the problems faced under such circumstances. . . .

Paintings had been hung in various palaces, but Josephine's favorite palace, Malmaison, which was her private property, contained an especially fine collection. Its most famous contents were the pictures brought from Cassel in 1806, forty-eight according to the records, but only thirty-six were admitted by Josephine to have arrived, the others being lost. Napoleon later ordered Denon to take these paintings to the Louvre, but he never succeeded in getting them, as Josephine insisted that they had been given her as an outright gift. When the Hessians went to Malmaison in 1815 to get their paintings from the heirs of Josephine, they were told that the finest pieces in the collection had been sold to Tsar Alexander for 940,000 francs. It is not clear whether this had happened just before or just after her death on May 29, 1814. The tsar refused to give them up, and many of them adorn the Hermitage in Leningrad today. This remarkable coup explains the tsar's stubborn refusals to join his allies in their efforts to return art treasures to the original owners. . . .

Some of the finest galleries in Europe contain paintings which were purchased in Paris at this time. The Glyptothek of Munich consisted at first almost entirely of articles from the confiscated collection of the Villa Albani, purchased in Paris. The treasures of the Giustiniani gallery found their way to Prussia, also via Paris. Others went to England, and the Leningrad collection has already been mentioned. As a dispersal of art treasures, no previous upheaval could rival it in quantity, at least during a similar period of time.

COMMENTS

1. In the excerpts from *Trophy of Conquest,* Gould states, "Tinet . . . was careful . . . to stick to the letter of the law." What does he mean by this?

2. As in the case of the Elgin Marbles, the French plunder of Europe through military force excited strong feelings. Poets declaimed and intellectuals argued. Some emphasized the benefit to a larger public of mounting and publicly displaying so great a concentration of important works of art that had formerly been widely dispersed, often among private holders, and visible only to the few. The French defended their behavior on a variety of grounds: compensation for the blood and toil of French soldiers; the cultural superiority of France, which made it only right that great art be brought and kept there; if France did not "give a home" to Italian cultural treasures they would be acquired by England or the tsar through purchase; they had been ceded to France in treaties and they were now legally French; and so on. Others referred to the French actions as those of "a band of practiced robbers" and "hordes of thieves." For a discussion of the varying reactions, see Wilhelm Treue, *Art Plunder: The Fate of Works of Art in War and Unrest* (New York: John Day, 1961), pp. 175ff.

3. What effect should express cession of artworks in peace treaties with the Italian states have had on the question whether Napoleon (and France) was ethically or legally entitled to take those works to Paris? This raises the more general problem of the effect to be given treaties of peace following armed conflict. Until recently the rule was that although the capitulating nation was coerced by superior armed force into the agreement it was nonetheless bound by it under international law. However, the view now is that a new rule has emerged as the result of post–World War I international agreements outlawing aggressive war (see Articles 2 and 51 of the United Nations Charter). Under this view a treaty imposed by an aggressor nation would not be legally binding on the loser.

4. Does the emergence of this new rule of international law mean that works of art acquired by aggressor nations under the old rule must now be returned? The generally acknowledged authority on this subject—the Vienna Convention on the Law of Treaties—seems to answer no. The convention was adopted on May 22, 1969, by the United Nations Conference on the Law of Treaties. Article 64 says that if a new "norm of general international law emerges, any existing treaty which is in conflict with that norm becomes void and terminates." But Article 71(2) says that such a termination does not in any way affect "the legal situation of the parties created through the execution of the treaty prior to its termination." The Convention is reprinted in *International Legal Materials,* vol. 8 (1969), pp. 679ff.

5. What were Napoleon's motives in plundering Europe? Would you describe them as "worthy motives"? Is the magnificent collection of works in the Louvre (even after partial restorations to the plundered nations) its own justification, an achievement that rises above the offenses to morals, if not to international law, committed by the French armies? In a conflict between art and morals, which should prevail?

THE EINSATZSTAB ROSENBERG

The most recent case of systematic art-looting on a large scale was carried out by the German Nazis in World War II. They began with the wholesale appropriation and destruction of so-called "degenerate" or "depraved" art within Germany itself. (The definition of degenerate art [*entarte kunst*] was broad enough to include works by many of the best contemporary artists, works by Jewish artists, and works in Jewish collections. The episode is described more fully in Chapter 4.) As the German armies invaded and occupied other nations, this policy was extended, first to the property of Jews and then indiscriminately to works that Nazi party officials, principally Hitler and Göring, directed to be seized and transported to Germany. The operation was placed in the hands of a "special unit" (*Einsatzstab*) directed by another high Nazi official, Alfred Rosenberg, which was separate from the German military and uninhibited by the military's policy against art looting. The quantity of material taken and shipped to Germany was enormous. Rosenberg produced an illustrated catalog of thirty-nine volumes, with about 2,500 photographs, of works seized. If the entire body of loot had been photographed and cataloged it would have run to about three hundred volumes. The story is told at length in Wilhelm Treue, *Art Plunder: The Fate of Works of Art in War and Unrest* (New York: John Day, 1961), pp. 238ff., and in the following materials.

The trial of major war crimes by the victorious Allied powers, held in Nuremberg, Germany, following World War II, was an important event in the development of public international law. Up to that time the theory had been that only states were subjects of international law and that hence only states were responsible. Individuals might be civilly or criminally liable for their actions under national laws, but public international law did not deal with them. The Allied powers in the Nuremberg Trials (and later in the trials of Japanese war criminals) announced and applied a different principle: certain acts in violation of the laws of war would be charged to the responsible individuals.

Alfred Rosenberg was one of the defendants at Nuremberg. The catalog of offenses charged against him was substantial. We here set out only those portions of the indictment and judgment directly relevant to the Nazi appropriation and destruction of art and cultural treasures.

Indictment in the Nuremberg Trials*

All the defendants, with divers other persons, during a period of years preceding 8 May 1945, participated as leaders, organizers, instigators, or accomplices in the formulation or execution of a common plan or conspiracy to commit, or which involved the commission of, Crimes against Peace, War Crimes, and Crimes against Humanity, as defined in the Charter of this Tribunal, and, in accordance with the provisions of the Charter, are individually responsible for their own acts and for all acts committed by any persons in the execution of such plan or conspiracy. . . .

In the development and course of the common plan or conspiracy it came to embrace the commission of War Crimes, in that it contemplated, and the defendants determined upon and carried out, ruthless wars against countries and populations, in violation of the rules and customs of war, including as typical and systematic means by which the wars were prosecuted, murder, ill-

*From *Trial of the Major War Criminals Before the International Military Tribunal* (Nuremberg, 1948), vol. 1, pp. 29, 55–56, 58–60.

treatment, deportation for slave labor and for other purposes of civilian populations of occupied territories, murder and ill-treatment of prisoners of war and of persons on the high seas, the taking and killing of hostages, the plunder of public and private property, the indiscriminate destruction of cities, towns, and villages, and devastation not justified by military necessity. . . .

PLUNDER OF PUBLIC AND PRIVATE PROPERTY

The defendants ruthlessly exploited the people and the material resources of the countries they occupied, in order to strengthen the Nazi war machine, to depopulate and impoverish the rest of Europe, to enrich themselves and their adherents, and to promote German economic supremacy over Europe.

The defendants engaged in the following acts and practices, among others:

   . . . .

8. In further development of their plan of criminal exploitation, they destroyed industrial cities, cultural monuments, scientific institutions, and property of all types in the occupied territories to eliminate the possibility of competition with Germany.

   . . . .

These acts were contrary to international conventions, particularly Articles 46 to 56 inclusive of the Hague Regulations, 1907, the laws and customs of war, the general principles of criminal law as derived from the criminal laws of all civilized nations, the internal penal laws of the countries in which such crimes were committed and to Article 6(b) of the Charter.

Particulars (by way of example and without prejudice to the production of evidence of other cases) are as follows:

1. Western Countries:

There was plundered from the Western Countries, from 1940 to 1944, works of art, artistic objects, pictures, plastics, furniture, textiles, antique pieces, and similar articles of enormous value to the number of 21,903. . . .

LOOTING AND DESTRUCTION OF WORKS OF ART

The museums of Nantes, Nancy, Old-Marseilles were looted.

Private collections of great value were stolen. In this way Raphaels, Vermeers, Van Dycks, and works of Rubens, Holbein, Rembrandt, Watteau, Boucher disappeared. Germany compelled France to deliver up "The Mystic Lamb" by Van Eyck, which Belgium had entrusted to her.

In Norway and other occupied countries decrees were made by which the property of many civilians, societies, etc., was confiscated. An immense amount of property of every kind was plundered from France, Belgium, Norway, Holland, and Luxembourg. . . .

2. Eastern Countries:

During the occupation of the Eastern Countries the German Government and the German High Command carried out, as a systematic policy, a continuous course of plunder and destruction including:

On the territory of the Soviet Union the Nazi conspirators destroyed or severely damaged 1,710 cities and more than 70,000 villages and hamlets, more than 6,000,000 buildings and made homeless about 25,000,000 persons.

Among the cities which suffered most destruction are Stalingrad, Sevastopol, Kiev, Minsk, Odessa, Smolensk, Novgorod, Pskov, Orel, Kharkov, Voronezh, Rostov-on-Don, Stalino, and Leningrad. . . .

As is evident from an official memorandum of the German command, the Nazi conspirators planned the complete annihilation of entire Soviet cities. In a completely secret order of the Chief of the Naval Staff (Staff Ia No. 1601/41, dated 29. IX. 1941) addressed only to Staff officers, it was said:

The Führer has decided to erase from the face of the earth St. Petersburg. The existence of this large city will have no further interest after Soviet Russia is destroyed. Finland has also said that the existence of this city on her new border is not desirable from her point of view. The original request of the Navy that docks, harbor, etc. necessary for the fleet be preserved—is known to the Supreme Commander of the Military Forces, but the basic principles of carrying out operations against St. Petersburg do not make it possible to satisfy this request.

It is proposed to approach near to the city and to destroy it with the aid of an artillery barrage from weapons of different calibers and with long air attacks. . . .

The problem of the life of the population and the provisioning of them is a problem which cannot and must not be decided by us.

In this war . . . we are not interested in preserving even a part of the population of this large city.

The Germans destroyed 427 museums, among them the wealthy museums of Leningrad, Smolensk, Stalingrad, Novgorod, Poltava, and others.

In Pyatigorsk the art objects brought there from the Rostov museum were seized.

Stealing of huge dimensions and the destruction of industrial, cultural, and other property was typified in Kiev. . . . A large number of artistic productions and valuables of different kinds were stolen and carried away.

Many valuable art productions were taken away from Riga.

The Germans approached monuments of culture, dear to the Soviet people, with special hatred. They broke up the estate of the poet Pushkin in Mikhailovskoye, desecrating his grave, and destroying the neighboring villages and the Svyatogor monastery.

They destroyed the estate and museum of Leo Tolstoy, "Yasnaya Polyana," and desecrated the grave of the great writer. They destroyed in Klin the museum of Tchaikovsky and in Penaty, the museum of the painter Repin and many others. . . .

Judgment in the Nuremberg Trials*

. . . The evidence relating to war crimes has been overwhelming in its volume and its detail. It is impossible for this Judgment adequately to review it, or to record the mass of documentary and oral evidence that has been presented. The truth remains that war crimes were committed on a vast scale, never before seen in the history of war. They were perpetrated in all the countries occupied by Germany, and on the high seas, and were attended by every conceivable circumstance of cruelty and horror. There can be no doubt that the majority of them arose from the Nazi conception of "total war," with which the aggressive wars were waged. For in this conception of "total war," the moral ideas underlying the conventions which seek to make war more humane are no longer regarded as having force or validity. Everything is made subordinate to the overmastering dictates of war. Rules, regulations, assurances, and treaties, all alike, are of no moment; and so, freed from the restraining influence of international law, the aggressive war is conducted by the Nazi leaders in the most barbaric way. Accordingly, war crimes were committed when and whenever the Führer and his close associates thought them to be advantageous. They were for the most part the result of cold and criminal calculation. . . .

Public and private property was systematically plundered and pillaged in order to enlarge the resources of Germany at the expense of the rest of Europe. . . .

In addition to the seizure of raw materials and manufactured articles, a wholesale seizure was made of art treasures, furniture, textiles, and similar articles in all the invaded countries.

The Defendant Rosenberg was designated by Hitler on 29 January 1940 head of the Center for National Socialist Ideological and Educational Research, and thereafter the organization known as the "Einsatzstab Rosenberg" conducted its operations on a very great scale. Originally designed for the establishment of a research library, it developed into a project for the seizure of cultural treasures. On 1 March 1942, Hitler issued a further decree, authorizing Rosenberg to search libraries, lodges, and cultural establishments, to seize material from these establishments, as well as cultural treasures owned by Jews. Similar directions were given where the ownership could not be clearly established. The decree directed that Rosenberg's activities in the West were to be conducted in his capacity as Reichsleiter, and in the East in his capacity as Reichsminister. Thereafter, Rosenberg's activities were extended to the occupied countries. The report of Robert Scholz, Chief of the special staff for Pictorial Art, stated:

During the period from March 1941 to July 1944 the special staff for Pictorial Art brought into the Reich 29 large shipments, including 137 freight cars with 4,174 cases of art works.

The report of Scholz refers to 25 portfolios of pictures of the most valuable works of art collections seized in the West, which portfolios were

* From *Trial of the Major War Criminals Before the International Military Tribunal* (Nuremberg, 1948), vol. 22, pp. 469–470, 484–486, 539, 540, 541, 588.

presented to the Führer. Thirty-nine volumes, prepared by the Einsatzstab, contained photographs of paintings, textiles, furniture, candelabra, and numerous other objects of art, and illustrated the value and magnitude of the collection which had been made. In many of the occupied countries private collections were robbed, libraries were plundered, and private houses were pillaged.

Museums, palaces, and libraries in the occupied territories of the U.S.S.R. were systematically looted. Rosenberg's Einsatzstab, Ribbentrop's special "Battalion," the Reichskommissare, and representatives of the Military Command seized objects of cultural and historical value belonging to the people of the Soviet Union, which were sent to Germany.

Thus, the Reichskommissar of the Ukraine removed paintings and objects of art from Kiev and Kharkov and sent them to East Prussia. Rare volumes and objects of art from the palaces of Peterhof, Tsarskoye Selo, and Pavlosk were shipped to Germany. In his letter to Rosenberg of 3 October 1941 Reichskommissar Kube stated that the value of the objects of art taken from Bielorussia ran into millions of rubles. The scale of this plundering can also be seen in the letter sent from Rosenberg's department to Von Milde-Schreden in which it is stated that during the month of October 1943 alone, about 40 box-cars loaded with objects of cultural value were transported to the Reich.

With regard to the suggestion that the purpose of the seizure of art treasures was protective and meant for their preservation, it is necessary to say a few words. On 1 December 1939, Himmler, as the Reich Commissioner for the "strengthening of Germanism," issued a decree to the regional officers of the Secret Police in the annexed eastern territories, and to the commanders of the Security Service in Radom, Warsaw, and Lublin. This decree contained administrative directions for carrying out the art seizure program, and in Clause 1 it is stated:

To strengthen Germanism in the defense of the Reich, all articles mentioned in Section 2 of this decree are hereby confiscated. . . . They are confiscated for the benefit of the German Reich, and are at the disposal of the Reich Commissioner for the strengthening of Germanism.

The intention to enrich Germany by the seizures rather than to protect the seized objects, is indicated in an undated report by Dr. Hans Posse, director of the Dresden State Picture Gallery:

I was able to gain some knowledge on the public and private collections, as well as clerical property, in Kraków and Warsaw. It is true that we cannot hope too much to enrich ourselves from the acquisition of great art works of paintings and sculptures, with the exception of the Veit Stoss altar and the plates of Hans von Kulmbach in the Church of Maria in Kraków . . . and several other works from the National Museum in Warsaw.

. . . .

Rosenberg is responsible for a system of organized plunder of both public and private property throughout the invaded countries of Europe. Acting under Hitler's orders of January 1940 to set up the "Hohe Schule," he organized and directed the "Einsatzstab Rosenberg," which plundered museums and libraries, confiscated art treasures and collections, and pillaged private houses. His own reports show the extent of the confiscations. In "Aktion-M" (Möbel), instituted in December 1941 at Rosenberg's suggestion, 69,619 Jewish homes were plundered in the West, 38,000 of them in Paris alone, and it took 26,984 railroad cars to transport the confiscated furnishings to Germany. As of 14 July 1944, more than 21,903 art objects, including famous paintings and museum pieces, had been seized by the Einsatzstab in the West. . . .

The Tribunal finds that Rosenberg is guilty. . . .

THE PRESIDENT: In accordance with Article 27 of the Charter, the International Military Tribunal will now pronounce the sentences on the defendants convicted on this Indictment:

. . . .

Defendant Alfred Rosenberg, on the Counts of the Indictment on which you have been convicted, the Tribunal sentences you to death by hanging.

COMMENTS

1. In Janet Flanner's three-part article in the *New Yorker*, February 24, March 1, and March 8, 1947, there is an excellent journalistic account of the Nazis' art destruction and confiscation actions and of the group of Americans known as MFA&A (for Monuments, Fine Arts, and Archives) in the SHAEF (Supreme Headquarters, Allied Expeditionary Force), who had the dual task of first trying to prevent destruction and looting by U.S. forces and second

locating, identifying, and returning confiscated works. On Hitler's taste in art and what he "collected" for a museum in Linz, Austria, to honor his mother and rival the Louvre, see Charles de Jaeger, *The Linz File: Hitler's Plunder of Europe's Art* (Exeter, England: Webb & Bower, 1981). For an interesting account of the recovery of some of the most valuable Nazi art loot from occupied countries, see "A Heavenly Treasure" in Milton Esterow, *The Art Stealers,* rev. ed. (New York: Macmillan, 1973), pp. 88ff.

2. For a detailed and depressing account of Austria's postwar custody of thousands of works of art looted by the Nazis, see Andrew Decker, "A Legacy of Shame," *ARTnews,* December 1984, p. 54; "Austria Will Auction "Heirless" Art" *ARTnews,* February 1985, p. 96; "A Promise of Justice," *ARTnews,* March 1985, p. 90; "Austria to List Art Confiscated by Nazis," *New York Times,* July 26, 1985, p. 13; "Austria Accepts New Claims for Looted Art," *ARTNews,* February 1986, p. 113.

3. On Polish art treasures sent to Canada to keep them from the Nazis, and for subsequent difficulties (eventually resolved) about returning them to the postwar socialist government of Poland, see Sharon Williams, "The Polish Art Treasures in Canada, 1940–1960," *Canadian Yearbook of International Law 1977,* p. 146; Stanislaw E. Nahlik, "The Case of the Displaced Art Treasures," *German Yearbook of International Law 1980,* p. 255.

4. Before World War II most of the great Berlin museums were located in the eastern section of the city. During the war the paintings were stored in salt mines. After the war was over, the four Allied powers had unilateral control of the museums in their sections. The salt mines were in the American zone, and the U.S. Army retrieved the paintings. Shortly after the Russians began to pillage the museums of Dresden and East Berlin as cultural reparations, the United States brought two hundred of the salt-mine paintings to Washington, D.C., to be kept in "protective custody" in the basement of the National Gallery. The MFA&A squad opposed the action, as did many in the art world. Eventually the National Gallery mounted an exhibition of the paintings, which traveled to several prominent U.S. museums. Following the tour, the paintings were returned to West Germany. The removal to the United States and uncertainty about their eventual fate produced a letter of protest by officers of the Monuments, Fine Arts and Archives squad. See materials in *Magazine of Art,* vol. 39 (February 1946), pp. 42, 73–75, 79–80.

5. *German War Art.* In 1942, Hitler established the Artists Staff in the Propaganda Division of the Wehrmacht High Command. The Staff grew to eighty artists and produced a large body of work depicting combat scenes and other military subjects. Immediately after the German surrender, the U.S. Army confiscated the bulk of this collection of "German war art" and sent it to the U.S. Army Center for Military History in Alexandria, Virginia, in pursuance of the Allied program of denazification and demilitarization of Germany (the Center also acquired four watercolors by Hitler himself). Portions of the collection have been shown in exhibitions, and a substantial number are on display in army museums and hospitals and schools. Some decorate offices and corridors in the Pentagon and on Capitol Hill. The justification for this kind of retention and display, instead of destruction or return, of the German war art has never been clear, although with the growth of Germany as a NATO ally the demilitarization note is seldom sounded. On March 18, 1982, President Reagan signed Public Laws 95-155 and 95-517, authorizing the return of most of the collection to Germany. The United States will keep (but not destroy?) any art that tends to glorify Hitler or the Nazis, plus another more than two hundred works for Army and Navy permanent art collections and the Hitler watercolors. The justification for the retention is unclear. See Ilana A. Dreyer, "The American Collection of Nazi Art: An Analysis Regarding the American Position" (1982), and Elisabeth Mikosch, "Confiscated German War Art and Its Return to the Federal Republic of Germany" (1982), both student research papers in the authors' files; John Paul Weber, *The German War Artists* (Columbia, S.C.: Cerburus Book Co., 1979); "Nazi Furor," *ARTnews,* May 1982, p. 20.

6. *The Crown of St. Stephen.* In the year 1000 Pope Sylvester II gave as a Christmas present to Hungary's first king, Stephen I, a magnificent crown for his coronation. For almost a thousand years the Crown of St. Stephen remained in Hungary, worn by fifty kings, a symbol of nationhood and political legitimacy. As the Russians were entering Hungary at the end of World War II, a Hungarian colonel, charged with the custody of the crown and other royal accessories, gave them to the United States for safekeeping. The royal treasures remained in U.S. custody in Fort Knox until November 1977, when President Jimmy Carter returned them to Hungary, much to the delight of the communist regime and the dismay of most Hun-

garians in exile. While not all Hungarians outside that country disapproved of Carter's decision, many felt a deep betrayal. The crown's display in Budapest seemed to indicate American legitimizing of communist rule and acceptance of the continued Russian presence after thirty years. Senator Robert Dole failed in his attempt to have a federal court block Carter's move until the U.S. Senate had approved it. Was it illegal for the United States to keep custody of the crown for so long, as the *San Francisco Chronicle* said it was in an editorial of November 5, 1977 (". . . The United States makes amends for years of unlawfully withholding what never belonged to us")?

7. In 1940, anticipating Nazi repression and confiscation, an official of the Hochschule für die Wissenschaft des Judentums in Berlin secretly entrusted a valuable group of Hebrew books and manuscripts to Dr. Alexander Guttman, a faculty member who was leaving Germany for the United States. The Hochschule was closed by the Nazis and the books and manuscripts were presumed to have been destroyed—until they appeared at auction at Sotheby's in New York in 1984. Amid the resulting outcry, both the attorney general of New York State and the commissioner for consumer affairs of New York City became involved. Dr. Guttman, the consignor, and Sotheby's maintained that the books and manuscripts were given to him. Jewish organizations and the attorney general took the position that he was merely entrusted with them for safekeeping. See the series of articles by Douglas C. McGill in the *New York Times* of July 10, 1984 (p. 22); July 15, 1984 (p. E9); August 14, 1984 (p. 1); August 16, 1984 (p. 28); August 28, 1984 (p. 24); and August 30, 1984 (p. 15). See also related articles: Bonnie Burnham and Linda E. Ketchum, "World War II Art Losses Still Surfacing," *Stolen Art Alert,* October 1984, p. 1; Nancy Miller, "Who Owns Jewish Art," *Reform Judaism,* Spring 1985. On July 16, 1985, Sotheby's and the state attorney general, Robert Abrams, agreed to a complex settlement that involved (1) recalling from the buyers at auction the works that are not duplicated in public collections, and distributing them to institutions where they would be available for viewing by the public, and (2) paying Dr. Guttman $900,000 (about half the total raised by the sale). See Douglas C. McGill, "Sotheby's to Recall Hebrew Books It Sold," *New York Times,* July 17, 1985, p. 20; "Judge Approves a Settlement in Sotheby's Sale of Hebraica," *New York Times,* August 15, 1985, p. 14.

8. In 1937 American artist Lyonel Feininger fled Germany, leaving forty-eight paintings with a German friend, Herman Klumpp. Feininger died in 1956 and his widow died in 1970. The executors of her estate, New York attorneys Ralph Colin and Ralph Colin Jr., then sought to recover the paintings from Klumpp, who was still living in East Germany and who claimed that he now owned them. Eventually, with the help of the East German government, the paintings were awarded to the estate and returned to the United States. See "Feininger Paintings' Odyssey," *New York Times,* March 15, 1984, Arts and Entertainment section.

9. The settlement of the Feininger case came soon after two Dürer portraits long sought by East Germany were ordered returned to Dresden in *Kunstsammlungen zu Weimar v. Elicofon,* 678 F.2d 1150 (2d Cir. 1982). The *Elicofon* case is set out in Chapter 2.

10. Art plunder and destruction have often been mixed with political, religious, and racial motives. Thus the suppression of the Aztec religion by zealous Spanish clerics was accomplished in part by the deliberate burning of almost the entire body of Aztec literature (codexes). Where religious objects were composed of valuable materials such as gold, avarice and religious zeal combined to justify melting them down and appropriating the metal. Temples and other religious structures were defaced and ruined. See Charles Samuel Braden, *Religious Aspects of the Conquest of Mexico* (Durham, N.C.: Duke University Press, 1930). Were the Nazi actions in Europe comparable in any way to the Spanish appropriations and suppressions of Aztec art? Were Napoleon's actions in looting Europe to fill the Louvre significantly different in ethical or legal quality from the Nazi actions?

THE ACT OF STATE DOCTRINE AND RELATED MATTERS

Some of the works of art confiscated by the *Einsatzstab* Rosenberg eventually found their way into the hands of private individuals. It may be assumed that these new owners had acted in reliance upon the validity of the government's title to the works. But suppose that the original owner of a confiscated work of art brings an action against the new owner for recovery of the work, claiming that the forced confiscation did not legally terminate his rights of ownership. Should the original owner be allowed to recover? The answer depends in part upon the willingness of the court to examine the validity of the confiscation. In certain well-defined cases, the court is precluded from any inquiry by the Act of State Doctrine. This doctrine applies to a taking of property by a foreign sovereign government (1) when the foreign government is recognized by the United States at the time of the lawsuit and (2) when the taking of the property occurred within the foreign sovereign's own territorial boundaries. In effect, the Act of State Doctrine requires the court to enforce the act of a foreign sovereign, even when that act might not be valid under the laws of the forum state. The source of the doctrine is in the principles of equality and independence of states before international law. For a fuller discussion of these underlying principles, see *Oppenheim's International Law,* ed. Sir Hersch Lauterpacht, 8th ed. (New York: Longman, Green & Co., 1955), vol. 1, pp. 263–270.

In *Menzel v. List,* 49 Misc. 2d 300, 267 N.Y.S.2d 804 (1966), the plaintiff sought to recover a painting by Marc Chagall which she and her husband had left in their apartment in Brussels when they fled in March 1941 before the oncoming Nazis. Treated by the Nazis as "decadent Jewish art," the painting was seized by the *Einsatzstab* Rosenberg on March 31, 1941. The Menzels settled in the United States and searched for the painting after the war was over. They were unable to locate it until 1962, when it was discovered in the possession of defendant Albert A. List, a well-known art collector. The defendant asserted, among other things, that "the painting was lawfully requisitioned by German authority, as an occupying power in the prosecution of the law and as confiscation of the property of its nationals," and that therefore the Act of State Doctrine prevented the court from questioning whether that confiscation was valid. The court, however, held that the doctrine did not apply in this case because the taking was not by a foreign sovereign but by an organ of the Nazi party; because the taking was in Brussels, not within the territorial limits of the government; and because the foreign government was not recognized by the United States at the time of the lawsuit. The plaintiff then was granted recovery of the painting or its value, because the court classified the seizure as illegal "plunder and pillage" rather than "lawful booty of war."

In other cases, where the Act of State Doctrine applies, the plaintiff has no opportunity to prove that the act of confiscation was invalid. The following case involves the expropriation of works of art in the USSR by a decree of the Soviet government in 1921.

Stroganoff-Scherbatoff v. Weldon
420 F.Supp. 18 (S.D.N.Y. 1976)

BONSAL, District Judge.

Plaintiff George Stroganoff-Scherbatoff commenced these actions alleging conversion of . . . a painting known as *Portrait of Antoine Triest, Bishop of Ghent* [Triest Portrait], by Sir Anthony Van Dyck, of the value of $50,000, . . . and a bust of Diderot by Houdon, . . . with a property value of $350,000. . . .

It appears undisputed that both the Triest Portrait and the Diderot bust were sold in Berlin in 1931 at the Lepke Kunst-Auctions-Hause (hereinafter "Lepke Auction") by order of the Handelsvertretung or Trade Consulate of the U.S.S.R. The Triest Portrait was purchased by the Frank T.

Sabin Gallery in London which later sold it to the Alfred Brod Gallery, Ltd. in London. In 1963, defendant Weldon acquired the painting from the Brod Gallery and remains the present owner. It is unclear from the record who purchased the Diderot bust at the Lepke Auction; however, Charles B. Wrightsman later acquired the bust in June, 1965 from French & Company, Inc., a New York art dealer, and later donated it to the Metropolitan Museum of Art on or about November 14, 1974.

Plaintiff alleges that he is the direct descendant of Count Alexander Sergevitch Stroganoff, the original owner of both works of art, and that he is the rightful owner of these works of art by reason of familial succession. . . .

Here, the record shows that the works of art, whether in the Stroganoff Palace or in the Imperial Hermitage Museum, were appropriated by the Soviet Government under either Decree No. 111 of the Council of People's Commissars published on March 5, 1921, which nationalized all movable property of citizens who had fled the Soviet Union, or Decree No. 245 of March 8, 1923, promulgated by the All Russian Central Executive Committee and the Council of People's Commissars, which nationalized property housed in State Museums. In addition, at the time of the Lepke Auction in Berlin, plaintiff's mother, Princess Stroganoff-Scherbatoff, wrote a public letter of protest stating that:

This collection remains entirely my property. *The Soviet republic has taken possession of this collection in a way that sets at defiance every principle of international law.* [Emphasis added by Judge Bonsal.] *New York Herald Tribune*, May 13, 1931, at 15.

While plaintiff contends that the "taking" did not occur within the territory of the Soviet Union but in Berlin at the Lepke Auction and, under such circumstances, the Act of State Doctrine is inapplicable, the record indicates that the works of art were appropriated in Russia, prior to the Lepke Auction, and were transported to Berlin by the Soviet Government solely for the purpose of the public sale.

In *Princess Paley Olga v. Weisz* [1929] 1 K.B. 718, the British Court of Appeal was faced with a case involving similar facts. There, a Russian refugee noble, Princess Paley Olga, instituted an action in the British courts to recover certain furniture and art objects that had been in the Paley Palace, near St. Petersburg, and which were sold by the Soviet Government to the defendant in 1928. Relying in part on Decree No. 111 of the Council of People's Commissars published on March 5, 1921, and Decree No. 245 promulgated by the All Russian Central Executive Committee and of the Council of People's Commissars in March 1923, the defendant Weisz contended that the articles in question had ceased to be the property of the plaintiff and were in the possession of the Soviet Government as public property. Since

that Government was the Government of a foreign sovereign State, and had been recognized as such by the English Government in 1924, defendant contended that the plaintiff could not dispute the validity of the appropriation of the articles by the Soviet Government in the British courts. In affirming the lower court's decision that plaintiff's action must fail, the Court of Appeal (Scrutton, L. J.) held:

Our Government has recognized the present Russian Government as the de jure Government of Russia, and our Courts are bound to give effect to the laws and acts of the Government so far as they relate to property within that jurisdiction when it was affected by those laws and acts. *Id.* at 725.

Here it appears that the Triest Portrait and the Diderot bust were transported to Berlin for public sale in May 1931 at the direction of the Soviet Government. The Soviet Government had been recognized by the United States as the *de jure* government of Russia in 1933. Whether the works of art had been appropriated under Decree No. 111 of March 5, 1921 or Decree No. 245 of March 8, 1923 appears to be immaterial. The sale of the Stroganoff Collection was held by order of the Handelsvertretung and as such was carried out under the direction and with the consent of the Soviet Government. While the actual sale of the works of art occurred in Berlin, the property had been seized in Russia by the Soviet Government.

Unlike the situation in *Menzel v. List*, 49 Misc. 2d 300, 267 N.Y.S.2d 804 (1966), where the taking was by an organ of the Nazi Party, not a sovereign state, and the Act of State Doctrine was held inapplicable, here, the Soviet Government, by official decrees of its political organs, had acquired the works of art in Russia prior to their public sale in Berlin in 1931. Moreover, in *Menzel v. List*, the appropriation of the painting was in Belgium and the Government of the Kingdom of Belgium, although in exile at the time, was still the recognized government of Belgium. Here, the appropriation was by the Soviet Union and occurred within the territorial boundaries of the Soviet Union.

Thus, it seems clear that, on this record, plaintiff is precluded from recovery by reason of the Act of State Doctrine. . . .

COMMENTS

1. A similar case arose in France, with a similar result. An exhibition in Paris in 1954 included thirty-seven Picassos from Soviet museums. These paintings had been confiscated

by the Soviet government in 1917 from a Russian national. The daughters of the original owner sued in the French courts to sequester the paintings while their title was being determined. The petition was denied, in part because of the incompetency of the French courts to judge the sovereign acts of a foreign state. See *DeKeller v. Maison de la Pensée Française*, 82 *Journal du Droit Int.* (Clunet) 119 (Civ. Trib. of Seine, July 12, 1954).

2. The Act of State Doctrine follows logically from basic premises of international law, but as the above cases show, the result is to deny a judicial hearing of a possibly meritorious claim. Nonrecognition of a foreign government can have a similar effect. In *Kunstsammlungen zu Weimar v. Elicofon*, 478 F.2d 231 (2d Cir. 1973), the owner, an East German state museum, was at first denied standing to appear because the United States had not recognized the East German government. It was only after the United States recognized East Germany that the museum was allowed to intervene in the case, which it eventually won. See *Kunstsammlungen zu Weimar v. Elicofon*, 678 F.2d 1150 (2d Cir. 1982), reproduced in Chapter 2.

3. The judicial deference paid to the acts of foreign sovereigns recognized by the United States has become the pivotal issue in many different kinds of lawsuits. An unusual example is *Farcasanu v. Commissioner of Internal Revenue*, 436 F.2d 146 (D.D.C. 1970). Mrs. Farcasanu, an American citizen, had lived for many years in Rumania. When World War II broke out, she was forced to flee the country, leaving behind many valuable works of art. Sometime after 1945, her property was confiscated by the new government of Rumania, under a general nationalization program. Advised by the U.S. Department of State, Mrs. Farcasanu submitted a claim for compensation for her lost property to the Foreign Claims Settlement Commission. She was eventually awarded much less than she claimed. In her tax return for 1959, she entered a deduction for the difference between her original claim and the figure finally awarded, an amount of $192,271.50. The ground for her deduction was Section 165(c)(3) of the Internal Revenue Code, which allows deductions for losses of property from theft. The International Revenue Service, however, contested this deduction and won, on the theory that because the confiscations were "under color of decrees" issued by the recognized government of Rumania, they did not constitute theft.

DESTRUCTION OF WORKS OF ART

THE 1954 HAGUE CONVENTION

Following World War II and the Nuremberg Trials an international conference called by UNESCO at the initiative of Italy and attended by the representatives of eighty-six nations produced the following Convention.

Convention for the Protection of Cultural Property in the Event of Armed Conflict*
The Hague, May 14, 1954

The High Contracting Parties,

Recognizing that cultural property has suffered grave damage during recent armed conflicts and that, by reason of the developments in the technique of warfare, it is in increasing danger of destruction;

Being convinced that damage to cultural property belonging to any people whatsoever means damage to the cultural heritage of all mankind, since each people makes its contribution to the culture of the world;

Considering that the preservation of the cultural heritage is of great importance for all peoples of the world and that it is important that this heritage should receive international protection;

Guided by the principles concerning the protection of cultural property during armed conflict, as established in the Conventions of The Hague of 1899 and of 1907 and in the Washington Pact of 15 April, 1935;

Being of the opinion that such protection cannot be effective unless both national and inter-

* *United Nations Treaty Series*, vol. 249 (1956), pp. 240–266, 358.

national measures have been taken to organize it in time of peace;

Being determined to take all possible steps to protect cultural property;

Have agreed upon the following provisions:

Chapter 1

GENERAL PROVISIONS REGARDING PROTECTION

Article 1

DEFINITION OF CULTURAL PROPERTY

For the purposes of the present Convention, the term "cultural property" shall cover, irrespective of origin or ownership:

(a) movable or immovable property of great importance to the cultural heritage of every people, such as monuments of architecture, art or history, whether religious or secular; archaeological sites; groups of buildings which, as a whole, are of historical or artistic interest; works of art; manuscripts, books and other objects of artistic, historical or archaeological interest; as well as scientific collections and important collections of books or archives or of reproductions of the property defined above;

(b) buildings whose main and effective purpose is to preserve or exhibit the movable cultural property defined in sub-paragraph (a) such as museums, large libraries and depositories of archives, and refuges intended to shelter, in the event of armed conflict, the movable cultural property defined in sub-paragraph (a);

(c) centres containing a large amount of cultural property as defined in sub-paragraphs (a) and (b), to be known as "centres containing monuments." . . .

Article 4

RESPECT FOR CULTURAL PROPERTY

1. The High Contracting Parties undertake to respect cultural property situated within their own territory as well as within the territory of other High Contracting Parties by refraining from any use of the property and its immediate surroundings or of the appliances in use for its protection for purposes which are likely to expose it to destruction or damage in the event of armed conflict; and by refraining from any act of hostility directed against such property.

2. The obligations mentioned in paragraph 1 of the present Article may be waived only in cases where military necessity imperatively requires such a waiver.

3. The High Contracting Parties further undertake to prohibit, prevent and, if necessary, put a stop to any form of theft, pillage or misappropriation of, and any acts of vandalism directed against, cultural property. They shall refrain from requisitioning movable cultural property situated in the territory of another High Contracting Party.

4. They shall refrain from any act directed by way of reprisals against cultural property.

5. No High Contracting Party may evade the obligations incumbent upon it under the present Article, in respect of another High Contracting Party, by reason of the fact that the latter has not applied the measures of safeguard referred to in Article 3.

Article 5

OCCUPATION

1. Any High Contracting Party in occupation of the whole or part of the territory of another High Contracting Party shall as far as possible support the competent national authorities of the occupied country in safeguarding and preserving its cultural property.

2. Should it prove necessary to take measures to preserve cultural property situated in occupied territory and damaged by military operations, and should the competent national authorities be unable to take such measures, the Occupying Power shall, as far as possible, and in close co-operation with such authorities, take the most necesssary measures of preservation.

3. Any High Contracting Party whose government is considered their legitimate government by members of a resistance movement, shall, if possible, draw their attention to the obligation to comply with those provisions of the Convention dealing with respect for cultural property.

Article 6

DISTINCTIVE MARKING OF CULTURAL PROPERTY

In accordance with the provisions of Article 16, cultural property may bear a distinctive emblem so as to facilitate its recognition.

Article 7

MILITARY MEASURES

1. The High Contracting Parties undertake to introduce in time of peace into their military regulations or instructions such provisions as may ensure observance of the present Convention, and to foster in the members of their armed forces a spirit of respect for the culture and cultural property of all peoples.

2. The High Contracting Parties undertake to plan or establish in peacetime, within their armed forces, services or specialist personnel whose purpose will be to secure respect for cultural property and to co-operate with the civilian authorities responsible for safeguarding it.

Chapter II

SPECIAL PROTECTION

Article 8

GRANTING OF SPECIAL PROTECTION

1. There may be placed under special protection a limited number of refuges intended to shelter movable cultural property in the event of armed conflict, of centres containing monuments and other immovable cultural property of very great importance, provided that they:

(a) are situated at an adequate distance from any large industrial centre or from any important military objective constituting a vulnerable point, such as, for example, an aerodrome, broadcasting station, establishment engaged upon work of national defense, a port or railway station of relative importance or a main line of communication;

(b) are not used for military purposes.

2. A refuge for movable cultural property may also be placed under special protection, whatever its location, if it is so constructed that, in all probability, it will not be damaged by bombs.

3. A centre containing monuments shall be deemed to be used for military purposes whenever it is used for the movement of military personnel or material, even in transit. The same shall apply whenever activities directly connected with military operations, the stationing of military personnel, or the production of war material are carried on within the centre.

4. The guarding of cultural property mentioned in paragraph 1 above by armed custodians specially empowered to do so, or the presence, in the vicinity of such cultural property, of police forces normally responsible for the maintenance of public order shall not be deemed to be used for military purposes.

5. If any cultural property mentioned in paragraph 1 of the present Article is situated near an important military objective as defined in the said paragraph, it may nevertheless be placed under special protection if the High Contracting Party asking for that protection undertakes, in the event of armed conflict, to make no use of the objective and particularly, in the cast of a port, railway station or aerodrome, to divert all traffic therefrom. In that event, such diversion shall be prepared in time of peace.

6. Special protection is granted to cultural property by its entry in the "International Register of Cultural Property under Special Protection." This entry shall only be made, in accordance with the provisions of the present Convention and under the conditions provided for in the Regulations for the execution of the Convention.

Article 9

IMMUNITY OF CULTURAL PROPERTY UNDER SPECIAL PROTECTION

The High Contracting Parties undertake to ensure the immunity of cultural property under special protection by refraining, from the time of entry in the International Register, from any act of hostility directed against such property and, except for the cases provided for in paragraph 5 of Article 8, from any use of such property or its surroundings for military purposes.

Article 10

IDENTIFICATION AND CONTROL

During an armed conflict, cultural property under special protection shall be marked with the distinctive emblem described in Article 16, and shall be open to international control as provided for in the Regulations for the execution of the Convention.

Article 11

WITHDRAWAL OF IMMUNITY

1. If one of the High Contracting Parties commits, in respect of any item of cultural property

under special protection, a violation of the obligations under Article 9, the opposing Party shall, so long as this violation persists, be released from the obligation to ensure the immunity of the property concerned. Nevertheless, whenever possible, the latter Party shall first request the cessation of such violation within a reasonable time.

2. Apart from the case provided for in paragraph 1 of the present Article, immunity shall be withdrawn from cultural property under special protection only in exceptional cases of unavoidable military necessity, and only for such time as that necessity continues. Such necessity can be established only by the officer commanding a force the equivalent of a division in size or larger. Whenever circumstances permit, the opposing Party shall be notified, a reasonable time in advance, of the decision to withdraw immunity.

3. The Party withdrawing immunity shall, as soon as possible, so inform the Commissioner-General for cultural property provided for in the Regulations for the execution of the Convention, in writing, stating the reasons.

Chapter III
TRANSPORT OF CULTURAL PROPERTY

Article 12
TRANSPORT UNDER SPECIAL PROTECTION

1. Transport exclusively engaged in the transfer of cultural property, whether within a territory or to another territory, may, at the request of the High Contracting Party concerned, take place under special protection in accordance with the conditions specified in the Regulations for the execution of the Convention.

2. Transport under special protection shall take place under the international supervision provided for in the aforesaid Regulations and shall display the distinctive emblem described in Article 16.

3. The High Contracting Parties shall refrain from any act of hostility directed against transport under special protection.

Article 13
TRANSPORT IN URGENT CASES

1. If a High Contracting Party considers that the safety of certain cultural property requires its transfer and that the matter is of such urgency that the procedure laid down in Article 12 cannot be followed, especially at the beginning of an armed conflict, the transport may display the distinctive emblem described in Article 16, provided that an application for immunity referred to in Article 12 has not already been made and refused. As far as possible, notification of transfer should be made to the opposing Parties. Nevertheless, transport conveying cultural property to the territory of another country may not display the distinctive emblem unless immunity has been expressly granted to it.

2. The High Contracting Parties shall take, so far as possible, the necessary precautions to avoid acts of hostility directed against the transport described in paragraph 1 of the present Article and displaying the distinctive emblem.

Article 14
IMMUNITY FROM SEIZURE, CAPTURE AND PRIZE

1. Immunity from seizure, placing in prize, or capture shall be granted to:

(a) cultural property enjoying the protection provided for in Article 12 or that provided for in Article 13;

(b) the means of transport exclusively engaged in the transfer of such cultural property.

2. Nothing in the present Article shall limit the right of visit and search.

Chapter IV
PERSONNEL

Article 15

As far as is consistent with the interests of security, personnel engaged in the protection of cultural property shall, in the interests of such property, be respected and, if they fall into the hands of the opposing Party, shall be allowed to continue to carry out their duties whenever the cultural property for which they are responsible has also fallen into the hands of the opposing Party.

. . . .

Chapter VI

SCOPE OF APPLICATION OF THE
CONVENTION

Article 18

APPLICATION OF THE CONVENTION

1. Apart from the provisions which shall take effect in time of peace, the present Convention shall apply in the event of declared war or of any other armed conflict which may arise between two or more of the High Contracting Parties, even if the state of war is not recognized by one or more of them.

2. The Convention shall also apply to all cases of partial or total occupation of the territory of a High Contracting Party, even if the said occupation meets with no armed resistance.

3. If one of the Powers in conflict is not a Party to the Present Convention, the Powers which are Parties thereto shall nevertheless be bound by it in their mutual relations. They shall furthermore be bound by the Convention, in relation to the said Power, if the latter has declared that it accepts the provisions thereof and so long as it applies them.

Article 19

CONFLICTS NOT OF AN INTERNATIONAL
CHARACTER

1. In the event of an armed conflict not of an international character occurring within the territory of one of the High Contracting Parties, each party to the conflict shall be bound to apply, as a minimum, the provisions of the present Convention which relate to respect for cultural property.

. . . .

Article 28

SANCTIONS

The High Contracting Parties undertake to take, within the framework of their ordinary criminal jurisdiction, all necessary steps to prosecute and impose penal or disciplinary sanctions upon those persons, of whatever nationality, who commit or order to be committed a breach of the present Convention. . . .

PROTOCOL

The High Contracting Parties are agreed as follows:

I

1. Each High Contracting Party undertakes to prevent the exportation, from a territory occupied by it during an armed conflict, of cultural property as defined in Article 1 of the Convention for the Protection of Cultural Property in the Event of Armed Conflict, signed at The Hague on 14 May, 1954.

2. Each High Contracting Party undertakes to take into its custody cultural property imported into its territory either directly or indirectly from any occupied territory. This shall either be effected automatically upon the importation of the property or, failing this, at the request of the authorities of that territory.

3. Each High Contracting Party undertakes to return, at the close of hostilities, to the competent authorities of the territory previously occupied, cultural property which is in its territory, if such property has been exported in contravention of the principle laid down in the first paragraph. Such property shall never be retained as war reparations.

4. The High Contracting Party whose obligation it was to prevent the exportation of cultural property from the territory occupied by it, shall pay an indemnity to the holders in good faith of any cultural property which has to be returned in accordance with the preceding paragraph.

II

5. Cultural property coming from the territory of a High Contracting Party and deposited by it in the territory of another High Contracting Party for the purpose of protecting such property against the dangers of an armed conflict, shall be returned by the latter, at the end of hostilities, to the competent authorities of the territory from which it came.

COMMENTS

1. The United States has never become a party to the 1954 Hague Convention. In this connection, consider the following correspondence.*

Richard M. Nixon
The President of the United States
The White House
Washington, D.C.

Dear Mr. President:

The following resolution was passed at the annual meeting on January 27, 1972, of the College Art Association of America, an organization of almost 7,000 individual and institutional members devoted to the encouragement of scholarship, teaching and production of art in America.

Resolved

The members of the CAA being deeply concerned with the protection and preservation of cultural property support in principle the purposes of the Hague Convention of 1954 for the Protection of Cultural Property in the Event of Armed Conflict. They are greatly disturbed by the repeated failure to submit the Convention to the United States Senate for ratification.

The CAA urges that the Convention promptly be submitted for ratification and that there be a full and public explanation of the military and security considerations which have caused the Secretary of Defense to oppose its ratification.

It is further resolved that the President of the Association be directed to communicate the substance of this resolution to appropriate Government officials.

We sincerely hope that you will give this resolution your full consideration.

Mrs. Anne Coffin Hanson
President, College Art Association of America

A similar letter was sent to Melvin Laird, Secretary of Defense.

From the Department of State:

Mrs. Anne Coffin Hanson
College Art Association of America
432 Park Avenue South
New York, New York 10016

Dear Mrs. Hanson:

I am writing in response to your letter of March 22 to President Nixon, concerning the 1954 Hague Convention on the Protection of Cultural Property in the Event of Armed Conflict.

We think that the Convention contains many important and worthwhile provisions. If we were to become a party, we would have to be sure that we could live up to all of the provisions of the Convention under all circumstances. The major difficulty is that adherence to the Convention would seriously limit the options of the United States in the event of nuclear war or even in some cases of conventional bombardment. We hope as fervently as you undoubtedly do that these situations will not occur, but if we are to limit our options, it is our view that this ought to be done in a straightforward manner and not under the guise of providing certain protection for cultural property. We can understand that certain other nuclear powers have for one reason or another become party to this Convention, but we seriously doubt that they would in fact be ready to live up to it in all circumstances. For our part, the United States Government has, by its actions, shown itself

*From Hanson-Bettauer Correspondence, *Art Journal,* vol. 31 (Summer 1972). Copyright © by the College Art Association of America. Reprinted by permission.

ready to take all possible measures to provide protection to important cultural property. We have often expressed our concern for the preservation of important cultural property situated in areas of armed conflict. Our military instructions are clear in this regard, and the Department of State has used appropriate diplomatic channels to seek to influence others to take similar care that important cultural property be preserved. We have also supported the efforts of UNESCO in this area under the provisions of Article 23 of the 1954 Hague Convention.

We appreciate having received a copy of your January 27 resolution on this topic, and we shall certainly take the views contained in it into account in any future reconsideration of our position on this Convention.

Ronald J. Bettauer
Attorney, Office of the Legal Adviser Department of State

2. What is your reaction to the explanation given for the failure of the United States to accede to the 1954 Hague Convention? In this connection, consider Article 11(2), which was added to the Convention at the insistence of the United States. Could the fact that the inquiry was made while the United States was at war in Southeast Asia, where there are many vulnerable cultural monuments and works of art, be a factor?

3. Suppose the Hague Convention had been in force at the time. Would it have applied to the actions of Lord Elgin in Greece? of Napoleon in Italy? of the Nazis in Germany? of the Nazis in France?

4. The preamble to the Hague Convention states: "Being convinced that damage to cultural property belonging to any people whatsoever means damage to the cultural heritage of all mankind, since each people makes its contributions to the culture of the world. . . ." Historically this is an extraordinary statement. Until this century there was no recognition of world art as we know it today. It was largely the effort of artists that validated the arts of China, Japan, Southeast Asia, Africa, pre-Columbia, and the American Indian that theretofore had been considered curiosities or artifacts. The establishment of the United Nations and UNESCO after World War II undoubtedly contributed to this recognition.

5. The 1954 Hague Convention was the most significant *general* international effort of its kind in the years following the Hague Convention and Rules of 1907. However, there was an intermediate inter-American effort, called the Washington Declaration of 1935 (reproduced in Bevans, *Treaties and Other International Agreements of the United States of America, 1776–1949* [Washington, D.C.: U.S. Government Printing Office, 1969], pp. 254–255), which has been obscured by events and is for most purposes a dead letter. Most recently a Convention for the Protection of the World Cultural and Natural Heritage was adopted by the General Conference of UNESCO in 1972. It is reproduced in *International Legal Materials*, vol. 11 (1972), pp. 1358ff. Its purposes are to (1) define the individual nation's obligations of "identification and rehabilitation" of its own cultural heritage and (2) to enlist international aid to help individual nations do so. Article 6 of the Convention contains language echoing that of the preamble to the 1954 Hague Convention: "The States Parties to this Convention recognize that such heritage constitutes a world heritage for whose protection it is the duty of the international community as a whole to cooperate." The United States is a party to the Convention. See Vickie A. Rochelle, "The World Heritage Treaty: A Means to Federally Regulate Private Property for the Preservation of Cultural and Natural Heritage," *Arizona Law Rev.*, vol. 23 (1981), pp. 1033ff.

BOMB THE CHURCH?

Are there any conditions under which protection of art justifies loss of human life? Pro-life forces will immediately respond in the negative and affirm that the preservation of any work of art is not worth the loss of a single human life. It has meant no disrespect for life on the part of thoughtful people that in this century this question posed a serious dilemma.

To appreciate the importance of great works of art and other symbols of a nation's culture, consider the German burning of the magnificent library of Louvain and the bombardment of the Cathedral of Reims in August 1914. Both were calculated acts intended to terrorize Germany's enemies. Belgium had been conquered and Reims had been proclaimed an open city before the deliberate destruction of these buildings. As Barbara Tuchman points out in her book *The Guns of August*, "By the end of August people of the Allied nations were persuaded that they faced an enemy that had to be beaten, a regime that had to be destroyed, a war that must be fought to the finish." It was no secret to the Germans that the library and cathedral represented the national genius of Belgium and France. (For centuries the kings of France had been crowned at Reims.) It is fair to say that the Germans sought to destroy the spirit of both nations by these barbaric acts. It is equally fair to say that the memory of the consequences of this destruction had not been forgotten by World War II and contributed to General Dwight D. Eisenhower's directives, which unfortunately seem to have applied only in countries to be liberated.

EISENHOWER'S VIEW

On December 29, 1943, General Eisenhower issued the following statement:

> Today we are fighting in a country [Italy] which has contributed a great deal to our cultural inheritance, a country rich in monuments which by their creation helped and now in their old age illustrate the growth of the civilization which is ours. We are bound to respect those monuments so far as war allows.
>
> If we have to choose between destroying a famous building and sacrificing our own men, then our men's lives count infinitely more and the buildings must go. But the choice is not always so clear-cut as that. In many cases the monuments can be spared without any detriment to operational needs. Nothing can stand against the argument of military necessity. That is an accepted principle. But the phrase "military necessity" is sometimes used where it would be more truthful to speak of military convenience or even of personal convenience. I do not want it to cloak slackness or indifference.
>
> It is a responsibility of higher commanders to determine through AMG Officers the locations of historical monuments whether they be immediately ahead of our front lines or in areas occupied by us. This information passed to lower echelons through normal channels places the responsibility on all commanders of complying with the spirit of this letter. [*Report*, pp. 48, 49.]*

On December 17, 1943, General Alexander ordered "that every officer brings continually to the notice of those serving under him our responsibility and obligation to preserve and protect these objects [art treasures and monuments] to the greatest extent that is possible under operational conditions. [*Report*, p. 61.]"

Pisa was one of the most damaged of Italian cities. From the point of view of military necessity the splendid monuments of its past were thrown into shadow by the fact that it was the most important railway and highway junction in western Tuscany and was situated astride the Arno, serving as an anchor in the German line before the Apennines. The city was heavily bombed and was the center of a bitter contest during July and August. [*Report*, p. 83.] . . .

At least ninety-five percent of the damage inflicted to major monuments was caused by air bombardment. It is difficult to estimate how far the comparative immunity of the greater cathedrals of France from damage was due to efforts of the Allied Air Force based on information supplied by Supreme Headquarters, Allied Expeditionary Force [SHAEF], but certainly

---

* *Report of the American Commission for the Protection and Salvage of Artistic Monuments in War Areas* (Washington, D.C.: U.S. Government Printing Office, 1946), pp. 48–49. Hereafter cited as *Report*.

such information was sought by the air staff and supplied, and except for Rouen, the great Gothic monuments of France have escaped comparatively lightly. [*Report,* pp. 98–99.] . . .

The need for specific instructions concerning historical monuments and works of art, which would be issued by command of SHAEF to all echelons, similar to those issued in Italy, was felt long before operational commitment [in France, Belgium, and the Netherlands]. It was realized that in northern Europe, as in Italy, the feeling of the nations for their monuments made it imperative, for the sake of good relations with the peoples of Allied countries, that the Allies show the utmost respect for their national treasures . . . it was essential that the policy in respect to historical monuments should be binding for all Allied personnel. . . ." [*Report,* p. 101.]

On May 26, 1944, General Eisenhower issued the following amplification of his directive for Italy:

> Shortly we will be fighting our way across the Continent of Europe in battles designed to preserve our civilization. Inevitably, in the path of our advance will be found historical monuments and cultural centers which symbolize to the world all that we are fighting to preserve.
>
> It is the responsibility of every commander to protect and respect these symbols whenever possible.
>
> In some circumstances the success of the military operation may be prejudiced in our reluctance to destroy these revered objects. Then as at Cassino, where the enemy relied on our emotional attachments to shield his defense, the lives of our men are paramount. So, where military necessity dictates, commanders may order the required action even though it involves destruction to some honored site. [*Report,* p. 102.]

The SHAEF Civil Affairs Directive for France, Belgium, and Luxembourg, May 25, 1944, directed all commanding generals to "take such steps as might be consistent with military necessity to insure that no unnecessary or wanton damage was done to such structures and to make such regulations as they thought fit to insure that full respect was paid by the troops [to the monuments]. [*Report,* p. 102.]"

An extract from the report of the MFA&A officer, First U.S. Army, for February 1, 1945, shows the unforeseen emergencies encountered as a result of the Battle of the Bulge:

> The damage to protected monuments by American troops described below can be ascribed to the following unavoidable combination of circumstances. The town was occupied by opposing troops, within a range of yards from each other for nearly a month. Fighting was unremitting and ferocious. Civilian authorities in the town at the time were either too frightened or too harassed by other problems to make representations to military authorities regarding the use of the Hotel de Ville and Museum. The military authorities, on the other hand, were not inclined to abandon, even temporarily, their urgent duties. Weather was such as to make any kind of cover and insulation the optimum. [*Report,* pp. 111–112.]
>
> The situation described above illustrates . . . the greatest single problem encountered by MFA&A officers in the field in the liberated countries—that of the billeting of troops in historical buildings, both those on the lists and those omitted from them. The reasons: incomplete knowledge of the existence of a definite policy for the protection of historic and artistic monuments, or the official lists, among tactical commanders who were sometimes not apprised of Civil Affairs plans and who were not included in the distribution of such directives; overriding emergencies in which the need for troop accommodation outweighed any other considerations; lack of instruction and discipline of some units, who, in the urgency of combat were understandably disinclined to respect historic edifices; . . . and the logical but sometimes unfortunate assumption by U.S. forces that buildings which had been occupied for four years by German units were in effect captured and consequently open to immediate use. [*Report,* pp. 112–113.]

In response to this kind of problem, General Eisenhower, in General Order No. 68, December 29, 1943, had commanded:

> No building listed in the section "Works of Art in the Zone" handbooks of Italy issued by the Political Warfare Executive to all Allied Military Government Officers will be used without explicit permission. . . . Commanders are reminded that buildings containing art collections . . . should not be occupied when alternative accommodations are available. [*Report*, p. 62.]

COMMENTS

1. In 1945, when the Allied armies crossed the Rhine into the homeland of the enemy, there does not seem to have been the same consideration about protecting "honored sites." Cologne Cathedral and the historic monuments of Dresden, for example, were repeatedly bombed and in the latter case destroyed totally, without invoking military necessity.

2. The Abbey of Monte Cassino lies near Rome. In February 1944, Allied forces, believing that the fortress-like monastery was a German stronghold, dropped 500 tons of explosive on it, killing several hundred refugees (the bombing took place a day earlier than had been stated in leaflets dropped by the Allies) and turning the magnificent buildings into rubble. There were no Germans in the abbey; they occupied fortified positions below it. This tragic mistake was also a tactical error. After the bombing, crack German paratroops did use the ruined buildings as an effective strategic position, from which they were finally ousted only in May, after five months and a cost of ten thousand lives. (Michele McCormick, "The Abbey of Misfortune," *International Herald Tribune*, July 8, 1983.)

ANOTHER VIEW

Sir Harold Nicolson (1886–1968) was a British author, lecturer, diplomat, and statesman. He had access to the inner chambers and confidences of the great leaders of his time as a result of his privileged social status and his personal qualities. The following statement by him appeared in the *Spectator* under the title "Marginal Comment" on February 25, 1944.

SIR HAROLD NICOLSON *Bombing Works of Art**

During the past few weeks there has been much discussion, in the Press and elsewhere, of the problem whether military necessity can justify the destruction of buildings of religious, historical or artistic importance. Those who regard the mortal as more important than the immortal fail to separate eternal values from momentary hopes and affections: whereas those who consider art to be more important than individual lives are unable to distinguish between what is desirable and what is practical. I am not among those who feel that religious sites are, as such, of more importance than human lives, since religion is not concerned with material or temporal things; nor

should I hesitate, were I a military commander, to reduce some purely historical building to rubble if I felt that by so doing I could gain a tactical advantage or diminish the danger to which my men were exposed. Works of major artistic value fall, however, into a completely different category. It is to my mind absolutely desirable that such works should be preserved from destruction, even if their preservation entails the sacrifice of human lives. I should assuredly be prepared to be shot against a wall if I were certain that by such a sacrifice I could preserve the Giotto frescoes; nor should I hesitate for an instant (were such a decision ever open to me) to save St. Mark's even if I were aware that by so doing I should bring death to my sons. I should know that in a hundred years from now it would matter not at all if I or my children had survived; whereas it would matter seriously and permanently if the Piazza at Venice had been reduced to dust and ashes either by the Americans or ourselves. My attitude would be governed by a principle which is surely incontrovertible. The irreplaceable is more important than the replaceable, and the loss of even the most valued human life is ultimately less disastrous than the loss of something which in no circumstances can ever be created again.

I consider the above to be a logical statement of a desirable aim. I am aware, however, that my logic is not unassailable and that the desirable must always be governed and controlled by the practicable. Were I pressed, for instance, to define what I meant by "a work of major artistic value" I might discover that what I really meant were those objects and buildings which I happened to like myself. Is the Torre Mangia at Siena, for instance, more important (when it comes to paying for it in human lives) than the Oratory of San Bernadino at Perugia? It would be very easy for a trained logician to shake my premises under this heading. What again do I mean by "human lives"? Do I mean ten men, or thirty men, or thirty thousand, or three million? Do I mean the abstention from some purely local engagement or the prolongation of the whole war? Here again I should find myself in difficulties. If I were willing to give my life for the Giotto frescoes would I also give my life for those of Sodoma? Certainly not. But if not, then my logic is reduced to a mere statement of personal predilection. And let the barrage thunder therefore, undeterred by high-brow whimpers, from Assisi to Perugia.

I know, moreover, that those of us who feel deeply and desperately about such matters constitute but an infinitesimal minority of the British, American and Russian peoples. Nor is it any use blaming the proletariates. It would be unreasonable to suppose that a Russian who has watched the church of Novgorod flaming round its golden domes, who has picked his way across the charred parquets of Peterhof, should have any feeling at all for the Palazzo del Te at Mantua. It is not sensible to reprove a doughboy from Iowa for caring nothing about Or San Michele. Nor should I hope to convince the mothers of Kettering or Luton that their sons should be exposed to a higher percentage of danger in order to preserve for posterity the balustrades and fountains of the Villa d'Este. We must face the fact that the British public are not merely unaware of aesthetic values, but are actually prejudiced against them. To the ordinary British citizen the artistic treasures of Italy represent, either nothing at all, or else the curious pleasures of the idle rich. It is impossible to persuade such people that Vicenza or Venice are a part of their own cultural heritage. The smoke-cloud of class rancour drifts across their eyes and they would dismiss as reactionary, even as ultramontane, those who urged our commanders to spare Bernini's Colonnade. Thus an aim which to a minority appears obviously, absolutely and eternally desirable, appears to the majority as some pampered pose. And since it is to the majority that our rulers must lend an ear, we of the minority must recognize that the desirable in this matter is in practice unattainable.

Our anger would to some slight extent be mitigated did we feel convinced, first that the allied statesmen and commanders were conscious of the importance of the issues involved, and secondly that the Italian front was likely to prove decisive. We are not so convinced. The dusty answers returned from time to time by the Secretary of State for War are not encouraging. It is not sufficient comfort to us to know that an elderly archaeologist has gone out to Italy to "do what he can." Were I a Catholic and one who felt sensitive to the religious associations of St. Peter's it would be almost intolerable for me to reflect how different, how very different, would be the attitude of the Government were it not Rome, but Mecca, or even the shrine of the Imam Reza at Meshed that was involved. The India Office and the Foreign Office would combine in panic to prevent the outrage to Moslem opinion which would be caused by any violation of the Holy Places of Islam; but since only Christian sensibilities are wounded by the threat to St. Peter's our anxiety can be dismissed as sectarian. If Perugia's Collegio del Cambio were the London Stock Exchange, if San Domenico were Canterbury Cathedral, or San Lorenzo York Minster, the Government would be forced to show greater solicitude. But as it is, neither the people of this country nor their Government pause for one moment to consider what the world will think of them a hundred years from now.

It would be some comfort to me also did I feel convinced that the prosecution of the Italian campaign to a ghastly conclusion would decisively shorten the war. I am strategically illiterate but even to my innocent mind it seems improbable that upon so narrow a peninsular front sufficient armies can be engaged on either side to force a conclusive military decision. I recognize the important advantages which we have gained by securing Sicily, Sardinia and Corsica as well as a wide base upon the Italian mainland. I recognize the serious strategic and political importance of Rome and the Campagna. But when I watch the sledge-hammer methods of our armies in Italy, when I realize that within a few months this devastating bull-dozer may be crunching into Tuscany, my mind turns sick with apprehension. I think of Siena, Volterra, Rimini, Ravenna, Verona, Padua and Venice. I think of the small towns, the farms and convents of Tuscany and Etruria. And I am sickened by the thought that two thousand years of artistic genius may be sacrificed to a side-show.

It is indeed a catastrophe that the most destructive war that Europe has ever witnessed should have descended upon the loveliest things that Europe ever made. It is a reproach to democratic education that the peoples of Britain and America should be either indifferent, or actually hostile, to these supreme expressions of human intelligence. It is a reflection upon our leaders that they have shown but a perfunctory awareness of their real responsibilities. And it will be a source of distress to our grandchildren that we, who might have stood firm as the trustees of Europe's heritage, should have turned our faces aside. To hope for a change of heart among the people or their rulers is, however, to hope for something which is quite impracticable: all we can do is to induce in them a slight uneasy and recurrent sense of shame.

COMMENTS

1. Do you agree with General Eisenhower or with Sir Harold Nicolson? Difficult as it would be, how could the consensus suggested by Nicolson be obtained? Should art history be a required course at our military academies?

2. Suppose you were a military commander in the field—say in Greece in 1940. You were certain beyond any doubt that there were German artillery spotters on the Acropolis, that their position and activities there would claim the lives of some of the men and women you command, and that the only effective way to deal with them was by aerial bombing or artillery fire which were likely to damage and perhaps to destroy the Parthenon. Would you or would you not bomb the Acropolis? Why or why not? Suppose, instead of the Acropolis, it were the Cologne cathedral. Would your answer be different?

CULTURAL REPARATIONS

The war ends and the victors draw up the terms of the peace treaty. What shall be said in it about cultural reparations? There seems to be little doubt that works stolen by the losers during the hostilities to which the treaty applies should be returned. But is it clear that "restitution" of specific works that found their way into the loser's hands before hostilities began is proper? What of reparations in kind for cultural damage inflicted by the loser? More generally, is it proper or desirable to denude the loser of artworks and cultural monuments? to turn it into a cultural desert? What is the proper approach to the question of cultural reparations? The Treaty of Versailles (1919), formally bringing World War I to a close, includes the following provisions.

WORLD WAR I

Treaty of Versailles*

Article 245. Within six months after the coming into force of the present Treaty the German Government must restore to the French Government the trophies, archives, historical souvenirs or works of art carried away from France by the German authorities in the course of the war of 1870–1871 and during this last war, in accordance with a list which will be communicated to it by the French Government; particularly the French flags taken in the course of the war of 1870–1871 and all the political papers taken by the German authorities on October 10, 1870, at the chateau of Cerçay, near Brunoy (Seine-et-Oise) belonging at the time to Mr. Rouher, formerly Minister of State.

Article 246. Within six months from the coming into force of the present Treaty, Germany will restore to His Majesty the King of the Hedjaz the original Koran of the Caliph Othman, which was removed from Medina by the Turkish authorities and is stated to have been presented to the ex-Emperor William II.

Within the same period Germany will hand over to His Britannic Majesty's Government the skull of the Sultan Mkwawa which was removed from the Protectorate of German East Africa and taken to Germany.

The delivery of the articles above referred to will be effected in such place and in such conditions as may be laid down by the Government to which they are to be restored.

Article 247. Germany undertakes to furnish to the University of Louvain, within three months after a request made by it and transmitted through the intervention of the Reparation Commission, manuscripts, incunabula, printed books, maps and objects of collection corresponding in number and value to those destroyed in the burning by Germany of the Library of Louvain. All details regarding such replacement will be determined by the Reparation Commission.

Germany undertakes to deliver to Belgium, through the Reparation Commission, within six months of the coming into force of the present Treaty, in order to enable Belgium to reconstitute two great artistic works:

(1) The leaves of the triptych of the Mystic Lamb painted by the Van Eyck brothers, formerly in the Church of St. Bavon at Ghent, now in the Berlin Museum;

(2) The leaves of the triptych of the Last Supper, painted by Dierick Bouts, formerly in the Church of St. Peter at Louvain, two of which are now in the Berlin Museum and two in the Old Pinakothek at Munich.

WORLD WAR II

Most of the items specified in the above "reparations" provisions of the Treaty of Versailles were in Germany long before World War I. More recently, at the end of World War II, the question of reparations arose again, this time in the context of much more extensive plunder and destruction than in World War I.

It was generally agreed that Germany would have to give back everything it had looted or forcibly "bought," but in addition some people suggested that Germany be made to reimburse other countries for its destruction of their cultural and artistic heritages with its own art treasures. Thus Germany would pay cultural reparations to every country it had bombed or looted. The following excerpts summarize the principal arguments.

---

*From *Treaties, Conventions, International Arts, Protocols, and Agreements between the United States of America and Other Powers* (Washington, D.C.: U.S. Government Printing Office, 1910–38), vol. 3, pp. 3329ff.

DOUGLAS RIGBY *Cultural Reparations and a New Western Tradition**

Twenty-four years ago in Paris, while hard-boiled political representatives of the victorious Allies sat in conference debating the complex problem of what "reparations" should be exacted from the Central Powers, there arose in French and Belgian intellectual circles a vociferous demand that the principle of payment "in kind" be extended from ships and cattle to works of art and other cultural objects.

It was urged, with apparent justice, that while nothing could ever make good the loss of such treasures as the Library of Louvain or the five hundred historic French buildings and public monuments obliterated or badly damaged as a result of the struggle, some compensation at least might be found in taking from German and Austrian museums the best of the French and Belgian art in their possession.

A generation later, anticipating the peace terms of World War II, American newspapers carry reports from London that the United Nations have already agreed upon a plan to exact restitution from the Nazis for every bit of wartime loot and destruction inflicted. Included in the plan, cultural objects take their place with more material forms of national wealth. One member of the House of Lords has demanded that the existence of this scheme be broadcast to the Third Reich as a "solemn warning of the day of reckoning to come"; and even the former Axis partner, Italy, is crying out, after the "crime of Naples," that the Germans must be compelled "to pay with their own art objects for the losses suffered by Italian museums and art galleries."

Yet in 1919 the demands of France and Belgium were denied in principle by their own peace commissioners, and granted in but three exceptional instances. . . .

While the test of the law always remains at the mercy of the strongest, it was during peacetime that the Western nations agreed to a united front against cultural plunder. International agreements, first drawn up in 1874 and later confirmed and amplified at The Hague conferences of 1899 and 1907, expressly forbade such practices in what was in effect a Magna Charta not for man himself but for his finest achievements, for those objects which mark his ascendancy, dignity, and purpose. Yet it was for 1919 to decide whether or not the concept of the victor's "right" to such spoils should receive a truly telling blow. It was then that the new tradition met its greatest test, when, in contrast to the partially accidental turn of events a century before, the writers of the World War treaties exercised conscious and enlightened volition to prevent the retaliative looting of cultural objects. . . .

It will be said, and with reason, that Germany this time has been not only a looter but the willful destroyer of vast portions of the intellectual patrimony of other nations. What more just than that she be stripped of her own possessions in payment?

The details of the problem are, of course, far too voluminous to discuss here. There can be no question that all retrievable looted objects must be returned to their owners. But what about reparations for those lost or destroyed? The recommendation that these be paid for in full might seem just enough, but there are times when justice cannot be made to coincide with realism.

To put it flatly, Germany will have no ability to pay. She will be completely bankrupt, and most of her industries will have been bombed out of existence. There remain, then, two possibilities: reparations in manpower and reparations in cultural objects. Wrecked buildings and other monuments of historic value in some cases can be restored by conscripted German specialists, as President Roosevelt has suggested; but when it comes to payment "in kind" for cultural objects, it is clear that these can be at most no more than token payments. In Germany's legitimate store of foreign objects some restitution in kind can be found; her native hoard is another matter. Even though the last German manuscript and bronze bust of Frederick the Great were removed, how could these things compensate Russia for the loss of her Tolstoi shrine? What restitution "in kind" is possible to Poland or Czechoslovakia, where presumably all is vanished; and what could be given Naples in exchange for priceless books and manuscripts wantonly burned in the libraries of the University and the Royal Society?

*From Douglas Rigby, "Cultural Reparations and a New Western Tradition," *American Scholar*, vol. 13, no. 3 (Summer 1944), pp. 273, 278–284. Copyright © 1944 by the United Chapters of Phi Beta Kappa. Reprinted by permission.

Rehabilitation without benefit of new armaments is envisaged instead. The matter of rehabilitation of individuals, as the practitioner so well knows, is not confined to three square meals, some work, and a place to sleep. There are roots of self-respect to be considered, and in this regard there is a strong analogy to the group: by clipping away those symbols of peaceful aspiration which identify a nation with its past, rehabilitation becomes a word without meaning. It would seem, therefore, that we must at least make a distinction between cultural objects of foreign origin possessed by Germany and those which she herself has produced. Indeed, these may in the future serve to remind her that her greatest contributions of this sort to the world society were made long before the recurrent idea of a "greater Germany" first burst into destructive flame.

To help disentangle postwar chaos in the field, the United States has established under the auspices of the State Department a "Commission for the Protection and Salvaging of Artistic and Historic Monuments in Europe," an outgrowth of work initiated and still being carried on by the American Council of Learned Societies. Made up of highly experienced men, this commission now has trained representatives attached to the Allied Military Government at the front where, in addition to its efforts to prevent as much further loss as possible, the commission is conducting extensive research into the destruction and looting that has occurred. It has powers of recommendation on cultural reparations, and according to its own stated objectives is expected in certain instances to advocate "restitution in kind." . . .

The hope remains, however, that when unconditional surrender becomes a fact the commission's recommendations and the final decrees of the treaty-makers may be tempered by the historic background. If ultimately it should be decided that exceptional circumstances demand cultural reparations, where possible forfeitures might be collected from objects native to the country to be compensated and the bulk of Germany's own intellectual patrimony left intact: in a hundred years the fate of a thousand factories will be forgotten but not the seizure of a single treasured relic.

Should we here insist upon harsh retribution, however "just," we shall be presenting the defeated foe with a rallying point for future aggressions which we hope to avoid. Rather, the wisdom of the new tradition should be kept alive and dedicated as a worthy legacy to the future.

PEYTON BOSWELL *Art as Reparations**

Should the art treasures of a defeated people be utilized as reparations for damage done to the victor? In the battle heat of total war the short-viewed decisions would undoubtedly be in the affirmative, but as the cold dawn of a precarious peace brings realization of the necessity of ethics in One World, we are forced to revise our opinion. You cannot strip a people of the best of its cultural heritage and expect it to recover its moral and political balance. Such a program, once begun on even a small scale, is too apt to get out of hand, as when Napoleon filled the Louvre with loot, not to mention the Elgin marbles. At the moment America, which has a clean record, despite the salt-mine petition of some of our scholars, is in danger of participating in this injustice of robbing the future for the sins of the past.

In the peace treaties with Italy, Hungary, Romania and Bulgaria appears a clause which at first glance seems just and proper, but upon careful study has implications abhorrent to civilized people. It reads the same in each treaty, save for the name of the country:

If, in particular cases, it is impossible for (Italy) to make restitution of objects of artistic, historical or archaeological value, belonging to the cultural heritage of the United Nation from whose territory such objects were removed by force or duress by (Italian) forces, authorities or nationals, (Italy) shall transfer to the United Nation concerned objects of the same kind as, and of ap-

*Originally published as Peyton Boswell, "Art as Reparations," *Art Digest,* vol. 21 (September 14, 1947), pp. 7ff. Reprinted by permission.

proximately equivalent value to, the objects removed, in so far as such objects are obtainable in (Italy).

A personal (not official) letter from my brother-in-law, Richard Foster Howard, chief of the U.S. Government bureau charged with returning displaced art in Germany, contains these comments which should be brought forcibly to the attention of the treaty makers:

It is probable that such an eye-for-eye, tooth-for-tooth policy will not greatly affect the satellite nations whose treaties have been signed and ratified. Should this policy be included in the draft of the German treaty, it would produce a situation of the gravest danger to the entire cultural heritage of Germany, and presage a wholesale rape of that country. Claims may be expected to pour in for every object which has not been found, in direct ratio to the volume of looting and destruction in any particular country formerly occupied by German forces.

Certainly the Germans did much damage. Certainly they stole and looted in a manner not to be condoned in any way. Certainly they should pay. But two wrongs do not make a right. It would be reasonable to require reparations for lost treasures, but to *use* treasures *as* reparations is contrary to the principles of international law, violates the Hague conventions of 1907, and makes the United Nations no better than the Nazis.

The Council of Foreign Ministers does not meet again until November, but preliminary conversations are undoubtedly proceeding now. It would be intelligent for Americans with wide-angle vision to communicate with the State Department. Germany is beaten, many of her monuments and cultural treasures are already lost. She is guilty, but nothing will be gained by stripping her completely of her cultural heritage. Now is the time for those same salt-mine scholars to stand up and be counted.

COMMENT

Although the Western Allies exacted substantial reparations from Germany, it appears that cultural property was not included. See "Berlin (Potsdam) Conference," *Treaties and Other International Acts Series,* 3 (Washington, D.C.: U.S. Department of State, 1945): 1213, 1231.

Chapter Two

THE ILLICIT INTERNATIONAL TRADE IN ART:

Who Owns the Past?

BEFORE the twentieth century the answer to the question of who owns the past was simple: "To the victor go the spoils." For some today, the answer is still simple: "To the richest and the brightest belong all the arts of mankind." To thinking people who have a regard for history, law, and ethics, there is no simple answer to this question that for years has remained the most important, explosive, and complex one before the international art world.

Historically the background to the question, and the source of the problems associated with owning art from the past, depend upon such modern phenomena as the concept of a national cultural patrimony, the emergence of art museums, the staggering growth of private art collections, the expansion of the international trade in art, and global education in the history of art. These are all interconnected with one another, as well as with politics and economics.

If the reader has any doubt about art's worldwide historical, cultural, and financial importance, this chapter will help remove uncertainty, but if the reader is searching for easy solutions to the myriad problems attending legitimate ownership of the past, the chapter may be discouraging. What we offer are an introduction to the problems, existing and proposed solutions, and analyses that could help clarify issues and rectify wrongs.

Among the major problems addressed is that of the many art-rich but financially poor countries that have inflexible export laws for their antiquities and that encourage illegal excavations and smuggling. A major subject of the chapter is attempts to curtail theft and illicit international traffic in art. Another issue, arising out of the discussion in Chapter 1, is the recent phenomenon of countries demanding repatriation of national treasures that they claim have been illegally removed from their territories.

The problems in this chapter will be with us far beyond the life of this book. As nations begin to reach reasonable agreements among themselves to solve some of these problems, still new ways are discovered to steal art, such as the revolutionary airborne technology of satellite photographs that penetrate jungle cover and surface soils to reveal lost archaeological sites. For $3,000 a would-be bootleg archaeologist or Indiana Jones can now obtain an incredibly detailed satellite photo map of 100 square miles anywhere on earth. Why such unscrupulous people will always have clients to buy their ill-gotten gains is discussed in the readings that follow.

TWO OVERVIEWS OF THE PROBLEM

HUGUES DE VARINE *The Rape and Plunder of Cultures**

Writers, doctors and psychologists have said repeatedly that one of the essential causes of the catastrophic development in the scale of drug trafficking and use lies in a certain disintegration

*From Hugues de Varine, "The Rape and Plunder of Cultures: An Aspect of Deterioration of the Terms of Cultural Trade Between Nations" (translated from the French), *Museum*, vol. 139, no. 3 (1983), pp. 152ff.

of post-industrial society, above all among the young. Is there not a similar problem at the root of the sudden increase in the illicit trading in and thefts of art objects, antiquities and other cultural goods throughout the world today? What we shall endeavour [here] is not to map the development of a trend but to apprehend a contemporary situation, one that is more complex than it at first appears since it is not one phenomenon but several that we shall have to take into consideration.

The primary phenomenon—one that in fact governs the others—is the emergence of the concept of cultural goods or property. Paradoxically, it is only when goods have been divested of their intrinsic purpose, losing their primary functional utility, that they are termed cultural property, providing they are considered worthy to be preserved, admired, i.e. used for another, secondary function. Such may be the fate of a crucifix, the music of a ritual dance, a steam engine or an *incunabulum.* This concept of cultural property is closely linked with those of "traditional values," the concern for continuity, the search for "cultural roots." It is this very combination that has given rise to most public and private collections, the listing of monuments and the creation of learned historical societies. Moreover, the very rarity of these vestiges of the past leads to their enhancement both in intellectual terms ("what is rare is beautiful") and in economic terms ("what is rare—or scarce—is dear").

Here, a question arises. Do what are customarily termed cultural goods not undergo a process of cultural transformation? Is a thing created by man for a specific purpose and then discarded not re-created by another man (or by society) for another purpose? It is at this point that the museum and its role must be considered. There are two types of museum: those that present artefacts isolated from their context (generally—and significantly—referred to as "works") and those that, artificially but as honestly as possible, re-create complete units that may be termed ecological units. The transformation which occurs in the former case has every likelihood of prompting the viewer to interpret the artefact as having a "sacred" value, thus resulting in the twin forms of enhancement referred to above. If, then, this line of reasoning is accepted, the museum (which in fact reflects the main trend of present-day education in the fields of art, literature and history) merely creates a new consumer item, of which only the material substance is derived from the vestige of the past that it had been intended to present. . . .

The second phenomenon, also of an essentially modern kind, is the rapid development of the international circulation of persons and goods, which enables an ever-broader and untrained public to gain an insight into societies and cultures that would otherwise have remained for it swathed in the mists of legend. Such exchanges, so conducive to understanding, coexistence and co-operation among individuals and peoples, nevertheless have their negative features, even if these have, for obvious reasons, hitherto been kept out of the public eye wherever possible. This is in our view a mistaken attitude inasmuch as it is always wise to learn as much as possible about what cannot be prevented, in order to devise appropriate remedies or palliatives.

The third phenomenon, a direct consequence of colonization, at first of a political and subsequently of an economic and cultural kind, might briefly be defined as an artificial acculturation of the exotic. The two phenomena already referred to have resulted in a profound failure on the part of the Europeans to understand the real values enshrined in non-European cultures, combined with the ever-more pronounced rejection of these same values by non-Europeans, themselves subjected to an intensive bombardment of concepts and techniques imported in the name of development. This has led to a sudden discovery of 'primitive art" at the very moment when its creators are turning away from it in a search for the symbols of so-called modern civilization. The trend to invest cultural goods with materialistic values, which began in Europe and the United States, is thus spreading rapidly to the rest of the world. . . .

Thus we may fairly say, at the risk of oversimplifying a complex problem, that cultural property as a whole passes from the cultural to the economic sphere and, accordingly, is henceforth subject to the laws of the latter.

THE DEMAND

Naturally, the demand for cultural goods, essentially in liberal capitalist countries, has in principle no direct bearing upon the licit or illicit nature of the supply. We may even regard it as being essentially normal and honest, the result of a series of causes and circumstances as described above. This demand is generated by certain sorts of people.

First, research workers need materials that they can use directly if they are to accomplish their work: artefacts and specimens, works of art, documents collected on the site, manuscripts, etc. These researchers tend to try to have the materials they collect as primary documents shipped home to their usual place of residence and work in order to study them in the best possible intellectual and technical conditions. This sometimes leads to their resorting to illicit practices. However, it is the intensification of research that must above all be taken into account. A discovery concerning the Anatolian Neolithic, a tribe in the Philippines or a Maya site, which formerly would have remained limited to a very small number of specialists, all of them scientists, is known almost immediately today by thousands or even millions of people whose interest in it is no longer purely professional but is prompted above all by curiosity and sometimes by greed or snobbery.

Secondly, museums closely associated with research and with the various scientific disciplines, are in much the same situation, but are far more open to public curiosity. They play a much more extensive role in transmitting information and moulding the public's taste. Most (one is tempted to say, almost all) have little chance of enriching their collections except through occasional purchases at public sales, from dealers, or thanks to donations by collectors. Indeed, it must be recognized that the museum is the normal final resting-place for all cultural goods that have been shorn of their sacred and functional properties.

Thus while museums alone account for only a tiny and virtually negligible proportion (in quantity if not in quality) of the overall demand for cultural goods, they nevertheless are, in a way, its justification. This is true more especially in the United States thanks to the particularly favourable conditions from which donations benefit in terms of tax relief. From this it should not be concluded that museums have no direct impact upon demand. Their impact is in fact exercised in three ways: through field research or by making the type of purchases described above; through the publicity which they give to certain art forms and certain cultures, in particular by means of exhibitions and public relations campaigns; and through their relations with private collections, particularly, but not solely, in the case of private museums (i.e. in the United States).

Thirdly, collectors are by far the most important factor serving to swell demand, particularly for illicitly obtained goods. They constitute an increasingly large and, in social, economic and cultural terms, relatively diversified international caste. Their motives are many and varied, but

whatever the source of their drive, virtually all collectors are, in this respect, self-centred: the sole criteria by which they are guided, within the limit of their financial resources, are their own pleasure and interest. Such collectors are for us of the greatest importance in so far as they are concerned by the licit or illicit nature of their acquisitions only if they run a major risk. Moreover, being generally neither scholars nor scientists, they do not require any precise identification, certificate of origin or related documentation.

In the rich countries, and in the upper social classes of the poor countries, collectors represent a considerable market on their own, whose operation is little known. One will finance clandestine excavations in Peru in order to stock a private museum with gold artefacts culled from tombs (at the cost of totally destroying the rest of the funerary furniture). Another collector in the Philippines is known to have approached village priests with an offer to exchange comparable pieces of deal or plywood furniture of recent make for more or less worm-eaten but ancient, sacred church furnishings. Yet another, at the beginning of the century, paid peasants to plough up the earth in the Fairies' Grotto in Arcy-sur-Cure in order to extract the finest specimens of Palaeolithic tools, thereby disrupting for ever an outstanding stratigraphy.

The social status of these individuals is frequently their best guarantee of impunity before the law. It also means that practices sanctioned by success and profitability are held up as examples to be followed. The fact is that collectors are regarded as patrons of the arts, without whom so many works of art or archaeological units would either have been destroyed or overlooked. The sequence can be easily re-established on the basis of these premises: from the financing of reprehensible or truly criminal acts the collector progresses easily to the encouragement of such acts, then to the ready agreement to spontaneous offers. The risk for the collector himself dwindles, happily compensating for the rising prices he is required to pay. If, in addition, it is borne in mind that the same people who collect on their own account are frequently members of museum boards or other cultural institutions, creators of philanthropic foundations, diplomats, fashionable lecturers or respected intellectuals, it is easy to show how complex is the problem and how virtually impossible it is effectively to combat a trade in which they play the leading role.

Fourthly, tourists, although themselves generally not collectors, today represent a nursery and school for them. Once the traveller has gone beyond the stage of the tasteless souvenir, he immediately starts to hanker after "genuine" old artefacts, which will acquire a prestige value upon his return home. The countries which encourage tourism are partly responsible for this by failing to ensure that the quality of modern craftwork is maintained, allowing it to degenerate into the "airport art" so pilloried by the best specialists, but still flourishing. Naturally, the ancient artefact purchased at a market in Mexico City, Lagos, Delhi or even in southern Italy or Istanbul is more often than not just a skilful fake. Nevertheless, the phenomenon persists, and the intention of purchase is the same.

To this satisfaction of bringing back a high-quality souvenir is added the guilty pleasure (for the tourist frequently suspects the illegal nature of his action) of spiriting a prohibited article past customs officers who, when not snowed under with work, are either insufficiently informed or corrupt.

Collectors and museums only seldom have an opportunity to acquire items at source, partly, indeed, because such acquisition is illegal and because they do not possess the logistic infrastructure required for clandestine operations. While in some cases, as was witnessed in 1969 during the affair of the Raphael painting sold and apparently transported by members of the Boston Museum staff, no intermediary is involved, it is generally with specialized dealers that the purchaser must do business. Accordingly, while the dealers essentially constitute one of the main cogs in the machinery—which will be studied below—that keeps the trade going, they are also one of the components of the demand for cultural goods. Possessing, as they do, substantial resources, they are frequently the "creators of trends in taste." The best known of them are also collectors, patrons of the arts, members of academies and of museum boards, and can afford without undue risk to turn a blind eye to the law, if not of their own country, then at least of others. They do not dirty their hands by engaging in shady dealing and appear as (or make themselves out to be) benefactors of mankind intent on bringing cultures and works of art to the notice of the general public.

Together with museums, the dealers have become the true promoters of this demand which, in liberal economies, operates as the driving force of all markets. Naturally, they are also—since the concept of scientific research conducted in the field is both unfamiliar and unthinkable to

them—the agents of the transformation of cultural items into consumer goods. For them, the artistic, ethnographic or archaeological object is what the fillet of veal is to the butcher or the necklace to the jeweller: an article to be sold, for profit, even though the one is considered nobler than the other. . . .

THE SUPPLY

. . . Most of the poorest countries in the world today happen to be the richest in cultural terms, by virtue both of the complexity of their still vital spiritual and human values and of the stratification of civilizations that have succeeded one another for hundreds and indeed thousands of years. However, precisely because of their constantly evolving present-day cultures, these countries have not yet acquired the urge to "sacralize" the past, which as we have seen leads straight to the "monetization" of cultural goods. For the majority of Africans, Asians and Latin Americans, an object shorn of its functions or, *a fortiori,* one that is found buried in the ground, loses all meaning and may be re-used however one pleases, either to form part of a treasure trove possessing symbolical or mythical virtues or, more frequently, for some entirely new purpose. For example, the stones of a temple may be used to build modern houses, or the ancestral tombs may be plundered for their gold, as occurred throughout the ancient Mediterranean civilizations. In no case does the artefact acquire a cultural significance. It is in a way destroyed. Likewise, brutal changes of political regime bring considerable destruction in their wake as a result of the imposed transformation of cultural values.

Such acts have a cultural value in themselves, man having a perfect right to rework his own materials in order to build a new edifice which will mark a stage in his evolution. There is no suspicion here of artefacts being placed on any market, either national or, *a fortiori,* international. By contrast, the phenomenon which we are analysing here is altogether more serious because it is of an essentially negative kind; moreover, it is occurring at a time when the relative poverty of the Third World countries is increasing at such a vertiginous rate, above all where the poorest sectors of their populations are concerned. When such a situation is compounded by the existence of a pressing demand, it is only to be expected that objects of no practical value are offered for sale in vast numbers, since there is no natural moral law against it. Why invoke national laws, about which people usually know—or can find out—little or nothing, or the alleged duty to protect the national heritage—an invention of intellectuals? Such criteria cannot penetrate the world of the poor and the illiterate. Can a peasant be asked to give up, for legal or ethical reasons, the opportunity to boost his annual income through the occasional sale of items of pottery turned up by his plough? Now, it is only a step from the lucky, and profitable, find to the systematic collection of such objects, a step that is quickly taken when the middleman from the city or the collector "boss" is constantly clamouring to buy ever more. So it happens that tens of thousands of peasants in Costa Rica find it more remunerative to devote their energies to clandestine archaeology than to traditional crop-farming; that Peruvian highland-dwellers are busily destroying thousands of Inca tombs, bringing the gold jewels plundered from them to the millionaire Mujica Gallo, whose famous Gold Museum is so admired by tourists, themselves indifferent to the mountains of documents and artefacts thrown onto the rubbish heap; and that the ritual sculptures of the Yoruba of Nigeria become the temporary property of Hausa traders in Ibadan.

To this it will be retorted that museum staff themselves, from the director to the attendant, sometimes sell off the collections in their charge. What is astonishing, however, is not that such dishonest stewards exist, but rather that there are so few of them. It should not be forgotten that there are still museum directors who earn less than $20 a month, even when their duties and responsibilities are of a higher level than those of a university lecturer. Let no one say, with the placid logic born of a clear conscience: "What hope is there, since those people sell off their own museums? Their artefacts would be better preserved and more highly respected in our countries."

It is therefore quite in the normal order of things not only that poor countries should be exploited for their cultural heritage but also that their people should become the accomplices of this exploitation. We ourselves have on several occasions noticed, in Africa, in the Middle East and elsewhere, the contempt shown by local officials and intellectuals, all trained in Europe, for their own traditional cultures, which they regard as being at once unworthy to be shown abroad and an obstacle to the modernization of their societies. To be sure, these same worthies do not hesitate at international meetings to chant the time-honoured slogans about the illicit export of cultural property. But once they return home, what do they do to stop it, to show their pride in the past, and to carry along their peoples in that continuous process by which man creates himself, a process compounded of traditions, external influences and useful technology, and which is the only true development process? . . .

To conclude by way of a tentative moral judgement, it would seem proper to emphasize the fundamental responsibility of the countries, museums and collectors that form the demand, a responsibility that cannot be attenuated by the fact that the suppliers also exist. There will always be suppliers, whenever an opportunity arises to make quick profit, one that appears unlikely to have any serious consequences. The rule whereby, in any society in which liberal capitalism prevails, it is the supply that generates the demand for consumer goods through advertising cannot be applied to cultural goods. In the case with which we are concerned here, there is, indeed, advertising of cultural goods directed at potential consumers, but this is carried out by the museums and dealers in their own countries, under the pretext of providing education in the case of the former, and of carrying on normal commercial promotion operations in the case of the latter.

PAUL M. BATOR *The International Trade in Art**

. . . In the fall of 1969 Dr. Clemency Coggins, an art historian specializing in pre-Columbian art, published a short article in *Art Journal*. Titled "Illicit Traffic of Pre-Columbian Antiquities," the article began:

In the last ten years there has been an incalculable increase in the number of monuments systematically stolen, mutilated and illicitly exported from Guatemala and Mexico in order to feed the international art market. Not since the sixteenth

---

*From Paul M. Bator, "An Essay on the International Trade in Art," *Stanford Law Review,* vol. 34 (1982), p. 275. Copyright © 1982 by Stanford Law Review. Reprinted by permission.

century has Latin America been so ruthlessly plundered.

The publication of Dr. Coggins's article represents an important milestone in the recent history of concern about illegal trade in art treasures.

That there existed such an illegal trade was, of course, no secret when Dr. Coggins wrote. Everybody has heard of Lord Elgin and remembers Byron's angry poem. Amateurs of the arts have always known that many antiquities find their way into private and public collections from sources that are "underground" in more ways than one. Complaints from classical archaeologists about the looting of sites in the Mediterranean region are an old story. And throughout the 1960s specialists were becoming increasingly aware of an impending crisis in the field of Maya art.

Nevertheless, Dr. Coggins's article dramatized and cast new perspectives on the problem. In the first place, her article was not the usual impressionistic account and denunciation of illicit pot hunting. Appended to it was a 2-page fine-print list of specific monumental sculptures and reliefs, most of them acknowledged masterpieces of pre-Columbian civilization, which could be documented as recently stolen from Mexico or Guatemala. This was not, in other words, a question of obscure pots pilfered from unknown graves; this was a question of known monuments from known sites, some already fully excavated and completely published, some actually registered as national monuments.

Dr. Coggins's article brought to public attention a second and tragic feature of the problem. Because the monuments involved are enormous, thieves cannot remove them without mutilation. The large intricately carved "stelae," some of them as tall as forty feet and weighing five tons, must be "thinned"—that is, sawed, hacked, split apart with crowbars, or simply smashed into movable pieces—before they are ready for the art market. Dr. Coggins thus established that aesthetic values, as well as scientific and scholarly ones, were in peril. Greed for art was destroying it.

Third, the loss to science and scholarship was itself special in this case. Understanding Maya civilization depends on our coming to understand the still largely undeciphered and extremely complex Maya hieroglyphic system. Since virtually no Maya books exist, this body of writing survives principally in the form of inscriptions—containing historical, religious, and astronomical data—carved into the great ceremonial stelae, usually around the edges and back. Deciphering the language requires the survival of these inscriptions; it requires, also, knowing their source and placing (and even the location of a stela within a particular site), so that inscriptions can be cross-related with pictures and with each other. For purposes of the commercial art market, however, these "glyphs" are much less valuable than pictorial carvings; they are consequently lopped off in the process of thinning the stelae for transport and sale. Looting, in other words, was threatening to destroy the most important records we have of a great civilization.

Fourth, and most important, Dr. Coggins's detective work traced a substantial portion of this stolen and mutilated art from the jungles of Central America into some of America's most respectable museums. Included were institutions as eminent as the Cleveland Museum of Art, the Houston Museum of Fine Arts, the Minneapolis Institute of Art, the Brooklyn Museum, Nelson Rockefeller's Museum of Primitive Art, and the St. Louis City Art Museum. Other looted pieces were traced to private dealers, collectors, and European museums.

The cat was thus out of the bag. The respectable part of the art world could no longer pretend that the looting of ancient art was a matter involving only a few obscure peasants, corrupt local officials, and unscrupulous dealers. Splendid national treasures, stolen and mutilated, could within a few years find their way into the halls of America's most sumptuous museums. As Dr. Coggins said, "to a specialist in the pre-Columbian field, this is rather like finding your local museum has just bought the Arch of Titus."

Dr. Coggins's account of the "Maya crisis" played an important role in giving credibility to the contention that the illegal traffic in art treasures is a problem that has to be taken seriously. Its publication was, further, roughly contemporaneous with other events and trends focusing world attention on the problem. Within the United States a number of highly publicized scandals involving major American museums and well-known collectors—including Boston's Museum of Fine Arts and its Raphael, the Metropolitan Museum and its "calyx crater," and Mr. Norton Simon and his million-dollar Hindu sculpture (the "Nataraja")—made "smuggled art" a matter of front page news. Some journalism of unusual depth devoted to this issue also appeared in the early 1970s. On the diplomatic front, the United

States came under increasing pressure from other countries to help stem an alleged flood of looted antiquities and stolen art finding its way into the United States. And the international community, in the form of the member countries of UNESCO, met in the spring of 1970 to draft an international convention on the "means of prohibiting and preventing the illicit import, export and transfer of ownership of cultural property"; the resulting Convention was adopted by UNESCO in November, 1970.

Throughout the 1970s developments in the United States and the rest of the world responded to this heightened sense of concern. (a) A virtually unanimous consensus emerged that the Maya situation constituted a genuine emergency. Consequently in July 1970 the United States signed a treaty with Mexico assuring the cooperation of the United States in the repatriation of Mexican cultural property illicitly exported, and in October 1972 Congress passed legislation prohibiting the import into the United States of monumental pre-Columbian sculpture and fresco which was exported illegally from its country of origin. (b) In August 1972 the U.S. Senate gave its consent to American adherence to the UNESCO Convention. The House of Representatives passed an implementing statute in 1977, but the further progress of this legislation has been stalled ever since. (c) Legal action has been taken against Americans guilty of complicity in the illegal art traffic. In an unprecedented action, the Guatemalan Government sued an American art dealer in 1971 for return of a stolen stela; in 1973 the same dealer was convicted in federal court of conspiracy to transport stolen goods in interstate and foreign commerce. Another such federal conviction—a highly controversial one—was upheld by the U.S. Court of Appeals for the Fifth Circuit in 1979. (d) The threat of possible legal action—or at least of embarrassing scandal—persuaded some museums to return looted art treasures to their country of origin. Thus the Brooklyn Museum returned a stela fragment stolen from Piedras Negras to Guatemala. (e) A number of American museums have voluntarily adopted new policies designed to bar the acquisition of illicitly exported art. And an international effort to facilitate the "repatriation" of national art treasures has been recently mounted by UNESCO. . . .

COMMENTS

1. The Bator article is an excellent legal and policy discussion of the topics in this chapter. It has been republished as a monograph, *The International Trade in Art* (Chicago: University of Chicago Press, 1982). There is an enormous amount of writing on the topic, which Bator cites and discusses. Sharon A. Williams, *The International and National Protection of Movable Cultural Property: A Comparative Study* (Dobbs Ferry, N.Y.: Oceana Publications, 1978), is another useful legal discussion. Karl Meyer, *The Plundered Past* (New York: Atheneum, 1973), is still the best work on the topic for the general reader.

2. Although the world's imagination was captured by the problem of Mayan sites, a much wider variety of objects from ancient and modern cultures are involved in the traffic. Analytically, there are three principal variations in illicit international traffic in art:

1. The law of a European country prohibits the export of privately owned works of art that are classified as "national treasures." X owns an old master painting that is so classified. He sells it to Y, who smuggles it out of the country, and the painting next appears in a major museum in the United States. This is an "illegal export" case.

2. A German museum owns an important painting. It is stolen and subsequently appears in a private collection in the United States. This is a "simple theft" case.

3. By the law of a Central American nation all ancient monuments, the contents of tombs, and other relics of earlier civilizations found in or built on the earth are the property of the state. Works stolen from sites in this nation frequently appear in major public and private collections in other nations. This is a "national theft" case.

Of the three, "simple theft" cases are ethically and legally the least complicated; most would agree that the theft of works of art from their owners should be discouraged. All legal systems do prohibit and punish such theft, and the private international law concerning the right of stolen works when found in other nations is reasonably clear. The "illegal export" and "national theft" variations raise thornier ethical issues, and the applicable law is far less clear or simple. We begin with illegal export.

NATIONAL RETENTION POLICIES

Most nations (the United States and Switzerland are two major exceptions) attempt to prevent or restrict the export of works of art and other cultural property, usually but not always limited in application to works more than fifty or a hundred years old and excluding the works of living artists. Although the national laws vary widely in detail, the types of regulation fall into four general categories.

1. One is the total prohibition of sale or exchange. That is the position, for example, in Mexico and Guatemala for pre-Columbian works. As a result, the international market for pre-Columbian objects from these countries can only be satisfied illegally.
2. In other nations, such as France and Italy, one finds total prohibition of export of listed works of great national importance plus the requirement of a permit for other works. In both nations, applying for a permit involves delay, confrontation with a bureaucracy, paperwork, and, in Italy, payment of an export tax (unless the object is being exported to a Common Market nation). In other words, for listed works there is no licit international market. For other works the process of legal export is burdened with delay, expense, and procedural difficulty.
3. In a third category, represented by Canada and Great Britain, an export permit is required for broad classes of artworks but is in most cases routinely awarded without substantial bureaucratic confrontation or unreasonable delay. For a small number of works a permit is temporarily withheld to allow institutions within the exporting country to acquire the work at a fair value. If none does so within the allotted time, the permit is then issued.
4. The fourth category is represented by the United States, which places no limitations on export.

For fuller descriptions of national laws, see P. J. O'Keefe and Lyndel V. Prott, *Law and the Cultural Heritage,* vol. 1: *Discovery and Excavation* (Oxford: Profession Books, Ltd., 1984) (this excellent study is the first of a projected five-volume series); Halina Niec, "Legislative Models of Protection of Cultural Property," *Hastings Law Journal,* vol. 27 (1976), pp. 1089ff; Bonnie Burnham, *The Protection of Cultural Property: Handbook of National Legislations* (Paris: International Council of Museums, 1974).

What are the purposes of laws prohibiting or limiting the export of cultural property? The following excerpt responds to that question.

J. H. MERRYMAN AND A. E. ELSEN *Interests of Exporting Nations**

SPECIFIC CULTURAL VALUE

The interests at play in exporting nations are relatively obvious. There is, first of all, the con-cern one hears about wrenching a work of art from the culture in which it is embedded, thus

*From J. H. Merryman and A. E. Elsen, "Hot Art: A Reexamination of the Illegal International Trade in Cultural Objects," *Journal of Arts Management and Law,* vol. 12, no. 3 (Fall 1982), pp. 8–11. Copyright © 1982. Reprinted by permission of the Helen Dwight Reid Educational Foundation.

depriving the society of benefits that are real, even though they may be difficult to measure and even though their articulation requires the use of vague terms like "cultural importance." A recent notorious example is the Afo-A-Kom, a statue of religious and cultural importance to the Kom (a tribe in French Cameroon), which appeared in a New York dealer's shop in late 1973 and was after much publicity returned to the tribe. The words of the First Secretary of the Cameroon Embassy in Washington convey the point:

It is beyond money, beyond value. It is the heart of the Kom, what unifies the tribe, the spirit of the nation, what holds us together.

The Afo-A-Kom for the Kom, the Crown of St. Stephen for Hungarians, the Liberty Bell for Americans, are merely obvious and extreme examples of objects that have cultural contemporary importance for one society quite distinct from their value as works of art, as antiquities, or as materials of scholarship. Most works of art and archaeological monuments and artifacts share this quality to some extent, although seldom so obviously or intensely as in the examples just given. They have something to do with cultural specification. They tell a people who they are, remind them of what they have in common. They help to satisfy a basic need for identity, symbolize shared values and experience. Like the Afo-A-Kom, they "unify the tribe, represent the spirit of the nation, they are what hold us together."

Specific cultural value of this kind is not neutral; it lends itself to a variety of uses, some benign, others less so. Thus, the symbols that bind a nation together can also be used in the service of aggressive and invidious nationalism, of claimed cultural or racial superiority—as recent world history (e.g. Nazi Germany) amply illustrates. In a culturally plural new nation (e.g. Cameroon) such symbols (e.g. the Afo-A-Kom) can strengthen tribal identity and thus impede the process of nation building.

THE ARCHAEOLOGICAL INTEREST

A second identifiable interest grows out of the desire to prevent destruction of the records of civilization. . . . The argument is that the best remaining record of the Mayan civilization—which is little understood and whose writing is not yet deciphered—is integral to the monumental architecture and sculpture of Mayan sites, deriving much of its significance and revealing much of its

information to scholars only while it remains in place. The mere fact of removal of a part takes it out of context and diminishes its meaning as a record of a civilization. In the case of Mayan stelae, the act of removal causes physical destruction to remaining parts of the site and often, because of the crudeness of the methods employed, to the stelae themselves. The sites frequently have not been fully excavated, photographed and documented. What is lost is irretrievably lost: destroyed in the process of looting, defaced by amputation, removed from its context, made anonymous by the unscholarly nature of its removal, by the lack of documentation of its origin, by the clandestine nature of its movement in the national or international art market.

We will argue that the archeological interest is of high international importance. All of mankind is impoverished by destruction of the records of such civilizations.

INTEGRITY OF THE WORK OF ART

A third interest, also illustrated by the Mayan case, is in preservation of the integrity of the work of art. It refers to the desire to keep the parts of a work together, in the belief that some of its value is lost if it is dismembered—even if it is carefully dismembered. At the heart of this interest is the belief that the whole of a work of art is greater than the sum of its parts. A famous example is the Parthenon in Athens, most of whose marble sculpture is in the British Museum in London. Other considerations aside, all would agree that the marbles should be reunited with the temple, in the interest of the integrity of the Parthenon as a work of art. That could, of course, be remedied by transporting the rest of the temple to the British Museum, and there reuniting it with the sculptures, but removal of the Parthenon would destroy the integrity of the Acropolis, and no one has seriously suggested that the entire Acropolis be transported to London. Accordingly, if integrity of the work of art were the only consideration, then the argument for return of the Elgin marbles to the Parthenon would be clear. There are, however, other interests at play.

PHYSICAL SAFETY OF THE WORK OF ART

The most fundamental of these other interests is the physical safety of the work of art itself. Returning to the Elgin marbles for the moment, one often hears as a justification for their removal that they might have been destroyed or badly damaged—by the action of the elements, more recently by the smog of Athens—if they had been left in place. Taking them to the British Museum, according to this argument, has preserved them. This argument can be employed with greater or less force in a variety of situations. Thus, it has been used to attempt to justify removal of Mayan stelae from their sites, even to justify the theft of paintings from decrepit churches and seedy provincial museums in southern Europe. While we do not give undue credit to such self-serving appeals to the art preservation interest, we do call attention to the fact that its application depends on the facts of the case. In most cases, concern for the safety of the work of art justifies limiting its movement. One of the arguments against the looting of Mayan sites is the fearful damage that is done to the works themselves in the process. That is a powerful argument. Still, there may be cases in which concern for the safety of the work will argue for, rather than against, its removal.

THE ECONOMIC INTEREST

Artworks have two kinds of economic worth: intrinsic and extrinsic. The intrinsic economic worth can be measured by the price the work would bring on an open world market. If the work is removed without payment of that price into the national economy (e.g. if the work is stolen) the nation is so much the poorer. If the price is paid, the removal will not impair the exporting nation's interest in the work's intrinsic economic worth. The uniform international rule that the courts of any nation are open to an owner seeking to recover a stolen article or its value from a thief (subject to rules protecting good faith purchasers) is a clear recognition of this kind of interest. Works of art, however, often also have substantial extrinsic economic worth. Their presence in the nation attracts tourists and their money and thus enriches the nation's economy. It is unlikely that such value would be fully recovered if the work were offered for sale on an open market. The extrinsic value is to some extent external to ownership of the work, not fully captured on its sale. In fact, there is nothing like an open market in such works, and the intention of national laws and proposed international regulations is to limit the market. We shall argue be-

low that the result often is to insure that the exporting nation, as a result, loses rather than captures economic value.

THE ARTISTIC INTEREST

There is also an important national artistic interest in retaining works of art. . . . The presence of art from the past of their homeland can be an inspiration to living artists. This is dramatically apparent in countries such as Japan, where recent art has often taken inspiration from the great Japanese tradition of painting and woodcuts. The governments of Indonesia and many African republics are interested in developing cultural nationalism and want their artists to be exposed to great models of the past. The history of modern art gives important evidence of the influence of a society's older art in inspiring new creativity. The sculptor Brancusi drew ideas from Rumanian folk art. The early Russian abstract artists, such as Kandinsky, were influenced by the example of great icon artists in their country. Many German Expressionists were fired by examples of late medieval woodcarving in their museums and churches. In America members of the Abstract Expressionist movement such as Jackson Pollock, Adolph Gottlieb, and Barnett Newman at critical moments in their careers were drawn to the art of American Indians. More basically, such works enrich the lives of those who view them. The power and beauty of great art contribute to the quality of life. They satisfy the basic human need that all the arts satisfy. A society deprived of its artworks is an impoverished society.

THE DISTRIBUTION INTEREST

Some people in some nations perceive it to be in the national interest that the achievements of their culture be widely distributed among the world's museums. Thus, it has been argued that the sale of Jackson Pollock's "Blue Poles" to the Australian National Museum was good for American art and that our nation should encourage the widest possible distribution of such works. We believe that this interest is shared widely among art-rich nations but that it is too frequently submerged by a process which overvalues competing national interests. Still, there are exceptional cases in which the distribution argument works in favor of strict controls in the exporting nation.

Thus, for example, few would argue that Nigeria should encourage the export of Benin bronzes.

MERE RETENTION

Finally, there is the *merely retentive* attitude that works within the nation should stay there. We are tempted to call this the "hoarding" instinct and deny it the dignity of classification as a national interest. It is exemplified in those nations that have acquired and retain huge stocks of duplicate material that is not exploited at home but is not made available for sale or trade.

THE AFO-A-KOM CASE

The tale of the Afo-A-Kom, which begins in New York and ends in Africa, is a story of theft, commerce, and goodwill. An October 25, 1973, *New York Times* article by Fred Ferretti told about this statue that "embodies the spiritual, political and religious essence of the 35,000 people of the West African kingdom of Kom in Cameroon." A little over 5 feet tall, made of rough wood, the statue represents a man standing behind a stool or small throne, holding in his hands a scepter and wearing a headdress or crown. The sackcloth-covered figure and part of the stool are decorated in brown and blue beads, and the face is covered in copper.

The statue was being shown in an exhibit at Dartmouth College, on loan from the Furman Gallery in New York, where it was on sale for $60,000. It had vanished six years before from a royal compound, Ngumba House, in Laikom, Kom, where it had been kept with two similar female statues with which it was said to be displayed once a year to the people as symbolic of the royal dynasty and in the presence of which the king was "enstooled" after ceremonies and meditation. Aaron Furman was first reported as saying that he was "not inclined to return it nor sell it back" because it had been bought from an "impeccable" dealer in good faith.

Officials of the Cameroon Embassy said that, after years of searching, the discovery of the whereabouts of the statue was good news and that "we shall do everything to retrieve it." In the meantime, the State Department cabled the American Embassy in Cameroon to determine what authorities there wanted the U.S. government to do.

With publicity about the discovery came comments from specialists in the field. A former missionary who had lived in Kom for several years, Gilbert Schneider, a professor of linguistics at Ohio University, said, "Aaron perhaps didn't know what an emotional, highly charged piece of African art he has. This is a national treasure. It ought to be returned." Dr. Ray Sieber, professor of art history at Indiana University, said, "It ought to go back." D. Frank Willet, of Northwestern University, also an art historian, whose area of specialization was African art, said, "Too often the collecting of traditional African art is scandalous, not an interest in art, but in bank balances and safe deposits." Karl Meyer, a journalist who has written on the looting of pre-Columbian sites, remarked that the Afo-A-Kom incident was "just a sad illustration of an unconscionable problem. That anyone would dream of buying a piece with such a suspect history is as much a commentary on our national morality as anything we've heard in Washington."

On the other hand, the visiting curator who put together the show at Dartmouth, Tamara Northern, asked, "Stolen in whose eyes? A willing buyer connotes a willing seller. The fact that Mr. Furman has the statue does not exclude the fact that someone in authority, for whatever reason, for whatever amount of money, disposed of it."

Only a few days had passed, however, before Furman cabled the king of Kom: "Your highness, In deep sympathy with you and the people of Kom, you will be happy to know that arrangements for the permanent return of the Afo-A-Kom to its homeland have been under discussion for the past week with Warren Robbins of the Museum of African Art in Washington."

Indeed, institutions and private individuals had stepped forward to volunteer their aid in returning the statue. Conversations were begun with Mr. Furman and his attorney, and Warren Robbins became the agent for the negotiations. A member of the museum's national council, Laurence Gussman, a New York businessman, a collector of African art, and president of the Schweitzer Hospital in Gabon, made it known that he would be willing to buy the statue in order to return it. The Warner-Lambert Pharmaceutical Company, a New York film producer, and the Buffalo Museum of Science all made pledges of support. Mr. Furman's attorney reported that the dealer wished only to cover his expenses, although he had received offers from collectors "who don't give a damn." Mr. Furman wanted assurances that the statue would remain with the Kom people. The writers for the *New York Times* had been told by various experts that in the past when an important African piece had been discovered in a museum and had been returned, it sometimes would appear on the market again. The *Times* had also learned that Paris was the prime depot for African art and that in many cases theft or the bribery of local government officials had been involved.

It was later reported that the Afo-A-Kom had in fact been taken from its sacred sanctuary by a son and nephew of Fon Alo-ah, who was said to have died shortly after its disappearance. The new king, Fon Nsom Ngwe, was enstooled with a new statue carved by a local artist.

The tale of the return of the original statue, however, is one of uncertain moral. The *National Geographic* of July 1974 carried a brief report by William S. Ellis, and *Esquire* of May 1974 had a long and colorful report by Sophy Burnham. It appears that the officials of the Cameroon government were not as delighted with the return of the object as had been expected. When a *Times* reporter telephoned the president of that country upon discovery of the statue he responded, in French, "The what? What is it? Where is Kom?"

When a party accompanying the statue back to Cameroon arrived in Douala, a young business-suited African remarked, "I come from only fifty miles from Kom. I never heard of the Afo-A-Kom. Was it really for sale for sixty thousand dollars?" This was a response heard repeatedly by members of the party as they went through about seven ceremonies conducted for the press to present the statue to the Cameroon government. In fact, the party, which included, among others, Gussman, two representatives of the Museum of African Art in Washington, one of them Warren Robbings, and three men from the National Geographic Society, was told at one point that they would not be allowed to present the statue to the Fon because it was the property of the nation. The difficulty appeared to be that it was a tribal totem and that presenting it back to the Kom people in fact reinforced clan loyalty at a time when the government was attempting to solidify a nation that included two hundred tribes with twenty-four languages, as well as French and English, and which had itself been in existence only fourteen years. The Americans insisted, however, and in the village of Fundong, where the statue was finally uncrated before him, the Fon declared, "This is the Kom thing." At a second ceremony Gussman was presented with the Cameroon Medal of Honor First Class, and the representatives of the Museum of African Art each received the Medal of Honor Second Class—depicting a black man hoeing a pineapple field. The Afo-A-Kom was recrated and sent back to the royal compound in Laikom.

In 1985 a major exhibition of art from Cameroon, including the Afo-A-Kom, traveled to several U.S. museums, setting to rest rumors that it had again appeared on the international art market.

COMMENTS

1. The Afo-A-Kom case seems clear. It was right to go to some trouble to have it returned to the Kom. Why? What interests, among those set out in the previous excerpts, were served by the return? What interests, if any, were endangered by the return?

2. What should be one's attitude toward Italy's claim that a painting by a French artist, Matisse, painted in France about fifty years earlier, part of a private art collection in a private home in Milan, is an important part of Italy's cultural heritage? See *Jeanneret v. Vichy,* set out later in this chapter.

3. In 1979 the Argentine owner of a valuable collection of Impressionist and modern paintings, including works by Degas, Renoir, Manet, Gauguin, Toulouse-Lautrec, Matisse, and Picasso, sent it to London for auction. According to a report in the March 19, 1979, *New York Times,* the Argentine government announced that it would use "diplomatic and legal channels" to stop the auction and recover the collection, which it said was "illegally taken out of Argentina." Which of the interests described in the previous excerpt does Argentina have in such a collection? As a matter of policy, should foreign nations take the Argentine government's claim seriously?

4. In November 1979 the Getty Museum acquired a bronze statue, believed to be by the fourth-century B.C. Greek artist Lysippus, for $3.9 million—the highest known price ever paid for a statue. The life-size bronze, probably of a victorious athlete, was found by fishermen in the Adriatic Sea near Rimini (although it is unclear whether it was found within or outside Italian territorial waters). After being secretly taken to an Italian village near Rimini, the bronze found its way to Germany for restoration and eventually to Malibu, California. Italian authorities claimed that the statue was the property of the Italian state because it had been found on Italian property, and they eventually prosecuted and convicted several Italians allegedly involved in its concealment and sale. Since the statue itself was never produced as evidence, however, the convictions were reversed by the Rome Appeals Court. The museum claims that its legal title to the Lysippus is in order, despite Italy's charge that it was illegally exported. For an inconclusive but lively account of its discovery and subsequent adventures, see Bryan Rostron, "Smuggled!" *Saturday Review,* March 31, 1978, pp. 25–30. What is the nature of Italy's interest in this bronze?

5. The Getty bronze, found in the Adriatic Sea, raises a variety of legal problems specific to underwater archaeology. These questions, among many others, were considered at a series of United Nations conferences on the law of the sea, and their major product, the 1982 Convention on the Law of the Sea, was signed by 117 countries (not including the United States). Articles 149 and 303 of the Convention apply to underwater archaeology. See P. J. O'Keefe and L. V. Prott, *Law and the Cultural Heritage,* vol. 1: *Discovery and Excavation* (Oxford: Professional Books, Ltd., 1984), secs. 317ff.; "Archaeological and Historical Objects: The International Legal Implications of UNCLOS III," *Virginia Journal of International Law,* vol. 22 (1982), p. 777.

6. *The Getty Factor.* The effectiveness of the British and Canadian export control systems depends on the right of national institutions to purchase particularly significant objects offered for sale by their owners. Many such objects, though foreign in origin (e.g., Italian Renaissance paintings), have been in British private collections for centuries. There have been widespread fears that the immense financial resources of the Getty trust may affect the ability of British institutions to deal with the flood of offers for important pictures at "Getty enhanced values." In 1983, for example, the Getty Museum was reported to have offered a British private collector £5.5 million (about $8.1 million) for a Rembrandt portrait whose highest reasonable value could be put at £3.5 million ($5.3 million), according to a statement made by Lord Normanby, chairman of the British Charitable National Art Collections Fund (*ARTnewsletter,* July 24, 1983, p. 6). Timothy Clifford, director of the Manchester City Art Gallery, proposed that a list of the top two thousand works of art remaining under private ownership in Great Britain should be drawn up, with a total export prohibition placed on them. Would such a prohibition be justified?

However, another "Getty factor" has entered the picture. J. Paul Getty II, who lives in England, helped England retain a Duccio di Buoninsegna painting with a gift of $524,000 to the Manchester City Art Gallery (*ARTnewsletter,* September 4, 1984, p. 1). Subsequently Mr. Getty made a gift ($64 million according to one report, $75 million according to another) to the National Gallery in London, which will enable it to compete on more even terms for works offered for export.

RETENTION VS. PROTECTION

The discussion of hot art is frequently carried on in euphemistic terms, particularly in international meetings and in the work of international organizations. There the talk often is of "protection" of cultural property, when what is really being discussed is retention. It is obvious that the national interest in retention may not concur with preserving "the cultural heritage of all mankind" (the language of the preamble to the 1954 Hague Convention, set out in Chapter 1). Consider the case of Peru, which is only one example of a common problem.

*Peru's Campaign to Halt Trade in Stolen Art**

The Peruvian Government is waging an urgent campaign to halt a billion-dollar trade in stolen art treasures that is ravaging the country's cultural heritage.

Diplomatic efforts culminated in the signing of an agreement with the United States in mid-September to facilitate the return of stolen works of art recovered by United States authorities.

At the same time, the Public Prosecutor's Office has launched an investigation into the activities of Peruvian dealers and collectors who are said to act as the agents for foreign buyers.

The export of artwork has been prohibited since 1929. But the law has failed to stop a boom in the trading of gold and silver objects, colonial-era paintings and centuries-old pottery.

"In the past 10 years, the illegal trade has flourished, especially toward the United States and Europe," a senior official of the National Institute of Culture said recently.

"Most of our best pieces are already abroad and if it continues, Peru will be left with only a mediocre collection of its own antiques," he said.

Clients are wealthy, cultured and demanding. "They want only the best," he said, "which is why the finest pieces disappear."

Furious at the appearance of Peruvian treasures in foreign auctioneers' catalogues, the Government decided earlier this year to take action to halt the trade.

It achieved an immediate success when the New York branch of Sotheby Parke Bernet, the art auctioneers, withdrew from a sale seven colonial paintings that the Peruvian Government charged had been stolen from Peruvian churches and museums.

Six were returned to Peru after the Government presented documentary evidence to back its claim. It is now seeking to recover 46 more earmarked for auction.

Cultural officials said the recovery marked an important precedent and had apparently already discouraged some collectors from buying Peruvian works.

A longer-term achievement was the signing of the agreement with the United States Government to speed up repatriation of stolen antiques.

The agreement, similar to one signed between the United States and Mexico in 1970, will allow the Peruvian Government to bypass the courts and obtain quick recovery of treasures if they can prove they have been stolen.

"Legal proceedings are lengthy and costly," one cultural official said. "While they go on, the antiques deteriorate because they are not properly stored."

The Institute of Culture said more than 5,000 works of art were stolen last year, and the main targets were churches in the region of Cuzco, the ancient capital of the Incas 365 miles east southeast of Lima. The Incas dominated the region at the time of the Spanish conquest in 1532, and the area is filled with Incan and colonial relics, which have made it one of the most famed archeological regions of the continent.

Most of the region's 305 chapels and churches have been pillaged of their finest treasures and archeological sites have been cleared by clandestine digging.

The local authorities are installing burglar alarms in 18 of the most important churches.

Mayor Willy Monzon said the budget of less

*Originally published as "Peru Wages Campaign to Halt Trade in Stolen Art Treasures," *New York Times*, October 4, 1981, p. 13.

than $25,000 was not enough to provide adequate security in the cathedral, which overlooks Cuzco's central square and was built in 1564.

"The only protection our churches has is the good faith of the local people," he said. "Unfortunately, that is no longer sufficient."

Mr. Monzon charged that local people carried out the robberies on the orders of outside dealers. "They are as well organized as the drug traffickers," he said.

Government officials agree. "The financing and organization comes from abroad and the locals are used for the dirty work," one official said.

The Government is also taking action at home. Official sources said the public prosecutor would shortly bring charges against a number of prominent people involved in the illicit trade.

The National Institute of Culture is also speeding up cataloguing of works held in museums, churches and private collections and tightening security in public buildings.

EDWARD SCHUMACHER *Peru's Antiquities Crumbling in Museums**

Pre-Columbian works of art and artifacts of major historical interest, some dating to 6,000 years before Christ, are rotting, crumbling or being stolen in museums [in Peru].

Museum curators and archeologists say that up to half of the priceless ceramics, textiles and other objects in Peru's more than 250 public and private museums have been lost or irreparably damaged in recent years.

"Each day we are losing more," said Luis Guillermo Lumbreras, a leading Peruvian archeologist and former director of the National Archeology and Anthropology Museum. "It's tragic."

Sylvio Mutal, head of Unesco's cultural preservation programs in Latin America, said a Unesco study completed last month on Peru's museums concluded that after years of meager budgets, "they can no longer cope" with their problems.

The decay of antiquities is a problem shared by many developing nations, but Peru's problem is especially critical. Peru was one of the most advanced centers of ancient civilization in the Western Hemisphere, and it holds an interest for museum curators, archeologists and prehistorians matched only by Egypt and China.

In addition, an unusually great number of artifacts have survived from ancient Peru because civilization here developed around oases along the narrow desert wedged between the Pacific Ocean and the Andes Mountains. Much of this desert is dryer than the Sahara, and the lack of humidity, the relatively cool underground temperature and the chemical neutrality of the soil preserved the remains largely intact.

THE CATALOGUE OF DAMAGE

The trouble began after objects were removed from the ground and put in museums and storehouses without humidity controls. Moisture in the air draws out ground salts in the ceramics and causes them to attack surface paint. Some brittle ceramics, such as pre-Christian, foot-high human figures with small arms and legs, have turned into dust, curators said. Insects and fungi have also done untold damage.

But Peru, which is one of the poorest nations in South America with a per capita income of only about $1,000 a year, cannot afford the controlled environment that would assure the preservation of the relics.

A recent stockroom tour of the more than half million pieces in the national museum, an expanded farmhouse, showed the holdings to be riddled with termites, infested with rats and attacked by fungi. The museum lacks climate controls and is seriously understaffed.

Wooden totems dating back 3,000 years were filled with termite holes. Half the face of a four-foot image of a person from the Chimu culture that curators said dates back 500 to 900 years had been eaten away in the museum.

Several hundred thousand ceramic vases,

*Originally published as "Peru's Rich Antiquities Crumbling in Museums," *New York Times,* August 15, 1983, p. 14.

bowls and figures 4,000 years old are crammed on to shelves. Curators are so unsure how many there are that estimates vary widely. Many vases are stacked, which weakens and cracks those on the bottom.

INSECTS EAT MUMMIES' HAIR

Many colorful painted ceramics have turned dull in storage. Among these are rows of 2,500-year-old Nazca polychrome vases depicting stylized cats and birds that are now faded and lifeless.

There are mummies in the museum, too. Peru's many ancient cultures—the Chavín, Paracas and Inca, which began emerging 8,000 years ago—mummified their dead and buried them with ceramics, weavings, seeds and food.

While mummies thousands of years old have been exposed on storage shelves, insects have eaten the hair. Buckets of bare skulls sit in the dirt courtyard outside. So do soggy cardboard boxes where researchers keep their shards and other study pieces. The research takes place in wooden shacks with large holes in the roofs. One archeology student said she has to quit work when it rains.

The museum is backed up in its effort to open and study the thousands of mummy bundles on its shelves; some of those still unopened were acquired in the 1940's, curators said, and rats have chewed holes in them.

But it is the deterioration of the woven fabrics that archeologists consider the greatest tragedy. Some date back 8,000 years and are among the oldest known to man.

The ancient Peruvians were perhaps the first to achieve tight weaves and strong fabrics, mixing fibers such as wool and alpaca. They also used an unusually wide range of dyes and created masterly designs on works up to 50 yards long.

Some of the weavings have been so harmed by fungi and insects while in the museum that curators say blowing on them makes them disintegrate.

Restorers working with microscopes are trying to restitch one textile that is in better condition than many. This 2,500-year-old weaving from the Paracas culture depicts a series of geometric human figures in red, orange and yellow. All that remains of it is a 4-foot-by-2-foot fragment.

Other textiles pulled out of drawers by Edu-

ardo Versteylen, the musuem's head conservator, were partly in threads.

GOOD INTENTIONS GONE AWRY

The loss of many of the weavings is particularly poignant because the Rockefeller family donated money 30 years ago specifically to conserve them. But the weavings were stored on top of cotton cloths laid over wooden shelves or placed under glass. The wood and cotton, being organic, attracted insects and fungi. The weavings placed under glass also decomposed.

Five years ago, the museum built its only climate-controlled room to house its nearly 40,000 weavings. It decontaminated many of the textiles by washing them in glycerine and put them on treated cotton in metal drawers. Thousands of the weavings still remain in cardboard boxes, however.

Thieves, meanwhile, broke into the museum two years ago and stole 34 gold and silver relics, including a two-pound, solid gold ceremonial knife that was a national symbol displayed on tourist posters. The knife, called a tumi, was recovered but had been mutilated.

The museum staff is pained by the deterioration it sees but is limited by a budget that last year was less than $200,000, Mr. Rosas said. That amount barely covered the salary of the museum's 89 staff members, including guards and secretaries. The staff is so small that only one curator and an assistant work with the several hundred thousand ceramics.

"We just get enough to survive as an institution," Hermilio Rosas La Noire, the museum's longtime assistant director, said.

The national budget for the nearly 250 public museums, including the national museum, is only $600,000, and Peru, like all of Latin America, has little tradition of private philanthropy.

AMBITIOUS SOLUTION PROPOSED

The Government of President Fernando Belaúnde Terry has been more sensitive than most to the problem. Its proposed solution is a new $40-million archeology museum to replace the current one.

The new museum is to be totally climate-controlled and will have more storage space, conservation laboratories, protected disply areas and facilities for an expanded staff.

Construction has begun in anticipation of an Inter-American Development Bank loan of $20 million next month. Mr. Belaúnde Terry has budgeted $10 million in Government money.

"You have to pay attention to cultural and spiritual needs even in times of crisis," Senator Manuel Ulloa, a former Prime Minister who heads a committee overseeing the project, said.

The project, however, is still shy $10 million, which the Government hopes will be provided by contributions from abroad. And even if finished, it would not completely solve the problem of the deterioration of Peru's cultural patrimony.

According to the experts and to the Unesco study, most museums in the country are in even worse condition than the national museum.

Peruvian curators have been loath to acknowledge the state of their museums, and many have been reluctant to open their storerooms to journalists. The reason, in many cases, has to do with the fact that thousands of pre-Columbian objects have been smuggled out of the country despite Peruvian laws which make the export of antiquities illegal.

One rationale of some of those who trade in or collect pre-Columbian antiquities is that "they are better off outside the country."

Some Peruvian archeologists, such as Mr. Lumbreras, say the Peruvian laws against the export of antiquities work against better conservation. By authorizing the sale of more common artifacts, he said, Peru could raise money for its museums. But sensitivity here is so acute that a change in the law is unlikely.

COMMENTS

1. Distribution and access are additional considerations. If all Aztec antiquities were kept in Mexico, that part of "the cultural heritage of all mankind" would be, in practical terms, inaccessible to most of mankind. Because the world is organized into sovereign nation-states, the Mexican government certainly has the power to provide that nothing shall leave the national territory, but should it do so? Art is a good ambassador, and many would suppose it to be advantageous to Mexico to have achievements of its many cultures fully represented in the world's great museums.

2. Many art-rich nations lack the resources and the organization to deal adequately with their cultural patrimony. How should this affect national policy toward export?

THE EFFECTS OF LEGAL CONTROLS

One important assumption behind national (and international) controls is that they will be effective. But is the assumption correct? Will the traffic in art and antiquities subside at the passage of a law? These questions are explored in the following excerpts.

J. H. MERRYMAN AND A. E. ELSEN *The Importance of a Licit Market**

There is a strong international interest in a licit market in the products of the world's cultures. If it is indeed true that the culture of any people is a part of the culture of all mankind, if it is true that international understanding is advanced by access to the products of other peoples, then unduly restrictive national policies lose much of their legitimacy. Why should the international community of nations actively lend its support to national policies that offend an important international interest? The availability of a licit market in works of the sort that the nation of origin wishes to control accordingly becomes an important consideration.

*From J. H. Merryman and A. E. Elsen, "Hot Art: A Reexamination of the Illegal International Trade in Cultural Objects," *Journal of Arts Management and Law,* vol. 12, no. 3 (Fall 1982), pp. 15–18. Copyright © 1982. Reprinted by permission of the Helen Dwight Reid Educational Foundation.

. . . It is Mexico's right to decide what should be permitted with respect to cultural objects in its jurisdiction, and . . . everyone should respect that decision. Such a position, though formally correct, is unrealistic because it ignores the existence of an international market for such works. If the market cannot be supplied through legal means, it will be supplied illegally. Indeed, the absence of a licit market insures the existence of an illicit one, with the usual consequences: loss of control over a traffic that, if licit, could be regulated; criminalization of the traffic; enrichment of the criminal element who exploit the illicit market; official bribery and other forms of corruption; the list can easily be extended. Further, such a situation becomes self-defeating. If the purpose is to preserve and protect national cultural heritage, the lack of a licit market insures the opposite. Clandestine excavation and removal in hasty circumstances by amateurs leads to loss of archaeologial information, physical damage to the sites, physical damage to the works removed, plus economic and cultural loss to the nation.

In the Mexican case, it is clear that the alternative of a licit market is possible. It is generally known that Mexico possesses large quantities of antiquities that are simply hoarded. They duplicate works already fully represented in Mexican museums; they are not exhibited; they are not needed for and, in any case, are not available for study. They are and will remain unused and anonymous. Such works could be sold to satisfy the market for them among foreign museums and private collections. They could be traded abroad for works that would enrich Mexican museums.

Such a licit traffic would deflate the indiscriminate demand for such works in the illicit market and reduce the danger to Mexican sites.

We know that these arguments have been made before. Efforts within the United Nations to obtain international agreement on programs that would encourage freer international trade in cultural properties continue. The point we wish to emphasize here, however, is the interrelation between the absence of a licit market and the attitude of the international community toward the illicit market. There is no internationally persuasive argument for vigorous support of a national policy that seems to be overbroad and, in any case, unenforceable. The international interest does not coincide with the Mexican position and perceives that the Mexican scheme is, in fact, contrary to Mexico's own interest. . . .

THE QUALITY OF ART PROTECTION AND DEVELOPMENT PROGRAMS IN ART EXPORTING NATIONS

We turn now to another important consideration: some poor countries are art-rich and some art-importing nations are, perhaps by definition, wealthy. How should these facts affect our interest analysis? One of the arguments for international action to control the traffic in stolen and smuggled art is that this will help the exporting nation to protect a national resource that it is too poor to protect by its own efforts. The argument has superficial appeal but is fundamentally defective. The defect is in the assumption that the illicit market can be eliminated or substantially reduced by international controls. We have already indicated our view that one effect of national controls is to drive the traffic into illicit channels, with a variety of undesirable consequences for the national and international interests. We are equally pessimistic about the primary and secondary consequences of rigorous international controls. While we favor the transfer of wealth to art-rich nations to assist their efforts to identify, preserve and study their cultural heritage, we oppose the attempt to impose stricter limitations on the art traffic. The belief that it is possible to preserve undeveloped art resources by such limitations is unjustified by experience. National resources must be invested in the identification, appropriation, preservation and display of such works if they are to receive true protection. The nation that both prohibits a licit market and pleads poverty as an excuse for failure to develop and protect its cultural property is acting inconsistently. On the contrary, it would advance the national, as well as the international, interest if the art-rich nation were to treat its cultural treasure as an exploitable national resource. The art wealth of the nation could be "mined" as a source of income. The prices paid in the international market for such works would finance further exploration, preservation and scholarship. Uniquely important works could be retained for the national patrimony. The creation of a licit market would take the profit out of the illicit traffic and place the identification, excavation, and distribution of works taken from sites with people who are responsible, professionally qualified and able to be supervised. This change, in turn, would advance the national and international archaeological, integrity and safety interests. In short, the relative poverty of the art-rich exporting country seems to us to be an argument against, rather than for, stricter national and international control of the art traffic.

At bottom is the view that it is in the national interest, as well as in the international interest, for the artifacts of a culture to be identified, appropriated, documented, displayed and widely distributed among the world's museums. The archaeological, integrity and safety interests are superior, as is the desire of a nation to retain articles uniquely important to its history and culture. Exploitation of the national art patrimony, subject to these principles, is in our view the preferable policy for the nation and for the international community. . . .

DWIGHT B. HEATH *Bootleg Archaeology in Costa Rica**

Everyone with a sincere interest in archaeology shares a deep concern for the irreparable damage that looting causes. Science loses by it; diplomacy suffers and ill will is aroused among peoples. As an historian of culture and sometime archaeologist, I deplore as much as anyone the illicit excavation of and traffic in antiquities. But I am also a social anthropologist and as such I am convinced that any human practice so widespread and durable must be filling some need. . . .

Rightly or wrongly, archaeological artifacts have become commercial goods and it makes sense to look at the ways in which this special market functions, even though such an approach may at first seem crass. Illicit artifacts, just like foodstuffs or clothing, are produced, distributed and consumed—"produced" by clandestine diggers or bootleg archaeologists, "distributed" by dealers and "consumed" by collectors and museums. . . .

It might at first seem that the producers of archaeological "goods" could be easily accounted for in terms as simple as "easy money." But on the basis of research done in Costa Rica, studies conducted over the course of a year from 1968 to 1969, I have come to feel that this explanation is inadequate. . . . In Costa Rica, a poor agrarian nation with a low subsistence level, the trade in illicit artifacts is more than a peripheral, rich-man's business; it is, in fact, an economic mainstay, accounting per annum for nearly one percent of the nation's total income and involving roughly 4,400 people—more than twice the number of people in the nation's medical, paramedical and pharmaceutical professions combined. Obviously bootleg archaeology is big business elsewhere, but rarely is it so open and widespread. There has been little effort made—in contrast, say, to Mexico—to educate Costa Ricans in the irreplaceable nature of the artifacts they deal in, and the practice has been illegal for only the last few years. Illicit excavation is an offense against the Republic; so is the exportation of antiquities without a permit. Export permits, exacting a small tax, are easy to get. But despite this, 95 percent of the foreign trade I learned about was conducted through smuggling.

In the eyes of the *huaqueros,* the artifacts buried in the soil of their country are part of "the national patrimony"—meaning not that they are to be treasured as inviolable or invaluable, but rather that they are a resource to be exploited. Thus looting of the past is seen as a form of mining, harmful to no one, a "crime without victims" if indeed a crime at all. This reasoning, to the outsider, may seem absurdly egocentric, perhaps even charmingly specious, but in fact it is basically neither, and when objections are voiced—as, during a 1969 crackdown—that restrictions on excavation are economically unsound, the huaqueros have a point; this is especially true in the impoverished rural northwest where so many people depend on excavations for all or part of their income that the activity cannot be rigidly restricted. . . .

During my year of research, the illicit trade artifacts totaled, by my estimate, at last a half-million dollars—an intake matched only by one tenth of the country's manufacturing establishments. . . .

Of the Costa Ricans involved in huaquerismo, nearly 4,330 are directly involved in digging for antiquities. I arrived at this figure by counting permits issued by the National Museum to huaqueros a few years ago (for then permits were

---

*From Dwight B. Heath, "Bootleg Archaeology in Costa Rica," *Archaeology,* vol. 26 (July 1973), pp. 217–219. Copyright ©1973 by the Archaeological Society of America. Reprinted by permission.

easily obtained), and by extrapolating with conservative indices developed from extensive and intensive interviews with a select sample of 75 huaqueros. In that small country, about 4,400 people make over half their total income from the sale of antiquities. . . .

Graft and dishonesty are common with the profession, and it is not unusual for the foreman of a dig to pay various employees to withhold good objects from the excavation's "sponsor," while the sponsor pays the local police to ignore the digging or bribes a customs agent to mislabel a shipment for export.

The huaqueros not only explained the tricks of their trade but also provided me with an extraordinarily rich account of the historical, geographical and social background of the antiquities market. It was this experience with the people and their needs that brought me to understand what an important role this market plays in the country's economy and its national spirit. For there can be no doubt that the rewards of huaquerismo are partly spiritual. The men involved in the trade highly prize their independence, the pleasure of the "hunt," and the aesthetic ramifications of their business. A kind of freemasonry prevails among their numbers; they enjoy talking at great length about their technical expertise, about the various "types" of huaqueros, and even trace the genealogy of teacher-apprentice relationship. Many have a philosophical bent and, very often, a very considerable knowledge of archaeological detail. All of them recognize the rather grim fact that making a living is easier this way: the alternatives available in the Costa Rican economy are not as plentiful as one might like.

The commercial antiquities business, then, is a communal affair, an intricate network of profits and connections—and not infrequent losses—that encompasses a broad spectrum of Costa Rican citizenry. But the Costa Ricans cannot be made to take the whole blame, for the network extends outward, across several oceans, to high-profit outlets in Paris and Zurich, to museums and private collectors in New York and elsewhere, to entrepreneurs in New Orleans and Los Angeles who offer seaborne "expeditions" to Costa Rica for fun and profit. I do not for a moment condone the damage done by these bootleg archaeologists. But they are certainly no more blameworthy than the collectors and curators whose competition sustains, even inflates, the international market, or the dealers who profit far more while risking far less.

Scientific archaeology will continue to lose out to bootleg archaeology until the complex problem of protecting archaeological resources is solved. And I do not believe we can work out a truly effective solution without recognizing that this activity serves important economic and other functions for many people in areas where opportunities are sharply limited. This is one reason why it is difficult to assign culpability to those who actually do the damage, with shovel in hand. It is also a reason why restrictions can probably be more effectively imposed among consumers than producers. After all, the consumer has the choice in what he buys.

COMMENT

Does the economic importance of the illegal art market within a nation provide an argument in favor of its continuance? Are the huaqueros merely mining their own national patrimony? How can the needs of the living be reconciled with protection of the past? In this connection, consider what happens in Italy.

THE TOMBAROLI IN ITALY

Since World War II the number of reported art robberies in Italy escalated from 300 in 1957 to 10,952 in 1974, so that by 1977 about 44,000 art thefts had been reported. Thieves did not appear to be deterred by either the age or size of their quarry, as, for example, in 1977, twelve priceless frescoes were taken from the walls of Pompeii, where 164 men and four dogs but no lighting or alarm system protected the extensive ruins. In addition, no photographs of the frescoes exist in Italian state archives, making identification difficult. In 1975 the theft of a Raphael painting and two Piero della Francesca paintings from the Ducal Palace in Urbino and twenty-eight paintings from the Main Gallery of Modern Art spurred the newly created Ministry of Cultural Property to increase funding for museum guards and curators, as well as for alarm systems, although adequate protection was slow in coming.

Sometimes only the difficulty of disposing of well-known works allows their recovery. There are, however, cases where stolen works grace prominent private collections or public buildings, such as the Lorenzo Monaco painting stolen in Milan and shown in the Stuttgart Museum, or the Veronese painting of a Madonna taken by the German armies in 1943 and still, in 1974, to be seen in a German government building. Furthermore, it has been suggested in a publication of the office of the premier of Italy, *Vita Italiana,* that the thieves rely on international art experts and that the investment plans of some European banks include the purchase of stolen artworks.

While it is said that the archaeological museum of Brindisi and the civic museum of Termini Imerese have been virtually emptied of their ancient coins, statues, and vases, tomb robbers do a brisk business in objects ravaged from clandestine excavations. From 1970 to 1974 about 42,000 antiquities were recovered by Italian police, although many find their way out of the country. The average Italian may not agree that any antiquity found on Italian soil is the property of the state, and amateur scavengers have been active in the Forum and the Appia Antica.

Furthermore, lack of funds means not only ill-protected museums and sites and a poor recovery rate by police, but also neglected museums. Rome's Torlonia Museum has been closed for decades, while elsewhere thousands of works lie in basements or storerooms, unavailable to the public. It seems fair to say it is almost impossible to maintain properly Italy's 30,000 churches, 600 museums, and 20,000 castles, let alone the innumerable archaeological sites.

DOUGLAS J. STEWART *Two Cheers for the Tombaroli**

FLORENCE

The long war among governments, museums, collectors, art thieves, archaeologists and the Catholic church is changing character. . . .

Art thieves every year steal an enormous number of unguarded paintings from churches, usually of middle-level importance, while tombaroli regularly loot Etruscan graves of desirable art and artifacts, usually Greek in origin, like the Euphronius vase. The fact that these two classes of thief seem so hard to discourage should not lead anyone to hasty conclusions, however, either about the intelligence of the government or the character of Italians.

Thieves who steal from churches are hardly in a class with tombaroli. It takes little skill and involves even less danger to steal a painting from many an Italian church. Tombaroli work hard at their trade, lay claim to considerable archaeological skills of their own, and face a good deal of danger. (I can testify to the latter, having naively entered a lot of Etruscan sites unguided and then found myself in considerable discomfort, if not positive danger, getting out again.) The latter, moreover, aren't necessarily destructive, ruining the entire situs of a grave for the recovery of one or two salable items. Many tombaroli truly love what they find, and keep back for their private delectation more than they sell. In any case, Italian public opinion, forgetting the government's official position on "national" art treasures, is remarkably lenient in its attitude toward thieves and tombaroli alike, and the reasons are not hard to find. Italians love their art treasures, but are discouraged because acres of medieval and renaissance paintings and frescoes are mouldering away on the walls of churches with no one to care

*From Douglas J. Stewart, "Two Cheers for the Tombaroli," *New Republic,* April 28, 1973, pp. 21–22. Reprinted by permission.

for them, and hundreds of archaeological sites go unexploited because of both the limited supply of "qualified" archaeologists, and government red tape in granting permits for new expeditions (though Italy is the soul of hospitality compared to Greece). Church robbers reasonably argue that the paintings they steal end up in the hands of people far more ready and able to care for them than the church, while the tombaroli assert that an archaeological site isn't a site until someone discovers it, and that they are far better—and what's more quicker—at it than professionals.

The central fact, however, is the one universally ignored. That fact is Italy. There is scarcely a rural farmhouse that does not own a piece or two of ancient sculpture or metalwork, and whose owner cannot find more. Scarcely a village which does not include a building or two with at least romanesque foundations, plus a church or two with important paintings or frescoes. What the world of collectors, museums and universities seems to misunderstand is the Italian attitude toward its art treasures, an attitude best shown in an article . . . published in La Nazione by the chief engineer of the city of Florence. Deploring the fact that a wayside shrine with a fresco by a student of Giotto's had been allowed to pass through several private owners' hands while rotting in wind and rain, the author ended with a passionate plea Per piacere, rubatelo, "Please someone steal it!" Like the real mother in the story of Solomon's wisdom, Italians, I'm convinced, love their treasures, but not to the point of wanting to see them ruined.

If there is a serious international will to do something about depradations of art, rifling of archaeological sites and general deterioration, it could be done by developing an international subscription fund, which could be made available to Italy for various clearly stated purposes: adequate patroling of exposed sites like the Roman Forum; the acquisition and restoration of art works going to pieces in churches; guarding those which can't be moved. And, finally, for enlisting tombaroli on the side of history and enlightenment, by bidding for their services at prices higher than they receive from the black market at their end of the smuggling chain, which are not all that high.

The last idea might seem like making crime pay well. But we already know how well crime pays the higher-ups, who lack their skills. Why not harness them to legitimate searches; hire them to look for everything they can find, and pay a good bonus for every site they uncover, letting them help exploit the site in cooperation with archaeologists, and then splitting the take between them and the government on all objects deemed salable and unnecessary for retention in Italy for further historical study or for the "national treasure." Depredations will not stop until collectors and museums are effectively frozen out of the primary market for archaeological materials and are forced to bid in open competition for all objects passed through, say, an Italo-UN clearing house. . . .

COMMENTS

1. For a realistic description of the Italian situation, see Giovanna Luna, "The Protection of the Cultural Heritage: An Italian Perspective," *The Protection of the Artistic and Cultural Heritage,* United Nations Social Defense Research Institute (UNSDRI) (Rome: UNSDRI, Publication #13, March 1976), pp. 21ff.

2. In 1963 the Superintendent of Antiquities of Western Sicily undertook an unusual experiment in the town of Selinunte. He hired all the tombaroli of a necropolis to work as professional diggers. The following excerpt taken from the above cited UNSDRI report at pp. 48–52, describes this experiment.

SELINUNTE—AN EXPERIMENT OF
CONVERSION AS ADVERTISED BY THE
AUTHOR

Immediately after my appointment as Sovraintendente of the Antiquities of Western Sicily in March 1963, I devoted my efforts to the solution of

the problem of the illegal excavations, which was particularly serious in Selinunte where, for a considerable period of time, the huge and almost endless necropolis had attracted the attention of many illegal excavators, who were able to work undisturbed and to sell their findings all over the world. This presented a great problem, which was up to the Department of Antiquity to solve—thus to me, in my capacity as Head of the Department.

I moved to Selinunte where I remained for some time making lengthy and careful inspections. Regrettably I had to acknowledge the damage done by the illegal excavators to our historical and artistic heritage. From a rough calculation I may say that as many as 80,000 to 100,000 tombs have been destroyed.

I concentrated my attention on the general environmental situation. The illegal excavators fled every time they met me, whereas I wanted to make their acquaintance. Eventually, on a radiant May morning in 1963, I was able to meet these people. It was 7:00 A.M. and I had been walking for over two hours. The *clandestini* had commenced work even earlier; there were 17 of them. I was escorted by my assistant and a guardian. We took the group by surprise. We sat down together and had a long and frank conversation.

They were excavating the tombs in order to earn their daily bread, they told me. From this and succeeding meetings I realized that the problem was mainly a social, human one. These men lived in Marinella di Selinunte, a small village just below the archaeological area. They had families to support and their only means of making a living was by searching the Greek tombs. They were actually fishermen but could earn very little from that source, mainly because of the lack of a small bay or a little harbour. From the human point of view we must try to remember that the residents of Marinella consider themselves as the legitimate heirs to the ancient inhabitants of Selinunte; they consider that these tombs contain the bodies of their ancestors and they are therefore entitled to the contents.

Of course they were aware of the existence of certain laws, but we all know how little thought is given to the law by certain social groups. Taking all these factors into consideration I came to the decision that the only way to deal with the problem was to take the work of the *clandestini* under our supervision. In other words, it would be our job to excavate the necropolis employing those people who were actually already working on it; we thought that the employment of other workers would have been both dangerous and unfair. We had to start working immediately, but we lacked funds. The existing regulations, which

are, in my opinion, absolutely inadequate anyway, were an almost unsurmountable obstacle to the realization of my plan. We had to submit an accurate and detailed estimate and once approved we had to work within it on contract. Nonsense! Worse still, we were not allowed to accept any extra financial assistance. It became extremely urgent to break this vicious circle and to start working so as to put a stop to the plundering by the illegal excavators; otherwise we might as well give up and admit failure. I suggested to the Ministry of Education to entrust the excavations to the Mormino Foundation of the Banco di Sicilia and obtained their agreement. It was then decided that the excavations should be carried out under the direction of the Department of Antiquity, a quarter of the findings would be the property of the bank, and no material could, under any circumstances, be sold or given away. Further, it was the responsibility of the Banco to preserve and exhibit the findings in their own building, and to ensure that the exhibition was open to the public.

The excavations started in May 1963 and ended in 1967 after four years of uninterrupted work; perhaps no excavation had ever lasted so long. The results were quite satisfactory with regard to the quality and the quantity of the findings, and also from a strictly historical point of view. A new necropolis was discovered and those already opened were more carefully searched so as to have a better knowledge of the whole area. The operation was satisfactory for everybody; the Ministry of Education rendered its official appreciation and the Banco di Sicilia had been given the opportunity to participate in something culturally and socially important; the Department of Antiquity, but above all the workers, the former illegal excavators from Marinella, could finally do openly what they had been doing secretly for such a long time: that is, bringing to light the remains of their ancestors. They also learned that although authority involves taxes and sometimes even trouble, it could also provide work and daily bread.

In order to reaffirm this principle, which in my opinion should be the guiding principle in our role of civil servants (particularly in Sicily), I tried to speed as much as possible the administrative operations required to pay to the owners of the land on which the excavations had taken place the indemnity and premium established by the law. As a result, the landowners are now co-operating with us in the fight against illegal excavations. It would be untrue to say that the problem is definitely and completely solved; at times some *clandestini* from Castelvetrano or other villages are caught in the necropolis, but these are just sporadic cases of very little relevance; actually the problem is certainly approaching a definite solution.

THE SELINUNTE EXPERIENCE IN RETROSPECT

Driving to Selinunte, I ask the Professor how, in the prevailing climate of mutual mistrust, absenteeism and blind bureaucratic legitimism he was able to put into effect the "revolutionary" experiment of Selinunte and whether such an experiment was actually as easy, smooth, rosy and well-accepted as it appeared from the two publications he had given me to read the day before. He smiles and tells me stories of borbonic resistance, threats and boycotts. From the Selinunte days, his career stopped, his promotion was withheld.

In spite of these difficulties Professor B. has succeeded in making Selinunte an archaeological and environmental site of rare beauty; by expropriating 224 hectares of privately-owned land and by requisitioning a stretch of beach around the temple area, he has created the first archaeological park of the island, covering a total of 270 hectares.

"*Professore,* how could you do all this with all the obstacles you found within the Fine Arts Administration?"

"Because I am a Sicilian and I know my people. I enjoy personal support and I have no interest in the state career. I love Selinunte and I am determined to preserve it from ministerial idiocy. There remains a lot to do there: the old town has not as yet been excavated, but I will start this in October; it will take years to do, but I want to complete it before I retire."

While he talks his enthusiasm is visible, and the pride of the scholar is easily detected. Nonetheless, I sympathize with this man who is not hampered by bureaucratic rigidity.

Now, away from the Sovraintendenza offices, there is an opportunity for free informal talk and a few risky questions can be ventured.

"*Professore,* apart from the Selinunte case, illegal excavations are popular throughout the island to such an extent that I wonder whether instead of shedding tears of false national pride whenever a Greek terracotta is known to have crossed the Swiss border, one should not seriously think of a programme of economic diversification for the people engaged in this so-called 'illegal' activity."

"It is clear that you do not know Sicily; the words 'planification' or 'infrastructure' have no meaning here: in certain parts of the island the state presence is manifested only in the street signs." . . .

COMMENT

It is clear that national laws like those of Italy do not effectively prevent or control the international traffic in art treasures and antiquities. The flow of cultural treasures out of Mexico and Central America, Africa, the Middle East, Asia, and Europe appears to grow, rather than diminish. One problem may be that the resources invested in effective enforcement of national legal systems as they affect the illegal export and theft of cultural treasures are so low as to ensure that these systems of regulation will be ineffective. According to this line of reasoning, the problem, if it is a problem, is simply one of national enforcement of national law. It seems more likely, however, that even the most rigorous enforcement of national law would fail to stem the traffic. The principal reason for this conclusion is that the major market for stolen and illegally exported antiquities is outside the exporting nation. There is, of course, also an internal market, but it is generally small by comparison. As long as there exists a large market in the art-importing nations, with buyers prepared to pay large sums, we can expect that means will be found to evade the controls enacted in exporting nations, even if they are more vigorously enforced. In such a situation, the principal effect of vigorous enforcement may be to increase the price to the ultimate purchaser (an additional effect is to further criminalize those who engage in the thieving and smuggling). As Karl E. Meyer comments in *The Plundered Past* (New York: Atheneum, 1973), pp. 41–42:

> Nearly every country rich in antiquities has legislation that seeks to restrict the export of rare works of art. In Mexico, for example, there is virtually no legal market in pre-Columbian antiquities. But because Mexico has thousands of archeological sites, because

much of the country is poor, and because prices for pre-Columbian art are high, the law is about as effective as the Prohibition Amendment was in America.

THE DEMAND SIDE

We have seen something of the supply side of the market. How about the demand side? According to the *New York Times* of March 2, 1973, the curator of ancient art of the Cleveland Museum, John D. Cooney, has said that 95 percent of ancient art in the United States has been smuggled in. If an object is declared at Customs, its entry is legal. Cooney said that many works have entered the United States from Switzerland, which does not prohibit illegal export of art works. He added, "Unless you're naive or not very bright, you'd have to know that much ancient art here is stolen." He seems to be concerned only that the artwork enter this country legally, while, "even if I know it's hot, I can't be concerned about that. If the museums in this country begin to send back all the smuggled material to their countries of origin, the museum walls would be bare." He went on to say that competition for art encouraged smuggling and that "the day of great acquisitions will have to end if we no longer smuggle art works."

The curator of Greek and Roman art at the Metropolitan Museum, hearing of these statements, called them "odd. And it's so crude."

Cooney predicted that museums would become cagier if the President and Congress ratify the Convention of the U.N. Educational, Scientific, and Cultural Organization (UNESCO), which outlaws illicit traffic in art. "They'll have to devise new methods of getting art works if they want to secure the best," he is quoted as saying.

Edward H. Merrin, a New York dealer, is quoted in the *New York Times* of March 27, 1973, as saying,

> If you talk to a policeman in Mexico and ask for a Mayan relief, he would probably take you to his house. The problem is obviously not an American problem—it is a Mexican problem. Prohibition never worked and never will work. I am against the destruction of monuments, but if you ask would I rather have a wall collapse at a Mayan site or have it in New York, I would rather have it in New York.

This statement represents the point of view of many dealers and museum curators, who feel that buying these objects means that they will be preserved and that the rest of the world will be able to enjoy them.

According to Abraham Lerner of the Hirshhorn Collection, "Almost every museum has pre-Columbian pieces without the approval of the Mexican Government. Without this trading, we would not have any representation of pre-Columbian art in this country."

Lee Moore, of South Miami, has said, "If objects are not dug up, they are going to sit there for the next 1,000 years," and he suggested that archaeologists would merely put the art in "catalogues that nobody will ever see." In response to a question about the fact that illicit excavations may destroy objects as well as their historical and scientific value, he replied, "Maya burials are all basically the same—they are not going to learn a lot more seeing another burial." He also contended that he had seen Mexican workers damage or destroy ancient ruins. In addition, he claimed to know of objects that were confiscated from smugglers in Mexico that later found their way to the New York art market, presumably to the profit of Mexican officials.

The curator of pre-Columbian art at the Princeton Art Museum, Gillette Griffin, appeared to agree with this attitude when he said, "Everything will go to European collectors, and American scholars will be more out of it. People who sit up on high perches are missing huge amounts of material."

At the height of the concern about the illegal trade in cultural objects in the early 1970s, several U.S. museums (particularly those concerned about retaining access to sites in foreign countries) and organizations like the International Council of Museums (ICOM) and the College Art Association adopted resolutions imposing or urging self-restraint. The Harvard statement, adopted in November 1971, is as follows.

The Harvard Statement on Self-Restraint, November 1971

. . . We therefore recommend that the President and Fellows adopt the following general principles to govern the University with respect to the acquisition (whether by gift, bequest, or purchase, or through the activities of scientific or archaeological expeditions) of works of art and antiquities:

1. The museum director, librarian, curator, or other University officer (hereinafter to be referred to as "Curator") responsible for making an acquisition or who will have custody of the acquisition should assure himself that the University can acquire valid title to the object in question. This means that the circumstances of the transaction and/or his knowledge of the object's provenance must be such as to give him adequate assurance that the seller or donor has valid title to convey.

2. In making a significant acquisition, the Curator should have reasonable assurance under the circumstances that the object has not, within a recent time, been exported from its country of origin (and/or the country where it was last legally owned) in violation of that country's laws.

3. In any event, the Curator should have reasonable assurance under the circumstances that the object was not exported after July 1, 1971, in violation of the laws of the country of origin and/or the country where it was last legally owned.

4. In cases of doubt in making the relevant determinations under paragraphs 1–3, the Curator should consult as widely as possible. Particular care should be taken to consult colleagues in other parts of the University whose collecting, research, or other activities may be affected by a decision to acquire an object. The Curator should also consult the General Counsel to the University where appropriate; and, where helpful, a special panel should be created to help pass on the question raised.

5. The University will not acquire (by purchase, bequest, or gift) objects that do not meet the foregoing tests. If appropriate and feasible, the same tests should be taken into account in determining whether to accept loans for exhibition or other purposes.

6. Curators will be responsible to the President and Fellows for the observance of these rules. All information obtained about the provenance of an acquisition must be preserved, and unless in the opinion of the relevant Curator and the General Counsel to the University special circumstances exist in a specific instance, all such information shall be available as a public record. Prospective vendors and donors should be informed of this policy.

7. If the University should in the future come into the possession of an object that can be demonstrated to have been exported in violation of the principles expressed in Rules 1–3 above, the University should, if legally free to do so, seek to return the object to the donor or vendor. Further, if with respect to such an object, a public museum or collection or agency of a foreign country seeks its return and demonstrates that it is a part of that country's national patrimony, the University should, if legally free to do so, take responsible steps to cooperate in the return of the object to that country. . . .

COMMENTS

1. Certain museums are considering repatriation (which we will discuss below) of objects, as well as being more cautious about purchases. E. John Bullard of the New Orleans Museum of Art has said he is discussing with Guatemala the possibility of restoring legal title to an important stela if that country would permit the museum to display it as a long-term loan. Bullard said about purchases, "In the future we hope to be much more careful. It may mean the museum will not collect at all in this area."

Samuel Sachs of the Minneapolis Institute of Arts said about that museum's Guatemalan stela from Piedras Negras, "We've been considering the possibility of repatriating it, but I am not sure we'd be doing the Guatemalan heritage any good. Their heritage is better protected in European and American museums." Philippe de Montebello of the Houston Museum said he had no intention of returning a similar stela. "We'd be serving no one. We would just be depriving American audiences." He went on to say, however, "A common front should be presented so that it is not done anymore."

2. It appears that while dealers, curators, and scholars differ widely in their attitudes toward the commerce in pre-Columbian art, they seem to agree that this trade will not cease unless the countries involved permit surplus objects to be sold and exported legally.

3. *What price glory?* Is it a justification for American museums acquiring outstanding works of art, notably antiquities, which encourages smuggling, that museums have an obligation to the public—in John Cooney's words—"to obtain the first and best of everything?" Do you agree with the argument that we should not let this initiative pass to other countries that do not control imports?

4. *Who should protect the past?* What are the merits in the arguments for and against the view that art dealers and museums who buy pre-Columbian artifacts are preserving objects that otherwise might never be recovered, or that they can do the job better than countries such as Guatemala? . . .

5. *What price scholarship?* Can scholars morally condone their collaboration with dealers and museums who have illegally exported or smuggled works, on the grounds that if they did not these works would go to private or European collections and American scholarship would be the loser?

6. In 1977, Representative Abner Mikva, who sponsored legislation to implement the 1970 UNESCO Convention (see pp. 91–97), said, "We're either a moral nation or we're not." Andre Emmerich, a prominent New York dealer in both contemporary art and antiquities, responded in a letter to the *Washington Post*.

Letter to the Washington Post, *July 6, 1977*

I would like to take this opportunity to explore the implications of the statements of Congressman Mikva quoted in the *Washington Post* for May 18, 1977 in an article headlined "The Pillaging of Global Art Treasures," in which he said, "We're either a moral nation or we're not. . . ."

All decent Americans, most especially including the art dealers of my acquaintance, are very much committed to the concept that ours is a moral nation. As a matter of fact, it has been my experience that art dealers not only tend to feel this very deeply but that they have widely and consistently acted on their beliefs by making their galleries available to a series of benefit shows on behalf of good and moral causes. . . .

The point, it seems to me, is not whether this country is a moral one or not: we are unequivocally agreed that it should be. The point is rather just *where* morality lies. And as in so many debates, it comes down to a question of defining and understanding one's terms.

For example, the *Post* article begins with the headlined phrase "The Pillaging. . . ." According to the *Oxford English Dictionary*, the word means "1. to rob, plunder, sack (a person, place, etc.):

esp. as practiced in war; to rifle, 2. to take possession of or carry off as booty; to make a spoil of; to appropriate wrongfully, 3. to take booty, to plunder; to rob with open violence."

However, the art treasures which the State Department aspires to block from entry into this country are by no means necessarily "pillaged," as the *Post* states.

Indeed, Congressional spokesmen such as Congressman Mikva do not advance the proposition that the United States should limit the importation of art which is shown to be "pillaged" or "looted" in the dictionary sense of these words. On the contrary, they argue that, if a foreign nation chooses to label art which originates within its territory as "pillaged" or "looted," we should not inquire into the meaning of the label, but should unhesitatingly defer to the wishes of the foreign nation and ban the importation of that art into our own country.

That approach overlooks the fact that many art-rich nations wish to maintain a monopoly of art originating in their territory, do not wish to share it with the world, and denounce as "pillaged" or "looted" or "stolen" *any* work of art thought to be from their soil which enters the international art market. I do not think that it is particularly "moral" for the United States to ally itself with the efforts of art-rich nations to enforce this sort of cultural nationalism.

The point is that the art treasures which the State Department aspires to block from entry into this country are by no means necessarily "pillaged." The art which would be subject to State Department exclusion are archaeological and ethnological works. . . .

Essentially, archaeological material is material which is discovered below the earth. Neglect, weathering and erosion, wars and revolutions, all conspire to destroy the overwhelming majority of artifacts left above ground by earlier civilizations. The only objects that survive are those buried by acts of nature and by acts of man. The acts of nature are rare: Pompeii and Herculaneum are famous exceptions. Early man, however, had a vivid belief in a concrete afterlife. Therefore, the tombs of notables were richly filled with the accoutrements of wealth and the symbols of rank. To insure proper service in the afterlife, slaves and wives were killed in very early times but, happily, in later and higher cultures, effigy statues were placed in the tombs in lieu of living retinue. Such tomb furnishings form the overwhelming bulk of the archaeological material which is found today in museum and private collections and in dealers' galleries.

These art-laden tombs are located on land which is usually used for agriculture or other purposes by the present day owners of the ground. In my experience such tombs are generally found by accident during construction or due to the sudden subsiding or shifting of soil. Of course, excavations are inevitably carried out by the owners of the land, the farmers and their families. Under U.S. law subsoil rights belong to the owner of the land.

When one uses the term "pillaged" in referring to these objects, he clearly applies a special, highly tendentious foreign label which is clearly contrary to our sense of equity and property rights. Americans have until now consistently refused to accept such labels in this country when they ran counter to basic U.S. tenets. For example, we refuse to apply foreign censorship laws in this country and gladly allow foreigners to publish here writings which are forbidden and labeled "seditious" in their own countries.

Why should we then apply the foreign term "stolen" to property which may be considered stolen under a legal principle in a foreign country but which is clearly the land owner's, and therefore the original seller's, right to own and sell as he pleases under U.S. law and tradition?

The term "pillaging" is also used by some professional field archaeologists (as opposed to those archaeological scholars who are less involved in actual excavations but who concentrate on studying and interpreting the objects found in official and unofficial excavations).

These field archaeologists urge that archaeological sites are a nonrenewable, exhaustible, natural resource that should be preserved for exploration by trained professional scientists. Theoretically and abstractly they are, of course, right. Unfortunately, however, their view of an ideal world remains in the realm of fantasy. The population explosion, intensified farming, construction activities, advancing industrialization, topped by governmental neglect in once backward parts of the world, all conspire to destroy remaining archaeological sites at a far faster rate than the widely deplored depredations of independent explorers.

This sad but little publicized fact has been attested to quietly by archaeologist after archaeologist. To protect physically and police all of the literally tens of thousands of sites in just one country such as Mexico would require an army—probably literally the entire existing army of each of the archaeologically rich countries.

In practice these archaeological sites will be destroyed for the reasons outlined above, reasons deeply embedded in the fabric of the life of the countries involved. All that we can do is to encourage the preservation of those works of art and artifacts which miraculously survive the inevitable depredations of our advancing contemporary civilization. In the real world which exists—as opposed to the utopia which some academics dream—this is best done by endowing such objects with sufficient monetary value to ensure their preservation.

All societies preserve the things they value and allow to be destroyed those which they do not value. The great contribution which this country's free enterprise economy has made to the entire field of archaeology has been exactly this aspect of enhancing the value of ancient art and thereby ensuring its preservation from otherwise certain neglect and destruction. This is also, of course, the practical morality.

The other kind of material to which H.R. 5643 [the legislation sponsored by Mikva] addresses itself is "ethnological material." In practice, this consists largely of abandoned tribal ritual art such as masks, shields and other ceremonial objects which have outlived their religious function. If they were not sold to foreign markets, such objects would simply be left to rot. Essentially, those who deal in ethnological material trade in the abandoned garbage of other cultures and civilizations. In virtually all cases the material salvaged by dealers, collectors and museums continues to exist at all only because of these acts of salvage.

Therefore, where lies the side of morality?

It is my great fear that well meaning, honorable citizens are now being misled about the issue of right and wrong in this matter through the misuse of such terms as "stolen art" and "pillaged global art treasures."

It seems to me that a clear distinction must be made by the Congress between objects which are indeed stolen and pillaged according to our own legal concepts, and objects which are arbitrarily so labelled by foreign jurisdictions. (In some countries, such as Mexico, *all* objects, including stamp and coin collections, modern paintings, etc., are considered "pillaged" if they are exported without an export license, a permit which in practice is virtually *never* granted.) . . .

COMMENTS

1. On another occasion Emmerich asked:

Do the descendants of the Turks who drove out the Greeks from Asia Minor have a better right to the art made by the ancestors of the Greeks? Do the destroyers of the Maya civilization [have more right] to its remnants than we do? I propose that it's a basic moral question. I beg the obvious fact that the art of mankind—the art of ancient mankind—is part of mankind's cultural heritage, and does not belong exclusively to that particular geographic spot where ancient cultures flourished. I think that this country more than any other has a special claim to the arts of all mankind. . . . American institutions have bought the objects they have acquired, and have not only paid with money, but we have paid the debt with scholarly contributions.

2. Dealers and collectors are not the only problem. Art historians are another danger. André Malraux, author of *Museum Without Walls* and later French minister of culture, was arrested and convicted in 1924 for stealing (with the help of saws and chisels) buffalo carts full of sculpture from Angkor Wat in Cambodia. Malraux and his wife had come to Cambodia for the purpose of stealing the sculptures to sell in order to rebuild their fortune. See Robert Payne, *A Portrait of André Malraux* (Englewood Cliffs, N.J.: Prentice-Hall 1970), pp. 61ff.

3. And beware the visiting museum curator and director! In *King of the Confessors* (New York: Simon & Schuster 1981), Thomas Hoving describes how he (then a curator, later director) and James Rorimer (then director) of the Metropolitan Museum of Art acquired a marble relief for the museum in Italy, clearly intending that it would be smuggled out for delivery to the museum. The relief was one of a set of seven; the other six were in place on the pulpit in the Church of San Lorenzo. One of Hoving's rationalizations is classic: "Italy had six reliefs. A seventh would only cause administrative confusion" (ibid., p. 88). For reactions to the Hoving book, which contains other horrors, see John Richardson, "The Mantle of Munchausen," *N.Y. Review of Books,* January 21, 1982, p. 17; J. H. Merryman, Review of *King of the Confessors* by Thomas Hoving, *Houston Journal of International Law,* vol. 4 (1982), p. 213.

BIG QUESTION

The Big Question can be variously phrased. "Who owns the past?" is as good as any. The purpose is to require ourselves, authors and readers, to think hard about the hot-art trade, to question prevailing attitudes, to make the necessary distinctions, to participate in forming defensible policies and enforceable laws. The readings so far in this chapter illustrate the complexity and difficulty of the hot-art problem. We now focus for the moment on some concrete issues.

SHOULD THE UNITED STATES LIMIT ART EXPORT?

The United States is one of the few nations that do not restrict the export of cultural property (and that impose no duty on imports—although, as we shall see, some kinds of cultural objects are not legally importable). Should the United States enact a law prohibiting export, so that Mimbres pots and paintings by Jackson Pollock cannot legally be acquired by foreign museums (as were Jackson Pollock's "Blue Poles" and a great De Kooning and other abstract works by Australia)? Was the "loss" of these works a national tragedy or, as art critic John Canaday suggested at the time, is it better that American art be spread around abroad?

The United States has not generally been thought of as an archaeological art-exporting nation. However, as the international distribution of wealth shifts and as collecting tastes extend to previously ignored cultural artifacts, the possibility of a strong foreign market for the relics of earlier cultures grows. Suppose for a moment that the United States became a relatively poor nation, that great wealth was concentrated in, say, Brazil and Mexico, and that there was a strong market for the relics of earlier U.S. cultures in those nations. Would you expect a smuggling trade in such objects to develop?

Analogous domestic problems arise entirely within the United States under federal and state legislation dealing with the sites and artifacts of native cultures and structures and objects having historical value. See "Looting of Indian Graves Widespread in West," *New York Times,* September 19, 1982, p. 132; and *U.S. v. Smyer,* 596 F.2d 939 (10th Cir. 1979) (the defendants were convicted of looting Mimbres pots, worth thousands of dollars on the market, from a Mimbres culture site in New Mexico). In 1979 Congress enacted the Archaeological Resources Protection Act (ARPA), Public Law No. 96-95, 93 Stat. 721, 16 U.S.C. §470 (1979) (only the latest in a series of federal statutes), which prohibits excavation or removal of "any archaeological resource located on public lands or Indian lands" without a permit. For discussions of the ARPA, see L. D. Northly, "The Archaeological Resources Protection Act of 1979: Protecting Prehistory for the Future," *Harvard Environmental Law Review,* vol. 6 (1982), p. 61; and Ronald H. Rosenberg, "Federal Protection for Archaeological Resources," *Arizona Law Review,* vol. 22 (1980), p. 70. Since the ARPA applies only to federal and Indian lands, areas outside them are governed by state and local laws. However, the ARPA has enforcement provisions (in addition to criminal and civil penalties for excavating, removing, etc., without a permit) that extend beyond federal and Indian territory. It is a crime to "sell, purchase, exchange, transport, receive or offer" any article removed in violation of the act. Most significant, it is an offense to traffic in an object acquired in violation of "any provision, rule, regulation, ordinance, or permit in effect *under state or local law*" (emphasis added). The ARPA thus could be used to prosecute persons who transported or sold such objects outside the United States—a form of illegal export. Further, articles involved in any of the three categories of offense may be forfeited. It takes little imagination to see how the ARPA might be made the basis for a nationwide system of export controls indistinguishable from those in other nations.

Section 2 of the ARPA states:

(a) The Congress finds that—

(1) archaeological resources on public lands and Indian lands are an accessible and irreplaceable part of the Nation's heritage;

(2) these resources are increasingly endangered because of their commercial attractiveness;

(3) existing Federal laws do not provide adequate protection to prevent the loss and destruction of these archaeological resources and sites resulting from uncontrolled excavations and pillage; and

(4) there is a wealth of archaeological information which has been legally obtained by private individuals for noncommercial purposes and which could voluntarily be made available to professional archaeologists and institutions.

(b)The purpose of this Act is to secure, for the present and future benefit of the American people, the protection of archaeological resources and sites which are on public lands and Indian lands, and to foster increased cooperation and exchange of information between governmental authorities, the professional archaeological community, and private individuals having collections of archaeological resources and data which were obtained before the date of the enactment of this Act.

The Northly article, cited above, is a good review of the journalism, professional literature, statutes, and case law out of which the ARPA emerged. Here again it is clear that the problems with which the law seeks to cope closely parallel international concerns.

Should the U.S. have a patrimony act? In this connection consider this statement by Norton Simon:

> The time has come for every country including the United States to protect its art. More and more art that has been owned by Americans has been leaving the country. I believe that the United States should adopt a policy similar to that of England or France which allows museums or foundations to have a first refusal to buy the art before it leaves the country. [Press release, August 11, 1976.]

Art critic John Canaday, writing in the *New York Times* of December 2, 1973, made a strong case for the wide distribution of art among different nations and cultures. Although it is understandable that a work that is still an object venerated in the religion it represents, such as the Afo-A-Kom, might be returned to its original owners, artworks help make an individual culture vivid and comprehensible elsewhere. Canaday argues that a fine Eakins painting hanging in the Louvre adjacent to a Degas, or a Church or Cole landscape next to a Constable, could offer French or English audiences a new perspective on American art and sensibility. He similarly believes that in Great Britain the Elgin Marbles have been ambassadors for the Greek spirit, which has become an international heritage. In this vein, he argues that rather than limiting the export of works such as Jackson Pollock's "Blue Poles" or examples of American pop art, so popular in Germany and Switzerland, we should welcome such foreign purchases, which will serve as missionaries, if good, or if not, will be forgotten.

In connection with the question whether there should be further legislation to protect this country's cultural heritage, consider the proposal by James J. Fishman in "Protecting America's Cultural and Historical Patrimony," *Art & the Law,* vol. 3, no. 3 (July 1977), pp. 1, 2–4. Inspired by the recent sale at auction to foreign purchasers of a gold sword of honor presented by the Continental Congress in 1779 to General Lafayette, and a white marble bust of Benjamin Franklin by Jean-Antoine Houdon done in Paris in 1779, Fishman argues that these are serious losses to our culture and portend others because there are almost no American export controls on works of art. He proposes a statute much like those in England and Canada, which grant export permission if no local institution buys the work.

Where do you stand on the Big Question? Should the United States try to keep its cultural property? If so, how?

THE LAW

The following materials describe and illustrate the way the law has been used to deal with stolen and illegally exported works. We begin with a famous case involving documents of the Medici family.

King of Italy v. De Medici

34 T.I.R. 623 (CH. 1918)

In this case the Italian Government, with whom the King of Italy had been joined as co-plaintiff, asked for an injunction to restrain the defendants from selling or disposing of, or permitting to be sold or otherwise disposed of, the manuscripts, letters, records, books, and other documents known as the Medici archives.

Mr. Hughes, K.C., and Mr. Bruce appeared for the plaintiffs; Mr. Maugham, K.C., and Mr. J. F. Carr for the defendants.

Mr. Hughes said that the documents were books and papers extending from the latter part of the 11th century to a period in the 18th century, and they had been collected by the distinguished Medici family. There were altogether about 800 lots, and of these about 400 were State papers, originally of the State of Florence. They belonged successively to several States, until ultimately they vested in the State of Italy, and they were now the property of that State. All these documents were of historical and archaeological importance, and Italy was very jealous about the exportation of such documents. There was a law which prohibited their exportation without a permit, and there was a heavy export duty even when a permit was granted. The State had also the right to purchase these documents.

There were several letters which passed between Lorenzo the Magnificent and an envoy of the Republic, and it was said by the defendants that, although the letters to Lorenzo were State papers, the letters from him were not. That was based on the fact that Lorenzo, while really head of the State, had taken up the position that he was simply a citizen of Florence. According, however, to Italian lawyers, these were State papers.

The defendants also said that papers were not protected unless they had been in the public archives. There were, however, several Italian cases to the contrary. He cited *Emperor of Austria v. Day and Kossuth,* . . . a case concerning the printing of notes for Kossuth when he was a refugee in England, to show that a foreign Sovereign could sue in this country for any wrong done to his subject.

With regard to prescriptive right, the statute did not begin to run until the Italian authorities made the demand for the return of these documents. . . .

Mr. Maugham submitted that the motion was hopelessly misconceived. He said that the wrong committed abroad must be of such a kind that it would be a wrong if committed in this country, and what the defendants had done would be no wrong in this country. The right of pre-emption claimed by the plaintiffs was unknown to English law, and would not be enforced here. This claim must fail under the Statute of Limitations. After 400 years the claim was stale, and would not be enforced by English law. In the admitted circumstances of the case it was in the highest degree improbable that the claim would succeed at the trial of the action. There was no instance where an action of the kind succeeded in this country. The Court was asked to enforce a foreign law, and that it would not do.

Mr. Hughes, in reply, said that it would be highly inconvenient if the injunction were not granted. The documents might be taken out of England, or possibly sold, and that would, in effect, decide the case without its being brought to trial. On the other hand, it was most improbable, in the circumstances, that the defendants could find a purchaser, and they would have no undertaking in damages.

Mr. Justice Peterson, in giving judgment, said that this was a motion of considerable interest and of considerable difficulty. The Italian Government claimed these documents because they were State papers and because they were of historical importance. He would assume as a fact that they were removed from Italy in contravention of the law of 1909, and that they were of historical importance within the meaning of that law. It was said by the plaintiffs that the State papers were communications between the authorities of Florence and their Ambassadors and Envoys, and that they never belonged to the holders, but were held throughout for the State; that they had been allowed to be retained by the holders, and that the authorities were content to let them so remain until there was an attempt to sell them. Whether that contention could be established at the trial of the action he did not know. He was asked to keep these documents intact until the trial. Now it seemed to him that there was evidence which raised a *prima facie* case on the part of the plaintiffs, that the documents belonged, not to the defendants, but to the Italian State, and if that were so the Italian Government was entitled to prevent the disposition of their property by someone who was not entitled to it. On this part of the motion then, as there was a *prima facie* case, there must be an injunction to prevent the defendants from dealing with these documents.

There remained a considerable block of documents which were not State papers, but were of historical interest, and came under the law of 1909, by Article 1. Article 2 provided that such documents were inalienable when they belonged to the State, to communes, &c. These documents therefore did not come under Article 2. Article 9 prohibited their exportation, but it was manifest that this only applied so long as they remained in Italy.

The question arose whether there was any probability, at the trial of the action, that these documents, apart from the State papers, would be ordered to be returned to Italy. He did not think that the Court would undertake such a burden.

The result therefore was that there would be an injunction in respect of the State papers, but no injunction would be granted in respect of the documents of historical interest. If, however, Messrs. Christie's sold these documents they might, as the result of the trial of the action, be liable to heavy damages, and the purchasers might also find themselves in great difficulties.

COMMENTS

1. The distinction made by the court between property owned by the Italian government and property owned by private individuals is obvious but fundamental. Although removal of the privately owned papers from Italy violated Italian law, the English court would not assist the Italian government in obtaining their return.

2. The importance of the distinction lies in the fact that much of the illegal international traffic has been in works that the nation of origin did not own but whose removal from the national territory was contrary to law. Although the offended nation could punish the smuggler, if it could catch him, and might have the power to confiscate the illegally exported article if it should be returned to the national territory, it could not expect the foreign nation to punish the smuggler or seize and return the object.

As we shall see, the major effort of art-rich nations concerned about "cultural drain" has been to change the illegal export rule or to evade its effects. The "Boston Raphael" case is an example of a successful evasion that became possible only because the importers made a foolish mistake.

CLIVE F. GETTY *The Case of the Boston Raphael**

THE UNVEILING

Shortly before noon on Thursday, January 7, 1971, a group of four Customs agents, led by Assistant U.S. Attorney Willie J. Davis, entered the Boston Museum of Fine Arts and confiscated a small (10½" x 8½") painting entitled *Portrait of a Young Girl* by Raphael on the grounds that it had been smuggled into the United States. The background for and the ensuing legal drama which resulted from this confiscation will be explored in this paper.

On Tuesday, December 16, 1969, the Boston Museum of Fine Arts proudly unveiled the *Portrait of a Young Girl* by Raphael which had been put on display in the Museum's place of honor, the great rotunda. The importance of the event was underlined by the fact that there are only a handful of Raphaels in the United States and that the painting was one of a very few in existence which date from the artist's early period. People naturally were curious where such a hitherto unknown Raphael came from, how it became part of an American museum's collection and what its undoubtedly high price tag had been. In public statements to the press, Mr. Perry Townsend Rathbone, Director of the Boston Museum of Fine Arts as well as the Acting Curator of the Department of Paintings, revealed only the following: the work had come from "an old European

*From Clive F. Getty, "The Case of the Boston Raphael" (student paper in the authors' files, 1972), pp. 1–2, 4–14.

The so-called "Boston Raphael" now in the possession of the Italian government. (Reproduction is of a postcard issued by the Boston Museum of Fine Arts in anticipation of the painting's acquisition.)

private collection" after three years of negotiations for a price of "Let's call it somewhere in six figures, but not seven." Mr. Rathbone said that the only condition of the sale was that the identity of the source not be disclosed. He added that the previous owner had also wished the painting to "come to a distinguished museum rather than to another private collection or a lesser art institution." Art authorities maintained that the painting, if placed on public auction, "would have commanded a price perhaps as high as $1.5 million." Funds for the Museum's acquisition of the painting came from a recently available 1923 bequest of Charles H. Bayley which stipulated that it be used for the purchase of a "very important painting."

What came to be known as the "Boston Raphael" did not escape the usual controversy of authenticity which revolves around a newly rediscovered painting, particularly one by an Old Master. Dr. John Shearman of the Courtauld Institute of Art at the University of London provided the strongest support for the authenticity of the painting in his generally acknowledged capacity as the ultimate authority on Raphael in the world. He identified the painting as a portrait of Eleanora Gonzaga, the daughter of the Duke of Mantua, which had been created in about 1505. . . .

The dispute over the painting's authenticity did arise as expected. As early as April 1970, John W. Pope-Hennessy, director of the Victoria and Albert Museum in London and world-renowned expert in Italian Renaissance art, expressed skepticism about the Raphael's authenticity. Mr. Sidney Sabin, a London art dealer, described the work as "chocolate-boxy" and in a statement printed in *The Times* declared it to be a 20th century fake. Neither side has conceded in the dispute and it presumably continues.

On January 23, 1970, Rodolfo Siviero, the Italian Foreign Ministry's Delegate for the Retrieval of Works of Art "announced that he had begun an inquiry as to how the museum acquired the High Renaissance portrait. Under Italian law, all works of art held to be an important part of the country's heritage are banned from export unless the government grants specific authorization." If such authorization fails to be obtained, the exportation is ipso facto illegal, constituting a criminal offense. Receipt of illegally exported goods is punishable under Article 648 of the Italian Penal Code. "Receiving is defined by Article 648 . . . as the purchase, receipt or concealment for the sake of profit of

valuables originating from a crime. The offense carries a penalty of up to six years in prison on conviction." When the Boston Raphael was seized by Customs officials, Assistant U.S. Attorney Willie J. Davis stated that in fact no authorization had been obtained from the Italian government for the painting's export. . . .

The Boston Raphael was seized on January 7, 1971, because it had not been declared at U.S. Customs.

Mr. Davis [Assistant U.S. Attorney] said that the Italian Government had discovered the painting missing sometime in 1969 and had requested an investigation after hearing it was in Boston. "We just discovered last week that the painting was smuggled into this country without being declared," Mr. Davis added. (*New York Times*, January 8, 1971.)

The events leading up to the seizure of the Raphael are quite clear: (1) "sometime in 1969" the Italian Government discovered the painting missing, (2) on January 2, 1970, Rodolfo Siviero announced he had begun an inquiry into how the Boston Museum of Fine Arts had acquired the work, (3) sometime during the week of December 28, 1970, it was learned that the painting had not been declared at (i.e. had been smuggled through) U.S. Customs, (4) on January 7, 1971, the painting was seized by U.S. Customs agents. . . . Anyone assessing this sequence of events cannot help but conclude that the seizure of the painting was imminent due to pressure exerted by Italian authorities, and that U.S. officials were impatiently awaiting the discovery of an infraction of U.S. law which would implement the seizure and give it the air of a purely internal matter.

The *New York Times* succinctly appraised the smuggling question: "As a work of art, according to customs law, the painting . . . could have been brought into this country duty-free. It would, however, have to be declared; failure to do so—that is, smuggling—is a civil and a criminal offense." It was the Tariff Act of 1913 which allowed for the free importation of works of art; Article 652 specifically lists "original paintings in oil, mineral, water, or other colors" under duty-free imports. Under Section 545 of Title 18 of the *United States Code Annotated*, it states that whoever smuggles goods into the United States "shall be fined not more than $10,000 or imprisoned not more than five years, or both" and that the "merchandise introduced into the United States in violation of this section" shall be recovered from that person and "forfeited to the United

States." In *U.S. v. Twenty-Five Pictures*, "failure of the importer . . . to declare the character or value of the merchandise was sufficient to establish a fraudulent importation, regardless of whether or not the merchandise was in fact dutiable." Thus, despite the fact that the Raphael was not dutiable, failure to declare it constituted smuggling and made it liable to seizure.

THE ALLEGED SMUGGLERS

That the Boston Raphael was smuggled into the United States had been firmly established, but who did the smuggling? From a compilation of sources, the voyage of the painting from Italy to the United States went something like this. Mr. Perry T. Rathbone, Director of the Boston Museum of Fine Arts and Acting Curator of the Department of Paintings, along with Dr. Hanns Swarzenski, the Museum's Curator for the Department of Decorative Arts and Sculpture, visited Genoa in the summer of 1969 and bought the painting from a local art dealer, Ferdinando Ildebrando Bossi; Mr. Bossi had purportedly acquired the work from the aristocratic Fieschi family in Genoa for a very small sum of money in 1947. From Italy, the painting went to Switzerland. It was quite likely in that country that Mr. Swarzenski gained possession of the Raphael and took a flight to Logan Airport where he spirited it past Customs agents "probably in his briefcase or under his coat." The Customs hurdle cleared, there was nothing to keep the painting from entering the Boston Museum of Fine Arts.

Mr. Rathbone and Dr. Swarzenski ran the danger of being prosecuted on the charge of receiving illegally exported goods according to Article 648 of the Italian Penal Code, as outlined earlier. On March 21, 1971, a Genoese district attorney, Deputy Prosecutor Luigi Meloni, stated that he had officially notified Mr. Rathbone and Dr. Swarzenski directly by mail that "they were considered suspects in a penal investigation and might face charges of receiving the Raphael illegally" and had "advised them to establish legal domicile in Italy, which they could do by retaining counsel."

While Mr. Meloni independently conducted his criminal investigations, Mr. Siviero pushed for official involvement of the Italian Government in the case of the Boston Raphael; he presumably wanted to guarantee that Mr. Rathbone and Dr. Swarzenski not escape the long arm of Italian law

by hiding behind the national boundaries of the United States. Mr. Siviero gained the support of the Fine Arts Department of the Italian Education Ministry. "On February 23, 1971, the Education Ministry's Superior Council of Fine Arts, in a resolution, deplored what it termed the Boston Museum's 'manifest violation' of Italian laws." By March 22, 1971, the Foreign Ministry was formally requsted to take the necessary diplomatic steps to recover the painting. . . . On June 25, 1971, an agreement was signed between Mr. George Seybolt, President of the Museum's Board of Trustees, and Mr. Siviero while the latter was on a secret visit to Boston. It states, in part:

1. Mr. Seybolt as representative of the Board of Trustees of the Museum of Fine Arts consigns to the Italian Government in the person of Signor Siviero the Portrait of a Young Girl attributed to Raphael, a portrait which without the knowledge of those responsible as members of the Board of Trustees came to the Museum through irregular channels. . . .

3. In the name of the Italian Government, Signor Siviero declares:

(a) That his Government is completely satisfied and has no further claim against the Museum of fine Arts in Boston or its Board of Trustees or any of its personnel.

(b) That no claim whatever can be made by anyone else against the Museum in connection with the acquisition of the painting (whether for the balance of the purchase price or otherwise), since any obligation assumed by representatives of the Museum is null and void under the provisions of the Italian law of June 1, 1939, Number 1089, Article 61 on the protection of the artistic patrimony of Italy.

It should be emphasized that Section 3a absolves from any blame not only the Museum and its Board of Trustees but also "any of its personnel," i.e. Mr. Rathbone and Dr. Swarzenski. The agreement in addition provides for an exhibition of Italian art at the Museum sometime in the future "in return for the voluntary restitution of the Raphael painting." The Museum, but not necessarily its personnel, were also absolved in the smuggling in a statement issued by Eugene T. Rossides, Assistant Secretary of the Treasury, on September 10, 1971.

On the evening of September 10, 1971, the Raphael was handed over to an Italian consular official in Boston under Customs supervision. It immediately was placed on a flight to Rome, escorted by Gino Gobbi, Italian vice consul in

Boston. Upon arrival in Rome on the following day, "hand-picked personnel of the Government's Fine Arts Department gingerly unloaded the painting—which was carefully packed and highly insured—and whisked it to the office of the Foreign Ministry's special Delegate for the Retrieval of Works of Art, Rodolfo Siviero."

With the Boston Museum of Fine Arts' complete absolution in the case and with the safe return of the painting to Italy, the question which next arises is, "What happened to the money versed out of the Charles H. Bayley bequest to pay for the painting?" The answer to that question, as well as to the one of to whom the painting will ultimately be returned in Italy, rests with the outcome of a rather complicated Italian court case. The *New York Times* gives an appraisal of the legal tangle as of September 11, 1971:

According to one trustee, there is some possibility that the museum will recover the $340,000 it has so far paid toward the painting's purchase price [$600,000]. The work was bought in Genoa from Ildelrando Bossi, a local art dealer, who subsequently died. The money was paid to his daughter, but the Italian Government, charging illegal sale and export of the work, has sequestered the Bossi family's assets.

A judicial inquiry is still pending as to how the painting, once owned by the Fieschi family of Genoa, came into Mr. Bossi's hands. Members of the Fieschi family have stated that they never sold it to Mr. Bossi. Italian legal experts said yesterday that the status of the painting after its return to Italy, and possibly claims to a refund of the purchase price, would depend on final disposition of the Genoa case.

. . . The following additional information, learned from an article written for the *New York Times* by Grace Glueck, is all I have been able to find. Dr. Swarzenski has retired from his post as Curator of Decorative Arts and Sculpture, but still works at the Museum as a senior research fellow. Mr. Rathbone, who was scheduled to retire from his position as Director of the Museum in July, 1972, announced his early retirement in December, 1971. In his letter to Mr. George Seybolt, the Museum's President, he stated:

Last July, I reached my sixtieth birthday. It is a time for pause and reflection in any man's life. My own serious thought at this time persuades me that I should seek early retirement, in order to write and pursue independent research.

Ms. Glueck thinks that the early retirement was a direct consequence of the dispute over the Raphael: "it is known that the board of trustees, which appointed a special committee to look into the museum's acquisition of the Raphael, was dissatisfied with the role played by Mr. Rathbone in procuring the painting." . . .

COMMENTS

1. The painting now hangs in an Italian national museum, where it is identified as "The Boston Raphael." During the process of cleaning and restoration after its return to Italy, it was found to be so heavily overpainted that little, if any, of the work can with confidence be attributed to Raphael, thus supporting the judgment of those experts who had questioned its authenticity at the time of its acquisition by the Boston Museum of Fine Arts.

2. The museum brought an action to recover the amount it had paid the seller, a dealer in Genoa, but with no success. It is estimated that the museum's loss attributable to this unfortunate transaction, when attorney's fees and other expenditures incurred are added to the amount paid to the seller, approached $1 million.

3. How did the painting become the property of the Italian state? The Genoese dealer who sold it to the museum and who was not fully paid for it brought an action claiming title to the painting when it was returned to Italy in the custody of Minister Siviero but lost. One reason for this result could have been that the Italian statute forbidding the export of such works provides for their confiscation by the state. . . . An equally plausible reason could be that the U.S. government acquired ownership of the painting when it confiscated it as contraband. When the U.S. government returned the painting to Italy, it transferred ownership to the Italian government.

4. Given the organization of boards of trustees into committees on acquisitions and on finance, is it possible that one or more members of the board of trustees of the museum knowingly condoned or played a more active role in acquiring the painting, knowing that its export from Italy was legally prohibited and could only be accomplished by smuggling?

5. The Rodolfo Siviero mentioned in the Boston Raphael case, now deceased, was chief of the Delegation for the Retrieval of Works of Art of the Italian Foreign Ministry and an inde-

fatigable art sleuth who recovered many valuable works for Italy. For an account, see Alan Leog, "Italy's Supersleuth for Art," *ARTnews,* February 1983, pp. 104–108.

6. In 1981 the Cleveland Museum bought a Poussin painting that the French insist was illegally exported from France because no application for an export license was made, although Sherman Lee, then director of the museum, claimed that no export license was required under French law. In fact, the French law on the point is unclear, but Lee's position is a tenable one. The painting was imported into the United States by a dealer who declared it at entry but falsely stated that it was "in transit" and that its value was $0, which is technically sufficient to permit seizure by Customs, confiscation, and return to France, as in the Boston Raphael case. The U.S. government has not acted against the museum, since it is satisfied that there was no wrong done by it, and has accordingly rejected a French diplomatic request for assistance in recovering the painting. In 1984 the French issued an "international warrant" for Lee's arrest for "complicity in exporting contraband." Such a warrant has no effect in the United States, though some other nations will honor it. The case is complicated by a long-standing debate over the authenticity of the work. There are two closely similar versions of the painting: "The Holy Family on the Steps," the other belonging since 1949 to the National Gallery in Washington, D.C. For full accounts of the Cleveland Poussin controversy, see Lisbet Nilson, "Poussin's Holy Family Feud," *ARTnews,* February 1982, p. 78; and "Dispute over Cleveland Museum Poussin Flares Again," *ARTnewsletter,* July 10, 1984, p. 3.

7. Why did the Boston Museum of Fine Arts officials smuggle the Raphael through Customs? Such works enter duty-free, and the fact of illegal export would give Customs no power to seize it. Why would the dealer who imported the Poussin report its value as $0 and thus expose himself to criminal liability and the painting to possible seizure and confiscation?

8. A jeweled gold monstrance of great value (estimated at $3 million) was illegally exported from Colombia and brought by its owner to the United States, where the owner tried to sell it. A curator at the San Antonio Museum of Art became suspicious and investigated. Eventually U.S. Customs personnel seized the monstrance because of false statements in Customs documents. See Linda E. Ketchum, "Curator Refuses Treasure Slipped Out of Colombia," *Stolen Art Alert,* vol. 4, no. 4 (June 1983), p. 1.

9. Returning from Lima, a young American named David Bernstein had four suitcases full of textile fragments, pottery, a feather cape, and other antiquities that were illegally taken from Peru. His declaration at Customs properly described the objects as pre-Columbian antiquities but misstated a total value of $1,785. In fact, according to the curator of Andean archaeology at the Smithsonian, Clifford Evans, the objects were worth hundreds of thousands of dollars. Bernstein was arrested and charged with falsifying a Customs declaration (a misdemeanor), and the objects were seized by Customs and returned to Peru. See Bonnie Burnham, "Peru Marks a Milestone in the Antiquities Trade," *Museum News,* February 1983, p. 7; Richard L. Burger, "The Theft of Peru's Past," *Art Research News,* vol. 2, no. 4 (1983), p. 7.

THE JEANNERET V. VICHEY DECISION

If a work is returned to the nation from which it was illegally exported it can be seized, even though it has been acquired by a good faith purchaser. The following case deals with the suggestion that the possibility of seizure by officials of the nation of the work's origin creates a "cloud" on the purchaser's title.

JEANNERET v. VICHEY
693 F.2d 259 (2d Cir. 1982)

FRIENDLY, Circuit Judge.

This appeal . . . involves novel issues concerning the application of foreign laws requiring the obtaining of licenses or permits for exports of works of art. . . .

Plaintiff Marie Louise Jeanneret, a citizen of

Switzerland, is a well-known art dealer in Geneva. Defendants Anna and Luben Vichey, wife and husband, are citizens of the United States. Anna's father, Carlo Frua DeAngeli, had an extensive and internationally recognized private collection of paintings in Milan, Italy. One of these was a painting, Portrait sur Fond Jaune, by the renowned French post-impressionist, Henri Matisse, who was born in 1869 and died in 1954. The date of the painting is disputed; we shall have more to say about this below.

Carlo Frua DeAngeli died on July 30, 1969, and his property passed by will to his wife and three children. As a result of a settlement, evidently concluded after July 24, 1970, title to the Matisse painting ultimately vested in Anna Vichey.

The date and circumstances of the painting's exit from Italy are unclear. A letter from the Bank Gut Streiff in Zurich dated July 24, 1970, acknowledged Mrs. Vichey's one-third interest in nine paintings by famous artists deposited with the bank, as well as in a Carpaccio painting and a tapestry which the bank had sent to a New York art dealer. However, there are some references in the record to the painting's possible arrival in the spring or early summer. It is uncontroverted that no export license or permit was obtained from the Italian government; whether any such official document was needed is in dispute. Later in 1970 the Matisse painting was brought to the Vicheys' apartment in New York City.

In January 1973 Mme. Jeanneret began negotiations for the purchase of the painting, and an agreement was reached for its sale for 700,000 Swiss francs, then equivalent to approximately $230,000. Luben Vichey delivered the painting to plaintiff in Geneva in March 1973. . . .

Mme. Jeanneret included the Matisse painting in a large exhibit of 20th century masters at her gallery in Geneva. The catalogue listed the Matisse as having been painted "vers 1924" and stated its provenance as the former collection Frua DeAngeli in Milan and a private collection in New York. The asking price was 1,300,000 Swiss francs. She received at least three offers for the painting—one for 900,000 Swiss francs, another for 1,000,000 and still another for 1,100,000, the last partly in cash and partly in exchange for another painting, but declined all as inadequate. The painting was also exhibited in Paris and Basel but again remained unsold at the price Mme. Jeanneret was asking.

In November 1974 plaintiff went to Rome.

While there she encountered Signora Bucarelli, superintendent in charge of the export of paintings. . . . As a result of the conversation Mme. Jeanneret telephoned Anna Vichey in the United States to ascertain the latter's knowledge as to how the painting had been exported from Italy. Anna referred plaintiff to her husband Luben who was in Milan. Luben in turn referred her to Dr. Magenta, the personal representative of the DeAngeli family, and to Mr. Diener, the Swiss bank officer who handled the paintings for the Bank Gut Streiff. According to plaintiff Dr. Magenta referred her back to Luben or the other heirs of Carlo Frua DeAngeli.

There followed a letter from Mme. Jeanneret to Anna Vichey dated November 21, 1974. This reported that Signora Bucarelli was looking for the Matisse painting because she suspected its illegal exportation, and that as a professional art dealer plaintiff could not "sell it anymore nor show it." Mme. Jeanneret proposed that the deal be annulled; she would bring the painting to New York and the Vicheys would repay the purchase price. On January 5, 1975, Luben Vichey wrote plaintiff rejecting her proposal. Other attempts to induce Mrs. Vichey to take back the painting were equally unsuccessful. This action, brought in July, 1977, was the result. The complaint was founded on breach of express and implied warranties of title, false and fraudulent misrepresentation, breach of contract, and a claim that defendants "used" plaintiff in a scheme of tax evasion. Mme. Jeanneret sought to recover not merely the $230,000 paid for the painting but the higher value it would command absent the alleged defect in title and also damages for loss of business and reputation, which, with the usual addition of a claim for punitive damages, brought the total *ad damnum* to $5,000,000.

II

After Judge Cannella had denied a motion by the defendants for summary judgment, the case proceeded to trial before himself and a jury. There was much testimony on the Italian law concerning the exportation of works of art. Two different sets of provisions were involved. The first are the Regulations for the Execution of Law No. 364 of June 20, 1909 . . . (hereafter "the 1913 regulations"). Art. 129 of these required anyone desiring to export objects of historical, archaeological, paleontological, artistic or numismatic interest to present them to a royal office for the exportation of antiquities and art objects. Those seeking export licenses were required to file a declaration of the value of the objects to be exported. Royal officials, after examining the objects, had discretion to ban their exportation and could exercise a right of compulsory purchase at the declared value. The 1913 regulations also provided in Art. 130 that:

Paintings, sculpture and any works of art made by living artists or not more than fifty years old, including copies and imitations, must be submitted to Export Offices or to the offices specifically set up pursuant to Art. 46 of Law No. 386 of June 27, 1907, in order to obtain an export permit.

The formalities involved in obtaining an export permit, as opposed to a license, appear to have been mainly fiscal in character. No declaration of the value of the object to be exported was required, and the export officer had no authority to deny a permit. . . .

The second set of provisions drawn to the attention of the court are contained in a statute of the Mussolini regime entitled "Protection of items of artistic or historical interest," Law No. 1089 of June 1, 1939 (hereafter, "the 1939 Law"). Art. 1 of this law lists, in slightly greater detail, the objects of interest covered by Art. 129 of the 1913 regulations. However, Art. 1 expressly excludes works by living artists or which are not more than fifty years old.

Art. 2 of the 1939 law establishes a process of notification by which the Minister of Public Instruction gives formal administrative notice to owners, proprietors and holders of art works determined to be of particular interest to the Italian Government. Such notification is kept on record and binds any successor in ownership, holder, or possessor of a beneficial interest in a work of art.

Art. 35 of the 1939 law prohibits the exportation from Italy of objects falling within the scope of Art. 1 when the items are of such importance that their export would represent a tremendous loss to the national patrimony protected by the law. Art. 36 requires anyone desiring to export objects specified in Art. 1 to apply to the Export Office for a license and to declare the market value of each object. . . . Within a period of two months after the declaration, the Minister is empowered under Art. 39 to purchase objects of particular interest to the national patrimony at their declared value. . . .

Much of the debate among the experts concerned the question whether the provisions of the 1913 regulations with respect to works of art by living artists or less than fifty years old survived the enactment of the 1939 law. The answer was agreed to lie in Art. 73 of the 1939 law, entitled Transitional Provisions, which read as follows:

The provisions of the regulations approved under Royal Decree No. 363(3) of January 30, 1913, shall remain in force, insofar as they are applicable, until such time as the regulations to be issued in execution of this law take effect.

Although one would suppose the issue would long since have been resolved, by decision or practice, the district court was presented with conflicting opinions. Five treatises by Italian lawyers and one by Professor Merryman of the Stanford Law School took the view that, as stated by him, "a work no more than fifty years old is freely exportable." . . . Two Italian attorneys submitted affidavits to the same effect. To the contrary, opining that works by living artists or less than 50 years old at the time of export continued to be subject to the 1913 regulations, were two earlier Italian treatises, an affidavit by an Italian lawyer, the live testimony of another, and, at least inferentially, the live testimony of Dr. Carlo Bertelli, Superintendent in the Ministry of Cultural Heritage and Director of the Brera Gallery in Milan. The only relevant judicial decision cited, Corte cass., No. 3325, Aug. 5, 1957, 1958 Fori It. I 1940, gives a featherweight of support to the latter view.

III

. . . John Tancock, a vice-president of Sotheby Parke Bernet auction house and head of its Department of Impressionist and Modern Painting and Sculpture, testified that, but for the question of illegal exportation, he would appraise the painting at $750,000. On the other hand, if the painting lacked "the necessary export documents from any country where it had been located," his opinion was that it would be impossible to sell the painting since "[n]o reputable auction house or dealer would be prepared to handle it." Hence "on the legitimate market its value is zero." He would date the painting "early 1920's, 1919, 1922, something like that." Nancy Schwartz, an art dealer associated with the Spencer Samuels & Company gallery in New York, testified that the gallery having received a number of requests for paintings by Matisse, she communicated with Mme. Jeanneret as to sending the painting to

New York. Before any arrangements could be made, Ms. Schwartz wrote Mme. Jeanneret on May 1, 1975 that she would not be able to sell the painting as plaintiff had proposed to her in Geneva in February; "I had a client who was ready to buy it, but as you said that the painting left Italy clandestinely I realized that this painting cannot be sold." Graham Leader, an independent art dealer, identified letters he had written to Mme. Jeanneret from London in June and November 1974. In the former he stated that he expected a client in the next few days to whom he had indicated a price of 1,100,000 Swiss francs for the painting; in the latter he confirmed a telephone conversation announcing his refusal to consider handling the painting or advising one of his best clients to buy it "from the moment that I learned that the painting had been clandestinely exported from Italy by its former owner, Mme. Vichey-Frua DeAngeli and that it could thus be subject to suit by any authority." Finally, Dr. Bertelli, whose position we have already described, testified that Dr. Enrico Vitali, Mme. Jeanneret's lawyer, had called him to ask whether there was any record that the Matisse painting had been issued export documents after 1969 and that Dr. Bertelli had found no evidence that it had. On March 28, 1979, the Assistant Minister of Culture issued a notification pursuant to Art. 3 of the law of June 1, 1939, declaring the painting, "an important work by the French painter Henri Matisse, datable between 1920 and 1923," to be of "particular artistic and historical interest" within the meaning of the 1939 law and "therefore subject to all the regulations regarding custody included therein."[1] The decree was to "be notified through administrative channels to the present owner, possessor or holder of this painting," to wit, Mrs. Vichey, in care of Dr. Magenta

in Milan. Dr. Bertelli also testified that on September 17, 1981, just before he had left Milan to attend the trial, the Attorney General of Italy had shown him a memorandum indicating that a penal proceeding had been instituted against Anna Frua DeAngeli, that Interpol had been requested to recover the painting, and that the Chief of the Italian Delegation for Retrieving Works of Art had been asked to present the request of the Italian Government to the United States authorities.

The defendants' evidence was sparse. Mrs. Vichey professed ignorance of the details of the exportation. Luben Vichey testified on direct examination that he had first seen the Matisse painting at the Bank Gut Streiff in Zurich; that he had not known it was to be taken out of Italy; and that Dr. Magenta, Mrs. Vichey, and at least one of her brothers also didn't know this. On cross-examination he asserted that the paintings taken to Switzerland did have export documents for which Dr. Magenta had arranged.

The final defense witness was Kenneth Silver, an associate professor in the art history department at Columbia University. An effort was made to show that the painting was included in a catalogue of the Gallery of Bernheim Jeune, Matisse's Paris dealer, in a show held in 1922–23, but the ineptness of defendants' counsel resulted in this not getting to the jury.[2] He thought the painting was almost certainly "a '20s Matisse . . . anywhere from early '20s, '22, '23, '24, maybe as late as '28. I don't think later than 1928." He would not date it as early as 1920 without doing research. Later he dated the picture as at the earliest "[a]bout 1921; I am not saying it is impossible to be '20 but I think it more likely to be at the earliest '21."[3]

---

1. The somewhat surprising conclusion that exportation of a painting by a prolific French post-impressionist master would represent a "tremendous loss to the national heritage" of Italy was sought to be justified on the grounds that it had been shown at the Venice Biennale in 1952 "in the large exposition dedicated to art" and "because it is part of the era of 'a return to normalcy' which pervaded all Europe at the end of the first world war, characterized by a return to classic and Renaissance motifs particularly evident in this balanced, well composed painting by a master of contemporary art and specially rare among Italian collections of significant works of that period." One is tempted to wonder why if Italian collectors do not care enough for Matisse to buy his paintings, one of these, not claimed to be an outstanding masterpiece, should be thought to constitute such an important part of the Italian national heritage.

2. The judge properly ruled that defendants had not sufficiently established the authenticity of the catalogue to qualify it for admission as an ancient document under F.R.E. 803(16). Defendants' counsel apparently did not urge admissibility under F.R.E. 803(17). Of course, the catalogue would be only marginally relevant in the absence of evidence, which may well be available in the form of treatises or otherwise but was not offered, that at this stage of his career Matisse generally sold his paintings shortly after they were completed.

3. It is ironical that defendants' counsel should have staked their effort to establish the date of the painting on the opinion testimony of an expert which, in the absence of a date on or datable objects in the painting, could only be approximate, when they were aware of a document which, if adduced in evidence and uncontradicted, would have established that Matisse painted this work during the season of 1922–23. In the course of pretrial discovery, defendants' counsel elicited that Mme. Jeanneret had received a letter dated July 20,

IV

The district judge charged the jury, over objection by the defendants, that "[t]he mere casting of a substantial shadow over the title, regardless of the ultimate outcome of that dispute, is sufficient to violate a warranty of good title." . . .

The jury returned a verdict for defendants on the first cause of action (breach of express warranty), and the third cause of action (fraudulent misrepresentation). It returned a verdict of $1,688,000 for plaintiff on the second and fourth causes of action (breach of implied warranty of title and breach of contract).

Defendants moved for judgment notwithstanding the verdict or for a new trial. By a memorandum and order, 541 F.Supp. 80, Judge Cannella denied the motion for judgment n.o.v. but granted the motion for a new trial unless plaintiff consented to a reduction of the amount awarded from $1,688,000 to $938,000. Plaintiff accepted the remittitur. Judgment was entered dismissing the causes of action based on breach of express warranty, fraudulent misrepresentation and tax evasion and adjudging that, subject to her obligation to return the painting and execute such documents as might be necessary to transfer title, plaintiff should recover $938,000 from Anna and Luben Vichey. This appeal followed.

V

We begin by expressing surprise that defendants' counsel did not move to set aside the verdict as reflecting passion and prejudice. . . .

1977, from Paris from Matisse's daughter, Mme. Marguerite Duthuit, whom Mme. Jeanneret had characterized as a great authority on Matisse's work. Mme. Duthuit's letter stated without equivocation that the painting had been painted "during the 1922–23 season. By this I mean between the month of October, when Matisse arrived in Nice, and the months of April–May following when he left that city before the heat-wave common in that region at those times." Mme. Duthuit offered to remain at Mme. Jeanneret's disposition to maintain this. For reasons not explained, defendants' counsel did not take Mme. Duthuit's deposition. Indeed, they did not even interrogate Mme. Jeanneret at trial about her receipt of the Duthuit letter, which would have been permissible for the purpose of arguing that Mme. Jeanneret should have used the letter and any further information Mme. Duthuit could have supplied in an effort to convince the Italian authorities that exportation of the painting did not violate the 1939 law since it was not yet 50 years old in the spring of 1970. Defendants' counsel did request plaintiff to admit the authenticity of the letter but plaintiff never responded, and the matter was left at that.

When we inquired of appellee's counsel what rational basis there could have been for a verdict of $1,688,000, the only answer was that the excess over the figure allowed by the judge might represent compensation for loss of business or of reputation. As to the former, the judge's $4,000 figure seems to be liberal; as to the latter there was no evidence. Seemingly the jury doubled Tancock's $750,000 appraisal to $1,500,000 and added $184,000 for interest and $4,000 for other damages. The jury could well have been inflamed by some of Mme. Jeanneret's letters and the testimony that a penal proceeding had been instituted against defendant Anna Vichey and that Interpol had become involved. However, defendants' counsel did not raise this point either below or here, and we therefore cannot consider it.

Both sides have assumed that defendants' liability is governed by the law of New York, where the negotiations for the sale of the painting occurred, rather than by the law of Switzerland, where it was delivered and payment received. We shall follow them in that assumption.

Section 2-312 of the Uniform Commercial Code as adopted in New York, Laws, 1962, c. 553, provides:

(1) Subject to subsection (2) there is in a contract for sale a warranty by the seller that
   (a) the title conveyed shall be good, and its transfer rightful; and
   (b) the goods shall be delivered free from any security interest or other lien or encumbrance of which the buyer at the time of contracting has no knowledge. . . .

The Official Comment on this section states in part:

1. Subsection (1) makes provision for a buyer's basic needs in respect to a title which he in good faith expects to acquire by his purchase, namely, that he receive a good, clean title transferred to him also in a rightful manner so that he will not be exposed to a lawsuit in order to protect it. . . .

There is nothing to show that defendants breached the warranty described in §2-312 (1)(a). No one denies that Carlo Frua DeAngeli was the lawful owner of the painting and that it passed by rightful succession to Anna Vichey. While Art. 61 of the 1939 Law provides that any transfers, agreements and legal acts in general carried out contrary to the law are null and void, no transfer, agreement, or comparable legal act occurred by virtue of the exportation to Switzerland; the heirs of Carlo Frua DeAngeli were exporting to themselves. The rights of the Italian

Government were neither a "security interest" nor, in the normal meaning of language, an "other lien or encumbrance," especially if any weight is to be given here to the maxim *ejusdem generis*.

None of the cases from New York or other states cited by the district court deals with a situation such as is presented here. The cases holding that the buyer can recover simply by showing "[t]he mere casting of a substantial shadow over his title, regardless of the ultimate outcome" . . . deal with what would be deemed defects in title or with liens or encumbrances in the ordinary meanings of those terms. Professor Nordstrom's seemingly apposite remarks anent a hypothetical sale of a painting in his Handbook of the Law of Sales 186 (1970) ("The buyer did not purchase a lawsuit. He purchased a painting.") lose force with respect to this case when it is realized that the author was discussing a true claim of lack of title.

The argument that there was no breach of the implied warranty created by §2-312(1)(b) is strengthened by the terms of the Italian law and customary international law. Although Art. 66 of the 1939 Law says that the item may be confiscated, it goes on to say that confiscation is carried out in accordance with the Customs laws and regulations pertaining to smuggled goods, which can be done only in Italy. Professor Bator, in an important article, An Essay on the International Trade in Art, 34 Stan.L.Rev. 275, 287 (1982), has declared the "fundamental general rule" to be that "illegal export does not itself render the importer (or one who took from him) in any way actionable in a U.S. court; the possession of an art object cannot be lawfully disturbed in the United States solely because it was illegally exported from another country." He adds that "[t]his general rule apparently obtains in all other major art-importing countries, including England, France, Germany, and Switzerland." Art. 64 of the 1939 Italian law makes clear that even when an item more than fifty years old has been exported from Italy, liability to pay the State the value of the exported item and any fine rests on the exporter, not on a purchaser. It is thus reasonably plain that so long as Mme. Jeanneret or any purchaser from her did not bring the painting back into Italy, it could not be confiscated and neither she nor a purchaser from her would be subject to monetary liability to Italy. There would seem no reasonable prospect that the United States or any other government would act on Italy's request for help in securing the return of the painting. This is especially true in light of the tenuous nature of the claim that a not especially notable painting by a French twentieth-century master who was testified to have left a thousand paintings constituted an important part of Italy's artistic patrimony, see note 6, *supra*. Matisse's Portrait sur Fond Jaune bore no such relation to Italy as a Raphael or a Bellini Madonna.

Against all this, however, we have the testimony of Mme. Jeanneret and of the three art dealers, Tancock, Schwartz, and Leader, here uncontradicted, that the painting could not be sold to any reputable art dealer or auction house. When we add to this evidence §1-102(1) of the Uniform Commercial Code providing that

This Act shall be liberally construed and applied to promote its underlying purposes and policies. . . .

we find it somewhat hard to reject the common-sensical view of the district judge that an art dealer who has bought a painting which, according to the usages of her trade, she cannot sell through ordinary channels is under a heavy cloud, indeed.

We are reluctant to decide so serious a question, of particular importance to New York where so many of the country's art transactions take place, on such an unsatisfactory record and without even the slightest clue from the New York courts. Although we may ultimately be forced to decide the question without the benefit of further guidance from New York cases, defendants have at least made out a case for a new trial which may avoid the need for such a decision on our part.

We say this because in our view the court's instruction was erroneous in several respects. One was in saying that if the painting were returned to Italy, the "owner, even if he purchased the painting in good faith, could be required to pay customs duties and/or fines." We see nothing in the Italian law that imposes any such liability on a purchaser as distinguished from the exporter. Much more important, the charge failed to focus the jury's attention adequately on the age of the painting when it was exported from Italy. . . .

There must therefore be a new trial at which, one would hope, more definitive evidence of the date of the painting can be provided unless, of course, the Italian Government should see fit to withdraw its notification or the parties should adjust their differences.

The judgment is reversed and the case remanded for further proceedings consistent with this opinion.

COMMENTS

1. The trial court decision in *Jeanneret v. Vichey* was characterized as "a decision to send chills down the spines of all owners of imported works of art" ("Caveat Vendor," *Stolen Art Alert,* vol. 3, no. 1 [January–February 1982]: p. 1).

2. Actually, the decision created more of a problem for sellers, including dealers. A dissatisfied purchaser could allege that the work was illegally exported, might easily arrange for the foreign government to make such a claim, and make a profit on the transaction.

3. Note that according to the trial court, the Italian claim of illegal export need not have been valid in order to constitute a cloud on title.

4. Judge Friendly's opinion reversing the trial court makes it clear that the trial decision and jury verdict were unfortunate accidents, unlikely to be repeated.

5. Suppose, however, that several major art-importing nations enact legislation prohibiting the importation and providing for seizure and return of illegally exported cultural property. Canada has already done so, and as other art-importing nations become parties to the 1970 UNESCO Convention, the number will grow. How much does the market for such works have to shrink before a court will properly find that there is a cloud on the title?

6. In 1972, under a marine insurance policy issued in Hamburg, the insured sought to recover in a German court for the loss at sea of three crates of African masks and figures, including six Nigerian bronzes. The insurer's defense was that there was no "insurable interest" (a requirement for the validity of an insurance contract in all Western legal systems) because the works were exported contrary to Nigerian law. This, the insurer argued, was against an international public policy evidenced by the 1970 UNESCO Convention (see pp. 91–97), which treats illegal export as "illicit." The *Bundesgerichtshof* (the German Federal Supreme Court in civil and criminal matters) agreed. It held that "in the interest of decency in the international trade in cultural objects" it should not enforce the contract (BGHZ 59, 82 [1972]; 35 NJW 1575 [1971]; Hans W. Baade, "The Legal Effects of Codes of Conduct for Multinational Enterprises," *German Yearbook of International Law 1979,* p. 40). The authors are not aware of any further applications of this doctrine, the consequences of which for international trade could be enormous, in Germany or elsewhere.

7. Karl E. Meyer, author of *The Plundered Past,* suggested in the *New York Times* of May 31, 1984, that the Internal Revenue Service should deny deductions for gifts to museums of "plundered art." His argument is that deductibility is a tax benefit that should be withheld in such cases. Is this a good idea?

U.S. LEGISLATION

In 1972 the United States enacted the following statute.

Regulation of Importation of Pre-Columbian Monumental or Architectural Sculpture or Murals
Public Law No. 92-587, 19 U.S.C.A. §§2091ff (1972)

Sec. 201. The Secretary, after consultation with the Secretary of State, by regulation shall promulgate, and thereafter when appropriate shall revise, a list of stone carvings and wall art which are pre-Columbian monumental or architectural sculpture or murals within the meaning of paragraph (3) of section 205. Such stone carvings and wall art may be listed by type or other classification deemed appropriate by the Secretary.

Sec. 202 (a) No pre-Columbian monumental or architectural sculpture or mural which is exported (whether or not such exportation is to the United States) from the country of origin after the effective date of the regulation listing such sculpture or mural pursuant to section 202 may be imported into the United States unless the government of the country of origin of such sculpture or mural issues a certificate, in a form acceptable to the Secretary, which certifies that such exportation was not in violation of the laws of that country.

(b) If the consignee of any pre-Columbian monumental or architectural sculpture or mural is unable to present to the customs officer concerned at the time of making entry of such sculpture or mural—

(1) the certificate of the government of the

country of origin required under subsection (a) of this section;

(2) satisfactory evidence that such sculpture or mural was exported from the country of origin on or before the effective date of the regulation listing such sculpture or mural pursuant to section 202;or

(3) satisfactory evidence that such sculpture or mural is not covered by the list promulgated under section 202;

the customs officer concerned shall take the sculpture or mural into customs custody and send it to a bonded warehouse or public store to be held at the risk and expense of the consignee until such certificate or evidence is filed with such officer. If such certificate or evidence is not presented within the 90-day period after the date on which such sculpture or mural is taken into customs custody, or such longer period as may be allowed by the Secretary for good cause shown, the importation of such sculpture or mural into the United States is in violation of this title.

Sec. 203. (a) Any pre-Columbian monumental or architectural sculpture or mural imported into the United States in violation of this title shall be seized and subject to forfeiture under the customs laws.

(b) Any pre-Columbian monumental or architectural sculpture or mural which is forfeited to the United States shall—

(1) first be offered for return to the country of origin and shall be returned if that country bears all expenses incurred incident to such re-turn and complies with such other requirements relating to the return as the Secretary shall prescribe; or

(2) if not returned to the country of origin, be disposed of in the manner prescribed by law for articles forfeited for violation of the customs laws.

Sec. 204. The Secretary shall prescribe such rules and regulations as are necessary and appropriate to carry out the provisions of this title.

Sec. 205. For the purposes of this title—

(1) The term "Secretary" means the Secretary of the Treasury.

(2) The Term "United States" includes the several States, the District of Columbia, and the Commonwealth of Puerto Rico.

(3) The term "pre-Columbian monumental or architectural sculpture or mural" means—

(A) any stone carving or wall art which—

(i) is the product of a pre-Columbian Indian culture of Mexico, Central America, South America, or the Caribbean Islands;

(ii) was an immobile monument or architectural structure or was a part of, or affixed to, any such monument or structure; and

(iii) is subject to export control by the country of origin; or

(B) any fragment or part of any stone carving or wall art described in subparagraph (A) of this paragraph.

(4) The term "country of origin," as applied to any pre-Columbian monumental or architectural sculpture or mural, means the country where such sculpture or mural was first discovered.

COMMENTS

1. This statute obviously changes the law. A limited category of works, if illegally exported from specified countries, will now be seized and returned to the nations of origin even though they are not technically stolen and even though they are correctly declared at Customs on entry.

2. The statute provides that if the articles are not returned to the country of origin, they shall be disposed of by customs "in the prescribed manner." Title 19 U.S.C.A. §§1603ff. governs the disposition of items seized by U.S. Customs. First, a report is made to the U.S. Attorney in the district where the violation occurs, and the items seized are stored in custody of U.S. Customs. The goods are then appraised for their current value in the United States. If their value is less than $2,500, notice is given that the items will be sold. Claims may be made at this time. If there is no claimant, the seized merchandise is sold at public auction. When the value of the items is more than $2,500 the U.S. Attorney is notified and condemnation proceedings are instituted.

Any person claiming the seized materials must show that he has a substantial interest therein. He may recover the goods upon payment of their appraised value. If the claim is made after the goods are sold, the claimant may recover part or all of the proceeds of sale. In other cases, the proceeds are deposited in the U.S. Treasury.

3. Regulations issued under this statute, as provided in Section 202, are published in the Code of Federal Regulations, Title 19, §§12.105–12.109.

4. In the early 1970s, U.S. Customs officials began an intensive effort to identify looted archaeological artifacts being brought into the United States illegally. Under the 1972 statute set out above, Customs has been watching closely artifacts from countries that regulate exports, including Guatemala, Panama, Peru, Venezuela, Costa Rica, Belize, Bolivia, Honduras, Colombia, El Salvador, the Dominican Republic, and Mexico.

John A. Grieco, senior special agent of the Customs Service's Offices of Investigation, was placed in charge of these efforts. Special agents not only familiarized themselves with the laws of other countries but also took courses in art history to be better able to identify the works in question. A book on pre-Columbian art was made available to agents in nearly seventy ports where such importation was likely. . . .

The special Customs agents work with other investigative agencies, such as the FBI and Interpol, and private groups, such as the Art Dealers Association of America. These officials can scrutinize the importation of any object that they have reason to believe came into this country in violation of Customs law and seize any object they think was imported with a false declaration. In addition, in the New York Port area, there are two art import experts who examine entering shipments in light of value, country of origin, and descriptions of stolen or looted artworks, and they inform the special agents when there appears to be a question of smuggling.

It has been suggested that in some countries government officials can be bribed to allow the export of national treasures. One of the art import experts was quoted as remarking, "We can only work effectively according to the degree of cooperation we get from other countries. If many of these countries really wanted to stop illegal exports, they could."

5. Where the country of origin is Mexico, the 1972 federal statute must be read in conjunction with the 1971 Mexico–U.S. Treaty of Cooperation, discussed later in this chapter.

6. It has been suggested that the 1972 statute and the 1971 treaty were parts of a deal with Mexico to enlist that country's active support in controlling traffic in drugs—the United States would keep out their pre-Columbian monumental artifacts if they would help us keep out their marijuana, cocaine, and/or heroin. Assuming that such a deal was made, what is your reaction? Is this the way policy about cultural property should be made?

MULTILATERAL APPROACHES

Theft and illegal export have been topics of general international concern, particularly in recent years. Three successive draft conventions were prepared under the auspices of the Intellectual Cooperation Organization of the League of Nations prior to World War II. None was ever adopted. They are reproduced in U.S. Department of State, *Documents and State Papers,* vol. 1, no. 1 (April 1948): "Texts of Draft International Conventions for the Protection of National Collections of Art and History," pp. 865–871.

After World War II, efforts at international legislation in this field revived. Out of this effort have come the European Convention on the Protection of the Archaeological Heritage of 1969, European Treaty Series, no. 66; and the 1985 European Convention on Offences Relating to Cultural Property, set out and explained in Council of Europe Document N. AS/Cult/ AA(36)10; the 1976 Convention on Protection of the Archaeological, Historical, and Artistic Patrimony of the American Nations (Convention of San Salvador), OAS Treaty Series, no. 47; and the 1970 UNESCO Convention on the Means of Prohibiting and Preventing the Illicit Import, Export, and Transfer of Ownership of Cultural Property.

THE 1970 UNESCO CONVENTION

Of these, the 1970 UNESCO Convention is much the most influential and most widely adopted. It is the only one to which the United States is a party. Here are its relevant provisions.

UNESCO Convention on the Means of Prohibiting and Preventing the Illicit Import, Export, and Transfer of Ownership of Cultural Property*

The General Conference of the United Nations Educational, Scientific and Cultural Organization, meeting in Paris from 12 October to 14 November 1970, at its sixteenth session,

Recalling the importance of the provisions contained in the Declaration of the Principles of International Cultural Co-operation, adopted by the General Conference at its fourteenth session,

Considering that the interchange of cultural property among nations for scientific, cultural and educational purposes increases the knowledge of the civilization of Man, enriches the cultural life of all peoples and inspires mutual respect and appreciation among nations,

Considering that cultural property constitutes one of the basic elements of civilization and national culture, and that its true value can be appreciated only in relation to the fullest possible information regarding its origin, history and traditional setting,

Considering that it is incumbent upon every State to protect the cultural property existing within its territory against the dangers of theft, clandestine excavation, and illicit export,

Considering that, to avert these dangers, it is essential for every State to become increasingly alive to the moral obligations to respect its own cultural heritage and that of all nations,

Considering that, as cultural institutions, museums, libraries and archives should ensure that their collections are built up in accordance with universally recognized moral principles,

Considering that the illicit import, export and transfer of ownership of cultural property is an obstacle to that understanding between nations which it is part of Unesco's mission to promote by recommending to interested States, international conventions to this end,

Considering that the protection of cultural heritage can be effective only if organized both nationally and internationally among States working in close co-operation,

Considering that the Unesco General Conference adopted a Recommendation to this effect in 1964,

Having before it further proposals on the means of prohibiting and preventing the illicit import, export and transfer of ownership of cultural property, a question which is on the agenda for the session as item 19,

Having decided, at its fifteenth session, that this question should be made the subject of an international convention,

Adopts this Convention on the fourteenth day of November 1970.

Article 1. For the purposes of this Convention, the term "cultural property" means property which, on religious or secular grounds, is specifically designated by each State as being of importance for archaeology, prehistory, history, literature, art or science and which belongs to the following categories:

(a) Rare collections and specimens of fauna, flora, minerals and anatomy, and objects of palaeontological interest;

(b) property relating to history, including the history of science and technology and military and social history, to the life of national leaders, thinkers, scientists and artists and to events of national importance;

(c) products of archaeological excavations (including regular and clandestine) or of archaeological discoveries;

(d) elements of artistic or historical monuments or archaeological sites which have been dismembered;

(e) antiquities more than one hundred years old, such as inscriptions, coins and engraved seals;

(f) objects of ethnological interest;

(g) property of artistic interest, such as:

(i) pictures, paintings and drawings produced entirely by hand on any support and in any material (excluding industrial designs and manufactured articles decorated by hand);

(ii) works of statuary art and sculpture in any material;

(iii) original engravings, prints and lithographs;

(iv) original artistic assemblages and montages in any material;

---

*From 823 United Nations Treaty Series, reprinted in *International Legal Materials,* vol. 10 (1971), p. 289.

(h) rare manuscripts and incunabula, old books, documents and publications of special interest (historical, artistic, scientific, literary, etc.) singly or in collections;

(i) postage, revenue and similar stamps, singly or in collections;

(j) archives, including sound, photographic and cinematographic archives;

(k) articles of furniture more than one hundred years old and old musical instruments.

Article 2. 1. The States Parties to this Convention recognize that the illicit import, export and transfer of ownership of cultural property is one of the main causes of the impoverishment of the cultural heritage of the countries of origin of such property and that international cooperation constitutes one of the most efficient means of protecting each country's cultural property against all the dangers resulting therefrom.

2. To this end, the State Parties undertake to oppose such practices with the means at their disposal, and particularly by removing their causes, putting a stop to current practices, and by helping to make the necessary reparations.

Article 3. The import, export or transfer of ownership of cultural property effected contrary to the provisions adopted under this Convention by the States Parties thereto, shall be illicit.

Article 4. The States Parties to this Convention recognize that for the purpose of the Convention property which belongs to the following categories forms part of the cultural heritage of each State:

(a) Cultural property created by the individual or collective genius of nationals of the State concerned, and cultural property of importance to the State concerned created within the territory of that State by foreign nationals or stateless persons resident within such territory;

(b) cultural property found within the national territory;

(c) cultural property acquired by archaeological, ethnological or natural science missions, with the consent of the competent authorities of the country of origin of such property;

(d) cultural property which had been the subject of a freely agreed exchange;

(e) cultural property received as a gift or purchased legally with the consent of the competent authorities of the country of origin of such property.

Article 5. To ensure the protection of their cultural property against illicit import, export and transfer of ownership, the States Parties to this Convention undertake, as appropriate for each country, to set up within their territories one or more national services, where such services do not already exist, for the protection of the cultural heritage, with a qualified staff sufficient in number for the effective carrying out of the following functions:

(a) Contributing to the formation of draft laws and regulations designed to secure the protection of the cultural heritage and particularly prevention of the illicit import, export and transfer of ownership of important cultural property;

(b) establishing and keeping up to date, on the basis of a national inventory of protected property, a list of important public and private cultural property whose export would constitute an appreciable impoverishment of the national cultural heritage;

(c) promoting the development or the establishment of scientific and technical institutions (museums, libraries, archives, laboratories, workshops . . .) required to ensure the preservation and presentation of cultural property;

(d) organizing the supervision of archaeological excavations, ensuring the preservation "in situ" of certain cultural property, and protecting certain areas reserved for future archaeological research;

(e) establishing, for the benefit of those concerned (curators, collectors, antique dealers, etc.) rules in conformity with the ethical principles set forth in this Convention; and taking steps to ensure the observance of those rules;

(f) taking educational measures to stimulate and develop respect for the cultural heritage of all States, and spreading knowledge of the provisions of this Convention;

(g) seeing that appropriate publicity is given to the disappearance of any items of cultural property.

Article 6. The States Parties to this Convention undertake:

(a) To introduce an appropriate certificate in which the exporting State would specify that the export of the cultural property in question is authorized. The certificate should accompany all items of cultural property exported in accordance with the regulations;

(b) to prohibit the exportation of cultural property from their territory unless accompanied by the above-mentioned export certificate;

(c) to publicize this prohibition by appropriate means, particularly among persons likely to export or import cultural property.

Article 7. The States Parties to this Convention undertake:

(a) To take the necessary measures, consistent with national legislation, to prevent museums and similar institutions within their territories from acquiring cultural property originating in another State Party which has been illegally exported after entry into force of this Convention, in the States concerned. Whenever possible, to inform a State of origin Party to this Convention of an officer of such cultural property illegally removed from that State after the entry into force of this Convention in both States;

(b) (i) to prohibit the import of cultural property stolen from a museum or a religious or secular public monument or similar institution in another State Party to this Convention after the entry into force of this Convention for the States concerned, provided that such property is documented as appertaining to the inventory of that institution;

   (ii) at the request of the State Party of origin, to take appropriate steps to recover and return any such cultural property imported after the entry into force of this Convention in both States concerned, provided, however, that the requesting State shall pay just compensation to an innocent purchaser or to a person who has valid title to that property. Requests for recovery and return shall be made through diplomatic offices. The requesting Party shall furnish, at its expense, the documentation and other evidence necessary to establish its claim for recovery and return. The Parties shall impose no customs duties or other charges upon cultural property returned pursuant to this Article. All expenses incident to the return and delivery of the cultural property shall be borne by the requesting Party.

Article 8. The States Parties to this Convention undertake to impose penalties or administrative sanctions on any person responsible for infringing the prohibitions referred to under Articles 6(b) and 7(b) above.

Article 9. Any State Party to this Convention whose cultural patrimony is in jeopardy from pillage of archaeological or ethnological materials may call upon other States Parties who are affected. The States Parties to this Convention undertake, in these circumstances, to participate in a concerted international effort to determine and to carry out the necessary concrete measures, including the control of exports and imports and international commerce in the specific materials concerned. Pending agreement each State concerned shall take provisional measures to the extent feasible to prevent irremediable injury to the cultural heritage of the requesting State.

Article 10. The States Parties to this Convention undertake:

(a) To restrict by education, information and vigilance, movement of cultural property illegally removed from any State Party to this Convention and, as appropriate for each country, oblige antique dealers, subject to penal or administrative sanctions, to maintain a register recording the origin of each item of cultural property, names and addresses of the supplier, description and price of each item sold and to inform the purchaser of the cultural property of the export prohibition to which such property may be subject;

(b) to endeavour by educational means to create and develop in the public mind a realization of the value of cultural property and the threat to the cultural heritage created by theft, clandestine excavations and illicit exports.

Article 11. The export and transfer of ownership of cultural property under compulsion arising directly or indirectly from the occupation of a country by a foreign power shall be regarded as illicit.

Article 12. The States Parties to this Convention shall respect the cultural heritage within the territories for the international relations of which they are responsible, and shall take all appropriate measures to prohibit and prevent the illicit import, export and transfer of ownership of cultural property in such territories.

Article 13. The States Parties to this Convention also undertake, consistent with the laws of each State:

(a) To prevent by all appropriate means transfers of ownership of cultural property likely to promote the illicit import or export of such property;

(b) to ensure that their competent services cooperate in facilitating the earliest possible restitution of illicitly exported cultural property to its rightful owner;

(c) to admit actions for recovery of lost or stolen items of cultural property brought by or on behalf of the rightful owners;

(d) to recognize the indefeasible right of each State Party to this Convention to classify and declare certain cultural property as inalienable which should therefore *ipso facto* not be exported, and to facilitate recovery of such property by State concerned in cases where it has been exported.

Article 14. In order to prevent illicit export and to meet the obligations arising from the implementation of this Convention, each State Party to the Convention should, as far as it is able, provide the national services responsible for the protection of its cultural heritage with an adequate budget and, if necessary, should set up a fund for this purpose.

Article 15. Nothing in this Convention shall prevent States Parties thereto from concluding special agreements among themselves or from continuing to implement agreements already concluded regarding the restitution of cultural property removed, whatever the reason, from its territory of origin, before the entry into force of this Convention for the States concerned.

Article 16. The State Parties to this Convention shall in their periodic reports submitted to the General Conference of the United Nations Educational, Scientific and Cultural Organization on dates and in a manner to be determined by it, give information on the legislative and administrative provisions which they have adopted and other action which they have taken for the application of this Convention, together with details of the experience acquired in this field.

Article 17. 1. The States Parties to this Convention may call on the technical assistance of the United National Educational, Scientific and Cultural Organization, particularly as regards:

(a) Information and education;

(b) consultation and expert advice;

(c) co-ordination and good offices.

2. The United Nations Educational, Scientific and Cultural Organization may, on its own initiative, conduct research and publish studies on matters relevant to the illicit movement of cultural property.

3. To this end, the United Nations Educational, Scientific and Cultural Organization may also call on the co-operation of any competent non-governmental organization.

4. The United Nations Educational, Scientific and Cultural Organization may, on its own initiative, make proposals to State Parties to this Convention for its implementation.

5. At the request of at least two State Parties to this Convention which are engaged in a dispute over its implementation, Unesco may extend its good offices to reach a settlement between them.

COMMENTS

1. The United States participated in drafting the Convention and supported its adoption by the General Conference of UNESCO in 1970. Paul Bator, who was a member of the U.S. delegation that helped draft it, discusses the Convention and its background in "An Essay on the International Trade in Art," *Stanford Law Review,* vol. 34, (1982), pp. 275, 370ff. In 1972 the Convention was ratified by the United States, subject to one "reservation" and six "understandings," as follows:

The United States reserves the right to determine whether or not to impose export controls over cultural property.

The United States understands the provisions of the Convention to be neither self-executing nor retroactive.

The United States understands Article 3 not to modify property interests in cultural property under the laws of the states parties.

The United States understands Article 7(a) to apply to institutions whose acquisition policy is subject to national control under existing domestic legislation and not to require the enactment of new legislation to establish national control over other institutions.

The United States understands that Article 7(b) is without prejudice to other remedies, civil or penal, available under the laws of the states parties for the recovery of stolen cultural property to the rightful owner without payment of compensation. The United States is further prepared to take the additional steps contemplated by Article 7(b)(ii) for the return of covered stolen cultural property without payment of compensation, except to the extent required by the Constitution of the United States, for those states parties that agree to do the same for the United States institutions.

The United States understands the words "as appropriate for each country" in Article 10(a) as permitting each state party to determine the extent of regulation, if any, of antique dealers and declares that in the United States that determination would be made by the appropriate authorities of state and municipal governments.

The United States understands Article 13(d) as applying to objects removed from the country of origin after the entry into force of this Convention for the states concerned, and, as stated by the Chairman of the Special Committee of Governmental Experts that prepared the text, and reported in paragraph 28 of the Report of that Committee, the means of recovery of cultural property under subparagraph (d) are the judicial actions referred to in subparagraph (c) of Article 13, and that such actions are controlled by the law of the requested State, the requesting State having to submit necessary proofs.

2. The "reservation" emphasizes the fact that the United States does not control the export of cultural property and accepts no obligation to do so under the Convention. The "understandings" reflect (a) the division of power between state and federal governments under the U.S. Constitution; (b) the fact that most American museums are private, nonprofit organizations, rather than government entities; (c) protection of property rights and opposition to retroactive laws under the U.S. Constitution; and (d) existing property law within the United States.

3. In addition, the "understanding" that the Convention is non-self-executing meant that it would have no legal force within the United States until implementing legislation was enacted by Congress. Such legislation was eventually enacted in 1983 (Public Law No. 97–446, 96 Stat. 2351, 19 U.S.C.A. §§2601–2613) as the Convention on Cultural Property Implementation Act, set out below (pp. 97–107).

4. As of July 23, 1985, fifty-six nations were parties to the Convention. By far the greater number are art-exporting nations. Of the major import nations, only Canada (which is both an exporter and an importer) and the United States are parties. Interest in the Convention has been stimulated among other importing nations by U.S. enactment of an implementation act (pp. 97–107, below), and steps toward ratification have been taken in Australia, France, the Netherlands, Norway, and West Germany.

5. The withdrawal of the United States from UNESCO does not affect U.S. legal obligations under the Convention or the Implementation Act, according to a report in *ARTnewsletter,* vol. 9, no. 11, January 24, 1983, p. 5.

6. Observe that the UNESCO Convention has three key provisions. Article 7(a) deals with illegally exported cultural property and commits the United States to "take the necessary measures . . . to prevent museums" from acquiring property illegally exported from another nation that is a party to the Convention. Given the "understandings" set out and discussed in notes 1 and 2, above, this affects only federal museums. Article 7(b) deals with stolen property and commits the United States to prohibit its import and to help recover and return it (with compensation to good-faith purchasers). As we shall see below, in the discussion of "simple theft," under U.S. law the foreign owner may recover its stolen property by judicial action in state courts without paying compensation to a good-faith purchaser. The Convention is in this sense less favorable to the owner than ordinary U.S. law. Article 9 is the "crisis" provision. It contemplates concerted international action, including controls over illegally exported property, when a party nation's "cultural patrimony is in jeopardy from pillage." The significance of these three provisions for the United States is elucidated in the following materials.

JAMES R. McALEE *Implementing Legislation**

From 1973 until late in 1981, a dispute raged about how best to implement the UNESCO Convention. . . .

The representatives of the State Department, and later the International Communications Agency, urged that the Executive Branch should

*From James R. McAlee, "The McClain Case, Customs, and Congress," *NYU Journal of International Law and Politics,* vol. 15 (1983), pp. 813–815. Copyright © 1983 by New York University. Reprinted by permission.

be vested with a broad discretion to ban the importation of ancient and ethnographic art. Under the bills proposed by the administration, this power to embargo could be invoked whenever the executive considered that "the cultural patrimony of [a] State Party is in jeopardy from the pillage of archaeological or ethnological materials . . ." and that the application of import restrictions "would be of substantial benefit in deterring a serious situation of pillage. . . ."

Without endorsing pillage or the destruction of any nation's cultural patrimony, opponents of the bills made the point that words have varying meanings and that one man's routine digging may be another man's plunder. Museums, collectors and dealers sought to impose a check on the discretion of the Executive. Opponents of the bills also emphasized that the proposed legislation exceeded the requirements of the UNESCO Convention itself. The Convention called for a "concerted international effort" to help deter pillage. In contrast, under the bills proposed by the Executive, the United States was empowered to act unilaterally in imposing restrictions. Opponents of the bill argued that, if the United States acted alone in imposing import restrictions, "it [would] not put an end to world trade in the art which it embargoes but [would] succeed only in rerouting the flow of such art from the United States to such countries as Switzerland, West Germany, England, France and Japan."

During the course of this long and often acrimonious dispute, none of the parties appearing before Congress urged that the UNESCO Convention should not be implemented or that there were not occasions in which at least multinational import restrictions might be needed to curb a critical situation of looting. All parties appearing before Congress sought a rational United States policy with respect to art imports. In late 1982, under the leadership of Senators Dole, Moynihan and Matsunaga, the interested parties agreed upon a compromise bill which was subsequently passed by Congress and signed into law. The long-standing controversy over legislation to implement the UNESCO Convention seemed to have reached a happy conclusion, and passage of what was labeled the Convention on Cultural Property Implementation Act was generally applauded. . . .

COMMENT

McAlee's law firm represented the American Association of Dealers in Ancient, Oriental, and Primitive Art in opposing early drafts and supporting the version that was finally enacted. This fact should be kept in mind when reading his evaluative comments.

The Convention on Cultural Property Implementation Act of 1983
Public Law No. 97–446, 96 Stat. 2350, 19 U.S.C.A. §§2601ff.

SEC. 302. DEFINITIONS

For purposes of this title—
(1) The term "agreement" includes any amendment to, or extension of, any agreement under this title that enters into force with respect to the United States.
(2) The term "archaeological or ethnological material of the State Party" means—
(A) any object of archaeological interest;
(B) any object of ethnological interest; or
(C) any fragment or part of any object referred to in subparagraph (A) or (B);
which was first discovered within, and is subject to export control by, the State Party. For purposes of this paragraph—

(i) no object may be considered to be an object of archaeological interest unless such object—
(I) is of cultural significance;
(II) is at least two hundred and fifty years old; and
(III) was normally discovered as a result of scientific excavation, clandestine or accidental digging, or exploration on land or under water; and
(ii) no object may be considered to be an object of ethnological interest unless such object is—
(I) the product of a tribal or nonindustrial society, and
(II) important to the cultural heritage of

a people because of its distinctive characteristics, comparative rarity, or its contribution to the knowledge of the origins, development, or history of that people.

(3) The term "Committee" means the Cultural Property Advisory Committee established under section 206.

(4)The term "consignee" means a consignee as defined in section 483 of the Tariff Act of 1930 (19 U.S.C. 1483).

(5) The term "Convention" means the Convention on the means of prohibiting and preventing the illicit import, export, and transfer of ownership of cultural property adopted by the General Conference of the United Nations Educational, Scientific, and Cultural Organization at its sixteenth session.

(6) The term "cultural property" includes articles described in article 1 (a) through (k) of the Convention whether or not any such article is specifically designated as such by any State Party for the purposes of such article.

(7) The term "designated archaeological or ethnological material" means any archaeological or ethnological material of the State Party which—

(A) is—

(i) covered by an agreement under this title that enters into force with respect to the United States, or

(ii) subject to emergency action under section 304, and

(B) is listed by regulation under section 305.

(8) The term "Secretary" means the Secretary of the Treasury or his delegate.

(9) The term "State Party" means any nation which has ratified, accepted, or acceded to the Convention.

(10) The term "United States" includes the several States, the District of Columbia, and any territory or area the foreign relations for which the United States is responsible.

(11) The term "United States citizen" means—

(A) any individual who is a citizen or national of the United States;

(B) any corporation, partnership, association, or other legal entity organized or existing under the laws of the United States or any State; or

(C) any department, agency, or entity of the Federal Government or of any government of any State.

SEC. 303. AGREEMENTS TO IMPLEMENT ARTICLE 9 OF THE CONVENTION

(a) AGREEMENT AUTHORITY.—

(1) IN GENERAL.—If the President determines, after request is made to the United States under article 9 of the Convention by any State Party—

(A) that the cultural patrimony of the State Party is in jeopardy from the pillage of archaeological or ethnological materials of the State Party;

(B) that the State Party has taken measures consistent with the Convention to protect its cultural patrimony;

(C) that—

(i) the application of the import restrictions set forth in section 307 with respect to archaeological or ethnological material of the State Party, if applied in concert with similar restrictions implemented, or to be implemented within a reasonable period of time, by those nations (whether or not State Parties) individually having a significant import trade in such material, would be of substantial benefit in deterring a serious situation of pillage, and

(ii) remedies less drastic than the application of the restrictions set forth in such section are not available; and

(D) that the application of the import restrictions set forth in section 307 in the particular circumstances is consistent with the general interest of the international community in the interchange of cultural property among nations for scientific, cultural, and educational purposes;

the President may, subject to the provisions of this title, take the actions described in paragraph (2).

(2) AUTHORITY OF PRESIDENT.—For purposes of paragraph (1), the President may enter into—

(A) a bilateral agreement with the State Party to apply the import restrictions set forth in section 307 to the archaeological or ethnological material of the State Party the pillage of which is creating the jeopardy to the cultural patrimony of the State Party found to exist under paragraph (1)(A); or

(B) a multilateral agreement with the State Party and with one or more other nations (whether or not a State Party) under which the United States will apply such restrictions, and the other nations will apply similar restrictions, with respect to such material.

(3) REQUESTS.—A request made to the United States under article 9 of the Convention by a State Party must be accompanied by a written statement of the facts known to the State Party that relate to those matters with respect to which determinations must be made under subparagraphs (A) through (D) of paragraph (1).

(4) IMPLEMENTATION.—In implementing this subsection, the President should endeavor to obtain the commitment of the State Party concerned to permit the exchange of its archaeological and ethnological materials under circumstances in which such exchange does not jeopardize its cultural patrimony.

(b) EFFECTIVE PERIOD.—The President may not enter into any agreement under subsection (a) which has an effective period beyond the close of the five-year period beginning on the date on which such agreement enters into force with respect to the United States.

(c) RESTRICTIONS ON ENTERING INTO AGREEMENTS.—

(1) IN GENERAL.—The President may not enter into a bilateral or multilateral agreement authorized by subsection (a) unless the application of the import restrictions set forth in section 307 with respect to archaeological or ethnological material of the State Party making a request to the United States under article 9 of the Convention will be applied in concert with similar restrictions implemented, or to be implemented, by those nations (whether or not State Parties) individually having a significant import trade in such material.

(2) EXCEPTION TO RESTRICTIONS.—Notwithstanding paragraph (1), the President may enter into an agreement if he determines that a nation individually having a significant import trade in such material is not implementing, or is not likely to implement, similar restrictions, but—

(A) such restrictions are not essential to deter a serious situation of pillage, and

(B) the application of the import restrictions set forth in section 307 in concert with similar restrictions implemented, or to be implemented, by other nations (whether or not State Parties) individually having a significant import trade in such material would be of substantial benefit in deterring a serious situation of pillage.

(d) SUSPENSION OF IMPORT RESTRICTIONS UNDER AGREEMENTS.—If, after an agreement enters into force with respect to the United States, the President determines that a number of parties to the agreement (other than parties described in subsection (c)(2)) having significant import trade in the archaeological and ethnological material covered by the agreement—

(1) have not implemented within a reasonable period of time import restrictions that are similar to those set forth in section 307, or

(2) are not implementing such restrictions satisfactorily with the result that no substantial benefit in deterring a serious situation of pillage in the State Party concerned is being obtained,

the President shall suspend the implementation of the import restrictions under section 307 until such time as the nations take appropriate corrective action.

(e) EXTENSION OF AGREEMENTS.—The President may extend any agreement that enters into force with respect to the United States for additional periods of not more than five years each if the President determines that—

(1) the factors referred to in subsection (a)(1) which justified the entering into of the agreement still pertain, and

(2) no cause for suspension under subsection (d) exists.

(f) PROCEDURES.—If any request described in subsection (a) is made by a State Party, or if the President proposes to extend any agreement under subsection (e), the President shall—

(1) publish notification of the request or proposal in the Federal Register;

(2) submit to the Committee such information regarding the request or proposal (including, if applicable, information from the State Party with respect to the implementation of emergency action under section 304) as is appropriate to enable the Committee to carry out its duties under section 306(f); and

(3) consider, in taking action on the request or proposal, the views and recommendations contained in any Committee report—

(A) required under section 306(f)(1) or (2), and

(B) submitted to the President before the close of the one-hundred-and-fifty-day period beginning on the day on which the President submitted information on the request or proposal to the Committee under paragraph (2).

(g) INFORMATION ON PRESIDENTIAL ACTION.—

(1) IN GENERAL.—In any case in which the President—

(A) enters into or extends an agreement pursuant to subsection (a) or (e), or

(B) applies import restrictions under section 204,

the President shall, promptly after taking such action, submit a report to the Congress.

(2) REPORT.—The report under paragraph (1) shall contain—

(A) a description of such action (including the text of any agreement entered into),

(B) the differences (if any) between such action and the views and recommendations contained in any Committee report which the President was required to consider, and

(C) the reasons for any such difference.

(3) INFORMATION RELATING TO COMMITTEE RECOMMENDATIONS.—If any Committee report required to be considered by the President recommends that an agreement be entered into, but no such agreement is entered into, the President shall submit to the Congress a report which contains the reasons why such agreement was not entered into.

SEC. 304. EMERGENCY IMPLEMENTATION OF IMPORT RESTRICTIONS

(A) EMERGENCY CONDITION DEFINED.—For purposes of this section, the term "emergency condition" means, with respect to any archaeological or ethnological material of any State Party, that such material is—

(1) a newly discovered type of material which is of importance for the understanding of the history of mankind and is in jeopardy from pillage, dismantling, dispersal, or fragmentation;

(2) identifiable as coming from any site recognized to be of high cultural significance if such site is in jeopardy from pillage, dismantling, dispersal, or fragmentation which is, or threatens to be, of crisis proportions; or

(3) a part of the remains of a particular culture or civilization, the record of which is in jeopardy from pillage, dismantling, dispersal, or fragmentation which is, or threatens to be, of crisis proportions;

and application of the import restrictions set forth in section 307 on a temporary basis would, in whole or in part, reduce the incentive for such pillage, dismantling, dispersal or fragmentation.

(b) PRESIDENTIAL ACTION.—Subject to subsection (c), if the President determines that an emergency condition applies with respect to any archaeological or ethnological material of any State Party, the President may apply the import restrictions set forth in section 307 with respect to such material.

(c) LIMITATIONS.—

(1) The President may not implement this section with respect to the archaeological or ethnological materials of any State Party unless the State Party has made a request described in section 303(a) to the United States and has supplied information which supports a determination that an emergency condition exists.

(2) In taking action under subsection (b) with respect to any State Party, the President shall consider the views and recommendations contained in the Committee report required under section 306(f)(3) if the report is submitted to the President before the close of the ninety-day period beginning on the day on which the President submitted information to the Committee under section 303(f)(2) on the request of the State Party under section 303(a).

(3) No import restrictions set forth in section 307 may be applied under this section to the archaeological or ethnological materials of any State Party for more than five years after the date on which the request of a State Party under section 303(a) is made to the United States. This period may be extended by the President for three more years if the President determines that the emergency condition continues to apply with respect to the archaeological or ethnological material. However, before taking such action, the President shall request and consider, if received within ninety days, a report of the Committee setting forth its recommendations, together with the reasons therefor, as to whether such import restrictions shall be extended.

(4) The import restrictions under this section may continue to apply in whole or in part, if before their expiration under paragraph (3), there has entered into force with respect to the archaeological or ethnological materials an agreement under section 303 or an agreement with a State Party to which the Senate has given its advice and consent to ratification. Such import restrictions may continue to apply for the duration of the agreement.

SEC. 305. DESIGNATION OF MATERIALS COVERED BY AGREEMENTS OR EMERGENCY ACTIONS

After any agreement enters into force under section 303, or emergency action is taken under section 304, the Secretary, after consultation with the Director of the United States Information Agency, shall by regulation promulgate (and when appropriate shall revise) a list of the archaeological or ethnological material of the State Party covered by the agreement or by such action. The Secretary may list such material by type or other appropriate classification, but each listing made under this section shall be sufficiently specific and precise to insure that (1) the import restrictions under section 307 are applied only to the archaeological and ethnological material covered by the agreement or emergency action; and (2) fair notice is given to importers and other persons as to what material is subject to such restrictions.

SEC. 306. CULTURAL PROPERTY ADVISORY COMMITTEE

(a) ESTABLISHMENT.—There is established the Cultural Property Advisory Committee.

(b) MEMBERSHIP.—

(1) The Committee shall be composed of eleven members appointed by the President as follows:

(A) Two members representing the interests of museums.

(B) Three members who shall be experts in the fields of archaeology, anthropology, ethnology, or related areas.

(C) Three members who shall be experts in the international sale of archaeological, ethnological, and other cultural property.

(D) Three members who shall represent the interest of the general public.

(2) Appointments made under paragraph (1) shall be made in such a manner so as to insure—

(A) fair representation of the various interests of the public sectors and the private sectors in the international exchange of archaeological and ethnological materials, and

(B) that within such sectors, fair representation is accorded to the interests of regional and local institutions and museums.

(3)(A) Members of the Committee shall be appointed for terms of two years and may be reappointed for 1 or more terms.

(B) A vacancy in the Commission shall be filled in the same manner in which the original appointment was made.

(c) EXPENSES.—The members of the Committee shall be reimbursed for actual expenses incurred in the performance of duties for the Committee.

(d) TRANSACTION OF BUSINESS.—Six of the members of the Committee shall constitute a quorum. All decisions of the Committee shall be by majority vote of the members present and voting.

(e) STAFF AND ADMINISTRATION.—

(1) The Director of the United States Information Agency shall make available to the Committee such administrative and technical support services and assistance as it may reasonably require to carry out its activities. Upon the request of the Committee, the head of any other Federal agency may detail to the Committee, on a reimbursable basis, any of the personnel of such agency to assist the Committee in carrying out its functions, and provide such information and assistance as the Committee may reasonably require to carry out its activities.

(2) The Committee shall meet at the call of the Director of the United States Information Agency, or when a majority of its members request a meeting in writing.

(f) REPORTS BY COMMITTEE.—

(1) The Committee shall, with respect to each request of a State Party referred to in section 303(a), undertake an investigation and review with respect to matters referred to in section 303(a)(1) as they relate to the State Party or the request and shall prepare a report setting forth—

(A) the results of such investigation and review;

(B) its finding as to the nations individually having a significant import trade in the relevant material; and

(C) its recommendation, together with the reasons therefor, as to whether an agreement should be entered into under section 303(a) with respect to the State Party.

(2) The Committee shall, with respect to each agreement proposed to be extended by the President under section 303(e), prepare a report setting forth its recommendations together with the reasons therefor, as to whether or not the agreement should be extended.

(3) The Committee shall in each case in which the Committee finds that an emergency condition under section 304 exists prepare a report setting forth its recommendations, together with the reasons therefor, as to whether or not emergency action under section 304 should be implemented. If any State Party indicates in its request under section 303(a) that an emergency condition exists and the Committee finds that such a condition does not exist, the Committee shall prepare a report setting forth the reasons for such finding.

(4) Any report prepared by the Committee which recommends the entering into or the extension of any agreement under section 303 or the implementation of emergency action under section 304 shall set forth—

    (A) such terms and conditions which it considers necessary and appropriate to include within such agreement, or apply with respect to such implementation, for purposes of carrying out the intent of the Convention; and

    (B) such archaeological or ethnological material of the State Party, specified by type or such other classification as the Committee deems appropriate, which should be covered by such agreement or action.

(5) If any member of the Committee disagrees with respect to any matter in any report prepared under this subsection, such member may prepare a statement setting forth the reasons for such disagreement and such statement shall be appended to, and considered a part of, the report.

(6) The Committee shall submit to the Congress and the President a copy of each report prepared by it under this subsection.

(g) Committee Review.—

(1) In general.—The Committee shall undertake a continuing review of the effectiveness of agreements under section 303 that have entered into force with respect to the United States, and of emergency action implemented under section 304.

(2) Action by committee.—If the Committee finds, as a result of such review, that—

    (A) cause exists for suspending, under section 303(d), the import restrictions imposed under an agreement;

    (B) any agreement or emergency action is not achieving the purposes for which entered into or implemented; or

    (C) changes are required to this title in order to implement fully the obligations of the United States under the Convention;

the Committee may submit a report to the Congress and the President setting forth its recommendations for suspending such import restrictions or for improving the effectiveness of any such agreement or emergency action or this title.

(h) Federal Advisory Committee Act.—The provisions of the Federal Advisory Committee Act (Public Law 92-463; 5 U.S.C. Appendix I) shall apply to the Committee except that the requirements of subsections (a) and (b) of section 10 and section 11 of such Act (relating to open meetings, public notice, public participation, and public availability of documents) shall not apply to the Committee, whenever and to the extent it is determined by the President or his designee that the disclosure of matters involved in the Committee's proceedings would compromise the Government's negotiating objectives or bargaining positions on the negotiations of any agreement authorized by this title.

(i) Confidential Information.—

(1) In general.—Any information (including trade secrets and commercial or financial information which is privileged or confidential) submitted in confidence by the private sector to officers or employees of the United States or to the Committee in connection with the responsibilities of the Committee shall not be disclosed to any person other than to—

    (A) officers and employees of the United States designated by the Director of the United States Information Agency;

    (B) members of the Committee on Ways and Means of the House of Representatives and the Comittee on Finance of the Senate who are designated by the chairman of either such Committee and members of the staff of either such Committee designated by the chairman for use in connection with negotiation of agreements or other activities authorized by this title; and

    (C) the Committee established under this title.

(2) Governmental information.—Information submitted in confidence by officers or employees of the United States to the Committee shall not be disclosed other than in accordance with rules issued by the Director of the United States Information Agency, after consultation with the Committee. Such rules shall define the categories of information which require re-

stricted or confidential handling by such Committee considering the extent to which public disclosure of such information can reasonably be expected to prejudice the interests of the United States. Such rules shall, to the maximum extent feasible, permit meaningful consultations by Committee members with persons affected by proposed agreements authorized by this title.

(j) No Authority To Negotiate.—Nothing contained in this section shall be construed to authorize or to permit any individual (not otherwise authorized or permitted) to participate directly in any negotiation of any agreement authorized by this title.

SEC. 307. IMPORT RESTRICTIONS

(a) Documentation of Lawful Exportation.— No designated archaeological or ethnological material that is exported (whether or not such exportation is to the United States) from the State Party after the designation of such material under section 305 may be imported into the United States unless the State Party issues a certification or other documentation which certifies that such exportation was not in violation of the laws of the State Party.

(b) Customs Action in Absence of Documentation.—If the consignee of any designated archaeological or ethnological material is unable to present to the customs officer concerned at the time of making entry of such material—

(1) the certificate or other documentation of the State Party required under subsection (a); or

(2) satisfactory evidence that such material was exported from the State Party—

(A) not less than ten years before the date of such entry and that neither the person for whose account the material is imported (or any related person) contracted for or acquired an interest, directly or indirectly, in such material more than one year before that date of entry, or

(B) on or before the date on which such material was designated under section 305, the customs officer concerned shall refuse to release the material from customs custody and send it to a bonded warehouse or store to be held at the risk and expense of the consignee, notwithstanding any other provision of law, until such documentation or evidence is filed with such officer. If such documentation or evidence is not presented within ninety days after the date on which such material is refused release from customs custody, or such longer period as may be allowed by the Secretary for good cause shown, the material shall be subject to seizure and forfeiture. The presentation of such documentation or evidence shall not bar subsequent action under section 310.

(c) Definition of Satisfactory Evidence.—The term "satisfactory evidence" means—

(1) for purposes of subsection (b)(2)(A)—

(A) one or more declarations under oath by the importer, or the person for whose account the material is imported, stating that, to the best of his knowledge—

(i) the material was exported from the State Party not less than ten years before the date of entry into the United States, and

(ii) neither such importer or person (or any related person) contracted for or acquired an interest, directly or indirectly, in such material more than one year before the date of entry of the material; and

(B) a statement provided by the consignor, or person who sold the material to the importer, which states the date, or, if not known, his belief, that the material was exported from the State Party not less than ten years before the date of entry into the United States, and the reasons on which the statement is based; and

(2) for purposes of subsection (b)(2)(B)—

(A) one or more declarations under oath by the importer or the person for whose account the material is to be imported, stating that, to the best of his knowledge, the material was exported from the State Party on or before the date such material was designated under section 305, and

(B) a statement by the consignor or person who sold the material to the importer which states the date, or if not known, his belief, that the material was exported from the State Party on or before the date such material was designated under section 305, and the reasons on which the statement is based.

(d) Related Persons.—For purposes of subsections (b) and (c), a person shall be treated as a related person to an importer, or to a person for whose account material is imported, if such person—

(1) is a member of the same family as the importer or person of account, including, but not

limited to, membership as a brother or sister (whether by whole or half blood), spouse, ancestor, or lineal descendant;

(2) is a partner or associate with the importer or person of account in any partnership, association, or other venture; or

(3) is a corporation or other legal entity in which the importer or person of account directly or indirectly owns, controls, or holds power to vote 20 percent or more of the outstanding voting stock or shares in the entity.

SEC. 308. STOLEN CULTURAL PROPERTY

No article of cultural property documented as appertaining to the inventory of a museum or religious or secular public monument or similar institution in any State Party which is stolen from such institution after the effective date of this title, or after the date of entry into force of the Convention for the State Party, whichever date is later, may be imported into the United States.

SEC. 309. TEMPORARY DISPOSITION OF MATERIALS AND ARTICLES SUBJECT TO TITLE

Pending a final determination as to whether any archaeological or ethnological material, or any article of cultural property, has been imported into the United States in violation of section 307 or section 308, the Secretary shall, upon application by any museum or other cultural or scientific institution in the United States which is open to the public, permit such material or article to be retained at such institution if he finds that—

(1) sufficient safeguards will be taken by the institution for the protection of such material or article; and

(2) sufficient bond is posted by the institution to ensure its return to the Secretary.

SEC. 310. SEIZURE AND FORFEITURE

(a) In General.—Any designated archaeological or ethnological material or article of cultural property, as the case may be, which is imported into the United States in violation of section 307 or section 308 shall be subject to seizure and forfeiture. All provisions of law relating to seizure,

forfeiture, and condemnation for violation of the customs laws shall apply to seizures and forfeitures incurred, or alleged to have been incurred, under this title, insofar as such provisions of law are applicable to, and not inconsistent with, the provisions of this title.

(b) Archaeological and Ethnological Material.—Any designated archaeological or ethnological material which is imported into the United States in violation of section 307 and which is forfeited to the United States under this title shall—

(1) first be offered for return to the State Party;

(2) if not returned to the State Party, be returned to a claimant with respect to whom the material was forfeited if that claimant establishes—

(A) valid title to the material,

(B) that the claimant is a bona fide purchaser for value of the material; or

(3) if not returned to the State Party under paragraph (1) or to a claimant under paragraph (2), be disposed of in the manner prescribed by law for articles forfeited for violation of the customs laws.

No return of material may be made under paragraph (1) or (2) unless the State Party or claimant, as the case may be, bears the expenses incurred incident to the return and delivery, and complies with such other requirements relating to the return as the Secretary shall prescribe.

(c) Articles of Cultural Property.—

(1) In any action for forfeiture under this section regarding an article of cultural property imported into the United States in violation of section 308, if the claimant establishes valid title to the article, under applicable law, as against the institution from which the article was stolen, forfeiture shall not be decreed unless the State Party to which the article is to be returned pays the claimant just compensation for the article. In any action for forfeiture under this section where the claimant does not establish such title but establishes that it purchased the article for value without knowledge or reason to believe it was stolen, forfeiture shall not be decreed unless—

(A) the State Party to which the article is to be returned pays the claimant an amount equal to the amount which the claimant paid for the article, or

(B) the United States establishes that such State Party, as a matter of law or reciprocity, would in similar circumstances recover and return an article stolen from an institution in the United States without requiring the payment of compensation.

(2) Any article of cultural property which is imported into the United States in violation of section 308 and which is forfeited to the United States under this title shall—

(A) first be offered for return to the State Party in whose territory is situated the institution referred to in section 308 and shall be returned if that State Party bears the expenses incident to such return and delivery and complies with such other requirements relating to the return as the Secretary prescribes; or

(B) if not returned to such State Party, be disposed of in the manner prescribed by law for articles forfeited for violation of the customs laws.

SEC. 311. EVIDENTIARY REQUIREMENTS

Notwithstanding the provisions of section 615 of the Tariff Act of 1930 (19 U.S.C. 1615), in any forfeiture proceeding brought under this title in which the material or article, as the case may be, is claimed by any person, the United States shall establish—

(1) in the case of any material subject to the provisions of section 307, that the material has been listed by the Secretary in accordance with section 305; and

(2) in the case of any article subject to section 308, that the article—

(A) is documented as appertaining to the inventory of a museum or religious or secular public monument or similar institution in a State Party, and

(B) was stolen from such institution after the effective date of this title, or after the date of entry into force of the Convention for the State Party concerned, whichever date is later.

SEC. 312. CERTAIN MATERIAL AND ARTICLES EXEMPT FROM TITLE

The provisions of this title shall not apply to—

(1) any archaeological or ethnological material or any article of cultural property which is imported into the United States for temporary exhibition or display if such material or article is immune from seizure under judicial process pursuant to the Act entitled "An Act to render immune from seizure under judicial process certain objects of cultural significance imported into the United States for temporary display or exhibition, and for other purposes," approved October 19, 1965 (22 U.S.C. 2459); or

(2) any designated archaeological or ethnological material or any article of cultural property imported into the United States if such material or article—

(A) has been held in the United States for a period of not less than three consecutive years by a recognized museum or religious or secular monument or similar institution, and was purchased by that institution for value, in good faith, and without notice that such material or article was imported in violation of this title, but only if—

(i) the acquisition of such material or article has been reported in a publication of such institution, any regularly published newspaper or periodical with a circulation of at least fifty thousand, or a periodical or exhibition catalog which is concerned with the type of article or materials sought to be exempted from this title,

(ii) such material or article has been exhibited to the public for a period or periods aggregating at least one year during such three-year period, or

(iii) such article or material has been cataloged and the catalog material made available upon request to the public for at least two years during such three-year period;

(B) if subparagraph (A) does not apply, has been within the United States for a period of not less than ten consecutive years and has been exhibited for not less than five years during such period in a recognized museum or religious or secular monument or similar institution in the United States open to the public; or

(C) if subparagraphs (A) and (B) do not apply, has been within the United States for a period of not less than ten consecutive years and the State Party concerned has received or should have received during such period fair notice (through such adequate and accessible publication, or other means, as the Secretary shall by regulation prescribe) of its location within the United States; and

(D) if none of the preceding subparagraphs apply, has been within the United States for a period of not less than twenty consecutive years and the claimant establishes that it purchased the material or article for value without knowledge or reason to believe that it was imported in violation of law.

SEC. 313. REGULATIONS

The Secretary shall prescribe such rules and regulations as are necessary and appropriate to carry out the provisions of this title.

SEC. 314. ENFORCEMENT

In the customs territory of the United States, and in the Virgin Islands, the provisions of this title shall be enforced by appropriate customs officers. In any other territory or area within the United States, but not within such customs territory or the Virgin Islands, such provisions shall be enforced by such persons as may be designated by the President.

COMMENTS

1. The statute is tricky, the result of ten years of lobbying and legislative drafting and compromise (by U.S. government agencies, dealers, museums, collectors, and academics, as well as by art-rich nations of origin). We can see how it works with respect to illegally exported objects by considering two hypothetical examples.

2. Suppose Italy wanted to recover the Matisse painting involved in *Jeanneret v. Vichey.* Would this statute help? Although the painting clearly is cultural property under Section 302(6), it was not stolen, so Section 308, which deals with the seizure and return of stolen cultural property, would not apply. The painting does not meet the definition of "archaeological or ethnological material" in Section 392(2). It is not 250 or more years old; it was not discovered by excavation, digging, or exploration; it is not the product of "a tribal or pre-industrial society"; and it is not important to the cultural heritage of Italians. Hence Sections 303–305 and 307, which provide for seizure and return of illegally exported objects, are not applicable. Since those are the only categories of protected property, the statute provides no help for Italy.

3. Suppose Guatemala asks the United States to seize some pots that were looted from an undeveloped Mayan site in the jungle and are believed to be headed for the United States. Guatemala is a party to the UNESCO Convention. Would this statute apply? It seems clear that Section 308, dealing with stolen property, is not applicable, even if Guatemala claims ownership, since these pots are not "documented as appertaining to the inventory of a museum . . . or similar institution." (The language of Section 308 is obviously open to interpretation. The Report of the Senate Committee on Finance, Report No. 97-564, states at p. 31: "This provision will apply to items of cultural property stolen from a broad range of institutions and public monuments. . . . In addition to public museums, the language is intended to cover cathedrals, temples, shrines, and other edifices or sites open for public visitation or scientific study. Examples include the Wailing Wall in Jerusalem; Pompeii, Italy; Teotihuacán, Mexico; Angkor Wat, Cambodia; the Colosseum, Rome; the Arc de Triomphe, Paris, etc." While this language does not bind future decision-makers, it is part of the legislative history of the statute and will be influential.)

4. How about Section 303 or Section 304? In order for Section 303 to apply, a number of things must happen first. The government of Guatemala must ask the U.S. government to act under Article 9 of the Convention. The President of the United States must publish notification of the request to the Cultural Property Advisory Committee (established by Section 306). If the committee reports to the President within 150 days, the President shall "consider its views and recommendations."

5. To act under Section 303 of the statute, the President must make the findings indicated in Section 303(1)(A), (B), (C), and (D). Paragraph (A) echoes the language of Article 9 of the Convention—the so-called "crisis provision"—indicating that Section 304 is to be invoked only in unusual situations, justifying use of such terms as "pillage" and "cultural pa-

trimony . . . in jeopardy." Paragraph (C) is the extremely important provision for "concerted action," also found in Article 9 of the Convention: The United States should act only when other important nations take similar action. Otherwise the United States, in acting alone, would simply divert the traffic to other nations. Paragraphs (B) and (D) are potentially very important provisions whose meaning is at present far from clear.

6. If all the preceding procedural steps are taken and the necessary findings are made, the President is authorized to enter into an agreement with Guatemala to apply the import restrictions set out in Section 307. In doing so, the President "should endeavor" to obtain Guatemala's commitment to permit the exchange of its archaeological and ethnological materials.

7. Section 304 of the statute sets out a less complex and less lengthy process which may be used in "emergency" conditions. Here the Committee has only ninety days to report, there is no requirement of concerted action by other importing nations, and so on.

8. It should be clear that there is little room for speedy action under the statute. The Guatemalan pots would long since have entered the United States before the President could respond. The statute contemplates deliberation and eventual action to deal with a *process* of cultural drain, not quick action to stop a single shipment at the U.S. border. Unless the whole process had taken place earlier and had produced a negotiated agreement with Guatemala under Section 303, this statute would not serve Guatemala's purpose.

9. Incidentally, the 1972 statute set out earlier in this chapter would not help Guatemala because pots are not monumental sculpture or murals.

10. On October 2, 1985, Canada became the first nation to request an agreement with the U.S. under the Convention and the Act. At this writing the request is unpublished and kept confidential by the U.S. and Canadian authorities.

Your authors have examined what we are reliably informed is a copy of the Canadian request. In our opinion, it falls far short of providing the basis for U.S. action under the Act, since there is no showing that a serious practice of "pillage" exists, as required by Article 9 of the Convention and Article 303 of the Act in order to show that Canada's cultural patrimony is under threat demanding U.S. attention.

Why would Canada file such a toothless request? We are reliably informed that it was made in response to an "informal request" by U.S. Information Agency officials who wanted Canada to be a "guinea pig." But why would the USIA encourage an unconvincing application? To sabotage the Act? To see how far they can stretch the Act's terms? Or is the USIA beefing up the application for Canada, in order to produce a version that will support U.S. action (and to fill an otherwise empty bureaucratic agenda)?

11. The regulations called for by the statute were published in *Federal Register,* vol. 50, no. 122 (June 25, 1985): pp. 26193–26197.

SIMPLE THEFT

Kunstsammlungen zu Weimar v. Elicofon
678 F.2d 1150 (2d Cir. 1982)

MANSFIELD, Circuit Judge.

In this diversity suit involving two foreign countries (East Germany and West Germany), a foreign national, and an American citizen, we are asked to determine the ownership of two priceless Albrecht Duerer portraits executed around 1499. They were stolen in 1945 from a castle located in what is now East Germany and fortuitously discovered in 1966 in the Brooklyn home of Edward I. Elicofon, an American citizen, where they had been openly displayed by him to friends since his good-faith purchase of them over 20 years earlier without knowledge that they were Duerers. The search for an answer to the deceptively simple question, "Who owns the paintings?" involves a labyrinthian journey through 19th century German dynastic law, contemporary German property law, Allied Military Law during the post-War occupation of Germany, New York State law, and intricate conceptions of succession and sovereignty in international law.

The Grand Duchess of Saxony-Weimar

("Grand Duchess"), who intervened as plaintiff in the lawsuit, which was initiated in 1969 by the Federal Republic of Germany ("FRG"), the government of West Germany, claims that the paintings were and remain the private property of the successive Grand Dukes of Saxony-Weimar and that title to the paintings was assigned to her by her husband Grand Duke Carl August. Kunstsammlungen zu Weimar ("KZW"), or the Weimar Art Collection, also intervened as plaintiff representing the interests of the German Democratic Republic ("GDR"), the government of East Germany, claiming that title to the paintings passed to the GDR as a successor in interest to the public property of predecessor sovereignties. Elicofon claims title based on his good faith purchase and uninterrupted possession of the paintings for 20 years.

In separate opinions, Judge Jacob Mishler of the Eastern District of New York granted summary judgment in favor of KZW and dismissed the claims of both intervenor-plaintiff Grand Duchess and defendant Elicofon. We affirm, substantially for the reasons stated in Judge Mishler's thorough and carefully reasoned opinions.

The two Duerer paintings had been in the possession of successive Grand Dukes of Saxony Weimar since at least Goethe's time in 1824. They were part of what was known as the Grossherzogliche Kunstsammlung, or the "Grand Ducal Art Collection." By 1913 the paintings along with other art objects were displayed in the Grand Ducal Museum in Weimar. Notwithstanding the failure of the 1913 Museum catalogue to designate the Duerer paintings as privately owned by the then Grand Duke (Wilhelm Ernst), the Grand Duchess maintains that they were his personal property and continued to be the personal property of his successors. KZW contends, to the contrary, that the paintings were public property on the basis of 19th century dynastic law, a 1921 settlement between the Grand Duke Wilhelm Ernst and the newly established Territory of Weimar (the successor sovereign of the Grand Duchy), and a 1927 settlement with the Land of Thuringia, successor to the Territory of Weimar.

Under German dynastic law in the nineteenth and early twentieth century property held by royal heads of state (e.g., grand dukes, princes, etc.) in their capacities as sovereigns was distinguished from property held in their private capacities. Personally-owned property could be disposed of freely, while property held as sovereign could be disposed of only with the express authorization of the Landtag (i.e., the Diet or Parliament) and normally passed upon the death of a grand duke to his eldest son as successor sovereign. KZW contends that the Grand Ducal Art Collection, which included the two Duerer paintings, constituted "Krongut" (roughly, "crown goods"), held by the Grand Duke of Saxony Weimar as sovereign only and not in his personal capacity as private property. Therefore, it urges, when Grand Duke Wilhelm Ernst abdicated his sovereignty in November 1918 upon Germany's defeat, any rights he formerly exercised as sovereign regarding the Grand Ducal Art Collection automatically passed to the Territory of Weimar.

The Grand Duchess responds that in 1848 the Grand Ducal Art Collection was declared to be a "Kronfideikomiss" (roughly, "family trust"), in which title was vested in the Grand Ducal family until the male line became extinct, thereby removing the Collection from the domain of property held as sovereign. However, according to KZW's German law expert, the terms "Krongut" and "Kronfideikomiss" were used interchangeably and both were subsumed under the broader classification "Kammervermoegen" (or property of the chamber), which denotes the aggregate of the property held by the sovereign in his official capacity. Under this view, title to the Duerer paintings passed to the Territory of Weimar automatically in 1918.

Subsequent to his abdication the Grand Duke Wilhelm Ernst in 1921 entered into an "Auseinandersetzungsvertrag" or settlement agreement ("1921 Agreement") with the Territory of Weimar, which defined their respective rights and obligations with respect to property held as "Kammersvermoegen" and that held by him privately. Section 1 of that Agreement provided:

The former sovereign, Grand Duke Wilhelm Ernst of Saxony, having, on November 9, 1918, for himself and his family, renounced the throne and succession to the throne in Saxe-Weimar-Eisenach for all time, the Grand Duke acknowledges a simultaneous renunciation of the payment of the civil list for the period on and after January 1, 1919 and that the entire Kammervermoegen, inclusive of the Krongut, is the exclusive property of the Territory of Weimar or its legal successor, insofar as not otherwise hereinafter expressly provided. (Citation omitted.)

With respect to artwork privately owned by the Grand Duke, §8 provided that he

shall continue, as heretofore, to permit the public view of the objects d'art belonging to him and his family that are presently situated in public institutions and museums. . . .

Under §9 these privately-owned art objects, would become the property of the Territory of Weimar upon the extinction of his male line. Other sections provided for the surrender and reservation of certain rights and privileges. Section 17 provided for a lump sum payment and annuities to descendants.

Subsequent to the 1921 Agreement it became apparent that the Grand Duke had surrendered physical possession of only a part of the former Grand Ducal Art Collection, including the Duerer paintings, but had improperly retained a portion, some of which had been destroyed or lost. The Land of Thuringia, which had succeeded to the Territory of Weimar, therefore commenced an arbitration proceeding pursuant to §34 of the 1921 Agreement against the heirs of Grand Duke Wilhelm Ernst (who had died in 1923 or 1924) seeking the withheld portion. After lengthy negotiations in which the Grand Duke's widow, acting on her own behalf and for her minor children, maintained that the former Ducal Art Collection had always been and still was the Grand Duke's private property, the parties reached a settlement in 1927 ("1927 Agreement"). Section 1 of that Agreement provided:

The arbitration defendants [Grand Duke's widow and heirs] acknowledge the property of the Land of Thuringia in the so-called Grand Ducal Art Collection. They surrender [give up] this collection, insofar as it is not already in the direct possession of the Land of Thuringia, and insofar as exceptions are not herein provided to the Land.

An exchange of correspondence between the parties clearly reveals that the phrase "so-called Grand Ducal Art Collection" was meant to encompass both those paintings previously surrendered, including the Duerers, and those that had been improperly retained.

The annuities under the 1921 Agreement were paid to the Grand Duke's heirs until 1945, when payments ceased. In 1948 the right to the annuities was extinguished by expropriation through an Act passed by the Langtag of Thuringia.

KZW maintains that the Duerer paintings became public property in any of three ways: (1) the 1918 abdication of Wilhelm Ernst, (2) the 1921 Agreement, and (3) the 1927 Agreement, and that KZW acquired title as the successor to the Land of Thuringia. The Grand Duchess maintains, apparently in the alternative, either that the

paintings were private property whose title never passed to the Land because male heirs remain extant even today, or that although title may have passed, she *regained* it when the annuities were improperly terminated in 1945. She thus demands either the return of the paintings or the payment by the GDR of past due and future annuities.

Elicofon's claim of ownership arises out of his uninterrupted possession of the Duerer paintings from the time of his good-faith purchase of them in 1946 from an American serviceman in Brooklyn to his discovery in 1966 of the identity of the paintings. Until 1943 the Duerer paintings had remained on exhibit in a museum in Weimar, Thuringia, known as the Staatliche Kunstsammlungen zu Weimar, the predecessor to the intervenor-plaintiff KZW. To protect the exhibited artworks from anticipated bombardment, they were in 1943 stored in a nearby castle, the Schloss-Schwarzburg, located in the District of Rudolstadt in the Land of Thuringia. They remained there until stolen some time between June 12 and July 19, 1945. Their disappearance coincided with the withdrawal of the temporary American occupation forces which were replaced by the Russian Army on July 2, 1945. Dr. Scheidig, the Director of the Weimar Museum from 1940 to 1967, who discovered the theft on an inspection of the castle, immediately reported the theft and thereafter engaged in diligent efforts to locate the paintings. These efforts included contacting various German museums and administrative organs, the Allied Control Council, the Soviet Military Administration, the United States State Department, and the Fogg and Germanic museums at Harvard (which were active in locating stolen art), all to no avail.

In the meantime, unbeknownst to Dr. Scheidig or the art world generally, Elicofon purchased the unsigned Duerer paintings in the spring of 1946 for $450 from a young American ex-serviceman who appeared at his Brooklyn home and claimed to have purchased the paintings in Germany. Elicofon framed and displayed them on the wall of his home along with his many other collected art objects. In the years that followed his house was used for numerous charity functions and other large gatherings and his collection was viewed by many people, including some who were knowledgeable about art.

In May of 1966 Elicofon discovered the identity of the Duerer paintings through a friend who had recently seen them listed in a German book describing stolen art treasures of W.W. II. His discovery was publicized in a front-page article in the *New York Times* of May 30, 1966, and was described by one official of the Metropolitan Museum as the "discovery of the century." Thereafter the FRG, the Grand Duchess and KZW all demanded the return of the paintings; KZW's demand was made in September 1966. These demands were refused.

In January 1969 the FRG commenced this litigation, seeking "custody of the possession of the Duerer paintings in order ultimately to restore them to the person or party who is truly and rightfully entitled to their possession." The United States submitted a "Suggestion of Interest," noting that the GDR was barred from suing since it was still not recognized by the United States, and stating that it recognized the FRG as "entitled in this litigation to represent the Weimar Museum as trustee of its interests."

In March 1969 the Grand Duchess sought and was granted leave to intervene as a plaintiff. In April 1969 KZW also moved to intervene but was denied permission to do so on the ground that it was "an arm and agency" of the then unrecognized GDR government and therefore barred from suing in our courts. . . .

On September 4, 1974, the United States formally recognized the GDR goverment, and in February 1975 Judge Mishler vacated his earlier order and permitted KZW to intervene as plaintiff. As a result, the FRG in December 1975 was granted leave to withdraw and discontinue its claim with prejudice on the ground that "prior impediments to the ability of Kunstsammlungen zu Weimar to pursue this action" had been removed. Also as a result of KZW's entry, the Grand Duchess on April 9, 1975, filed an amended complaint adding certain cross-claims against KZW for the payment of past-due and future annuities allegedly owing under the 1921 Agreement.

By decision and order dated August 24, 1978, Judge Mishler granted KZW's motion for summary judgment dismissing the Grand Duchess' claim and denied her request for an order compelling additional discovery. On the central question of title, Judge Mishler held that the 1927 Agreement, standing alone, "unequivocally established that at least from that time forward" the paintings were owned by the State. He explicitly left unresolved KZW's claims that title passed automatically in 1918 upon the Grand Duke's abdication and by virtue of the 1921 Agreement. He based his view of the 1927 Agreement on (1) the

terms of §1 of that Agreement, (2) an exchange of correspondence demonstrating that the 1927 Agreement covered the Duerer paintings, and (3) a 1973 judgment by the highest court of the FRG regarding certain other paintings in the same posture as the Duerers, which rejected the Grand Duchess' claim that the Grand Ducal Art Collection was private property.[1] . . .

As a result of these dispositions, the only claims that remained to be adjudicated were those between Elicofon and KZW. By decision and order dated June 12, 1981, Judge Mishler denied Elicofon's motion for summary judgment dismissing the complaint and granted KZW's motion for summary judgment in its favor, thereby terminating the litigation. Judge Mishler found that the paintings were stolen between June 12 and July 19,1945, that the GDR is entitled to assert ownership as a successor in interest to the property of either the Land of Thuringia or the Third Reich, and the KZW is a validly authorized juristic person with legal capacity to prosecute this claim on behalf of the GDR. On the central issue of title, Elicofon had claimed that the obtained good title at the time of his purchase since the paintings were initially sold by a custodian of the paintings who under German law could convey good title even though not himself in possession of good title.[2] In the alternative Elicofon

1. . . . In 1973 the Grand Duchess sued the FRG to recover three paintings stolen from the Weimar Museum in April 1921. Subsequent to their theft they were discovered in the United States, seized under the Trading With the Enemy Act, 50 U.S.C.App. §§1, *et seq.*, and in 1966 pursuant to an Act of Congress delivered to the FRG in trust for the Weimar Museum. An Act to amend the Trading with the Enemy Act to provide for the transfer of three paintings to the Federal Republic of Germany in trust for the Weimar Museum, Pub. L. No. 89-619, 80 Stat. 871 (1966) (codified at 50 U.S.C.App. §39(e)). In November 1973 the Bundesgerichtshof (FRG Supreme Court) held that the two paintings that were part of the former Grand Ducal Art Collection (the Tischbein and Terborch) became public property under the 1927 Agreement, and therefore could not be claimed by the Grand Duchess as her private property. With respect to the third painting, a Rembrandt, that was not part of the Grand Ducal Art Collection, the German Supreme Court held that it was private property inherited by the former Grand Duchess Sophie and was specifically reserved to her by §§8 and 9 of the 1921 Agreement. *In the Lawsuit of the Archduchess Elizabeth of Saxony Weimar Eisenach v. Federal Republic of Germany* (Nov. 28, 1971).

2. Elicofon advanced the theory that the paintings may have been removed from the castle by Fassbender, a German architect who lived on the grounds and was allegedly a *de facto* custodian of the stored artwork.

claimed that he acquired good title some time subsequent to his purchase, either under the German doctrine of "Ersitzung," under which a good faith purchaser gains title to a stolen object upon 10 years' possession without notice of defect in title, or because the New York statute of limitations had run and therefore barred KZW from bringing this suit. Judge Mishler rejected both theories and held that KZW was entitled to the paintings as their lawful owner by succession. . . .

. . . Judge Mishler's holding that the State's ownership of the paintings was established by the 1927 Agreement is fully supported and indeed strengthened by the earlier occurrences, including the 1918 abdication and the 1921 Agreement, which unequivocally rebut the erroneous assumption underlying the Grand Duchess' interpretation of the 1927 Agreement, namely, that the Grand Ducal Art Collection was originally private property and not Krongut or Kammervermoegen, and is therefore governed by §§8 and 9 rather than by §1 of the 1921 Agreement. Moreover, it is undisputed that the 1913 Museum Catalogue, which clearly designates those objects owned privately by the Grand Duke, failed to designate the Duerer paintings as privately owned. Thus the Collection as a whole constituted Krongut or Kammervermoegen and not private property. We hold, therefore, that the paintings, as acknowledged by §1 of the 1921 Agreement and §1 of the 1927 Agreement, were the "exclusive property" of the Territory of Weimar. . . .

ELICOFON'S CLAIMS

Elicofon . . . contends that the GDR is not a successor in interest entitled to possession of the paintings. Judge Mishler held that the GDR did succeed to the paintings as property of the Land of Thuringia, either directly by an act of the GDR in 1952 or indirectly as a successor within its territorial jurisdiction to the rights of the Third Reich, to whom the Land's property rights passed. Second, Elicofon argues that subsequent to his

Elicofon maintained that under German law Fassbender could have conveyed good title even though he himself did not have title, and that the good faith purchaser or transferee could in turn have transferred good title to Elicofon. Judge Mishler discussed the German law issues at length and dismissed the argument on the grounds of German legal doctrine and the fact that evidence of Fassbender's role "is so insubstantial [that it] does not raise a genuine issue of fact." We agree.

purchase he acquired title under the German doctrine of Ersitzung, which awards title to the holder upon 10 years uninterrupted good faith possession. Judge Mishler held that New York's interest in regulating the transfers of property located within its border (in this case for over 30 years) overrides any interest the GDR may have in applying the policy of Ersitzung to extraterritorial transactions. . . . Thus applying New York's choice of law rules, Ersitzung is inapplicable and New York law governs, under which a purchaser cannot acquire good title from a thief. We affirm both rulings, substantially for the reasons stated in the district court's opinion.

Elicofon's third argument is that KZW is barred by New York's statute of limitations from suing to recover the paintings. The essential facts are that in October 1966 Elicofon refused to comply with KZW's demand for the return of the paintings and in April 1969 KZW moved to intervene in this action, which was begun by FRG, thereby commencing KZW's action. . . . The applicable New York statute provides a three (3) year limitation period. . . . The question is when the limitation period began to run, or, in other words, when KZW's claim against Elicofon accrued. If it accrued only upon Elicofon's refusal in 1966, then the suit was timely commenced. If, on the other hand, it accrued in 1946, when Elicofon bought the paintings, the action would be barred by the then-applicable limitation period of six years unless it was tolled by a subsequent disability before it expired. Judge Mishler held that under New York law KZW's claim accrued in 1966 and that, even if it accrued earlier in 1946, the then-applicable period was tolled under New York's judicially-created "non-recognition" toll because the United States did not recognize GDR until 1974, which precluded the KZW from intervening until then. We agree with both conclusions.

Under New York law an innocent purchaser of stolen goods becomes a wrongdoer only after refusing the owner's demand for their return. Until the refusal the purchaser is considered to be in lawful possession. . . .

Directly on the point is a New York decision applying these principles to a case involving a *bona fide* purchaser of stolen art works, holding that the cause of action accrues only after demand and refusal. In *Menzel v. List* . . . the Appellate Division clearly held that the owner's demand on a *bona fide* purhaser is substantive . . . and that the statute of limitations begins to run only upon the purchaser's refusal to return the property. . . .

Applying these principles here, KZW's cause of action did not accrue until October 1966 when Elicofon refused to comply with the demand for the return of the paintings. Since the action was begun in 1969, within the three-year limitation period, it is not barred. . . .

Even were we to assume that under New York law KZW's cause of action accrued in 1946, we would affirm Judge Mishler's holding that the statute of limitations was tolled under New York's judicially created "non-recognition" toll until 1974, when the United States first recognized the GDR. . . .

Since the then-applicable limitation was at least six years, the statute of limitations had not run by 1949, when the GDR government was founded, and it was thereafter tolled by our non-recognition of the GDR. . . .

Elicofon responds that the non-recognition toll is inapplicable since from 1949 until 1974 this country recognized the FRG government as the only government entitled to speak for the entire German people. Therefore, his argument goes. . . . the statute of limitations was not tolled since the U.S. courts were available to the FRG as the recognized sovereign of the German State. . . .

We reject the premise of this argument. The United States itself recognized the FRG only "as sovereign over its own territory and not over that of East Germany" and as not "having any territorial jurisdiction, either *de facto* or *de jure*, over East Germany." . . . The view of the United States is consistent with that taken by the government of West Germany, which "did not purport to exercise sovereign authority with regard to matters in East Germany, either *de jure* or *de facto*."

Notwithstanding the GDR's disability to sue from 1949 onward, Elicofon maintains that the statute of limitations nevertheless began to run uninterrupted from 1946 because at all times thereafter the United States' courts were available to parties competent to sue *on behalf* of the GDR. He claims that from 1945 to 1949 the Allied Powers acting through the Allied Control Council, and from 1949 the FRG government, could have brought suit to assert the GDR's claim to the paintings on its behalf. We find no support for the proposition that the Allied Council could have brought suit in American courts to assert the interests of the predecessor of the GDR within its territorial boundary; Elicofon concedes that he is aware of no such suits. In any event the six-year limitations period would not have run by 1949, when the Allied Control Council ceased acting as the government of occupied Germany, in view of

the Soviets' withdrawal from the Council. The Soviets had been empowered to act with respect to its "zone of occupation," which included Weimar. Moreover, in any such hypothetical suit the state of war that officially remained in effect until 1951 would have cast serious doubt upon the Allied Council's capacity to sue since at least technically it would be viewed as a military government in charge of an enemy and the recognized procedure for recovery of German-owned property in the United States was governed by the Trading with the Enemy Act. . . .

Even if the Allied Council could have brought suit on behalf of the GDR's predecessor, and it is clear that the FRG could have sued and in 1969 did sue on behalf of the GDR, at most they would have been acting as trustees for the GDR's interests. FRG's complaint, for instance, expressly states that it was suing merely to obtain "custody of the possession of the Duerer paintings in order ultimately to restore them to the person or party who is truly and rightfully entitled to their possession." The United States' "Suggestion of Interest" submitted in this litigation states that it recognizes the FRG as "entitled in this litigation to represent the Weimar Museum [i.e., KZW] *as trustee of its interest*." (emphasis added).[3] Under New York law the commencement of a prior action by a trustee or guardian does not thereby lift the disability toll accorded the beneficiary. . . . *A fortiori* the rule governs here, where Elicofon's only claim is that the Allied Council or the FRG *might or could have* sued as trustee between the years 1946 and 1969. We hold, therefore, that even if the cause of action accrued in 1946 the statute of limitations was tolled and KZW's suit is timely. . . .

Accordingly, we affirm the district court's holding that KZW is entitled to possession of the paintings, and order that the judgment entered below be enforced.

---

3. Indeed, the 1966 Act amending the Trading with the Enemy Act to transfer to the FRG the three paintings that later were the subject of the 1973 German Supreme Court decision (see n. 1, *supra*) is consistent with the view of FRG as trustee for the GDR. The amending Act added §39(e) to the Trading with the Enemy Act, and reads in relevant part as follows: "(e) . . . the Attorney General is hereby authorized to transfer the three paintings . . . to the Federal Republic of Germany, to be *held in trust* for eventual transfer to the Weimar Museum, Weimar, State of Thuringia, Germany, in accord with the terms of an agreement to be made between the United States and the Federal Republic of Germany. 50 U.S.C.App. §39(e)." (Emphasis added.)

COMMENTS

1. The Dürer portraits have been returned to Weimar. There is a comment on the decision in *Harvard International Law Journal,* vol. 23 (1983), p. 466. For an interesting attempt by an investigative reporter to reconstruct the theft, see Leslie Maitland, "From Schwarzburg to Flatbush: The Mysterious Journal of Hans and Felicitas Tucher," *ARTnews,* September 1981, pp. 78ff. For a [West] German comment on the case, see Ulrich Drobnig, "Amerikanische Gerichte zum internationalen Sachenrecht auf dem Hintergrund der Teilung Deutschlands," *IPRax,* vol. 4 (March–April 1984), p. 61.

2. Once the West German government removed itself from the case and the court rejected the countess' claim, the case became a classic dispute between the owner and a good-faith purchaser from a thief. This is the eternal triangle of property law: A owns something; B steals it and sells it to C, who buys in good faith. Can A recover the painting from C? In U.S. law the general rule (to which there are exceptions not applicable in this case) is that A can recover. Buyer C is left to his remedy against B (if he can find him and if B can be made to pay, as to which the odds are not good). A similar rule prevails in other common-law countries (e.g., England, Canada, Australia, and New Zealand).

3. In civil-law nations (e.g., all of Europe, all of Latin America) the law is kinder to the good-faith purchaser and less so to the owner; the exact rules vary from nation to nation. In the Dürer case, observe that the East German plaintiff successfully argued that the U.S. rule should apply, while the American defendant wanted the court to apply the German approach.

4. In *Winkworth v. Christie Manson and Woods Ltd.,* [1980] All E.R. 1121, works of art were stolen from the plaintiff in England and taken to Italy, where they were sold to an Italian collector, who bought them in good faith. The Italian sent them to Christie's, the auctioneers, in London for sale. The plaintiff brought an action to have the works declared his property. The court held that the legal effects of the sale to the collector were determined by Italian law and that under that law the good-faith purchaser became the owner. It thus held for the collector, even though under the law of England the good-faith purchaser would not have acquired good title against the owner.

5. Since the U.S. rule is less favorable to purchasers, it has been suggested that civil-law nations should adopt the U.S. rule (for cultural property) as a way of discouraging art theft. (Stefano Rodota, "The Civil Law Aspects of the International Protection of Cultural Property" [Report presented to the Council of Europe's XIII Colloquy on European Law, 1983]. [Copy in the authors' files].) A similar suggestion was made to the European Economic Community Commission in 1976 by Professor Jean Chatelain of France in a study entitled "Means of Combating the Theft and Illegal Traffic in Works of Art in the Nine Countries of the EEC," Doc. No. XII/757/76 (1976). The International Institute for the Unification of Private Law, in Rome, is studying the proposal.

6. The remaining question in the Dürer case concerned the passage of time. All legal systems have rules of prescription, statutes of limitation, and so on. Such rules respond to the difficulty of reconstructing ancient events and to the tendency of people to rely on the existing state of affairs. To allow old transactions to be questioned is to invite fraud and perjury and to unsettle the affairs of the present. The applicable statutes vary widely from one country to another (and, within the United States, one state to another). Here again the German rule would have helped Elicofon, but the court applied New York law, which favored the plaintiff.

7. In part as a reaction against the *Elicofon* decision, bills were introduced in Congress and in New York to set special time limitations on actions to recover stolen cultural property. At hearings on January 9, 1986, on a bill sponsored by Senators Mathias and Bentsen that would reduce the period to two years on works "displayed, publicized or cataloged and housed in a museum," opposition was strongly expressed by the Department of Justice, the State Department, the U.S. Information Agency and the Society for American Archaeology, among others. They argued that the bill would make the United States a "pirate's cove" and would encourage the traffic in looted art. The bill was not reported out of committee at this writing. See Andrew Decker, "Is Possession Nine-tenths of the Law?" *ARTnews,* April 1986, p. 21. A comparable bill was adopted by the New York legislature but was vetoed by Governor Cuomo on July 28, 1986. The Governor said the bill would make New York "a haven for cultural property stolen abroad."

8. Suppose you were the Director of the Metropolitan Museum. Would you support such

"cultural property repose" legislation? Apparently the Museum stimulated and supported the New York bill (*Artnewsletter,* Sept. 2, 1986, p. 4).

9. Note the power of ownership. A museum that is an agency of a socialist bloc nation wins in a U.S. court against an American citizen, and two masterpieces leave the United States forever, because the court finds that the foreign museum is the owner.

10. In "Foreign Claims to Stolen Art," *Stolen Art Alert,* vol. 4, no. 3 (May 1983), p. 3, Linda Ketchum reports that the East German (GDR) government spent about $1 million on legal fees to recover the Dürers. When a Tintoretto painting that disappeared from the Dresden Art Gallery during World War II turned up in the United States and was seized by Customs because of false statements in the Customs declaration, the U.S. Department of State urged the GDR to sue for its return, but the GDR refused. Ketchum reports that the GDR may have found American justice "too dear."

NATIONAL THEFT

We now turn to ways in which nations use the power of the "ownership" concept to deal with the traffic in illegally exported cultural property and to related matters. We begin with a case in which New Zealand seeks to assert "ownership" over illegally exported Maori relics, arguing that under New Zealand law the act of illegal export automatically forfeited the works to the state.

Attorney General of New Zealand v. Ortiz and Others
[1983] 2 All E.R. 93 (House of Lords)

LORD BRIGHTMAN. My Lords, the facts . . . are as follows. In or about 1972 one Manukonga found in a swamp in the province of Taranaki a valuable Maori relic, described as a series of five carved wood panels that formed the front of a food store. In 1973 Manukonga sold the carving to Mr Entwistle, who was a dealer in primitive works of art. The carving was to the knowledge of Mr Entwistle a historic article within the meaning of the Historic Articles Act 1962 of New Zealand. Later in the same year the carving was exported from New Zealand by or on behalf of Mr Entwistle. No permission under the Historic Articles Act 1962 authorising the removal of the carving from New Zealand had been obtained by him. In the same year Mr Entwistle sold the carving to Mr Ortiz for $65,000. In 1978 Mr Ortiz consigned the carving to Messrs Sotheby Parke Bernet & Co (Sothebys) in England for sale by auction.

In June 1978 the Attorney General of New Zealand (suing on behalf of Her Majesty the Queen in right of the government of New Zealand) issued proceedings against Mr Ortiz and Sothebys and Mr Entwistle. The New Zealand government claims a declaration that the carving is the property of Her Majesty the Queen, as against Mr Ortiz and Sothebys an order for delivery up of the carving, and as against Mr Entwistle damages for conversion.

Under a consent order Sothebys retain possession of the carving pending the outcome of the action, and proceedings against them have been stayed. . . .

It is not in dispute that the carving was exported in breach of the 1962 Act. The resolution of the first issue depends on whether, on the true construction of §12 of the 1962 Act, incorporating certain provisions of the Customs Act, the carving was forfeited immediately it was unlawfully exported, so that it thereupon became vested in the Crown, or whether the unlawful export of the carving merely rendered it liable to forfeiture in the future, the forfeiture taking effect only on the seizure by the New Zealand customs or police, which has not taken place.

So, as it seems to me, the position of the Crown and the wrongdoer under the 1962 Act is clear. The offence is created by §5(1). The pecuniary penalty is defined by §5(2). The penalty "in rem" is created by §12(2). The process of forfeiture is regulated in accordance with the provisions of the 1966 Act, in particular, the necessity of seizure (to be followed by actual or deemed condemnation) before the forfeiture is completed, at which stage it relates back to the accrual of the right to forfeit. There being no seizure in the instant case, the conclusion is inescapable that the ownership of the carving and the right to possession thereof have not become vested in the Crown.

Counsel for the New Zealand government sought to argue that sub-§(2) of §12 imposed automatic forfeiture for a "knowing" export of a historic article, as a remedy additional to condition forfeiture for an "unknowing" but illegal export under the Customs Act 1966 as applied by sub-§(1). He accepted that there could be no forfeiture without seizure in the case of an "unknowing" export or attempted export, but he argued that there was no reason in the case of a "knowing" export or attempted export to introduce into a sub-§(2) forfeiture the requirement of seizure before the forfeiture takes effect. . . .

In my opinion there is a fatal flaw in the argument of counsel. There is no offence committed under the 1962 Act by the export of a historic article unless it is done "knowingly." No cause of forfeiture is capable of arising by reason of an "unknowing" export of a historic article. . . . It is not in my opinion possible to reach any conclusion save that (a) the penalty of forfeiture of a historic article as such is imposed only for an offence under §5(1) of the 1962 Act and (b) such forfeiture is not complete until seizure.

I have every sympathy with the New Zealand government's claim. If the statement of claim is correct, New Zealand has been deprived of an article of value to its artistic heritage in consequence of an unlawful act committed by the second respondent. I do not, however, see any way in which, on a proper construction of the 1962 Act and in the events which here happened, the Crown is able to claim ownership thereof. . . .

COMMENTS

1. Observe that since the plaintiff lacked ownership (there had been no seizure of the Maori carving) the remedy was denied. This was merely a case of illegal export.

2. Omitted portions of the decision indicate doubt that a statute automatically vesting ownership in the government on illegal export would be given effect by English courts even if that intention were clear.

3. The strategy of attempting to convert illegal export into theft at the moment of export, illustrated in this case, is unusual. The more common strategy is for a nation to enact a law declaring that all objects of a described kind are property of the state. Mexico and Guatemala, and a growing number of other nations, have such laws. If such an object is taken without permission, it then becomes stolen property. The state can sue for its recovery on the theory that it is the owner.

4. A stela, Machaquila 2, from the El Peten region of Guatemala, was put on view at the Los Angeles County Museum in 1976, on a one-year loan with an option for a second, from the Guatemalan government. The stela was recorded in the 1960s by Ian Graham, an archaeologist from Harvard University. It was subsequently cut into more than a dozen pieces and flown to Miami from British Honduras. The stela was seized by federal agents at a private home in Los Angeles. The price being asked for it was $300,000.

The museum's deputy director, Rexford Stead, had negotiated with the legal advisers to the Guatemalan government concerning the restoration of the stela, then in pieces in a warehouse, and its loan to the museum. The conservation center at the museum reconstructed the stela by embedding it in concrete, although some of its glyphs had been previously damaged. The advisers to the Guatemalan government and museum officials believed exhibiting the work would call attention to the fact that laws are being enforced to recover stolen art objects. Stead was quoted as saying that while he was pleased that scholars had inquired about the stela and millions of people would see it before its repatriation, "I must say we'll feel some regret when the stela must be returned."

The Machaquila stela was central to two very important cases. One was a *civil* action in which the government of Guatemala sued a California art dealer to recover the stela or its value. The theory of the action was that the stela was national property, that it had been stolen from its owner (the nation of Guatemala) by the defendant Hollinshead and others, that it was in Hollinshead's possession, and that Hollinshead refused to return it. The situation thus was treated as one in which the owner sues to recover stolen property from the thief. This action ended when defendants returned the stela (by way of the Los Angeles County Museum) as part of a settlement with the plaintiff. The second case, *U.S. v. Hollinshead*, is discussed below, pp. 118 (note 1), 120.

5. Suppose that the case of *Guatemala v. Hollinshead* had not been settled and had gone to trial. Counsel for Guatemala would have to prove, among other things, that Guatemala owned the Machaquila stela. Should evidence that Guatemala had enacted a law that in generic terms nationalized all Mayan remains in Guatemala be sufficient? Suppose Hollinshead's counsel sought to prove that the Machaquila site was open and unprotected, that no Guatemalan official or agency had specifically identified it as national property or had instituted proceedings to expropriate it from the owner of the land on which it sits, and so on. Should such evidence be admissible?

THE U.S.-MEXICO TREATY OF COOPERATION

The following treaty with Mexico was adopted in 1971.

Treaty of Cooperation between the United States of America and the United Mexican State Providing for the Recovery and Return of Stolen Archaeological, Historical, and Cultural Properties
22 U.S. Treaty Series 494, T.I.A.S. No. 7088 (1971)

The United States of America and the United Mexican States, in a spirit of close cooperation and with the mutual desire to encourage the protection, study and appreciation of properties of archaeological, historical or cultural importance, and to provide for the recovery and return of such properties when stolen have agreed as follows:

Article I

1. For the purposes of this Treaty, "archaeological, historical and cultural properties" are defined as

(a) art objects and artifacts of the pre-Columbian cultures of the United States of America and the United Mexican States of outstanding importance to the national patrimony, including stelae and architectural features such as relief and wall art;

(b) art objects and religious artifacts of the colonial periods of the United States of America and the United Mexican States of outstanding importance to the national patrimony;

(c) documents from official archives for the period up to 1920 that are of outstanding historical importance;

that are the property of federal, state, or municipal governments or their instrumentalities, including portions or fragments of such objects, artifacts, and archives.

2. The application of the foregoing definitions to a particular item shall be determined by agreement of the two governments, or failing agreement, by a panel of qualified experts whose appointment and procedures shall be prescribed by the two governments. The determinations of the two governments, or of the panel, shall be final.

Article II

1. The Parties undertake individually and, as appropriate, jointly

(a) to encourage the discovery, excavation, preservation, and study of archaeological sites and materials by qualified scientists and scholars of both countries;

(b) to deter illicit excavations of archaeological sites and the theft of archaeological, historical or cultural properties;

(c) to facilitate the circulation and exhibit in both countries of archaeological, historical and cultural properties in order to enhance the mutual understanding and appreciation of the artistic and cultural heritage of the two countries; and

(d) consistent with the laws and regulations assuring the conservation of national archaeological, historical and cultural properties, to permit legitimate international commerce in art objects.

2. Representatives of the two countries, including qualified scientists and scholars, shall meet from time to time to consider matters relating to the implementation of these undertakings.

Article III

1. Each Party agrees, at the request of the other Party, to employ the legal means at its disposal to recover and return from its territory stolen archaeological, historical and cultural properties that are removed after the date of entry into force of this Treaty from the territory of the requesting Party.

2. Requests for the recovery and return of designated archaeological, historical and cultural properties shall be made through diplomatic offices. The requesting Party shall furnish, at its expense, documentation and other evidence necessary to establish its claim to the archaeological, historical or cultural property.

3. If the requested Party cannot otherwise effect the recovery and return of a stolen archaeological, historical or cultural property located in its territory, the appropriate authority of the requested Party shall institute judicial proceedings to this end. For this purpose, the Attorney General of the United States of America is authorized to institute a civil action in the appropriate district court of the United States of America, and the Attorney General of the United Mexican States is authorized to institute proceedings in the appropriate district court of the United Mexican States. Nothing in this Treaty shall be deemed to alter the domestic law of the Parties otherwise applicable to such proceedings.

Article IV

As soon as the requested Party obtains the necessary legal authorization to do so, it shall return the requested archaeological, historical, or cultural property to the persons designated by the requesting Party. All expenses incident to the return and delivery of an archaeological, historical or cultural property shall be borne by the requesting Party. No person or Party shall have any right to claim compensation from the returning Party for damage or loss to the archaeological, historical or cultural property in connection with the performance by the returning Party of its obligations under this treaty.

Article V

Notwithstanding any statutory requirements inconsistent with this Treaty for the disposition of merchandise seized for violation of laws of the requested Party relating to the importation of merchandise, stolen archaeological, historical or cultural property which is the subject matter of this Treaty and has been seized, or seized and forfeited to the requested Party, shall be returned to the requesting Party in accordance with the provisions of this Treaty. The Parties shall not impose upon archaeological, historical or cultural property returned pursuant to this Treaty any charges or penalties arising from the application of their laws relating to the importation of merchandise.

COMMENTS

1. Observe that the treaty works both ways, that is, Mexico undertakes obligations with respect to works from the United States. How significant in Mexico's obligation under this treaty at the present time?

2. Because Mexico could already sue in a U.S. court to recover its property, how does this treaty change the law? Observe that this treaty does not define the key term, "stolen." Article III places an obligation on the executive to act, including filing suit if necessary, but the law applied by the court in an eventual suit would under Article III(3) be the same. The 1972 statute set out above, where applicable, is a far more significant innovation.

3. Executive agreements (not technically treaties, but with many of the same operative effects) similar to the U.S.-Mexico treaty set out above have been made with Ecuador, Guatemala, and Peru.

THE McCLAIN DECISION

In the following case, smugglers of Mexican artifacts were convicted under U.S. laws.

United States v. McClain et al.
593 F.2d 658 (5th Cir. 1979)

GEE, Circuit Judge:

Again before us come Patty McClain, Mike Bradshaw, Ada Simpson and William Simpson, challenging their second round of convictions for having received, concealed and/or sold stolen goods in interstate or foreign commerce and also for conspiracy to do the same, violations of 18 U.S.C. §§371, 2314 and 2315. The goods in which they dealt are pre-Columbian artifacts, and in neither this nor the prior trial was there evidence that the appellants or anyone else had taken the items from the personal possession of another. The legal theory under which the case was tried was that the artifacts were "stolen" only in the sense that Mexico generally has declared itself owner of all pre-Columbian artifacts found within its borders. Thus, anyone who digs up or finds such an item and deals in it without governmental permission has unlawfully converted the item from its proper owner.[1] . . .

I. THE APPELLANTS' DEALINGS IN PRE-COLUMBIAN ARTIFACTS

In May 1973, Joseph Rodriguez, a resident of Calexico, California, arrived at a Dallas motel with a collection of pre-Columbian artifacts for display and sale. He sold pieces at least to a local art dealer and to a law professor who was staying in the same motel. He thereafter moved his wares to a San Antonio motel, apparently as a result of

his dealings with the professor, who taught in San Antonio. From the new location Rodriguez contacted prospective buyers, including Alberto Mejangos, who unbeknownst to Rodriguez was director of the Mexican Cultural Institute, an educational outpost of the Mexican government located in San Antonio. Suspecting Rodriguez of illicit dealings, Mejangos and Adalina Diaz-Zambrano, the librarian of the institute, visited Rodriguez to see the collection of fine artifacts, many of which were caked with mud and straw. When he was asked how it was possible that he had all these ancient artifacts, Rodriguez said that he had five squads working in various Mexican archaeological zones and that the objects were passed, a few at a time "by contraband" to his Calexico store, which served as a front for his operation. When he amassed enough objects, he said, he would sell them in different localities. He priced the items he showed Mr. Mejangos and Mrs. Diaz-Zambrano at figures ranging between $5,000 and $20,000, explaining that the prices had gone up as a result of the February 1972 presidential agreement between the United States and Mexico. He said he now had to give more money to the people who were passing the objects to him. . . .

Simpson and appellant Mike Bradshaw contacted William Maloof of Cleveland, Ohio, a college friend of Bradshaw. . . . They told Maloof that the items had been "stolen" or "smuggled" out of Mexico.

. . . Simpson and Bradshaw told Maloof that they planned to take most of the objects to Europe, "auction" them off, and then return them to the United States. This process would yield bills of sale from European art dealers, which would facilitate later resale. . . . Simpson replied that he had approximately 150 pieces already in San Antonio and was in Calexico awaiting a new shipment from the diggings. He described a "conduit" by which the items were taken from the diggings to the archaeological institute in Mexico, where documents or permits were forged or backdated.

---

1. Only one other reported conviction has resulted from application of the National Stolen Property Act to dealings in pre-Columbian artifacts. In *United States v. Hollinshead*, 495 F.2d 1154 (9th Cir. 1974), Clive Hollinshead of Los Angeles, California, was successfully prosecuted for transporting into the United States a known and cataloged Guatemalan stela. Hollinshead was on probation for this offense during the events leading to the instant prosecution. At least appellants Simpson and Bradshaw knew Hollinshead and were aware of his conviction and probation. Hollinshead was to have supplied several of the artifacts that appellants were selling when they were arrested.

The items were then trucked in disguise to the border at Calexico before distribution to various cities in the United States, particularly San Antonio. Simpson stated that what they were doing "is illegal, but really not illegal, because if the Mexican authorities knew basically what we were doing, they would take them away from us, because the Mexicans really claim all of the items belong to them." Simpson explained further that the backdating of the papers was due to a new "presidential law" that had gone into effect in Mexico, prohibiting private ownership of artifacts after its effective date. . . .

There was evidence at trial that none of the items . . . bore the indicia of registration with the Archaeological Registry maintained by the Mexican government since 1934—a permanent, coded number placed with indelible ink on an inconspicuous area of the piece. Nor were any documents of registration for these pieces in the names of either Rodriguez, or any of the appellants found in the registry. Additionally, no export permits had been obtained for the items. In fact, since 1897 the Mexican government has issued only temporary export permits, and those are issued exclusively to cultural institutions or universities. Permits have never been issued to private individuals or for commercial purposes.

II. APPLICATION OF N.S.P.A. TO DEALINGS IN PRE-COLUMBIAN ARTIFACTS

Appellants attack the application of the N.S.P.A. [National Stolen Property Act] to their conduct under two different theories. They first argue that Congress never intended the N.S.P.A. to reach items deemed "stolen" only by reason of a country's declaration of ownership. In any event, they claim, the N.S.P.A. was superseded by the 1972 Law on Importation of Pre-Columbian Monumental or Architectural Sculpture or Murals, . . . which provides only the civil penalty of forfeiture for importation of certain types of pre-Columbian artifacts. Second, they and their amicus argue that due process is violated by imposing criminal penalties through reference to Mexican laws that are vague and inaccessible except to a handful of experts who work for the Mexican government.

. . . Though appellants articulated their theories in a slightly different manner in the first appeal, they provoked a square holding that, in addition to the rights of ownership as understood by the common law, the N.S.P.A. also pro-

tects ownership derived from foreign legislative pronouncements, even though the owned objects have never been reduced to possession by the foreign government. . . . Moreover, the earlier panel had considered evidence of the 1972 statute, its legislative history and UNESCO negotiations, holding nevertheless that neither statute nor treaty nor our historical policy of encouraging the importation of art more than 100 years old had the effect of narrowing the N.S.P.A. so as to make it inapplicable to artifacts declared to be the property of another country and illegally imported into this country. . . . Appellants' attempt to raise these points again on appeal is therefore foreclosed. . . .

Our study of the statute and its scant legislative history persuades us that appellants' reading of it is not correct. Both the Report by the House Ways and Means Committee and the Report by the Senate Finance Committee explicitly refer to the presence of other unspecified sanctions: "While legal remedies for the return of such objects are available in U.S. courts in some cases, these procedures can be extremely expensive and time consuming and do not provide a meaningful deterrent to the pillage of pre-Columbian sites now taking place." Moreover, the Act covers objects imported from all the countries of Latin America. These countries may have acted quite differently to protect their cultural heritages, some by declaring national ownership and others merely by enacting stringent export restrictions. Since it covers artifacts from such a large number of countries, the Act is better seen not as an indication that other available penalties were thereby precluded, but rather as a recognition that additional deterrents were needed. . . .

III. JURY INSTRUCTIONS REGARDING MEXICAN LAW, SUFFICIENCY OF EVIDENCE

At appellants' first trial a deputy attorney general of Mexico testified as an expert witness, and the trial court subsequently instructed the jury that Mexico had, since 1897, vested itself with ownership of all pre-Columbian artifacts found in that country. As mentioned above, its independent review of translations of the various Mexican statutes convinced the earlier panel that Mexico had not unequivocally claimed ownership of *all* such artifacts until 1972. The earlier Mexican statutes seemed only to have claimed national ownership of immovable monuments and such movable artifacts as were found on, and possibly in, the immovable objects. Movable objects not in the above classes seemed capable of being privately owned and conveyed, though the Mexican government required that such objects be registered and retained the right to acquire items of great cultural or archaeological value by purchase at a fair price. Certain other provisions referred to in the petition for rehearing seem to have established a presumption against private ownership of any movable not registered within the applicable time limits. In view of the complicated and gradual nature of Mexico's apparent declarations of ownership, the earlier panel ruled that the defendants were entitled to a new trial because of the prejudice that may have resulted from the erroneous instruction that Mexico owned all artifacts as early as 1897. Its analysis of the changes in Mexican law convinced the panel that the jury should have been told to determine when the artifacts had been exported from Mexico and to "apply the applicable Mexican law to that exportation." . . .

The 1972 statute, on the other hand, is clear and unequivocal in claiming ownership of all artifacts. Deferring to this legitimate act of another sovereign, we agree with the earlier panel that it is proper to punish through the National Stolen Property Act encroachments upon legitimate and clear Mexican ownership, even though the goods may never have been physically possessed by agents of that nation. . . .

. . . The evidence presented to the jury amply showed that appellants' conspiracy was much broader than an intent to deal in the single collection already in the United States for an unspecified length of time. It is abundantly clear that they conspired to bring in at least one other load, and most likely a continuing stream of articles that, owing to a broken drive shaft and appellants' subsequent arrest, never arrived. Their plans regarding those loads—and the conduit itself—were clearly illegal under any view of Mexican law, including that presented by their own witnesses. The evidence is massive that appellants knew and deliberately ignored Mexico's post-1972 ownership claims. . . .

Accordingly, appellants' convictions on the conspiracy count are AFFIRMED, and the convictions on the substantive court are REVERSED.

COMMENTS

1. The earlier case of *U.S. v. Hollinshead,* which first applied the Interstate Stolen Property Act to a foreign "theft" of cultural property, is cited and described in the footnote in the *McClain* opinion. *Hollinshead* caught the art world unprepared, but by the time of the prosecution in *McClain,* the American Association of Dealers in Ancient, Oriental, and Primitive Art had been formed and appeared as *amicus curiae* (friend of the court) in support of the defendants.

2. The *Hollinshead* and *McClain* decisions shook the American art world. Application of the Interstate Stolen Property Art to such cases was totally unexpected. Scholars were intrigued by the notion that the act could be used to convert a crime against the people of Mexico or of Guatemala into a crime against the people of the United States, arguably contrary to the settled rule of private international law that one nation will not enforce the criminal laws of another. See William J. Hughes, "United States v. Hollinshead: A New Leap in Extraterritorial Application of Criminal Laws," *Hastings International and Comparative Law Review,* 1 (1977), p. 1.

3. The most interesting question raised by these decisions concerns the proper effect to be given to the declaration of a foreign state that works in undiscovered or unprotected sites and works in private collections are state property. Where such a declaration is made, whether in the form of a statute or of an executive decree, it clearly is part of the law of the foreign state. But what else has occurred? If the unknown site remains unknown, if the unprotected site remains unprotected, if objects in private collections are left there, if no expropriation proceedings are brought and no compensation is paid or promised, little has happened.

4. The troubling thought arises that such a declaration of state ownership might be meant primarily for foreign consumption. It is easy and relatively costless to issue a decree stating that all pre-Columbian artifacts are property of the state. All that has changed is a few words in the *Gaceta Oficial.* If no effort is made to give it internal effect, then no private owner of artifacts can raise legal questions about expropriation procedure and compensation (questions, incidentally, that McClain and Hollinshead were unable to raise in their cases). If no

steps are taken to identify sites, to protect them, restore objects in them, to study and exhibit such objects, and so on, then the declaration of state ownership begins to look like an empty form of words. It is not clear why art-importing nations should give such "rhetorical laws" substantial consequences when they have none at home.

5. *The "Blank Check" Objection.* If importing nations enforce an exporting nation's declaration of ownership without question, the exporting nation has in effect been given extensive power to affect the outcome of legal proceedings—including criminal trials, as the *McClain* and *Hollinshead* cases show—in the importing nation. This is the so-called "blank check" objection.

6. The problem posed by such laws has been resolved in the 1970 UNESCO Convention, Article 7(b), in a pragmatic way: the obligations of parties in the case of stolen property extend only to property "stolen from a museum or a religious or secular public monument or similar institution." In the Convention on Cultural Property Implementation Act of 1982, the language of Section 308 is similar but more explicit, referring to "cultural property documented as appertaining to the inventory of a museum or religious or secular public monument or similar institution." Although such language is open to interpretation, the clear intention is to restrict the category of stolen property to objects that were actually in the possession of the individuals or institutions from which it is claimed that they were stolen. If that interpretation had been placed on the word "stolen" in the *McClain* and *Hollinshead* cases, the defendants would have been acquitted.

7. The *McClain* case was prominent in the minds of the museum, collector, and dealer interests that participated in the process of drafting and compromise that produced the Cultural Property Implementation Act. As stated in James F. Fitzpatrick, "A Wayward Course: The Lawless Customs Policy Toward Cultural Properties," *N.Y.U. Journal of International Law and Politics,* vol. 15 (1983), pp. 837ff, "The agreement reached by the parties cleared the way for prompt enactment of the law" (p. 859). According to Fitzpatrick, the agreement had three key elements. One, embodied in the text of the statute, was the insistence in all but exceptional cases that the United States act only in concert with other importing nations. The second, also embodied in the statute, was the power to act unilaterally in emergencies. As to the third, Fitzpatrick states (at pp. 862–864):

> The third key element in the compromise was that legislation to overturn the *McClain* decisions would be introduced promptly and that the various parties to the compromise would support, or at least not oppose, passage of the legislation. . . .
>
> The Senate Finance Committee recognized that "[m]any [persons] question whether the court's interpretation of *McClain* . . . is overly broad as a matter of national policy." Thus, under the agreement, the *McClain* doctrine was to be modified legislatively to the extent necessary to bring it into accord with the Cultural Property Law. As Senator Dole stated, "it is important for the Congress to insure that the potential application of existing law (i.e., NSPA) is consistent with our national policy, that will be substantially established by H.R. 4566, with respect to illicitly traded cultural materials."
>
> The Agreement to overturn *McClain* was the linchpin of the compromise. The parties concurred that the Cultural Property Law, rather than the National Stolen Property Act, was to be the basis for the implementation of U.S. policy in the cultural property area. This decision led to the prompt introduction by Senator Dole of a bill to overturn *McClain*. He was joined by the two other Senators influential in the passage of the Cultural Property Law, Senators Spark Matsunaga (D.-Hawaii) and Daniel P. Moynihan (D.-N.Y.). The *McClain* legislation was not expected to pass in the Ninety-Seventh Congress, but was considered to reflect a continuing commitment into the next Congress on the part of congressional leaders.

8. The bill to overturn *McClain* did not pass in the 97th Congress. It was reintroduced in the 98th Congress (S. 605) by Senators Moynihan and Dole and at this writing seemed unlikely to pass because officials of the State Department and the U.S. Customs opposed it (reneging, according to one source, on their original agreement to support it). See *New York Times,* May 23, 1985, p. 22.

JAMES R. McALEE *The McClain Case, Customs, and Congress**

In 1981, the United States Customs Service— perhaps weary of the continuing congressional debate on the UNESCO implementing legislation—moved to obtain by indirection the authority to control the importation of ancient and ethnographic art which had thus far been denied to it by Congress. It did so by construing the *McClain* case as an instrument of Customs' enforcement, employing along the way procedures for which it had highly questionable authority. Customs has now succeeded in creating a de facto embargo on the importation into the United States of ancient art from a number of countries which assert legislative claims of ownership.

Customs' attitude toward the *McClain* case evolved slowly. It began as early as November 15, 1977 when an "Advisory Memorandum" on the subject of pre-Columbian art was prepared by the Office of the Regional Counsel of the Service in San Francisco. In effect, the memorandum apprised its readers of the theory of the National Stolen Property Act as espoused in the *McClain* case and discussed that theory in light of the laws of a number of Central and South American nations. . . .

The memorandum concluded that, wholly apart from violations of specific Customs statutes or treaty provisions, the importation of pre-Columbian art into the United States might involve violations of the National Stolen Property Act as construed in the *McClain* case and that, under those circumstances, Customs agents should consider seizure of the material. Customs is authorized by statute to seize material which is "introduced into the United States in any manner contrary to law." The memorandum apparently assumes that a *McClain* theory violation of the National Stolen Property Act is an importation "contrary to law." In addition, the memorandum asserts that a breach of the National Stolen Property Act also likely constitutes a breach of 18 U.S.C. §545, one of the criminal laws administered by Customs. This law provides as follows:

Whoever fraudulently or knowingly imports or brings into the United States any merchandise *contrary to law,* or receives, conceals, buys, sells, or in any manner facilitates the transportation, concealment, or sale of such merchandise after

importation, knowing the same to have been imported or brought into the United States contrary to law. . . . [Emphasis added by McAlee.]

Indeed, probably not coincidentally, just eight days after the Advisory Memorandum, an indictment was filed against one Daniel Weiner in the Eastern District of California, charging violations of both the National Stolen Property Act and Section 545 and seeking forfeiture of pre-Columbian art valued in excess of $100,000, which was alleged to have been brought illegally into the United States from Panama, Peru, Costa Rica and Mexico. The *Weiner* case was apparently settled with a guilty plea and the return of the objects in question to their putative countries of origin. . . .

Then, early in 1981, there was a flurry of Customs activity in Miami. This Customs activity was of an unanticipated and surprising nature since it involved neither violations of the National Stolen Property Act nor routine Customs violations. Customs "detained" Peruvian antiquities which Mr. David Goldfarb sought to import into the United States, even though Mr. Goldfarb was apparently handling the antiquities in good faith and with full disclosure to Customs. Customs was apparently satisfied that Mr. Goldfarb had no knowledge of any Peruvian laws claiming ownership of pre-Columbian antiquities. Nevertheless, Customs continued to detain the antiquities for several months and then filed an interpleader action in federal court in which it joined Peru and the importer as defendants and, in effect, asked the court to determine who was entitled to the antiquities. Faced with the prospect of long and costly litigation, Mr. Goldfarb settled the case by returning the antiquities to Peru. At about the time that Customs detained Mr. Goldfarb's shipment, another Florida dealer was told that he should discontinue importing pre-Columbian antiquities from Guatemala; otherwise, Customs would institute similar action. The word spread, and, as a practical matter, the Port of Miami was effectively closed to pre-Columbian art. . . .

Not surprisingly, what had started in Miami spread to other ports of entry, and there was a well-publicized spate of Customs investigations and criminal actions directed against art importers. . . .

*From James R. McAlee, "The McClain Case, Customs, and Congress," *NYU Journal of International Law and Politics,* vol. 15 (1983), pp. 813, 829ff. Copyright ©1983 by New York University. Reprinted by permission.

In one case, Customs "detained" Peruvian gold objects which were being returned to the United States from Australia. The objects had been "registered" with Customs so that, when they were shipped back to the United States, Customs would have proof that the antiquities were being reintroduced to this country. Despite this "registration," Customs not only detained the material but also interpleaded Peru when the dealer sued Customs for their return. Again, rather than engage in protracted litigation, the dealer agreed to return the objects to Peru.

Subsequently, the writer attempted to obtain an assurance from Customs that another dealer would not similarly be treated if he sent ancient Peruvian textiles to Japan for exhibition. Customs took the position that the only way for the dealer to protect himself would be to establish to Customs' satisfaction, prior to shipping the materials to Japan, that the textiles had left Peru before the enactment of the Peruvian legislation claiming ownership, which was apparently in 1929. The textiles had been in the United States for some years, but the burden of proving that they had left Peru before 1929 was insuperable. As a result, the textiles were never sent to Japan for exhibition. This seems a particularly unfortunate and even a bizarre application of the theory of the *McClain* case. . . .

Just how far down the line Customs wanted to go may have been answered when, on October 5, 1982, Customs issued a supplement to its Policies & Procedures Manual entitled *Seizure and Detention of Pre-Columbian Artifacts.* The Supplement contains a number of directives to Customs agents, all applicable to pre-Columbian objects not subject to the explicit statutory import restrictions. . . .

Overall, the Supplement appears to direct that *all* pre-Columbian materials should be detained by Customs until it determines whether the country of origin asserts such a claim, then it appears that Customs will, if necessary, file an inter-

pleader action in the case of Peru or Mexico and will "consider" doing so in the case of other Central and South American countries. Where there is a misdescription or undervaluation of the objects or evidence of a violation of the National Stolen Property Act, Customs will seize rather than merely detain the pre-Columbian material and presumably will return it to the Central or South American country asserting ownership. . . . The catalyst is a legislative claim of ownership by a Central or South American nation. . . .

Customs has undertaken to regulate art imports on a basis inconsistent with the scheme of regulation adopted by Congress in the Cultural Property Act. . . .

Under the policy established by Congress in the Cultural Property Act, the executive must carefully investigate the facts and determine among other things that import restrictions on ancient or ethnological art, if applied on concert with similar restrictions implemented by other major art-importing nations, would be of substantial benefit in deterring a serous situation of pillage. Under congressional policy, it is only on this basis that the importation of ancient or ethnographic art will be restricted. Under Customs' policy, on the other hand, the importation of ancient art will be restricted simply on the basis that it is pre-Columbian and the nation or origin asserts a legislative claim of ownership.

Customs' policy on art imports is not only inconsistent with that of Congress, but thwarts the goals which the United States sought to advance in the UNESCO Convention. . . . The United States fought long and hard to avoid handing the art-exporting countries a "blank check" which Customs and the Fifth Circuit together have now handed to Central and South American countries. If these nations adopt statutes containing the appropriate incantatory claim to national ownership, Customs will enforce their export restrictions for them, whatever the motive or need for such restrictions. . . .

COMMENTS

1. As Mr. McAlee points out, his firm represents dealers who are affected by the Customs policy, and his views reflect their interests and attitudes. For another discussion of the directive see *ARTnewsletter,* vol. 8, no. 11, January 25, 1983, p. 1.

2. Still, there seems to be a clear divergence between the approach taken by Congress in the Cultural Property Implementation Act of 1983 and the approach taken simultaneously by the Customs Service in its directive and its actions. Should we care?

3. Observe that the Customs Service, by the threat of civil and criminal litigation and its seizure of objects, exercises great de facto power. The tendency of the importer faced with

that sort of threat and the expense and delay it entails is to give in. Consider the cases that McAlee decribes, and try to make allowances for his partisanship. Is there potential for abuse of government power in such situations? Should we worry about it if there is? After all, the end (frustrating the illegal traffic in cultural property) is admirable, isn't it?

4. If legislation to overrule the *McClain* case were enacted, much of the basis for the Customs policy would be cut away, but as we have seen, that legislative effort is stalled, in part because of Customs opposition to it.

REPATRIATION OF CULTURAL PROPERTY

"Repatriation" of cultural property can mean different things. We have already seen one kind of repatriation in the case of *Kunstsammlungen zu Weimar v. Elicofon* (above), where an agency of the East German government, having established ownership, recovered two stolen Dürer paintings in a civil action in a U.S. court. We have also seen examples of the seizure and repatriation of illegally exported works by the U.S. Customs Service. In this part we focus on a different set of questions. Suppose that some important cultural objects—for example, the Elgin Marbles—are beyond the reach of any such process, that the country of origin has no right to their return under the existing law. Still, the country wants them back. Under what circumstances, if any, should they be returned?

One way to deal with such a situation, when there is no convenient legal remedy, is through self-help. Thus a patriotic Mexican (a lawyer!) stole a rare Aztec Codex (only four are known to exist; most of them were burned by zealous Spanish priests in Cortéz's wake) from the Bibliothèque Nationale and "repatriated" it to Mexico. The Mexican government, claiming that it was stolen from Mexico in the nineteenth century, confiscated the Codex, asserted ownership, and rejected French demands for its return (*San Francisco Chronicle,* August 19, 1982, p. 41).

Self-help, however, is the antithesis of law. We need a more civilized approach to repatriation than that.

Another approach to repatriation is through purchase, but many of the most important objects are in the permanent collections of museums and are not for sale. Those that do appear on the market, if genuinely important, attract competitive interest from wealthy collectors and museums, and the nation of origin may be unwilling to compete with them for something it believes belongs to it. If the resources of the nation of origin are subject to heavy alternative demands, the purchase of cultural objects is an economically difficult decision to make. Accordingly, although purchases for the purpose of repatriation do occur, the principal effort takes other forms.

Most of the repatriation transactions that have received publicity in recent years could be classified as "bilateral," that is, as specific arrangements worked out between two parties: officials of the returning institution or nation, on one side, and the responsible parties in the nation of origin, on the other. The actual motivations (to be distinguished from the public rhetoric) of such transactions are not always evident. Some returns may conceivably, if improbably, be altruistically motivated solely by sympathy with the state of cultural deprivation of the nation of origin.

Others express the professional attitudes and ethics of museum curators or archaeologists, who may be professionally interested in having good relations with, and acquiring or retaining access to, the nation of origin. Thus, for example, the curator of the Semitic Museum at Harvard will be inclined to share objects from and scholarship about Ur with Iraq in order to have Iraq's cooperation, including continued access to its archaeological sites.

Some repatriations are outright deals. For example, Norton Simon agreed in 1974 to return an important Nataraja (a bronze of Shiva dancing) to the government of India in return for India's agreement to drop its lawsuit against Simon and to leave the Nataraja with the Norton Simon Museum on loan for ten years. The case of the Teotihuacán murals, discussed later in this chapter, is another example of a deal. Some deals, like the Norton Simon Nataraja, are cultural property-related on both sides and for that reason seem reasonable and unalarming. But the opportunity and temptation to use repatriation as a bargaining chip in a totally unrelated context—for permission to install a military base; for assistance in controlling narcotics; for help in extraditing a wanted criminal—must occasionally arise. Should that kind of deal be discouraged—or do we care?

RECENT REPATRIATIONS

Here are examples of a few recent, well-publicized repatriations.

In 1976 the Peabody Museum of Harvard University returned to the Mexican government about six hundred jade pieces that had been found in a sacrificial well or *cenote* at Chichén Itzá. The priceless jade objects had originally come to Harvard as a gift of archaeologist Edward H. Thompson, who discovered them between 1904 and 1909 on a 30,000-acre hacienda he owned. Mexican courts had ruled that he had the right to the objects he found, although some legal experts have claimed that such rulings are invalid, and subsequent Mexican law prevents the removal of such objects without specific government permission.

Belgium and Zaire entered into a bilateral agreement that took effect in March 1970, in which Belgium agreed to a policy of restitution of important cultural objects which had been taken from Zaire after it gained its independence in 1960. The agreement provided for Belgian assistance to Zaire in the form of specialized scientific and technical personnel, to aid in the establishment and organization of a museum network and to aid in the conservation and preservation of artifacts. Also in accordance with the agreement, Belgium has undertaken and assisted with the transfer of important art collections to Zaire. See Huguette Van Geluwe, "Belgium's Contribution to the Zairian Cultural Heritage," *Museum*, vol. 31, no. 1 (1979), p. 32.

The Netherlands and Indonesia have also worked out a cooperative program of restitution of objects of major historical and cultural importance to Indonesia. Many such objects were removed from Indonesia during its period of colonization under the Netherlands. Delegations from both countries devised a number of joint recommendations at a conference in November 1975. These recommendations essentially provide for the transfer of state-owned objects of great importance to Indonesia and for the facilitation by the Netherlands of the transfer of such privately owned objects, both presently known and later discovered. The recommendations also propose establishment of a program of visual documentation for ethnological and archaeological objects of cultural importance. Since those recommendations have been accepted by both governments, a number of important artifacts have been transferred to Indonesia.

The Australian Museum has returned objects to Papua New Guinea and to the Solomon Islands and has persuaded a private collector to return a number of objects to Melanesia (Jim Specht, "The Australian Museum and the Return of Artifacts to Pacific Island Countries," *Museum*, vol. 31, no. 1 (1979), pp. 28ff).

The head of the Iraqi Organization of History and Antiquities, Dr. Mauye Said Damergi, was quoted by Marvin Howe in a *New York Times* article (February 17, 1980, p. 2) as saying, "There is a new awakening among the Iraqis, a pride in their history and bitterness that their sons cannot see here the art of their ancestors." Accordingly, the Iraqi government is pressing for the return of many great works of ancient art, such as the Ishtar Gate of Babylon housed in the Pergamon Museum in East Berlin, the famous engraved stele containing the Law Code of King Hammurabi in the Louvre, and the British Museum's Nineveh reliefs and Gate of Balawat. A few museums, including the British Museum and that of Harvard, have already returned some objects after negotiations begun by correspondence and through UNESCO. One irony of the situation is that the late famous British archaeologist, Sir Charles Leonard Wooley, whose great excavations at Ur in the 1920s did so much to educate the Iraqis and the world into that country's ancient history, is now bitterly condemned for having "stolen" all the gold, silver, and jewels from the royal tombs and giving them to the British Museum, which along with that of the University of Pennsylvania sponsored his expeditions. Iraq, which has 10,000 registered archaeological sites to 3,000 in Egypt, no longer shares the finds with the archaeologists who excavate them, but will lend certain discovered pieces for study.

In addition to the above and Greece's request for return of the Elgin Marbles, discussed later in this chapter, Great Britain is receiving numerous other demands for the return of cultural property. Egypt has informally asked for the Sphinx's Beard, now in a British Museum storeroom, and has also requested the return of Cleopatra's Needle, once at the Temple of Karnak and now on the Thames embankment in London. Egypt is also demanding return of the bust of Nefertiti, originally taken by German archaeologists and now in the West Berlin Museum. The Nigerians would like to have back the Benin bronzes in the British Museum, while Ghana would like to see the return of some Ashanti gold, also in that institution. Sri Lanka has requested repatriation of the five-foot-tall statue of the goddess Tara and thirty-four other treasures in the British Museum, which were sent to England in 1815 by Sir Robert Brownrigg, then governor of Ceylon. And both India and Pakistan claim the Kohinoor Diamond in the Tower of London, reputedly the largest diamond in the world. (*ARTnewsletter,* vol. 7, no. 14, March 2, 1982, pp. 203ff.)

There have also been a number of demands by American Indians for the return of articles in the Smithsonian Museum, the Museum of the American Indian, and others, to Indians. See, for example, the letter by Michael A. Bush in the *New York Times,* March 24, 1985, p. 22E.

Such examples are only a very small tip of a very large iceberg.

THE ROLE OF INTERNATIONAL ORGANIZATIONS

Since World War II an additional player has entered the repatriation arena. Beginning in the United Nations General Assembly and spreading to UNESCO, the International Council of Museums (ICOM), and the Council of Europe, nations of origin (most but not all of them Third World nations) have used international organizations both to legitimize their repatriation claims and to press them. To give the flavor, here is a statement from the Director-General of UNESCO, issued in 1978.

AMADOU-MAHTAR M'BOW, DIRECTOR-GENERAL OF UNESCO *A Plea for the Return of an Irreplaceable Cultural Heritage**

. . . On behalf of the United Nations Educational, Scientific and Cultural Organization which has empowered me to launch this appeal,

I solemnly call upon the governments of the Organization's Member States to conclude bilateral agreements for the return of cultural prop-

*Amadou–Mahtar M'Bow, "A Plea for the Return of an Irreplaceable Cultural Heritage to Those Who Created It," *Museum,* vol. 31 (1979), pp. 58ff. Reprinted by permission.

erty to the countries from which it has been taken; to promote long-term loans, deposits, sales and donations between institutions concerned in order to encourage a fairer international exchange of cultural property, and, if they have not already done so, to ratify and rigorously enforce the Convention giving them effective means to prevent illicit trading in artistic and archaeological objects.

I call on all those working for the information media—journalists of press and radio, producers and authors of television programmes and films—to arouse world-wide a mighty and intense movement of public opinion so that respect for works of art leads, wherever necessary, to their return to their homeland.

I call on cultural organizations and specialized associations in all continents to help formulate and promote a stricter code of ethics with regard to the acquisition and conservation of cultural property, and to contribute to the gradual revision of codes of professional practice in this connection, on the lines of the initiative taken by the International Council of Museums.

I call on universities, libraries, public and private art galleries and museums that possess the most important collections to share generously the objects in their keeping with the countries that created them and which sometimes no longer possess a single example.

I also call on institutions possessing several similar objects or records to part with at least one and return it to its country of origin, so that the young will not grow up without ever having the chance to see, at close quarters, a work of art or a well-made item of handicraft fashioned by their ancestors.

I call on the authors of art books and on art critics to proclaim how much a work of art gains in beauty and truth, both for the uninitiated and for the scholar, when viewed in the natural and social setting in which it took shape.

I call on those responsible for preserving and restoring works of art to facilitate, by their advice and actions, the return of such works to the countries where they were created and to seek with imagination and perseverance for new ways of preserving and displaying them once they have been returned to their homeland.

I call on historians and educators to help others to understand the affliction a nation can suffer at the spoliation of the works it has created. The power of the *fait accompli* is a survival of barbaric times and a source of resentment and discord which prejudices the establishment of lasting peace and harmony between nations.

Finally, I appeal with special intensity and hope to artists themselves and to writers, poets and singers, asking them to testify that nations also need to be alive on an imaginative level.

Two thousand years ago, the Greek historian Polybius urged us to refrain from turning other nations' misfortunes into embellishments for our own countries. Today when all peoples are acknowledged to be equal in dignity, I am convinced that international solidarity can, on the contrary, contribute practically to the general happiness of mankind.

The return of a work of art or record to the country which created it enables a people to recover part of its memory and identity, and proves that the long dialogue between civilizations which shapes the history of the world is still continuing in an atmosphere of mutual respect between nations.

Since 1973 the United Nations General Assembly has adopted an annual series of resolutions on the subject of cultural property. These are described in the following excerpt.

JAMES A. R. NAFZIGER *The New International Framework for the Return, Restitution, or Forfeiture of Cultural Property**

. . . Although they have differed in wording, the essential provisions each year have been the following: to affirm the salutary implications of international cooperation in the restitution of cultural property to countries of origin; to invite states to take adequate measures to prohibit and

* From James A. R. Nafziger, "The New International Framework for the Return, Restitution, or Forfeiture of Cultural Property," *New York University Journal of International Law and Politics,* vol. 15 (1983), pp. 789–802. Copyright ©1983 by New York University. Reprinted by permission.

prevent illicit trafficking in *objets d'art;* to invite states to prepare national inventories; to invite states to become parties to the UNESCO Convention; to strengthen museum infra-structures; and to marshall professional expertise, the media and public opinion in favor of programs of restitution.

The trend during a decade of such resolutions is illuminating. Very simply, they have become less strident and more accommodating of the interests of the target states. At first they were crude and unconditional; now they are refined and moderate. For example, the 1975 version affirmed the need for *prompt* restitution of cultural property, *without charge,* as *just reparation for dam-age;* none of the italicized working appears in the 1981 version. The 1975 resolution called upon "those States concerned which have not already done so to proceed to the restitution of" cultural property; the 1981 version merely invites states to deter illegal trafficking. Finally, the later versions eliminate a reference in the 1975 version that recognized a "special obligation" of countries advantaged by their "rule over or their occupation of foreign territory." The result of such revisions has been to strengthen the influence of the resolutions and to disarm much of the initial opposition to the unconditional wording of the first versions.

In 1979 a study prepared under the auspices of the International Council of Museums (ICOM) at the request of UNESCO, appeared. Its conclusion follows.

AD HOC COMMITTEE APPOINTED BY THE EXECUTIVE COUNCIL OF THE ICOM *Study on the Principles, Conditions, and Means for the Restitution or Return of Cultural Property in View of Reconstituting Dispersed Heritages**

CONCLUSION

38. The reassembly of dispersed heritage through restitution or return of objects which are of major importance for the cultural identity and history of countries having been deprived thereof, is now considered to be an ethical principle recognized and affirmed by the major international organizations. This principle will soon become an element of *jus cogens* of international relations.

39. Finally, one should recall the principle which is constantly emphasized during meetings devoted to this problem, i.e. that the restitution or return of cultural property to the country of origin should be determined in each case through bilateral negotiations. These would take place at different levels of responsibility, often at the very highest. It should be emphasized, none the less, that in many cases mere discussions and agreements between museums concerned and other scientific institutions of the countries in question will lead to positive results without it being necessary to call systematically on governmental authorities.

40. It is a matter of course that this latter mechanism of negotiation cannot be isolated from the general context in which the problem of restitution or return is placed and that international organizations, governmental or non-governmental, will play a major role in this cause. It will be up to them, in particular, not only to ensure co-ordination and coherence, which are indispensable for success in this type of policy, but also to make sure that the fundamental principles of cultural accessibility and the preservation of works are respected and that the latter are facilitated and reinforced. And finally, it will be their role to help improve mutual understanding by the parties concerned of their respective problems. Such has been the desired general philosophy of the principles and means of action indicated in this report.

*From Ad hoc Committee appointed by the Executive Council of the ICOM, "Study on the Principles, Conditions, and Means for the Restitution or Return of Cultural Property in View of Reconstituting Dispersed Heritages," *Museum,* vol. 31 (1979), p. 62. Reprinted by permission.

COMMENT

Meanwhile, beginning in 1976, a UNESCO/ICOM committee began to take form and was established in 1978 as the Intergovernmental Committee for Promoting the Return of Cultural Property to Its Countries of Origin or Its Restitution in Case of Illicit Appropriation. The Committee held its first meetings in 1980 and 1981. Also in 1981, the Secretary General issued a "Report . . . on the Return or Restitution of Cultural Property" (UNESCO Document A/36/561 Annex), which includes the recommendations of the committee adopted at its second meeting (the recommendations adopted at its first meeting are reproduced in *Museum,* vol. 33 [1981], p. 119).

THE COUNCIL OF EUROPE

In 1983 the Council of Europe Parliamentary Assembly adopted the following resolution.

COUNCIL OF EUROPE PARLIAMENTARY ASSEMBLY *Resolution on Return of Works of Art*
35th Ordinary Sess., Res. 808 (1983)

The Assembly,

1. Having noted the reports of its Committee on Culture and Education on the movement and return of art objects (Docs. 5110 and 5111);

2. Aware of the imbalance that exists at world level in the distribution of cultural property, a disproportionate amount of which is concentrated in major collections in Europe and North America;

3. Particularly concerned at the lack of representative national collections in certain countries, and recognising the reasonableness of the wish of these countries to recover their cultural heritage;

4. Wishing to encourage all moves to co-operate in the negotiated return of certain items of cultural property to their country of origin;

5. Supporting in particular the work of the UNESCO Intergovernmental Committee to help identify representative items missing from national collections and provide a satisfactory basis for their return and display;

6. Noting that the displacement of cultural property, whether from its place of origin or through its return, or for preservation, must be viewed as a historical act;

7. Noting also the cultural value of art collections containing pieces from other countries in permitting broader access by scholars and the general public to the diversity of cultural traditions;

8. Stressing the unity of the European cultural heritage within a historical context of the frequent movement of individual art objects;

9. Believing that claims for the return of cultural property within the European cultural area must be considered differently from claims for the return of property outside this area,

10. Calls on the governments of member states to recognise that the European cultural heritage belongs to all Europeans, and to ensure that the diversity of this heritage remains easily accessible in each country;

11. Asks member governments to co-operate fully on a bilateral basis, and where appropriate through the mechanisms provided by UNESCO, for the return of certain cultural property to countries outside the European area.

CULTURAL NATIONALISM

All these United Nations, UNESCO, ICOM, and Council of Europe pronouncements share a premise—sometimes assumed and sometimes asserted. The premise is that cultural property belongs at the place, or among the descendants of the culture, of its origin. This translates in most cases into the claim that the nation that includes that geographic area, or whose people are descendants of that culture, rightfully claim the objects. This gives every repatriation proposal a political component. For example, people who favor returning the Elgin Marbles to Greece might have opposed returning them when the colonels were in power (just as some Americans opposed returning the Crown of St. Stephen to Socialist Hungary).

Politics aside, cultural nationalism is a form of nationalism and for that reason is subject to all the usual concerns: the tendency to become invidious, to breed rivalry, misunderstanding, and war, and to divide rather than unite. The 1954 Hague Convention spoke of "the cultural heritage of all mankind" in a spirit of internationalism. Repatriation advocates express the spirit of nationalism, which these international organizations and officials support. Is there a paradox here? An inconsistency?

In its truest and best sense, cultural nationalism is based on the relation between cultural property and cultural definition. For a full life and a secure identity, people need exposure to their history, much of which is represented or illustrated by objects. Such artifacts are important to cultural definition and expression, to shared identity and community. They tell people who they are and where they come from. In helping to preserve the identity of specific cultures, they help the world preserve texture and diversity. Works of art civilize and enrich life. They generate art (it is a truism among art historians that art comes from art) and nourish artists. Cultural property stimulates learning and scholarship. A people deprived of its artifacts is culturally impoverished. The difficulty comes in relating the notion of cultural deprivation to physical location. We will explore that problem when we return to the Elgin Marbles later in this chapter.

There is a sense in which the repatriation movement owes its influence to a poet. Shelley (*In Defense of Poetry*) said: "Poets are the unacknowledged legislators of Mankind." In the field of cultural property, Byron is definitely the unacknowledged legislator. The French (with the crucial if unacknowledged assistance of Byron) coined the term "Elginisme" to refer to the wrongful removal of cultural property from its site. "Byronism" might serve as the term for the kind of romantic nationalism that Byron expressed in his poetic attack on Elgin in *Childe Harold* and *The Curse of Minerva.* Byronism lies at the base of widely accepted attitudes toward cultural property. It is strongly built into Western culture.

The repeated assumption, or assertion, of the premise supporting repatriation gives it a growing momentum. As consensus grows, law may not be far behind. Thus, in paragraph 38 of the ICOM study (earlier in this chapter) confidence is expressed that "this principle will soon become an element of *jus cogens* of international relations," and in paragraph 8 there is an even stronger assertion: "The community of nations now considers as an element of *jus cogens* the right of all people to recover property which forms an integral part of their cultural identity." (*Jus cogens* is a term of international law and is sometimes translated as "peremptory" or "nonderogable" norm, i.e., as a rule that is clearly accepted in and fundamental to the international order.) Nafziger characterizes this claim as "disputable" and "very doubtful" (James A. R. Nafziger, "The New International Framework for the Return, Restitution, or Forfeiture of Cultural Property," *N.Y.U. Journal of International Law and Politics,* vol. 15 (1983), pp. 789, 805–806). While there may be substantial consensus among nations of origin that such a principle is right and should be law, other nations take a different view. As in other such matters, First World / Third World and socialist/nonsocialist politics play a prominent part.

APPROACHES TO REPATRIATION PROBLEMS

The following two cases illustrate two quite different approaches to repatriation problems. The Teotihuacán Murals case was resolved quietly at the professional level by discussion and cooperation between museum directors, curators, and conservators, with law involved less as the basis for the solution than as a means for expediting and memorializing it. The Elgin Marbles case, on the contrary, has occupied the headlines. Each side argues that the law favors its side, and the debate goes on.

THE TEOTIHUACÁN MURALS: JOINT CUSTODY

A variety of issues arise when a museum is considering the return of works of art to the country of origin. The case of the Teotihuacán Murals illustrates how complicated the situation can become. Note the interplay of U.S. and Mexican laws and international principles and the special interests of museum curators and conservators in the object of art.

In 1976 the M. H. de Young Memorial Museum in San Francisco was left more than seventy fragments of murals by the will of a local architect, Harold Wagner. The murals were from the world-famous Aztec site of Teotihuacán, outside Mexico City. The architect bought the murals in Mexico and brought them into the United States. The collection is the largest known collection of such pre-Columbian murals outside Mexico. The de Young Museum was both delighted by and concerned about the gift.

Under Mexican law the murals were property of the nation, and an export license would have had to be obtained to remove them from Mexico. Neither the estate nor the museum was able to show that a license had been obtained. A second and related problem concerned the treaty of March 24, 1971, between the United States and Mexico concerning the recovery and return of stolen archaeological, historical, and cultural properties, set out above, pp. 116–17.

In accordance with the provisions of the treaty, the government of Mexico requested the Attorney General of the United States to look into and obtain the return of the murals. Under Article II, Section 3, of the treaty, the Attorney General has the power to file a civil action in U.S. District Court on behalf of the government of Mexico. (Note that the treaty does not change U.S. law, but only requires the Attorney General to use the means at his disposal to effect return of the object.) One American law seems directly applicable to the mural situation: the 1972 statute prohibiting the importation of illegally exported monumental and archaeological pre-Columbian art from Mexico and other Central American nations to the United States, set out earlier in this chapter, pp. 89–91.

Harold Wagner appears to have been prescient. In 1971, one year before the enactment of the statute, Wagner prepared a sworn affidavit that the murals had entered the United States before 1972. In addition, witnesses declared that they had seen the murals in San Francisco during the 1960s. The Attorney General, on the other hand, was unable to come up with any evidence that the murals entered after 1972.

The Wagner will was probated in a California state court, and the U.S. Attorney's office requested that the proceedings be removed to federal district court. This would have allowed the federal government to litigate the issues in the hope of returning the murals to Mexico. Unfortunately for the federal government, only a defendant can remove an action to federal district court from a California state court. Since the United States was not a defendant in the state court proceedings, removal was denied.

At this point, the de Young Museum began private negotiations with Mexico for partial return of the murals to Mexico. The de Young is a part of the Fine Arts Museums of San Francisco. Personnel at the Fine Arts Museums cited several reasons for the decision to negotiate. First, ownership of the murals was complicated: under U.S. law, the museum owned them; under Mexican law, the Mexicans owned them. In addition, the museum accepted the Mexican claim that the murals were of cultural significance to Mexico. The moral and ethical solution to the problem seemed to rise above national laws. Further, the museum does not specialize in Mexican or pre-Columbian art, so the Mexicans could provide the museum with important assistance in the conservation of the murals. On their side, the Mexicans had nothing to lose. The murals were at the museum, and under U.S. law it appeared that they would stay there.

One way to rise above the laws was to set aside the issue of ownership. Strangely enough, even if it wanted to, the museum was not in a position to grant Mexico ownership of the murals. The Fine Arts Museums are a public agency. Since under U.S. law it appeared that the murals were their property, giving the murals to Mexico would have constituted giving away public property, which is illegal. As Thomas K. Seligman, deputy director of exhibits and education at the Fine Arts Museums, noted, "Sometimes we can lock horns about something that will never be solved. If we tried to force ownership, we would never have gotten anywhere because our law says we own it and their law says they own it."

Instead of addressing ownership, a joint custody arrangement was negotiated. Representatives of the Fine Arts Museums of San Francisco met with representatives of the National Institute of Anthropology and History (INAH), the arm of the Mexican government responsible for the care of national monuments. After three years, the following agreement was reached.

Agreement Relating to the Return of the Teotihuacán Murals

DECLARATIONS

I. "The Institute" [the National Institute of Anthropology and History] declares that it is the organism of the Mexican Government which, by virtue of the Federal Law relative to Archeological, Artistic and Historical Monuments and Zones, is charged with the conservation, protection and study of the archeological and historical monuments of Mexico. In accordance with the authority vested by the Institute's Organic Law, the Institute, acting by and through its General Director, possesses the legal capacity to enter into this agreement.

II. "The Museum" [the Fine Arts Museums of San Francisco] declares that it is the department of the City and County of San Francisco responsible for the care and management of the City's art museum and their collections and that its Director possesses the legal authority to represent the museum in this agreement.

III. "The Museum" declares that it acquired the Teotihuacán murals which are the subject of this agreement as a testamentary legacy from Mr. Harold Wagner.

IV. "The Institute" declares that the Teotihuacán Murals that were willed to the Museum are originally from the San Juan Teotihuacán archeological zone and are authentic archeo-logical monuments according to the determinations made by the archeological expert appointed for the purpose of authentication.

V. "The Institute" and "The Museum" together declare that, within the scope of their respective powers, they shall unite their efforts and respective capacities for the purpose of preserving these Teotihuacán Murals and reintegrating those which have an essential socio-cultural value into the cultural patrimony of which they are a part in accordance with the study on the principles, conditions and means for the restitution or return of cultural property in view of reconstituting dispersed heritages prepared for UNESCO by the Ad Hoc Committee appointed by the Executive Council of ICOM, a copy of which is attached hereto and is referred to hereafter as the UNESCO report.

In consideration of these declarations, the parties . . . agree to the following:

CLAUSES

First.—"The Museum" agrees to return to the Institute a minimum of 50% of the Teotihuacán Murals which were donated by way of Mr. Harold

Metope from the Parthenon showing
a struggle between a Lapith and a
Centaur. (British Museum.)

Metope until recently on the Parthenon showing the ruined condition
of a horse and rider. (Acropolis Museum, Athens.)

Wagner's testamentary legacy. The selection of the Murals to be returned to the Institute shall be made by the Museum in accordance with the principles set forth in the UNESCO report and in consultation with representatives of the Institute and other scholars. The Institute will be responsible for the cost of packing and shipping the Murals which will be returned.

SECOND.—"THE INSTITUTE" agrees to send to the Museum persons who are qualified in the subject of restoration, for the purpose of assisting the Museum in restoring the Murals.

THIRD.—"THE MUSEUM" agrees to pay the expenses of the restoration of the Murals if funds can be raised for this purpose. The Institute will loan the Museum experts who will train people to perform the restoration. The living expenses of the experts who will be selected by THE INSTITUTE for travel to San Francisco for the restoration work shall be included as a cost of the restoration.

FOURTH.—"THE INSTITUTE" agrees to exhibit the Teotihuacán Murals that are returned to Mexico in a location which will provide maximum protection and public accessibility for the Murals and to give credit for said return to The Fine Arts Museums of San Francisco.

FIFTH.—"THE MUSEUM" agrees that it shall exhibit the Murals retained in San Francisco and that it shall give suitable credit to THE INSTITUTE for its assistance with the restoration of the Murals.

COMMENTS

1. It was not decided which murals would be returned to Mexico and which would remain at the museum. This was intentional. It was believed that the conservation efforts would be enhanced if workers were not deliberately or unintentionally differentiating between the two sets of murals. Note that Declaration V of the agreement refers to the ICOM Study on Principles, Conditions, and Means for the Restitution or Return of Cultural Property in View of Reconstituting Dispersed Heritages, set out earlier in this chapter (pp. 000–000). Clause 12 of that study provides that "only those objects which have an essential socio-cultural value for the countries in question should be subject to a request for restitution or return," words that are incorporated in the agreement.

2. The delicate process of restoration of these fragile murals went on in the de Young Museum as a kind of "live exhibition." The restorers worked in a room with windows through which museum visitors could watch. The murals will eventually be on display both in Mexico and in San Francisco. Both Mexicans and Americans will be able to appreciate an aspect of Mexican culture. The parties believe that they have reached an unprecedented cooperative agreement for joint custody of a spectacular collection of pre-Columbian murals.

3. The participants attribute the success of the project to its removal from the political process. Although the National Institute of Anthropology and History is a branch of the Mexican government, the people involved were museum professionals. The murals were the primary concern of the negotiators. The results might have been quite different, and possibly less satisfactory, if the Mexican government and the U.S. government had done the negotiating.

4. For additional background on the Teotihuacán Murals case, see Barbara Braun, "Subtle Diplomacy Solves a Custody Case," *ARTnews,* Summer 1982, p. 100.

BIG QUESTION: SHOULD THE ELGIN MARBLES BE RETURNED TO GREECE? WHY OR WHY NOT?

In Chapter 1 we discussed the removal of the Elgin Marbles from the point of view of international law and morality. Here we return to the Marbles with a different question: Should they be returned to Greece, even if the removal were not illegal or immoral? Greek minister of culture Melina Mercouri has no doubt: "The British say they saved the Marbles. Well, thank you *very* much. Now give them back." The following excerpts discuss the question in more detail.

ROBERT BROWNING *The Case for the Return of the Parthenon Marbles**

. . . From the beginning, voices were raised in England both to condemn Elgin's action and to urge that the marbles be returned to Greece. Byron in *Childe Harold's Pilgrimage* (1812) called their removal an act of shameless vandalism and to the end of his life maintained that their proper place was on the Acropolis. Edward Dodwell, the traveller and archaeologist, who was present when the sculptures were taken from the Parthenon, lamented the disastrous lack of judgement and taste which had prompted such an act. Hugh Hammersley, a member of the Parliamentary Committee set up to consider what to do with the marbles, proposed that they be held by the British Museum on trust, to be returned to Athens as soon as Greece attained independence, but failed to persuade his parliamentary colleagues. Later in the nineteenth century men as different in their views as the novelist and poet Thomas Hardy, Sir Roger Casement, the Irish Nationalist, and Frederic Harrison, Liberal historian, jurist, and editor of the influential *Nineteenth Century,* all wrote in favour of returning the marbles to Greece. In the present century, others have taken up the same cause. Harold Nicolson, diplomat and historian, urged the first Labour government to break with the policy of its predecessors and offer the Parthenon sculptures to Greece. In 1941, during the grimmest days of the Second World War, it was proposed in the House of Commons that when the war ended the marbles should be returned as a tribute to Britain's ally, but the government rejected the proposal as premature. Since then the matter has been raised many times in the Commons or the Lords. The answer of successive governments has been an unyielding refusal even to discuss the marbles. Only Harold Macmillan as Prime Minister admitted that this was a question which might sometime be looked into.

Today the stage of individual protest has been passed. Relations between the great powers and the smaller nations are no longer as one-sided as they were. International organizations are actively concerned with the restitution or return of cultural property. The Greek Government has announced its intention to make a formal request for the return of the marbles. And in the United Kingdom, a British Committee for the Restitution of the Parthenon Marbles has been working since autumn 1982 to spread information and stimulate discussion of the arguments for return.

These arguments are basically two. The first is the argument of integrity. The Parthenon sculptures are not portable antiquities, like an icon or a manuscript. They were not conceived and executed to pass into the possession of a patron or to be bought and sold on the art market. Nor are they a decoration applied externally to a building after it has been completed. They were and are an integral part of the Parthenon, which in its turn is part of the landscape, natural and manmade, in which it is set. It is not merely that the architect and sculptor designed the building together, but that the sculptures are often a part of the structure; thus the metopes were placed in position before the construction of the cornices, which locked them in their place. If the head of a statue is in one museum and the torso in another, the argument for reuniting them is a strong one. How much stronger is the case for reuniting the disjointed parts of this unique building. Had an occupying power authorized the removal of the ceiling of the Sistine Chapel to a foreign museum, there would certainly be irresistible pressure for it to be returned to its original setting.

The second argument turns on the concept of cultural property, the claims of which may on occasion override those of juridical property. Cultural property has been defined by the Director-General of Unesco as a people's "irreplaceable cultural heritage, the most representative works of a culture, which the dispossessed regard as of highest importance, and the absence of which is psychologically most intolerable." The Intergovernmental Committee for the return or restitution of cultural property speaks of "objects charged with cultural significance, the loss of which deprives a culture of one of its dimensions." That the Parthenon has been since the foundation of the Greek state a principal symbol of the cultural identity of the Greek people and of its links with its own past is scarcely in doubt. It is sometimes suggested that this symbolism is recent and factitious and results from the influence of the Western Enlightenment and the Romantic

*From Robert Browning, "The Case for the Return of the Parthenon Marbles," *Museum,* vol. 36, no. 1 (1984), p. 38. Reprinted by permission.

movement. Even if this were wholly true, it would not diminish the force of the argument. Symbols are human inventions and the result of historical processes. Cultural values are not eternal. But in fact the objection is only partially true. . . .

It remains only to answer briefly the arguments which have been advanced against the return of the marbles to Greece. We are told, quite correctly, that the British Museum is prevented by an Act of Parliament of 1963 from alienating objects in its possession. But what Parliament resolved Parliament can repeal, especially since it was Parliament that originally entrusted the marbles to the British Museum. A proposal to amend the Act is likely to come before the House of Lords during the present session, which will at least lead to an informed debate.

Then we are asked: "Why take the marbles from one museum only to put them in another? It would be a different matter if they could be replaced on the building." To Greek ears this is a strange objection, since the main reason why they cannot be so replaced is the damage caused by their removal, as is shown by comparison of drawings made before Elgin's operations and later photographs. The sculptures can be better understood and appreciated in close proximity to their original site, in the same climate and light and with the possibility of moving to and fro between temple and sculptures. The Greek Government has declared its intention to build a new museum at the foot of the Acropolis—a few minutes' walk from the Parthenon—which will have every modern aid to conservation. Whether the sculptures can or should ultimately be replaced, in originals or copies, is a question for the technology and taste of posterity.

It is often argued that atmospheric pollution is a bar to the return of the marbles. This is rather a case of the pot calling the kettle black. The atmosphere of London was notoriously polluted by smoke until the 1950s and is now heavily affected by the by-products of the internal combustion engine. On a more serious level, it must be said that pollution is a general problem of large cities and essentially a transitory one. It will be solved when it becomes more costly to hospitalize and care for its human victims than to eliminate its sources. In the meantime, much is being done in Athens in general and in the Acropolis area in particular to reduce the level of pollution. Active research on the effects of atmospheric pollution on marble and on means of counteracting them is going on in the Technical University of Athens under the direction of Professor Theodore Skoulikides, an internationally recognized expert in the field, and in collaboration with the Department of Antiquities. If pollution is the reason why the marbles cannot be returned, then an agreement can easily be reached to return them when the pollution is reduced to an agreed level.

Little need be said about the other arguments against the return, such as that they are more accessible in London than in Athens—more accessible to whom?—or that the Greek Government is "picking on Britain" although parts of the Parthenon sculptures are held in other countries. As for the argument that this is "the thin end of the wedge" and that if the marbles go, the great museums of the world will be emptied, all one can say is that other countries are already requesting the return of their cultural property and will go on doing so, whether or not the Parthenon marbles are returned to Greece, and that Unesco and its organs are working hard to establish national and practical guidelines for this process which will ensure that museums are not emptied.

The case for the return of the Parthenon marbles is a powerful one, which demands serious consideration by all parties concerned. It will not be forgotten or allowed to go by default. A magnanimous recognition by the British Government of the justice of the Greek request would cement the long-standing friendship between two old allies and provide an example for the rest of the world.

COMMENTS

1. The British have from the beginning presented the Elgin Marbles openly and candidly as the work of Greek artists of extraordinary genius and refinement. Presented as they are, spectacularly mounted in their own fine rooms in one of the world's great museums, the Marbles honor Greece and Greeks. No visitor to the British Museum could come away with any other impression. By their removal to London and exposure in the British Museum, they have brought admiration and respect for the Greek achievement. In the most important sense, has the Greek cultural heritage not been preserved, arguably enhanced, by the British acquisition and display of the Marbles?

2. Is it clear that enjoyment of *cultural* value (as distinguished from economic and political value) requires possession of the Marbles? Greeks need access to their cultural heritage, and access would be easiest and most direct if the Marbles were in Athens, but they are widely published, exact plaster casts have been made of the Marbles, and they are available (to the British as well as the Greeks) through reproductions. Is there some cultural magic inherent in the authentic object, and not in an accurate reproduction that should determine the *situs* of the Marbles? Should the Greeks—or the British—be content with reproductions?

3. The argument for possession as an aspect of cultural nationalism has an instinctive appeal. We see that appeal in its most compelling form in cases like that of the Afo-A-Kom, a statue whose possession was said to be essential for the Kom people in Cameroon (see above, pp. 56–58). The words of the First Secretary of the Cameroon Embassy in Washington at the time are eloquent: "It is beyond money, beyond value. It is the heart of the Kom, what unifies the tribe, the spirit of the nation, what holds us together." In that case a belief was at work. Physical removal of the artifact threatened the welfare of the tribe or village. Disaster would befall. Return of the object was essential. There is an analogous kind of mystical element in the attitude of some Greeks toward the Marbles: something essential is missing; there is a cultural wound. In earlier times conquerors took the cultural property of the losers in the belief that the *mana,* or cultural identity and strength of the conquered, was embodied in those objects. Such Greeks want these powerful symbols of their cultural identity returned. Should such beliefs be respected? Should they serve as a basis for the international allocation of cultural property?

4. Economically, whoever has the Marbles had something of value: they would command an enormous price if they were offered for sale, and their presence in a public collection nourishes the tourist industry. Possession is obviously necessary in order to enjoy the economic value, and Britain has the Marbles. We have already seen, however, that the law seems to support the British acquisition and thus to sanction British enjoyment of the economic value. Is there a non-legal argument for giving Greece the economic value?

5. If one accepts the claim that works of importance to a culture belong at that culture's site, does it follow that the Marbles should return to Athens? They have been in England for more than a century and a half, and in that time have become part of the British cultural heritage. The Elgin Marbles and other works in the British Museum have entered British culture, help define the British to themselves, inspire British arts, give Britons identity and community, civilize and enrich British life, stimulate British scholarship. While one may argue that in these terms the Greek claim is more (or less) powerful than that of the British, is it unreasonable to perceive the two positions as roughly equivalent?

6. The Hague Convention of 1954, set out in Chapter 1, speaks of "the cultural heritage of all mankind." Are there considerations from the point of view of cultural internationalism (which this language expresses) that indicate the proper way to allocate the Marbles? The authors believe that there are three such considerations: preservation, integrity, and distribution. Preservation takes priority for obvious reasons. If the Marbles are destroyed, people of all cultures will be deprived of an important part of their cultural heritage, and the problem of allocation disappears. Damage short of destruction—whether through inadequate care, the action of the elements, or the hazards of war, terrorism, or vandalism—threatens the same values. It clearly is essential that the specific objects comprising the Elgin Marbles be protected from damage or destruction, but it can hardly be argued that they are exposed to such danger in London. On the contrary, they are well mounted, well maintained, and well guarded. There is no reason to suppose that they would be safer in Athens. Indeed, if one compares the record of care of works on the Acropolis and in the British Museum since 1816, it is clear where the greater danger has lain. The sculptural reliefs remaining on the Parthenon, and the caryatids on the Erechtheion, have all been badly eroded by exposure to a variety of hazards, including the smog of Athens. The Marbles in the British Museum have fared much better. If one had to make a decision based solely on a pre-1980 concern for the physical preservation of the Marbles, it would be difficult to justify moving them to Athens. (Since 1980 the Greeks have taken great care to preserve the art on the Acropolis.) Even if, as is probable, they would be placed in a museum there, rather than reinstalled on the Parthenon, what reason would there be to expose them to the danger, however slight, involved in removal and transport? What reason would there be to expect that they would be safer in Athens over the next 170 years than they have been in London over the past 170 years?

7. The second international concern is for the integrity of the work of art—for restoration

of the parts of "dismembered masterpieces" (see Patricia Failing, "The Case of the Dismembered Masterpieces," *ARTnews,* September 1980, pp. 68ff.). If we think of the intact Parthenon as an integrated work of art, so that the parts together have more beauty and significance than the sum of the dismembered pieces, then it makes sense to argue that the sculptures should be reinstalled on the temple. That could be achieved by removing the remains of the Parthenon to London and there reuniting it with the sculptures. But the Acropolis itself is a part of our cultural heritage, with it own integrity, and who can imagine the Acropolis without the Parthenon? Accordingly, the integrity argument favors the Greek position. There is, however, a serious objection. The Marbles cannot be reinstalled on the Parthenon without exposing them to almost certain damage from the elements and smog of Athens. The preservation and integrity interests are in direct conflict, and in that case should not the preservation interest prevail? Is not the masterpiece better dismembered than destroyed or seriously damaged? At a time when the caryatids of the Erechtheion have had to be taken indoors by the Greek authorities to preserve them from further damage, can it seriously be argued that the Marbles should be restored to their places on the temple? The Greek proposal is not to restore the Marbles to the Parthenon but to transfer them to a museum near the Parthenon (within 200 yards, according to Minister Mercouri), where they would be joined with the remaining Parthenon Marbles. Is that the same as restoration of the integrity of the Parthenon?

8. There is another kind of integrity argument that goes like this. Phidias was in charge of the entire sculptured "program" for the Parthenon, and it would be a great advantage to connoisseurs and scholars if all surviving parts of the program—the frieze, motopes, and pedimental figures—were in one place for convenient study. Proximity to the Parthenon itself and to sites to which they refer argues for the assembly of the sculptures in Athens rather than in London. Convincing?

9. The other international interest is distributional—a concern for an appropriate international distribution of the common cultural heritage, so that all of mankind has a reasonable opportunity for access to its own and other people's cultural achievements. How should this distribution/access consideration affect the allocation of the Marbles? It is true that Greek antiquities can be found in major museums and private collections throughout the world, and that some of the greatest Greek antiquities are found abroad, but it is difficult to argue that Greece itself is in this sense impoverished. One of the reasons people go to Greece is to enjoy its wealth of antiquities. One of the informed and concerned traveler's preoccupations is with the future of many works that remain in Greece. Like most art-rich nations, Greece faces enormous problems of expense and cultural organization in order to protect, conserve, and display what it has. The distribution interest actually has another and quite different aspect. There is an international interest in the accessibility of cultural property—"the cultural heritage of all mankind"—to all people. That policy is advanced by distribution, rather than concentration in one place, of the works of a culture. As a general matter it seems difficult to argue convincingly for the return of the Marbles to Athens on distributional grounds. If we focus instead on the question of access, is there any reason to suppose that the Marbles would be more accessible to the world's people in Athens than they are in London?

CONCLUDING NOTE ON THE RETENTION AND REPATRIATION OF CULTURAL PROPERTY

Many art-rich nations prohibit export and urge repatriation of cultural property. How well do such claims bear critical examination? Is it possible that some of them, perhaps many of them, will on examination turn out to express prejudice and sentiment at the expense of reason and principle? Do some of them justify policies that endanger, rather than protect, the cultural heritage? Do some claims promote or frustrate an appropriate distribution and accessibility of the cultural heritage? In the international political climate of the 1960s and 1970s such questions have been avoided. In the United Nations, at UNESCO, and in the Council of Europe the justice of the claim of the nation of origin for retention or repatriation is often accepted without question. In such an atmosphere the cultural heritage of mankind may be in greater danger than from the combined efforts of all the tombaroli and hauqueros and their local equivalents in art-rich nations. Byron has much to answer for.

The authors hope that the dialogue about cultural property can move to a higher level. The stakes are high. The world is full of undiscovered, unexplored sites. Uncounted millions of artifacts await discovery. Other millions, already discovered, lead a precarious existence while they wait to be properly preserved, studied, and displayed. We need them to tell us who we are and where we came from, to nourish creativity and enrich our lives, to discredit myths of racial and national superiority in cultural achievement, to demonstrate our common humanity. That, in the end, is what the law and politics of cultural property should be about: the cultural heritage of *all* mankind.

Chapter Three

THE ARTIST'S RIGHTS
IN THE WORK OF ART

THE history of artists' rights has yet to be written. Throughout most of history, artists' rights were restricted to those of a subject or citizen. In ancient times, what may have been the first example of artists actually claiming a right, that of authorship, occurred when Greek artists began to sign their sculptures and paintings in the seventh century B.C. Thereafter, until the nineteenth century, artists won certain rights through their organizations, beginning with the ancient collegia and then the medieval guilds, followed by the academies that emerged in reaction to the restrictive practices of the guilds. These organizations determined who could be an artist and where that artist could and could not practice. Giovanni Battista Paggi earned fame among artists all over Europe when in 1590 he won from the government of Genoa his case against the Genoese painters' guild and was allowed to practice painting without joining the guild. (The City of Genoa decided in Paggi's favor on the grounds of the public interest, because it wanted to encourage people of high birth to become artists and add to the city's glory.)

When artists began to employ legal agreements with commissioners, at least by the thirteenth century in the case of Nicola Pisano and the Cathedral of Pisa, and shortly thereafter by Duccio with the Cathedral of Siena, artists were able to obtain contractual rights for specific undertakings. Unquestionably an artist's fame and the laws of supply and demand contributed to important artists obtaining privileges and occasionally rights from rulers who sought their services. Emperor Charles V decreed that any artist wishing to depict him had to use Titian's portrait as a model (a curious inversion of what we today know as copyright for the artists). Dürer's widow obtained the right from the town council of Nürnberg to prevent other artists from using her late husband's monogram on its prints. The beginnings of copyright go back to the sixteenth century in Venice and the eighteenth century in England; printers of prints and fine books were the initial beneficiaries.

In retrospect, the most important right sought by artists from the time of the Renaissance was that of authorship and the protection of their individuality. Until the nineteenth century, in France, artists had no protection for the physical integrity of their art. Once a work was sold, the owner could do as he pleased with it. When we remember that artists contributed at times to the mutilation and destruction of religious art, and that the monopolies of the guilds restricted the freedom of an artist's movement and practice, it would appear that artists were often their own worst enemies when it came to rights and freedom. It remained for the modern state to give all artists the now-familiar group of artists' rights, as described in this chapter.

The artist who creates a tangible work of art has made something to which the law of property applies, just as it applies to automobiles, home appliances, or items of furniture. We do not deal with such matters in this chapter. The interested reader may consult Ray Andrews Brown, *The Law of Personal Property,* 3rd ed. (Chicago: Callaghan, 1975), for a thorough discussion.

Our interest here is in three kinds of rights that accrue to the artist because the object he has made is a work of art: *moral right* (a literal translation of the French term *droit moral*), *copyright,* and *proceeds rights.* Of these, only the second—copyright—is fully available to the artist under U.S. law. There is a reasonable equivalent of one component of the moral right (the right of divulgation) in our "common-law copyright" (now federalized under the Copyright Act of 1976). But the most important aspect of the moral right, the right of integrity, which is available under the law of most foreign nations, exists presently in only three states: California, Massachusetts, and New York. A version of the proceeds right has been enacted in California, but efforts to follow the California example in other states and in Congress have met substantial resistance. Thus, most American artists have fewer legal rights in their works after they part with them than do artists in France, Germany, and Italy, or in Argentina, Colombia, Mexico, and Venezuela.

This sharp difference between U.S. law and that of other nations provides an interesting exercise in comparison and raises certain questions. Why is there such a contrast in the law of artists' rights? What difference does it make? Which is the preferable system, and why? What, if anything, should be done? All these good questions will be considered in this chapter.

THE MORAL RIGHT

INTRODUCTION

JOHN HENRY MERRYMAN *The Refrigerator of Bernard Buffet**

The French artist Bernard Buffet was invited to decorate a refrigerator to be auctioned in Paris for the benefit of charity. He did so by painting a composition composed of six panels: three on the front, one on the top, and one of each side of the refrigerator. He considered the six panels parts of one painting and signed only one of them. The refrigerator was duly auctioned along with nine others, decorated by nine other artists, at the Galerie Charpentier. Six months later the catalog for another auction included a "Still Life and Fruits" by Bernard Buffet, illustrated and described as a painting on metal. Inspection showed that the painting was one of the panels decorating the front of the refrigerator. The artist brought an action against the owner-consignor to prevent the separate sale of the panel, and the court so ordered.

Guille, a painter, agreed to deliver to Colmant, a dealer, his entire future production for a period of ten years, at a rate of at least twenty paintings a month. The contract provided that the works furnished to the dealer would be signed with a pseudonym and that the painter would not sign the earlier works still in his possession. There was

no evidence that the artist entered the agreement under duress or that he lacked capacity to contract. A dispute eventually arose, and the dealer sued the artist for breach of contract. The Court of Appeals of Paris held that the dealer could not prohibit the artist from using his real name in connection with works he created, despite the terms of the contract.

In 1893 Lord Eden commissioned the American artist James McNeill Whistler, then living in Paris, to paint Lady Eden's portrait. Through intermediaries they agreed on a price "between 100 and 150 guineas." Whistler eventually completed the portrait, which he exhibited (with Eden's approval) at the Salon du Champs de Mars with the title "Brown and Gold, Portrait of Lady E. . . . ." Meanwhile Lord Eden had sent Whistler a check for 100 guineas, which Whistler took as an insult (although he cashed it). On the return of the painting to his studio after the exhibition, Whistler painted out Lady Eden's head, and painted in another, and refused to deliver the painting to Lord Eden, who sued to require the restoration of the portrait, delivery, and damages. The trial court held for Eden on all counts, but, in

*From John Henry Merryman, "The Refrigerator of Bernard Buffet," *Hastings Law Journal,* vol. 27, no. 5 (May 1976), pp. 1023–1028. Copyright © 1976 by the Hastings College of the Law. Reprinted by permission.

the court of Appeal, that part of the judgment ordering restoration and delivery was reversed. Lord Eden was entitled to restitution of the 100 guineas he had paid and damages for breach of contract, but he could not compel restoration of the portrait or its delivery. The Cour de Cassation agreed.

These three decisions illustrate three principal components of "the moral right of the artist," a right that has had its major development in France but that is a part of the law of most European and some Latin American nations. The moral right of the artist is usually classified in civil law doctrine as a right of *personality,* and in particular is distinguished from patrimonial or property rights. Copyright, for example, which is available to artists in civil law countries as well as in the United States and other common law countries, is a patrimonial or property right which protects the artist's pecuniary interest in the work of art. The moral right, on the contrary, is one of a small group of rights intended to recognize and protect the individual's personality. Rights of personality include the right to one's identity, to a name, to one's reputation, to one's occupation or profession, to the integrity of one's person, to privacy, etc.

It is interesting to note that the moral right of the artist in French law is entirely judicial in origin. This is in itself remarkable, since one of the most treasured tenets of the conventional wisdom about the civil law is that law is made by legislators and executives, not by judges. The development of the moral right of the artist is merely another example of the extent to which this tattered brocard is inapplicable to France.

Although judicial in origin, the moral right of the artist has been put into statutory form in France and in many other civil law nations, and is regularly included in international conventions on the topic of copyright and related rights of authors and artists. Like other statutory rights, it continues to grow and develop through judicial interpretation and application, and it is probably accurate to say that the moral right of the artist, still comparatively young even in the nation of its origin, has not reached anything like its full development.

The moral right of the artist is actually a composite right. The Bernard Buffet case involved one of those components: the right of integrity (of the work of art), also sometimes called the right to respect of the work. The notion is that the work of art is an expression of the artist's personality. Distortion, dismemberment or misrepresentation of the work mistreats an expression of the artist's personality, affects his artistic identity, personality and honor, and thus impairs a legally protected personality interest. To treat one of the six panels of the refrigerator-painting as a separate work distorted and misrepresented the artist's intention. The owner of the refrigerator could keep and enjoy it. He could dispose of the entire painting. He was not permitted to take it apart and dispose of it piece by piece.

The Guille case involved a second component of the moral right, the right of paternity. This is the right of the artist to insist that his work be associated with his name. In France and in some other nations the artist cannot waive this right so that, as in the Guille case, the artist can insist that his paintings be attributed to him even though he has contracted to the contrary. The artist can also insist that his name not be associated with works that are not his creation.

The Whistler case is an example of the artist's right to withhold the work, sometimes referred to as the right of divulgation. This component of the moral right gives the artist the absolute right to decide when (and whether) a work of art is complete, and when (and whether) to show it to the public. Even though knowledgeable third persons might conclude that a work of art is for all practical purposes complete, and even if their judgment is supported by the artist's conduct with respect to the work, the artist still can insist that the work not be shown or treated as complete.

In addition to these three components (the right of integrity, the right of paternity, and the right of divulgation) French commentators usually mention other interests commonly treated as aspects of the more general moral right. Of these the "right to repent or to retake" is the most important and consists of the right of the artist to withdraw the work from its owner on payment of an indemnity. Related to this right, and sometimes treated as an aspect of it, is the "right of modification." These rights are usually considered primarily applicable to literary works, although their potential utility in connection with works of visual art is apparent.

COMMENTS

1. The Rationale for the Moral Right:

A. *Privacy-Personality Right.* The primary justification for the protection of moral rights is the idea that the work of art is an extension of the artist's personality, an expression of his innermost being. To mistreat the work of art is to mistreat the artist, to invade his area of privacy, to impair his personality.

B. *Publicity-Property Right.* French writers, and most other commentators, reject any pecuniary-property basis for the moral right, although they recognize that, as in the world of commerce, the artist relies on his reputation in the art market. One writer summed up the need for economic protection in this way:

> As any artist can attest, in the art world with its network of galleries and specialized channels for disposition of works of art, the artist must be able to dissociate himself from work which has been so badly altered that it no longer expresses his creative efforts. Further, to mount exhibitions, especially retrospective ones, he should have access to works he has created earlier in his career. To do so, he must be able to locate the owners of the works and to prevent destruction of the works. To effectuate the right to restrain destruction, the artist should have the right to repair damaged works so that careless abandonment does not put the work of art beyond redemption.

C. *Public Rights.* The idea that the public has an interest in preserving the integrity of cultural property is not new, but it has only recently become prominent in moral-right legislation. The California statutes discussed below are the most recent example, but the 1941 Italian statute also expresses a public interest by providing for enforcement of the right of integrity by a public official.

2. Observe that the moral right of the artist conflicts with the traditional right of the owner of the work of art to use or abuse his property as he pleases. Property rights are never absolute, and the moral right can be seen as just another application of the principle *sic utere tuo ut alienam non laedas* (use your own property so as not to injure others). No one else is hurt if you take an axe to your computer in rage and frustration, but if you deface a work of art you wrong the artist (and, arguably, everyone else). Convincing?

3. One argument against the need for a "public" moral right is that the matter can safely be left in private hands. The owner has an economic interest in preserving the work, and the artist or his heirs can use the "private" moral right in the unusual case in which the owner acts irrationally. Convincing?

ILLUSTRATIVE TREATY AND STATUTE PROVISIONS

Berne Convention for the Protection of Literary and Artistic Works

Article 6bis. (1) Independently of the author's economic rights, and even after the transfer of the said rights, the author shall have the right to claim authorship of the work and to object to any distortion, mutilation or other modification of, or other derogatory action in relation to, the said work, which would be prejudicial to his honor or reputation.

(2) The rights granted to the author in accordance with the preceding paragraph shall, after his death, be maintained, at least until the expiry of the economic rights.

France, Law of March 11, 1957, No. 296

Article 6. The author shall enjoy the right to respect for his name, his authorship, and his work. This right shall be attached to his person.

It shall be perpetual, inalienable and imprescriptible.

It may be transmitted *mortis causa* to the heirs of the author.

The exercise of this right may be conferred on a third person by testamentary provisions.

Article 19. The author alone shall have the

right to divulge his work. He shall determine the method of divulgation, and in the case of cinematographic works shall fix the conditions thereof, subject to the provisions of Article 17.

Article 25. Under any matrimonial regime, and notwithstanding any contrary clauses included in the marriage contract, the right to disclose a work, to fix the conditions of its exploitation, and to defend its integrity shall belong to the spouse who is the author or to the spouse to whom such rights have been transferred. This right cannot be included in dowry (*en dot*), nor can it be brought into the marriage as community property (*acquis par la communauté*), or become after-acquired community property (*acquis par une societé d'acquêts*).

Germany, Law of September 9, 1965

CONTENTS OF COPYRIGHT

Article 11. —Copyright shall protect the author with respect to his intellectual and personal relations to the work, and also with respect to the utilization of the work.

Article 12. The Right of Dissemination—(1) The author shall have the right to determine whether and how his work is to disseminated.

(2) The right of publicly communicating the contents of his work or a description thereof is reserved to the author, provided that neither the work, nor its essence, nor a description thereof has previously been publicly disseminated with his consent.

Article 13. Recognition of Authorship—The author shall have the right of recognition of his authorship of the work. He can determine whether the work is to bear an author's designation and what designation is to be used.

Article 14. Distortion of the Work—The author shall have the right to prohibit any distortion or any other mutilation of his work which would prejudice his lawful intellectual or personal interests in the work.

Italy, Law of April 22, 1941, No. 633

Section II

PROTECTION OF RIGHTS IN THE WORK CONCERNING THE DEFENSE OF THE PERSONALITY OF THE AUTHOR (MORAL RIGHT OF THE AUTHOR)

Article 20. Independently of the exclusive rights of economic utilization of the work referred to in the provisions of the preceding Section, and even after the assignment of such rights, the author shall retain the right to claim authorship of the work and to oppose any distortion, mutilation or any other modification thereof capable of prejudicing his honor or reputation.

However, in the case of works of architecture, the author may not oppose modifications found necessary in the course of construction. He may not, moreover, oppose other modifications which may be necessary in any such completed work. However, if the work is recognized by the competent State authority as having an important artistic character, the author shall be entrusted with the study and execution of such modifications.

Article 21. The author of an anonymous or pseudonymous work shall at all times have the right to reveal his identity and to have his position as author recognized by judicial procedure.

Notwithstanding any prior agreement to the contrary, persons who have derived title from an author who has revealed his identity shall be required to indicate the name of the author in publications, reproductions, transcriptions, performances, recitations and diffusions, or in any other form of manifestation or announcement to the public.

Article 22. The rights indicated in the preceding Articles shall be inalienable. However, if the author was aware of and accepted modifications in his work, he shall not be entitled to intervene to prevent the performance thereof or to demand its suppression.

COMMENTS

1. Notice that in the French statute the moral right is "perpetual." In Article 23, the Italian statute provides that the right can be asserted "without limit of time." In Germany, however, the moral right has the same duration as copyright, and the Berne Convention accepts this as the minimum. Which approach to duration is preferable? Why?

2. The French statute provides that the moral right passes to the artist's heirs or may be conferred on a third person by the artist's will. The Italian statute also provides, in Article 23, for transfer of the right on death. These provisions were thought necessary because the generally applicable laws of wills and inheritance in these nations deal with property rights, and the moral right, as a right of personality, is by definition not property.

3. The Italian statute provides for enforcement of the artist's moral right by a public official as well as by the artist or his successors in interest. The German statute makes no such provision for enforcement of the moral right by a public official. Eric Marcus, "The Moral Right of the Artist in Germany" (paper in the authors' files, 1975) states that such enforcement was rejected in Germany because it offered the possibility that the government would "steer" culture, a sore point in Germany under the Nazis.

4. Notice that in the French statute the moral right is "inalienable" and "imprescriptible." Article 22 of the Italian statute also states that the right is inalienable, but immediately qualifies that statement. French courts have similarly qualified the statutory inalienability of the moral right. The obvious legislative purpose is paternalistic—to protect the artist, who is assumed to be an easy victim of collectors and dealers.

5. The United States is not a party to the Berne Convention, which has been adopted by more than seventy nations. Professor Melvin Nimmer states that resistance to the moral-right provision by U.S. "user groups"—primarily the motion picture and television interests—is one reason for U.S. abstention (Melvin Nimmer, "Implications of the Prospective Revision of the Bern Convention and the United States Copyright Law," *Stanford Law Review*, vol. 19 [1967], pp. 499, 524). The United States is a party to the Universal Copyright Convention, which includes no moral right provision.

SOME CASES

Vargas v. Esquire
164 F.2d 522 (7th Cir. 1947)

Major, Circuit Judge.

. . .

Plaintiff, an artist, sued to enjoin the reproduction of certain pictures made by him and delivered to defendant, a publisher, upon the ground that the same were wrongfully used in that they were published without the signature of plaintiff and without being accredited to him. . . . Defendant moved to dismiss on the ground that the plaintiff at the time of publication had no property right in the pictures and no right to control or to direct their disposition.

The facts alleged by the complaint center about and relate largely to two contracts of which the plaintiff and defendant were parties. The complaint sets forth that in June, 1940, the parties entered into a contract . . . whereby plaintiff was employed as an artist for three years, to produce art work for use by defendant in its publication and also for use in publications of a commercial nature, for a certain monthly compensation and in addition thereto a certain percent of the proceeds realized by defendant for work of a commercial nature. Under this contract plaintiff made and delivered certain pictures, one of which was reproduced each month, beginning October 1, 1940, in the magazine *Esquire*, published by defendant. Plaintiff also made and delivered twelve pictures each year, beginning in the fall of 1940, for a calendar published and sold the following year by defendant.

At first the pictures furnished bore plaintiff's name or signature, "Vargas," and they were reproduced and published with his name thereon. Later, by agreement of the parties, the name "Vargas" was changed to "Varga." Thereafter, the pictures . . . were called "Varga Girls," and the name of the plaintiff appearing thereon was

"A. Varga." The name was used only in connection with pictures made by plaintiff and was thus used by the defendant until March 1, 1946. No name was on the pictures when they were furnished by plaintiff to the defendant.

The contract . . . expired on June 30, 1943, but plaintiff continued to furnish pictures to defendant without a contract, which were published in the same manner as when the contract was in force, until May 25, 1945, when the parties entered into a second contract. . . .

On or about January 14, 1946, plaintiff notified the defendant that he was no longer bound by the contract . . . and refused to longer furnish it with pictures. Defendant at that time had twenty pictures made by plaintiff which had not as yet been published. On February 11, 1946, plaintiff caused to be instituted in the United States District Court an action by which he sought a cancellation of such contract. On May 20, 1946, the court entered its decree, allowing the relief sought by the plaintiff, finding among other things that the contract had been fraudulently obtained by defendant and ordering the same cancelled and set aside. . . .

The complaint alleged that on March 1, 1946, the defendant published its magazine, *Esquire,* which contained a two-page reproduction of a picture made by the plaintiff. At the top thereof instead of the words, "The Varga Girl," appeared the words, "The Esquire Girl." The reproduction did not bear plaintiff's signature, "A. Varga," or any other signature. The supplemental complaint made a similar allegation as to a picture produced by plaintiff appearing in *Esquire* for the month of May, 1946. It was also alleged in the supplemental complaint that on October 1, 1946, defendant published a certain calendar enclosed in an outside envelope on which appeared the words and figures, "The 1947 Esquire Calendar 35¢ Copyright Esquire Inc. 1946 Printed in U.S.A." On the envelope was a reproduction of a picture painted for defendant by plaintiff. The calendar contained in said envelope was composed of the reproduction of twelve pictures plaintiff made intended to be used for the Varga Esquire 1947 calendar. Each of the said pictures bore the words, "The Esquire Girl Calendar." None of such pictures carried plaintiff's name or any name, word or legend indicating them to be the work of plaintiff or any other person.

All the pictures used by the defendant both in its magazine and in connection with its 1947 calendar were furnished by plaintiff to the defendant in accordance with the terms of "Exhibit B," prior to the time that plaintiff gave notice of its cancellation. All of such pictures had been paid for by the defendant in accordance with the terms of the contract, and as to those used in defendant's magazine, plaintiff had no further monetary interest. As to those used in connection with defendant's calendar, plaintiff was entitled to a share of the proceeds derived from the sale thereof. There is no allegation, however, and no claim that defendant had refused to pay or is likely to refuse to pay to plaintiff his share of such proceeds. . . .

In a preamble to [the second contract] it is stated that Vargas for approximately three years had been preparing and furnishing to *Esquire* drawings for use by *Esquire* in connection with its publications and other printed merchandise:

In connection with certain of these drawings, the name "Varga," "Varga Girl," and similar names have been given national publicity by *Esquire* and have become well known to the public. Vargas acknowledges that the success of the drawings has been due primarily to the guidance which *Esquire* has given him and to the publicity given them by *Esquire's* publications.

The contract, after expressing the desire of the parties to enter into an agreement defining their mutual rights and obligations, contains a paragraph around which this controversy revolves and which we think is determinative of the issues involved. It provides:

Vargas agrees for a period of ten years and six months, beginning January 1, 1944, as an independent contractor, to supply *Esquire* with not less than twenty-six (26) drawings during each six-months' period. . . . *The drawings so furnished, and also the name "Varga, "Varga Girl," "Varga, Esq.," and any and all other names, designs or material used in connection therewith, shall forever belong exclusively to Esquire, and Esquire shall have all rights with respect thereto, including (without limiting the generality of the foregoing) the right to use, lease, sell or otherwise dispose of the same as it shall see fit,* and all radio, motion picture and reprint rights. *Esquire* shall also have the right to copyright any of said drawings, names, designs or material or take any other action it shall deem advisable for the purpose of protecting its rights therein. [Emphasis added by Judge Major.]

. . . As already shown, we think there is no ambiguity in the granting language of the contract, nor can there be an implied intention from the language thus employed of an intention of the parties of any reservation of rights in the grantor. The parties had been dealing with each other for a number of years, and the fact that no reservation was contained in the contract strongly indicates that it was intentionally omitted. Such a reservation will not be presumed; it may be expressed and clearly imposed. . . .

Plaintiff advances another theory which needs little discussion. It is predicated upon the contention that there is a distinction between the economic rights of an author capable of assignment and what are called "moral rights" of the author, said to be those necessary for the protection of his honor and integrity. These so-called "moral rights," so we are informed, are recognized by the civil law of certain foreign countries. In support of this phase of his argument, plaintiff relies upon a work by Stephen P. Ladas entitled "The Inter-

national Protection of Literary and Artistic Property" (page 575, et seq.). It appears, however, that the author's discussion relied upon by plaintiff relates to the law of foreign countries. As to the United States, Ladas in the same work states (page 802):

The conception of "moral rights" of authors so fully recognized and developed in the civil law countries has not yet received acceptance in the law of United States. No such right is referred to by legislation, court decision or writers.

What plaintiff in reality seeks is a change in the law in this country to conform to that of certain other countries. We need not stop to inquire whether such a change, if desirable, is a matter for the legislative or judicial branch of the government; in any event, we are not disposed to make any new law in this respect.

Crimi v. Rutgers Presbyterian Church
89 N.Y.S.2d 813 (Sup. Ct. 1949)

LOCKWOOD, Official Referee.

In 1937 the Rutgers Presbyterian Church invited members of the National Society of Mural Painters to enter a competition to design and execute a mural to be placed on the rear chancel wall of its edifice on West Seventy-third Street, Manhattan.

Some twenty artists competed, and after study the committee in charge unanimously selected the plans and sketches of the well-known Alfred D. Crimi for a fresco mural painting twenty-six feet wide by thirty-five feet high.

A contract in which the church is designated as "Owner" and Mr. Crimi as "Artist" was prepared by the attorney for the church and the attorney for Mr. Crimi, and signed by the chairman of the board of trustees of the church and by the artist on February 4, 1938.

The work was completed in time, as per contract, and the agreed price of $6,800 paid in full.

The manner in which the work was done is described by Mr. Crimi as follows:

The fresco had to be built over the existing wall which had a metal lath base suspended four inches over the brick structure on steel channels running perpendicularly. Holes were cut through the wall and the existing channels were reinforced in order that they could carry the weight of the new structure. New channels were then fastened horizontally over the existing ones and in turn were furred with metal lath over which the plaster was laid. To avoid contact between the new and existing wall, after holes were replastered, a heavy coat of asphalt was applied over the old. This also served as water-proofing, eliminating the possibility of dampness penetrating through the brick structure.

Fresco painting is done on wet plaster. The color adheres to the plaster through chemical action—the union of carbonic acid gas and lime oxide producing carbonate of lime as the water evaporates on the surface of the plaster. In fresco no binding agent need be mixed with the pigment as in other painting processes; the pigments are simply well ground in water and applied to the wet surface. As the plaster dries, *the color is actually incorporated in the plaster* and—if the work is properly executed—the painting is assured a permanence surpassing that achieved in any other method of wall decoration. (Emphasis supplied.)

The contract provides that the executed fresco mural, as soon as affixed to the chancel wall, would become a part of the church building. Also that the work of the artist was to be copyrighted and such copyright duly and properly assigned to the owner—the church. This was done.

The mural, signed by the artist, was dedicated November 20, 1938. At the service a leaflet was distributed to the congregation, reading in part:

Alfred D. Crimi. Lower section of Rutgers Presbyterian Church mural now covered over. (Photo courtesy ARTNews Associates.)

Thus the desires and hopes and the thoughtful study, over a period of twelve years, of a difficult aesthetic and deeply religious problem comes to consummation on this twentieth day of November, 1938. Whether the committee and the artist have done well is not for them to say. They have done their best. The verdict must be left to the present congregation, to the successive generations of worshippers who will look upon the fresco, and to Him whose glory is all in all. . . . With the passage of time the mural will grow less brilliant but richer in color.

Plaintiff says that the Reverend Ralph W. Key, former pastor of the church, told him that some parishioners objected to the mural, feeling that a portrayal of Christ with so much of His chest bare placed more emphasis on His physical attributes than on His spiritual qualities.

The number of those objecting evidently increased, for in 1946, when the church was redecorated, the mural was painted over without first giving notice to plaintiff.

Upon learning what had been done, plaintiff brought this proceeding, alleging three causes of action for equitable relief:

1. To compel the defendant to remove the obliterating paints on the fresco mural.

2. In the alternative, to permit the plaintiff to take the fresco mural from the defendant's church at the cost and expense of the defendant.

3. In the event that the fresco mural cannot be thus removed, for judgment against the defendant for $50,000 on each of the three alleged causes of action.

Defendant has denied plaintiff's requests that the obliterations be removed or that he be given the right to take away the mural.

Plaintiff contends that "Defendant's obliteration of the mural constituted a branch of the custom and usage considered part of the contract of commission; violates plaintiff's continued, albeit limited, proprietary interest therein; constitutes irreparable damage to plaintiff; and constitutes an anti-social act and one against public policy."

Defendant asserts:

a. That the mural, under the terms of the contract, became part of the building owned by the church.

b. That the church is not a public or semi-public building.

c. That the contract between an artist and his patron is basically and essentially a service contract.

d. That when the artistic work has been completed and delivered to the patron and accepted and paid for by the patron there is no right whatever in and to the subject matter of the painting reserved to the artist in the absence of a specified agreement providing therefor.

e. That the contract here contains no such reservation.

Thus, the question presented is whether the sale by an artist of a work of art wipes out any interest he might have therein.

Certain general customs and usages are claimed between artists and those who contract with them for the creation of a work to which the artist's name and reputation will be attached—more specifically between mural artists and public or semi-public institutions open to the public. The gist of this claimed custom is that the work, if accepted as being of high artistic standard, will not be altered, mutilated, obliterated or destroyed.

The existence of these customs and usages, their universality, and their acceptance by the public was testified to by leading artists, art critics and art experts.

Plaintiff also pleads that, aside from the question of custom and usage, the artist has a continued limited proprietary interest in his work after its sale, to the extent reasonably necessary to the protection of his honor and reputation as an artist, and that within this limited ambit of protection was the right to have the work continue without destruction, mutilation, obliteration or alteration.

The fact that artists, as distinguished from artisans and mechanics, have peculiar and distinctive rights in their work has been accepted in some countries of the Continent of Europe, where it has been given the appellation "droit moral" (see "The International Protection of Literary and Artistic Property," by Stephen P. Ladas, 1938 ed.).

The extent to which such doctrine has been adopted in common-law jurisdictions is considered by Martin A. Roeder in 53 Harvard Law Review, p. 554, "The Doctrine of Moral Right: A study in the Law of Artists, Authors and Creators," in which (p. 557) the author distinguishes the protection provided by the copyright laws from that provided by the "droit moral."

When an artist creates, be he an author, a painter, a sculptor, an architect or a musician, he does more than bring into the world a unique object having only exploitive possibilities; he projects into the world part of his personality and subjects it to the ravages of public use. There are possibilities of injury to the creator other than merely economic ones. . . . Nor is the interest of society in the integrity of its cultural heritage protected by the copyright statute.

However, this author discussing the Bern Convention as revised at Rome in 1928, says, at page 569 of his article:

The right to prevent deformation does not include the right to prevent destruction of a created work. The doctrine of moral right finds one social basis in the need of the creator for protection of his honor and reputation. To deform his work is to present him to the public as the creator of a work not his own, and thus make him subject to criticism for work he has not done, the destruction of his work does not have this result. Thus even in France, in *Lacasse et Welcome c. Abbé Quénard* . . . it was held that the artist could not recover when murals painted by him on the walls of a church were destroyed, without notice, by the abbe.

The Bern Convention, the International Copyright Union, article 6, reads:

1. Independently of the patrimonial rights of the author, and even after the assignment of the said rights, the author retains the right to claim the paternity of the work, as well as the right to object to every deformation, mutilation or other modification of the said work, which may be prejudicial to his honor or to his reputation.
2. It is left to the national legislation of each of the countries of the Union to establish the conditions for the exercise of these rights. The means for safeguarding them shall be regulated by the legislation of the country where protection is claimed.

The United States of America was not a signatory to these conventions held at Bern and Rome.

Plaintiff concedes "there is a decided paucity of legal authority" on the question in this country. He quotes from Stephen P. Ladas' work (International Protection of Literary and Artistic Property, vol. 1, §287, p. 603):

The author may demand respect for the integrity of his work. This applies only to cases in which his work has been presented to the public. It does not extend to the personal or private use of a reproduction of his work by the purchaser thereof, but it does when the original work of the author is involved. This is particularly the case with works of art, the nature of which calls for exhibition by the purchaser. The latter is not permitted to violate its integrity but is he permitted to destroy the work of art? A decision of the Court of

Appeals of Paris has recognized the right of a purchaser of a work of art to destroy it. While this may be justified on a strict interpretation of the legal position based on the general law of property, it is questionable whether it should be admitted in the case of works of art. *Modern legislation and court decisions have admitted several limitations of the property right in cases where public or social interests are involved. The maintenance and preservation of a work of art is invested with the public interest in culture and the development of the arts.* (Italics supplied.)

In a footnote Ladas cites *Lacasse et Welcome c. Abbé Quénard*, . . . where "the Court reversed the decision of the Tribunal Civil de Versailles and held that the proprietor of a church containing wall paintings may destroy the latter without advising the artist and permitting him to remove them." The author severely criticizes this holding in the language italicized above.

Ladas cites Nicola Stolfi and Hermann Otavsky (foreign authors) for the proposition that the owner may not destroy a work of art because of the "intention of the parties at the time of purchase, and . . . claims that such intention is limited to the transfer of the work for the purpose of its being used according to its nature, and not for the purpose of destruction" (Ladas, op. cit. supra, p. 604). Thus Ladas, Stolfi and Otavsky are all in agreement that the owner should not have the right to destroy the work of art, Ladas on the ground of public policy and Stolfi and Otavsky on the ground of original intent of the parties.

Counsel overlooked the statement at page 802, section 363, Volume II, where Ladas writes:

The conception of "moral right" of authors, so fully recognized and developed in the civil law countries, has *not yet received acceptance in the law of the United States. No such right is referred to by legislation, court decisions or writers.* (Italics supplied.)

This comment is supported by *Vargas v. Esquire, Inc.,* . . . at page 526, where the court said:

The conception of "moral rights" of authors so fully recognized and developed in the civil law countries has not yet received acceptance in the law of the United States. No such right is referred to by legislation, court decision or writers.

What plaintiff in reality seeks is a change in the law in this country to conform to that of certain other countries. We need not stop to inquire whether such a change, if desirable, is a matter for the legislative or judicial branch of the government; in any event, we are not disposed to make any new law in this respect.

And by *Yardley v. Houghton Mifflin Co.,* . . .

When a man, hereinafter referred to as a patron, contracts with an artist to paint a picture for him, of whatever nature it may be, the contract is essentially a service contract, and when the picture has been painted and delivered to the patron and paid for by him, the artist has no right whatever left in it.

Whilst the artist in such a case may by contract reserve the right of reproduction, and so reserve his right of copyright, *Werckmeister v. Springer Lithographing Co.,* C.C., 63 F. 808, 809, if the sale is not shown to have been thus limited, the patron becomes the sole owner and has all the rights in the picture, including the right to reproduce it, and the artist employed to make the picture cannot derogate from his patron's rights by taking out a copyright thereon without his patron's permission.

In *Pushman v. New York Graphic Society, . . .*

In this case the absolute sale and delivery of the painting without any condition, reservation or qualification of any kind, to a state-owned public institution where it has been displayed for a long period of time, constitute an abandonment of all the plaintiff's rights and a publication and dedication to public use free for enjoyment and reproduction by anybody.

Our Court of Appeals, affirming, . . . in a unanimous decision by Desmond, J., stated in part:

Our conclusion is that under the cases and the texts, this unconditional sale carried with it the transfer of the common law copyright and right to reproduce. Plaintiff took no steps to withhold or control that right. "The courts cannot read words of limitation into a transfer which the parties do not choose to use." . . .

[1] Thus, the claim of this plaintiff that an artist retains rights in his work after it has been unconditionally sold, where such rights are related to the protection of his artistic reputation, is not supported by the decision of our courts.

This court does not agree with the contention that the destruction of the mural to which plaintiff's name had been publicly attached constitutes a "body blow" to plaintiff's artistic reputation. It merely shows that those representing the 1938 congregation of this church thought highly of the fresco mural, while those representing the 1946 congregation did not like it.

The cases cited involving literary productions—authors of plays, attempts to restrain modifications of paintings in public or semi-public buildings, and the maintenance and preservation of works of art presented to public authorities, are not in point. . . .

[2] Plaintiff designed and executed this fresco mural as part and parcel of the wall of the church building—on part of the real estate.

Thus, any interest, proprietary or otherwise, claimed to have arisen by custom and usage as part of the contract of commission, or in any manner, would have to be in writing, or it would violate section 242 of the Real Property Law.

[3] The time for the artist to have reserved any rights was when he and his attorney participated in the drawing of the contract with the church. No rights in the fresco mural were reserved, and, by the terms of the written agreement between the parties, signed February 4, 1938, the artist plaintiff sold and transferred to defendant all his right, title and interest in the mural.

Shostakovich v. Twentieth Century-Fox Film Corp.

196 Misc. 67, 80 N.Y.S.2d 575 (Sup. Ct. 1948), aff'd, 275 App. Div. 695, 87 N.Y.S.2d 430 (1st Dept. 1949)

KOCH, Justice.

Plaintiffs are composers of international renown. They are citizens and residents of the Union of Socialist Soviet Republics. Defendant, a domestic corporation, has produced a picture known as "The Iron Curtain" which is now being exhibited in theatres throughout this country. In the public mind, this title has come to indicate the boundary between that part of Europe which is under the sovereignty of, occupied by or under the influence of the U.S.S.R., as distinguished from the rest of the continent. The picture depicts recent disclosures of espionage in Canada attributed to representatives of the U.S.S.R. There is shown, preliminarily, but not as part of the picture proper, as is customary in the showing of motion pictures, the names of the players, the producer, the cameramen, and similar informative data. Included is this statement: "Music—From the Selected Works of the Soviet Composers— Dmitry Shostakovich, Serge Prokofieff, Aram Khachaturian, Nicholai Miashovsky—Conducted by Alfred Newman." Such practice in the theatrical, advertising and kindred businesses is known as giving a "credit line." During the picture, music of the several plaintiffs is reproduced, from time to time, for a total period of approximately 45 minutes. The entire running time of the film is 87 minutes. The use of the music can best be described as incidental, background matter. Aside from the use of their music neither the plot nor the theme of the play, in any manner, concerns plaintiffs. In addition to the use of their names on the "credit lines" the name of one plaintiff is used when one of the characters in the play is shown placing a recording of this particular plaintiff's music on a phonograph. Again this is incidental, the name is mentioned in an appreciative, familiar fashion, the impression given being that the character has come upon a record of a composition which he recognizes and appreciates hearing. All the music, it is conceded, for the purposes of this motion, is in the public domain and enjoys no copyright protection whatever. . . .

There is no longer any doubt that the deliberate infliction of a wilful injury without just cause is actionable. . . . The wrong which is alleged here is the use of plaintiff's music in a moving picture whose theme is objectionable to them in that it is unsympathetic to their political ideology. The logical development of this theory leads inexcapably to the Doctrine of Moral Right. . . . There is no charge of distortion of the compositions nor any claim that they have not been faithfully reproduced. Conceivably, under the doctrine of Moral Right the court could, in a proper case, prevent the use of a composition or work, in the public domain, in such a manner as would be violative of the author's rights. The application of the doctrine presents much difficulty however. With reference to that which is in the public domain there arises a conflict between the moral right and the well established rights of others to use such works. . . .

So, too, there arises the question of the norm by which the use of such work is to be tested to determine whether or not the author's moral right as an author has been violated. Is the standard to be good taste, artistic worth, political beliefs, moral concepts or what is it to be? In the present state of our law the very existence of the right is not clear, the relative position of the rights thereunder with reference to the rights of others is not defined nor has the nature of the proper remedy been determined. Quite obviously therefore, in the absence of any clear showing of the infliction of a wilful injury or of any invasion of a moral right, this court should not consider granting the drastic relief asked on either theory. The motion is accordingly denied in all respects.

COMMENT

At the time that the Shostakovich case was under litigation in New York, a companion case was going on in Paris: *Soc. Le Chant de Monde v. Soc. Fox Europe et Soc. Fox Americaine Twentieth Century* (1954) D. Jur. 16, 80 (Cour d'Appel de Paris). The French court reached precisely the opposite conclusion.

Meliodon v. Philadelphia School District
328 Pa. 457, 195 Atl. 905 (1938)

On November 28, 1933, the plaintiff filed his bill, covering 24 pages of typewritten matter, against the School District of Philadelphia, a corporation. . . .

Condensing the averments of the bill and the prayer thereof, it appears that plaintiff, a sculptor, was engaged by School District in 1932 to do certain artistic work in the preparation of models to be placed upon the building of the Board of Education. The defendant avers that the plaintiff having performed his work, which was accepted by the School District, has been paid in full and, having accepted payment, he now files this bill in equity seeking money damage in the amount of $500,000 for the loss of and for irreparable damage to his reputation as a sculptor and modeler of distinction. The plaintiff avers that his models were so changed, by direction of the superintendent of buildings of the Board of Education, Mr. Catherine, that "as a result of the attribution of said sculptural units and groups to your orator and the general belief amongst artists and connoisseurs of art that said units and groups are actually the creations and work of your orator, he has been subjected to the ridicule and contempt of all artists and connoisseurs of art who are familiar with the sculptural units and groups on the exterior of said Board of Education Building. As a further result thereof, your orator has found it difficult to obtain other contracts for sculptural works in the United States of America, in some cases, as in that of the new Custom House Building to be erected in Philadelphia by the Government of the United States of America, having been refused the right even to enter a bid for the sculptural work, and in other cases, as in that of the new Post Office Building to be erected in Philadelphia by the Treasury Department of the United States of America, having had his contract rescinded after he had been awarded the same on the strength of his sketch models and had posted his bond guaranteeing completion of the work. Your orator estimates, and will be able to prove to your Honorable Court, that his monetary loss due to the rescinding of this contract with the Treasury Department of the United States of America, was $3,062."

The plaintiff further asks that the School District be required to tear down the sculptural work performed by the plaintiff and paid for by the defendant and to prevent the defendant's officers and agents from declaring that the work done under the plaintiff's contract was performed by him.

The questions raised by the bill and defendant's preliminary objections thereto are: (1) Whether, under the facts averred in the bill, the School District of Philadelphia would be liable to the plaintiff in a suit in equity for damages to his reputation as an artist; and (2) whether, under the facts averred in the bill, the court can compel the school district to tear down the sculptural work in question.

A school district is a state agency, performing governmental functions, and is not liable for the negligence or malfeasance of its officers or agents. . . .

A careful reading of the averments in the bill reveals that the principal damage alleged is to the reputation of the plaintiff, for which he claims the sum of $500,000. This is in the nature of a tort, wherein the plaintiff has an adequate remedy at law, and the school district is not liable for the torts of its agents, and the prayer for relief and the award of $500,000 damages is not the subject of equitable relief.

The plaintiff further prays that the defendant be directed to tear down the sculptural units or groups in question and that the court decree that the plaintiff be permitted, "at the sole expense of the defendant," to replace all said units or groups to his own satisfaction. Apparently the granting of such power would place the disposition of the entire case in the hands of the plaintiff to determine which groups were satisfactory. The Act of April 8, 1846, P.L. 272, 17 P.S. §299, provides that: "No courts within the city and county of Philadelphia shall exercise the powers of a court of chancery in granting or continuing injunctions against the erection or use of any public work of any kind, erected or in progress of erection, under the authority of an act of the legislature, until the questions of title and damages shall be submitted, and finally decided by a common-law court." In the instant case no question of title is involved, and, as we have heretofore indicated, for damage to his reputation the plaintiff has an adequate remedy at law. We are of opinion that the plaintiff has not set forth any right justifying the issuance of an injunction and the relief prayed for by the plaintiff.

COMMENTS

1. A son of the painter Millet intervened in a suit between two publishers over which had the right to publish a "reproduction" of Millet's "The Angelus." He claimed that both versions distorted and falsified his father's work and violated the artist's moral right. The French court agreed and prohibited publication of both versions (Millet, Tribunal civil de la Seine, 20 May 1911. Amm. 1911. 1. 271).

2. A granddaughter of Henri Rousseau sued to stop a Paris department store from using "reproductions" (which employed altered images and different colors) of the painter's work in its window decorations. The court found this a violation of the artist's moral right (*Bernard-Rousseau v. Soc. des Galeries Lafayette*, Tribunal de grand instance de Paris, 3ᵉ ch., 13 March 1973 [unpublished]). Do you agree? What effect would omission of the artist's name from the "reproductions" have on your opinion?

3. The French artist Fernand Léger was engaged to design sets for the opera *Bolivar* by Darius Milhaud. He completed the commission, and the opera was performed in 1950. It was performed again in 1952, but with scene 3 of act 2, "The Crossing of the Andes," omitted. Léger brought an action for damages and an order to reestablish the settings in their entirety. The court agreed with the artist that the settings constituted a work of art to which the moral right attached, but said that the composer and the producer also had rights, including the right to control the production. Still the court thought it wrong to make a cut both without the artist's permission and without notice to the public, and it ordered that all advertising for future incomplete performances include a statement that a part of the stage settings would not be shown because that scene was omitted. *Léger v. Reunion des Theatres Lyriques Nationaux* (1955) 6 R.I.D.A. 146 (Tribunal civil de la Seine).

4. Does the moral right protect against total destruction of a work of art? The Roeder article, quoted in the *Crimi* case, states that it does not. This statement in this very influential article is routinely quoted by the other writers and has become accepted doctrine in the United States. Note, however, that Roeder cites as authority the *Lacasse* case. Lacasse was commissioned by the local priest to paint frescoes in a chapel in a small town in France. Eventually the bishop heard that there were complaints about the completed work. He inspected the frescoes, found them in questionable taste, decided that even modification would not make them acceptable, and ordered them defaced. The artist objected and litigation followed. The court held for the bishop. (*Lacasse et Welcome c. Abbé Quénard,* Cour d'Appel de Paris, 1ʳᵉ ch., 27 April 1934; D.H. 1934. 385; Gaz. pal. 1934. 2. 165.) *Lacasse* is flimsy authority for Roeder's proposition, for two reasons. First, a fresco on the wall of a building is a special case. The conflict is between the artist and the owner of the building. Second, the local priest who commissioned the fresco was not the owner of the chapel. The bishop was the owner, and the French court held that he had the right to obliterate a fresco he did not commission or approve.

5. Compare the *Sudre* case, decided two years later. Sudre was commissioned to decorate a public fountain in his native village and did so by making a statue of a woman wearing the local costume. The sculpture was installed, but not well maintained. It was abused by birds and schoolboys. Finally the city council decided, without a serious attempt at restoration, to have the sculpture removed and destroyed. On a visit to the village, Sudre found that pieces of his broken statue had been used to fill holes in the road. He brought an action for damages based on moral right and won. (*Raymond Sudre v. Commune de Daixas,* Conseil d'Etat, 3 April 1936; Dall. 1936. III. 56.)

6. The owner of a house commissioned a mural. Some time after its completion he had nude figures in the mural clothed by another painter. The artist claimed that this violated his moral right. The German court agreed, stating that the work could not be altered without the artist's consent. In the course of its opinion, however, the court suggested that the mural might be completely effaced, as distinguished from altered, without liability (*Felseneiland mit Sirenen,* 79 RGZ 397, 8 June 1912). In the *de Chirico* case (described in note 9, below) the Court of Appeals of Venice opined that total destruction of a work of art violates the artist's moral right. Both these statements are dicta. But in a later German case, "*Hajed v. ADAC,*" *Film und Recht* 9 (1982), p. 510, the Munich Landgericht (trial court of general jurisdiction) first held for the artist and then, on reconsideration, against him, in a dispute with the German Automobile Club concerning a renovation of the club's headquarters building resulting in the destruction of works by the artist. The court directly held that under the circumstances of the case the club could destroy the artist's works.

7. The authors know of no moral right case holding that a separate work of art not part of a building may be destroyed. Whether destruction should be permitted in such a case depends on one's view of the purpose of the right of integrity. If the artist's personality interest is emphasized, then destruction seems less offensive than the continued existence of an altered work that misrepresents the artist. Even so, if an important work is lost, the artist's total *oeuvre* is misrepresented. If emphasis is instead placed on the public interest in preserving the culture, then destruction clearly impairs that interest.

8. Destruction of a work of art deprives the artist of any prospect of exploiting the resale proceeds right (discussed below). It also prevents reproduction and exploitation of other derivative rights by the copyright owner. Should this affect our position on whether destruction violates the moral right?

9. In 1950 the Venice Biennale arranged a retrospective exhibition of the work of Italian

painter Giorgio de Chirico, with works lent from public and private collections. De Chirico brought an action to prohibit the exhibition, arguing that the show misrepresented him by overincluding his earlier paintings and underincluding the later ones. Although the trial court held for the artist, the Court of Appeals of Venice reversed (*Ente autonomo "La Biennale" di Venezia c. De Chirico,* 25 March 1955; Foro It. 1955. I. 717.) In this connection it is interesting to note that Article 9 of the Spanish law of Intellectual Property of January 10, 1879, provides that "the transfer of a work of art does not constitute a transfer . . . of the right of public exposition of the work . . . unless there is agreement to the contrary."

MORAL RIGHT IN THE UNITED STATES

As the preceding materials show, U.S. law until recently contained no direct equivalent of the moral right, and U.S. courts resisted suggestions that they adopt one. This is so even though legal scholars had optimistically suggested that existing legal remedies, if imaginatively employed, might lead to protection approximating the moral right. In particular, breaches of implied agreement, copyright, unfair competition, libel, intentional injury to business relations, intentional infliction of emotional stress, violation of the right of privacy, and possibly others were listed to show that U.S. law did not need to import the moral right. See James M. Treece, "American Law Analogies of the Author's 'Moral Right,'" *American Journal of Comparative Law,* vol. 16 (1968), p. 487; "Toward Artistic Integrity: Implementing Moral Right Through Extension of Existing Legal Doctrines," *Georgetown Law Journal,* vol. 60 (1972), p. 1539 and "The Doctrine of Droit Moral: Its Place in American Copyright Law," *Harvard Law Review,* vol. 16 (1971), p. 589.

In practice, these theoretical "equivalents" of the moral right did not come close. Until enactment of the California statutes, there was no basis for assuming that an American court would have enjoined the sale of the Buffet panel or publication of one or the other Millet reproduction, that it would have required published notice of the omission of one scene from the Léger stage settings, or that it would have suppressed the Rousseau reproductions. Relief that would be routinely granted in Europe was denied in the Vargas, Crimi, Shostakovich, and Meliodon cases. Thus, although there was some degree of protection under U.S. law, "these similarities should not be overstated" (Paul Goldstein, "Adaption Rights and Moral Rights in the United Kingdom, the United States, and the Federal Republic of Germany," *International Review of Industrial and Copyright Law,* vol.14 [1983], pp. 43ff).

ABUSE OF PUBLICLY FUNDED WORKS: SOME HORRIBLE EXAMPLES

1. In 1960 sculptor Elio Benvenuto was commissioned by Santa Clara County (California) to create a fountain, which was installed in the courtyard of the county government center in 1962. In 1972, during the course of modifications to the government center, the fountain was moved to the West Valley Storage Yard of the Transportation Agency without notification to the artist. One San Francisco reporter described the scene of the abandoned sculpture:

> Covered with a patina of pale green, the once-proud bronze fountain that sprayed jets of dancing water onto the fountain in front of the old County Administration Building at 70 West Hedding Street lies humbly on its side. It leans at a crazy angle, its mass crushing an old tire as it dies an ignominious death of decay and tarnish. [*San Francisco Chronicle,* November 14, 1976.]

A second reporter was more blunt: "Eli Benevenuto's sculpture was at Santa Clara's Civil Center, now it's in a junkyard" (*San Francisco Chronicle,* November 19, 1976).

2. Another example of mistreatment by a government body occurred at the Empire State Mall, a complex of office buildings in New York's state capital. A number of major contemporary paintings were installed in the mile-long concourse in the late 1960s, but despite the value of the exhibit the paintings were outrageously neglected. "Via Ochre," by Kenneth Noland, was abused when installers took the canvas off its stretcher, cropped its edges, and using white lead as an adhesive fixed it permanently to the concourse wall. In addition, the piece was continuously mistreated. It served as background for a variety of meetings and festivals. In one such festival, an ethnic food fair, price tags for various foods were actually stuck to the canvas. Another painting, by Al Held, was also taken off its stretchers and similarly glued permanently to the wall. The painting, composed of three panels, was not mounted according to Held's plans; the edges of the panels did not meet on the wall, and strange jumps in the lines and planes of the work appeared. The artist attempted to correct the situation for three years, offering to travel to Albany to repaint and repair the painting—all to no avail. These paintings and others suffered abrasions and scratches left by chairs and other displays that leaned against the pictures. Additional indignities included splashes from cleaning and detergent fluids, and the scrapes, bruises, and batterings that accompany unprotected public displays. Some of the work also began to peel away or became soiled. (Thomas Hess, "The Mess in Albany," *New York,* November 28, 1977, p. 83.)

3. Another case involving the destruction of publicly funded works of art occurred in 1980 at the Holly Court Housing Project in San Francisco's Bernal Heights district. The housing project's tenants had arranged for a HUD grant to fund the painting of murals along the central corridor of their housing project. The tenants actually sought the aid of the Art Commission, which helped them run a contest to select the most suitable muralists for the job. Two artists, Michael Moscher and Claire Josephson, were hired and worked closely with the tenants. The muralists spent six months creating murals, which depicted interracial harmony in large Hispanic, black, and Caucasian faces. Less than four months after the work was completed, the two artists were shocked to learn that the murals had been whitewashed. The Holly Court residents had had a change of heart and painted over the murals without notifying the artists. (See "Whitewashing Mural Art," *Community Murals,* Fall 1981, p. 55.)

4. Consider the 1980 destruction of two Art Deco sculptures on the Bonwit Teller building in New York City. The two stone bas-relief sculptures were embedded in the facade of the eleven-story building between the eighth and ninth floors when it was erected in 1928. The building was being razed by a developer to make way for a sixty-two-story complex, and the pieces had been sought with enthusiasm by the Metropolitan Museum of Art. In fact, the developer had agreed to donate them if removal costs were not prohibitive. Ultimately, however, the sculptures were smashed by jackhammers. The developer reasoned that, although the actual costs of removal were not excessive (an estimated $32,000), the costs in terms of delay were prohibitive. The unexpected destruction of the sculptures stunned disappointed officials, all of whom had urged their preservation. (See Robert D. McFadden, "Bonwit Art Deco Sculptures Ruined," *New York Times,* June 6, 1980, p. JE6.)

5. The case of "Shinto," by Isamu Noguchi, one of the world's foremost sculptors, helped arouse sentiment in favor of moral-right legislation in New York. In 1975 the Bank of Tokyo in New York City commissioned Noguchi to design a sculpture for the lobby of its U.S. headquarters near Wall Street. Specifically designed for the space, the 1,600-pound aluminum sculpture was a large, 17-foot-long rhomboid hung point downward from the lobby's ceiling. In 1980 the bank decided to remove the sculpture after comments about its guillotine appearance from uneasy customers and employees. The sculpture, which was too large to pass through doors or windows in the bank, was cut into pieces and shipped to a warehouse. In an interview by a *New York Times* reporter, Noguchi expressed his shock at what he called

Isamu Noguchi. Shinto, *1976, stainless steel. Formerly in the Bank of Tokyo, New York City. (Photo by Ezra Stoller. Reproduced by courtesy of the artist.)*

an "act of vandalism" and emphasized his dismay at not being notified before the destruction. Even so, he felt that he was legally powerless to obtain redress for the act because he had sold the work and assumed that all rights had been transferred with its title. (See Glueck, "Wall Street Bank Cuts up Noguchi Sculpture," *New York Times,* April 19, 1980, p. 1.)

6. Alexander Calder, known for his large-scale mobiles and stabiles, has been the victim of insensitive abuse by a number of public entities. In 1958 one of his mobiles, "Pittsburgh," was donated by a private collector to Allegheny County, Pennsylvania, and was to be installed in the Greater Pittsburgh International Airport. Before its installation and without Calder's knowledge, the county of Pittsburgh immobilized the work (an immobile mobile!) and re-painted it from black and white to the official county colors: green and gold. Calder was understandably furious, but despite his continuing protests the work was never properly re-stored in the remaining eighteen years of his life. Only later, after the situation had received national publicity, did the county finally return the mobile to its original condition. (See Barbara Rose, "Calder's Pittsburgh: A Violated and Immobile Mobile," *ARTnews,* January 1978, p. 39.)

A more upsetting abuse of Calder's work was the treatment of his "Hello Girls" by the Los Angeles Museum. The piece consisted of three mobiles-cum-stabiles designed by the artist to be activated by jets of water in a fountain. When the fountain fell into disuse in 1975, the museum drained its moat and moved the three elements of the work to dry land. Any inter-action between the reinstalled components was lost because they were separated by trees and even by a totally separate sculpture placed between the second and third elements. All this was done without Calder's approval.

If these instances of abuse are not shocking enough, take the case in which the curator (of all people!) of the Wichita State Art Museum allegedly painted some of Calder's unpainted maquettes to increase their appraisal value (unpainted Calders have a lower market value). The donor wanted a large tax deduction for its charitable contribution to the museum and therefore urged the painting, which was done, so that the new appraisal was higher.

7. Consider what might politely be called the "disassembly" of a sculpture by means of a chain saw. In 1974 a 25-foot-high sculpture by Bernard Langlais was installed at the entrance to the Samoset Resort in Rockport, Maine. A change of ownership at the resort in 1979 brought a decision to remove the piece. The manner of "disassembly" was particularly dis-concerting to local residents, and especially Langlais's widow, who was not informed in ad-vance that the work would be disassembled. Mrs. Langlais emphasized that the use of the chain saw made accurate reassembly extremely difficult. After the "chain saw massacre," the fragments of the sculpture were piled up and left uncovered at the rear of Samoset's main entrance, where they remained through a summer and fall. (See *ARTnews,* Dec. 1979, p. 12.)

8. Consider Jean Dubuffet's confrontation with Renault, the huge French automobile com-pany. In 1973 Renault invited Dubuffet to construct a 2,000-square-yard environmental sculpture, or garden, for the courtyard of its super-modern new headquarters at Boulogne-Billancourt on the outskirts of Paris. The project, entitled "Salon de Eté," would have been the biggest and most ambitious of Dubuffet's sculptural projects. Seven months after the com-mission, the artist produced a 20-foot-by-18-foot model, one-tenth the envisioned size, which was approved by Renault, and construction began in November 1974. In 1975 a new president, Bernard Venier-Palliez, took over at Renault. He was not as enthusiastic about the project as his predecessor, and he ordered construction halted (at that time the structure was a little over half completed). All Dubuffet's work was to be junked and the site covered with a smooth new lawn.

At the age of seventy-five, an outraged Dubuffet sued the giant state-owned company to prevent destruction of the monument it had commissioned and to compel its completion.

Though he had been paid the agreed fee, he insisted on completion and offered to put up his own money to help fund the project. In June 1978 a lower French court found against him. He lost again in the Court of Appeal, but in the Supreme Court of Cassation he won his case, and after eight years of litigation Renault was ordered to start construction from scratch and complete the monument. Having made his point, Dubuffet decided not to build the structure after all. He explained that he did not want to force Renault's people to build something they did not want, and thereupon bid the matter adieu.

9. The case of the Winston Churchill portrait, painted by Graham Sutherland during Churchill's life and presented to him by Parliament, presents an interesting problem. Both Churchill and his wife detested it, though as a work of art it was generally considered excellent, one of Sutherland's best. After Churchill died, his widow had the portrait destroyed. Should the moral right require the subject of a hated portrait who owns it to permit it to survive?

PROTECTING THE PUBLIC INTEREST AND THE ARTIST'S REPUTATION

Who cares? What difference does it make to anyone that an artist's work has been revised without his consent? At a minimum, it seems reasonable to suggest the following.

JOHN HENRY MERRYMAN *The Refrigerator of Bernard Buffet**

On the level of individual interest there is more at stake than the concern of the artist and his heirs for the integrity of his work. There is also the interest of others in seeing, or preserving the opportunity to see, the work as the artist intended it, undistorted and "unimproved" by the unilateral actions of others, even those with the best intentions and the most impressive credentials. We yearn for the authentic, for contact with the work in its true version, and we resent and distrust anything that misrepresents it.

The machinery of the state is available to protect "private" rights in part because there is thought to be some general benefit in doing so. Thus the interests of individual artists and viewers are only a part of the story. Art is an aspect of our present culture and our history; it helps tell us who we are and where we came from. To revise, censor, or improve the work of art is to falsify a piece of the culture. We are interested in protecting the work of art for public reasons, and the moral right of the artist is in part a method of providing for private enforcement of this public interest.

It might be argued that the artist can always protect the interest involved in the right of integrity by including appropriate provisions in the original agreement of a sale of the work, and indeed some artists try to do so. However, for most artists that is not a workable suggestion. They do not, as a general rule, execute formal agreements on the sale of their work. (Perhaps they should do so, but at present few attempt it.) Most have never thought of doing such a thing and would not know how to go at it if the problem were in their minds; others shrink from negotiations and bargaining. Nor is the artist, particularly when young and unknown, in a very powerful bargaining position. If the buyer (or the artist's dealer) resists, it is hard for the artist to insist.

An additional problem grows out of the fact that works of art change hands. Even if the first owner expressly agrees to respect the work, there is no way of securely binding his successors. The notion of a servitude of the sort attached to land by private agreement depends for its effectiveness on notice to subsequent takers; a purchaser without notice of the restriction takes free of it. Such a system of servitude works reasonably well for land both because of the system of public records

Hastings Law Journal, vol. 27, no. 5 (May 1976), pp. 1023–1028. Copyright © 1976 by the Hastings College of the Law. Reprinted by permission.

(and the notion of "record notice") and because of the apparentness of many kinds of servitudes to one who physically inspects the land. But there is no equivalent system of public records of transactions affecting paintings, drawings, and sculpture. And most works of art would be unacceptably defaced by any attempt to attach notice of restrictions to them in some permanent and indelible, and at the same time reasonably apparent, way.

Despite this difficulty, agreements protecting against the destruction, alteration, or inappropriate use of works of art were at one time widely circulated. The first of these was the "Artists Reserved Rights Transfer and Sale Agreement," the "Projansky Contract." Others included a milder sequel proposed by Charles Jurrist, and the contract used and advocated by artist Ed Kienholz. These contracts are reproduced in John Henry Merryman and Albert E. Elsen, *Law, Ethics and the Visual Arts* (New York: Matthew Bender, 1979), pp. 4-143ff. They are not in wide use today.

There was a flurry of excitement about the case of *Gilliam v. American Broadcasting Company,* 538 F.2d 14 (2d Cir. 1976). There the defendant was sued to enjoin further broadcasts of tapes of *Monty Python's Flying Circus* that the defendant had "edited" (i.e., cut in order to provide more time for advertisements) without Monty Python's knowledge or consent. The plaintiff alleged that the resulting tapes "truncated" and "garbled" the originals. The court held for the plaintiff on two grounds. First, the editing exceeded the terms of license granted by the copyright owner, and thus was an infringement of copyright. (The basis for and implications of the notion that a copyrighted work "is infringed when something is deleted from it" are explored in Stephen R. Barnett, "From New Technology to Moral Rights: Passive Carriers, Teletest, and Deletion as Copyright Infringement—The WGN Case," *Journal of the Copyright Society,* vol. 31 [1984], pp. 427ff. Second—and this is what caused the excitement—Section 43(a) of the Lanham Act (15 V.S.C. 1125(a)) provided that

> Any person who shall affix, apply, or annex, or use in connection with any goods or services, . . . a false designation of origin, or any false description or representation . . . and shall cause such goods to enter into commerce . . . shall be liable to a civil action by any person . . . who believes that he is or is likely to be damaged. . . .

The majority opinion by Judge Lumbard held that "the mutilation of Monty Python's work" was actionable under this statute, and mentioned the moral right several times in passing. The separate concurring opinion of Judge Gurfein rested on the first ground, finding "no need" to discuss possible relief under the Lanham Act. The case is discussed in "The Monty Python Litigation: Of Moral Right and the Lanham Act," *University of Pennsylvania Law Review,* vol. 125 (1977), p. 611; and in J. T. McCarty, *Trademarks and Unfair Competition* vol. 2, 2d ed. (Rochester, N.Y.: Lawyers Cooperative Pub. Co., 1984), pp. 374ff. The authors know of no case in which the Lanham Act has been used to provide a moral right type of protection to a work of visual art. However, *Visual Artists and Galleries Association v. Various John Does,* 80 Civ. 4487 (S.D.N.Y. 1980), discussed in Tim Jensen, "The Selling of Picasso: A Look at the Artist's Rights in Protecting the Reputation of His Name," *Art & the Law,* vol. 6 (1981), p. 77 comes close. There Picasso's signature appeared on T-shirts without authorization of the artist's heir, and an action was brought to enjoin the manufacture, distribution, or sale under Section 43(a) of the Lanham Act. As Jensen points out, the purpose of the action was not to protect the artist's reputation but to protect the economic value of Picasso's signature as a trademark.

LEGISLATIVE APPROACHES

Federal bills dealing specifically with rights of integrity and paternity, which would have taken the form of amendments to the Copyright Act, have been proposed: H.R. 2908, 97th

Cong., 1st Sess., 127 Cong. Rec. H217 (daily ed. March 30, 1981), introduced by Congressman Frank of Massachusetts; and H.R. 288, 95th Cong., 2d Sess., 125 Cong. Rec. 164 (1979), introduced by Congressman Drinan of Massachusetts. Both bills died in the Judiciary Committee. Texas also attempted moral-right legislation, which failed in 1981 (see H.B. 2101).

In 1979 California broke the ice and enacted the Art Preservation Act (Cal. Civ. Code §987) and in 1982 added the Cultural and Artistic Creations Preservation Act (Cal. Civ. Code §989). New York followed in 1983 with the Artists' Authorship Rights Act, and in 1985 Massachusetts adopted a modified version of the California law (Mass. Ann. Laws, ch. 231, §85S; and ch. 260, §2C). All these statutes are set out below.

There are two distinct approaches to the moral right issue in this legislation. The New York statute seeks to secure the protection of the *artist's reputation* by isolating and emphasizing the right of attribution, the issue being whether the artist's good name has been harmed. The work of art itself is not protected from alteration unless damage to the artist's reputation is "reasonably likely" (Section 228(n)). The California statute, as its title indicates, directly prohibits the alteration of art (see Section 1(c)(1)). Its preamble states that the act serves the dual purpose of protecting the artist's reputation and of protecting the *public interest* in preserving the integrity of cultural and artistic creations. The idea that the public has an interest in art is not novel. Both the French and Italian moral right laws contemplate enforcement by public officials. The California law is simply more explicit in its public purpose, which was advanced in 1982 by the enactment of Section 979 of the Civil Code, which permits an art-promoting organization to intervene to preserve or restore the integrity of works of art. The Massachusetts statute follows the California pattern.

Substantive differences in the laws result from these distinct approaches. For example, the New York statute applies only to works on "public display," on the assumption that an artist's reputation cannot be harmed by actions that occur in private. By contrast, the California law applies to any work of fine art, whether it is in the public eye or not. Yet it must be of "recognized quality," and the statute specifically directs that the fact finder hear expert testimony to determine whether the threshold quality criterion has been met. The provision seems to be in line with the goal of the California law to protect works that are of agreed-on cultural significance and therefore presumably important to the public. The New York statute does not protect against the total destruction of a work, the rationale being that a work that has ceased to exist cannot prejudice the honor or reputation of an artist.

The California Art Preservation Act (1979)
Cal. Civ. Code §987

§987 (a) The Legislature hereby finds and declares that the physical alteration or destruction of fine art, which is an expression of the artist's personality, is detrimental to the artist's reputation, and artists therefore have an interest in protecting their works of fine art against such alteration or destruction; and that there is also a public interest in preserving the integrity of cultural and artistic creations.

(b) As used in this section:

(1) "Artist" means the individual or individuals who create a work of fine art.

(2) "Fine art" means an original painting, sculpture, or drawing, or an original work of art in glass, of recognized quality, but shall not include work prepared under contract for commercial use by its purchaser.

(3) "Person" means an individual, partnership, corporation, association or other group, however organized.

(4) "Frame" means to prepare, or cause to be prepared, a work of fine art for display in a manner customarily considered to be appropriate for a work of fine art in the particular medium.

(5) "Restore" means to return, or cause to be returned, a deteriorated or damaged work of fine art as nearly as is feasible to its original state or condition, in accordance with prevailing standards.

(6) "Conserve" means to preserve, or cause to be preserved, a work of fine art by retarding or preventing deterioration or damage through appropriate treatment in accordance with prevailing standards in order to maintain the structural integrity to the fullest extent possible in an unchanging state.

(7) "Commercial use" means fine art created under a work-for-hire arrangement for use in advertising, magazines, newspapers, or other print and electronic media.

(c) (1) No person, except an artist who owns and possesses a work of fine art which the artist has created, shall intentionally commit, or authorize the intentional commission of, any physical defacement, mutilation, alteration, or destruction of a work of fine art.

(2) In addition to the prohibitions contained in paragraph (1), no person who frames, conserves, or restores a work of fine art shall commit, or authorize the commission of, any physical defacement, mutilation, alteration, or destruction of a work of fine art by any act constituting gross negligence. For purposes of this section, the term "gross negligence" shall mean the exercise of so slight a degree of care as to justify the belief that there was an indifference to the particular work of fine art.

(d) The artist shall retain at all times the right to claim authorship, or, for just and valid reason, to disclaim authorship of his or her work of fine art.

(e) To effectuate the rights created by this section, the artist may commence an action to recover or obtain any of the following:

(1) Injunctive relief.

(2) Actual damages.

(3) Punitive damages. In the event that punitive damages are awarded, the court shall, in its discretion, select an organization or organizations engaged in charitable or educational activities involving the fine arts in California to receive such damages.

(4) Reasonable attorneys' and expert witness fees.

(5) Any other relief which the court deems proper.

(f) In determining whether a work of fine art is of recognized quality, the trier of fact shall rely on the opinions of artists, art dealers, collectors of fine art, curators of art museums, and other persons involved with the creation or marketing of fine art.

(g) The rights and duties created under this section:

(1) Shall, with respect to the artist, or if any artist is deceased, his heir, legatee, or personal representative, exist until the 50th anniversary of the death of such artist.

(2) Shall exist in addition to any other rights and duties which may now or in the future be applicable.

(3) Except as provided in paragraph (1) of subdivision (h), may not be waived except by an instrument in writing expressly so providing which is signed by the artist.

(h)(1) If a work of fine art cannot be removed from a building without substantial physical defacement, mutilation, alteration, or destruction of such work, the rights and duties created under this section, unless expressly reserved by an instrument in writing signed by the owner of such building and properly recorded, shall be deemed waived. Such instrument, if properly recorded, shall be binding on subsequent owners of such building.

(2) If the owner of a building wishes to remove a work of fine art which is a part of such building but which can be removed from the building without substantial harm to such fine art, and in the course of or after removal, the owner intends to cause or allow the fine art to suffer physical defacement, mutilation, alteration, or destruction, the rights and duties created under this section shall apply unless the owner has diligently attempted without success to notify the artist, or, if the artist is deceased, his heir, legatee, or personal representative, in writing of his intended action affecting the work of fine art, or unless he did provide notice and that person failed within 90 days either to remove the work or to pay for its removal. If such work is removed at the expense of the artist, his heir, legatee, or personal representative, title to such fine art shall pass to that person.

(3) Nothing in this subdivision shall affect the rights of authorship created in subdivision (d) of this section.

(i) No action may be maintained to enforce any liability under this section unless brought within three years of the act complained of or one year after discovery of such act, whichever is longer.

(j) This section shall become operative on January 1, 1980, and shall apply to claims based on proscribed acts occurring on or after that date to works of fine art whenever created.

(k) If any provision of this section or the application thereof to any person or circumstance is held invalid for any reason, such invalidity shall not affect any other provisions or applications of this section which can be effected without the invalid provision or application, and to this end the provisions of this section are severable. . . .

Cultural and Artistic Creations Preservation Act (1982)
Cal. Civ. Code §989

§989 (a) The Legislature hereby finds and declares that there is a public interest in preserving the integrity of cultural and artistic creations.

(b) As used in this section:

(1) "Fine art" means an original painting, sculpture, or drawing, or an original work of art in glass, of recognized quality, and of substantial public interest.

(2) "Organization" means a public or private not-for-profit entity or association, in existence at least three years at the time an action is filed pursuant to this section, a major purpose of which is to stage, display, or otherwise present works of art to the public or to promote the interests of the arts or artists.

(3) "Cost of removal" includes reasonable costs, if any, for the repair of damage to the real property caused by the removal of the work of fine art.

(c) An organization acting in the public interest may commence an action for injunctive relief to preserve or restore the integrity of a work of fine art from acts prohibited by subdivision (c) of Section 987.

(d) In determining whether a work of fine art is of recognized quality and of substantial public interest the trier of fact shall rely on the opinions of those described in subdivision (f) of Section 987.

(e)(1) If a work of fine art cannot be removed from real property without substantial physical defacement, mutilation, alteration, or destruction of such work, no action to preserve the integrity of the work of fine art may be brought under this section. However, if an organization offers some evidence giving rise to a reasonable likelihood that a work of art can be removed from the real property without substantial physical defacement, mutilation, alteration, or destruction of the work, and is prepared to pay the cost of removal of the work, it may bring a legal action for a determination of this issue. In that action the organization shall be entitled to injunctive relief to preserve the integrity of the work of fine art, but shall also have the burden of proof. The action shall commence within 30 days after filing. No action may be brought under this paragraph if the organization's interest in preserving the work of art is in conflict with an instrument described in paragraph (1) of subdivision (h) of Section 987.

(2) If the owner of the real property wishes to remove a work of fine art which is part of the real property, but which can be removed from the real property without substantial harm to such fine art, and in the course of or after removal, the owner intends to cause or allow the fine art to suffer physical defacement, mutilation, alteration, or destruction the owner shall do the following:

(A) If the artist or artist's heir, legatee, or personal representative fails to take action to remove the work of fine art after the notice provided by paragraph (2) of subdivision (h) of Section 987, the owner shall provide 30 days' notice of his or her intended action affecting the work of art. The written notice shall be a display advertisement in a newspaper of general circulation in the area where the fine art is located. The notice required by this paragraph may run concurrently with the notice required by subdivision (h) of Section 987.

(i) If within the 30-day period an organization agrees to remove the work of fine art and pay the cost of removal of the work, the payment and removal shall occur within 90 days of the first day of the 30-day notice.

(ii) If the work is removed at the expense of an organization, title to the fine art shall pass to that organization.

(B) If an organization does not agree to remove the work of fine art within the 30-day period or fails to remove and pay the cost of removal of the work of fine art within the 90-day period the owner may take the intended action affecting the work of fine art.

(f) To effectuate the rights created by this section, the court may do the following:

(1) Award reasonable attorney's and expert

witness fees to the prevailing party, in an amount as determined by the court.

(2) Require the organization to post a bond in a reasonable amount as determined by the court.

(g) No action may be maintained under this section unless brought within three years of the act complained of or one year after discovery of such act, whichever is longer.

(h) This section shall become operative on January 1, 1983, and shall apply to claims based on acts occurring on or after that date to works of fine art, whenever created.

(i) If any provision of this section or the application thereof to any person or circumstances is held invalid, such invalidity shall not affect other provisions or applications of this section which can be given effect without the invalid provision or application, and to this end the provisions of this section are severable. . . .

The Artists' Authorship Rights Act
New York Arts and Cultural Affairs Law 14.51 – 14.59 (1983)

SECTION 14.51: DEFINITIONS

Whenever used in this article, except where the context clearly requires otherwise, the terms listed below shall have the following meanings:

1. "Artist" means the creator of a work of fine art;

2. "Conservation" means acts taken to correct deterioration and alteration and acts taken to prevent, stop or retard deterioration;

3. "Person" means an individual, partnership, corporation, association or other group, however organized;

4. "Reproduction" means a copy, in any medium, of a work of fine art, that is displayed or published under circumstances that, reasonably construed, evinces an intent that it be taken as a representation of a work of fine art as created by the artist;

5. "Work of fine art" means any original work of visual or graphic art of any medium which includes, but is not limited to, the following: painting; drawing; print; photographic print or sculpture of a limited edition of no more than three hundred copies; provided however, that "work of fine art" shall not include sequential imagery such as that in motion pictures.

. . . .

SECTION 14.53: PUBLIC DISPLAY,
PUBLICATION, AND REPRODUCTION OF
WORKS OF FINE ART

Except as limited by section 14.57 of this article, no person other than the artist or a person acting with the artist's consent shall knowingly display in a place accessible to the public or publish a work of fine art of that artist or a reproduction thereof in an altered, defaced, mutilated or modified form if the work is displayed, published or reproduced as being the work of the artist, or under circumstances under which it would reasonably be regarded as being the work of the artist, and damage to the artist's reputation is reasonably likely to result therefrom. . . .

. . . .

SECTION 14.55: ARTISTS'
AUTHORSHIP RIGHTS

1. Except as limited by section 14.57 of this article, the artist shall retain at all times the right to claim authorship, or, for just and valid reason, to disclaim authorship of his or her work of fine art. The right to claim authorship shall include the right of the artist to have his or her name appear on or in connection with the work of fine art as the artist. The right to disclaim authorship shall include the right of the artist to prevent his or her name from appearing on or in connection with the work of fine art as the artist. Just and valid reason for disclaiming authorship shall include that the work of fine art has been altered, defaced, mutilated or modified other than by the artist, without the artist's consent, and damage to the artist's reputation is reasonably likely to result or has resulted therefrom.

2. The rights created by this section shall exist in addition to any other rights and duties which may now or in the future be applicable.

. . . .

SECTION 14.57: LIMITATIONS
OF APPLICABILITY

1. Alteration, defacement, mutilation or modification of a work of fine art resulting from the

passage of time or the inherent nature of the materials will not by itself create a violation of section 14.53 of this article or a right to disclaim authorship under subdivision one of section 14.55 of this article; provided such alteration, defacement, mutilation or modification was not the result of gross negligence in maintaining or protecting the work of fine art.

2. In the case of a reproduction, a change that is an ordinary result of the medium of reproduction does not by itself create a violation of section 14.53 of this article or a right to disclaim authorship under subdivision one of section 14.55 of this article.

3. Conservation shall not constitute an alteration, defacement, mutilation or modification within the meaning of this article, unless the conservation work can be shown to be negligent.

4. This article shall not apply to work prepared under contract for advertising or trade use unless the contract so provides.

5. The provisions of this article shall apply only to works of fine art knowingly displayed in a place accessible to the public, published or reproduced in this state. . . .

. . . .

SECTION 14.59: RELIEF

1. An artist aggrieved under section 14.53 or section 14.55 of this article shall have a cause of action for legal and injunctive relief.

2. No action may be maintained to enforce any liability under this article unless brought within three years of the act complained of or one year after the constructive discovery of such act, whichever is longer. . . .

The Massachusetts Law (1985)
Mass. Ann. Laws ch. 231, §85S; ch. 260 §2C

Chapter 231

§85S. FINE ART; PHYSICAL ALTERATION OR DESTRUCTION; RIGHTS OF ARTISTS; COMMENCEMENT OF ACTIONS; REMOVAL FROM BUILDINGS

(a) The general court hereby finds and declares that the physical alteration or destruction of fine art, which is an expression of the artist's personality, is detrimental to the artist's reputation, and artists therefore have an interest in protecting their works of fine art against such alteration or destruction; and that there is also a public interest in preserving the integrity of cultural and artistic creations.

(b) As used in this section, the following words shall, unless the context clearly requires otherwise, have the following meanings:—

"Artist," the natural person who actually creates a work of fine art but not to include such art as is created by an employee within the scope of his employment. In case of a joint creation of a work of art, each joint creator shall have the rights of an artist with respect to the work of fine art as a whole.

"Fine art," any original work of visual or graphic art of any media which shall include, but not be limited to, any painting, print, drawing, sculpture, craft object, photograph, audio or video tape, film, hologram, or any combination thereof, of recognized quality.

"Gross negligence," the exercise of so slight a degree of care as to justify the belief that there was an indifference to the particular work of fine art.

"Public view" means on the exterior of a public owned building, or in an interior area of a public building.

(c) No person, except an artist who owns or possesses a work of fine art which the artist has created, shall intentionally commit, or authorize the intentional commission of any physical defacement, mutilation, alteration or destruction of a work of fine art. As used in this section, intentional physical defacement, mutilation, alteration, or destruction includes any such action taken deliberately or through gross negligence.

(d) The artist shall retain the right to claim and receive credit under his own name or under a reasonable pseudonym or, for just and valid reason to disclaim authorship of his work of fine art. Credit shall be determined in accord with the medium of expression and the nature and extent of the artist's contribution to the work of fine art.

(e) The artist or any bona fide union or other artists' organization authorized in writing by the artist for such purpose may commence an action in the superior court department of the trial court of the commonwealth without having as prerequisites to a suit any need for: (1) damages already incurred, (2) a showing of special damages, if any, or (3) general damages in any monetary amount to recover or obtain any of the following (i) injunctive relief or declaratory relief, (ii) actual damages, (iii) reasonable attorneys' and expert witness fees and all other costs of the action, or (iv) any other relief which the court deems proper.

(f) In determining whether a work of fine art is of recognized quality the court shall rely on the opinions of artists, art dealers, collectors of fine art, curators of art museums, restorers and conservators of fine art and other persons involved with the creation or marketing of fine art.

(g) The provisions of this section shall, with respect to the artist, or if any artist is deceased, his heir, legatee, or personal representative, continue until the fiftieth anniversary of the death of such artist, continue in addition to any other rights and duties which may now or in the future be applicable, and except as provided in paragraph (1) of subdivision (h) may not be waived except by an instrument in writing expressly so providing which is signed by the artist and refers to specific works with identification and such waiver shall only apply to work so identified.

The attorney general may, if the artist is deceased, assert the rights of the artist on the artist's behalf and commence an action for injunctive relief with respect to any work of art which is in public view.

(h)(1) If a work of fine art cannot be removed from a building without substantial physical defacement, mutilation, alteration, or destruction of such work, the rights and duties created under this section, unless expressly reserved by an instrument in writing signed by the owner of such building and properly recorded, prior to the installation of such art shall be deemed waived. Such instrument, if recorded, shall be binding on subsequent owners of such building.

(2) If the owner of a building wishes to remove a work of fine art which is a part of such building but which can be removed from the building without substantial harm to such fine art, the rights and duties created under this section shall apply unless the owner has diligently attempted without success to notify the artist, or, if the artist is deceased, his heir, legatee, or personal representative, in writing of his intended action affecting the work of fine art, or unless he did provide notice and that person failed within ninety days either to remove the work or to pay for its removal. If such work is removed at the expense of the artist, his heir, legatee, or personal representative, title to such fine art shall be deemed to be in such person. . . .

Chapter 260

§2C. FINE ART; ALTERATION OR DESTRUCTION; LIMITATION OF TWO YEARS AFTER CAUSE OF ACTION ACCRUES OR ONE YEAR AFTER DISCOVERY OF ACT

Actions commenced under the provisions of section eighty-five S of chapter two hundred and thirty-one shall be commenced only within two years next after the cause of action accrues, or within one year next after the discovery of the act, whichever is later. . . .

COMMENTS

1. There is no reported litigation under the California legislation, but one case has received journalistic publicity. It has to do with San Diego artist Viki Cole and her multimedia collage entitled "When It Comes to Small Change, Baby . . . the Buck Stops Here." The work, which was described by Cole's attorney as a "cynical commentary on personal relationships, men, and money," consisted of fifty-four one-dollar bills sewn together and the phrases "As a Woman I Feel Bound to Tell You . . ." followed by "There Will Be Substantial Penalties for Early Withdrawal." It was originally purchased for $350 in a San Diego television station auction. The first purchaser then donated the piece to another benefit auction in San Diego, but this time it sold for $120. After each purchase, it should be noted, the buyers had asked Cole to buy back her own work. Cole declined these offers, but let the second buyer put the work up for sale in one of her shows, where it did not sell. The buyer went to the gallery and, without interference from its director, opened the painting by removing the nailed bars that held the encasing Plexiglas frame and cover in place, removed the rag paper, tore the canvas from its backing, and walked off with the fifty-four dollar bills.

These acts clearly violated the California law—unless it could be argued that the piece was not "fine art" of "recognized quality." On this point both purchasers had decided to give the piece away after attempting to get Cole to buy it back. Though valued at $800 in the first auction, it sold for $120 in the second, and the destructive act itself arguably amounted to an expression that to its owner the piece was not worth more than the fifty-four dollar bills. If monetary worth were an appropriate indicator of artistic merit, the artist might lose, but that is obviously not the measure of quality. An unusual defense raised by the purchaser was that the use of the dollar bills in the piece was a violation of federal currency laws because the bills were taken out of circulation.

Another interesting facet of the case was the question of damages and how much the artist could recover. It was argued that Cole could have mitigated damages by simply replacing the dollar bills, to which she responded that the bills were specially selected, partly for their serial numbers. (See Peter H. Karlen, "Art Destruction—The Viki Cole Case," *Artweek*, December 10, 1983, p. 3.) At this writing the case is unresolved.

2. The New York statute is involved in the case of *Newmann v. Delmar Realty Co.* (*New York Law Journal*, June 11, 1984, p. 1), in which artist Robert Newmann obtained a court order that would allow him to complete his mural pending the outcome of further litigation. Newmann's work is an experimental project in which he attempts to coax a variety of tones out of a brick wall by sandblasting it at fixed intervals. He claims to have searched Manhattan for six months looking for a wall suitable for the project. Finally, with the help of the Public Art Fund, a private nonprofit organization that aids the public display of art, he negotiated an agreement with the owner of the Palladium, Delmar Realty, and its tenant, Ron Delsener, a rock music promoter, in February 1982. The owner authorized the installation and wall treatment on the theater's rear wall, and also provided that if a new lease were negotiated he would use his best efforts to persuade the new tenant to agree to the project. Apparently the owner was unsuccessful, for a new tenant, the Muidalp Corporation, stopped the work in April 1983 despite Newmann's claim that he could complete the $6,200 project in a matter of days. Muidalp planned to paint the rear wall black and install a new entrance in it. (See "Manhattan Wall Spurs Test Case over Art," *New York Times*, March 3, 1984, p. 13.)

In his decision, Judge Wilke held that questions raised about the terms of the original agreement with Newmann, the lease with the Muidalp Corporation, and the effects of the latter on the former would require a trial in order to decide, among other things, whether Muidalp could legally efface Newmann's work. This would take time, and meanwhile Newmann's unfinished artwork, because it was unfinished, would fall within the terms of the new Artists' Authorship Rights Act. Accordingly, Judge Wilke enjoined Muidalp from altering or defacing the work and ordered it to permit Newmann to finish the work—if the artist choose to do so—recognizing that when the case was finally decided Muidalp might have the right to eradicate it.

In a later development in the Newmann case, the artist sought a contempt of court order against Muidalp for punching two holes in the wall near the artwork. Judge Wilke denied the motion. (See *ARTnewsletter*, November 27, 1984, p. 5.)

3. Opposition to moral right legislation in New York came from major museums, for instance, the Metropolitan Museum of Art and the Whitney Museum. One expressed concern was that the process of conservation and restoration of works of art, in which judgment is exercised and disagreements were frequent, could lead to litigation. In this connection, note the requirement that alteration be "intentional" under the California law, Section 987(c)(1), except in cases involving "framers, restorers, and conservators," who are liable for "gross negligence" (Section 987(c)(2)). Notice that the New York statute explicitly provides that "conservation shall not constitute alterations" (Section 14.57(3)), while the Massachusetts law makes no special provision for conservators, and subjects all potential defendants to liability for gross negligence as well as for deliberate acts.

4. The California laws do not protect works of art that are so integral to a building that they cannot be removed without "substantial physical defacement, mutilation, alteration, or destruction" (Section 987(h)(1)). It has been suggested that this actually helps artists, because developers will continue to commission works of art without fearing that substantial liability could arise if the building were renovated or demolished. Similarly, the strict "intentional" standard is claimed to help artists. Any lesser standard, it is argued, would be accompanied by a severe disincentive to the purchase of art because of the potential suits that could be brought based on mere negligence or accidental damage. (See Stephen Weil, "The Moral Right Comes to California," *ARTnews*, December 1979, p. 91.)

5. These statutes all apply only to actions occurring after enactment. However, the protected work of art may have been created before that time. How long before? Look closely at the California statutes, which appear to create two remedies—one in favor of the artist and

his successors, limited to the artist's life plus fifty years (Section 987(g)(1)), the other a public right in favor of "organizations" (Section 989(c)). Both remedies are expressly applicable to "works of fine art, whenever created" (Sections 987(j) and 989(h)). It seems clear that the rights of the artist expire fifty years after his death, so that no work more than about seventy-five to one hundred years old would be protected by *this* provision. But there appears to be no comparable limit on the public right under Section 989. Thus it would be possible for the Committee for Art at Stanford, which clearly qualifies as an "organization," to sue the de Young Museum for gross negligence in restoring an early Renaissance painting or a Teoti-huacan mural or in conserving a Greek pot, if the actions complained of occurred after January 1, 1983, and the action were brought within the time specified in Section 989(g). Thus the *organization's* or *public's* moral right is perpetual, as in France (where, however, the artist's right is also perpetual). This is consistent with the California concern for art preservation.

Although the language of the Massachusetts statute is less clear, a reasonable construction of Section 55(g) would produce the same result. The New York law, on the contrary, would appear to limit relief to the life of the artist, since only the artist may sue (Section 14.59).

6. The three state statutes apply only to conduct falling within their jurisdictions. This means, for example, that someone who acquires a painting by a California artist can freely take it to another state (other than Massachusetts or New York), alter it, and publicly display it there. Conversely, the artist need not be a Californian, and the work need not have been created in California, to be entitled to protection against acts performed in California (or New York or Massachusetts).

7. The most controversial aspect of the California statute is the provision limiting protection to "fine art" of "recognized quality" (Section 987(b)(2)). This provision and Section 987(f), directing the use of expert testimony on these questions, were inserted because of a concern expressed by members of the California legislature. They feared misuse and trivialization of the law to protect children's finger-paintings, the products of "art club" and "Sunday" artists, and so on. Stephen E. Weil, commenting on these provisions, states: "While this may invite the traditional battle of the experts, . . . the law cannot accord a special status to art without also providing some mechanism for tracing its boundaries" ("The 'Moral Right' Comes to California," *ARTnews,* December 1979, pp. 88, 90). For a critical view, see Peter H. Karlen, "Moral Rights in California," *San Diego Law Review,* vol. 19 (1982), pp. 675, 996ff.). Both the New York statute and the Massachusetts statute are much less restrictive, containing no "quality" provisions and expressly including photographs, prints, and multiples and, in Massachusetts, "craft objects."

8. To fall within the protections afforded by the California statute, the work in question must also be an "original" and cannot be work that was prepared "under contract for commercial use in advertising, magazines, newspapers or other print and electronic media" (Section 987(b)(7)). The New York statute (Section 14.57(4)) and the Massachusetts statute (Section 85S(b)) contain comparable "work for hire exceptions."

9. Notice that the California statute permits the artist to waive his rights by an instrument in writing (Section 987(g)(3)). French moral rights, by contrast, are "inalienable" (although under some circumstances they turn out to be alienable as the result of judicial decisions). This accords with legal biases in the United States in favor of freedom of contract and the marketability of resources. The lack of any protection against excessive criticism, which exists at least in theory in other nations, is also American. Constitutional protection of free speech and concern about a "chilling effect" on criticism would block any proposal for a right against excessive criticism.

10. The California and Massachusetts statutes protect only against *physical* defacement, and it would be reasonable to read the New York statute as similarly restricted, although the term "physical" does not appear in it. Consider the following examples of arguably offensive but remediless actions (and recall the attempt of Italian artist Georgio de Chirico to prevent an exhibition of his works because he did not like the selection, above, pp. 156–57).

    a. Suppose a painting or sculpture is used as background for a fashion photograph or a whiskey advertisement with the permission of the owner but without the artist's consent.

    b. A group of artists who called themselves the Los Angeles Fine Art Squad were hired by the owner to do an enormous mural covering the entire side of a building, which was then effectively blocked from view when the owner of the neighboring lot erected a large building on it.

c. In 1975 sculptor Carl Andre was invited to participate in the Whitney Museum's "200 Years of American Sculpture" show. He visited the museum to survey areas that might be suitable for his "Twelfth Copper Corner" and decided on a corner spot on the fourth floor of the museum, which he understood to be the agreed-on location. Two days before the opening of the show, Andre visited the museum and to his surprise discovered his work in a location that he found unpalatable. Instead of being set against plain walls, his copper piece was flanked by a trapezoidal window and a fire door, complete with a lighted "Exit" sign and a red alarm box. He wrote to the museum director and asked that the piece be put in the originally intended location or removed from the exhibition altogether. The following day the work was removed and replaced by a smaller Andre piece, "29th Copper Cardinal," which had been earlier acquired by the Whitney. Andre decided he did not want the museum exhibiting any of his works and offered to buy back "29th Copper Cardinal" at its original price plus 10 percent. The offer was not accepted. Andre then arranged an alternative exhibition of "Twelfth Copper Corner" and of a duplicate of "29th Copper Cardinal" (which was in his view the original, since he had disavowed authorship of the Whitney's work). Announcing the opening of the exhibition, Andre described his "Twelfth Copper Corner" as "rescued from mutilation at the Whitney Museum" and "29th Copper Cardinal" as "liberated from property bondage there." In addition, he purchased one hundred Whitney catalogs and stamped "Mutilated by Whitney Museum" on each catalog photo of "Twelfth Copper Corner."

11. The California and Massachusetts statutes, with their emphasis on preservation, both protect against destruction of the work of art (note that both clearly state that destruction is detrimental to the artist's reputation). The New York law, limited in intent to preventing harm to the artist's reputation, merely prohibits public display of any "altered, defaced, mutilated or modified" work. Compare the discussion of destruction in the notes on p. 176 above.

12. Although we have focused on the "right of integrity," all three statutes also create "rights of paternity" by giving the artist the right to claim or disclaim authorship. On this point the New York statute spells out the right of paternity in detail (Section 14.55), while the other two say it only in sketchy terms. In interpreting the California and Massachusetts statutes, courts will probably find the New York provision useful and persuasive.

13. A potentially troublesome problem with moral right legislation in the United States is determination of its proper locus in state or federal law. Under the federal copyright power, it is arguable that the matter is one for federal legislation, and the common tendency in treaties (e.g., the Berne Convention) and in legislation (e.g., France, Germany, and Italy) to include moral right provisions in comprehensive "author's rights" laws is consistent with that approach. If so, a federal moral right law would preempt the field, and state legislation would be nullified. This topic is explored in Roberta Rosenthal Kwal, "Copyright and the Moral Right: Is an American Marriage Possible?" *Vanderbilt Law Review,* vol. 38 (1985), p. 1.

APPLYING THE LAW

It is instructive to consider how the New York and California statutes would apply in the following case.

ROSALIND KRAUSS *Changing the Work of David Smith**

Among the sculptures that are still in the estate of the artist [David Smith], several have been deliberately stripped of paint—sandblasted, allowed to rust, then glossily varnished. Others have simply been left outdoors, unprotected over the years; their surfaces are flaking off under the pressures

---

*From Rosalind Krauss, "Changing the Work of David Smith," *Art in America,* vol. 30 (September–October 1974), p. 31. Copyright © 1974 by Art in America, Inc. Reprinted by permission.

of heat and cold, rain and sun. Given the identity of the executors of the Smith estate—Clement Greenberg, a well-known critic; Robert Motherwell, a well-known artist; and Ira Lowe, a Washington lawyer—all this becomes particularly disturbing. . . .

Whatever one feels—as art historian, critic or simply admirer of Smith's art—about this situation, it is eminently clear what Smith himself would have felt, for a dramatic example of unauthorized alteration of one of his painted sculptures occurred during his lifetime. Outraged, Smith wrote letters to *Art News* (Summer 1960) and *Arts* (June 1960) magazine. The *Art News* letter read:

Since my sculpture, *17 h's* (44¾ inches high), 1950, painted cadmium aluminum red, during the process of sale and resale, has suffered a willful act of vandalism. . . , I renounce it as my original work and brand it a ruin.

My name cannot be attributed to it, and I shall exercise my legal rights against anyone making this misrepresentation.

All persons involved in this act of vandalism will be, to the best of my ability, prohibited from acquiring any more of my work.

I declare its value to be only its weight of 60 lbs. of scrap steel.

The letter to *Arts* ran under the heading "A Protest Against Vandalism":

My sculpture *17 h's*, made in 1950, painted with six coats of cadmium aluminum red, has been partially destroyed by one or more persons involved in its sale and donation to a collection.

This willful work of vandalism causes me to deny this work and refuse any future sale to any of those connected with this vandalism.

I tried to repurchase this work but was refused. There seems to be little legal protection for an artist in our country against vandalism or even destruction. Lacking full proof, I cannot name the guilty participants; but I ask other artists to beware. Possibly we should start an action for protective laws. . . .

HILTON KRAMER *Questions Raised by Art Alterations**

At what point in the life of a work does a technical alteration constitute an artistic revision? Under what, if any, conditions is it permissible for the heirs or executors of an artist's estate—or anyone else, for that matter—to authorize posthumous alterations in the work? And how are such changes, once executed, to be regarded? Should a work of art that is altered after the artist's death still be considered a legitimate part of his oeuvre?

These are some of the questions that are being pondered by artists, critics, collectors, dealers, museum curators and others in the wake of a report that Clement Greenberg, the well-known art critic who is also an executor of the estate of David Smith, authorized changes in the visual appearance of certain Smith sculptures after the artist's death in 1965.

As reported in the *New York Times* yesterday, Mr. Greenberg acknowledged that he ordered the removal of white paint from a number of Smith's painted sculptures in the open air so that their

painted surfaces would be eroded by the natural effects of the weather.

Mr. Greenberg was responding to charges in the current issue of Art in America magazine that some "startling alterations" have occurred in certain Smith sculptures since his death.

One can safely say that, in principle at least, no serious art authority would endorse the idea of allowing anyone to impose either technical or artistic revisions on an artist's work after his death—or indeed, during his lifetime, without the artist's consent. Smith himself was clearly adamant on the subject. In the Art in America article that sparked the controversy—"Changing the Work of David Smith," by Prof. Rosalind Krauss of Hunter College—Smith is quoted as saying that he felt the removal of the painted surface from one of his earlier works resulted in its being "partially destroyed." He was referring to a 1960 episode in which unidentified parties had the red surface of a sculpture called "17h's" stripped after its purchase. . . .

*From Hilton Kramer, "Questions Raised by Art Alterations." *New York Times*, September 14, 1974. Copyright © 1974 by The New York Times Company. Reprinted by permission.

The stripping of a painted surface, either by sandblasting or natural erosion, represents the imposition of a critical judgment that significantly alters our experience of the work. That it may also represent a sincere "reading" of the artist's intentions does not lessen the magnitude of the revision.

There is no doubt, at least in my mind, that Mr. Greenberg sincerely believes that the removal of the painted surfaces from some of Smith's later works results in an improvement of their esthetic quality, and he is certainly not alone in that belief. But this belief is precisely that: a subjective judgment that has no warrant in the artistic practice that governed the artist's ambitions in his later years.

Much of Smith's work, which I am not alone in regarding as the greatest single oeuvre produced by an American sculptor, owes its distinctive character to . . . the use of direct, unembellished metal craft for expressive purposes. But Smith's was a complex mind, and among its complexities was a burning ambition to take constructed sculpture a step beyond . . . to join the syntax of constructed sculpture to the esthetics of color, and thus produce a sculpture in which both construction and color were given co-equal power.

The opinion among people who have studied the matter is that, although he produced some extraordinary work in the process, Smith never really succeeded in realizing his ambition. The fact that he was, in his later years, constantly painting, stripping, and repainting these works suggests that Smith himself was rarely satisfied with the results.

But it is one thing to feel that a high artistic aspiration has not been realized: it is quite another to implement, without the artist's consent, an alternative realization. This, in effect, is what Mr. Greenberg has done in authorizing the stripping of Smith's later sculpture. He has taken a body of work designed to be a part of Smith's color-sculpture, and transformed it into still another part of the Gonzales inheritance. He has thus revised not only certain works but the esthetic scenario of Smith's last period.

My own view is that the paint Smith applied to the surfaces of these works, whether it consists of a white primer or other colors, is, at the very least, a faithful expression of Smith's desire to create a sculpture that combined the resources of both color and construction. All evidence of that desire, which so consumed the artist in his later years, has been obliterated with the sandblasting or erosion of the painted surface. In a choice between Smith's partial realization of his ambition and Mr. Greenberg's radical revision of it, one naturally wants the artist's own version. Even an incomplete work is preferable to the revisions of an alien hand.

COMMENTS

1. It seems clear that deliberately stripping "17h's" and sandblasting works in the artist's estate violate their integrity, but what could Smith or his heirs, or a representative of the public, do about it?

2. In New York, during his life, Smith could have "prevent[ed] public display" of the stripped "17h's" "as his work or under circumstances under which it would reasonably be regarded as being his work," if he showed to the court's satisfaction that "damage to his reputation was likely to result" (Section 14.53). He would also, under Section 14.55, have the right to prevent "his name from appearing on or in connection with the work as its artist," if he showed "reasonable likelihood of damage to his reputation." He could also, under Section 14.55, disclaim authorship. Some obvious questions arise. For one, the statute obviously contemplates that some "altered, defaced, mutilated or modified" works can be publicly exhibited without damaging the artist's reputation. Was this meant merely to screen out trivial changes in the work (a nick in a sculpture, an unflattering frame on a drawing)? If something else is involved, what must the artist prove to show the likelihood of harm? Suppose the owner of "17h's" removes Smith's name from it. Can he now display it publicly without liability? What of Smith's right to claim authorship? Questions of this kind will be settled only through judicial interpretation and legislative amendment.

3. In any case, it seems clear that under the New York statute Smith's remedies died with him. His heirs would have no remedy either for the stripping of "17h's" or for the changes made in works in the estate by his executors.

4. Under the California statutes, Smith could compel restoration of "17h's" and get such

other relief as the court deemed proper, without proving public display or likelihood of harm to his reputation. That right would survive him. His successors could exercise it up to fifty years after his death, and a qualifying organization under Section 989 could compel restoration at any time. Both the artist's successors and a qualifying organization could correct the executor's actions. The Massachusetts statute provides comparable remedies.

5. If one considers the applicability of the three states' legislation to the "horrible examples" of abuse of publicly funded artwork (above, pp. 157–61), these striking differences in the type and duration of legal protection between the New York law and the California and Massachusetts statutes emerge even more clearly.

6. The stripped sculptures will probably bring higher prices when sold by the estate than they would have if the paint had not been removed. (One reason is the influence of Clement Greenberg, who as an influential critic constantly has denigrated the painted works and preferred the unpainted ones.) Suppose a beneficiary under Smith's will had demanded that the executors strip the painted sculptures in the estate so they would sell at a higher price. The law is that the executor must maximize the assets in the estate. It could be argued that an executor who refused to strip the sculptures out of regard for the artist's intentions and the integrity of his work would be liable to the heirs for the difference. If such a case should arise, the executor would be well advised to ask the court of probate jurisdiction for instructions. This passes the buck to the probate judge and absolves the executor from possible liability. But in a legal system that does not recognize a right of integrity, how should the judge rule?

SELECTED READINGS ON MORAL RIGHT

Because moral right fascinates American lawyers and law students a large literature, quite out of proportion to the amount of legislative and judicial activity on the topic, has grown up. In addition to the works already cited, the following selective list should satisfy the most voracious appetite for further reading.

Amarnik, P. "American Recognition of the Moral Right: Issues and Options," *Copyright Law Symposium,* vol. 29 (1983), p. 83.

"An Artist's Personal Rights in His Creative Works: Beyond the Human Cannonball and the Flying Circus," *Pacific Law Journal,* vol. 9 (1978), p. 855.

"Artworks and American Law: The California Art Preservation Act," *Boston Law Review,* vol. 51 (1981), p. 1201.

"The Author's Moral Right: Can Louisiana Adopt the Doctrine?" *Tulane Law Review,* vol. 51 (1977), p. 309.

Bostron, C. "The Moral Rights of Artists: Museums and the Law," *Museum News* (April 1984), p. 46.

"Copyright—Moral Right: A Proposal," *Fordham Law Review,* vol. 43 (1975), p. 793.

Damich, J. "The New York Artists' Authorship Rights Act: A Comparative Critique," *Columbia Law Review,* vol. 84 (1894), p. 1733.

DaSilva, R. "Droit Moral and the Amoral Copyright," *Bulletin of the Copyright Society,* vol. 28 (1980), p. 1.

Diamond, S. "Legal Protection for 'Moral Rights' of Artists and Other Creators," *Trademark Reporter,* vol. 68 (1978), p. 244.

Katz, A. "The Doctrine of Moral Right and American Copyright Law: A Proposal," *Southern California Law Review,* vol. 24 (1951), p. 375.

Maslow, J. "Moral Right and the Lanham Act," *George Washington Law Review,* vol. 48 (1979–1980), p. 377.

McDonough, B. "The California Art Preservation Act: Statutory Protection of Artwork Against International Alternation or Destruction," *University of Cinncinnati Law Review,* vol. 49 (1980), pp. 49–87.

McNabb, C. "Moral Right and the American Court," *Houston Law Review,* vol. 13 (1976), p. 781.

Petrovich, J. "Artists' Statutory Droit Moral in California: A Critical Appraisal," *Loyola of Los Angeles Law Review,* vol. 15 (1981), p. 29.

Stromholm, S. "Droit Moral: The International and Comparative Scene from a Scandinavian Viewpoint," *International Review of Industrial Property and Copyright Law,* vol. 14 (1983), p. 1.

On the moral right in Canada, see D. Vaver, "Authors' Moral Rights in Canada," *International Review of Industrial Property and Copyright Law,* vol. 14 (1983), p. 329.

COPYRIGHT

Copyright, unlike moral right, is a property right. It allows an artist (or one to whom he transfers the right) to prevent unauthorized copying, publishing, exhibition, or other use of his copyrighted work. In effect, the artist is given a monopoly over the use of his work for a limited period of time. The idea is that art is worth promoting and that the best way to promote it is to guarantee the prospective creator, for a limited time, the exclusive opportunity to benefit from his own work.

COPYRIGHT PROTECTION IN THE UNITED STATES

Before January 1, 1978, copyright protection in the United States was administered under two different systems: common-law copyright, in the states, and statutory copyright (the 1909 act), in federal law. The newest version of the federal Copyright Act (the 1976 act) went into effect on January 1, 1978, but the 1909 act is still important: works created before January 1, 1978, continue to be governed by the 1909 act, and the new act was written with the older one in mind. Therefore, the older act will be useful in understanding the operation of the new one, especially in the early years, when it has not yet been widely tested in court.

The source of copyright in the United States is the Constitution, Article I, Section 8, Clause 8: "Congress shall have the power to promote the progress of science and the useful arts, by securing for a limited time to authors and inventors the exclusive right to their respective writings and discoveries." Some doubt may linger about the constitutional basis for federal statutes giving copyright protection to the fine arts, but as a practical matter the question is settled. Dicta in a number of judicial decisions interpret the constitutional language to extend to the fine arts (e.g., *Bleistein v. Donaldson Lithographing Co.*, 188 U.S. 239 (1903)). The Supreme Court in *Goldstein v. California*, 412 U.S. 546, 561 (1983), specifically stated that "writings" include "any physical rendering of the fruits of creative, intellectual or aesthetic labor." Moreover, Congress has acted as though it believes it has the constitutional power in enacting legislation specifically applicable to copyright of the fine arts (e.g., Act of May 31, 1970, ch. 15, 1 Stat. 124). The current Copyright Act expressly includes protection of the fine arts. In short, the question is more hypothetical than real.

As the passage from the Constitution suggests, there are limitations to the monopoly in copyrighted works. The concern is that too powerful a monopoly in one work of art will discourage other closely related creations. The current Copyright Act provides for a number of important limitations, including the following:

1. The duration of the copyright is set at life of the artist plus fifty years.
2. A work of art is entitled to copyright at all only if it is "original."
3. The copyright in a work of art extends only to the "expression" of an idea, not the idea itself.
4. The work must be fixed in a "tangible medium of expression."

Anything outside these limitations is considered to be in the "public domain," that is, freely available to anyone. A work of art, otherwise copyrightable, will enter the public domain if the artist fails to comply with the copyright laws.

The 1976 Copyright Act purports to eliminate the previous dual system by absorbing the state common-law copyright into the federal statutory copyright. Thus, the statutory copyright now attaches automatically to a work of art from the moment of creation in a tangible form, regardless of whether the work has been published.

Consider three situations: (1) artist has made and has not published a painting without copyright notice on it; (2) artist has made and published a painting without copyright notice on it; (3) artist has made and published a painting with copyright notice on it. Many of the operational effects under the 1901 and 1976 copyright acts are the same in Case 1. The artist is protected. Before the 1976 act the protection was by "common-law copyright" under state law. Since 1978 the artist is protected under federal law. The common-law copyright was perpetual, and the statutory copyright terminates fifty years after the artist's death, so he was in this sense better off prior to 1978, as far as unpublished work was concerned.

For Case 2, the effects under the two laws are quite different. Publication terminated the common-law right under state law, and publication without notice destroyed the federal right under the 1901 law. Hence, the painting "fell into the public domain." Under the 1976 act, the artist has five years in which to correct the omission of copyright notice and is protected against all but those who in good faith are misled by the absence of notice on the published painting.

Case 3 is easy. The artist is protected under the respective copyright acts.

Registration is not necessary to acquire and retain copyright protection. All the artist need do is place (1) the copyright symbol © or the word "copyright" or the abbreviation "copr.," *plus* (2) the date, *plus* (3) his or her name on the work. Those three elements constitute "notice of copyright," and a work published with notice is fully protected. It is not necessary to "register," to file any papers, or to pay any fees. There are, however, definite advantages to registration. Statutory damages and attorneys' fees may be recovered from the infringer only by someone who registered before the infringement, although the ordinary remedies of injunction, compensatory damages, and so on would still be available. In any case, registration is always a prerequisite to suit.

"Publication" is a peculiar concept as applied to works of art and is discussed further infra. In practice, however, the artist should assume that when the work leaves the studio on loan, on consignment for sale, or is sold, publication takes place and the notice of copyright should be on it.

The copyright and the work of art are separate and may be separately owned. At the beginning, of course, the artist who creates the work (unless it is a "work for hire," discussed infra) owns both the work and the copyright. If the artist transfers the work—say, by selling it to a collector or a museum—he does *not* sell the copyright with it *unless the artist agrees in writing, signed, to do so.* (Under state common-law copyright the opposite presumption prevailed. *Pushman v. New York Graphic Society,* 25 N.Y.S.2d 32 [1941], held that the unconditional sale of a painting included the transfer of the copyright in that painting unless the reproduction rights were specifically reserved. This decision was criticized by Saul Cohen in "An Artist Sells a Painting: The Courts Go Astray," *UCLA Law Review,* vol. 5 [1957], p. 235. In 1966, New York enacted Article 12E of the General Business Law for the express purpose of overruling *Pushman.* California enacted a similar statute in 1975 [Civil Code §982]. The 1976 Copyright Act superseded all that.) In the normal case the artist thus retains the copyright when he transfers the work of art. Conversely, the artist can sell the copyright and keep the work of art, or the artist can transfer them to different people.

Why should the artist copyright the work? For two important reasons. First, if there is exploitation value in it (e.g., reproductions—think of the zillions of reproductions in all media of Robert Indiana's "L O V E") the artist who copyrights and retains the copyright on sale of the work owns the reproduction rights and can sell or license them on a royalty or fixed-sum basis. Robert Indiana did not get a cent, and art people sometimes say he was ripped off. Well, not really. All he had to do was put a copyright notice on the painting. Second, if the work is copyrighted the artist can prevent the preparation and distribution of inadequate reproductions, use of the image in inappropriate ways (e.g., as background for advertising; reproduction in connection with an ideologically offensive text), and so on. The artist who fails to copyright has given up both.

Articles and books that discuss the 1976 Copyright Act as it relates to artists include "Courting the Artist with Copyright: The 1976 Copyright Act," *Wayne Law Review,* vol. 24 (1978), p. 1685; A. Katz, "Copyright Preemption Under the Copyright Act of 1976," *George Washington Law Review,* vol. 4 (1978), p. 200; R. E. Duffy, *Art Law: Representing Artists, Dealers, and Collectors* (New York: Practicing Law Institute, 1977); Sandison, "Copyright Revision Bill's Impact on the Visual Artist," *Art & the Law,* vol. 2, no. 6 (September–October 1976), pp. 1–4; L. E. Duboff, *The Desk Book of Art Law* (Washington D.C.: Federal Publication, 1977); T. Crawford, *Legal Guide for the Visual Artist* (New York: Hawthorn Books, 1977); S. Weissman, "Can an Artist's Copyright Be Jeopardized?" *Art & the Law,* vol. 6 (1981), p. 66; T. Crawford, *The Visual Artists Guide to the New Copyright Law* (New York: Graphic Artists Guild, 1978). The leading treatise on copyright law is M. Nimmer, *Nimmer on Copyright* (New York: Matthew Bender, 1980).

WHAT CAN BE COPYRIGHTED

The new law hardly improved on the old in establishing the boundaries of what is copyrightable. It does not define originality and creativity or what constitutes a copy or reproduction, it does not say whether short-lived but tangible works are protected, and it does not state what protection is afforded functional works that are arguably also artistic—from lamps to architecture. The following materials help fill the gap.

THE KIESELSTEIN-CORD CASE: UTILITARIAN ARTICLES

Kieselstein-Cord v. Accessories by Pearl
632 F.2d 989 (2d Cir. 1980)

OAKES, Circuit Judge.

This case is on a razor's edge of copyright law. It involves belt buckles, utilitarian objects which as such are not copyrightable. But these are not ordinary buckles; they are sculptured designs cast in precious metals—decorative in nature and used as jewelry is, principally for ornamentation. We say "on a razor's edge" because the case requires us to draw a fine line under applicable copyright law and regulations. Drawing the line in favor of the appellant designer, we uphold the copyrights granted to him by the Copyright Office and reverse the district court's grant of summary judgment, 489 F.Supp. 732, in favor of the appellee, the copier of appellant's designs.

FACTS

Appellant Barry Kieselstein-Cord designs, manufactures exclusively by handcraftsmanship, and sells fashion accessories. To produce the two buckles in issue here, the "Winchester" and the "Vaquero," he worked from original renderings which he had conceived and sketched. He then carved by hand a waxen prototype of each of the works from which molds were made for casting the objects in gold and silver. Difficult to describe, the buckles are solid sculptured designs, in the words of district court Judge Goettel, "with rounded corners, a sculpted surface, . . . a rectangular cut-out at one end for the belt attachment," and "several surface levels." The Vaquero gives the appearance of two curved grooves running diagonally across one corner of a modified rectangle and a third groove running across the opposite corner. On the Winchester buckle two parallel grooves cut horizontally across the center of a more tapered form, making a curving ridge which is completed by the tongue of the buckle. A smaller single curved groove flows diagonally across the corner above the tongue.

The Vaquero buckle, created in 1978, was part of a series of works that the designer testified was inspired by a book on design of the art nouveau school and the subsequent viewing of related architecture on a trip to Spain. The buckle was registered with the Copyright Office by appellant's counsel on March 3, 1980, with a publication date of June 1, 1978, as "jewelry," although the appellant's contribution was listed on the certificate as "original sculpture and design." Explaining why he named the earlier buckle design "Winchester," the designer said that he saw "in [his] mind's eye a correlation between the art nouveau period and the butt of an antique Winchester rifle" and then "pulled these elements together graphically." The registration, which is recorded on a form used for works of art, or models or designs for works of art, specifically describes the nature of the work as "sculpture."

The Winchester buckle in particular has had great success in the marketplace: more than 4,000 belts with Winchester buckles were sold from 1976 to early 1980, and in 1979 sales of the belts amounted to 95% of appellant's more than $300,000 in jewelry sales. A small women's size in silver with "double truncated triangle belt loops" sold, at the time this lawsuit commenced, at wholesale for $147.50 and a larger silver version for men sold at wholesale with loops for $662 and without loops for $465. Lighter weight men's versions in silver wholesaled for $450 and $295, with and without loops respectively. The gold versions sold at wholesale from $1,200 to $6,000. A shortened version of the belt with the small Winchester buckle is sometimes worn around the neck or elsewhere on the body rather than around the waist. Sales of both buckles were made primarily in high fashion stores and jewelry stores, bringing recognition to appellant as a "designer." This recognition included a 1979 Coty American Fashion Critics' Award for his work in jewelry design as well as election in 1978 to the Council of Fashion Designers of America. Both the Winchester and the Vaquero buckles, donated by appellant after this lawsuit was commenced, have been accepted by the Metropolitan Museum of Art for its permanent collection.

As the court below found, appellee's buckles "appear to be line-for-line copies but are made of common metal rather than" precious metal. Appellee admitted to copying the Vaquero and selling its imitations, and to selling copies of the Winchester. Indeed some of the order blanks of appellee's customers specifically referred to "Barry K Copy," "BK copy," and even "Barry Kieselstein Knock-off." Thus the only legal questions for the court below were whether the articles may be protected under the copyright statutes. . . .

DISCUSSION

We commence our discussion by noting that no claim has been made that the appellant's work here in question lacks originality or creativity, elements necessary for copyrighting works of art. . . .

The thrust of appellee's argument, as well as of the court's decision below, is that appellant's buckles are not copyrightable because they are "useful articles" with no "pictorial, graphic, or sculptural features that can be identified separately from, and are capable of existing independently of, the utilitarian aspects" of the buckles. The 1976 copyright statute does not provide for the copyrighting of useful articles except to the extent that their designs incorporate artistic features that can be identified separately from the functional elements of the articles. See 17 U.S.C. §§101, 102.² With respect to this question, the law adopts the language of the longstanding Copyright Office regulations. . . . The regulations in turn were adopted in the mid-1950's, under the 1909 Act, in an effort to implement the Supreme Court's decision in *Mazer v. Stein.* . . .

The Court in *Mazer,* it will be recalled, upheld the validity of copyrights obtained for statuettes of male and female dancing figures despite the fact that they were intended for use and used as bases for table lamps, with electric wiring, sockets, and lampshades attached. *Mazer* itself followed a "contemporaneous and long-continued

2. 17 U.S.C. §101 provides in relevant part: "As used in this title, the following terms and their variant forms mean the following:
. . . 'Pictorial, graphic, and sculptural works' include two-dimensional and three-dimensional works of fine, graphic, and applied art, photographs, prints and art reproductions, maps, globes, charts, technical drawings, diagrams, and models. Such works shall include works of artistic craftsmanship insofar as their form but not their mechanical or utilitarian aspects are concerned; the design of a useful article, as defined in this section, shall be considered a pictorial, graphic, or sculptural work only if, and only to the extent that, such design incorporates pictorial, graphic, or sculptural features that can be identified separately from, and are capable of existing independently of, the utilitarian aspects of the article. . . .
". . . A 'useful article' is an article having an intrinsic utilitarian function that is not merely to portray the appearance of the article or to convey information. An article that is normally a part of a useful article is considered a 'useful article'."
17 U.S.C. §102 provides generally for copyright protection of "pictorial, graphic, and sculptural works."

construction" by the Copyright Office of the 1870 and 1874 Acts as well as of the 1909 Act, under which the case was decided.

. . . As Professor Nimmer points out, however, the Copyright Office's regulations in the mid-1950's that purported to "implement" this decision actually limited the Court's apparent open-ended extension of copyright protection to all aesthetically pleasing useful articles . . .

Ultimately, as Professor Nimmer concludes, none of the authorities—the *Mazer* opinion, the old regulations, or the statute—offers any "ready answer to the line-drawing problem inherent in delineating the extent of copyright protection available for works of applied art." Congress in the 1976 Act may have somewhat narrowed the sweep of the former regulations by defining a "useful article" as one with "*an* intrinsic utilitarian function," 17 U.S.C. §101 (emphasis added), instead of one, in the words of the old regulations, with utility as its "*sole* intrinsic function." . . .

We are left nevertheless with the problem of determining when a pictorial, graphic, or sculptural feature "can be identified separately from, and [is] capable of existing independently of, the utilitarian aspects of the article," 17 U.S.C. §101. This problem is particularly difficult because, according to the legislative history explored by the Court below, such separability may occur either "physically or conceptually," *House Report* at 55. . . .

As the late Judge Harold Leventhal observed in his concurrence in *Esquire, Inc. v. Ringer,* . . . legislative policy supports the Copyright Office's "effort to distinguish between the instances where the aesthetic element is conceptually severable and the instances where the aesthetic element is inextricably interwoven with the utilitarian aspect of the article." Examples of conceptual separateness as an artistic notion may be found in many museums today and even in the great outdoors. Professor Nimmer cites Christo's "Running Fence" as an example of today's "conceptual art": it "did not contain sculptural features that were physically separable from the utilitarian aspects of the fence, but the whole point of the work was that the artistic aspects of the work were conceptually separable." . . .

Appellee argues that the belt buckles are merely useful objects, which include decorative features that serve an aesthetic as well as a utilitarian purpose. And the copyright laws, appellee points out, were never intended to nor would the Constitution permit them to protect monopolies on useful articles. But appellee goes too far by further arguing that "copyrightability cannot adhere in the 'conceptual' separation of an artistic element." . . .

This assertion flies in the face of the legislative intent as expressed in the House Report, which specifically refers to elements that "physically or conceptually, can be identified as separable from the utilitarian aspects of" a useful article. *House Report* at 55. . . .

We see in appellant's belt buckles conceptually separable sculptural elements, as apparently have the buckles' wearers who have used them as ornamentation for parts of the body other than the waist. The primary ornamental aspect of the Vaquero and Winchester buckles is conceptually separable from their subsidiary utilitarian function. This conclusion is not at variance with the expressed congressional intent to distinguish copyrightable applied art and uncopyrightable industrial design, *House Report* at 55. . . .

Pieces of applied art, these buckles may be considered jewelry, the form of which is subject to copyright protection. . . .

Appellant's designs are not, as the appellee suggests in an affidavit, mere variations of "the well-known western buckle." As both the expert witnesses for appellant testified and the Copyright Office's action implied, the buckles rise to the level of creative art. Indeed, body ornamentation has been an art form since the earliest days, as anyone who has seen the Tutankhamen or Scythian gold exhibits at the Metropolitan Museum will readily attest. The basic requirements of originality and creativity, which the two buckles satisfy and which all works of art must meet to be copyrighted, would take the vast majority of belt buckles wholly out of copyrightability. The Copyright Office continually engages in the drawing of lines between that which may be and that which may not be copyrighted. It will, so long as the statute remains in its present form, always be necessary to determine whether in a given case there is a physically or conceptually separable artistic sculpture or carving capable of existing independently as a work of art.

We reverse the grant of summary judgment to the appellee and remand the case for consideration of whether appellant has satisfied the copyright notice requirements.

COMMENTS

1. The *Kieselstein-Cord* case is discussed in Gary I. Horowitz, "The Case for the Designer Belt Buckle: The Problem of Copyrighting Utilitarian Objects," *Art & the Law,* vol. 6 (1981), p. 59. Horowitz argues that the belt buckles in *Kieselstein* are not copyrightable under a strict reading of the 1976 statute (which was Judge Weinstein's position) but that allowing these articles to be copyrighted might be justified by the statute's public policy encouraging experimentation in the arts.

2. *Mazer v. Stein,* 347 U.S. 201 (1953), held that a statuette of a Balinese dancer intended for use as a lamp base was copyrightable, reasoning that an article's intended utilitarian purpose should not affect copyright protection. *Mazer* has been read broadly, as in the *Kieselstein-Cord* case, to allow utilitarian articles to be considered works of art subject to copyright protection. (See also *Esquire, Inc. v. Ringer,* 414 F.Supp. 939 (D.D.C. 1976), in which the Copyright Office was directed by the court to register a nontraditionally shaped outdoor light fixture whose form was essentially inseparable from its function.) *Mazer* has also been read narrowly to limit copyright protection to works of art that are separable parts of utilitarian objects, as was true of the *Mazer* statuettes. Outside the Second Circuit, the issue is not resolved.

3. "Works of Applied Art: An Expansion of Copyright Protection," *Southern California Law Review,* vol. 56 (1982), pp. 241ff, argues that under the cases applied art may be denied protection solely because of a judge's taste. The writer proposes that subjectivity be minimized by giving full copyright protection to any useful article meeting the originality requirement, even if the design and utilitarian aspects of the work are inseparable.

4. The court in *Kieselstein-Cord* cites Professor Nimmer's reference to Christo's "Running Fence" as an example of conceptual art because it "did not contain sculptural features that were physically separable from the utilitarian aspects of the fence." What "utilitarian aspects" do you see in a "fence" placed for two weeks over rolling pastureland with gaps for cattle crossings, roadways, and so forth?

5. Other useful discussions of the copyrightability of utilitarian articles include "Functional Works of Art: Copyright, Design Protection, or Both?" *Comm/Ent Law Journal,* vol. 3 (1980), pp. 83ff. Valerie Flugge, "Works of Applied Art," *Southern California Law Review,* vol. 56 (1982), pp. 241ff; Robert Denicola, "Applied Art and Industrial Design: A Suggested Approach to Copyright in Useful Articles," *Minnesota Law Review,* vol. 67 (1983), pp. 707ff.

COPYRIGHTING AN IDEA

Mazer v. Stein established firmly that copyright protects the expression of an idea but not the idea itself. This distinction is considered in the following case.

Franklin Mint v. National Wildlife Art Exchange, Inc.
575 F.2d 62 (3d Cir. 1978)

WEIS, Circuit Judge.

Nearly two centuries ago, Lord Mansfield identified the conflicting interests underlying copyright law in his oft quoted warning:

[We] must take care to guard against two extremes equally prejudicial; the one, that men of ability, who have employed their time for the service of the community, may not be deprived of their just merits, and the reward of their ingenuity and labour; the other, that the world may not be deprived of improvements, nor the progress of the arts be retarded. . . .

The necessity of balancing these divergent concepts is illustrated in this case in which we are asked to determine whether an artist infringed a copyright, which he had once owned, by painting another work portraying the same general subject matter. The district court found no infringement and, being in agreement, we affirm.

In a series of suits and cross suits, Albert Earl Gilbert and Franklin Mint Corporation were accused of infringing on the purported copyright of National Wildlife Art Exchange, Inc. to a painting, "Cardinals on Apple Blossom." After a bench trial, the district court found that the copyright was valid, but there had been no copying and, consequently, no infringement. . . .

In late July or early August 1972 Ralph H. Stewart began to implement a plan of organizing a business enterprise which would publish and market limited edition prints of wildlife. He telephoned Gilbert, a nationally recognized wildlife artist, and asked him to paint a water color of cardinals. Gilbert agreed and in the following months completed "Cardinals on Apple Blossom," using as source material color slides, photographs, sketches, and two stuffed cardinal specimens. He signed and dated the painting, and placed a copyright notice on it before August 25, 1972, the day when Stewart came to the artist's residence and approved the rendition. While there, Stewart gave Gilbert a check in the amount of $1,500, bearing on the back a notation, "For Cardinal painting 20 X 24 including all rights—reproduction etc." On the following day, Stewart and Gilbert discussed a proposal to incorporate National Wildlife Exchange, Inc. to market prints of Gilbert's future works. They agreed in general on the plan but it was understood that at a later date attorneys for both parties would draw up a contract in terms meeting their approval. Gilbert endorsed Stewart's check and cashed it on August 28, 1972. . . .

Gilbert and National ultimately were unable to agree upon terms of the business venture discussed in August of 1972, and in January, 1975, Gilbert agreed to paint a series of four water color birdlife pictures, including one of cardinals, for Franklin Mint Corporation. The series was completed in January of 1976, and included a work entitled "The Cardinal." Franklin made engravings of the four paintings which were sold as a group and not separately.

In painting "The Cardinal," Gilbert used some of the same source material he had utilized for "Cardinals on Apple Blossom," including preliminary sketches from his collection, photographs, slides, and a working drawing. In addition, however, he used other slides of foliage taken after completion of the earlier painting and sketches specifically developed for "The Cardinal," as well as a series of cardinal photographs. He did not use the stuffed bird specimens which had served as models for "Cardinals on Apple Blossom."

After hearing extensive testimony and viewing Gilbert's rendition of a cardinal painted in the courtroom during the trial, the district judge found that the artist had not copied "Cardinals on Apple Blossom" when he painted "The Cardinal." . . .

Since copyrights do not protect thematic concepts, the fact that the same subject matter may be present in two paintings does not prove copying or infringement. Indeed, an artist is free to consult the same source for another original painting. As Justice Holmes stated: "Others are free to copy the original [subject matter]. They are not free to copy the copy." . . .

Precision in marking the boundary between the unprotected idea and the protected expression, however, is rarely possible, the line between copying and appropriation is often blurred. . . .

Moreover, in the world of fine art, the ease with which a copyright may be delineated may depend on the artist's style. A painter like Monet when dwelling upon impressions created by light on the facade of the Rouen Cathedral is apt to create a work which can make infringement attempts difficult. On the other hand, an artist who produces a rendition with photograph-like clarity and accuracy may be hard pressed to prove unlawful copying by another who uses the same subject matter and the same technique. A copyright in that circumstance may be termed "weak," . . . since the expression and the subject matter converge. . . .

In contrast, in the impressionist's work the lay observer will be able to differentiate more readily between the reality of subject matter and subjective effect of the artist's work. The limitations imposed upon the artist by convention are also factors which must be considered. A scientific drawing of a bird must necessarily be more similar to another of the same nature than it would be to an abstract version of the creature in flight.

The "copying" proscribed by copyright law, therefore, means more than tracing the original, line by line. To some extent it includes the appropriation of the artist's thought in creating his own form of expression. In *Universal Athletic Sales Co. v. Salkeld* . . . we observed:

To establish a copyright infringement, the holder must first prove that the defendant has copied the protected work and, second, that there is a substantial similarity between the two works. . . . Phrased in an alternative fashion, it must be shown that copying went so far as to constitute improper appropriation, the test being the response of the ordinary lay person.

In that case, the district court had found copying but made no specific finding that would meet the second test—"that of substantial similarity in the sense of an appropriation of the original work." Copying which had been determined by dissection of the two works at issue was not sufficient, we said, because:

substantial similarity to show that the original work has been copied is not the same as substantial similarity to prove infringement. As the *Arnstein* case points out, dissection and expert testimony in the former setting are proper but are irrelevant when the issue turns to unlawful appropriation.

In the case *sub judice,* testimony was presented by experts for the respective parties to support and refute substantial similarity. There are indeed obvious similarities. Both versions depict two cardinals in profile, a male and a female perched one above the other on apple tree branches in blossom. But there are also readily apparent dissimilarities in the paintings in color, body attitude, position of the birds and linear effect. In one, the male cardinal is perched on a branch in the upper part of the picture and the female is below. In the other, the positions of the male and female are reversed. In one, the attitude of the male is calm; in the other, he is agitated with his beak open. There is a large yellow butterfly in "Cardinals on Apple Blossom," and none in "The Cardinal." Other variances are found in the plumage of the birds, the foliage, and the general composition of the works. Expert testimony described conventions in ornithological art which tend to limit novelty in depictions of the birds. For example, minute attention to detail of plumage and other physical characteristics is required and the stance of the birds must be anatomically correct.

There was also testimony on the tendency of some painters to return to certain basic themes time and time again. Winslow Homer's schoolboys, Monet's facade of Rouen Cathedral, and Bingham's flatboat characters were cited. Franklin Mint relied upon these examples of "variations on a theme" as appropriate examples of the freedom which must be extended to artists to utilize basic subject matter more than once. National vigorously objects to the use of such a concept as

being contrary to the theory of copyright. We do not find the phrase objectionable, however, because a "variation" probably is not a copy and if a "theme" is equated with an "idea," it may not be monopolized. We conceive of "variation on a theme," therefore, as another way of saying that an "idea" may not be copyrighted and only its "expression" may be protected.

The district court had the opportunity to hear the testimony from the artist and found credible his statement that he did not copy. For further support, Gilbert painted a third picture, "The Cardinal," while in the courtroom and without referring to either of his earlier paintings. The court determined that although some of the same source materials were used in all three paintings, similarity between the works necessarily reflected the common theme or subject and each painting was a separate artistic effort. . . .

Although evidence of access and similarity between the paintings constitute strong circumstantial evidence of copying, they are not conclusive. . . .

[W]e conclude that the district court did not err in finding that there was no copying.

Even if it be assumed that the trial court's finding was based only on an application of a mechanical standard of copying—a tracing concept—without consideration of the appropriation factor, we would affirm. We have examined the two paintings and based upon our own observations and impressions, we conclude that while the ideas are similar, the expressions are not. A pattern of differences is sufficient to establish a diversity of expression rather than only an echo. . . .

The similarities here are of a nature not calculated to discourage an artist in the development of a specialty yet sufficiently distinguishable to protect his creativity in that sphere. Just as Justice Holmes would not ban the ballerinas of Degas, we may not excommunicate the cardinals. . . .

We conclude that the district judge did not err in finding that there was no copyright infringement.

THE REQUIREMENT OF ORIGINALITY

Are copies and reproductions of art copyrightable? In Section 102(a) of the copyrighted statute the law requires that copyrightable pictorial, graphic, and sculptural works be "original." As used in the statute, "original" must be distinguished from "novel." Thus two people might independently produce identical images at different times, and both would meet the originality requirement. In this sense, "original" means "not copied." Even if the preexisting work is in the public domain, originality is still an issue, as the following case demonstrates.

L. Batlin & Son, Inc. v. Snyder
536 F.2d 485 (2d Cir. 1976), cert. denied, 429 U.S. 857 (1976)

OAKES, Circuit Judge.

. . . Uncle Sam mechanical banks have been on the American scene at least since June 8, 1886, when Design Patent No. 16,728 issued on a toy savings bank of its type. The basic delightful design has long since been in the public domain. The banks are well documented in collectors' books and known to the average person interested in Americana. A description of the bank is that Uncle Sam, dressed in his usual stove pipe hat, blue full dress coat, starred vest and red and white striped trousers, and leaning on his umbrella, stands on a four- or five-inch wide base, on which sits his carpetbag. A coin may be placed in Uncle Sam's extended hand. When a lever is pressed, the arm lowers, and the coin falls into the bag, while Uncle Sam's whiskers move up and down. The base has an embossed American eagle on it with the words "Uncle Sam" on streamers above it, as well as the word "Bank" on each side. . . .

Appellant Jeffrey Snyder doing business as "J.S.N.Y." obtained a registration of copyright on a plastic "Uncle Sam bank" as "sculpture" on January 23, 1975. According to Snyder's affidavit, in January, 1974, he had seen a cast metal antique Uncle Sam bank with an overall height of the figure and base of 11 inches. In April, 1974, he flew to Hong Kong to arrange for the design and eventual manufacture of replicas of the bank as Bicentennial items, taking the cast metal Uncle Sam bank with him. His Hong Kong buying agent selected a firm, "Unitoy," to make the plastic "prototype" because of its price and the quality of its work. Snyder wanted his bank to be made of plastic and to be shorter than the cast metal sample "in order to fit into the required price range and quality and quantity of material to be used." The figure of Uncle Sam was thus shortened from 11 to nine inches, and the base shortened and narrowed. It was also decided, Snyder averred, to change the shape of the carpetbag and to include the umbrella in a one-piece mold for the Uncle Sam figure, "so as not to have a problem with a loose umbrella or a separate molding process." The Unitoy representative made his sketches while looking at the cast metal bank. After a "clay model" was made, a plastic "prototype" was approved by Snyder and his order placed in May, 1974. The plastic bank carried the legend "© Copyright J.S.N.Y." and was assertedly first "published" on October 15, 1974, before being filed with the Register of Copyrights in January, 1975.

Appellee Batlin is also in the novelty business and as early as August 9, 1974, ordered 30 cartons of cast iron Uncle Sam mechanical banks from Taiwan where its president had seen the bank made. When he became aware of the existence of a plastic bank, which he considered "an almost identical copy" of the cast iron bank, Batlin's trading company in Hong Kong procured a manufacturer and the president of Batlin ordered plastic copies also. Beginning in April, 1975, Batlin was notified by the United States Customs Service that the plastic banks it was receiving were covered by appellants' copyright. In addition the Customs Service was also refusing entry to cast iron banks previously ordered, according to the Batlin affidavit. Thus Batlin instituted suit for a judgment declaring appellant's copyright void and for damages for unfair competition and restraint of trade. . . .

Appellant Snyder claims differences not only of size but also in a number of other very minute details. . . .

What the leading authority has called "the one pervading element prerequisite to copyright protection regardless of the form of the work" is the requirement of originality—that the work be the original product of the claimant. M. Nimmer, The Law of Copyright §10, at 32 (1975). This derives from the fact that, constitutionally, copyright protection may be claimed only by "authors." . . .

Thus "[o]ne who has slavishly or mechanically copied from others may not claim to be an author." . . .

Since the constitutional requirement must be read into the Copyright Act, 17 U.S.C. §1 *et seq.*, the requirement of originality is also a statutory one. . . .

The test of originality is concededly one with

a low threshold in that "[a]ll that is needed . . . is that the 'author' contributed something more than a 'merely trivial' variation, something recognizably 'his own.'" . . .

But as this court said many years ago, "[w]hile a copy of something in the public domain will not, if it be merely a copy, support a copyright, a distinguishable variation will. . . ."

A reproduction of a work of art obviously presupposes an underlying work of art. Since *Mazer v. Stein,* . . . it has been established that mass-produced commercial objects with a minimal element of artistic craftsmanship may satisfy the statutory requirement of such a work. . . . So, too, a toy which qualifies as a work of art such as the original Uncle Sam mechanical bank may qualify as a "work of art" under Section 5(g). . . .

The underlying work of art may as here be in the public domain. But even to claim the more limited protection given to a reproduction of a work of art (that to the distinctive features contributed by the reproducer), the reproduction must contain "an original contribution not present in the underlying work of art" and be "more than a mere copy." . . .

According to Professor Nimmer, moreover, "the mere reproduction of a work of art in a different medium should not constitute the required originality for the reason that no one can claim to have independently evolved any particular medium."

. . . Professor Nimmer refers to *Doran v. Sunset House Distributing.Corp.* . . . as suggesting "the ludicrous result that the first person to execute a public domain work of art in a different medium thereafter obtains a monopoly on such work in such medium, at least as to those persons aware of the first such effort."

We do not follow the *Doran* case. We do follow the school of cases in this circuit and elsewhere supporting the proposition that to support a copyright there must be at least some substantial variation, not merely a trivial variation such as might occur in the translation to a different medium.

Nor can the requirement of originality be satisfied simply by the demonstration of "physical skill" or "special training" which, to be sure, Judge Metzner found was required for the production of the plastic molds that furnished the basis for appellants' plastic bank. A considerably *higher* degree of skill is required, true artistic skill, to make the reproduction copyrightable. Thus in *Alfred Bell & Co. v. Catalda Fine Arts,* . . . Judge

Frank pointed out that the mezzotint engraver's art there concerned required "great labour and talent" to effectuate the "management of light and shade . . . produced by different lines and dots. . . ," means "very different from those employed by the painter or draughtsman from whom he copies. . . ."

. . . Here on the basis of appellants' own expert's testimony it took the Unitoy representative "[a]bout a day and a half, two days work" to produce the plastic mold sculpture from the metal Uncle Sam bank. If there be a point in the copyright law pertaining to reproductions at which sheer artistic skill and effort can act as a substitute for the requirement of substantial variation, it was not reached here.

Appellants rely heavily upon *Alva Studios, Inc. v. Winninger,* the "Hand of God" case, where the court held that "great skill and originality [were required] to produce a scale reduction of a great work with exactitude." . . . There, the original sculpture was, "one of the most intricate pieces of sculpture ever created" with "[i]nnumerable planes, lines and geometric patterns . . . interdependent in [a] multi-dimensional work." Originality was found by the district court to consist primarily in the fact that "[i]t takes 'an extremely skilled sculptor' many hours working directly in front of the original" to effectuate a scale reduction. *Id.* at 266. The court, indeed, found the exact replica to be so original, distinct, and creative as to constitute a work of art in itself. The complexity and exactitude there involved distinguishes that case amply from the one at bar. As appellants themselves have pointed out, there are a number of trivial differences or deviations from the original public domain cast iron bank in their plastic reproduction. Thus concededly the plastic version is not, and was scarcely meticulously produced to be, an exactly faithful reproduction. Nor is the creativity in the underlying work of art of the same order of magnitude as in the case of the "Hand of God." Rodin's sculpture is, furthermore, so unique and rare, and adequate public access to it such a problem that a significant public benefit accrues from its precise, artistic reproduction. No such benefit can be imagined to accrue here from the "knock-off" reproduction of the cast iron Uncle Sam bank. Thus appellants' plastic bank is neither in the category of exactitude required by *Alva Studios* nor in a category of substantial originality; it falls within what has been suggested by the amicus curiae is a copyright no-man's land.

Absent a genuine difference between the underlying work of art and the copy of it for which protection is sought, the public interest in promoting progress in the arts—indeed, the constitutional demand—could hardly be served. To extend copyrightability to minuscule variations would simply put a weapon for harassment in the hands of mischievous copiers intent on appropriating and monopolizing public domain work. Even in *Mazer v. Stein,* supra, which held that the statutory terms "works of art" and "reproduction of works of art" (terms which are clearly broader than the earlier term "works of the fine arts") permit copyright of quite ordinary mass-produced items, the Court expressly held that the objects to be copyrightable, "must be original, that is, the author's tangible expression of his ideas." . . . No such originality, no such expression, no such ideas here appear. . . .

Judgment affirmed.

MESKILL, Circuit Judge (dissenting) (with whom TIMBERS and VAN GRAAFEILAND, Circuit Juges, concur):

I respectfully dissent.

In the instant case the author has contributed substantially more than a merely trivial variation. "Any 'distinguishable variation' of a prior work will constitute sufficient originality to support a copyright if such variation is the product of the author's independent efforts, and is more than merely trivial." 1 Nimmer on Copyright §101 at 34.2. In accord with the purposes of the copyright law to promote progress by encouraging individual effort through copyright protection, we should require only minimal variations to find copyrightability. The independent sculpting of the mold for the plastic bank and the aggregated differences in size and conformation of the figurine should satisfy this standard. . . .

COMMENTS

1. Your authors favor the *Batlin* result because it discourages, by denying copyright protection to, exact reproductions of sculpture and other works of art. As an example of the dangers of the *Batlin* dissent, consider the Nelson Rockefeller collection of copyrighted Rodin *surmoulages* (bronze casts made from authentic bronze casts) that were so exact that they were indistinguishable to the ordinary eye from authorized casts. However, the foundry stamp on many of the copies, "NR," could be easily altered to "M.R.," the mark of the Musée Rodin in Paris, which alone can produce authorized casts. The Musée learned of the problem when one of the Rockefeller *surmoulages* was offered for sale as an original at an important Paris gallery just blocks from the Musée. The "NR" foundry mark on this cast had been obscured by shoe polish. See Albert E. Elsen and John Henry Merryman, *Legal and Illegal Counterfeiting of Art in America, Quaderni Di Scienze Criminali* 53 (Siracusa, Italy: Istituto Superiore di Scienze Criminale, 1983).

2. Gregg Oppenheimer, "Originality in Art Reproductions: 'Variations' in Search of a Theme," *Copyright Law Symposium,* vol. 27 (1983), p. 207 observes that courts have been inconsistent on the issue of the copyrightability of art reproductions. He attributes this inconsistency to the vagueness of the "more than a trivial variation" requirement of protectability.

3. To be eligible for copyright protection, a work must be "fixed in any tangible medium of expression," a requirement that would disqualify a ballet performance, for example. (The ballet could of course be protected by copyrighting a notated ballet score or a videotaped performance.) How long would a work have to be "fixed" in the "medium of expression"? The artist Christo—who hung an enormous orange curtain across Rifle Gap, Colorado, ran a "running fence" 24½ miles long north of San Francisco, wrapped miles of coastline in Australia, and surrounded islands in Tampa Bay, Florida, with enormous pink skirts (among many other projects)—typically dismantles his works in two weeks and meticulously restores each site to its pre-Christo state. Are two weeks enough? The House report accompanying the 1976 statute speaks of an "embodiment" that is "sufficiently permanent or stable to permit the work to be perceived, reproduced, or otherwise communicated for a period of more than transitory duration" (House Report No. 1476, 94th Cong., 2d Sess. 53 [1976]).

Chicago lawyer Scott Hodes relates that when he attempted to register Christo's "Valley Curtain" with the Copyright Office in 1972, the office's initial objection was that a curtain is a useful article. He convinced them that a bright orange 200,000-square-foot curtain hung outdoors in the gap between two promontories was not like other curtains, and registration was accepted as a work of art with no objection to the temporary nature of the installation.

(Hodes also reports that he did not attempt to copyright "Running Fence" because of the problem of placing adequate copyright notice on its 24½-mile length.) See Joan Infarinato, "Copyright Protection for Short-Lived Works of Art," *Fordham Law Review,* vol. 51 (1982), p. 90; Lisa Schilet, "A Look at the Copyright Revision Act Through the Eyes of the Art Collector," *Art & the Law,* vol. 6 (1981), p. 31.

4. Do works of architecture enjoy the protection of the federal Copyright Act? According to the House report accompanying the 1976 statute,

> A special situation is presented by architectural works. . . . Purely nonfunctional or monumental structures would be subject to full copyright protection under the bill, and the same would be true of artistic sculpture or decorative ornamentation, or embellishment added to a structure. On the other hand, where only elements of shape in an architectural design are conceptually inseparable from the utilitarian aspects of the structure, copyright protection for the design would not be available. [House Report No. 1476, 94th Cong. 2d Sess. 54 (1976)].

What elements of the architectural design of the Transamerica Building in San Francisco (the famous, or infamous, pyramid structure that dominates the skyline) are separable from the "utilitarian aspects of the structure"? For an interesting analysis of the application of copyright law to architecture, see Erika White, "Standing on Shaky Ground: Copyright Protection for Works of Architecture," *Art & the Law,* vol. 6 (1981), pp. 70ff.

5. For an interesting argument that art restorations, whether of buildings or of paintings, should be copyrightable, see Reid A. Mandel, "Copyrighting Art Restorations," *Bulletin of the Copyright Society of the U.S.A.,* vol. 28 (1981), p. 273.

FORMALITIES OF COPYRIGHT

"Publication with notice," as already explained, is an important concept in the law of copyright. Under the 1909 law, publication without notice had drastic consequences, as the following case shows. Under the 1976 statute, publication is not required to obtain copyright because copyright attaches at the moment of creation without any further action by the artist. Works will fall into the public domain only if the artist publishes without copyright notice and fails to take corrective action within five years. Still, others can with impunity copy and otherwise exploit works published without notice (unless they receive notice in some other way). So for most practical purposes, publication with notice is still essential to protection of the artist's copyright.

Letter Edged in Black Press, Inc. v. Public Building Commission of Chicago
320 F.Supp. 1303 (N.D. Ill. 1970)

NAPOLI, District Judge.

Plaintiff seeks a declaratory judgment invalidating defendant's copyright to the Pablo Picasso sculpture entitled "The Chicago Picasso." The defendant is the Public Building Commission of Chicago (Commission) and the plaintiff is a publisher who desires to market a copy of the sculpture. Pursuant to Rule 56 of the Federal Rules of Civil Procedure both parties have moved for summary judgment. Succinctly, plaintiff maintains that defendant's copyright is invalid because the sculpture is in the public domain. Defendant asserts that the Chicago Picasso has never been in the public domain.

STATEMENT OF FACTS

In 1963 certain of the Civic Center architects, representing the Commission, approached Picasso with a request to design a monumental sculpture for the plaza in front of the proposed Chicago Civic Center. By May, 1965, Picasso completed the maquette (model) of the sculpture. William E. Hartmann, the architect, who had been the chief liaison with Picasso, then had the maquette brought to the basement of the Art Institute of Chicago, without public notice. The design of the maquette was subjected to an engineering analysis to determine the feasibility of constructing the monumental sculpture and three Chicago charitable foundations undertook to finance the actual construction by contributing $300,000 toward the total cost of $351,959.17. An aluminum model of the design with some slight revisions was prepared as a guide to the construction of the sculpture, and Picasso approved a picture of this model on August 9, 1966.

The Commission, through its board, had been given a private viewing of the maquette. Subsequently, the Commission passed a resolution authorizing the payment of $100,000 to Picasso. This sum was intended as the purchase price for the entire right, title and interest in and to the maquette constituting Picasso's design for the monumental sculpture including the copyright, and copyright renewals. Hartmann proffered the $100,000 check to Picasso and asked the artist to sign a document referred to as the "Formal Acknowledgment and Receipt." Picasso refused to accept the money or to sign the document. He stated that he wanted to make a gift of his work. In accordance with Picasso's wish, counsel for the Commission and William Hartmann prepared the following "Deed of Gift" which Picasso signed on August 21, 1966:

The monumental sculpture portrayed by the maquette pictured above has been expressly created by me, Pablo Picasso, for installation on the plaza of the Civil Center in the City of Chicago, State of Illinois, United States of America. This sculpture was undertaken by me for the Public Building Commission of Chicago at the request of William E. Hartmann, acting on behalf of the Chicago Civic Center architects. I hereby give this work and the right to reproduce it to the Public Building Commission, and I give the maquette to the Art Institute of Chicago, desiring that these gifts shall, through them, belong to the people of Chicago.

In the fall of 1966 the Commission, the public relations department of the City of Chicago, the Art Institute of Chicago and the U.S. Steel Corporation, the latter being the prime contractor for the construction of the sculpture, began a campaign to publicize the Chicago Picasso. . . .

As part of the campaign at least two press showings were conducted. The first was held on September 20, 1966, when the maquette was placed on public exhibition at the Art Institute. No copyright notice was affixed to the maquette. The following notice was, however, posted in the Art Institute:

The rights of reproduction are the property of the Public Building Commission of Chicago. © 1966. All Rights Reserved.

Press photographers attended the showing at the invitation of the Commission and the Art Institute and later published pictures of the maquette and aluminum model in Chicago newspapers and in magazines of national and international circulation. In addition the Commission supplied photographs of the maquette and the uncopyrighted architect's aluminum model to members of the public who requested them for publication. The second showing took place in December of 1966 when the U.S. Steel Corporation, with the knowledge of the Commission, had completed a twelve-foot six-inch wooden model of the sculpture and invited the press to photograph the model. There was no copyright notice on the model and the pictures were published without copyright notice. U.S. Steel also hired a professional photographer to take pictures of the model and these pictures were used in the publicity drive.

The drive was seemingly successful for pictures of the Picasso design appeared in Business Week Magazine on May 6, 1967, and in Holiday Magazine in March, 1967. Fortune Magazine published three pages of color photographs about the Chicago Picasso including pictures of the U.S. Steel wooden model. The Chicago Sun Times Midwest magazine published a cover story on the sculpture with a drawing of the maquette on the cover of the magazine. And a picture of the maquette was printed in U.S. Steel News, a house organ with a circulation of over 300,000. None of the photographs or drawings that were published in the above named publications bore any copyright notice whatever.

From June, 1967, through August 13, 1967, the maquette was displayed at the Tate Gallery in London, England. In conjunction with the exhibit at the Tate, a catalog was published wherein a picture of the maquette appeared. Neither on the maquette itself nor on the photograph in the catalog did copyright notice appear. The Commission had knowledge of these facts for on July 6, 1967, Hartmann had sent to the Chairman of the Commission the catalog which was placed in the Commission files.

On August 15, 1967, the monumental sculpture, "The Chicago Picasso," was dedicated in ceremonies on the Civic Center Plaza. The sculpture bore the following copyright:

© 1967 PUBLIC BUILDING COMMISSION OF CHICAGO
ALL RIGHTS RESERVED

The Chairman of the Public Building Commission, in his speech of dedication to the approximately 50,000 persons assembled for the ceremony said:

It's an occasion we've all been anticipating—the dedication of this great gift to our city by the world-renowned artist, Pablo Picasso. . . .
. . . Pablo Picasso . . . as you know gave the creation of the sculpture to the people of Chicago and his maquette to the Art Institute of Chicago.
I dedicate this gift in the name of Chicago and wish it an abiding and happy stay in the City's heart.

In conjunction with the dedication a commemorative souvenir booklet of the Chicago Picasso dedication ceremonies was prepared by the Commission. The booklet which contained drawings and photographs of the maquette and the aluminum model was distributed to 96 distinguished men and women from all areas of Chicago life and to honored guests. Neither the booklet itself, nor any of the photographs shown therein, bore any copyright notice. Also, on the day of the dedication the United States Steel public relations office sent out a press release together with a photo of the monumental sculpture. The photograph bore no copyright notice.

Subsequent to the dedication, the Art Institute published its Annual Report which contained an uncopyrighted picture of the maquette. This publication had a circulation of 40,000 copies, including museums and libraries. The Art Institute also continued selling a photograph of the maquette on a postcard. Between October 1966 and October 1967, 800 copies of this postcard were sold. In 1967, however, the Commission asked the Art Institute to stop selling the postcard and the Art Institute complied with this request.

In October 1967, the Commission caused to be engraved in the granite base of the sculpture the following legend:

CHICAGO PICASSO
THE CREATION OF THE SCULPTURE WAS GIVEN TO THE PEOPLE OF CHICAGO BY THE ARTIST PABLO PICASSO
THE ERECTION OF THE SCULPTURE WAS MADE POSSIBLE THROUGH THE GENEROSITY OF WOODS CHARITABLE FUND, INC., CHAUNCEY AND MARION DEERING

McCORMIC FOUNDATION, FIELD FOUNDATION OF ILLINOIS
DEDICATED AUGUST 15, 1967 RICHARD J. DALEY, MAYOR

In November, 1967, the Commission stated its policy that no individuals shall be restricted from "full personal enjoyment of the sculpture, including the right to take photographs and make paintings, etchings, and models of the same for personal, non-commercial purposes." The Commission has also had a policy of granting licenses to copy the sculpture for commercial purposes. The Commission requires payment of a nominal fee and a royalty on copies sold. Several such licenses have been granted.

Finally, on January 12, 1968, the Public Building Commission filed its application with the Register of Copyrights asking a copyright in the monumental sculpture entitled "The Chicago Picasso." In due course a certificate of copyright registration was issued to defendant.

STATEMENT OF APPLICABLE LAW

Defendant submits that the attaching of notice to the monumental sculpture on August 4, 1967, and the later registration of the copyright were acts sufficient to obtain a statutory copyright under 17 U.S.C. §10 and 17 U.S.C. §11. This attempt to establish a statutory copyright must fail, however, if the Chicago Picasso was in the public domain prior to August 4, 1967. Such a conclusion is inescapable given the statutory admonition of 17 U.S.C. §8 that "[n]o copyright shall subsist in the original text of any work which is in the public domain. . . ."

To determine how a work comes to be in the public domain it is necessary to explore the basis of the copyright protection. The common law copyright arises upon the creation of any work of art, be it a first sketch or the finished product. This common law right protects against unauthorized copying, publishing, vending, performing, and recording. The common law copyright is terminated by publication of the work by the proprietor of the copyright. Upon termination of the common law copyright, the work falls into the public domain if statutory protection is not obtained by the giving of the requisite notice.

In some of the early English decisions there was debate as to whether publication did indeed divest its owner of common law protection. Arguing that divestment should not occur upon publication, because of the seeming irrationality of such a rule, Lord Mansfield observed: "The copy is made common, because the law does not protect it: and the law can not protect it because it is made common."

In the United States, however, it has been clear, from the date the question first reached the Supreme Court, that the common law copyright is terminated upon the first publication. And as Judge Learned Hand noted in *National Comics Publications v. Fawcett Publications*, citing *Donaldson v. Becket*, "It is of course true that the publication of a copyrightable 'work' puts that 'work' into the public domain except so far as it may be protected by copyright. That has been unquestioned law since 1774."

One justification for the doctrine, that publication *ipso facto* divests an author of common law copyright protection, can be found in the copyright clause of the United States Constitution. Protection is granted, but only "for limited times." The inclusion of this caveat in the Constitution makes manifest the right of society to ultimately claim free access to materials which may prove essential to the growth of the society. The copyright clause, however, does not impinge on the right of privacy of a creator. An author who refrains from publication and uses his work for his own pleasure may enjoy the common law copyright protection in perpetuity. Once a work is published, however, the Constitution dictates that the time for which the statutory copyright protection is accorded starts to run. An author is not allowed to publish a work and then after a period of time has elapsed choose to invoke statutory copyright protection. If the statutory protection is not acquired at the time of publication by appropriate notice, the work is lost to the public domain. Any other rule would permit avoidance of the "limited times" provision of the Constitution.

An exception to this rule is that a limited publication does not divest the holder of his common law protection. A good definition of limited publication can be found in *White v. Kimmell* wherein the court found that a limited publication is a publication "which communicates the contents of a manuscript to a definitely selected group and for a limited purpose, without the right of diffusion, reproduction, distribution or sale." For example, if an artist shows a painting to a selected group of his friends, for the limited purpose of obtaining their criticism, the publication will be said to be limited and thus not divestive of the artist's common law copyright.

Applying these general principles of copyright law to the facts of the case at bar the court is persuaded that the copyright to the work of art known as the "Chicago Picasso" is invalid. General publication occurred without the requisite notice. Accordingly, the common law protection was lost upon publication and the work was thrust into the public domain.

While this suit could have been resolved on any one of several distinct theories the court has decided to base its opinion on the proposition that the Chicago Picasso was placed into the public domain prior to the attachment of copyright notice on the monumental sculpture. Accordingly, only cursory reference will be paid to the other issues presented in this action. Even limiting the opinion in this fashion, however, multiple and rather sophisticated arguments of the defendant must be met in order to sustain the court's opinion.

DEFENDANT'S CLAIM THAT THE MODELS DID NOT NEED COPYRIGHT NOTICE

The defendant's basic contention is that the work of art is the properly copyrighted monumental sculpture not the models. In support of this thesis defendant correctly points out that what was always envisioned by the Civic Center architects and Picasso was a monumental sculpture for the Civic Center Plaza. There can only be one copyright in one work of art it is asserted, and that work allegedly is the sculpture in the Civic Center Plaza; not the various models used in its development. It is therefore concluded that copyright notice on the models was unnecessary before publication of the monumental sculpture.

The court takes a different view of the facts. When Picasso signed the deed of gift on August 21, 1966, there existed but a single copyright. Picasso had a common law copyright in the maquette. He gave the maquette itself to the Art Institute and the right to reproduce it to the defendant. The monumental sculpture did not exist at this point in time and accordingly there could be no copyright in the monumental sculpture, either common law or statutory. It is settled that a copyright can exist only in a perceptible, tangible work. It can not exist in a vision. When Picasso made his deed of gift the monumental sculpture was undeniably but a vision and thus not subject to copyright protection.

The maquette, however, was an original, tangible work of art which would have qualified for statutory copyright protection under 17 U.S.C. §5(g). The court finds that when the maquette was published without statutory notice Picasso's work was forever lost to the public domain. When the monumental sculpture was finally completed it could not be copyrighted for it was a mere copy, albeit on a grand scale, of the maquette, a work already in the public domain.

DEFENDANT'S CLAIM THAT DISPLAY OF THE MAQUETTE DID NOT CONSTITUTE GENERAL PUBLICATION

Three arguments have been submitted to the effect that display of the maquette did not constitute general publication. First, defendant urges that display of the maquette at the Art Institute was a "limited" publication and thus did not place the Chicago Picasso in the public domain. In support of this position the defendant's prime authority is *American Tobacco Co. v. Werckmeister.* . . .

In the case at bar there were no restrictions on copying and no guards preventing copying. Rather every citizen was free to copy the maquette for his own pleasure and camera permits were available to members of the public. At its first public display the press was freely allowed to photograph the maquette and publish these photographs in major newspapers and magazines. Further, officials at this first public showing of the maquette made uncopyrighted pictures of the maquette available upon request. Were this activity classified as limited publication, there would no longer be any meaningful distinction between limited and general publication. The activity in question does not comport with any definition of limited publication. Rather, the display of the maquette constituted general publication. . . .

DONALD M. MILLINGER *Copyright and the Fine Artist**

Time of publication was an appropriate test in early copyright laws, which were limited to books, maps, charts, and sheet music. The concept posed few problems to composers and authors, whose work is created with the goal of publication in mind. The publication of works such as music and books is also relatively simple to define and, hence, to comprehend. In addition, difficulties that do arise regarding what constitutes publication are less likely to be acute for authors and composers because they generally deal with publishing companies that are knowledgeable in copyright law. Moreover, the mechanics of publication do not create dissatisfaction among composers and authors because copyright notice on a page of sheet music or a book is not regarded as a debasement of the work's aesthetic value. Publication has proved to be an inappropriate concept, however, in the context of fine art. A basic difficulty is the lack of a precise definition of what constitutes a publication of a work of art. This problem is intensified because fine artists generally lack the sort of access to legal advice that is available to authors and composers. Moreover, to many fine artists who create singular works, commercial reproduction is a foreign or repugnant concept, and the word "notice" conjures up visions of offensive writing on a masterpiece. Thus, many fine artists would not comply with the notice requirement even if they were aware of its existence.

The 1909 Act did not define publication, it thus left unclear the law concerning publications of works of art. Generally, if an exhibitor enforced rules against copying and did not distribute reproductions of the work to the public, the painting or sculpture was not considered published. The work could be deemed published, however, if the exhibitor permitted unlimited public viewing and copying or if the general public had access to copies. In all of these circumstances, the work was discharged into the public domain unless the artist also had complied with the notice provisions of the 1909 Act. Many works of art consequently fell into the public domain because of confusion or lack of knowledge about publication and requisite notice. Fortunately, this result should occur less frequently under the new Act because it both deemphasizes the concept of publication and narrows the statutory definition of publication.

Though deemphasized, the concept of publication remains relevant for several provisions of the 1976 Act. The most significant provision of the 1976 Act that uses publication is the new notice requirement under section 401. Section 401 provides that whenever a work protected by the Act is "published," a notice of copyright is to be placed on "all publicly distributed copies." Section 101 defines "publication" as the "distribution of copies . . . to the public by sale, or other transfer of ownership, or by rental, leasing, or lending." Publication also occurs when the copyright owner offers to distribute copies to a group of persons for the purposes of further distribution or public display. The definition further clarifies prior law by explicitly stating that a "public . . . display of a work does not of itself constitute publication." Publication now consists entirely of distribution of copies to the public and certain offerings of distribution, whether or not in conjunction with public displays. Mere display, even with permissible copying, is not publication. An exhibition of a painting at a gallery, even though sale or lease is the ultimate goal, would not require notice on the work under the Act because public distribution has not yet occurred. Public distribution would occur when the sale or lease is actually consummated. Thus, notice would not be required during the display, but would only be required after the work leaves the artist's or gallery's possession. Even if a work is offered to a group for purposes of further distribution or public display, and therefore is considered published under section 101, notice is still not required until after the sale or lease of the work because section 401 requires notice on "public distribution," not on publication.

The Senate and House Reports state that references to "copies" in the Act are intended to include specifically that piece in which a work is originally fixed. Thus, if only one "copy"—the "original" in layman's terms—of an oil painting exists, that "copy" is subject to the notice requirement. The Universal Copyright Convention rejects this view. It defines a publication as a reproduction and a distribution of more than one "copy" of a work. The sale of a unique painting would not be a publication under the Convention and thus would not require notice to preserve the artist's copyright. Because it does not adopt this approach, the 1976 Act is directed more toward authors and composers, whose goal is mass distribution of copies of each work, than toward fine artists, whose goal is the production and sale of a single unique work or a limited edition. . . .

COMMENTS

1. As Millinger states, the 1909 statute did not define publication, but the courts had to deal with the concept. For example, in *American Tobacco Co. v. Werckmeister,* 207 U.S. 284 (1907), the defendant argued that it could validly distribute reproductions of the plaintiff's copyrighted painting by the English painter W. Dendy Sadler because that painting was "published without notice." The painting had been displayed before the press and in private showings during 1894 in the Royal Academy in London. In rejecting the defendant's claim, Justice Day noted that at best the exhibition was a "limited publication" that did not inject the work into the public domain. Day reasoned that the Academy's well-known policy, enforced by guards present in the galleries, of forbidding copying of exhibited works precluded a presumption that the work was a "general publication," that is, intended to be dedicated to the public. Justice Day then concluded:

> The rule is thus stated in Slater on the Law of Copyright and Trade Marks: "It is a fundamental rule that to constitute publication there must be such a dissemination of the work of art itself among the public as to justify the belief that it took place with the intention of rendering such work common property."
> And that author instances as one of the occasions that does not amount to a general publication the exhibition of a work of art at a public exhibition where there are by-laws against copies, or where it is tacitly understood that no copying shall take place, and the public are admitted to view the painting on the implied understanding that no improper advantage will be taken of the privilege.
> We think this doctrine is sound and the result of the best-considered cases. In this case it appears that paintings are expressly entered at the gallery with copyrights reserved.

There is no permission to copy; on the other hand, officers are present who rigidly enforce the requirements of the society that no copying shall take place.

Starting with the presumption that it is the author's right to withhold his property, or only to yield to a qualified and special inspection which shall not permit the public to acquire rights in it, we think the circumstances of this exhibition conclusively show that it was the purpose of the owner, entirely consistent with the acts done, not to permit such an inspection of his picture as would throw its use open to the public. We do not mean to say that the public exhibition of a painting or statue, where all might see and freely copy it, might not amount to publication within the statute, regardless of the artist's purpose or notice of reservation of rights which he takes no measure to protect. But such is not the present case, where the greatest care was taken to prevent copying.

2. The cases on whether and under what circumstances exhibition constitutes publication are inconsistent, unpredictable, and unconvincing. For a thorough discussion, see Randolf Jonakeit, "Do Art Exhibitions Destroy Common-law Copyright in Works of Art?" *Copyright Law Symposium,* vol. 19 (1971), pp. 81ff.

3. The 1976 statute attempts to define the term "publication" in Section 101:

Publication is the distribution of copies or phonorecords of a work to the public by sale or other transfer of ownership, or by rental, lease, or lending. The offering to distribute copies or phonorecords to a group of persons for purposes of further distribution, public performance, or public display constitutes publication. A public performance or display of a work does not of itself constitute publication.

In the same section, "copies" is defined to include the original work itself. The section further explains that to perform or display a work "publicly" means: "to perform or display it at a place open to the public or at any place where a substantial number of persons outside a normal circle of a family and its social acquaintances is gathered." This last clause would appear to include circumstances like those of the Royal Academy exhibition in Werckmeister.

The following case was decided under the 1909 statute, but its analysis is still valid under the 1976 act.

Scherr v. Universal Match Corp.
297 F.Supp. 107 (S.D.N.Y. 1967)

McGohey, District Judge.

The defendants in this copyright infringement action moved for summary judgment dismissing the complaint on the ground that the subject matter, a statue made at Government expense by soldiers assigned to do so while on active military duty, is a publication of the United States Government and thus is not copyrightable; and that in any event the claimed copyright is invalid for failure of the plaintiffs to affix an adequate notice of copyright to the statue. The latter depicts a charging infantryman in battle dress and is entitled "The Ultimate Weapon."

The action arises from defendant Universal's production and distribution, with the authorization of the Army, of books of matches bearing on the cover a picture of the statue and the legend: "Home of The Ultimate Weapon Fort Dix N.J."

The United States (the Government), not originally named as a defendant, intervened. It asks, additionally, that if the copyright is held valid, it be ordered assigned to the Government as an employer under the "works for hire" rule.

The court finds there is no genuine issue as to any material fact. Summary judgment in favor of the defendants is granted to the extent and for the reasons hereafter stated.

The plaintiffs are two ex-servicemen. Goodman served in the Army from April 1957 to April 1959; Scherr from October 1957 to October 1959. Both men, prior to induction, had had education and experience in the fine arts. They were assigned as illustrators to Headquarters Company at Fort Dix, New Jersey, where their duties included the preparation of visual training aids. During his free time, Goodman, using supplies given him by the post hobby shop, began to make a small model of an infantryman which was brought to the attention of the deputy post commander. The latter expressed interest in having constructed a larger statue of an infantryman which would serve as a symbol of Fort Dix. After some preliminary research as to the feasibility of such a project it was agreed that Goodman and Scherr would undertake it. Both men were thereupon relieved of their regular duties as illustrators and they set about to create the proposed statue. With the exception of a few "KP" details and barracks inspections, the plaintiffs devoted all of their regular duty hours, and some of their free time, to the work for a period of nine months.

In the design stage, the plaintiffs used other servicemen, assigned by the Army, as models and photographs of these men taken by Government furnished photographers. The first step in the actual construction of the statue was the making of an "armature" out of scrap metal obtained from various "dumps" located on the base. Sculpt-Metal, which was then applied to the armature, was molded to form the figure of a charging infantryman in battle dress and equipment. The body above the waist is bent forward and on the back, just over the belt, is a field pack. This is box-like in shape and appears to hang from suspenders which also support a belt. Its front and back panels are of equal size and almost square in dimension. Narrower panels joining the front and back form the other four sides of the box. The completed figure was sprayed with numerous alternate coats of bronze finish and clear lacquer. Most of this work was done in the heavy equipment section of the post engineers' shop at Fort Dix. . . .

The statue was unveiled on March 20, 1959, and remains on display at Infantry Park, Fort Dix, a site selected by the Army. The title of the statue was also selected by the Army. The claim of copyright in the names of plaintiffs was registered in June 1959, approximately three months after the unveiling.

The defendants next contend that the copyright notice is inadequate, that the claimed copyright is thus invalid and that "The Ultimate Weapon" is, therefore, in the public domain. The statue is twelve feet tall and stands on a pile of rocks about three feet high which, in turn, stands on a base about twelve feet high. Affixed to this base are two plaques, one of which bears the legend: "The Ultimate Weapon—The only indispen-

sible instrument of war—The fighting man." The smaller plaque bears the names of plaintiffs and of the two men who assisted them. Plaintiffs did not affix their notice of copyright to this base, either as part of one of the plaques or separately, because they feared the repercussions, real or imagined, of the Army. Before the unveiling, the statue, without the pack, was taken from the engineers' shop and placed in position on its base. Scherr, unknown to his superiors, then placed a notice of copyright in the proper form to the uppermost panel of the pack which he then attached firmly to the back of the soldier. The notice is located close to that back and about twenty-two feet from the ground. It is impossible for anyone standing on the ground to see the notice. In order to do so, one would have to get astride the back of the figure or, in some manner, get positioned above it.

Section 10 of the Copyright Act provides: "Any person entitled thereto by this title may secure copyright for his work by publication thereof with the notice of copyright required by this title. . . ." Section 19 of the Act provides, with respect to *copies* of works of art, that, "The notice of copyright required by section 10 . . . may consist of the letter C enclosed within a circle . . . accompanied by the initials, monogram, mark or symbol of the copyright proprietor; *Provided*, That on some accessible portion of such copies or of the margin, back, permanent base, or pedestal, or of the substance on which such copies shall be mounted, his name shall appear." Defendants do not contend that any of the requisite contents of the notice are missing, but rather that the notice is inadequate because it is improperly placed.

The present Act is silent as to where the notice should appear on works of art. However, the unquestioned purpose of the notice requirement is "to apprise anyone seeking to copy the article, of the existence of the copyright. . . ." This purpose was clearly frustrated by plaintiffs who, in their own words, sought to make the notice as inconspicuous as possible, an objective they achieved with singular success. Furthermore, although the Certificate of Registration obtained by plaintiffs is prima facie evidence of the validity of the copyright, the defendants have rebutted this presumption by showing that the notice did not fulfill the statutory purpose—a purpose which plaintiffs had no intention of fulfilling. Since its unveiling, "The Ultimate Weapon" has at all times been, and is today, on view at Infantry Park, a site open to the public. During this time there has never been any restriction, posted or otherwise, on the copying or photographing of the statue. Because the statue was displayed without restriction as to either persons or purpose and without adequate notice, it is concluded that there was a divestive publication under an invalid copyright such as to place "The Ultimate Weapon" in the public domain.

COMMENTS

1. The *Scherr* court also ruled against the plaintiff on the independent ground that the artist was hired by the government to create the sculpture and that therefore any rights he might have had in the work appertained to the government in a "work for hire" theory. Thus, since the government, by statute, cannot copyright art, the sculpture entered the public domain upon publication. For the current statutory provision on "work for hire," see Section 201(b) of the 1976 Copyright Act. Section 105 of the statute exempts government art from copyright protection.

2. In *Coventry Ware, Inc. v. Reliance Picture Frame Co.*, 288 F.2d 193 (2d Cir. 1961), the defendant admitted copying the plaintiff's design of decorative wall plaques and asserted as its sole defense that the copyright notice, which appeared on a small printed label attached to the back of the placques, was invalid under the 1909 statute and should have appeared on the front of the work. In ruling in favor of the plaintiff, the court noted the strong legislative trend to liberalize the requirements of notice location, adopting an approach (presaging the 1976 act) that it should be placed so as to give reasonable notice to the prospective copyist.

3. Section 401(c) of the 1976 statute provides:

> The notice shall be affixed to the copies in such manner and location as to give reasonable notice of the claim of copyright. The Register of Copyrights shall prescribe by regulation, as examples, specific methods of affixation and positions of the notice on various types of works that will satisfy this requirement, but these specifications shall not be considered exhaustive.

The new notice provision should encourage visual artists to seek copyright protection by permitting notice to be placed where it will not impair the work of art. Under the 1909 law there was a widespread unjustified belief that the copyright notice had to appear, for example, on the image of a painting or the body of a sculpture.

4. The power of the simple copyright notice requirements should not be underestimated. The Universal Copyright Convention, as revised at Paris on July 24, 1971, which came into force in the United States on July 10, 1974, provides, in Article III:

> Any Contracting State which, under its domestic law, requires as a condition of copyright, compliance with formalities such as a deposit, registration, notice, notarial certificates, payment of fees or manufacture of publication in the Contracting State, shall regard these requirements as satisfied with respect to all works protected in accordance with this Convention and first published outside its territory and the author of which is not one of its nationals, if from the time of the first publication all the copies of the work published with the authority of the author or other copyright proprietor bear the symbol © accompanied by the name of the copyright proprietor and the year of first publication placed in such a manner and locations as to give reasonable notice of copyright.

5. The argument is frequently advanced that the requirement of notice detracts from the work of art and serves no useful purpose. Strasburger points out that artists avoid using statutory copyright in part because of "incompatibility of the original statutory scheme, which was formulated to protect works of authorship in the print media, with the particular needs and concerns of the visual artist" (Alison Strasburger, "Copyright Notice Placement for the Visual Artist," *Art & the Law*, vol. 7 (1983), pp. 281, 282. Why have a notice requirement at all? Why not simply accord full copyright protection to all works of art, for the statutory period of life plus fifty years, as other nations do, so long as the artist's name appears somewhere on it? See Ellyn Sue Roth, "Is Notice Necessary?" *Copyright Law Symposium*, vol. 27 (1982), p. 245.

6. *Registration.* An artist who wishes to register a visual artwork for copyright must (1) complete registration "Form VA," (2) pay a $10 registration fee, and (3) deposit copies or

representations of the work with the Copyright Office and the Library of Congress. "Form VA" is a relatively simple two-page form available from the Register of Copyrights, Library of Congress, Washington, D.C., 20599. The form can be difficult to complete because the artist must state whether the work is "published" or "unpublished," must decide in whose name the copyright should be issued, and must cope with some other copyright terminology (e.g., whether the work is a "compilation" or "derivative" work). Still, in the simple case of a unique painting or sculpture, there should be no difficulty.

7. The deposit requirements of the copyright law can be confusing. For a unique work (a painting or a sculpture), photographs will do. For an edition of prints, examples from the edition are required. In addition, deposits of copies or representations must be placed with the Library of Congress, assuring the government a free contribution to its collections. Copyright Office Circulars R40a and R40b outline the deposit requirements for registration of visual works of art.

8. Why should an artist register his or her work? There are several advantages to registration. (1) Registration is a prerequisite to a suit for infringement of copyright. (2) Registration within five years of publication is prima facie proof of the copyright and of the validity of the facts stated in the certificate of registration, including the fact that the claimant owns the copyright. (3) Registration is a prerequisite to collecting statutory damages under Section 504 of the Copyright Act. (4) Registration is a prerequisite to the collection of attorney's fees under Section 505 of the act. (5) Registration is valuable, tangible evidence of copyright ownership to potential purchasers of the artist's work. (6) Registration serves to deter potential infringers.

The disadvantages of registration are the need to complete Form VA (which may require professional advice), the $10 fee, and the deposit requirements. Although a $10 fee may be an insignificant price to an artist who produces three or four sculptures a year, what about the artist who produces dozens of drawings or watercolors each year? Would he be well advised to pay the $10 fee to register each of his works, as well as file all those forms and send all those photographs?

9. Why should registration be required? Is the public value of the register of works of art sufficient to justify the unrealistic (for the majority of working artists) requirements of registration? Consider the following.

"Note," Courting the Artist with Copyright: The 1976 Copyright Act. *

. . . The registration requirements provide additional, although indirect, benefits for copyright holders and interested members of the artistic community. Because the art world lacks a formal recording system to keep track of the existence and transfer of various ownershp interests, information contained in the application for copyright registration assists dealers, exhibitors, and collectors in ascertaining the authenticity and desirability of a prospective purchase by giving them descriptive information and a copy or facsimile of the original work. In today's booming art market there are numerous opportunities for misrepresentation and forgery. Too many purchasers enter the market ill-equipped to cope with its complexities, and their desire to reflect social and financial accomplishments often supersedes any cautious appraisal of their prospective purchase. Access to copyright registration information, coupled with the use of catalogues in which relevant details of the artist's works are listed, assist collectors, and the dealers who sell to them, in ascertaining whether the object to be purchased or sold is an original or has been misrepresented or misappropriated.

Indirect benefits also flow to the copyright holder from the statutory requirement that all transfers of the copyright interest be in writing and recorded in the copyright office. These requirements afford parties interested in exhibiting or commercially reproducing an art work an expedient means of ascertaining the identity and location of the copyright holder. The exclusive right vested in the copyright holder is of little pecuni-

*From "Courting the Artist with Copyright: The 1976 Copyright Act," *Wayne Law Review,* vol. 24 (1978), pp. 1685, 1693–1698. Copyright © 1978 by Wayne Law Review. Reprinted by permission.

ary value if interested entrepreneurs cannot locate him to obtain the necessary permission to reproduce or exhibit the art work. These requirements are similarly beneficial to institutions and individuals seeking exhibition privileges since the 1976 Copyright Act imposes a requirement that the permission of the copyright holder be obtained prior to the public exhibition or display of an original work. Permission of the copyright holder is necessary when the individual, museum, or gallery has possession of the protected work through lease, loan, rental, or consignment. If the art work is owned by the person seeking to display it the Act does not require consent of the copyright holder since a right to display is inherent in ownership rights and reaffirmed by the Act. This requirement also benefits artists or other copyright holders by allowing them to refuse exhibition rights where the potential exposure is felt to be inappropriate or harmful to the art work or the artist's reputation. . . .

COPYRIGHT INFRINGEMENT

Because few artists actually bring infringement actions, there are few reported decisions on copyright infringement. However, some basic propositions are clear. Any unauthorized copying or reproduction of a validly copyrighted artwork can constitute an infringement, whether or not the copy or reproduction is sold or published. The plaintiff in an infringement action must prove that the copy is substantially similar to the plaintiff's copyrighted work, or that it is a substantial part of it. See Joseph G. Cook, "The Fine Arts: What Constitutes Infringement," *Copyright Law Symposium,* vol. 13 (1964), p. 65. The plaintiff must show that the defendant had access to the plaintiff's work and that the defendant's work was not independently created. Circumstantial proof may be offered to establish a prima facie case. See e.g., *Hollywood Jewel Manufacturing Co. v. Dushkin,* 136 F.Supp. 738 (1955) (fourteen out of fourteen items of the defendant's costume jewelry were identical to the plaintiff's).

It is important to note that it is only the work that is copyrighted, not the subject matter. For example, a photograph of an uncopyrighted painting may be copyrighted, but the copyright does not prevent another artist from making a photograph of the same work. The copyright only protects against copying the copy (*Pagano v. Chas. Beseler Co.,* 234 F. 963 (D.C.N.Y. 1916)).

Alva Studios, Inc. v. Winniger, 177 F.Supp. 265 (S.D.N.Y. 1959), involved a reproduction of a reproduction. The plaintiff, Alva Studios, was authorized by several museums to reproduce sculpture in the museums' collections. The defendant was a company that sold unauthorized reproductions. The plaintiff had prepared an authorized reproduction of Rodin's "The Hand of God," based on the sculpture owned by the Department of Fine Arts of the Carnegie Institute. The plaintiff registered this reproduction with the Copyright Office. The defendant also produced a reproduction of the Rodin sculpture. The court noted that "the test as to infringement of copyright is not the test of mere likeness, but the work claimed to constitute the infringement must be a copy, more or less servile, of the copyrighted work." The court found an infringement because the defendant produced its reproduction by actually copying the plaintiff's reproduction, sandpapering and smoothing a copy of the reproduction, and cutting off two inches from its base.

Your authors believe that the copyright law difficulties entailed by exact reproductions, with concomitant problems of increased forgery and devaluation of original art, are best avoided by entirely outlawing exact reproductions. Our suggested reproduction practices include proscribing copies within 20 percent of the size of the original, labeling the copy clearly as a reproduction, and eliminating foundry, signature, edition, or other "marks falling outside the image of the original" ("Art Replicas: A Question of Ethics," *ARTnews,* February 1979, p. 61).

Artists who seek judicial enforcement of copyright must observe the requirements of statutory notice and register their work properly with the Copyright Office before filing their infringement claim. Clever defendants will ask the court to have the plaintiff prove the validity of his copyright before the plaintiff can show that the defendant copied the work. In this context, consider the following case involving the designer Peter Max.

Goldsmith v. Max
25,248 CCH Copyright L. Dec. 16,441, (S.D.N.Y. Mar. 30, 1981)

Before PIERCE, District Judge.

OPINION AND ORDER

This is a copyright infringement action, pursuant to 17 U.S.C. §411, brought by Lynn Goldsmith ("Goldsmith"), a commercial photographer, against Peter Max ("Max"), a well-known artist. The gravamen of plaintiff's complaint is that Max created a collage by painting over and using parts of a poster of rock star Mick Jagger which was an enlargement of a Goldsmith photograph. . . .

THE PHOTOGRAPH

The photograph of Mick Jagger which forms the basis of this lawsuit was one of several taken by Goldsmith apparently without written permission or a release during a Jagger concert in New York's Madison Square Garden on July 25, 1972. The photograph depicts Jagger from the waist up, hands on hips, face in profile, wearing a white sequined open-necked collarless shirt with laces up the front in lieu of buttons, a black leather jacket open to the waist and a long red neck scarf.

Each party has introduced slides which contain the alleged copyrighted image. The first of these, plaintiff's Exhibit 2, is held in a slide jacket (a white cardboard holder approximately two inches square) which bears a stamped, virtually indistinct legend down the side reading "Photo Lynn Goldsmith, Inc. 16 East 61st St., N.Y.C." together with an unreadable zip code. The defendant has introduced three copies of the same slide contained in similar holders (Collectively Def. Exh. D). One has been stamped along the side with the name "Lynn Goldsmith" and "23 E. 63rd N.Y.C." The address has been changed by

hand to "23 E. 74th" and another address has been added by hand, "15 E. 61 St. N.Y. 10021." Along the bottom of the slide jacket is written "Mick Jagger." In the top left corner is written "PP78 Ti" and two letters which cannot be read. The remaining two slides introduced by the defendant merely contain the words "Duggal Color Projects" along the right side. None of the four slides introduced by the parties contains a statutory copyright notice. 17 U.S.C. §401. . . .

THE COPYRIGHT

The complaint in this action alleges that Max infringed copyright No. VA 36-881 which Goldsmith holds on the slide. The certificate bearing this registration number (Pl. Exh. 4), dated November 16, 1979, states that the work was first completed in 1972 and lists no information in the box entitled: "Date and Nation of First Publication." From the testimony at trial it appears that the plaintiff sought unsuccessfully to register the poster, the pillow and the Escapade magazine photo. On January 30, 1980, the Copyright Office, apparently acting *sua sponte,* cancelled the aforesaid registration No. VA 36-881 and returned a new registration certificate bearing No. VAU 13-741 (Pl. Exh. 5), a designation used to describe unpublished works. Significantly, neither the slide nor the slide jacket filed with the Copyright Office (Def. Exh. CC1-2) contains a copyright notice in Goldsmith's name. They merely state her name and address.

The defendant argues that the complaint herein was predicated upon Certificate No. VA 36-881 which has been cancelled, that No. VAU 13-741 covers an unpublished work which is not the image on the slide at issue, and that there is, therefore, no valid registration certificate in effect. Since the statute requires a valid registration certification as a condition precedent to maintaining an infringement action, 17 U.S.C. §411; the defendant argues that the complaint should be dismissed.

While the registration, cancellation and reissuance of the certificates for this work have occurred under wholly unclear circumstances, the failure to allege the proper registration number will not be deemed fatal to the complaint. . . . Moreover, since the Court finds, as outlined hereinbelow, that the alleged copyright on this photograph is invalid, the issue of the validity of the registration certificate is moot.

THE MAX SERIGRAPHS

In early 1973 defendant Max created a series of collages utilizing the Personality Poster copy of the Goldsmith photo. The poster contained a clear, albeit arguably invalid, copyright notice in the name of Personality Poster and a photo credit to Lynn Goldsmith. Nonetheless, without seeking approval from either party the defendant applied acrylic paint and collage materials to the poster. At the time Max did not intend to sell or otherwise reproduce the collage. . . .

INFRINGEMENT

To demonstrate copyright infringement the plaintiff must establish her ownership of a valid copyright and that the defendant copied her work. . . .

The central issue herein is whether plaintiff has demonstrated the existence and validity of her copyright, "for in the absence of copyright . . . protection even original creations are in the public domain and may be freely copied. Ownership and validity are generally established by introduction of the certificate of copyright registration which if "obtained within five years after first publication of the work shall constitute prima facie evidence of the validity of the copyright and of the facts stated in the certificate. . . ." 17 U.S.C. §410(c). . . .

The Court declines to afford the copyright registration a rebuttal presumption of validity. The initial registration certificate was issued on November 16, 1979 (Pl. Exh. 4). The Personality posters were distributed in 1972 and 1973 more

than five years earlier. Moreover, where, as here, the transactions with the Coypright Office "cast serious doubt on the question, validity will not be assumed."

The publication of a copyrightable work with authority from the owner will inject that work into the public domain unless it is protected by the giving of the requisite notice. . . .

Thus, under the 1909 Act the proprietor of a copyright would forfeit her rights in a work if she authorized its publication without the requisite notice. . . .

The central issue of this litigation is, therefore, whether Goldsmith's photograph entered the public domain—was published with her consent and without the proper statutory notice—before January 1, 1978. If it had entered the public domain there could be no copyright on the work and accordingly, no infringement.

The Goldsmith photo has been used to create at least three products which were distributed to the public—the Personality poster, the Escapade magazine page and the pillow. The Court will consider each of these distributions individually to determine which, if any, injected Goldsmith's work into the public domain.

THE POSTER

The focus of this litigation is clearly the reproduction of Goldsmith's photo on the poster which Max admittedly used to create his collage—the alleged infringing work. Goldsmith testified that in December 1972 she granted a license for her photograph to be reproduced in poster form by Personality Posters, Inc. For this she was to receive royalties and "an appropriate photo credit." She further testified that she entered into a written agreement with Personality (Tr. 146) which included a provision that the copyright notice was to be in the name of Personality Posters "for their line of posters" but that she "maintained [her] copyright to the photograph." Robert Schwartz, a principal of Personality, also testified that Goldsmith had told him she intended to keep her copyright. Significantly, the written agreement between Personality and Goldsmith which purportedly contained this reservation was not introduced.

The poster, widely distributed in 1972 and 1973, contained the following "copyright" notice: "c Personality Posters 641 Sixth Avenue New York, NY 10011 Printed in USA Photo/Lynn Goldsmith." The c was not encircled. Goldsmith testified that she saw the posters almost immediately after they were printed. Although she had immediate knowledge of the lack of copyright notice in her name, it was not until approximately one year after the posters were initially released that Goldsmith's attorneys drafted a complaint which was to have been filed in Supreme Court, New York County, against Personality (Def. Exh. I) charging failure to render royalty statements and pay royalties. That complaint alleged neither breach of contract nor failure to provide copyright notices. It referred to the royalty agreement which was purportedly annexed as Exhibit A. However, the document produced at trial had no royalty agreement attached. The complaint was apparently never filed and the matter was settled without intervention of the court. Personality agreed to stop distributing the Goldsmith poster and to pay royalties. Although there was testimony that the agreement between plaintiff and Personality was written, it was not introduced into evidence during the trial of the instant action. More importantly, Goldsmith testified that she saw copies of the poster after the agreement was signed but took no action to restrain distribution or to enforce the settlement agreement with respect to the copyright.

Notwithstanding plaintiff's testimony that she intended to safeguard her proprietary rights in the photo, 100,000 posters of the photo bearing no copyright in Goldsmith's name were printed and distributed with Goldsmith's knowledge.

There is insufficient credible evidence from which this Court can conclude that Goldsmith reserved her copyright rights in the claimed agreement by which she authorized Personality to use her slide. Moreover, there is nothing from which the Court may conclude that even if the rights were reserved, Goldsmith exercised those rights by promptly halting distribution of the posters. . . .

Lacking the presumption of copyright validity, the plaintiff must demonstrate that the publication of her work on the Personality poster without copyright notice was unauthorized. The Court finds that the plaintiff has not carried that burden. Schwartz and Goldsmith offered evidence to show that Goldsmith intended to protect her rights in the photo, yet the record is devoid of evidence from which it can be concluded that she in fact protected those rights. From the lack of reference to copyright protection in the plaintiff's state court complaint against Personality it is reasonable to infer, as the Court does, that the unavailable license or royalty agreement with Personality was silent on copyright protection.

Accordingly, the Court finds that the Personality poster of Mick Jagger which was developed from plaintiff's slide was published and distributed with the permission of the copyright proprietor—Goldsmith. Since the poster contained no copyright notice in plaintiff's name, the publication injected the subject work into the public domain and Goldsmith's rights in the work were thereby forfeited. . . .

COMMENTS

1. Assuming that an artist properly copyrights a work, how can he discover infringements of these rights? One suggestion is the adoption of blanket licensing for artists. See "Blanket Licensing: A Proposal for the Protection and Encouragement of Artistic Endeavor," *Columbia Law Review,* vol. 83 (1983), p. 1245. According to that article, artists are often unable to secure their artwork against infringement in spite of the federal copyright provisions: "Visual Artists, for example, experience problems stemming from the increasing popularity of design notecards and postcards. Stationery and gift items often embody reproductions of modern artwork . . . as cover designs. Manufacturers producing the cards frequently fail to secure the requisite licenses from the artists." This article suggests that because few individual artists have the resources to discover all unauthorized uses of their artwork, an organized national monitoring system is needed to detect infringements of an artist's copyright. It argues for the adoption of such a system for visual artists, which might function like the performing rights societies (such as the American Society of Composers, Authors, and Publishers) established by composers and lyricists to license their works and monitor against infringement. Who would be the blanket licensees under such a scheme?

2. The Visual Artists and Galleries Association, Inc. (VAGA), a New York entity, has set up a clearinghouse for artist and dealer licensing and reproduction rights along the lines of and supported by SPADEM, the archetypical French organization. However, the enormous task of establishing a blanket licensing scheme for the U.S. visual arts world still remains to be done.

Visual artists often feel they are at the mercy of members of the commercial world who do not respect their copyrights. Consider the following.

Excerpt from ARTnews *

Jerry Kaye was reading his copy of the *Los Angeles Times* not long ago when, at the bottom of the movie page, a lurid ad caught his eye. "I was leafing through the paper when all of a sudden I saw this picture. I couldn't believe it," says Kaye, a Los Angeles manufacturer's representative who has been an *ARTnews* reader for many years. "There was this ad for a film called *Doctor Butcher, M.D.* that was a rip-off of the Philippe Halsman photograph of Salvador Dali that was on the cover of the April 1980 *ARTnews*. I have a very good visual memory."

Kaye was right. Maniacally staring out from the newspaper page (with what Dali himself has called his "paranoia-critical" look) was a slightly altered version—a doctor's head mirror had been added—of the photograph of the artist taken by Halsman in 1972, which later appeared on *ARTnews'* cover. The film it was promoting, starring a cast of not exactly household-name actors and actresses, seemed to be one of those "exploitation" films most likely to be found in drive-ins or aging theaters with sticky floors. "*Dr. Butcher,*

M.D.—He Makes House Calls!" the ad copy read, as a suggestively clad woman fled beneath the doctor's crazed gaze. . . .

"Seeing that ad made me very angry," says Kaye. "I immediately wrote to the *L.A. Times*. It was the first time I've ever written to any publication. I thought the Halsman photo was so unbelievably good the way it expressed the mind and personality of Dali as a wild eccentric. I was outraged that some quick-buck types would use the *ARTnews* cover that way. A few days later I cooled down and began to think that Dali would probably have loved it."

Mrs. Philippe Halsman, the photographer's widow, sounded a serious note. "So many pictures are pirated in this way. This sort of thing has happened before, and it's always some obscure production company nobody ever hears from again. The photograph was copyrighted, of course, but there are always people who are dishonest and who disappear from the planet whenever there's a complaint."

Visual artists often complain of unauthorized uses of their works, as in the "Doctored Dali" example above. Ironically, however, artists themselves routinely and unreflectively infringe on their fellow artists' copyrights, as the following excerpt relates.

Gay Morris *Artists' Use of Photographs*†

In November 1976 San Francisco photographer Morton Beebe read a cover story on Robert Rauschenberg published in *Time* magazine. There, among the pages illustrating Rauschenberg's work, Beebe was astonished to see one of his own photographs incorporated into a Rauschenberg print. The photograph, entitled *Diver*, depicted a young man, arms outspread in a swan dive. The

shot was taken from above, looking down on the youth as he hurtled toward the water. It had been published in a number of magazines in the early '70s as part of a portfolio used in advertisements by the Nikon camera company.

Rauschenberg had incorporated Beebe's photograph into a print named *Pull*, made in 1974 at Gemini G.E.L., the Los Angeles graphics work-

*From *ARTnews*, May 1982, p. 19. Copyright © 1982 by ARTnews Associates. Reprinted by permission.

†From Gay Morris, "When Artists Use Photographs: Is It Fair Use, Legitimate Transformation, or Rip-off?" *ARTnews*, January 1981, p. 102. Copyright © 1981 by ARTnews Associates. Reprinted by permission.

shop. The print is part of the "Hoarfrost" series, considered by many critics to be among Rauschenberg's most important prints. It consists of two pieces of fabric, cheesecloth glued to silk taffeta, with the image of a boy in a swan dive silkscreened in the center. Around the edges, forming a border, are other offset-printed images, and there is a small paper bag glued to the fabric near the top of the print.

Beebe was particularly upset by this unauthorized use of his copyrighted image because he knew that Rauschenberg was a leader in the artists' rights movement who had devoted time and effort to bringing the needs of artists to the attention of legislators, the media and the public. Among the causes Rauschenberg has most ardently espoused is the controversial proceeds right—sometimes called the artists' royalty—which gives artists a portion of the money realized when their works are resold at a profit.

"You having been in the lead in protecting artists' rights," Beebe wrote to Rauschenberg, "I was stunned to see one of my images so obviously borrowed without recognition."

Rauschenberg replied, indicating that he was surprised at Beebe's reaction and commenting, "I have received many letters from people expressing their happiness and pride in seeing their images incorporated and transformed in my work."

Five months later, in June 1977, Rauschenberg was in San Francisco for the opening of an exhibition of his work, and Beebe met him at a party. They discussed the issue, but nothing concrete came of their talk, and eventually Beebe retained an attorney and brought suit against Rauschenberg and Gemini G.E.L. for copyright infringement. He asked for a minimum of $10,000 in damages, plus attorney's fees and court costs, and the profits from the sale of *Pull.* Twenty-nine copies of this print were made; it is currently valued at $10,000.

The case was settled out of court in September 1980. Beebe accepted $3,000, a copy of *Pull* and the promise that if the print were put on exhibition, Rauschenberg or Gemini would request the exhibitor to state in any accompanying catalogue: "The image of the Diver in *Pull* is after a photograph by Morton Beebe." Although the settlement was smaller than Beebe had originally sought, he says he agreed to it because his legal costs were mounting and he didn't want to risk losing the case on "a technicality." He says he is satisfied: "Any appearance of the piece will have to have proper recognition on it, and that's the important thing. I consider it a victory for myself and for photographers."

Rauschenberg could not be reached for comment, but a statement he made in his earlier letter to Beebe sheds light on his viewpoint. "Having used collage in my work since 1949," Rauschenberg wrote, "I have never felt that I was infringing on anyone's rights as I have consistently transformed these images sympathetically with the use of solvent transfer, collage and reversal as ingredients in the compositions which are dependent on reportage of current events and elements in our current environment, hopefully to give the work the possibility of being reconsidered and viewed in a totally new context."

Irwin Spiegel, attorney for Rauschenberg and Gemini G.E.L., emphasized that his clients admitted no wrongdoing in the settlement agreement. "It is the position of Mr. Rauschenberg and Gemini G.E.L. that an artist working in the medium of collage has the right to make fair use of prior printed and published materials in the creation of an original collage including such preexisting elements as a part thereof and that such right is guaranteed to the artist as a fundamental right of freedom of expression under the First Amendment of the Constitution of the United States of America." The only reason his clients chose to settle, Spiegel continued, was because they didn't want to spend any more time or money on the case—the same reason given by Beebe.

Although the unauthorized use of photographers' images doesn't always involve artists as prominent as Rauschenberg, it is by no means rare. Stuart Kahan, executive director of the American Society of Magazine Photographers (ASMP), says "the unauthorized use of photographers' work is extensive. I see it every day."

The difference between the point of view of the artist and that of the photographer was summed up in the course of a recent dispute between artist Larry Rivers and photographer Arnold Newman. Last summer *The New York Times* published an article by Grace Glueck called "How Picasso's Vision Affects American Artists" and illustrated it with a detail of a print by Rivers from a portfolio called "Homage to Picasso." The print incorporates part of Newman's celebrated photograph of Picasso. Newman wrote a letter to the *Times* protesting the publication and said: "In reproducing and using my interpretation of Picasso Larry Rivers has claimed creation of this image which is morally indefensible as well as illegal as it is an infringement of my copyright."

In his reply to the *Times,* Rivers invoked freedom of expression as a justification for using photographs in his work, but Newman answers that "freedom of expression doesn't give you the freedom to steal from others. Any photographer who values his work doesn't like to see it used without permission."

Rivers answered, "I've used photographs since the early '60s and no one has ever complained. The way I used it [Newman's image], it had a minor role in the whole. Some art necessitates the use of photography. In this case, it was just to give information about Picasso. I didn't even use the whole thing, only across the forehead and down to the nose. The rest is drawn in. It's like a quote, that's all. He says I didn't give him credit. Where am I supposed to put the credit? On the bottom? 'Eyes by Arnold Newman'?"

Rivers had given Newman a copy of the print, but Newman says, "I accepted it not as a payment. I thought it was just for my records. . . . Larry misunderstood and he thought I was accepting it as a payment."

The two have now "agreed to work things out," Newman says. They are planning to hold a symposium this year to "explore the problems of artists' using other artists' material." Both agree, Newman continues, that "there's a larger problem, a moral problem—where are the boundaries on the use of material that is not yours?" . . .

Andy Warhol has been involved in disputes with photographers many times. In all cases, the photographers said he settled with them when they complained, but not always to their satisfaction.

In 1965 New York photographer Patricia Caulfield discovered that Warhol had used her shot of flowers in the Everglades, published in *Modern Photography* magazine in 1964, for a series of paintings called "Flowers." "I was walking down Broadway," she remembers, "and I saw posters of flowers in a bookstore. I thought, 'My god, that looks familiar!' So I bought one and took it back to the office and compared it to tearsheets from the magazine. It was my photograph."

No one knows precisely how many "Flowers" were painted; the German art historian Rainer Crone, who had the artist's cooperation in the preparation of his book *Andy Warhol* (published by Praeger in 1970), estimates that there were over 900, in various sizes. Photographs of a 1964 installation at the Leo Castelli gallery in New York show the walls virtually papered with "Flowers."

For these works, the photographic image was silkscreened onto canvas and the flowers painted in bright colors. A professional painter did the silkscreening, and then the painting was done at Warhol's Factory. Crone quotes Warhol as saying that a number of his friends had helped with the painting.

Caulfield's attorney, Arthur Penn, obtained a settlement in which Warhol gave Caulfield two of the "Flowers" paintings (one went to Penn) and agreed to give her a royalty in the form of artwork or monetary compensation whenever he used the image again.

In 1970 Warhol made a print series, "Flowers," based on Caulfield's photograph. The portfolio consisted of ten prints of the same image printed in different colors. There were 250 portfolios, of which Caulfield received 12 (8 for herself, 4 for her attorney).

But despite the settlement, Caulfield remains upset by the experience. She maintains that she does not have the time, money or energy to pursue the matter further. "I'm not the kind of person to go out and *sue* people," she says. "Getting upset interferes with the rest of your work."

"The reason there's a legal issue here is because there's a moral one," Caulfield says. "What's irritating is to have someone like an image enough to use it, but then denigrate the original talent." There's nothing wrong with using or adapting someone else's work, she continues, if you get the other person's approval and you pay them for it. She is particularly upset because her image was used not just for a single work but for many—paintings, prints and posters. Warhol could not be reached for comment.

Photojournalist Charles Moore also discovered by accident that his work had been used by Warhol when his agent saw a *Time* magazine story on the artist in which *Red Race Riot* was illustrated. The painting, one of the series called "Race Riot" done in 1963–64, used three photographs of a man being attacked by police dogs that had been published in a photo-story on the Birmingham riots Moore had done for *Life* magazine in 1963. Moore and his agent arranged a meeting with Warhol. Moore says he told the artist, "I want it settled so you know, and other artists know, you can't just rip off a photographer's works." The disagreement was settled with Warhol's giving Moore a series of prints. It was "Flowers." . . .

Kahan believes that the problem sometimes stems from a lack of understanding of the copyright law, especially since a new federal law went into effect in 1978 which superseded the earlier law and in some ways changed it. The situation is made more complex by the fact that works created before 1978 are still governed by the old law. . . .

Many people assume that a photograph, especially one that appears in a magazine or newspaper, is in the public domain. The chances are, however, that it isn't. Even if the photographer hasn't copyrighted it, however, the new law gives him five years to correct the omission by registering the photograph with the Copyright Office. . . .

Part of the answer to limiting the incidence of unauthorized reproduction lies in increasing the public's awareness of the copyright laws and its respect for the work of photographers. "They think it's *just* a photograph." Arnold Newman says in answer to the question of why his work has been so much copied. It doesn't occur to people, he suggests, that there is a person behind a photograph just as there is a person behind a painting. "The ability to see," says Caulfield, is part of the photographer's art as well as the painter's.

COMMENTS

1. An important question that these cases raise but do not resolve is how the copyright doctrine of "fair use" should apply to fine art. "Fair use" is governed by Section 107 of the 1976 Copyright Act, as follows:

§107. Limitations on exclusive rights: Fair use.

Notwithstanding the provisions of section 106, the fair use of a copyrighted work, including such use by reproduction in copies or phonorecords or by any other means specified by that section, for purposes such as criticism, comment, news reporting, teaching (including multiple copies for classroom use), scholarship, or research, is not an infringement of copyright. In determining whether the use made of a work in any particular case is a fair use the factors to be considered shall include—

(1) the purpose and character of the use, including whether such use is of a commercial nature or is for nonprofit educational purposes;

(2) the nature of the copyrighted work;

(3) the amount and substantiality of the portion used in relation to the copyrighted work as a whole; and

(4) the effect of the use upon the potential market for or value of the copyrighted work.

2. How should such language apply to the Rauschenberg, Rivers, and Warhol cases? It seems clear that the uses these artists made of others' copyrighted works were not for purposes like criticism, comment, news reporting, teaching, scholarship, or research. Does that suffice, or is it still necessary to apply the additional four criteria—commercial or nonprofit educational purpose, nature of the copyrighted work, proportion copied, and market effect? Your authors would have no difficulty denying the claim of fair use in each of these cases, but there are no judicial decisions on the point.

3. What is your reaction to the argument, attributed to Rauschenberg's lawyer, that the right to appropriate the copyrighted work without permission of a fellow artist is guaranteed by the First Amendment? See *Zacchini v. Scripps-Howard Newspapers,* 433 U.S. 562 (1977).

4. Should Beebe be flattered at Rauschenberg's uncredited and unpermitted use of his photograph? Without even a credit, who would know who is being flattered? If the situation were reversed and Beebe had sold unauthorized photo reproductions of one of Rauschenberg's works, would Rauschenberg have been "flattered"?

5. Beebe's case is rare in that Beebe had been careful to preserve his copyright. His photograph appeared in a number of magazines in the early 1970s. Each publication of the photograph contained an appropriate copyright notice. Beebe subsequently had the copyright transferred to him from each of the magazines, and he registered his copyright claim in the U.S. Copyright Office. See *Morton Beebe v. Robert Rauschenberg,* Complaint for Copyright Infringement, U.S. District Court, Northern District of California, No. C79-3372. Beebe's complaint sought an injunction restraining infringement of his copyright, an accounting from the defendants for all gains derived from the sale of "*Pull,*" and an order directing defendants to pay Beebe statutory damages and all sums derived from the sales of "Pull." See also Gay Morris, "'Diver' v. 'Pull' Goes to Court," *Peninsula Times Tribune,* April 19, 1980, pp. A-1, A-12.

6. The more typical reaction of photographer Caulfield to the unauthorized use of her

copyrighted work goes far to explain why infringement of copyrighted artworks often goes unremedied: "I'm not the kind of person to go out and *sue* people," Caulfield said, further noting, "Getting upset interferes with the rest of your work."

REMEDIES FOR COPYRIGHT INFRINGEMENT

What does a copyright owner actually get when he wins a suit for infringement? The 1976 statute authorizes a broad range of remedies in Section 502-05: injunction, impounding, and destruction or other disposition of infringing articles; damages and profits; and costs and attorney's fees. In determining the amount of damages to be awarded, the copyright owner is permitted to choose between actual damages and statutory damages. The latter will be desirable in a case where it is difficult to show how much actual harm, if any, the owner has suffered as a result of the infringement. Costs and attorney's fees are awarded at the discretion of the court. It is important to remember, however, that the copyright owner is not eligible for statutory damages or attorney's fees unless he registered his work *before the infringement* commenced.

AMY ROTH *Copyright Remedies and the Fine Artist**

. . . Damages are awarded to compensate the copyright owner for losses from the infringement, and profits are awarded to prevent the infringer from unfairly benefiting from a wrongful act.

While damages and profits are appropriate remedies in cases of literary, musical, and commercial art infringement, they are entirely inapt remedies where the infringed work is fine art. The distinction lies in the nature of the profits of and the infringer's damage to the respective art forms.

"Mass artists" such as writers, composers, and commercial artists generally maximize their profits by selling reproductions of each work in the highest volume possible. The fine artist, by contrast, usually creates a single work, and much of his profit is directly related to the work's uniqueness. Where the mass artist's copyright is infringed, the monetary relief afforded by damages and profits is likely to be substantial and likely to be his primary motivation in bringing suit.

Where a fine artist's copyright is infringed, however, monetary relief will not compensate justly for the wrong, and possible financial gain is not the artist's motivation in bringing suit. The fine artist is compensated only when the infringing artwork is removed from display.

IMPOUNDING AND DISPOSITION OF INFRINGING ARTICLES

The plaintiff in an infringement suit has the right to request the seizure *pendente lite* of defendant's work and, upon successful prosecution of his action, the "destruction or other reasonable disposition" of the infringing work.

Impounding is discretionary and considered to be an "extraordinary" remedy. It has been little used and little litigated, except in cases where the infringed work is seasonal or short-lived, such as records and catalogs, where the delay involved in waiting for a final decree may amount to a denial of any effective relief.

INJUNCTION

Section 502(a) of the 1976 Copyright Act reasserts the discretionary power of the courts to grant preliminary or permanent injunctions to prevent or stop copyright infringement. The tripartite standard for a temporary injunction is a probability of success at trial, a special reason ("irreparable injury") for threshold relief, and a balance of hardships.

*From Amy Roth, "Copyright Remedies and the Fine Artist" (student paper in the authors' files, May 10, 1982). Reprinted by permission.

Probability of success at trial is the most important factor and is satisfied by the plaintiff's showing of a valid copyright and substantial copying by defendant. While courts usually do not require a detailed showing of irreparable injury, some evidence of irreparable harm must be presented to justify a preliminary injunction.

Once the tripartite standard is satisfied, the plaintiff is required, as a condition of the grant of injunctive relief, to give security for the costs and damages defendant incurs if he has been unlawfully enjoined. . . .

A court may waive the injunction bond requirement where plaintiff is indigent. The applicant need not be "absolutely destitute" to be granted relief; he need only state in an affidavit that he cannot "pay or give security for the costs." Thus, by waiving the bond requirement, a court may enable the impecunious fine artist to preliminarily enjoin a defendant from displaying infringing art.

Of course, there is always the risk that the defendant will incur substantial cost and damages during the injunction; however, the court can minimize this risk by ordering a short injunction term, and by carefully balancing the hardships before issuing the injunction. . . .

NOMINAL BOND

. . . A judge could require an artist to post a nominal bond, or in lieu of that, a court could require a financially strapped artist to post artworks as security. . . .

A lawyer may be unwilling to pursue a permanent injunction action for an infringed artist who has no prospect of substantial financial reward. Even if counsel pursues the action and prevails, his attorney's fee award—if granted—would likely be insufficient to make the effort worth his while. Fortunately, the infringed artist is not remediless: he may pursue a permanent injunction pro se, for "himself." . . .

Pro se is especially apposite in cases where the artist is seeking the removal of infringing art. Since such cases promise little monetary reward, the artist is likely to have difficulty retaining counsel; his choice may be to either represent himself or drop the action.

The successful pro se plaintiff, whether he is an attorney or not, may even win attorney's fees. The court in a recent copyright infringement suit awarded attorney's fees to a nonattorney, pro se plaintiff. The judge emphasized the importance of granting pro se attorney's fees in infringement suits. First, granting fees ensures that all litigants have equal access to the courts to vindicate their statutory rights; second, it prevents copyright infringements from going unchallenged where there is no financial means or incentive to challenge an infringement through expensive litigation.

Finally, if all legal avenues are blocked, the infringed artist may find relief by way of publicizing the infringement. Alerting local television talk shows or writing letters to newspaper editors might stir the public to demand removal of the infringing work. Unfortunately, such publicity may very well create amusement, not indignation, for the public and business, not boycotts, for the infringer. . . .

COMMENTS

1. The possibility that a successful plaintiff will be awarded attorney's fees is a powerful incentive for an artist to bring suit for infringement. However, there is authority for the view that attorney's fees will not be awarded in the absence of bad faith on the part of the copyright infringer, even though the language of the 1976 statute seems to contemplate fee awards as a form of reimbursing the winning artist complaining of infringement and to penalize the infringer. See *Edward B. Marks Music Corp. v. Continental Record Co.*, 222 F.2d 488 (2d Cir.), *cert. denied*, 350 U.S. 861 (1955). In any case, the award of attorney's fees is discretionary ("the court may also award a reasonable attorney's fee").

2. Still, to be eligible for any kind of copyright protection the artist must take action and use the rights made available under the 1976 statute. Most artists don't do so. Why not? Timothy M. Sheehan, "Why Don't Fine Artists Use Copyright?" *Bulletin of the Copyright Society of the United States*, vol. 22 (1975), p. 242, reports that a survey of 206 artists revealed that the great majority had never used copyright. Some of the reasons given were: lack of information about how to do it (or in some cases discouraging misinformation); unwillingness to deface the work of art with the copyright notice; dislike of seeming "commercial;" and concern that collectors will be less willing to buy copyrighted works.

3. The Sheehan article, written in 1975, concluded that there was little reliable literature available to the fine artist on copyright. The situation has since changed. There is now substantial literature. *Contracts for Artists* by William Gignilliat (Atlanta: Words of Art, 1983) provides "everyday contracts and forms" for use by artists and reproduces relevant provisions of the 1976 Copyright Act as well as the relevant applications and publications of the U.S. Copyright Office. Similar practical guides include *Contracts and Copyright* by Laurence Singer (Washington, D.C.: The Registry 1982) and *An Artist's Handbook on Copyright* by Robert Lower and Jeffrey Young, published by Volunteer Lawyers for the Arts, Inc. (Atlanta: Georgia Volunteer Lawyers for the Arts, 1981). See also Tad Crawford "The Visual Artist's Guide to the New Copyright Law," a concise booklet published by the Graphic Artists Guild of 30 East 20th Street, New York, New York 10003; and Robert Wade and Richard L. Stroup, "Safeguarding the Uniqueness of Your Work," in *The Business of Art*, ed. L. E. Caplin (Englewood Cliffs: Prentice-Hall, 1982). In addition, artists can easily obtain information and applications with respect to copyright protection through a new Copyright Office Forms Hotline, (202) 287-9100, and the Copyright Public Information Office, telephone (202) 287-8700.

Articles in art publications and the popular press also provide the artist with information about the copyright law. See, for example, Johnson, "Copyright is Cheap, Informal, and Effective," *Design*, no. 366 (June 1979), p. 91; "Copyright Law for the Artist," *Ceramics Magazine*, no. 27 (Fall 1979), p. 71; Hamish Sandison, "New Copyright Law: Its Impact on the Visual Artist," *National Sculpture Review*, vol. 26 (Spring 1977), p. 7; and J. Jevnikar, "Copyright Protection," *American Artists*, vol. 46 (June 1982), p. 16. See also the series of articles on copyright by P. H. Karlen in various issues of *Artweek* during 1980 and 1981.

4. One reason artists sometimes give for failing to copyright is their fear that collectors will be less likely to buy a copyrighted work. A major collector of contemporary art has stated that only 5 percent of his collection is copyrighted and that an artist's use or nonuse of copyright does not affect his acquisition decisions (Statement by "Hunk" Anderson to authors).

5. Another factor may be doubt that it is worth the effort to obtain copyright protection because artists rarely win. Take heart! Follow the example of Susan Emery Eisenberg, a Florida artist:

SUSAN EMERY EISENBERG *One Artist's Experience**

My experience began in December 1979. I was having a one-person show of my three-dimensional works in plastic and paint at the Barbara Gillman Gallery in Miami, Florida. During this exhibit a prominent local designer, Mr. C., came into the gallery and expressed an interest in commissioning a "Ribbons Series" wall sculpture for his clients. During the course of the conversation with Barbara Gillman, it was decided that I would make a maquette to show to Mr. C's clients, and if approved a 4-by-8-foot piece in red, yellow, black, and green at a cost of $1,800 would be commissioned.

In January 1980 the maquette was given to Mr. C. The maquette, entitled "Ribbons #12" was clearly marked with the copyright symbol ©, the date of completion, and my name. Mr. C. also received a slide of "Ribbons #12," which was also clearly marked with the copyright symbol.

Because this was my first dealing with a decorator, I decided to file a copyright form with the Copyright Office in Washington for added protection.

Upon receiving "Ribbons #12," C. took the 24-by-35-inch maquette to "S" Corporation, a plastics fabricating firm in Miami. At this time Mr. C. instructed "S" Corporation to make a copy in a 4-by-8-foot size.

The maquette remained at "S" Corporation for several weeks and was seen by numerous individuals known to Barbara Gillman and myself. When employees of "S" Corporation were questioned about "Ribbons #12," they said the maquette was being copied for Mr. C. and they attempted to solicit additional orders. The "S" copy was made in clear plastic because their fabricators do not work with paint. My works are all hand-painted with enamels or acrylics.

After several weeks and numerous attempts

*Letter from Susan Emery Eisenberg to the authors. Used by permission.

via telephone and letter, Mrs. Gillman finally made contact with Mr. C., who responded that his clients were not interested in this type of work and that there would be no commission for me.

My lawyer filed a lawsuit against "S" Corporation and Mr. C. in the U.S. District Court for the Southern District of Florida, Case Number 80-1014-CIV-EBD, asking for a judgment of actual and statutory damages of $50,000 for copyright infringement under the U.S. Copyright Act.

Two impressive affidavits were obtained from experts Eugene Massin and Leslie Judd Ahlander, which include excerpts such as: "Susan Emery Eisenberg has developed a unique style of plastic sculpture"; "easily recognized as an Eisenberg style"; and "striking similarity to the maquette, the only difference being the color or lack of it."

Less than a week before trial, Mr. C. settled out of court by paying me the sum of $23,000, a hefty price to pay for a piece of art that could have been commissioned two years earlier at a mere $1,800.

Section 106(5) of the 1976 Copyright Act gives the copyright owner the exclusive right "to display the copyrighted work publicly." This sounds better than it actually is, as the following excerpt explains.

LEE CORT *The Artist's Right to Control Public Display**

Among the exclusive rights granted to the copyright owner is the previously unprotected right of public display. That is, in the case of "pictorial, graphic or sculptural works" the owner of copyright has the exclusive right to display the copyrighted work publicly (Section 106(5)). To "display" a work means to show a copy of it, either directly or by means of a file, slide, television image, or any other device or process (Section 101). To display a work "publicly" means to display it (1) at a place open to the public or at any place where a substantial number of persons outside of a normal circle of a family and its social acquaintances is gathered or (2) to transmit or otherwise communicate a display of the work to a place specified by clause (1) or to the public, by means of any device or process, whether the members of the public capable of receiving the display receive it in the same place or in separate places and at the same time or at different times (Section 101).

Presumably this new right would enable the artist to prevent unauthorized exhibition (or obtain royalties for authorized exhibition) of his work by museums, galleries, etc. In fact, however, the right of public display offers precious little protection beyond that which would be secured by contractual means. This is due, in large part, to the fact that the Section 106(5) right of public display is subject to several critical limita-

tions. The most severe limitation is found in Section 109(b) which states:

Notwithstanding the provisions of section 106(5), *the owner of a particular copy* lawfully made under this title, or any person authorized by such owner, *is entitled, without the authority of the copyright owner, to display that copy publicly,* either directly or by the projection of no more than one image at a time, *to viewers present at the place where the copy is located.* [emphasis added by Cort.]

Subsection (c) of Section 109 clarifies that ownership of a copy (not possession by rental, lease, loan, or otherwise) alone is sufficient to afford the privilege prescribed by Section 109(b).

Section 109 evidences a distinction between ownership and possession of a copyrighted work. One who obtains ownership of the work (e.g., by sale) thereby acquires the right to display it publicly, whereas one who obtains mere possession of the work (by rental, lease, or loan) without acquiring ownership of it does not thereby acquire the right to display it. Thus a museum that purchased a painting would be free to display it, but the same museum could not do so without the copyright owner's permission if it held the painting on loan.

Obviously, Section 109(b) places a severe limitation on the exhibition rights of the artist. Pursuant to this section, the right to display is lost whenever the copyright owner transfers owner-

*From Lee Cort, "The Artist's Right to Control Public Display Under the Copyright Revision Act of 1976" (student paper in authors' files, 1978), pp. 2–6. Reprinted by permission.

ship of the copyrighted work to another person. This result stands in sharp contrast to the superior protections afforded by other exclusive rights of the copyright proprietor, such as the right to reproduce the work in copies. Thus, the ironic result obtains that the artist who retains his copyright in a painting, for example, yet transfers ownership of the painting to a collector, would retain the right to reproduce the painting on postcards or in lithographs, but would lose the right to control display of the painting at a museum or gallery. Clearly, Section 109(b) substantially curtails many of those protections afforded to the artist by the highly vaunted right to public display.

COMMENT

In fact, the "exclusive right to display the work publicly" is a statutory restatement of the right of divulgation. In other nations (e.g., France, Germany, and Italy) the right of divulgation is a moral right, as explained earlier in this chapter. In the United States, however, under "common law copyright," the artist had a comparable right to divulge or not to divulge. On "federalization" of the common-law copyright in the 1976 law, this statutory provision resulted. As with the common-law copyright, the right of divulgation does not survive a transfer of ownership of the work.

COPYRIGHT AND THE ART CONSUMER

We have been focusing on the rights of the artist under the copyright law. Now we turn briefly to artists' copyright from the point of view of two major groups of art consumers: museums and collectors.

NICHOLAS D. WARD *Copyright in Museum Collections* *

THE TRANSFER OF COPYRIGHT

THE TRANSFER OF THE WORK DOES NOT INCLUDE A TRANSFER OF THE COPYRIGHT

One of the most important aspects of the copyright law for museums concerns transfers. Since copyright, that proprietary right of the author to control certain uses of his work, is distinct from the work itself, the transfer of the material object in which copyright subsists, does not constitute a transfer of any coypright interest. Accordingly when a museum acquires a work subject to copyright, it will not acquire any of the rights of copyright unless those rights are conveyed specifically in a written agreement. There is an exception to this principle that involves the right of display. The lawful owner of the work or a copy of the work (the act tends not to distinguish between originals and copies) may display that copy or the original publicly without need of any license from the copyright holder. This right is not, however, afforded to one who acquires the work from the copyright owner by rental, lease or loan or otherwise without acquiring ownership of it. In other words one who borrows the work from the owner cannot, in the absence of a license, in turn lend to a third person and authorize that person to display the work.

THE TRANSFER OF THE COPYRIGHT MUST BE BY AN EXPRESS AGREEMENT

There are two ways that a museum can acquire a copyright in a work, by exclusive transfer or by non-exclusive license. An exclusive transfer of one of the rights of copyright would give the mu-

*From Nicholas D. Ward, "Copyright in Museum Collections: An Overview of Some of the Problems," *Journal of College and University Law,* vol. 7 (1980–1981), p. 297. Copyright © 1981 by National Association of College and University Attorneys. Reprinted by permission.

seum the right to exclude others from exercising a similar right. For example, if we obtain an exclusive right of reproduction then if another museum publishes a postcard without our permission they have infringed the copyright. Almost by definition, however, the holder of a non-exclusive license cannot sue for infringement. . . .

A SUGGESTED APPROACH TO SOLVING THE PROBLEMS

WHAT RIGHTS DO WE REALLY NEED?

There are four incidents of copyright ownership that are of potential interest to a museum, namely, the copyright owner's exclusive right to do or authorize the following: (i) to reproduce the copyrighted work in copies, (ii) to distribute copies of the copyrighted work to the public by sale, or other transfer of ownership or by rental, (iii) to adapt the work to a derivative work, and (iv) when the museum is not the owner of the work, to display the copyrighted work publicly. It is difficult to distinguish between the right of adaptation and the right of reproduction. The exclusive right to prepare derivative works "overlaps the exclusive right of reproduction to some extent;" however, it is a broader right nevertheless. A post card, for example, may involve both rights.

Abundance of caution suggests that both rights are desirable and that the specific usages proposed should accompany any grant of license. If the museum is unable to obtain either an exclusive or non-exclusive right to do the foregoing, except as the doctrine of fair use may provide the contrary, the museum will be restricted to merely showing the work in its gallery and will not be able safely to:

(1) Take a photograph of the work or allow others to do so.

(2) Include a photograph of the work in a catalogue or allow another to include such a photograph in another's catalogue.

(3) Sell any publications of the work in the museum shop.

(4) Lend the work to other museums for exhibition without the copyright owner's express permission unless the museum is the owner of the work.

Since there is no presumption that a transfer of the work itself constitutes a transfer of any of these proprietary rights, an express written assignment thereof is necessary.

Perhaps initially someone ought to try to classify works that are proposed for acquisition by purchase or loan to determine which rights it might wish to obtain, bearing in mind that minimal copying for a registrar's files and the like is probably permitted as a fair use. But once a decision to acquire is made and rights of copyright are not acquired such fact should be noted in the file so inadvertent but unlawful infringement does not occur.

A second question arises as to which is the preferable right to acquire, an exclusive transfer or a non-exclusive license. Essentially there are two differences. The holder of a non-exclusive license cannot exclude others and cannot license others, whereas the owner of a transfer of an exclusive license can exclude others and grant a license to another. Therefore, if you wish to organize a show and allow others to copy you would need an exclusive license. An alternative method would be to have a provision in the original grant of the non-exclusive license that would provide for the copyright owner's future additional grants of non-exclusive license to the grantee's nominees. Further, if the museum is unable to obtain an exclusive assignment of the right of reproduction, it will not be able to have the work reproduced in or on any kind of article, whether useful or otherwise, thereby being limited to reproduction solely for a catalogue and not for note paper, tote bags, etc. But, again, how important is this consideration?

A TESTAMENTARY GRANT IS NOT SUBJECT TO TERMINATION

Whenever a transfer or license is obtained, you have the opportunity to suggest that the artist bequeath that copyright interest to you. If the interest is valuable the artist's estate will obtain a charitable deduction in the Federal Estate Tax return based on the fair market value of the interest, and this testamentary disposition is not subject to the ordinary rule on termination of transfers and licenses. If the artist does not bequeath this copyright interest to a charity, he may subject his estate to increased taxation because his retention of the right of termination may either in and of itself be valuable or may, if worth 5% or more of the total value of the copyright, bring the whole copyright into his estate as a reversionary interest. The tax law is not clear on this one but it is your development officer's opportunity to make a reasonable pitch for support.

FAIR USE IS NOT THE PREFERABLE SOLUTION

An alternative to obtaining a specific license or transfer of a copyright interest may lie in reliance upon the doctrine of fair use, but it is not as desirable because it is uncertain and probably not sufficiently broad to provide extensive enough protection from claims for infringement.

Since fair use is a doctrine of defense to a claim for infringement and exists to mitigate against an unduly harsh result, it is a more flexible principle than others contained in the act. But, it is also vague. If the museum has a license from the copyright holder, it has a document specifying the extent of its rights. If the museum copies, adapts and distributes in reliance upon fair use, it has an argument only. It would there-

fore seem that a license or transfer would be preferable to reliance upon fair use. But what if a license or transfer cannot be obtained? Can fair use nevertheless be relied upon? If the license or transfer is denied, the museum is on notice that the artist will be looking carefully at any reproduction and the scope of fair use will perforce be diminished. If the license or transfer is not obtained because the copyright holder cannot be located then resort to fair use still makes sense.

In the planning stage before a work is acquired, it would be a good idea to review the proposed uses, the kinds of copyright interests that may be desired, including whether an exclusive transfer is preferred over of a non-exclusive license, and the prospects of which of the proposed uses might qualify as a fair use. At this point a negotiating strategy can be developed without risking the taking of the inconsistent position of asking for a license, because it is said to be necessary, and then upon the failure to obtain it, to copy on the tenuous grounds that it is a fair use anyway. . . .

COMMENTS

1. In 1982 Dorothy M. Weber of the Visual Artists and Galleries Association of the United States presented a report on "Museums and Copyright" (copy on file with the authors) to an international conference of copyright societies in Madrid, Spain. The report consisted of a survey of the copyright practices of seventeen American museums. The report concluded:

> We did anticipate that the results of this survey would show that the Museums are, in fact, abusing artists' rights. Unfortunately, the results show that the situation is far worse than originally anticipated. For the most part, every major museum is seeking a complete grant of rights from the artist. In addition, pressure is brought on the artist to sign these grants of copyright or risk having the Museum no longer acquire that artist's work.

2. In an article in *State of the Arts* (no. 35, May–June 1982), Tim Jahns noted:

> The Museum of Modern Art in New York [uses] . . . a limited nonexclusive license. . . . This license allows the museum to reproduce a work for the usual catalogs, postcards, slides, magazines and newspaper publicity or reviews, plus educational books and T.V. programs. . . . [By contrast,] the San Francisco Museum of Modern Art tries to obtain all rights when it acquires a contemporary artist's works.

3. The following comment by Albert Elsen appeared in Jahns's article: "To try to get the whole copyright from an artist is outrageous. Whether museum directors are principled people or not, that's an unprincipled act. They should get a restricted waiver or assignment of a limited right to do certain things with the work. . . . Artists shouldn't be pressured in any way to give up their rights." And in the Weber report Elsen commented: "I think the idea of a museum's trying to obtain the copyright from the artists is an outrageous thing. There is not reason they should get all the rights. This policy should be fought at all costs. It is hypocritical and should not be tolerated. Artists, art historians, and collectors should boycott any museum that has this policy until an acceptable policy is established."

4. See also Dorothy Weber-Karlitz, "Museums, Artists, and Copyrights," *Cardozo Arts and Entertainment Law Journal,* vol. 2 (1983), pp. 21ff.

The following article looks at copyright from the collector's point of view.

LISA SCHILIT *The Copyright Revision Act Through the Eyes of the Art Collector**

A federal copyright is like the proverbial sword and shield in the hands of its owner. As a sword, it arms the owner with the exclusive rights to reproduce and adapt the work, and to distribute and display his reproductions and adaptations. As a shield, it safeguards the owner from those who attempt to usurp his rights.

A collector who purchases a unique work for his personal pleasure or for investment purposes will rarely need to use copyright as a sword but he may need to use it as a shield in order to preserve the value of the work. His interests tend to overlap the artist's; for the most part, both will want to maintain the integrity of the work by controlling its exposure, barring offensive uses, and preventing inferior reproductions. Due to the substantial identity of the artist's and the collector's concerns, the collector may be content to entrust control over subsequent reproduction and adaptation to the artist. Nevertheless, the wise collector will ascertain whether the artist has a valid copyright in the work at the time of sale and insist on copyright protection as a condition of purchase.

In contrast, the collector who purchases a work with the intention of reproducing or adapting it will have a use for copyright both as a sword to produce and disseminate his copies and as a shield to block competition. If the artist were to retain copyright ownership, the collector would infringe upon the artist's rights by making his copies. To determine whether his intended use will constitute an actionable infringement, the collector will have to investigate the copyright status of the work. If the artist still owns the copyright, the collector will want to acquire it.

Under the new statute, the collector can obtain the copyright, in whole or part, through a written transfer signed by the artist. He should take any steps necessary to perfect the copyright and should record the instrument of transfer in the Copyright Office as soon as possible. Most copyright transfers are terminable thirty-five years after the date of their execution at the option of the artist or his heirs.

The tension between the artist and the collector should by now be apparent. Copyright law assigns to each certain rights in the same work, and the Revision Act expresses this fundamental premise in the following language:

Ownership of a copyright, or of any of the exclusive rights under a copyright, is distinct from ownership of any material object in which the work is embodied. Transfer of ownership of any material object . . . does not in itself convey any rights in the copyrighted work embodied in the object; nor, in the absence of an agreement, does transfer of ownership of a copyright or of any exclusive rights under a copyright convey property rights in any material object.

The statutory language borders on the metaphysical, but the reports that accompanied the bill through Congress explain it succinctly: "copyright ownership and ownership of a material object in which the copyrighted work is embodied are entirely separate things."

Conceptually, it is more accurate to view copyright ownership and ownership of the material object as correlative rather than "separate things" and to think of these "things" as bundles of legal rights. One who owns both a unique work of art and the copyright in it holds the maximum aggregate of property rights in the work. One who owns less holds correspondingly fewer rights. When ownership of the material object and ownership of the copyright are severed—when the collector acquires the copyrighted work from the artist— the rights of each owner are circumscribed by the rights of the other. . . .

The 1976 Act reverses the common law presumption that the artist intended to transfer his copyright together with his work by requiring the separate conveyance of the material object and the copyright in it. The collector gains no rights from the artist's inaction at the time of sale. If he desires the exclusive rights conferred by the statute, the collector must now bargain for them.

. . . One thing is clear: the collector who intends to reproduce or adapt the work should make every effort to obtain a transfer of copyright from the artist. But the outlook for the collector who has no need for reproduction or adaptation rights is not nearly so bleak. And regardless of his reason for acquiring the work, every collector can find solace in the fact that the artist who refuses to release his copyright in a unique work still loses two of his exclusive rights upon its sale.

This curtailment of the coypright owner's exclusive rights, which evolves from the common law aversion to restraints on alienation, was

*From Lisa Schilit, "A Look at the Copyright Revision Act Through the Eyes of the Art Collector," *Art & the Law,* vol. 6 (1981), p. 3L. Copyright © 1981 by Volunteer Lawyers for the Arts. Reprinted by permission.

known as the first sale doctrine under prior law. The Revision Act codifies the doctrine in section 109. The two rights affected are the right to distribute and the right to display.

Section 109(a) limits the artist's distribution right after sale of the unique art work: "the owner of a particular copy . . . lawfully made under this title, or any person authorized by such owner, is entitled, without the authority of the copyright owner, to sell or otherwise dispose of the possession of that copy." The provision effectively terminates the artist's right to distribute the original work after its sale because the collector, by virtue of his ownership, has the right to dispose of his tangible property as he sees fit. The congressional reports state unequivocally: "The copyright owner's exclusive right of public distribution would have no effect upon anyone who owns 'a particular copy . . . lawfully made under this title' and who wishes to transfer it to someone else or to destroy it."

At this juncture, it is interesting to note that the new copyright law does not purport to give the artist the right to prevent the destruction of a unique work after its sale, although his reproduction and adaptation rights might be impaired as a result.

Section 109 also limits the artist's right to display the work after sale. American coypright law has never explicitly recognized an exclusive right to display before; section 106, which enumerates the exclusive rights of the copyright owner, contains "the first explicit recognition . . . of an exclusive right to show a copyrighted work, or an image of it, to the public." The right is an important one to many artists, who desire greater control over the installation of their work and the environment in which it is exhibited. Yet the scope of the new right is not nearly so broad as many artists assume.

Since the right extends only to public display, the collector can exhibit the work privately without encroaching upon the rights of the artist. Section 109(b) further enlarges the collector's display right:

The owner of a particular copy lawfully made under this title, or any person authorized by such owner, is entitled, without the authority of the copyright owner, to display that copy publicly, either directly or by the projection of no more than one image at a time, to viewers present at the place where the copy is located.

The quoted language is broad enough to enable the collector to exhibit the work in a gallery, museum, or other public place without the consent of the artist. Some art periodicals have advised their readership that the owner of a work copyrighted under the new act must ask the artist's permission before lending the work for the purpose of exhibition. Their advice is erroneous. The artist cannot prevent the collector from displaying the work in an objectionable way unless the display involves projecting the work to distant viewers. The congressional reports confirm that section 109(b) is intended

to preserve the traditional privilege of the owner of a copy to display it directly, but to place reasonable restrictions on the ability to display it indirectly in such a way that the copyright owner's market for reproduction and distribution of copies could be affected.

. . . Thankfully, the act is far more successful in establishing the relative positions of the artist and the collector with respect to the reproduction and adaptation rights in a unique work.

Unless the work has fallen into the public domain, the copyright owner retains his reproduction and adaptation rights after sale. Although he owns the unique work, the collector has no power to prevent the artist from exploiting it other than that which he derives from his physical control over the master copy. . . .

COMMENTS

1. The artist and the collector both have interests in the artist's work being copyrighted, but who is the best party to own the copyright in light of the difficulties the artists have in enforcing their copyrights? Given transaction costs of obtaining permission to copy a work from the copyright owner, in whose hands is the copyright more valuable—the museum or gallery that displays the work, or the artist who may or may not be living nearby? Can the artist transferring his copyright obtain a premium in the purchase price to reflect the value of the copyright transfer and end the practice of museums accepting gratuitous transfers? Is ownership of copyright in the hands of the artist of more than pecuniary value?

2. As the owner of a work, the collector has a right to limit access to it. The value of this right to the collector is discussed in a footnote to the Schilit article excerpted above:

With respect to unique works of art, which exist in only one copy, "it is virtually impossible to make a reproduction of commercial quality without the owner" . . . [citing Brenner, "A Two-Phase Approach to Copyrighting the Fine Arts," *Bulletin of the Copyright Law Society,* vol. 24 (1976), pp. 85ff.] Even if the artist has a valid copyright in the work, he cannot compel the collector to permit reproduction of the master copy. . . . Here the collector can employ his ownership of the material object as a shield against the copyright owner.

3. It would seem reasonable to argue that the right to reproduce without the right of access for the purpose of reproduction is a valueless right (unless the artist made reproductions before transferring the work), that Congress must not be assumed to have created empty rights, and that reasonable access in order for the copyright owner to exercise his right to copy should be implied. There is no American authority on the point. In Italy, in *Garofalo v. Istituto Cavalieri della Carita,* 49 Diritto di Autore 601 (1975), on the basis of a similar argument, the court ordered the owner of the work to permit the artist to photograph it.

THE RESALE PROCEEDS RIGHT

The resale proceeds right (in French, *droit de suite;* in German, *Folgerecht*), like the copyright, is a patrimonial or property right of the artist, not a right of personality. It does not apply to the "primary market"—that is, to transfers of works by the artist who created them. But subsequent transactions (sometimes referred to as the "secondary market") are subject to the artist's right to share in the proceeds. Thus if Artist sells a painting to Collector, and Collector then sells it to Museum, the Collector–Museum transaction may, depending on the applicable law and the facts, be subject to the proceeds right.

The resale proceeds right was first established in France in 1920 and has since been adopted in varying forms in a number of other nations, though a greater number have rejected it. A UNESCO survey conducted in 1983 indicated that of fifty-one nations that responded twenty-one had resale proceeds right laws. In Europe these included Belgium, France, Germany, and Italy, but not the Netherlands, the Scandinavian countries, Spain, or Switzerland (*Propriété Artistique* [an information bulletin published by the Société de la Propriété Artistique et des Dessins et Modèls, or SPADEM, described below], nos. 9–10 [January–April 1984], p. 17). The right did not exist anywhere in the common-law world until its enactment in California in 1976.

SELECTED EUROPEAN STATUTES AND CONVENTIONS

France, Law of March 11, 1957, No. 296

Article 42. Authors of graphic and plastic works shall have, regardless of transfer of the original work, an inalienable right to participate in the proceeds of any sale of their works by public auction or through a dealer.

After the author's death, this *droit de suite* shall subsist to the benefit of the heirs and, for the usufruct provided by Article 24, to the benefit of the spouse, but excluding all legatees and transferees, for the current calendar year and fifty years thereafter.

The rate of the levy for this right shall be uniformly fixed at 3 per cent, applicable only on a sale price of more than 10,000 francs.

The levy shall be based on the sales price of each work and on the total sales price, without any deduction.

Ministerial regulations shall determine the conditions under which the authors shall assert their claims to the right recognized by the provisions of the present Article, in the case of the sales referred to in the 1st paragraph.

COMMENTS

1. The French established the proceeds right in 1920. It originally applied only to sale at auction. The extension to sales by dealers was part of a major revision of the law applicable to artists' rights in 1957. However, the statute requires implementing rules, and these have not been issued. The executive, which opposes extension, refuses to issue the rules and would like the reference to sales by merchants to be repealed. But the legislature, which favors extension, will not repeal. As a result, the French statute still is applied, in practice, only to sale at auction.

2. Sales at auction are the easiest to monitor. The sales are public, announced in advance, and often accompanied by widely distributed catalogs containing identification of the artists and descriptions and provenances of the works offered for sale. In France auctioneers are semi-public officials required to keep thorough, accurate records of all transactions. Sales by art dealers, even those who maintain art galleries and keep regular books, are less public and more difficult to monitor. As one moves to private dealers, who do not maintain galleries or put on exhibitions, and on to resale by private persons, the difficulty of effectively monitoring transactions becomes impressive, and the temptation to avoid payment of the resale proceeds right is sometimes irresistible. The French limitation of the proceeds right to public auction thus avoids the common problem of the unenforced or unenforceable statute that rewards the scofflaw by placing those who comply at a competitive disadvantage.

3. On the other hand, since auctioneers and dealers compete with one another, there is a certain logic to the auctioneers' complaint that the French statute, in operation, discriminates against them, since they have to pay the artist his 3 percent, while a dealer who makes a similar sale need pay the artist nothing.

4. As originally enacted, the French system required the artist or his representative to register his claim to future resale proceeds rights in a given work in the *Journal Officiel* (something like the *Federal Register* in the United States), and a copy of the registration statement was to be sent to the minister of fine arts. In this way it was intended that a public register of works of art, useful for a variety of purposes, including authentication, would be built up. In practice, however, the registration scheme did not work. Instead artists simply join SPADEM and generally assign the power to collect their proceeds rights to it. The statute obliges the auctioneer to pay the proceeds to the artist, but in practice the payment is made to SPADEM. Thus SPADEM, a private organization (roughly comparable to ASCAP for composers in the United States), dominates the process. See Rita Hauser, "The French Droit de Suite," *Copyright Law Symposium*, vol. 11 (1959), p. 1.

Germany, Law of September 16, 1965, No. 51

Article 26. (1) Should the original of an artistic work be resold and should such resale involve an art dealer or an auctioneer as purchaser, vendor or agent, the vendor shall pay the artist a participation at the rate of five per cent of the sale price. There shall be no such obligation if the sale price is less than one hundred German marks. (2) The artist may not in advance waive his right to the participation. The expectancy thereof shall not be subject to judicial execution; any disposition of the expectancy shall be without legal effect.

COMMENT

In 1980, after much discussion and litigation, the German Art Dealers Association (which includes auctioneers) entered into an agreement with Bild-Kunst, an artists' rights licensing and collection organization (similar to and associated with SPADEM, the archetypal French organization). Under this agreement the dealers and auctioneers pay 1 percent of their sales of twentieth-century art to Bild-Kunst and provide records of sales subject to the proceeds right, and Bild-Kunst uses this sum (1) to pay proceeds rights and (2) to pay over the excess to a special social security fund for artists ("Nouvelles d'Allemagne," *Propriété Artistique*, nos. 9–10, [January–April 1984], p. 15).

Italy, Law of April 22, 1941, No. 633

Article 144. The authors of works of art in the form of paintings, sculptures, drawings and prints shall be entitled to a percentage of the amount by which the price of the first public sale of original copies of such works exceeds the price of first alienation, and such excess shall be presumed.

The organizer of the sale, the vendor and the purchaser shall, however, be entitled to prove that such public sale was not preceded by any act of alienation for valuable consideration, or that the price of first alienation was not less than that obtained in the public sale.

Article 145. The authors of the works indicated in the preceding Article shall also be entitled to a percentage of the higher value that the original copies of their works ultimately acquire in successive public sales, such higher value being the difference between the price at the last public sale and the price at the public sale which immediately preceded it.

Article 146. The percentages specified in the preceding Articles shall be due only if the selling price is in excess of 1,000 lire in the case of drawings and prints, 5,000 lire in the case of paintings, and 10,000 lire in the case of sculptures. The percentages shall be payable by the owner selling the work.

Article 147. If the price of the original copy of the works specified in this Section, at any sale which is not deemed to be public under law, attains 4,000 lire in the case of drawings and prints, 30,000 lire in the case of paintings, and 40,000 lire in the case of sculptures, and also exceeds five times the price of first alienation, however effected, such increase in value shall be subject to a payment of 10% to the authors of the works, payable by the owner selling them.

Proof of the price paid for a work and of the conditions specified in this Article shall be the responsibility of the authors.

The percentage shall be reduced to 5% if the vendor proves, in turn, that he acquired the copy at a price not less than half of that realized by him.

The provisions of Article 145 shall apply for the purpose of determining the higher value.

Article 148. For the purposes of the protection specified in the foregoing Articles, replicas made by the author shall also be considered as original works, but not reproductions otherwise produced. In respect of prints, those which have been derived from original engravings, signed by the author, shall be considered as original works.

Article 149. For the purposes of this Law, the following shall be considered public sales:

(a) sales effected at shows and exhibitions, authorized within the meaning of Royal Decree Law of January 21, 1934, No. 454, which became the Law of July 5, 1934, No. 1607;

(b) sales by court order;

(c) sales effected by means of public auctions;

(d) sales of works offered by sale at public auctions, but withdrawn from such offering as the result of private negotiations;

(e) sales effected in connection with private exhibitions organized or carried out by third parties.

Article 150. The rights specified in Articles 144, 145, 146 and 147 shall belong to the author and, after his death, and in the absence of testamentary provisions, to his spouse and legitimate heirs to the third degree, according to the rules of the Civil Code; if there are no successors as above indicated, the rights shall devolve upon the insurance and assistance fund of the National Syndicate of Fine Arts (*Cassa di previdenza e di assistenza del Sindicato nazionale della belle arti*).

Such rights shall continue for the life of the author and fifty years after his death, and may not be the object of alienation or advance renunciation.

Article 151. The percentage due upon the price of the first public sale within the meaning of Article 144 shall be fixed at the level of 1% for amounts up to 50,000 lire; 2% for amounts exceeding that sum and up to 100,000 lire; and 5% for any further excess.

Article 152. The percentages due upon the increase in value determined in accordance with Article 145 shall be fixed as follows:

2% for increases in value not exceeding 10,000 lire
3% for increases in value in excess of 10,000 lire
4% for increases in value in excess of 30,000 lire
5% for increases in value in excess of 50,000 lire
6% for increases in value in excess of 75,000 lire
7% for increases in value in excess of 100,000 lire
8% for increases in value in excess of 125,000 lire
9% for increases in value in excess of 150,000 lire
10% for increases in value in excess of 175,000 lire

Article 153. The person who legally presides over the public sale of works of art referred to in this Section shall be obliged to deduct from the sale price of original copies the percentages due within the meaning of Articles 144 and 145, and to pay such amount to the Italian Authors' Rights Institute (EIDA) under the conditions specified in the Regulations.

Until such time as the payment is effected, the person who presides at the sale shall, for the purposes of law, be deemed to be the depository of the sums deducted.

Article 154. Works of art which, in a public sale, have attained at least the price indicated in Article 146, shall be notified to the Italian Authors' Rights Institute by the person who has lawfully directed the sale. Such person shall proceed to effect appropriate registration in the manner prescribed by the Regulations.

In the absence of any imputation of falsity, the registration effected shall constitute proof of the price obtained for the work.

COMMENT

For a thorough examination of the proceeds right in Italy, see Vittorio M. DeSanctis and Mario Fabiani, "The Right on the Increase in Value of the Works of Fine Arts in the Italian Copyright Law," in *Legal Rights of the Artist,* ed. M. Nimmer (Washington, D.C.: National Endowment on the Arts and Humanities, 1971). DeSanctis and Fabiani state that as early as 1950 the application of the Italian *droit de suite* legislation "came to a standstill."

Berne Copyright Union (1886) as Modified in Paris Act (1971), Art. 14

(1) The author, or after his death the persons or institutions authorized by national legislation, shall, with respect to original works of art and original manuscripts of writers and composers, enjoy the inalienable right to an interest in any sale of the work subsequent to the first transfer by the author of the work.

(2) The protection provided by the preceding paragraph may be claimed in a country of the Union only if legislation in the country to which the author belongs so permits, and to the extent permitted by the country where this protection is claimed.

(3) The procedure for collection and the amounts shall be matters for determination by national legislation.

COMMENTS

1. The United States is not a party to the Berne Convention, but it does adhere to the Universal Copyright Convention, which contains no resale proceeds right provision.

2. The art market in a country that has the resale proceeds right (e.g., France) is at a comparative disadvantage vis-à-vis one that does not (e.g., England, Switzerland). Sellers naturally prefer not to pay the artist a percentage of the sale price, and the mobility of most art (and of money) make it easy enough to send work to London or Berne for sale, rather than to Paris or Munich. Accordingly, French dealers and auctioneers would prefer to abolish the resale proceeds right, while SPADEM and Bild-Kunst would prefer to generalize it. SPADEM has been particularly active in promoting the resale proceeds right internationally and strongly supports action in the European Economic Community and UNESCO to this end.

3. The French and German statutes give the artist a percentage of the total resale price, whether the resale is at a profit or at a loss. However, the Italian statute gives the artist a percentage of the difference between the seller's purchase price and the resale price. It is clear that the Italian statute is more difficult to administer and enforce, and that may help explain its disuse. But it is fairer, and more consistent with arguments in support of the right, to restrict the artist to a portion of the profit, if any, on resale. Suppose the resale is at a loss. Should the artist compensate the seller?

4. The French, German, and Italian statutes and the Berne Convention all make the proceeds right inalienable. Moral right statutes, as we have seen, generally contain similar provisions. The artist's copyright, however, is not so restricted by statute. If, as is usually argued,

the vulnerable, impractical artist needs to be protected against more powerful and worldly dealers and collectors, it is difficult to justify excluding copyright from the protection.

5. Suppose a painting at auction fails to reach the reserve price. Is the artist entitled to his cut? Scholars in Italy seem to have decided that the right applies only to true sales, but an important French decision, dealing with a work by the Douanier Rousseau, takes a different direction. There the painting by Rousseau was bid in for the owner. The heirs of Rousseau demanded their percentage of the last bid. The court (Tribunal de la Seine, 21 January 1931, Gaz. du Palais 1931. 1. 301) held that they were entitled to payment. The decision, based in part on the court's view that the use of the secret reserve was illegal, is critized in Albert Wahl, "Le Droit des Artistes sur les Oeuvres Retirées d'une Vente Publique ou Adjugées au Profit du Vendeur," 1936 Rev. trim. dr. civ. 613.

6. One attempt to provide economic aid to unrecognized artists is the *"domaine public payant,"* which is sometimes confused with the proceeds right. The *domaine public payant* is a statutory requirement that royalties continue to be paid after the copyright expires. Such royalties are paid into a fund that is used to assist and encourage living creative artists. Such a system exists in both France and Italy. In a way it resembles the National Endowment for the Arts in the United States, but the funds come from royalties instead of from government grants. Questions about the proper methods of supporting working artists are pursued in Chapter 5.

7. The resale proceeds right is controversial both in the nations that have enacted it and in the nations in which its enactment is proposed. The California statute, discussed below, pp. 231–38, has excited a great deal of controversy, and attempts to enact the proceeds right in other states and in Congress have reignited the debate. The Canadian Government "after careful research" rejected it (*International Journal of Museum Management and Curatorship,* vol. 1, no. 3 [September 1982], p. 264).

ARGUMENTS FOR AND AGAINST THE RESALE PROCEEDS RIGHT

At a celebrated and now legendary auction of contemporary art held in New York in 1973, which was captured for posterity in a widely distributed documentary film, a collection of works owned by Robert and Ethel Scull was sold. One painting, by Robert Rauschenberg, sold for $85,000. Scull had bought the work some years earlier (for $960, according to one account). After the auction there was a celebrated encounter between Scull and Rauschenberg in which the latter is reported to have said, "I've been working my ass off just for you to make that profit. . . ." Since that episode the proceeds right has become a militant cause for Rauschenberg and a variety of artists and sympathizers in the art world. "From now on I want a royalty on the resales and I am going to get it," the artist is reported to have said. Rauschenberg's crusade has made good copy, producing articles in the *New York Times,* the *Wall Street Journal* and *Time* magazine, as well as in the art press. See Baruch D. Kirschenbaum, "The Scull Auction and the Scull Film," *Art Journal,* vol. 39 (Fall 1979), p. 50. We now turn to the arguments for and against the *principle* of the proceeds right. These arguments should be read skeptically. What assumptions do they make? Are they valid? Does the world they describe really exist, or is there some romance here?

CARL R. BALDWIN *The Artist's Royalty Problem**

Droit de suite, incorporated into French law in 1920, stipulated that a work of art sold at public auction would return to its author (or to his or her heirs and assigns, up to 50 years after the artist's death), from 1 to 3 percent of the total sales price (3 percent for works sold for 50,000-francs

*From Carl R. Baldwin, "Art and Money: The Artist's Royalty Problem," *Art in America* (March–April 1974), pp. 20–23. Copyright © 1974 by Art in America, Inc. Reprinted by permission.

or more). The law was revised in 1957 to stabilize the percentage at 3 percent, regardless of selling price, and to include sales made through dealers as well as auctions . . . .

In 1930s America, the economic squeeze sparked a good deal of speculation on the ways and means by which artists could regularize their participation in the economic workings of the art world, and of the larger social and political world as well. In 1934 a representative group called the Society of Painters, Sculptors, and Gravers, backed by the Artists' Union and its publication, *Art Front*, announced a rental plan which called upon museums to pay artists a fee for the public exhibition of their work. The charge was to be 10% of the fair value of the work per month, which the Society estimated would cost museums an average of $6.61 per work per month. The Society agreed with such infuriated museum men as Francis Henry Taylor (then of the Worcester Art Museum) and Duncan Phillips (Phillips Gallery, Washington, D.C.) that American museums as currently operated did not have that kind of money; but the Society insisted that museums would have adequate funds, if they spent their money in the right places: stop the single-minded acquisition of high-priced old masters, they urged, and put more money into works of living American artists. The notion that museums should pay artists for exhibiting their work may seem fanciful today, but at the time it won the support of Peyton Boswell, editor of *Art Digest*, and in 1935 was accepted by the Whitney Museum and about a dozen smaller museums around the country. Mrs. Juliana Force, Director of the Whitney, and Lloyd Goodrich, then associate curator, were its strongest supporters in the museum world (Goodrich informed me, in fact, that he still favors the idea). And during 1935, according to an unpublished dissertation on the Whitney by Daty Healy, the museum paid rental fees to all artists who exhibited there. The rental plan was dropped by the Whitney in 1936 because the other major museums were adamant in their opposition, and the Whitney could not afford to continue the plan in virtual isolation. Although not a Royalty Plan in the sense of a participation in sales proceeds, the Rental Plan of the '30s is an important—and largely forgotten—evidence of the self-assertiveness of artists as a collective group, bargaining for a fair share of art world resources. (It is interesting to note that as recently as 1972, Billy Al Bengston refused to exhibit at the Whitney because they would not pay a rental fee. See *Art in America*, no. 2 [1973].)

A full-fledged and audacious Royalty Plan was, interestingly enough, presented by Grant Wood in 1940 (and sympathetically reported in *Life*, February 19, 1940). Disgruntled at what he took to be collectors' speculation on *Daughters of Revolution*, which had quadrupled in value over a short period of time, Wood announced that his new work, *Parson Weems' Fable*, would be sold by his dealer, Associated American Artists, with the stipulation that subsequent sales would bring him 50 percent of the appreciated value. I have not yet been able to discover whether this agreement was ever put into effect. It provides, in any case, an illuminating instance of an artist's intention to write his own ticket—to be as tough and determined as American heroes of business and labor were expected to be, and were admired for being.

During the '40s and '50s, Royalty Plans were far from the minds of artists, perhaps because any well-disposed dealer or museum was revered as a godsend, not to be embarrassed by discussion of some notion of Artist Power that would have smacked of the denigrated radicalism of another age. It was not until the late 1960s, and coupled with a general disillusionment with allegedly benevolent hierarchies—whether governments or institutions—that artists, individually and collectively, began to consider alternatives to time-honored art world practices. Reproduction rights, rentals and royalties were all studied afresh. Positions adopted by the Art Workers Coalition (as summarized by Lucy Lippard in *Studio International*, November 1970) included: "(1) rental fees should be paid to artists or their heirs for all works exhibited where admissions are charged, whether or not the work is owned by the artist" (this latter provision goes beyond the '30s Rental Plan and incorporates the notion of "participation rights" in the European sense); "(2) a percentage of the profit realized on the resale of an artist's work shall revert to the artist or his heirs" (like *droit de suite*, but related to appreciated value rather than net receipts, and broader, by presumably including private sales). Both of these ideas were incorporated in modified form in a sample contract called "The Artist's Reserved Rights Transfer and Sale Agreement," composed by the dealer Seth Siegelaub and the attorney Robert Projansky, and published in *Artforum* and *Studio International* in 1971. To be signed by artist and dealer, or artist and first purchaser, it specified that artists would receive 15 percent of the appreciated value each time a work was resold, donated, exchanged or otherwise transferred. The artist would also have control over exhibition of the work and be entitled to a percentage of the proceeds in the event that an owner received remuneration from its exhibition. . . .

Another possibility is to try to have participation rights written into U.S. law. This was suggested in law journals by Dr. Rita A. Hauser (*Bulletin of the Copyright Society of the U.S.A.*, 1959) and attorney Diane B. Schulder (*Northwestern University Law Review*, 1966). Their ideas . . . involve the introduction of a variation of *droit de suite* in American law, perhaps by including it in the U.S. Copyright law. An important argument in this regard is that in other arts, such as literature and musical composition, the dissemination of the work to the public and its increasing renown and popularity bring concrete and proportional benefits to its creator, whereas in the visual arts increasing renown and popularity primarily benefit owners rather than creators. . . .

FRANÇOIS HEPP *The Origin of Droit de Suite in Copyright Law* *

If the painter or sculptor authorizes the reproduction of his work, he usually stipulates royalties. However—and this is curious—when he sells the original work itself, he usually exhausts all his rights. Although this method of sale—which after all relates to an object somewhat different from the manuscript of a book—may seem to be just and practical from the commercial viewpoint, it has been regarded by a number of European jurists as being far from equitable from the viewpoint of safeguarding the interests of the artist and his heirs. Why is this so? These are the points that require some explanation, as in the majority of the countries the attention of the legislators has not been directed toward the practical consequences of the present general usage.

Works of the fine arts have an economic value which varies considerably, according to the tastes of the public, fashion, and the evolution of artistic views. The greatest masterpieces of art have generally not been recognized at the time they were created. On the other hand, many artists whose works were fashionable at the time of their creation were completely forgotten after their deaths, and their names do not evoke any echo in the minds of subsequent generations.

Unrecognized artists are vindicated after their death. Their works, which they sold when they were poor to some competent art collector and for which they received only a very low price, acquire considerable value. This is a common phenomenon, well illustrated by much-publicized public auctions, in which works completely neglected at the time of their creation have been sold for tens, even hundreds, of thousands of dollars. Such sales, however fabulous the prices may be, mean no profit to the artist. He is dead; and his children, even poorer perhaps than he was himself, learn about the extraordinary results of such auctions in the newspapers.

This situation has aroused those jurists, particularly in France, who seek to improve copyright protection. They thought that it was perfectly equitable that the original buyer, who had had a sure enough artistic taste and also courage when he gambled his money on a work without any market value at the time of buying it, should benefit by the increase in value of the work. It is only just that his good taste and courage be rewarded through a good business deal. However, when the work passes into the hands of another buyer who may be nothing more than a simple businessman without any artistic taste, and who simply wants to make a good business deal by buying an article which is generally recognized to have a high value—would it not be just to give to the artist, old and poor, or to his children if he is dead, a small portion of the price which the buyer pays without taking any chances or showing any courage, because the work is now generally recognized as having a certain commercial value in the market for works of fine arts? It is from this idea, inspired both by feelings of equity and a desire to compensate for the variations in public taste, that the right—juridically not very correctly called the "droit de suite"—to royalties for the authors of works of fine arts is born. This expression was invented somewhat hastily by French jurists by a rather far-fetched analogy with mortgages on real property. It is not surprising that this expression is not quite understood by foreign jurists and causes them, for this very reason, to reject without further examination the concept behind the expression. But if the terminology is forgotten and the essence of the question is examined, it will be seen that what is instituted is not a new right but simply a method whereby the royalties they are now deprived of are granted to authors who sold their works under special circumstances—usually the presure of necessity—and without realizing the true value of their work.

If the problem is not one of justice, it certainly is one of equity, and deserves the most careful consideration. . . .

COMMENTS

1. Arguments like those in the Hepp article are sometimes referred to as the *La Boheme* or "starving artists' children" theory of proceeds right justification. Compare Randall K. Filer, "The 'Starving Artist'—Myth or Reality? Earnings of Artists in the United States," *Journal of Political Economy,* 56 (1986), p. 94. Professor Filer, an economist, examines 1980 census and other data and concludes that artists do not "earn any less on average than they would in other jobs."

2. In "The French Droit de Suite: The Problem of Protection for the Underprivileged Artist Under the Copyright Law," *Bulletin of the Copyright Society of the U.S.A.,* vol. 6 (1959), pp. 94ff. Rita E. Hauser identifies two legal theories that proponents use to justify the resale proceeds right: the German theory of intrinsic value and the French theory of compensation for exploitation. According to the theory of intrinsic value, any higher price achieved on resale merely recognizes the latent or intrinsic value of the work, due solely to the artist's labors and genius in creating it. The French theory is that the proceeds right compensates the artist for exploitation of the work, just as royalties are a payment to the author or composer for exploitation of his creation. The idea is that the normal form of exploitation of literary or musical compositions is through the publication and sale of copies or through public performance, and the author of the copyrighted work is entitled to demand payment, whether in a lump sum or royalties, in return for his permission to exploit. Reproduction and performance are not, however, the usual forms of exploitation of works of art. Hence something is needed to give visual artists parity of treatment with other creative people.

3. Paul Sherman, "Incorporation of the Droit de Suite into United States Copyright Law," *Copyright Law Symposium,* vol. 18 (1968), p. 50, describes a third, Belgian theory of a continuing relation between the artist and the purchasers of his works. According to this theory, the artist, by his continuing creativity and growing fame, continues to add value to works previously sold and should share in that added value.

4. With the support of SPADEM, a Visual Artists Rights Society has been formed in England and has issued the following statement.

*Statement by the Visual Artists Rights Society**

1. For some years there have been organisations at work, both here and on the continent, concerned with securing rights and benefits for artists on such matters as VAT, collection of artists' copyright dues, exchange of artists' works free of customs formalities and duties and the right of an artist to benefit from the exploitation and re-sale of his work by collectors, speculators and others. In short, protecting artists' material, moral and intellectual rights.

2. The Brussels Copyright Convention of 1948 dealt with copyright and re-sale rights and was signed, in Brussels, by all European Economic Community (EEC) countries *except* the United Kingdom, Irish, Greek and Netherlands Governments which for different reasons did not adhere to the particular provision dealing with artists' re-sale rights usually known as *droit de suite.*

3. The issue is shortly to be reconsidered. The EEC is preparing a Directive to this end to which it is hoped all member countries will adhere. This is therefore an opportune moment to try and influence our government to

*As quoted in the *International Journal of Museum Management and Curatorship,* vol. 1, no. 3 (September 1982), p. 264.

fall in line with other EEC countries for the benefit and protection of UK artists.

4. The case briefly is that as paintings and sculptures are frequently re-sold at prices many times those originally paid to the artist, the artist should be able to receive a small percentage of each re-sale. At present, in this country, the speculators, collectors, auctioneers and dealers benefit exclusively. While authors and composers receive royalties and musicians receive "performing rights" fees, visual artists receive nothing.

5. We believe this to be unjust. With the passage of time the value of an artist's work may be considerably enhanced or depressed. For example, an artist's earlier work for one reason or another (to give only one of many examples) may come to be valued at the expense of his later work. The same situation will face his or her heirs who do not benefit by subsequent re-sales.

6. What is proposed is that where the price of a re-sale exceeds a certain level, the artist, or his heirs, should receive a small percentage of this price or of the profits. This is the case in France, the Federal Republic of Germany, Belgium, Italy, Denmark, Luxembourg and in several countries outside the EEC.

7. In France there is a powerful organisation, SPADEM, which acts on behalf of artists for collection of copyright reproduction fees and artists' re-sale rights and we have been in close touch with them to profit by their experience.

8. The Visual Artists Rights Society (VARS) has been formed in the United Kingdom, in consultation with SPADEM, to act on behalf of artists in the collection of reproduction fees etc. It will also press the government to allow the introduction of artists' re-sale rights.

9. As this matter is soon to be reconsidered by the UK authorities, we believe that it is vital that artists make known their interest in the matter by calling on the government to agree to the institution of artists' re-sale rights when it comes up at international level in the near future.

ARGUMENTS AGAINST THE PROCEEDS RIGHT

In 1977 Congressman Henry Waxman became interested in the proceeds right and prepared a draft bill for introduction into the U.S. Congress. Comments on the draft were sought from interested people and institutions in the art world, and a number of them attended an informal meeting on Capitol Hill to discuss it. (This is in contrast to the California law enacted in 1976 at the initiative of one legislator, supported by a coterie of artist-enthusiasts, with little publicity and no solicitation of views from museums, collectors, or dealers.) After the discussion, Congressman Waxman drastically revised the bill, which he introduced in 1978 but did not actively support. The bill died in committee. Stephen E. Weil, deputy director of the Hirshhorn Museum, participated in the 1979 discussion. The following article is based on his statement.

STEPHEN E. WEIL *Resale Royalties: Nobody Benefits* *

That American artists should, through their own creative efforts, be able to sustain themselves—and to sustain themselves with greater dignity and more adequate means than many can do today—is not merely socially desirable. It is a national necessity. In an environment that increasingly stresses corporate accomplishment and technical skills, the importance of artists becomes correspondingly greater. They are among the last role models we have of free imagination, transcendent aspiration, and—above all—individual effort and responsibility. Beside whatever contributions their work can make to our accumulated cultural heritage, artists in their own selves are

*From Stephen E. Weil, "Resale Royalties: Nobody Benefits," *ARTnews*, March 1978. Copyright © 1978 by ARTnews Associates. Reprinted by permission. This article also appeared in Stephen E. Weil, *Beauty and the Beasts: On Museums, Art, the Law, and the Market* (Washington, D.C.: Smithsonian Institution Press, 1983).

more than ever vital to maintaining the balance of our national life.

Recognizing that artists require a more adequate support system than American society now provides, legislators at both the state and the federal level have shown increasing interest in finding other means to help them. One proposal, strongly championed by a number of artists and by many artists' groups, would do so by the establishment of resale royalties.

To question, as I shall, both the principles underlying this proposal and, regardless of the soundness of these principles, the utility of any legislation that would establish such royalties is to risk being misunderstood as indifferent or even hostile to the well-being of artists. I hope that I am neither, and I would hesitate to raise such questions publicly were I not convinced so strongly, first, that the establishment of resale royalties, far from helping artists or having only a neutral impact, would in fact be positively harmful to their interests and, second, that it is critically important that those who wish to help artists take advantage of this current surge of legislative interest by concentrating their efforts on alternative measures that would increase—rather than, as resale royalties threaten to do, diminish—the funds now available for the purchase of contemporary art.

Analogy and image. Underlying the proposal for artists resale royalties are an analogy and an image.

The analogy is to the means by which authors and composers have traditionally been compensated. Implicit is the suggestion that, by reason of their right to receive royalties, these other creative workers enjoy an advantage that visual artists are denied. This was clearly expressed in one of the seminal documents of the present campaign for resale royalties, the Art Proceeds Act proposed in 1966 by Diana B. Schulder in the *Northwestern University Law Review.* Section 2 provided: "Since a painter or a sculptor who creates a unique work of art does not benefit from the fruits of his labors as does an author or composer who derives royalties from the reproduction or performance of the work, this act, by allowing an economic right upon re-transfer, is intended to ensure to artists a parallel benefit."

The image coupled with this analogy is that of a collector who, having purchased a work of art for relatively little, resells it for a great deal more, pocketing the entire profit and leaving the artist, whose effort first created the work and whose subsequent accomplishments may have contributed to its increase in value, with no part of such increase. It is the image of Robert Rauschenberg and Robert Scull in tense confrontation after the 1973 auction at which Scull resold for $85,000, a work for which he had originally paid Rauschenberg less than $1,000.

If the establishment of resale royalties is to be founded upon some sound principle, then, at the outset, two questions must be asked. Is this underlying analogy correct, and does this underlying image—unquestionably distressing in its suggestion of a collector unjustly enriched at an artist's expense—reflect some common situation or only an occasional, albeit highly visible, anomaly in the market?

Painters, poets, and others. Would the grant to visual artists of some continuing economic interest in their work, the realization of which would be dependent on the resale or successive resales of such work, in fact be a "parallel benefit" to the royalty rights now enjoyed by other creative workers? Clearly, it would not. The royalties that authors and composers receive are based on the multiple initial sales of their infinitely reproducible efforts. For each additional copy of a novel printed and sold, the author may receive additional compensation. So may the composer for each additional performance of a musical composition. For that matter, so too may the visual artist who elects to sell additional copies of an infinitely reproducible *image* of a work of art rather than the unique object in which the work itself is embodied.

This is not the case with a resale royalty. In the case of a resale royalty, no additional example of the original work is being brought into being nor is the work itself being put to any broader use. The event that would cause the proposed royalty to be paid would, instead, be the substitution of one owner for another. It would be as if Norman Mailer could claim some further payment for each copy of *The Naked and the Dead* resold in the secondhand book market above the $4 price at which it was originally published in 1948 or as if an architect could claim some share of the proceeds when a house he designed was subsequently resold at a profit. No such right exists today.

What is proposed here, then, is the establishment of a *new* right—one very different from a royalty and one that does not extend naturally from existing concepts of property and ownership. Whether such a special right should be established for artists is a larger, open, and arguable question, but not one that can be answered by a simple analogy to the royalties payable to authors and composers.

Might the establishment of this special right be justified, then, on the ground that the traditional method by which artists have been compensated places them at a disadvantage to other creative workers? It might, if this were so. It appears, however, not to be so. If we exclude such supplementary income-producing activities as teaching, lecturing, or wholly unrelated employment—none of which relates to the question of royalties and some of which normally supplement the art-derived income of most creative individuals—and exclude as well the grotesquely inflated earnings of such mass-appeal entertainers as rock stars or gothic novelists, visual artists would seem to be consistently better compensated for their creative effort than their peers in the other arts.

To make such comparisons is awkward. Real names must be used, and virtually no one will agree with particular comparisons. Nevertheless, if you compared the probable art-derived income of creative individuals of comparable seriousness, achievement, and popularity, how well would visual artists fare? Consider Pablo Picasso in relation to Igor Stravinsky or Thomas Mann; Marc Chagall to Vladimir Nabokov or Béla Bartók; Henry Moore to Benjamin Britten or W. H. Auden; the fifth best earner of the Castelli Gallery to the fifth best earner among the Yale Younger Poets. Make your own comparisons. If you do it fairly, I believe you will find that the earnings of visual artists—no matter how inadequate such earnings may be in themselves or how poorly they may compare with those of individuals outside the arts—are nevertheless consistently above the earnings of those of their peers who are compensated by royalties.

There are reasons why this should be so. That a work of art is traditionally embodied in a tangible, physical object rather than—as in the case of literature or music—expressed through such infinitely reproducible media as words or sounds has more than aesthetic implications. Beyond the fact that their value is influenced—if not largely determined—by scarcity, works of art do not require the same level of demand as do works of literature or music to secure their creators a living. A painting needs no initial market larger than a single buyer in order to be sold. Two potential buyers, by themselves, can provide the

basis for a successful auction. A hard-core audience of two hundred faithful collector-buyers might guarantee an artist's livelihood. By contrast, a poet or novelist—able, perhaps, to realize a two-dollar royalty on the sale of each hardcover copy of a book—would require thousands, if not tens of thousands, of reader-buyers to earn any continuing support from the sale of his work.

If this is so—and if the difference in the way in which they have traditionally been compensated has been an advantage, rather than a disadvantage, to visual artists—then we must look elsewhere for some basis by which the establishment of a resale royalty might be justified.

The argument of unjust enrichment. We know that there are collectors who, from time to time, have made a great deal of money from buying and reselling works of art. We know too that some artists whose work has been involved in these transactions feel that they have been "ripped off" as a result. What we do not know, however, is whether this happens very often. That is only the tip of our ignorance. Confining our consideration to works of art by living American artists, we also do not know, for example:

- The annual dollar volume, number, and price level of primary sales (sales from the artist or dealer to a first collector).

- The ratio these bear to the overall market for art, antiques, antiquities, and other competing "collectibles."

- The number of those works sold in the primary market that are ever resold in the secondary market, and the interval between such sales.

- Of the works resold in the secondary market, the number that are sold at more and the number that are sold at less than their initial price and, in each case, the dollar volume involved.

Beyond this, we have only the haziest idea of how many American artists there are for whose work there even is a regular primary market, of how many of these artists also have a secondary market, of how many buyers "collect" art in any significant way, and of how many such buyers ever resell the works they buy.

We remain, thus, stalled at our original question: How common is the situation that provoked the Rauschenberg-Scull confrontation? Is it one that is constantly repeated across the country, with large numbers of collectors reaping "windfall" profits by reselling the work of a large number of artists? Or is the resale market for contemporary art confined largely to the work of a relatively small group of well-known artists whose work is bought and sold chiefly by "blue-chip" collectors?

Certainly, if it proved that some substantial number of transactions were involved, and if there were general agreement that the ability of collectors to reap such windfall profits had within it an element of unfairness, there might be some warrant for adopting national legislation that would impose some additional tax—which need not necessarily be one payable to artists—beyond the state and federal income taxes to which such profits are already subject.

Even here, though, it would be difficult to know what, except in the most extreme cases, would be meant by a "windfall" or even—always a problem in calculating taxes—what would be meant by a "profit." If, between the time he bought and resold it, the net after-selling-cost value of a painting in a collector's hands increased by no more than the current rate of inflation, was he unjustly enriched? What if the increase just equaled the interest paid on funds that he might have borrowed to purchase the painting in the first place? What if the increase just equaled the expenses incurred during ownership for insurance and/or conservation? What if he bought and sold two paintings by the same artist, profiting as much on one as he lost on the other?

And what if all of these—inflation, interest cost, the expenses of ownership, and offsetting gains and losses—occurred together? While something may be sensed as unfair in a collector buying a work of art for $10,000 and selling it the next year for $50,000, to what extent do we sense it unfair if a painting, or anything else with a secondhand value, is bought for $10,000 and resold for $15,000 some ten years later?

To justify a resale royalty on the basis that it would ameliorate some widespread injustice done by collectors to artists would require considerable information beyond what we now have. Moreover, to achieve acceptance as fair and reasonable, it would require a mechanism more sophisticated than those proposed thus far to determine when, and in what amount, such a royalty might be appropriate. If windfall profits from the sale of contemporary art are, in fact, a substantial problem, that problem should be addressed by some measured response and not by a dramatic gesture that, regardless of any immediate satisfaction it might give, could neither be justified to those it would affect nor be of benefit to those on whose behalf it was made. Frustration

and anger, real as they may be, are not a sound basis for national legislation.

The one-way connection. A further argument made in support of resale royalties is that their establishment would give legal recognition to—as well as symbolize—a continuing connection between the artist and a work of art after it had once been sold. In so doing, it would move American law closer to those Continental systems that recognize a *droit de suite,* from which the concept of resale royalties was first derived, as well as a *droit moral.* Their right to receive resale royalties would, in effect, be the "umbilical cord" through which artists would maintain an ongoing relationship with their work.

The justice of this argument fades, however, when we realize how one-sided this ongoing relationship would be. It would not require the artist to bear any part of a collector's ongoing expenses, such as those for insurance or conservation. Neither would it impose on the artist any greater liability than heretofore for the instability or failure of the materials or workmanship he might have employed in his work. Above all, the proposed umbilical cord would only carry gains, carefully filtering out any losses that collectors might incur on the resale of those works to which the artists would otherwise remain connected.

Certainly, no one seriously proposes that the artist—or the artist's heirs for fifty years after death—should be liable for a refund of five percent of the initial purchase price whenever a collector is unable to resell a work of art for the amount it originally cost. For many artists, the contingent liability might well exceed their total worth. At the same time, however, it is difficult to accept as just a proposed form of partnership in which one of the partners would bear all of the risks while the other enjoyed the luxury of sharing in profits only.

Art in a commodity market. To all of the foregoing, it may in some fairness be replied: so what? If resale royalties would, in reality, benefit artists generally, that fact alone, regardless of any infirmity in the supporting arguments, might be reason enough to consider their establishment. As I said at the outset, however, I have come to believe exactly the opposite: that resale royalties would be neither of any benefit nor even neutral in their impact but would in fact do enormous harm to the already not-very-well-being of contemporary artists.

Unpalatable as it may be to many, works of art—once out of an artist's hands—become commodities. They are articles of commerce. As such, the prices at which, and the numbers in which, they are bought and sold in both their initial and resale markets are influenced by those same considerations that affect the level of prices and sales of any commodity in any market.

No matter how else it may be characterized, a resale royalty would function as a tax. As a tax, it could—as we know from long experience with other taxes—substantially influence the behavior of those to whom it applied. If contemporary art were as much a necessity for collectors to buy as it is for artists to make, this might not matter. Unhappily, though, no matter how bravely we proclaim "ya gotta have art," nobody "gotta" have art, and especially contemporary American art.

If contemporary works of art are to be the subject of a discriminatory tax—one that would not be equally applicable to such alternative "collectibles" as nineteenth-century American art, twentieth-century European art, contemporary crafts, Ming vases, shares of IBM, or condominiums in the Bahamas—there is every reason to believe that some number of collectors would choose alternative investments. Ironically, these would most likely be those very same collectors who most distress artists by considering works of art primarily for their investment possibilities rather than as a personal commitment. Without greater knowledge of the art market, we do not know what this number and their impact might be. What we do know is that to impose a greater tax on one commodity than on another that can readily be substituted for it is to alter the pattern of demand and that, in any market, a reduction in demand must inevitably be followed by a reduction in either or both the level of prices and the volume of sales.

As it is, contemporary works of art are, for the most part, poor investments already. While some may increase in value, the greater number can never again be resold for what they initially cost. Those that do increase in value must increase substantially before any significant return can be realized. Unlike securities, for example—on which a stockbroker's commission may be less than 1 percent—the expense of reselling a work of art through a dealer or at auction will often be 15 to 25 percent. To this, before a profit can be realized, must be added any intermediate costs of ownership: insurance, conservation, and shipping. A security that increases in value by 20 percent can, on resale, yield its owner a profit. A work of art that increases by only the same amount will more likely yield its owner a loss. And, unlike a security, neither such loss nor any intermediate cost of ownership is generally deductible for tax purposes.

Into this already fragile situation, the resale royalty would introduce a further disincentive. Its impact—if calculated on the basis of gross proceeds rather than, as in the case of an income tax, on profit alone—would be far greater than the generally proposed figure of 5 percent at first suggests.

Assuming an average expense of 20 percent, a collector cannot—even before any resale royalty—resell a work of art for less than 125 percent of its original purchase price without incurring a net loss. By adding a resale royalty of 5 percent of gross proceeds, the minimum break-even point would rise to 133 percent. In the case of a painting bought for $10,000 and resold for $13,000, leaving a net of $10,400 after the payment of expenses, the collector—his remaining profit having been already wiped out—would have to pay a substantial portion of the $650 resale royalty directly from his own pocket.

As resale prices began to exceed 133 percent of the original purchase price, the impact of the royalty, while no longer confiscatory, would still remain high in comparison to other taxes. Thus, if the same painting were sold for $14,000, the resale royalty—$700, to be paid out of the net profit of $1,200 remaining to the collector after expense—would equal an income tax of 58 percent. If the painting were resold for $20,000, the royalty of $1,000 would—after deducting expenses of $4,000—still equal a tax on this profit of more than 15 percent. Even with a three-times appreciation—the original $10,000 painting resold for $30,000—the royalty, calculated on gross proceeds, would equal a tax of more than 10 percent of the net profit remaining after the cost of sale. Beyond this, the collector would still, of course, be required to pay state and federal income taxes on whatever remained.

To make contemporary American art so disfavored an investment can only affect the level of demand in its primary and secondary markets. While diminished demand might initially affect volume, it would sooner or later be reflected in prices as well. If the prices and sales of well-established artists were the first to weaken, then those of almost-as-well established artists would inevitably follow. The process would continue until it affected the sales and prices of the least established of all.

Less now, more later? Acknowledging that the market might be thus affected, some proponents of resale royalties have argued that artists would nevertheless make up, and ultimately surpass, any initial depression in their primary selling prices by the resale royalties they would earn in later years. Surely, there are some who might: the well-established artists, those with regular resale markets and, for the most part, substantial primary markets as well.

For the greater number, though—the 90 or 99 out of every 100 whose work never increases substantially in value, who may have no resale market at all, and who might far better be the focus of legislation intended to benefit artists— no subsequent royalties would make up for this initial deficiency. In the end, what the establishment of a resale royalty would do is what most regressive legislation does: the rich might—or might not—get richer, but the poor would certainly get poorer. As Monroe and Aimée Price concluded in their 1968 *Yale Law Journal* article analyzing the distribution of benefits under the comparable *droit de suite* legislation in France: "to those who have shall more be given."

When gross sales proceeds are used as the basis for computing royalties, this balance is tilted still further—to those who have the most shall the most be given. Artist A, young and unknown, sells a painting for $1,500. Several years later, primarily as a result of A's steadily growing accomplishments and reputation, the painting is resold for $15,000, a tenfold increase. At five percent, Artist A will receive a royalty of $750 to add to the $1,500 he received on the original sale. Artist B, mature and well established, also sells a painting. The price is $18,000. After the same several years, it too is resold. The price is $20,000, a moderate increase reasonably attributable to the intervening inflation. Artist B will receive a royalty of $1,000 to add to the $18,000 that he received on his original sale.

Results such as these are inherent in the gross proceeds formula. They make an awkward fit with the argument that justifies the establishment of resale royalties as rectifying an injustice done to artists when collectors sell their work at very large profits. In fact, the artists who already have the strongest primary markets, and generally the strongest secondary markets as well, would be those likely to benefit the most from this formula. For them, only a moderate percentage increase on resale would be necessary to trigger a substantial royalty. For newly established artists, a manyfold increase might not bring them nearly as much.

Alternatives. The most serious economic problem facing most contemporary artists is the lack of any broad initial market for their work—not such abuses as may occur in the resale market. What would benefit these artists most is an increase in the funds available to purchase works of art. This is the basic flaw in the resale royalty. It does not seek to increase these funds, but, at best, would merely redistribute—ostensibly from collectors to artists but, as a side effect, also from the less-established to the better-established artists— some portion of the inadequate funds already in the market. At worst, by imposing a discriminatory tax on contemporary art, it would reduce such funds.

In Europe, where it originated, the resale royalty has not produced any substantial returns for the great mass of artists. In some countries it has been rejected, in others it is unenforced, and, at its best, it favors only a few. In California, the resale royalty established last year [1977] has thus far served only as a divisive element within the art community and has produced virtually no tangible benefits for artists.

Given the limited, and possibly transient, attention that Congress can focus on this problem, it would be far bolder and more productive if artists and those who would help them channeled their energies behind legislation that would have an effect exactly opposite to that to be expected from royalties—that would increase, rather than diminish, the potential funds available for the purchase of contemporary art.

Most effective would be legislation that, instead of making art a less favored form of investment, would do just the contrary and give it a special and favored status. That is a route that other special-interest groups have taken with advantage. There might, for example, be a provision parallel to the present Section 1034 of the Internal Revenue Code, which defers to a later time any capital gains tax otherwise payable on the sale of a taxpayer's residence provided that the proceeds realized are used to purchase a new residence. By giving collectors an incentive to use the entire proceeds from the resale of a work of art—both their initial investment and any profit realized—to purchase additional works of art, substantial additional moneys could be brought into and kept in the market for contemporary art.

Such a provision could include many refinements. It might limit qualifying new purchases to the work of living American artists. It might require that all such purchases be made directly from artists and not in the secondary market. To benefit a broader group of artists, it might require that no single purchase could exceed some particular price of some particular portion of the amount to be reinvested. Whatever the formula, the object would be to provide an incentive for recycling back into the market—and thus back to artists—100 percent of the funds invested in every kind of art, ancient and modern, domestic and foreign—and not merely 5 percent of the resale proceeds from contemporary art.

Another alternative that has been suggested is the establishment of an art bank similar to that which now exists in Canada. Should an art bank be considered desirable, there is no reason why it need be, as some have suggested, connected with—or financed through—resale royalties. While no one has yet estimated what level of funding would be necessary to establish, supervise, and enforce a nationwide resale royalty, it must be considerable. Instead of using these funds to provide more jobs in Washington, why could the same funds not be used as the initial capital for an art bank? Its benefits could flow to artists immediately—not in five or ten years hence, as would be the case if resale royalties were to be used for its financing. Moreover, such funds would be "new money" in the market—not, as would be the case if an art bank were financed through royalties, simply a redistribution of the funds already there.

"Percent for art" legislation has only recently begun to receive the stronger backing that it deserves. Where it does not yet exist, it can be brought into being. Where it already exists, there may be the possibility of seeking higher percentages. At the federal level, Representative Gladys Spellman of Maryland has taken this course with the introduction [in 1977] of H.R. 7988, which would require the General Services Administration to double to 1 percent the percentage of construction funds to be used to commission or purchase works of art.

One enormous advantage of "percent for art" legislation is that it can coexist at the federal, state, county, and municipal levels. In some local jurisdictions, substantial percentages have been achieved. San Francisco has established a 2 percent rate, Miami Beach has a 1½ percent rate, and a 1 percent rate will become effective in Colorado this coming July [1978]. Above all, legislation of this kind at the local level offers the broadest group of artists not only the possibility of improving their livelihood through the sale of their work but, beyond that, the opportunity to see their work woven into the public fabric of the communities in which they live.

Whether these or other devices, alone or in combination, represent the best possible approach, what they share is the purpose of increasing the demand for contemporary works of art by injecting into the market new funds that could be channeled toward their purchase. Rather than serving to divide, such measures could enlist the enthusiastic support of all elements within the art community and, in the most practical way, offer what artists presumably want most from any legislation passed on their behalf: an increased opportunity to earn dignified livelihoods through their own creative efforts.

In the end, we would all be the beneficiaries.

Statement by the Society of London Art Dealers*

1. The Society of London Art Dealers has always been concerned about the economic position of the artist, and many of its members do their best to assist in the most obvious practical way they can by showing and selling the work of living painters and sculptors.

2. The recent retrenchment in Public Spending has accelerated the fall in the amount of art teaching available with consequent hardship for many artists. So the Society of London Art Dealers has embarked on a campaign with other interested bodies, to try and persuade the Government to change its attitude to artists.

3. The main objectives that we are attempting to achieve are:—

(a) The acceptance of "Artist" as a profession by the Department of Health and Social Security. This entails also the question of the definition of an "Artist."

* As quoted in the *International Journal of Museum Management and Curatorship*, vol. 1, no. 3 (September 1982), pp. 265ff.

(b) Acceptance of the idea of an unemployed artist and consequently his support during periods of unemployment.

(c) The problem of support for an artist, who has been trained as such at a state run art school, from the period of his leaving art school until his first successful exhibition. Acceptance by the state of some responsibility for him.

(d) Acceptance of the concept that during this period of working without selling the artist will be improving by practising his art and if alternative work is offered or insisted upon, this may prove detrimental to his development.

(e) Removal of VAT on first sales by living artists.

(f) Duty free movement for works of art anywhere within the EEC.

(g) More support and patronage from Industry and the introduction of the idea that a sum of money should be allocated to be spent on art as an accepted part of every building contract.

4. The Society of London Art Dealers feel that action as outlined above is far more likely to produce solid material benefits for artists especially for those young artists more likely to be in need, than the rather nebulous proposals for a Droit de Suite (Artists' Resale Right). There is now a strong lobby in this country for such a proposal although the idea is largely discredited among artists in EEC countries who have tried it out. Whilst being superficially attractive, the Society of London Art Dealers, after lengthy discussions both there and with their contacts in Europe, have decided against supporting it for the following reasons:—

(a) Although the avowed object of Droit de Suite is to help the poorer artist, it seems unlikely to do so; in fact the truth is that it will only make already successful artists richer. Not many works by unsuccessful artists appear in the sale rooms and even those by relatively successful ones often sell for less than the original price. Someone has calculated that barely 1% of works resell for even as much as their historic first purchase price, no account being taken of inflation. In fact proponents of Droit de Suite never mention inflation or any suggestion of its effect on prices.

(b) If Droit de Suite is to be introduced it will require machinery to register all sales including the first, as otherwise it will be largely ignored for the very good reason that most buyers will regard it as unfair. Machinery will be required to collect and pay over the percentage due to the artist or his heirs. Many members of the Society of London Art Dealers are well aware that it is difficult to sell contemporary work even without these kinds of strings attached.

(c) Many first time buyers of an artist's work have more than half an eye on an eventual price rise. They feel (and this includes many galleries, particularly in France) that in return for stockpiling an artist's work when he is young and unknown they should eventually benefit from their successes and use them to offset the amounts spent on their failures. Droit de Suite will certainly not help this process.

(d) In the period when an artist's success is being built up there are always a number of re-sales of his work made so-to-speak behind the scenes between collectors, dealers and speculators. These are a very necessary part of the construction of a solid market for the work and will be very much inhibited if a Droit de Suite has to be paid every time. Only such sales as show a sufficient profit to pay Droit de Suite will see the light of day.

(e) If, as in some quarters, is suggested, a resale percentage is paid to the artist on the resale price (whether greater or less than the original cost price), the obvious danger exists of spurious sales, through bogus first time buyers or alternatively of secret unrecorded buyers entering the chain of transaction.

5. For these reasons the Society of London Art Dealers consider that, far from helping unsuccessful artists, Droit de Suite will actually put off potential first time buyers. Quite apart from its adverse effect on the "market" on which the artists depend, the practical difficulties are immense. For instance, to be fair, a factor for inflation should be deducted from all notional profits made. A large number of civil servants will be required to run and police the collection of the sums involved and to distribute them to beneficiaries. The proponents of the scheme suggest that a computer could do the job quickly and easily. So it may, but preparing the figures to feed the computer will be immensely complicated and so will interpreting the result and distributing the money. In any case, will artists relish handing over so much personal data to a computer? Collectors will also be reluctant—another deterrent to sales!

6. However, the Society of London Art Dealers are very aware that young artists often do need, for a time, financial support and there are

sad cases of widows or children of artists who have left very little money in their wills but whose work sells after their death for much more than in their lifetime. The Society of London Art Dealers consider these people can much more fairly be helped from a central fund.

COMMENTS

1. For additional discussions questioning the principle of the resale proceeds right, see Monroe E. Price, "Government Policy and Economic Security for Artists: The Case of the Droit de Suite," *Yale Law Journal,* vol. 77 (1968), p. 1333; Michael Asimow, "Economic Aspects of the Droit de Suite," in *Legal Rights of the Artist,* ed. M. Nimmer (Washington D.C.: National Endowment on the Arts and Humanities, 1971); Simon Rottenberg, "The Remuneration of Artists," *Frontiers of Economics* (1975), p. 45; Ben W. Bolch, William W. Damon, and C. Elton Hinshaw, "An Economic Analysis of the California Art Royalty Statute," *Connecticut Law Review,* vol. 10 (1978), p. 692. Price is particularly telling when he describes what he calls "the theology of the *droit de suite*" as "the product of a lovely wistfulness for the nineteenth century." "The *droit de suite* is *La Boheme* and *Lust for Life* reduced to statutory form." But see Lewis D. Salomon and Linda V. Gill, "Federal and State Resale Royalty Legislation: 'What Hath Art Wrought?'" *UCLA Law Review,* vol. 26 (1978), p. 322.

2. Asimow, Rottenberg, and Bolch et al. all concentrate on the economics of the resale proceeds right. Asimow treats it as analogous to an excise tax on resale and concludes: "Thus the *droit de suite* . . . seems to be a 'bad' tax in the economic sense. It interferes seriously with the market, produces negligible revenue, is costly to administer, and is poorly accepted by the market." Rottenberg concludes: "Resale revenue-sharing laws make no artists better off and make some artists worse off." Bolch, Damon, and Hinshaw conclude: "The resale royalty law will result in only a small economic gain to a few and an economic loss to many. It should be repealed for the sake of the artists affected."

3. Note the argument that proceeds right laws discourage people from buying the work of living artists. Such an effect cannot be ignored. Still, even if the flow of money into the contemporary art market is not reduced, the redistributive effects of the proceeds right are an important consideration. This follows because the works of only a very few artists have any resale market at any price. Estimates vary, but 1 percent of living artists is generally considered an unrealistically high estimate.

4. A survey done for the authors in 1978 by Thomas Camp examined all sales of contemporary art at Sotheby Parke Bernet and Christie's in New York, the leading auction houses, from the Scull sale in October 1973 through 1977. In those four-plus years, works by 152 living American artists sold for $1,000 or more. (Observe that there is no information about how many of the resales were at a profit.) The 1970 census showed that there were then 107,476 artists in the United States. Although many other secondary sales take place through art dealers or in auctions, this sample is impressive.

5. On the basis of the survey, it seems clear that the proceeds right will result in payments to only a few artists, while the great majority will collect nothing. It seems obvious that those who will receive payment are those who are already successful, who are represented by major dealers, whose works have been acquired by major museums and collectors. That is why they have a secondary market.

6. Is there a free lunch? Weil's argument sounds persuasive. If the money spent on contemporary art decreases (or even if it remains the same) and more of that money goes to the few already successful artists, then less remains for the great mass who are unsuccessful. The money to pay the successful few has to come from somewhere. It is taken from the poor to give to the rich.

7. Here is a hypothetical but realistic example. Suppose that Dealer runs an art gallery in which he shows the work of promising but unknown artists. His commissions on sales at these shows are not sufficient to pay his overhead (a common situation). Thus his "front room," where these shows hang, must be subsidized. One way dealers subsidize the front room is by dealing profitably in the secondary market with works of established artists like Sam Francis, Jasper Johns, Robert Rauschenberg, Roy Lichtenstein, and Frank Stella. If Dealer's profit in the back room is reduced by the proceeds right payment he must make to those artists, his ability to subsidize the front room is reduced. Promising but unknown artists thus subsidize established successful artists.

8. Money is not the only consideration. Artists often believe that the proceeds right corrects injustice. It seems unfair to them that the Sculls paid only $960 for a painting that sold a few years later for $85,000. Clearly, they argue, Rauschenberg was underpaid for the painting. But if that was the going price at the time for his paintings in a fair market (Rauschenberg was already represented by Leo Castelli, one of the greatest of dealers, known for fair dealing with artists and extraordinary success in promoting them and their work), in what sense could it be said that the price was too low?

9. Where did the increase in value from $960 to $85,000 come from? In part it came from the continued activity of the artist in building a body of highly regarded work. How about Castelli's activity? How about the activities of critics, museum curators, and important collectors (like the Sculls)? How about the Venice Biennale, which awarded Rauschenberg its highly publicized first prize for painting in 1964? How about the auction house itself, which created the occasion on which so much money would be bid for that painting? How about inflation? The cost of money?

10. One way for artists to participate in the increasing value of their work (if indeed it does increase in value) is by investing in themselves. They can do this by retaining, rather than selling, some of their work. Thus if an artist paints twenty canvases in a year and sells only eighteen of them, retaining the other two, he can later cash in if they increase sharply in value. At the time of the Scull auction, Rauschenberg and his dealer still held works from the same period, and the prices were raised sharply the day after the auction. As someone remarked, "The Scull sale made Rauschenberg a millionaire."

THE CONTRACTUAL PROCEEDS RIGHT

One of the arguments occasionally made by some opponents of proceeds right laws is that they are unnecessary. The artist can, if he wishes, contract for such a right when he initially sells the work, and his desire to retain a proceeds right becomes one element in a bargaining process that affects the price paid for it. In most states, where there is no statutory proceeds right, the contract is the only available means for the artist who is convinced that he should have such a right.

In the early 1970s a form contract drafted by New York attorney Bob Projansky and dealer Seth Siegelaub, called "The Artist's Reserved Rights Transfer and Sale Agreement," was widely distributed and promoted by artists' rights activists. However, it was so hostile to collectors and dealers that few purchasers signed it. Other, more moderate and realistic form contracts have been proposed, one by lawyer Charles Jurrist and another by sculptor Ed Kienholz. None of these contracts is widely used, and none has proved to be effective as a vehicle for participation in the proceeds of resales. All are reproduced in John Henry Merryman and Albert E. Elsen, *Law, Ethics and the Visual Arts* (New York: Matthew Bender, 1979), pp. 4-144ff.

A major difficulty with contract provisions is that there is no way to make them legally binding on subsequent owners of the work of art. The artist can, by contract, bind only the person with whom he directly deals. Suppose Artist sells to Collector, Collector then sells to X, and X then sells to Y. Artist can rely on a contract provision to recover from Collector for the Collector–X transaction. But unless there is a separate agreement by X to pay Artist a percentage of X's resale price, Artist will have no recourse against X for the X–Y transaction or against subsequent parties for later transactions. Artist can extract a promise from Collector to include a proceeds right clause in favor of Artist in any resale contract, but suppose X refuses to accept such a provision or Collector neglects to require it. If the Collector–X sale goes ahead, X takes the painting free of any legal obligation to Artist.

One reason for this state of the law is concern for third persons who take without notice of restrictions—called "bona fide purchasers." Another concern is with the free and unrestricted movement of goods in commerce. These concerns combine to make it unlikely that any attempt to make a contractual provision—a proceeds right or any other—legally effective against "remote" parties (i.e., against persons who are not parties to the transaction) will work.

In the case of land it is possible to make agreements that *will* bind remote parties—so-called "covenants running with the land." The system of covenants running with land at law and equity relies for its effectiveness on the existence of a real property-recording system, on the legal concept of "record notice," and on the fact that most such servitudes are apparent to one who makes a reasonable inspection of the premises. There is no comparable system of records of art transactions and no equivalent of record notice of restrictions like proceeds right provisions. The Projansky and Kienholz agreements provide for notice of the artist's reserve to be attached to the work. Kienholz is a sculptor, and it seems possible that such notice might be given without marring his work. But it is not clear how such notice could be permanently and indelibly attached to paintings and drawings in such a way as to be both apparent to subsequent acquirers and yet so unobtrusive as to leave the work itself unimpaired. In this connection, recall the refusal of some artists to place copyright notices on their works because they believe the image would be impaired.

Thus the contract is a relatively ineffective way of giving the artist continuing rights in the work. If one wishes to argue against the statutory proceeds right on the ground that the artist can assure the right by contract, then it is obvious that such an argument is only partially valid. The artist can contract effectively for a proceeds right in the first resale, but not, under present law, in subsequent transactions.

A workable system of records and of notice to remote parties would be extremely difficult to devise and expensive to establish and maintain but might be possible—perhaps through the Register of Copyrights in Washington, D.C.—if it were thought important enough to have one. The French attempted something of the sort in their 1920 legislation but eventually gave it up.

An additional possible problem in trying to accomplish the objectives of the proceeds right by contract is the rule in New York and some other states, possibly applicable to works of art by analogy, that "provisions reserving to the grantor a portion of the proceeds of a resale by the grantee" of land "are . . . void and unenforceable" because they "clog alienation" and thus violate the public policy in favor of free alienability of land (and other resources?). See Annotation, 123 A.L.R. 1474 (1939); 45 New York Jurisprudence §94 (1973).

THE CALIFORNIA STATUTE

The following statute, enacted in 1976 to become effective on January 1, 1977, caught many California museums, collectors, and dealers, and some artists, by surprise. Assemblyman (later Senator) Alan Sieroty of Los Angeles, who introduced and managed the passage of a number of art-related statutes (including the California moral right law discussed previously) was the bill's author. It attracted little attention before passage and was enacted without consulting the art community beyond artists and enthusiasts who helped draft the bill and supported it. An additional element of surprise was that the California Legislative Counsel (the legislature's lawyer) had in a written opinion to Sieroty indicated that the law would be constitutional only as applied to sales occurring in California (the law also purports to apply to sales outside California, if the seller is a California resident) (Letter of August 30, 1976, to Sieroty from George H. Murphy, Legislative Council). The California Department of Finance had recommended to the governor that the bill be vetoed, estimating that it would be very expensive to administer (Sylvia Hochfeld, "Legislating Royalties for Artists," *ARTnews*, December 10, 1976, pp. 52, 54).

Enactment of the California Resale Proceeds Right Law immediately produced outcries from outraged museums, collectors, and dealers and equally vehement defenses by artists and artist-support organizations such as Artists' Equity, Bay Area Lawyers for the Arts, and Artists for Economic Action. For some of the flavor, see Sylvia Hochfeld, "Legislating Royalties for Artists," *ARTnews,* December 10, 1976, p. 52; William Bates, "Royalties for Artists: California Becomes the Testing Ground," *New York Times Art and Leisure Section,* August 14, 1977, p. 1; and Gay Weaver, "Controversy Stirred up over Artists' Resale Payments," *Palo Alto Times,* November 11, 12, and 13, 1976, pp. 14, 15, 16, respectively.

In 1982, in response to suggestions from all sides, Senator Sieroty introduced and managed the adoption of several amendments which are indicated in the text of the law by underlining.

The California Resale Proceeds Right Law
Cal. Civ. Code, §986 (Enacted 1976, Effective January 1, 1977, amended 1982)
[Underlining represents amendments enacted in 1982.]

(a) Whenever a work of fine art is sold and the seller resides in California or the sale takes place in California, the seller or the seller's agent shall pay to the artist of such work of fine art or to such artist's agent 5 percent of the amount of such sale. The right of the artist to receive an amount equal to 5 percent of the amount of such sale . . . may be waived only by a contract in writing providing for an amount in excess of 5 percent of the amount of such sale. An artist may assign the right to collect the royalty payment provided by this section to another individual or entity. However, the assignment shall not have the effect of creating a waiver prohibited by this subdivision.

(1) When a work of fine art is sold at an auction or by a gallery, dealer, broker, museum, or other person acting as the agent for the seller the agent shall withhold 5 percent of the amount of the sale, locate the artist and pay the artist.

(2) If the seller or agent is unable to locate and pay the artist within 90 days, an amount equal to 5 percent of the amount of the sale shall be transferred to the Arts Council.

(3) If a seller or the seller's agent fails to pay an artist the amount equal to 5 percent of the sale of a work of fine art by the artist or fails to transfer such amount to the Arts Council, the artist may bring an action for damages within three years after the date of sale or one year after the discovery of the sale, whichever is longer. The prevailing party in any action brought under this paragraph shall be entitled to reasonable attorney fees, in an amount as determined by the court.

(4) Moneys received by the council pursuant to this section shall be deposited in an account in the Special Deposit Fund in the State Treasury.

(5) The Arts Council shall attempt to locate any artist for whom money is received pursuant to this section. If the council is unable to locate the artist and the artist does not file a written claim for the money received by the council within seven years of the date of sale of the work of fine art, the right of the artist terminates and such money shall be transferred to the . . . council for use in acquiring fine art pursuant to the Art in Public Buildings program set forth in Chapter 2.1 (commencing with Section 15813) of Part 10b of Division 3 of Title 2, of the Government Code.

(6) Any amounts of money held by any seller or agent for the payment of artists pursuant to this section shall be exempt from . . . enforcement of a money judgment by the creditors of the seller or agent.

(7) Upon the death of an artist, the rights and duties created under this section shall inure to his or her heirs, legatees, or personal representative, until the 20th anniversary of the death of the artist. The provisions of this paragraph shall be applicable only with respect to an artist who dies after January 1, 1983.

(b) Subdivision (a) shall not apply to any of the following:

(1) To the initial sale of a work of fine art where legal title to such work at the time of such initial sale is vested in the artist thereof.

(2) To the resale of a work of fine art for a gross sales price of less than one thousand dollars ($1,000).

(3) <u>Except as provided in paragraph (7) of subdivision (a),</u> to a resale after the death of such artist.

(4) To the resale of the work of fine art for a gross sales price less than the purchase price paid by the seller.

(5) To a transfer of a work of fine art which is exchanged for one or more works of fine art or for a combination of cash, other property, and one or more works of fine art where the fair market value of the property exchanged is less than one thousand dollars ($1,000).

<u>(6) To the resale of a work of fine art by an art dealer to a purchaser within 10 years of the initial sale of the work of fine art by the artist to an art dealer, provided all intervening resales are between art dealers.</u>

<u>(7) To a sale of a work of stained glass artistry where the work has been permanently attached to real property and is sold as part of the sale of the real property to which it is attached.</u>

(c) For purposes of this section, the following terms have the following meanings:

(1) "Artist" means the person who creates a work of fine art <u>and who, at the time of resale, is a citizen of the United States, or a resident of the state who has resided in the state for a minimum of two years.</u>

(2) "Fine art" means an original painting, sculpture, or drawing, <u>or an original work of art in glass.</u>

<u>(3) "Art dealer" means a person who is actively and principally engaged in or conducting the business of selling works of fine art for which business such person validly holds a sales tax permit.</u>

COMMENTS

1. Key criticisms of the California statute were: (1) its application to sales outside of California; (2) nonwaivability of the artist's right; (3) application to sales by dealers and to private sales; (4) treating the difference between the purchase price and the resale price as "profit," with no recognition of commissions, expenses, or inflation; (5) giving the artist 5 percent of the gross resale price rather than a percentage of the profit, if any, on the resale; (6) application to resales of works acquired before enactment of the law.

2. In addition, California dealers, auctioneers, and collectors objected that by imposing an excise tax on California transactions, the law drove art business out of California. Indeed, Sotheby Parke Bernet Los Angeles, at that time the largest art auctioneer in California, immediately suspended sales of contemporary art. (It subsequently closed, but for a variety of reasons, of which this was only one.)

3. Some dealers who bought art from artists rather than taking it on consignment objected that the statute applied to first sales by them. (Section 986(b)(7)) was added in 1982 to deal with this problem.

4. As originally enacted, the statute operated to the benefit of foreign artists, even though critics argued that a California law should subsidize only California artists. The amendment to Section 986(c)(1) was a partial response. The reference to a "resident of the state who has resided in the state for a minimum of two years" is sometimes referred to as "the David Hockney clause." David Hockney, a prominent British artist, maintains a California residence.

5. Observe that the statute does not apply to the resale of fine prints or photographs. The reasoning was that artists can protect their interests in the appreciation of such works by retaining copies (e.g., artist's proofs).

6. A group calling itself CADRE (Collectors, Artists, and Dealers for Responsible Equity) was formed to back a constitutional attack on the law (the authors were members). The following decision finally disposed of the lawsuit. Note that two potential grounds for constitutional attack—preemption under the 1976 Copyright Act and impermissible interference with interstate commerce—were not before the court, as Judge Sneed is careful to emphasize. In the opinion of some observers, these were the most promising grounds for attack (recall the California legislative counsel's opinion on the interstate commerce question), although there is no certainty that either would have prevailed had the case properly raised them.

Morseburg v. Balyon
621 F.2d 972 (9th Cir. 1980)

SNEED, Circuit Judge.

Appellant is an art dealer. On March 24, 1977, he sold two paintings under such circumstances as to require him to pay royalties under the California Resale Royalties Act (California Act). . . . He thereupon brought suit challenging the Act's constitutionality, claiming that it is preempted by the 1909 Copyright Act and that it violates due process and the Contracts Clause of the Constitution. The lower court rejected these contentions. We affirm.

PREEMPTION UNDER THE 1909 COPYRIGHT ACT

Appellant's preemption argument has compelled us to review in some detail the preemption doctrine as applied by the Supreme Court and developments in copyright law during much of this century and, to some extent, even those of an earlier time. We shall not extend this opinion describing in detail our research but shall limit it to stating our reasoning in a direct and straightforward manner.

Before commencing this statement we emphasize that this case concerns the preemptive effect of the 1909 Act only. We do not consider the extent to which the 1976 Act, particularly section 301(a) and (b), 17 U.S.C. §301(a) and (b), may have preempted the California Act. It is unavoidable that certain of our reasons will be weighed and measured to determine their applicability to the 1976 Act. Nonetheless, our holding, as well as our reasons, to repeat, are addressed to the 1909 Act only.

Appellant utilizes as the foundation to his argument portions of sections 1 and 27 of the 1909 Act. The selected portion of section 1 reads:

Any person entitled thereto, upon complying with the provisions of this title, shall have the exclusive right: (1) To print, reprint, publish, copy, *and vend* the copyrighted work. [Italics added by Judge Sneed.]

The section 27 portion, after providing that the copyright was distinct from the object and that the latter's transfer did not of itself transfer the copyright, reads:

But nothing in this title shall be deemed to forbid, prevent, or *restrict the transfer* of any copy of a copyrighted work the possession of which has been lawfully obtained. [Italics added by Sneed.]

On this foundation appellant asserts that the California Act impairs the artist's ability *to vend* his "work of fine art" when it is a "copyrighted work" within the meaning of section 1 of the 1909 Act. He also asserts that the California Act "restricts the transfer" of a copyrighted "work of fine art" when in the hands of one who lawfully obtained it, such as a purchaser from the artist. It follows, appellant contends, that the California Act conflicts with the 1909 Act. Under these circumstances, appellant concludes, the California Act is preempted by the 1909 Copyright Act.

To evaluate appellant's position we shall describe briefly certain aspects of the "works of fine art" market place as well as our perception of the current attitude of the Supreme Court with respect to preemption generally.

ASPECTS OF THE MARKET PLACE FOR "WORKS OF FINE ART"

Turning to the market place for "works of fine art," it is frequently the case that such works are not copyrighted and that the sales proceeds realized by the artist upon its first sale are significantly less than the prices at which it subsequently changes hands. See Sheehan, *Why Don't Fine Artists Use Statutory Copyright?—An Empirical and Legal Survey,* 22 Bull. Copyright Soc'y 242 (1975); Price & Price, *Right of Artists: The Case of the Droit de Suite,* in Art Works: Law, Policy, Practice 67 (1974). There are several explanations for both circumstances. The failure to utilize copyright protection has its source in, among other things, ignorance, a distaste for legal details, weak bargaining power, and the desire to avoid defacing the work with a copyright symbol. See Note, *Courting the Artist with Copyright: The 1976 Copyrights Act,* 24 Wayne L.Rev. 1685–86 (1978). An increase in the price of an artist's works after they have left his hands may be the result of greater recognition of the artist, an increase in the overall demand for art works, inflation, unpredictable shifts in fashion and taste, or some combination of the above.

The California Act functions under these conditions. It is an American version of what the French call the *droit de suite,* an art proceeds right. See Emley, *The Resale Royalties Act: Paint-*

ings, Preemption and Profit, 8 Golden Gate Univ. L.Rev. 239, 240 n.9 (1978). It provides by force of state law a conditional economic interest of a limited duration in the proceeds of sales other than the initial one. Similar rights perhaps could be obtained by by contract. See Projansky & Siegelaub, *The Artist's Reserved Rights Transfer and Sale Agreement,* Art Works: Law, Policy, Practice, *supra* at 81. Opinions differ as to whether the existence of such an interest, without regard to its source, will increase the incentives to produce available to the young and not well known artist. See Katz, *Copyright Preemption Under the Copyright Act of 1976: The Case of Droit de Suite,* 47 Geo. Wash.L. Rev. 200, 220–21 (1978). Some argue that only a few artists will benefit, as appears to have been the French experience, while others believe such an interest prevents exploitation of the artist's creativity. See Hauser, *The French Droit de Suite: The Problem of Protection for the Underprivileged Artist Under the Copyright Law,* 6 Bull. Copyright Soc'y 94 (1959). See Merryman & Elsen, Law, Ethics and the Visual Arts, ch. IV *passim* (1979). Resolution of that dispute is not necessary for the purposes of this opinion.

Preemption and the Supreme Court

With respect to preemption the Supreme Court's emphasis varies from time to time. At times the preemption doctrine has been applied with nationalistic fervor while during other periods with generous tolerance of state involvement in areas already to some extent the subject of national concern. See Note, *The Preemption Doctrine: Shifting Perspectives on Federalism and the Burger Court,* 75 Colum.L.Rev. 623 passim (1975). Without regard to the emphasis of the period certain basic doctrinal notions repeatedly are used in applying preemption. Thus, the extent to which the federal law has "occupied the field" and the presence of "conflict" between the federal and state law have always been focuses of analytic attention. The nature of the Court's emphasis at a particular time is revealed by whether "occupation of the field" and "conflict" are easily found to exist or not. "Occupation" can require no more than the existence of a federal law generally applicable to a significant portion of the area in question to no less than an express statement demonstrating an intention to occupy the area duly enacted by Congress. "Conflict," likewise, can require no more than a mechanical demonstration of potential conflict between federal and state law to no

less than a showing of substantial frustration of an important purpose of the federal law by the challenged state law. When the emphasis is to protect and strengthen national power "occupation" and "conflict" are easily found while not so easily found when the emphasis is to promote federalism.

Although there is a discernable cyclical character in the Supreme Court's choice of emphasis, it is also true that, without regard to the particular point in the cycle at which a preemption issue arises, the choice of emphasis is heavily influenced by the area of the law in which the issue arises. Thus, when the area concerns foreign affairs . . . the emphasis, not surprisingly, is on the national interest, while when the area is protection of consumers of commodities . . . the emphasis understandably is upon the state's interest particularly and the imperatives of federalism generally. . . .

Fortunately, the Supreme Court provided clear guidance with respect to the emphasis proper for this case. This was done in *Goldstein v. California,* 412 U.S. 546, 93 S.Ct. 2303, 37 L.Ed.2d 163 (1973), in which the Court held valid a California statute making it a criminal offense to "pirate" recordings produced by others, an activity against which the copyright holder at that time had no protection. The interests of California in particular and of federalism in general were given emphasis. The court refused to read the Copyright Clause of the Constitution to foreclose the existence of all state power "to grant to authors the exclusive Right to their respective Writings." Also it held that the 1909 Copyright Act did not preempt the California statute. In support of this conclusion the Court observed that Congress had not exercised its full power under the Copyright Clause and that it was not required to do so. In addition, Congress had evidenced no intent, either expressly or impliedly, to bar the states from exercising their power. As a consequence, the area was not fully occupied by the federal government. This was supported additionally by the Court's explicit conclusion that no conflict between the national and state law existed because state law regulated a matter not covered by the federal Copyright Act of 1909 in a manner that did not disturb a careful balance struck by Congress between those matters deserving of protection and those things that should remain free. . . .

We hold that *Goldstein* governs this case. The Copyright Clause does not prevent the enactment by California of the Resale Royalties Act. Nor has the Copyright Act of 1909 explicitly forbidden the enactment of such an act by a state. A bar by implication cannot be found in the word "vend" in section 1 of the 1909 Act. Doubt concerning the correctness of this conclusion disappears when the rights of the artist who creates a work of fine art are analyzed. Prior to the initial sale he holds title to the work and, assuming proper steps have been taken, all rights given to him by reason of his copyright. None of these provide the right afforded to him by the California Resale Royalties Act. This is an additional right similar to the additional protection afforded by California's anti-pirating statute upheld in *Goldstein.* It is true that under the California Act the right it bestows cannot be waived or transferred. This limits the right created by state law but not any right created by the copyright law.

It would be proper to brand this conclusion as sophistry were it true that the right "to vend" provided by section 1 of the 1909 Act meant a right to transfer the works at all times and at all places free and clear of all claims of others. It is manifest that such is not its meaning. It merely means that the artist has "the exclusive right to transfer the title for a consideration to others. . . ."

The California Act does not impair this right; it merely creates a right in personam against a seller of a "work of fine art."

Nor can we conclude that section 27 of the 1909 Act by implication precludes the enactment of resale royalty acts by the states. Technically speaking such acts in no way restrict the transfer of art works. No lien to secure the royalty is attached to the work itself, nor is the buyer made secondarily liable for the royalty. The work can be transferred without restriction. The fact that a resale may create a liability to the creator artist or a state instrumentality and, at the same time, constitute an exercise of a right guaranteed by the Copyright Act does not make the former a legal restraint on the latter. It is true, of course, that the imposition of the royalty may well influence the duration of a purchaser's holding period of a work of fine art. To cover the royalty the holder may defer selling until the work's value has appreciated to a greater extent than otherwise might have been the case. The aggregate volume of business done by the relevant art markets may be diminished somewhat. Moreover, the possibility of the imposition by the state of very high royalty rates and more than one state "taxing" a single sale suggests that resale royalty acts under certain circumstances could make transfer of the work

of fine art a practical impossibility. Without regard to how the preemption argument should fare under those circumstances, we are not confronted with them here. We explicitly restrict our holding to the facts before us.

These observations permit us to conclude that the 1909 Copyright Act has not occupied the area with which we are concerned and that the California Act is not in conflict with it. A resale royalty is not provided by the 1909 Act; no hostility toward such a royalty is expressed by the Act; and, on the facts before us, the obligation to pay a resale royalty does not impermissibly restrict resales by the owners of works of fine art. The teaching of *Goldstein* is not limited to situations in which the matter regulated by state law is not covered by the 1909 Act. . . .

The crucial inquiry is not whether state law reaches matters also subject to federal regulation, but whether the two laws function harmoniously rather than discordantly. We find no discord in this instance. . . .

THE CONTRACTS CLAUSE AND DUE PROCESS ISSUE

Appellant also contends that even if the Resale Royalties Act is not preempted by federal copyright law, it violates either the Contracts Clause or the due process provisions of the Constitution. We hold otherwise.

The Contracts Clause Issue

The California Act with respect to initial sales by the artist subsequent to its enactment impairs only the power of the artist and his purchaser to contract. The exercise of the police power of states frequently has the effect and raises no Contracts Clause issue. . . .

With respect to initial sales prior to enactment of the California Act a Contracts Clause issue lurks sufficiently close by to require discussion.

The economic interest bestowed on an artist, who previous to the Act's enactment has parted with his work, can be viewed as a benefit conferred upon him by the state because of its desire to promote artistic endeavor generally. So viewed no Contract Clause issue emerges. Appellant, however, contends that the California Act rewrites his contract with the person from whom he acquired the work to require payment to the creator of the work or the California Arts Council. This is not a compelling characterization of the operation of the Act. However, without regard to whether the California Act can be said to rewrite all pre-California Act sales contracts, the inescapable effect of the Act is to burden such a buyer of a work of fine art with an unbargained-for obligation to pay a royalty to the creator of that work or the Arts Council upon resale. The buyer's obligation is increased, and such an alteration no doubt requires that the Act be scrutinized under the Contracts Clause. . . .

This scrutiny reveals no unconstitutional impairment. The Contracts Clause is not absolute. "One whose rights, such as they are, are subject to state restriction, cannot remove them from the power of the State by making a contract about them." . . .

Nor are all impairments of contracts improper. "The States must possess broad power to adopt general regulatory measures without being concerned that private contracts will be impaired, or even destroyed, as a result." . . .

The degree to which a state may impair the obligations of contract varies with the public need for that impairment. . . .

An insignificant impairment does not need the extensive justification that otherwise might be necessary. . . . Moreover, we should defer to the state legislature's determination of the public need whenever possible. . . .

However, an impairment that is severe, permanent, irrevocable and retroactive and which serves no broad, generalized economic or social purpose violates the Contracts Clause. . . .

If impairment there be, which we are not prepared to concede, it is not of that magnitude. The obligation of the appellant created by the California Act serves a public purpose and is not severe. Under these circumstances the California Act survives a Contracts Clause challenge.

THE DUE PROCESS ISSUE

Appellant's due process arguments fare no better. He asserts that he has lost a fundamental property right; that the Resale Royalties Act affects the very heart of the relationship between buyers and sellers of art; and that there is no public interest whatsoever to support such meddling. We reject these contentions.

We view the California Act, whatever its merits as a legislative matter, as economic regulation to promote artistic endeavors generally. "It is by now well established that legislative Acts adjusting the burdens and benefits of economic life come to the Court with a presumption of constitutionality, and that the burden is on one complaining of a due process violation to establish that the legislature has acted in an arbitrary and irrational way." . . .

The courts are not to act as "superlegislature[s] to judge the wisdom or desirability of legislative policy determinations made in areas that neither affect fundamental rights nor proceed along suspect lines. . . ."

We would ignore a national characteristic were we to say that an act modeled upon a French law lacked a rational basis. Nor need we do so. The required rational basis exists. Moreover, the California Act is neither arbitrary nor capricious. In its present form it does not affect fundamental rights.

Appellant emphasizes that the California Act is retroactive, removing it from the sphere of the usual economic regulation. This is arguable because it is only applicable to sales made subsequent to the passage of the California Act. In any event, "legislation readjusting rights and burdens is not unlawful solely because it upsets otherwise settled expectations."

Many laws upset some expectations regarding the legal consequences of prior conduct. Much legal business consists of assisting clients to adjust their affairs to the new laws. It has been said that "[o]nly when such retroactive effects are so wholly unexpected and disruptive that harsh and oppressive consequences follow is the constitutional limitation exceeded."

The consequences of the California Act in its present form are not of that magnitude.

Affirmed.

[The U.S. Supreme Court denied a hearing on this case on November 10, 1980.]

COMMENTS

1. Despite the 1982 provisions for assignability of the right to royalties (e.g., to a California equivalent of SPADEM or some existing artists' organization), attorneys' fees, and

extension of the right to the artist's successors for twenty years after his death, the statute appears to have had little impact on the activities of most museums, dealers, and collectors and seems to have generated little additional income for artists. See Barbara Isenberg, "The Art Royalties Act: The 5% Evasion," *Los Angeles Times,* December 21, 1980, Calendar Section, p. 1; and "Art Resales: Not a Pretty Picture," *Los Angeles Times,* November 21, 1982.

2. There are law review discussions of, or bearing on, the California Statute in Stephen S. Ashley, "A Critical Comment on California's Droit de Suite, Civil Code Section 986," *Hastings Law Journal,* vol. 29 (1977), p. 249; Sharon J. Emley, "The Resale Royalties Act: Paintings, Preemption and Profit," *Golden Gate University Law Review,* vol. 8 (1978), p. 239; Jennifer R. Clarke, "The California Resale Royalties Act as a Test Case for Preemption Under the 1976 Copyright Law," *Columbia Law Review,* vol. 81 (1981), p. 315; Lynn Warren, "Droit de Suite: Only Congress Can Grant Royalty Protection for Artists," *Pepperdine Law Review,* vol. 9 (1981), p. 111.

3. Should the United States adopt some form of the resale proceeds right? Efforts in Congress have failed twice: the Waxman bill, discussed above, and a hastily withdrawn toe in the water by Congressman Fred Richmond in 1981. Efforts in a number of state legislatures have also failed. It is tempting to assume that the idea has been judged to be a bad one and politically inexpedient (two quite different notions). Still, there are people who find the proceeds right immediately and instinctively appealing. It is a sentimental favorite and will probably rise again and again because it looks so good when you first see it. Indeed, it arose again in September 1986, when Senator Kennedy introduced it in S.2796 (the bill also includes a New York type of moral right provision, and it would again abolish the copyright notice requirement for works of art). The bill was not reported out of committee but will be reintroduced, in some form, in the 100th Congress.

Chapter Four

ARTISTIC FREEDOM AND ITS LIMITATION

INTRODUCTION

On February 20, 1796, the Danish painter Asmus Jakob Carstens wrote to the Prussian minister concerning the writer's dismissal for canceling an obligation to the Prussian Academy in order to remain indefinitely in Rome: "I must tell your Excellency that I belong to Humanity, not to the Academy of Berlin." As Lorenz Eitner pointed out, "The letter documents the emancipation of artists toward the end of the eighteenth century, not only from official patronage, but also from some of the social and legal restrictions which bind other men" (Lorenz Eitner's *Neoclassicism and Romanticism, 1750–1850,* vol. 1 [Englewood Cliffs, N.J.: Prentice-Hall, 1970], p. 109).

The concept of complete artistic freedom—the right of artists to choose and pursue their own purposes—is very recent in the history of art and is a legacy of the late eighteenth and nineteenth centuries. Throughout most of history the artist worked for the ruler and such institutions as the church and was in effect a public relations arm of the establishment. Leonardo spoke for countless artists before and after him when he said, "I serve the one who pays me." The artist accepted dogma he was to illustrate, whether or not he was a believer. As can be seen in the sections that follow, when he strayed from ideological orthodoxy punishment could be corporal and/or imprisonment and exile, as well as the alteration or destruction of his art. The ninth-century Byzantine artist Lazarus earns highest ranking in the artist's hagiography for dedication to his calling in the face of brutal censorship. Even with the emergence of the concept of genius, first ascribed to Michelangelo, many great artists did not know freedom from censorship.

> As in the disputes over heresy, so in those over decency, Michelangelo's *Last Judgment* came in for the most violent attacks. Its position in the Sistine Chapel gave it an importance which made it a good test case, and on the question of nudity it provided ample material for discussion. It was not only exposed to written attacks, but on several occasions was in danger of complete destruction and only escaped with serious mutilation. . . .
>
> Paul IV threatened to destroy the whole fresco and finally ordered Daniele da Volterra to paint draperies over some of the figures. Pius IV was still dissatisfied and had the draperies increased in number, while Clement VIII was only prevented from completely destroying the painting by the appeals of the Academy of St. Luke. Pius V also had some figures repainted; and it was on this occasion that El Greco offered to replace the whole fresco with one "modest and decent" and "no less well painted than the other." [Anthony Blunt, *Artistic Theory in Italy, 1450–1600* (Oxford: The Clarendon Press, 1940), pp. 118–119.]

Michelangelo lived long enough to see his magnificent painting altered. The great Venetian artist Veronese, whose defense against censorship was based on equating his activities with those of the more esteemed poets and court jesters, lost his case before the Council of Trent but won his war by changing the painting's title instead of its content. Until protected by recent laws, many censored artists had to fall back on the defense of sincerity, and that of the great sculptor Rodin is still in use today. Frequently criticized for creating licentious art, and having experienced actual censorship, Rodin argued:

> In art, immorality cannot exist. Art is always sacred even when it takes for a subject the worst excesses of desire. Since it has in view only the sincerity of observation, it cannot

debase itself. A true work of art is always noble, even when it translates the stirrings of the brute, for at that moment, the artist who has produced it had as his only objective, the most conscientious rendering possible of the impression he has felt. [*Antée,* June 1, 1907.]

This chapter documents some of the ruthless government censorship of art and artists during this century, not just in the USSR and Germany, but also in the United States during the McCarthy era. Less well known is the history of censorship by institutions, such as the guilds and academies, that were founded to give the artist security as well as education but that also served as reactionary forces against the artist's drive for independence. Leonardo was one of the earliest to decry the restrictions of the guild system of craft education and the need of the artist to inquire into art and science on his own. In the late eighteenth and nineteenth centuries the art academies and their strict canons were seen by many, such as Goethe, as inimical to genius. In 1791 the academically trained sculptor Antoine Quatremère de Quincy criticized the French Academy for the following defects:

The despotic authority of a material and moral kind which, by virtue of its power, it holds over the arts and the artists.

The pettiness and levelling influence of its teaching on the spirit of students and on the development of their talents.

The revolting inequality which results from the privileges, both practical and ideal, which the Academy possess, and which cause in those who benefit from them, as well as those who are deprived of them, passions that are inimical to the progress of art. [Eitner, *Neoclassicism and Romanticism,* p. 115.]

In an article that opened a new area of art historical research, Professor Linda Nochlin of Vassar argued that academies historically exercised an inhibiting influence on women artists:

The answer to why there have been no great women artists lies not in the nature of individual genius or the lack of it, but in the nature of given social institutions and what they forbid or encourage in various classes or groups of individuals. Let us first examine such a simple but critical issue as availability of the nude model to aspiring women artists, in the period extending from the Renaissance until near the end of the 19th century, a period in which careful and prolonged study of the nude model was essential to the training of every young artist, to the production of any work with pretensions to grandeur, and to the very essence of history painting, generally accepted as the highest category of art . . . central to the training programs of the academies since their inception in the late 16th and early 17th centuries, was life drawing from the nude, generally male, model. . . . The female nude was forbidden in almost all public art schools as late as 1850 and after. . . . [There was a] complete unavailability to the aspiring woman artist of any nude models at all, male or female. As late as 1893, "lady" students were not admitted to life drawing at the Royal Academy in London. [Linda Nochlin, "Why Have There Been No Great Women Artists?" *ARTnews,* January 1971, pp. 23–39.]

There have been many times when artists have been their own worst enemies, for the profession has a long history of censoring itself. Leo Tolstoy had definite views on banishing what he felt was considered "bad art." From the Middle Ages, artists manned the directorships of the guilds and academies, the juries of public exhibitions in Europe started in the eighteenth century, and it was an artist, Adolf Ziegler, who delivered Hitler's decree to German museums authorizing the confiscation of "degenerate" art. Before Ziegler certain avantgarde groups called for the burning of museums. In his essay "Contemporary Art and the Plight of Its Public," Leo Steinberg observed:

Whenever there appears an art that is truly new and original, the men who denounce it first and loudest are artists. Obviously, because they are the most engaged. No critic, no outraged bourgeois, can match an artist's passion in repudiation. The men who kept Courbet and Manet and the Impressionists and the Post-Impressionists out of the salons were all painters. They were mostly academic painters. But it is not necessarily the academic painter who defends his own established manner against a novel way of making pictures or a threatened shift in taste. The leader of a revolutionary movement in art may get just as mad over a new departure or betrayal in a revolutionary cause. And I think it was this sense of betrayal that made Matisse so angry in 1907 when he saw what he called "Picasso's hoax" ("Demoiselles d'Avignon"). It serves no useful purpose to forget that Matisse's contribution to early cubism—made at the height of his own creativity—was an attitude of absolute and arrogant incomprehension. In 1908, as juror for the avant-garde Salon d'Automne, he rejected Braque's new landscapes "with little cubes"—just as, by 1912, the triumphant Cubists were to reject Duchamp's "Nude Descending a Staircase." [Leo Steinberg, "Contemporary Art and the Plight of Its Public," in *Other Criteria: Confrontations with Twentieth Century Art* (New York and London: Oxford University Press, 1972), p. 4.]

The Nazis, as the Bolsheviks before them, found artists who willingly filled vacancies in art schools caused by the exiling and "neutralizing" of other artists, and in the United States during the McCarthy era there were large groups of artists who approved of and joined the witch-hunts in the art community. Pathetic and futile as it may seem to us today, German artist Oskar Schlemmer's letter of protest to Goebbels concerning the destruction of "degenerate" art was a genuinely heroic act by a man who died for his beliefs.

The artist's hard-won freedom has not been without the criticism that he nevertheless has an ethical obligation to be a voice of humanity in times of crisis. During World War II, for example, the great Russian sculptor Naum Gabo, an exile from the Leninist reaction against modern art, was criticized for continuing to make abstract sculptures that he viewed as personal models of a harmonious world. Here is his reply.

A world at war . . . may have the right to reject my work as irrelevant to its immediate needs. I can say but little in my defense. I can only beg to be believed that I suffer with the world in all the misfortunes which are now fallen upon us. Day and night I carry the horror and pain of the human race with me. Will I be allowed to ask the leaders of the masses engaged in a mortal struggle of sheer survival: ". . . Must I, ought I, to keep and carry this horror through my art to the people?"—the people in the burned cities and scorched villages, the people in the trenches, people in the ashes of their homes. . . . What can *I* tell *them* about pain and horror that they do not know? . . . I am offering in my art what comfort I can to alleviate the pains and convulsions of our time. I try to keep our despair from assuming such proportions that nothing will remain in our devastated life to prompt us to live. I try to guard in my work the image of the morrow we left behind us in our memories . . . and to remind us that the image of the world can be different. [Herbert Read and Leslie Martin, *Gabo: Constructions, Sculpture, Paintings, Drawings, and Engravings* (London: Lund Humphries Publishers, 1957), p. 172.]

In 1932 Picasso expressed the sentiments of most modern artists when he vowed, "I will never make art with the preconceived idea of serving the interests of the political, religious or military art of a country" (Dore Ashton, *Picasso on Art,* Documents of Twentieth Century Art, [New York: Viking Penguin, 1972], p. 148). In 1945, when Picasso joined the Communist Party, he was told that many journalists believed it was done out of whim and that for him art and politics had nothing in common. With the exceptions of "Guernica" and his "Charnal House," Picasso had not done paintings that were a commentary on specific historical events, and many took this as indifference to the fate of mankind. Picasso replied:

What do you think an artist is? An imbecile who only has eyes if he's a painter, ears if he's a musician, or a lyre in every chamber of his heart if he's a poet. . . . Quite the contrary, he is at the same time a political being constantly alert to the horrifying, passionate or pleasing events in the world, shaping himself completely in their image. . . . No, painting is not made to decorate apartments. It's an offensive and defensive weapon against the enemy. [Ashton, *Picasso on Art,* p. 149.]

Historically, censorship in art has resulted from acts by those legally empowered to alter, suppress, or destroy works of art and to prohibit artists from making certain kinds of art. (The best compilation of cases is Jane Clapp's *Art Censorship* [Metuchen, N.J.: Scarecrow Press, 1972].) Censors have been and continue to be officials or designated representatives of government, the church, and institutions having their own laws, such as academies, universities, professional societies, and art museums. Publications have their own rules governing what is and is not permissible. The censoring of art has been and continues to be based on ideological, moral, and aesthetic grounds, and more recently on a new concern about art's legality. The effect of censorship has been to deprive the artist of access to an audience or the public access to a work of art.

Actual censorship should be distinguished from the disinterested exercise of critical professional judgment such as occurs in serious art criticism. Censorship is not the same as the selection process by which artists compete for admission to an exhibition, a commission, or an award. When the decision has been made on artistic merit, those who have failed should not be considered censored. In the examples of Leo Steinberg, Matisse was exercising his right of professional critical judgment in denying the exhibition of Cubist works, and those works were shown elsewhere. On the other hand, censorship may have been involved when women were proscribed from studying the live nude model in art academies, for they were effectively prevented from making historical figure subjects. That the Soviet Union continues to withhold from its people on ideological grounds many works of its great pioneering modern artists between 1910 and 1925 can properly be called censorship.

Censorship that takes the form of altering a work of art is harmful to the integrity of the work and hence to truth. It is still not always recognized that a work of art can have integrity (this is discussed in the previous chapter in the section on moral right.) Today we accept the view that art's integrity means completeness, that none of its essential parts are missing. To an Egyptian pharaoh who beheaded all the statues of a despised predecessor, thereby censoring art, such an argument would have had little weight; as a god, he had little concern for artists' rights. Today we care about the artist's intent, no matter when he lived, and we expect to see the unadulterated original work as our right to the truth.

We care about censorship when it stifles creativity, as when the Nazis forbade German artist Emil Nolde to make art and when most of the creative artists in Russia had to leave their country in the 1920s to pursue their careers elsewhere. The worst cases in modern times have been the result of official censorship, when governments have denied artists their freedom to create as they pleased. Nevertheless, censorship today by a government, an academy, or a museum can be a badge of honor. The resulting publicity often leads to invitations for the censored artist to emigrate or exhibit elsewhere, as was the case of Hans Haacke.

The word "censorship" has become such an invidious term that to most people it signifies an unwarranted interference with an artist and is always bad. It is not popular to argue that censorship can be good under certain circumstances. Yet every day fair-minded people who are knowledgeable and sympathetic to art are faced with questions of justifiable censorship, as when a museum director, having contracted for a show, finds that the artist plans to incinerate a cage filled with live animals, or when a gallery owner discovers that the artist has set himself up in an electric chair that can be activated by a visitor to the gallery. As contemporary artists engage in "body art" and live performances often involving the public, a new set of ethical and legal problems has arisen. Do the claims of art always override the personal safety and mental health of those toward whom the artist directs his performances? After reading about the activities of such body artists as Chris Burden and Vito Acconci, one is surprised that to date there have been no legal challenges to their artistic freedom.

The contemporary artist in the Western world has been the beneficiary of laws that allow unprecedented if not total freedom of expression. It is paradoxical that the last and sometimes strongest curb on that freedom in our society may now come from the artist himself. "Freedom," says Picasso, "one must be very careful with that. In painting as in everything else. Whatever you do, you find yourself once more in chains. Freedom not to do one thing requires that you do another, imperatively. And there you have it, chains" (Ashton, *Picasso on Art*, p. 75).

SOME HISTORICAL EXAMPLES

THE ICONOCLASTS

History is full of examples of the destruction and disfigurement of works of art for religious or ideological reasons. The iconoclasts (literally "image breakers") are a prominent example.

CYRIL MANGO *The Art of the Byzantine Empire**

The cult of the icon assumed an ever-growing importance in Christian devotion from about the middle of the 6th century onward. In 726 (or 730) iconoclasm became the official doctrine of the Empire and remained in force until 780; it was revived once again in 814 and lasted until 842. Two remarks are worth making here. First, iconoclasm was not a purely Byzantine phenomenon, but extended into the Semitic and Caucasian world—in fact, the origin of Byzantine iconoclasm is attributed in our sources to the Arab court in Syria. Second, the adoption of iconoclasm by the Emperor Leo III occurred at a time when the fortunes of the Empire were at their lowest ebb, only a few years after the Arab siege of Constantinople in 717. There can be little doubt that the Emperor and his advisers attributed Byzantine reverses to the wrath of the Almighty caused by the growth of idolatry in the Christian Church.

It is difficult to determine how much Early Christian art perished in the 8th and 9th centuries. Judging by our meager sources, the period of serious destruction coincided with the reign of Constantine V (741–75), but even the Iconoclastic Council of 754 expressed serious reservations on this score, while prohibiting the manufacture of images in the future. . . .

The Iconoclasts held the cruder view concerning the nature of figurative art; to them, a true image had to be "consubstantial" with its model ("prototype"), a kind of magical double. From this they drew the conclusion that the only genuine image of Christ was the consecrated bread and wine of the eucharist. The Orthodox were clearly on more solid ground when they argued that an image was a symbol (*tupos*) which, by reason of resemblance, reproduced the "person" (*prosôpon*), but not the substance (*ousia* or *hupostasis*) of the model. Yet, in their appeal to the tradition of the Church—and this formed an important part of the argument—the Iconoclasts were closer to historical truth than their opponents in affirming that the early Christians had been opposed to figurative art. . . .

THE PAINTER LAZARUS

Inasmuch as the tyrant [Theophilus] had resolved that all painters of sacred images should be done away with, or, if they chose to live, that they should owe their safety to having spat upon [these images], and thrown them to the ground as something unclean, and trodden upon them; so he determined to bring pressure on the monk Lazarus who at that time was famous for the art

*From Cyril Mango, *The Art of the Byzantine Empire, 312–1453: Sources and Documents*, ed. H. W. Janson (New York: Prentice-Hall, 1972), pp. 149–159. Copyright © 1972 by Prentice-Hall, Inc. Reprinted by permission.

of painting. Finding him, however, to be above flattery and not amenable to his will, and having been reproved by him not once or twice, but several times, he subjected him to such severe torture that the latter's flesh melted away along with his blood, and he was widely believed to have died. When he [Theophilus] heard that Lazarus, having barely recovered in prison, was taking up his art again and representing images of saints on panels, he gave orders that sheets of red-hot iron should be applied to the palms of his hands. His flesh was thus consumed by fire until he lost consciousness and lay half-dead. Yet he was destined to be preserved by Grace as a spark of light for the following generation. For when he [Theophilus] was informed that Lazarus was on his deathbed, he released him from prison thanks to the supplication of the Empress and some of his closer associates, and Lazarus took refuge at the church of the Fore-runner called *tou Phoberou* where, in spite of his wounds, he painted an image of the Precursor that exists to this day and performs many cures. These things happened at that time; when, however, the Tyrant had died and True Faith shone forth once again, it was he who with his own hands set up the image of the God-man Jesus Christ at the Brazen Gate. Invited by the illustrious Theodora to grant and seek forgiveness for her husband, he replied, "God is not so unjust, O Empress, as to forget our love and labors on His behalf, and attach greater value to that man's hatred and extraordinary insanity." But that was later. . . .

DAVID FREEDBERG *The Structure of Byzantine and European Iconoclasm**

While Byzantine Iconoclasm has received much attention from scholars, European Iconoclasm, until very recently, has been a surprisingly neglected phenomenon. . . . Outbreaks of Iconoclasm in Europe have not always been minor and isolated events. In the Reformation it swept countries like England, Germany, France and the Netherlands—to say nothing of Eastern Europe—with a vigour that was as great as anything in the eighth and ninth centuries, and with a polemical backing that was perhaps greater. But the issues it raises parallel those of Byzantine Iconoclasm. . . .

In the first place, one simply asks: Why do men destroy images? That, in many ways, is a question which goes beyond the bounds of historical analysis, but it would beg too many questions to ignore the element of fear in men's attitudes towards images, and to overlook the associated problem of the magical properties supposed to inhere in them. Kitzinger's brilliant study of the Cult of Images before Iconoclasm provides a model analysis of the hold of the image on the popular imagination in a particular period, and it is helpful to assume that the common denominator of beliefs and practices which attribute magical properties to images is that the distinction between the image and the person represented is to some extent eliminated.

[T]here is an unspoken . . . awareness of this in that favourite argument of all defenders of images . . . that the honour paid to an image passes to its prototype. There is no question that when image and prototype become fused, images become prone to the abuses that characterize man's behaviour toward them. This is why images themselves and not only what they represent, work miracles. When one considers this along with the fact that it is usually only *holy* images, consecrated in one way or another, which work miracles, it is not surprising to find a potentially explosive situation. "As long as images remain in the sculptors workshop," claimed an anonymous but frequently reprinted Netherlandish Calvinist, "they can do no miracles—until they are brought into the Church." . . .

[I]t is important to distinguish between destruction and removal ordained from above, and spontaneous attacks from below. These are often concomitant phenomena, and frequently the orders from above simply provide the initial impulse, giving free rein to the expression of popular antipathy. Iconoclasm can be ordained by the ruler, as in Constantinople, and in England under

*From David Freedberg, "The Structure of Byzantine and European Iconoclasm," in *Iconoclasm: Papers Given at the Ninth Spring Symposium of Byzantine Studies, University of Birmingham, March 1975.* Footnotes omitted. (Birmingham, England: Centre for Byzantine Studies, 1977).

Henry VIII, Edward VII and during the Anabaptist uprising, by the Long Parliament once again in England, and during the French Revolution. It often almost always, has a significant political dimension. Although the question of the motivation of Byzantine Iconoclasm is a vexed one, even there it seems safe to say that it goes hand in hand with a reassertion of imperial authority. Images are symbols of a deposed ruling class, as in Florence and the French Revolution, or of a hated one, as in the Netherlands in 1566, where field preachers and the middle nobility group together to provoke and then organize that great iconoclastic outburst which marks the beginning of the revolt against Spain.

There is another aspect of motivation which is frequently mentioned in the anti-image polemics but all too often discounted as a real impulse to Iconoclasm. That is the resentment of the populace, especially in times of economic stress, against the expense represented by images. Such feelings are exploited by the polemicists, who repeatedly harp on the disgraceful wealth expended on making fine statues, paintings and other liturgical accessories, when the money could have been more usefully expended on clothing the poor—all of whom, after all, had been created in God's own image. . . .

Once the abuses and theological weaknesses of images are made clear, it is not difficult to suggest that the blame may be laid on them for various aspects of God's wrath, such as military setbacks—especially when images fail to fulfil their expected apotropaic or palladian function. . . .

Good accounts are given by the chroniclers of the actual destruction of images. We know in many cases from them what instruments were used, and how images in relatively inaccessible positions were brought down. For the Reformation we have some illustrations, in painting and engraving, showing Iconoclasm in action. . . . The violent wave of Iconoclasm in the Netherlands was long thought to be an outburst of popular anger against a repressive regime, but it is now clear that it was organized by field preachers and some of the lower nobility. Hired men often took the lead and showed the way to further destruction. The participation of clergymen and monks who had convinced themselves of the wrongfulness of images is well documented from Byzantium to the Reformation and the French Revolution. During the Byzantine Iconoclastic periods we know that there were Iconoclastic

monks and monasteries. In the reign of Edward VI a Bishop Nicholas Ridley not only preached against images but actively encouraged the destruction. Many lapsed clerics participated in the destruction in the Netherlands, even though hounding of the clergy usually went hand in hand with Iconoclasm. . . .

Perhaps even more surprising is the participation of artists themselves: one can only wonder at what must have passed through their minds as they turned their backs on the very concept which sustained their livelihood. During one of Savonarola's *bruciamenti*, Fra Bartolommeo and Lorenzo di Credi are supposed to have consigned some of their works to the flames; in the Netherlands van Mander recorded that Joos van Lier gave up painting altogether because of the strength of his religious beliefs, and even though artists were attacked for not recording the great events of the French Revolution, "no group seemed more anxious to join the iconoclastic crusade than the artists themselves." Soon after the opening of the National Convention, David himself demanded that the effigies of kings and cardinals in the Academy's school in Rome be destroyed. Such examples are worthy of attention not only because of modern idealistic notions about the integrity of artistic endeavour. There are indications that artists like these gave some thought to the problem of pursuing their calling in times when the validity of their productions was being undermined. Some gave up painting altogether. . . .

[I]t is clear that wholesale destruction was not always the aim. The aim is to render images powerless, to deprive them of those parts which may be considered to embody their effectiveness. This is why images are very often mutilated rather than wholly destroyed. Once deconsecrated they lose their power: they are deprived of their holiness. For that, they need only be removed from the context of the consecrated.

Relief sculptures and vessels embossed with figures are scraped down, the heads of saints broken off and the Infant Christ removed from the arms of the Virgin, which are then amputated, or her crown taken away. When John the Grammarian is removed to a monastery after the restoration of Orthodoxy, he displays his continued devotion to his principles by having the eyes of a picture cut out; in Münster the standards of medieval justice are purposefully applied to effigies by depriving them of their extremities or appropriate sense organs. There too, images of the upper class and of members of the previous administration, from bishops to court and treasury officials, have their heads defaced to emphasize the anonymous equality of the new order. In East Stoneham an image of St. Thomas Becket is turned into a female saint at the behest of Henry himself. Inscriptions are removed, seals destroyed. Obviously, when Iconoclasm is subsumed under attacks on imperial or royal power, images which personify it come under particular fire. Opponents of Elizabeth slashed her portraits, defaced her arms, even hanged her effigies. . . .

Before concluding, it is necessary to consider an important aspect of the reaction to Iconoclasm. To put it briefly, a certain form of rigoristic and moralistic zeal had characterized the attitude of the church towards imagery since its earliest days. This is what might be termed the Iconoclasm of the Orthodox, and if it is not Iconoclasm in the narrowest sense, it is certainly anti-art. One may refer . . . to suggested and actual restrictions such as those imposed by the Council of Elvira and the Quinisext Council of 692. Images could be mere distractions of the senses, or incitements to concupiscence, or simply historically inaccurate—as when painters represented St. Peter with short hair and St. Paul as bald. Standards of what might be called decorum fluctuate, and it is according to such standards that restrictions are imposed. . . .

Various ways are then devised of controlling such problems, and more restrictions imposed. . . .

After the first period of Byzantine iconoclasm, the Acts of the Council of Nicaea made it clear that the Church had to decide what could be represented. The same insistence on the ecclesiastical supervision of artistic activity was made by the Council of Trent's decree on religious imagery, a decree which was itself passed, only at the very final session of the Council, because of the pressing need to formulate an official stand on images in response to recent outbreaks of Iconoclasm in France. . . .

Thus, in the reaction to Iconoclasm, there lurks another form of antipathy towards images. It is perhaps one of the more depressing consequences of Iconoclasm, and although Iconoclasm sometimes had positive results in terms of the art that was produced afterwards, its effect was as frequently stifling. In the Netherlands after Iconoclasm, for example, there is a palpable loss in confidence on the part of both artist and patron, who are reluctant to produce or commission works which are ever liable to attack at the hands of those who are against images. And then, as soon as images are restored, official supervision inhibits artists: they become unsure not only of *what* to represent, but also of *how* they should represent things.

COMMENTS

On January 11, 1983, the *San Francisco Chronicle* carried an Associated Press story headlined "Wealthy Christian Smashes 'Pagan' Treasures to Bits." The dateline was Fort Worth, Texas:

> Wealthy businessman Cullen Davis, a born-again Christian, destroyed more than $1 million worth of gold, silver, jade and ivory art objects because they were associated with Eastern religions, evangelist James Robison said yesterday. Robison told the *Fort Worth Star-Telegram* that he and Davis used hammers to smash the carvings, which Davis had donated last September to help Robison pay off debts. The evangelist decided not to accept the gift after recalling a verse in Deuteronomy: "The graven images of their gods shall ye burn with fire: . . . for it is an abomination to the Lord thy God." Robison said he considered Davis' actions "a good testimony for his Christian faith."

THE INQUISITION

ELIZABETH GILMORE HOLT *Religious Art at the Council of Trent and During the Inquisition* *

THE COUNCIL OF TRENT AND RELIGIOUS ART

The Roman Catholic Church, in the sixteenth century, restated its old argument in favor of images and paintings, that pictures were "the Bible of the illiterate." At the same time it insisted that religious art should be the servant of the Church. This came in the wake of unsuccessful attempts to compromise with the Protestant reformers, who tended to regard all such art as idolatrous. The Roman Catholic restatement came as a decree from the twenty-fifth, and last, session of the Council of Trent, which terminated after eighteen stormy years on December 4, 1563.

This Council articulated for the first time the whole of medieval Catholic doctrine. When it discussed religious art its decisions were brief and to the point, so that it remained for self-appointed commentators to elaborate upon them. Through the decisions of the Council, art was made once again the handmaiden of the Catholic Church; humanism declined, artists turned for inspiration from the natural world to that of theory, from subjects of human significance to those with theological import. In a word, the results were nearer in spirit to the Middle Ages than to the Renaissance. Among the iconographic effects of the Council was the proscription of nudity in religious art, as in the case of Michelangelo's *Last Judgment,* although heroic and mythological nudity were tolerated.

THE COUNCIL OF TRENT'S DECREE "ON SACRED IMAGES"

The holy council commands all bishops and others who hold the office of teaching and have charge of the *cura animarum,* that in accordance with the usage of the Catholic and Apostolic Church, received from the primitive times of the Christian religion, and with the unanimous teaching of the holy Fathers and the decrees of sacred councils, they above all instruct the faithful diligently in matters relating to intercession and invocation of the saints, the veneration of relics, and the legitimate use of images. . . . Moreover, that the images of Christ, of the Virgin Mother of God, and of the saints are to be placed and retained especially in the churches, and that due honor and veneration is to be given them; not, however, that any divinity or virtue is believed to be in them by reason of which they are to be venerated, or that something is to be asked of them, or that trust is to be placed in images, as was done of old by the Gentiles who placed their hope in idols; but because the honor which is shown them is referred to the prototypes which they represent, so that by means of the images which we kiss and before which we uncover the head and prostrate ourselves, we adore Christ and venerate the saints whose likeness they bear. That is what was defined by the decrees of the councils, especially of the Second Council of Nicaea, against the opponents of images.

Moreover, let the bishops diligently teach that by means of the stories of the mysteries of our redemption portrayed in paintings and other representations the people are instructed and confirmed in the articles of faith, which ought to be borne in mind and constantly reflected upon; also that great profit is derived from all holy images, not only because the people are thereby reminded of the benefits and gifts bestowed on them by Christ, but also because through the saints the miracles of God and salutory examples are set before the eyes of the faithful, so that they may give God thanks for those things, may fashion their own life and conduct in imitation of the saints and be moved to adore and love God and cultivate piety. But if anyone should teach or maintain anything contrary to these decrees, let him be anathema. If any abuses shall have found their way into these holy and salutory observances, the holy council desires earnestly that they be completely removed, so that no representation of false doctrines and such as might be the occasion of grave error to the uneducated be exhibited. And if at times it happens, when this is beneficial to the illiterate, that the stories and narratives of the Holy Scriptures are portrayed

Paolo Veronese. Christ in the House of Levi *(Originally titled Christ in the House of Simon), 1573, 18'2" ×
42", oil on canvas. (Academy, Venice. Reproduced by courtesy of Photo Alinari.)*

and exhibited, the people should be instructed that not for that reason is the divinity represented in picture as if it can be seen with bodily eyes or expressed in colors or figures. Furthermore, in the invocation of the saints, the veneration of relics, and the sacred use of images, all superstition shall be removed, all filthy quest for gain eliminated, and all lasciviousness avoided, so that images shall not be painted and adorned with a seductive charm, or the celebration of saints and the visitation of relics be perverted by the people into boisterous festivities and drunkenness, as if the festivals in honor of the saints are to be celebrated with revelry and with no sense of decency. Finally, such zeal and care should be exhibited by the bishops with regard to these things that nothing may appear that is disorderly or unbecoming and confusedly arranged, nothing that is profane, nothing disrespectful, since holiness becometh the house of God. That these things may be the more faithfully observed, the holy council decrees that no one is permitted to erect or cause to be erected in any place or church, however exempt, any unusual image unless it has been approved by the bishop; also that no new miracles be accepted and no relics recognized unless they have been investigated and approved by the same bishop, who as soon as he has obtained any knowledge of such matters, shall, after consulting theologians and other pious men, act thereon as he shall judge consonant with truth and piety. But if any doubtful or grave abuse is to be eradicated, or if indeed any graver question concerning these matters should arise, the bishop, before he settles the controversy, shall await the decision of the metropolitan and of the bishops of the province in a provincial synod; so, however, that nothing new or anything that has not hitherto been in use in the Church, shall be decided upon without having first consulted the most holy Roman pontiff.

PAOLO VERONESE BEFORE THE INQUISITION TRIBUNAL

Paolo Veronese (1528–1588) was born in Verona. After working in Mantua he went to Venice in 1553 where he soon achieved great success and fame as a painter of large canvas on which, under the guise of any story, the brilliance and magnificence of sixteenth-century Venice was depicted. In 1573 he was called before the Tribunal of the Inquisition to answer to charges of having introduced secular elements unsuitable for religious painting into a so-called "Feast in the House of Simon" executed for the Refectory of SS. Giovanni e Paolo. He offered in defense the claim for poetic license for painting, and finally satisfied his accusers by changing the name of the picture, now in the Accademia in Venice, to "The Feast in the House of Levi," making it clear that the scene was neither the "Last Supper" nor the "Feast in the House of Simon."

[The questioning of Paolo Veronese is set down in the minutes of the July 18, 1573, session of the Inquisition Tribunal in Venice as follows.]

The minutes of the session of the Inquisition Tribunal of Saturday, the 18th of July, 1573. Today, Saturday, the 18th of the month of July, 1573, having been asked by the Holy Office to appear before the Holy Tribunal, Paolo Caliari of Verona, domiciled in the Parish Saint Samuel, being questioned about his name and surname, answered as above.

Questioned about his profession:

ANSWER. I paint and compose figures.

QUESTION. Do you know the reason why you have been summoned?

A. No, sir.

Q. Can you imagine it?

A. I can well imagine.

Q. Say what you think the reason is.

A. According to what the Reverend Father, the Prior of the Convent of SS. Giovanni e Paolo, whose name I do not know, told me, he had been here and Your Lordships had ordered him to have painted [in the picture] a Magdelan in place of a dog. I answered him by saying I would gladly do everything necessary for my honor and for that of my painting, but that I did not understand how a figure of Magdalen would be suitable there for many reasons which I will give at any time, provided I am given an opportunity.

Q. What picture is this of which you have spoken?

A. This is a picture of the Last Supper that Jesus Christ took with His Apostles in the house of Simon.

Q. Where is this picture?

A. In the Refectory of the Convent of SS. Giovanni e Paolo.

Q. Is it on the wall, on a panel, or on canvas?

A. On canvas.

Q. What is its height?

A. It is about seventeen feet.

Q. How wide?

A. About thirty-nine feet.

Q. At this Supper of Our Lord have you painted other figures?

A. Yes, milords.

Q. Tell us how many people and describe the gestures of each.

A. There is the owner of the inn, Simon; besides this figure I have made a steward, who, I imagined, had come here for his own pleasure to see how the things were going at the table. There are many figures there which I cannot recall, as I painted the picture some time ago.

Q. Have you painted other Suppers besides this one?

A. Yes, milords.

Q. How many of them have you painted and where are they?

A. I painted one in Verona for the reverend monks at San Nazzaro which is in their refectory. Another I painted in the refectory of the reverend fathers of San Giorgio here in Venice.

Q. This is not a Supper. We are asking about a picture representing the supper of the Lord.

A. I have painted one in the refectory of the Servi of Venice, another in the refectory of the San Sebastiano in Venice. I painted one in Padua for the fathers of Santa Maddalena and I do not recall having painted any others.

Q. In this Supper which you made for SS. Giovanni e Paolo, what is the significance of the man whose nose is bleeding?

A. I intended to represent a servant whose nose was bleeding because of some accident.

Q. What is the significance of those armed men dressed as Germans, each with a halberd in his hand?

A. This requires that I say twenty words!

Q. Say them.

A. We painters take the same license the poets and the jesters take and I have represented these two halberdiers, one drinking and the other eating nearby on the stairs. They are placed here so that they might be of service because it seemed to me fitting, according to what I have been told, that the master of the house, who was great and rich, should have such servants.

Q. And that man dressed as a buffoon with a parrot on his wrist, for what purpose did you paint him on that canvas?

A. For ornament, as is customary.

Q. Who are at the table of Our Lord?

A. The Twelve Apostles.

Q. What is St. Peter, the first one, doing?

A. Carving the lamb in order to pass it to the other end of the table.

Q. What is the Apostle next to him doing?

A. He is holding a dish in order to receive what St. Peter will give him.

Q. Tell us what the one next to this one is doing.

A. He has a toothpick and cleans his teeth.

Q. Who do you really believe was present at that Supper?

A. I believe one would find Christ with His Apostles. But if in a picture there is some space to spare I enrich it with figures according to the stories.

Q. Did any one commission you to paint Germans, buffoons, and similar things in the picture?

A. No, milords, but I received the commission to decorate the picture as I saw fit. It is large and, it seemed to me, it could hold many figures.

Q. Are not the decorations which you painters are accustomed to add to paintings or pictures supposed to be suitable and proper to the subject and the principal figures or are they for pleasure—simply what comes to your imagination without any discretion or judiciousness?

A. I paint pictures as I see fit and as well as my talent permits.

Q. Does it seem fitting at the Last Supper of the Lord to paint buffoons, drunkards, Germans, dwarfs and similar vulgarities?

A. No, milords.

Q. Do you not know that in Germany and in other places infected with heresy it is customary with various pictures full of scurrilousness and similar inventions to mock, vituperate, and scorn the things of the Holy Catholic Church in order to teach bad doctrines to foolish and ignorant people?

A. Yes that is wrong; but I return to what I have said, that I am obliged to follow what my superiors have done.

Q. What have your superiors done? Have they perhaps done similar things?

A. Michelangelo in Rome in the Pontifical Chapel painted Our Lord, Jesus Christ, His Mother, St. John, St. Peter, and the Heavenly Host. These are all represented in the nude—even the Virgin Mary—and in different poses with little reverence.

Q. Do you not know that in painting the Last Judgment in which no garments or similar things are presumed, it was not necessary to paint gar-

ments, and that in those figures there is nothing that is not spiritual? There are neither buffoons, dogs, weapons, or similar buffoonery. And does it seem because of this or some other example that you did right to have painted this picture in the way you did and do you want to maintain that it is good and decent?

A. Illustrious Lords, I do not want to defend it, but I thought I was doing right. I did not consider so many things and I did not intend to confuse anyone, the more so as those figures of buffoons are outside of the place in a picture where Our Lord is represented.

After these things had been said, the judges announced that the above named Paolo would be obliged to improve and change his painting within a period of three months from the day of this admonition and that according to the opinion and decision of the Holy Tribunal all the corrections should be made at the expense of the painter and that if he did not correct the picture he would be liable to the penalties imposed by the Holy Tribunal. Thus they decreed in the best manner possible.

FRANCE

JANE CLAPP *Art Censorship Under French King Louis Philippe**

1831, May 5

Charles Philipon, French journalist and caricaturist, edited and published *La Caricature,* a weekly satirical sheet that appeared in Paris each Thursday after the July Revolution of 1830, and carried one page of text and two pages of lithographs (225:106). *La Caricature,* first issued November 4, 1830, carried such "ferocious political cartoons" as a "weapon in the fight for the people and for liberty" in France that during the four years it was published government authorities seized the paper twenty-seven times.

English novelist William Thackeray, observing the French people's fight for social, political, and economic reforms—as reflected in *La Caricature*—described the contest sympathetically: "Half a dozen poor artists on one side, and His Majesty Louis Philippe, his august family, and the numberless placemen and supporters of monarchy, on the other." These "poor artists" whose work appeared in *La Caricature* included

the leading French painters and printmakers: Honoré Daumier, Denis Auguste Raffet, Grandville (Jean Gerard), Henri Monnier, Charles Travies de Villers, and Pigal. Philipon's cartoon "Soap Bubbles"—showing bursting bubbles as the French government's promises for social and political reform vanishing in thin air—appeared in *La Caricature* on May 5, and caused Guisquet's men (he was Chief of Paris Police) to seize the offending picture in a raid on the Aubert shop where the lithograph was printed (607:16).

1831, June 30

The paper *La Caricature* was ordered seized in Paris when Charles Philipon printed a cartoon showing King Louis Philippe refacing the July 1830 signs (that is, forgetting old promises).

1831, November 19

"Le Poire," a symbol invented by Charles Philipon to represent French Emperor Louis Philippe as a large Burgundy pear, was published frequently in his Paris papers *La Caricature* and *Le Charivari*—issued daily from 1832 to 1842, including a six month's period when the censors refused publication of many drawings and only the framed page appears in the paper, empty except for complaint about the censorship.

"Le Poire," as a symbol for "Le Roi Bourgeois" took its meaning from French slang (a "fathead"), and it became identified with and succeeded in ridiculing the King—and the French government—by associating them with "bourgeois stupidity" whenever it appeared in Philipon's satirical papers, or was chalked on walls and buildings by passers-by to attack the regime.

When Philipon was brought to trial November 14, 1831 "for crimes against the person of the King" for his insulting drawing, he denied "Le Poire" was a libel and claimed he had drawn only what he saw. As his defense in court against the charge of *lèse majesté*, the artist drew a pear (in the manner of his friend caricaturist Grandville), converting it with a few strokes into a likeness of the King: "The first looks like Louis Philippe, the last looks like the first, yet this last one . . . is a pear! Where are you to draw the line? Would you condemn the first drawing? In that case you would have to condemn the last as well, since this resembles the first and thus the King, too! . . ." "Can I help it if His Majesty's face is like a pear?"

The court found Philipon guilty, on November 19, 1831, and sentenced him to six months in prison—a term he began January 13, 1832—and fined him 2,000 francs. The famous sequence "Metamorphois of the Pear," Philipon drew in court—an analysis of the process of caricature—was published in *La Caricature*—the first time on November 24, 1831—and, in a variation, as a woodcut supplement to *Le Charivari*, on January 17, 1834. . . .

1832, February 23

In the atmosphere of repression and censorship of the July Monarchy in France—when prints required official approval prior to publication, and newspapers had to deposit bonds to be forfeited if they criticized the government—artist Honoré Daumier was brought to trial for his lithograph "Gargantua," along with the lithographer—Delaporte—and the printer—Aubert.

Lèse Majesté was charged, an offense to King Louis Philippe, and Daumier was also accused of "fomenting disrespect and hatred of His Majesty's Government." Scatalogical "Gargantua" drawn in December, 1831 for an issue of the Paris weekly *La Caricature* did not appear in the paper because police seized the stone (according to a December 29, 1831 article) before the picture could be run. Twenty-three-year-old Daumier had caricatured the King as Rabelais's giant Gargantua—gorging on the wealth of France: Seated on a throne (*chaise percée*—toilet seat) Louis Philippe devours the wealth of France—taxes represented by baskets of gold brought up a ramp to his mouth by tiny men, his ministers—and passes it on as favors, commissions, privileges and monopolies to the business classes and French peerage, in whose interest the government is conducted.

Daumier had already received one warning from French authorities for a "rash lithograph," and the court found him guilty as charged for drawing "Gargantua," sentencing him to six months imprisonment—to begin August 27, 1832—and fining him 500 francs. He spent five months in cell 102, Sainte-Pelagie Prison, Rue de la Clef, Paris. Political caricatures were forbidden by French censorship from 1835 to 1848, dictating a change in Daumier's subject matter from government to social comment.

THE ACADEMIES OF ART

NIKOLAUS PEVSNER *The Rebellion Against the Academies of Art**

The first indictments of academies of art are contained in Heinse's Letters on the Düsseldorf Gallery. But neither his condemnation nor the outbreaks of other young writers found any response among the artists themselves, a fact which corresponds to the almost complete lack

in painting, sculpture and architecture of any movement reflecting the mood of Sturm und Drang. An anti-academic campaign amongst artists did not set-in until 1790 and did not grow until after 1800.

There was, however, another ally who joined

---

*From Nikolaus Pevsner, *Academies of Art: Past and Present* (New York: Da Capo Press, 1973), pp. 191–92. Copyright © 1973 by Da Capo Press. Reprinted by permission.

from the start in the Sturm und Drang's hatred against academies—an ally who came from the camp of the very enemy. Voltaire and the Encyclopaedists questioned the value of academic organization with all the cold brilliancy and malicious poignancy of their scepticism. They did not fail to point out how academies are bound to foster pedestrian talent and to harm genius. "Nous n'avons pas un grand peintre, depuis que nous avons une Académie de Peinture, pas un grand philosophe, formé par l'Académie des Sciences." Voltaire's pupil, Frederick the Great, was in a position to translate these teachings into practice. Only a few years before his death he refused to do anything for the Berlin academy, because he "had not seen one student who had left it as a passable artist." Some of the arguments set forth by Voltaire and Diderot are strongly reminiscent of those used by Sturm und Drang writers. This can perhaps be accounted for by the one conception they had in common: their faith in the rights of the individual against any restrictions interfering with his subjective sphere. "Aucun ouvrage qu'on appelle académique, il a été en aucun genre un ouvrage de gënie," said Voltaire. The reason for this is according to Diderot that "les académies étouffent presque les hommes de cette trempe [i.e. of genius] en les assujettissant à une tâche réglée." And objections of this kind were by no means limited to the leaders of Enlightenment. Henry Bate, when he wished to praise his friend Gainsborough in the *Morning Herald* of 1788, made an unmistakable hit at the Royal Academy: "This great genius, schooled in nature's extensive study, and not in academies."

However, at bottom the meaning of Voltaire's and Young's attacks differed greatly. The writers of the Enlightenment used their weapons with a brilliant and superior lightness, fighting for the fun of the fight, whereas the preachers of the Sturm und Drang gospel tried to crush resistance by the use of their fists and anything they could lay hand on. The intellectual revolution grew into a revolution of passionate sentiment, and political and social revolutions were imminent. The first battles between young artists and academies were—this is highly characteristic—fought in Germany in the field of Weltanschauung, in France in the field of practical policy. In either case it was the most powerful artist of his nation who challenged the old régime: Carstens in Germany, David in France. Both belonged to the same generation, David being born in 1748 and Carstens in 1754. They are thus considerably younger than Winckelmann and Reynolds and represent exactly the age-group of Goethe.

COMMENTS

1. Do any of the motives of the Iconoclasts discussed by Freedberg have relevance in the twentieth century among those who have attacked modern art?

2. What was the basis of Veronese's defense? Under the circumstances, could you recommend a better one?

3. Rebellions of artists against academic taste and training are plentiful in the history of art. But can academies be accused of being censors when promoting education in the fine arts according to certain standards of style? Today's art colleges are the descendants of art academies—can one also consider them censors?

4. What are the significant differences among the sorts of "censorship" exercised by the iconoclasts, the Inquisition, the French king, and the academy? In the long run, which kind would you expect to be more influential?

CHRISTIAN ART

LEO N. TOLSTOY *What Is Art? (1898)* *

So there are only two kinds of good Christian art; all the rest of art not comprised in these two divisions should be acknowledged to be bad art, deserving not to be encouraged but to be driven out, denied, and despised as being art which does not unite, but divides, people. Such, in literary

*From Leo N. Tolstoy, "What Is Art?" in *Tolstoy on Art*, ed. Aylmer Maude (New York: Haskell House Publishers, 1973), pp. 117, 294–296. Copyright © 1973 by Haskell House Publishers, Inc. Reprinted by permission.

art, are all novels and poems which transmit Church or patriotic feelings, and also exclusive feelings pertaining only to the class of the idle rich such as aristocratic honor, satiety, spleen, pessimism, and refined and vicious feelings flowing from sex-love—quite incomprehensible to the great majority of mankind.

In painting we must similarly place in the class of bad art all the Church, patriotic, and exclusive pictures; all the pictures representing the amusements and allurements of a rich and idle life; all the so-called symbolic pictures, in which the very meaning of the symbol is comprehensible only to the people of a certain circle; and, above all, pictures with voluptuous subjects—all that odious female nudity which fills all the exhibitions and galleries. And to this class belongs almost all the chamber and opera music of our times, beginning especially from Beethoven (Schumann, Berlioz, Liszt, Wagner), by its subject matter devoted to the expression of feelings accessible only to people who have developed in themselves an unhealthy, nervous irritation evoked by this exclusive, artificial, and complex music. . . .

And just in this same way, in all branches of art, many and many works considered great by the upper classes of our society will have to be judged. By this one sure criterion we shall have to judge the celebrated *Divine Comedy* and *Jerusalem Delivered,* and a great part of Shakespeare's and Goethe's works, and in painting every represen-

tation of miracles, including Raphael's "Transfiguration," etc.

Whatever the work may be and however it may have been extolled, we have first to ask whether this work is one of real art or a counterfeit. Having acknowledged, on the basis of the indication of its infectiousness even to a small class of people, that a certain production belongs to the realm of art, it is necessary, on the basis of the indication of its accessibility, to decide the next question. Does this work belong to the category of bad, exclusive art, opposed to religious perception, or to Christian art uniting people? And having acknowledged an article to belong to real Christian art, we must then, according to whether it transmits the feelings flowing from love to God and man, or merely the simple feelings uniting all men, assign it to a place in the ranks of religious art or in those of universal art.

Only on the basis of such verification shall we find it possible to select from the whole mass of what in our society claims to be art those works which form real, important, necessary spiritual food, and to separate them from all the harmful and useless art and from the counterfeits of art which surround us. Only on the basis of such verification shall we be able to rid ourselves of the pernicious results of harmful art and to avail ourselves of that beneficent action which is the purpose of true and good art and which is indispensable for the spiritual life of man of humanity.

THE SOVIET UNION

HELLMUT LEHMANN-HAUPT *Art Under a Dictatorship**

The story of modern art in Russia under communist rule . . . cannot be understood without some knowledge of what happened early in the twentieth century. Russia had been in the *avant-garde* of modern art since 1911, but it was cut off completely from the western world with the beginning of the First World War in 1914. One of the very early collections of progressive French paintings, including those of Matisse, Picasso, and others, had been assembled in Moscow. It was Tschoukin, wealthy patron of the arts, who collected these paintings and established a gallery

that is still in existence. The gallery has been nationalized, and another collection, by Morosov, has been joined with it. It is now known as the Museum of Western Art.

In the early days artists such as Marinetti . . . came to Russia, Matisse painted murals [for] Tschoukin's mansion. The naturalistic, academic art of nineteenth-century origin was dying out in Russia before 1914. There was a whole new school of young, modern artists—cubists, futurists, and other groups—in St. Petersburg as well as in Moscow. These artists were progressive not

*From Hellmut Lehmann-Haupt, *Art Under a Dictatorship* (New York and London: Oxford University Press, 1954), pp. 219–230. Copyright © 1954 by Oxford University Press, Inc. Reprinted by permission.

only in their work but also in their whole way of thinking; even though they were not members of the communist party their sympathies were with the Revolution.

The Academy professors had run away with the White Army when the Revolution started, and the young, modern artists took their places. They started the "Vchutemas," workshop groups which attempted the integration of artistic creation and building construction. The school in Moscow became an important center where exhibitions, group discussions, and public non-political meetings were held.

The first communist leaders in Russia were people of Western education. Men such as Lunacharsky, who in 1918 became the commissar for cultural matters and education in Lenin's cabinet, were idealists. But there was a strong preoccupation with the civil war, and cultural matters were not given a very high priority. Lenin visited the art school in Moscow once, but he admitted quite openly that he did not understand modern art, that it was none of his business; he said that it was up to Lunacharsky to concern himself with these matters. Lunacharsky had enough intellectual tolerance to leave the artists alone and, for the time being, to let them do as they pleased. He had under him several commissars for the various branches of cultural activity, for the theater, music, and so on. The art commissar was D. Sterenberg. Lunacharsky met with strong opposition in the party. The majority of the party members were not in agreement with the modern artists, but they still tolerated them. Characteristic of the mounting opposition to Lunacharsky's aims were the difficulties Gabo and Pevsner experienced in the attempt to print a *Manifesto* in which they stated their artistic credo. They succeeded in getting it published only after surmounting the most serious obstacles.

Until 1921 the Moscow school went on working and maintaining its progressive standards, but after the White Army was beaten, a wave of refugees, including most of the Academy professors, came back and the communists liked their art. By the end of 1921 the workshops had been reorganized, the young, progressive artists had been pushed out, and the academic painters had replaced them. But even before this, there had developed a split within the ranks of the modern artists, with certain groups demanding art as propaganda.

Lunacharsky and Sterenberg planned an exhibition of contemporary Russian art in Berlin, which would help re-establish the lost contact with the western world and would show Russia's artistic contribution during the years of war and revolution. The preparations for this exhibition offered Gabo a welcome opportunity to go to Berlin. After a frank discussion with Lunacharsky, he left, six months before the opening of the show—never to return to his native land.

The exhibition opened in Berlin in the fall of 1922, at the Galerie van Diemen. We can see from the catalogue that a serious attempt was made to give fair representation to the great variety of schools then active in Russia. Along with some examples of traditional naturalism and of impressionism, we find expressionism, cubism, the beginnings of surrealism, abstraction, montage, and constructivism. We get a sense of variety, of freshness and vitality.

Commissar Sterenberg, in his foreword to the catalogue, called the exhibition "the first real step toward *rapprochement.*" There had been previous attempts in this direction, and the year before a book on contemporary Russian art had been published in Vienna, which featured works of Marc Chagall and Alexander Archipenko. Sterenberg explained in his foreword that

Russian art is still very young. It was only after the October Revolution that the broad masses of the population were able to approach it and thus to install new life into the official and dead art which in Russia as in the other countries was recognized as "Grande Art." At the same time the revolution has opened up new perspectives for Russia's creative forces, by giving the artist the opportunity to carry his creations out into the streets and the market places, thus enriching him with new ideas. The embellishment of the towns—their character completely changed by the Revolution—and the demands of new architecture necessitated as a matter of course new forms of construction, and, most important of all, the artists no longer worked each for himself, hidden in his corner, but they entered into the closest contact with the broad masses of the population, which accepted avidly what was offered them, sometimes with lively enthusiasm, sometimes with sharp criticism.

These were brave words, born of the same enthusiasm and utopian vision that had fired the imagination of the progressive artists of Germany after the 1918 Revolution. The Soviet commissars who came to visit the Berlin exhibition were annoyed. They went home and made their complaints. More to their liking was a very different statement about the function of the artist, pronounced during that same year, 1922, by the Association of the Artists of the Revolution. "It is our duty to mankind," so read their manifesto, "to perpetuate the Revolution, the greatest event in history, in artistic documents. We render a pictorial representation of the present day; the life of the Red Army; the life of the workers and peasants, the leaders of the Revolution, and the heroes of labor."

The growing rift between progressive art on the one side and incipient "social realism" on the other was accurately reflected three years later in the observations of Louis Lozowick.

Modern Russian artists [he wrote in 1925] are much bolder in their theorization owing to their leaning on the state. The Soviet government acted on the assumption that a new art can be the work of a new man, himself the product of a new social system. Their policy was based on this assumption and they attempted to solve the art problem in a practical way—perhaps in the only practical way possible—in the way implicit in the assumption. [Such efforts, however, were] not crowned with immediate success. External and internal complications . . . new economic policy, restoring to private property and initative certain of its former privileges [stood in the way]. . . . There is a growing demand for portraits, landscapes and genre pictures. The demand is met by the older schools, which are reorganizing their semi-defunct groupings, arranging exhibitions, and becoming in general assertive. All this had a decided effect on the radical artists, for though the Soviets still aid art and artists in various ways . . . such aid is of necessity more limited than formerly. Compelled to shift for themselves the less resolute among the radicals either have turned to other fields or have gone abroad to join the modernists' ranks in Berlin, Paris, Prague. Not a few, however, are still at their posts, certain that the present crisis in art is only temporary; that it is destined to be liquidated.

The reader will hardly need to be told that it was not the threat to modern art but modern art itself that was liquidated.

RETARDING INFLUENCES IN SOVIET CULTURAL DICTATORSHIP

It is true that the process was gradual. There were certain retarding and neutralizing influences at work, which for a time concealed the bitter truth. For instance, in an exhibition of Russian art held in Philadelphia in 1934−5 one could still see a few modern paintings alongside a number of canvases marking the transition toward social realism and a solid group of typical examples of this new trend.

In Soviet Russian art, as in the art of Nazi Germany, what could be called the "Law of varying susceptibility of various artistic media to ideological corruption" can be observed. In other words, we can notice in Russia as we did in Germany that ideological pressure was most effective on the free arts and less noticeable in the applied arts. Progressive tendencies in Soviet Russian art were more quickly and more thoroughly liquidated in painting and sculpture than in architecture or in the graphic arts. . . .

FORMULATION OF OFFICIAL DEMANDS

Now what about these official demands? What were they like, how were they formulated, and what did they prescribe? The interesting thing about the official aesthetics of the communist state is the fact that they are separated by such a wide gap from actual performance. As in Nazi Germany, there is a tremendous discrepancy between theory and practice, sometimes admitted, sometimes glossed over, sometimes denied.

One of the earliest available enunciations of the role of the artist in the new Soviet state is a conversation between Lenin and Lunacharsky, which took place probably in the winter of 1918−19. Lenin had summoned Lunacharsky and had asked him if there were not artists around who were hard up and needed support.

I am talking of sculptors and to a certain extent, perhaps, of poets and writers. The idea I am about to explain to you has been in my mind for some time. You remember that Campanella says in his *City of the Sun* that the frescoes which decorate the walls of his imaginary socialist city serve as an object lesson to youth in natural science and history, rouse their sense of citizenship, and, in short, play a part in educating and bringing up the younger generation. It seems to me that this notice is far from naïve and might, with certain modifications, be adopted by us and put into practice now.

Lunacharsky recalls: ". . . the idea of direction and using art for such a lofty purpose as the propaganda of our great ideas struck me at once as extraordinarily tempting."

Above all, Lenin wanted propaganda through monuments: "I regard monuments as still more important than inscriptions; we might have busts, figures, and, perhaps, bas-reliefs and groups." He recommended a series on the forerunners and theoreticians of Socialism: "Take a list like this and commission the sculptor to make temporary monuments—of plaster, even, or of concrete. The important thing is that they be understandable to the masses, that they catch the eye. . . ."

Lenin was aware of the great gap between the fulfillment of such ideas and the actual conditions he saw around him. Lunacharsky once again recalled some words of Lenin: "What do we lack in order to build our socialist state? Our land is vast and wide, the power belongs to us. What we lack is culture, culture among the leaders, culture among communists."

Lunacharsky quoted these words in an important speech, given toward the end of his life, in which he developed his own ideas and demands. This was no longer a tolerant and liberal expression but a sharp and forceful defense of state art in terms of a completely materialistic concept of culture. He asks:

Can the dictatorship of the proletariat influence culture, influence its tempo, direction, the character of its development? . . . Can culture whose development depends upon the pressure of the material process and which in its highest spiritual spheres has its own laws, be regulated by one of its parts, namely by organized human knowledge in the form of the state and again, in its acutest manifestations, in the form of the dictatorship of the proletariat?

After citing, and rejecting the objections to such a cultural dictatorship raised by the "bourgeois" and "capitalistic" critics, he clearly answers in the affirmative:

The proletarian state seeks to elevate to the level of socialist culture the backward toiling masses, to create for the first time an opportunity for a truly human culture. The effect of the proletarian state on art is beneficial. . . . All the aims of the Soviet state and of the Soviet state alone are creative aims, emancipative and constructive aims in the widest sense of the word. . . . To point out the direction in which the artistic forces, the artistic attention, the artistic talents should be directed is a natural conclusion from our entire system of planning. We thus are very well aware of the fact that we have the right to interfere in the development of culture, beginning with the development of machinery in our country and electrification as part of it, and ending with the direction of the subtlest forms of art. . . . All these measures we are employing to regulate creative art, both proletarian and the art of those following the proletariat, and to put a stop to artistic work among the direct enemies of the USSR—this entire school of

influences, from repression to the greatest care of the artist, to comradely concern about him, to giving him support, to penetration of his laboratory—all of them are good and necessary.

This speech is the clearest enunciation of the Soviet doctrine of state control of the arts that I have been able to find. The doctrine has remained basically unchanged through the days of the Cominform and its director, Andrei Alexandrovitch Zhdanov, and on to the present day—regardless of how many times and by whom it has been repeated and reinterpreted. The only things that have been added are specific and more detailed directions for each form of art fostered by the state, and prohibitions and liquidations of undesirable expressions.

THE TIGHTENING OF THE REINS

The early thirties, when Lunacharsky stated his ideas with such decisiveness, witnessed the same process of "tightening of the reins" that took place in Nazi Germany in 1937 after four years of the Hitler regime. This phase of heightened control and more stringent direction of the arts came correspondingly later in Soviet Russia, after about fifteen years. Its tardiness can probably be explained by the fact that, as was frequently admitted by Soviet leaders, the early years of the regime were so taken up with civil strife and basic economic rehabilitation that in the early days cultural control did not receive a very high priority.

A typical reflection of the stricter course of artistic regimentation is seen in the review of a 1933 exhibition, "Fifteen Years of Art in the USSR." It speaks frankly of "the backwardness of the art of painting as compared to the advancement of Socialist construction. . . . The national forms of the Socialist content of the paintings exhibited are very poorly developed. This is exceedingly regrettable." The article explains that during the early period of communism "the party had to throw all its forces into the then raging civil war and could pay only the most cursory attention to the fine arts. . . . Special organizations with a clear understanding of the foundations of art in the revolution were altogether lacking. . . . The party adopted a waiting policy with respect to the art of painting, as bourgeois influence was still strong. . . . The various schools of painting, the Futurist-Cubist's primarily, threw themselves into the breach with great enthusiasm." But "the vast majority of the artists had not the slightest conception of Marxist-Leninist teachings. . . ." They were not the only sinners, however. "The Realists, Naturalists, Impressionists of this period stood aloof from the daily struggle of the proletariat." Only a few painters are praised—Kustodiev, for instance. "In his *Mayday* the victorious march of the Leningrad workers, filled with the joy of life, is shown with splendid craftsmanship and coloring. His *Bolshevik,* symbolizing the party as the leader, guide, the central force of the revolution, in the full consciousness of his powers, waves the flag not only over the Soviet Union but over the entire world."

The note of increasing nationalism, coupled with demands for cultural world conquest, is present also in another document of the early thirties, an article entitled "Leninism and Art." Here we find the official lineage of Soviet aesthetics, the deliberate linking of the so-called art doctrines of Marx and Engels with those of Lenin and on to Stalin, with full references to official party documents, organization, and resolutions.

Of special interest in this article is a critical review of various artists' associations, which are denounced for having escaped "during the dismantling of the as yet not completely destroyed forces of the bourgeoisie and kulaks in literature and art, a process which it was necessary to carry on to a definite finish." We learn that "by the decree of the Central Committee of the Communist Party of 23 April 1932, all these organizations were liquidated, and instead of them were created single unions of writers, composers, and artists, with Communist factions in them."

We remember that it was only about a year later that Goebbels' Art Chamber was established in Nazi Germany. The Soviet policies from 1932 on show the same emphatic pressure, the same lavish encouragement, through official commissions and premiums, of one kind of art, and the fierce, relentless extinction of every other kind, which was so characteristic of the Nazi art policies after 1937.

Under Stalin You Could Have Been Shot*

A group of Soviet artists who decided to bring abstract art out of the ideological closet got a harsh dose of Socialist Realism when they attempted to set up their paintings in a vacant lot in Moscow's drab Smenovskoye suburb last September 15. As the artists and their friends began arranging the canvases on improvised stands, a man who called himself Ivan Ivanovich Ivanov (the Russian equivalent of John Doe) announced that he was leading a group of volunteer workers to turn the lot into a "park of culture." At a signal from Ivan, the "volunteers," some of whom were believed to be militiamen out of uniform, began grabbing the pictures, ripping canvases and shattering frames. At another signal, bulldozers and dump trucks roared onto the crowded lot and began churning the pictures into the mud. One truck backed into a group of spectators and almost buried a child under a load of mud. A bulldozer let loose a pile of heavy sewer pipes, and water trucks sprayed the crowd as it tried to escape.

Foreign diplomats and reporters who had retired to the sidelines were threatened by "volun-

teers." Christopher Wren of the *New York Times* had his camera shoved into his face and was punched in the stomach by one roughneck while two others held his arms. Other reporters, including a woman, were also beaten when they tried to come to his assistance. Uniformed militiamen and KGB agents stood by calmly and snapped pictures of the beatings. Five painters were arrested and charged with "petty hooliganism" for attempting to resist the bulldozers, but all were released a few days later, probably as a result of the worldwide publicity given to the event.

Soviet officials seemed genuinely surprised at the shocked reaction to their brand of no-holds-barred art criticism, which made headlines around the world. Semi-official sources stated that Soviet leaders had also been embarrassed by the image of bulldozers and vigilantes ripping up paintings. For domestic consumption, however, the Soviet press blamed the artists and foreign newsmen for the violence. An "inspired" letter from "four citizens" printed in the official newspaper of the Communist Paper's Central Commit-

*From "Under Stalin You Could Have Been Shot," *ARTnews,* November 1974, p. 72. Copyright © 1974 by ARTnews Associates. Reprinted by permission.

tee charged the nonconformist artists with staging a "deliberate political provocation" with the help of diplomats from capitalist countries.

But the Soviet government reversed its position, and, two weeks later, the artists finally had their outdoor show. It was probably the largest officially sanctioned exhibition of modern and unorthodox art by Soviet painters held in the Soviet Union since the 1920s.

The artists and their friends credited the government turnaround to Western pressure. "This is a classic example of the influence of détente," said Aleksandr Goldfarb, a scientist and friend of many of the artists. "This never would have taken place without the pressure of the West, and hard pressure at that."

The 10,000 Muscovites who packed what the artists ironically called the "Second Fall Outdoor Art Show" held children on their shoulders and called for the paintings to be held aloft because the crowd was so thick it was impossible to see. Most of the art was conservative by Western standards, but to Soviet viewers, most of them young and in a holiday mood, it was a revelation. "That's the new word, completely new," exclaimed a spectator of Vladislav Zhdan's *Dusk,* an impressionistic all-blue fantasy of a girl in a babushka emerging from a forest. The crowd also liked his surrealistic still life of Boris Pasternak, which featured a skull from which a tree of life emerged to entwine with a portrait of the poet. Another success was Dima Gordeyev, who paints gentle satires of the prudishness and formality of Russian public life. A picture of a young couple kissing in the sky above a drab cityscape drew appreciative laughter. But not everyone approved of the exhibition. One middleaged man pointed an accusing finger at an expressionistic painting by Oskar Robin and told the artist: "Under Josif [Stalin] you could have been shot for that one painting."

THE NAZIS

HELLMUT LEHMANN-HAUPT *Art Under a Dictatorship**

On 8 July 1937, quite without warning, Professor Adolf Ziegler arrived at the Kunsthalle in Mannheim with two assistants and brandished a piece of paper with Goebbels' signature on it. Professor Ziegler, Nazidom's number-one painter, was known to the opposite faction as "The Master of the Pubic Hair" for his meticulously detailed nudes. He was authorized by a special order from the Fuehrer to "secure" all paintings and sculptures of "degenerate" German art since 1910 that were in the possession of the Reich and of any of its Laender or individual municipalities.

What happened in Mannheim was typical of Professor Ziegler's procedure wherever he went. The confiscated items were to be shipped to Munich for an exhibition at which examples of "degenerate" art would be publicly displayed and derided. The party operators collected paintings, sculptures, and drawings by such men as Wilhelm Lehmbruck, Franz Marc, Max Beckmann, Carl Hofer, George Grosz, and Willi Baumeister, and also by foreigners such as André Derain, Edvard Munch, Alexander Archipenko, and Marc Chagall. The operation was nation-wide and wholesale. Sixteen thousand works of art—paintings, sculptures, drawings, and prints—by nearly 1400 different artists were gathered up. Complete and final destruction of a whole culture was the intention.

No specific definition of "degenerate art" was enunciated for this operation, but certain principles of selection are easy to recognize from the kinds of work that were condemned. The Nazis swept up the drawings and paintings of Jewish artists and any works depicting Jewish subject matter; they took any painting that betrayed pacifist sentiments and any war art not in line with the officially prescribed heroic spirit (they took Otto Dix, for instance); and they confiscated expressions of socialist or Marxist-doctrines; works showing "inferior racial types," such as the Barlach creatures or Otto Mueller's gypsies; all German expressionist painting and sculpture, including the work of their old party member Emil Nolde; abstract art, especially that done by the men who had been connected with the Bauhaus. "Impertinent attacks on our culture and our national art treasure, promoted by a number of

*From Hellmut Lehmann-Haupt, *Art Under a Dictatorship* (New York and London: Oxford University Press, 1954), pp. 78–87. Copyright © 1954 by Oxford University Press, Inc. Reprinted by permission.

swindlers motivated purely by political, propagandistic motives"—these were the words with which Hitler characterized modern art.

The exhibition of "degenerate art" opened in Munich in the summer of 1937 and was still open when the Fuehrer delivered his lecture on art at the Nuremberg Party Conference that year. Every possible device was used to pillory the exhibits. All the shameless tricks developed four years earlier in the Karlsruhe, Mannheim, and Nuremberg displays were now repeated on a grand scale. The pictures were hung without frames, closely jammed together to make a clutter, and the labels that were appended to them were of such a slanderous nature that even the Fuehrer is supposed to have ordered some of them changed after he had completed his own preview. Price tags showing the amounts paid for the pictures in drastically devaluated German currency were appended without explanation, in order to scandalize the taxpayers.

The exhibition attracted huge crowds, not only party members and masses of the curious and the casual but also large groups of friends of modern art, who could do no more than pass through the halls in utter silence with faces of stone. At least one wealthy collector, hitherto interested only in traditional values, was won over to modern art by the powerful appeal it exerted even in the hour of its deepest humiliation.

A catalogue was issued for the occasion, designed to underline the effect of the exhibition: provocative juxtapositions of pictures and slogans on the right hand pages and running comment and an excerpt from a Hitler art speech on the left. The most interesting thing about this catalogue is its fraudulent identification of progressive art and political radicalism. This is the avowed intention of the catalogue and the main point of attack. To prove the point there were reprinted statements on art by radical left-wing writers. Two things are interesting: not one of the people cited is a well-known or important artist; not one of the quotations is later than 1921; most of them are dated 1914 or 1915. In other words, these statements were garnered first from the period of infancy of the twentieth-century revolution in the arts, and second from the brief period of courtship between progressive art and political revolution. We have examined carefully this phase of the early years of the Weimar Republic and have seen how short-lived it was, how full of misunderstandings, how insignificant the political influence exercised by the artists as a group. But in 1937 there was no organ of public opinion left

inside Germany that could have pointed out the fallacy in this accusation against modern art. The exhibition was a resounding victory for the Nazis, not only at the time and in Germany but also, and more so, because of the long-range effects of this type of reasoning.

Professor Ziegler and his committee worked on a generous scale. They amassed more than a hundred works by the sculptor Lehmbruck; between two and three hundred examples each of Dix, Grosz, and Corinth; between three and four hundred by Hofer, Pechstein, Barlach, Feininger, and Otto Mueller; more than four hundred Kokoschkas, five hundred Beckmanns, six hundred Schmidt-Rottluffs and Kirchners, seven hundred Heckels, and more than a thousand Noldes. In addition they confiscated the works of some non-German artists—paintings by Cézanne, Picasso, Matisse, Gauguin, Van Gogh, Braque, Pisarro, Dufy, de Chirico, and Max Ernst.

Very few works of art in public collections escaped. At the Kronprinzen-Palais two of the floor attendants managed to hide Erich Heckel's much-attacked *Madonna of Ostende* between two doors, and after the raid was over they telephoned the artist to hide the painting away somewhere. Such occurrences were rare exceptions. Ziegler's men were extremely thorough. At the print gallery in Stuttgart the single leaves of each objectionable artist were fished out of otherwise neutral portfolios.

Museums in western Germany suffered the heaviest losses. The Folkwang Museum in Essen, the Municipal Collection in Duesseldorf, and the Hamburg Kunsthalle each lost more than nine hundred works of art. The National Gallery in Berlin, the Berlin Print Cabinet, and the museums in Frankfurt and Breslau each lost from five hundred to six hundred works.

But the Nazis had other motives besides the protection of German culture against "the poisoning influence upon public opinion" of this type of art. On 31 May 1938, some months after the collecting had been completed, a law was passed over the signatures of Hitler and Goebbels legalizing the seizures and making provisions for the further exploitation of the booty. They disposed of their loot with exactly the same cold-blooded calculation with which they utilized the gold fillings from the teeth and the ashes from the bones of their gas-chamber victims.

All items of international value were sold outside of Germany, and a final report was made to the Fuehrer by the Propaganda Ministry. It is possible that the figures were tampered with to con-

GEMÄLDE UND PLASTIKEN MODERNER MEISTER

AUS DEUTSCHEN MUSEEN

Braque, Chagall, Derain, Ensor, Gauguin, van Gogh, Laurencin, Modigliani, Matisse, Pascin, Picasso, Vlaminck, Marc, Nolde, Klee, Hofer, Rohlfs, Dix, Kokoschka, Beckmann, Pechstein, Kirchner, Heckel, Grosz, Schmidt-Rottluff, Müller, Modersohn, Macke, Corinth, Liebermann, Amiet, Baraud, Feininger, Levy, Lehmbruck, Mataré, Marcks, Archipenko, Barlach

AUSTELLUNG

IN ZURICH
Zunfthaus zur Meise, vom 17. Mai (Mittwoch) bis 27. Mai (Samstag) 1939

Eintritt: Fr. 3.—
Taglich geoffnet von 10–12 Uhr und-von 2–6 Uhr (Sountag nachmittag geschlossen)

IN LUZERN
Grand Hotel National, vom 30. Mai (Dienstag) bis 29. Juni (Donnerstag) 1939

Eintritt: Fr. 3. —
Taglieb geoffnet vom 10–12 Uhr und vom 2–6 Uhr (Sountag geschlossen)

AUKTION IN LUZERN

Grand Hotel National, Freitag, den 30. Juni 1939, nachmittags 2.15 Uhr

AUKTIONSLEITUNG: THEODOR FISCHER, GALERIE FISCHER, LUZERN

Text of poster for auction of confiscated art, Lucerne, Switzerland, June 1939.

ceal "unofficial" transactions, but according to the report they netted more than 10,000 pounds, nearly 45,000 dollars, and about 8000 Swiss francs. A major portion of the confiscated art was sold in Switzerland at a public auction held in the Theodor Fischer Gallery in Lucerne on 30 June 1939 [see poster, above]. Some of the proceeds were used to buy what the Party considered desirable examples of German national art for Hitler's Linz Museum—nineteenth-century Romantic pictures for the most part, with a dreamy landscape by Caspar David Friedrich as the star item. Other examples of nineteenth-century German art were acquired by barter. More than thirty paintings by members of the expressionist school, with nearly two hundred prints and sculptures thrown in for good measure, were bartered for a single painting by a man named Oehme. The "worthless" paintings, namely, those that seemed to have no barter or sale value, had already been sorted out. They were burned in the spring of 1939 by the Berlin Fire Brigade.

Before the disposal of the booty had actually got under way, Goering took a look at it. His haughty eye fell with favor on some paintings by Van Gogh, Gauguin, Marc, and Munch, and he made off with them for his private collection. Unlike Hitler, who practiced his preachments about the value of German art above all other art, Goering's digestion was never upset by the "international poison" that he himself devoured in such generous helpings.

There were several leaks; the meshes of the dragnet were rather wide. Professor Heise, whose museum in Luebeck did not escape the confiscations, said to me in 1950: "What I thought especially cheap in this operation was the fact that one was offered these pictures right away for repurchase. I was secretly offered virtually all the museum paintings confiscated in Luebeck. One or two of them I was able to buy, others I got friends to purchase."

What became of the "degenerate" artists themselves, the men who were considered enemies of the state and traitors to the national cause? Many more of them survived than one would have guessed, but they survived in isolation, cut off from other artists, unable to communicate with their friends, living constantly under the threat of the concentration camp, deprived of the tools of their trade and of space in which to work. They went underground. They found a few friends who continued to buy their work, a few dealers who secretly sold for them, a shopkeeper here or there who was willing to take risks to give them without ration cards a few paints and brushes, and sometimes a few disciples who wanted to learn. But the isolation from other painters and from any kind of appreciative public had a paralyzing effect: a damming up of the sources of creation.

Worse than actual danger and physical hardship was the feeling of living constantly as a suspect. This was what the artists complained about most bitterly after the war—this atmosphere of disapproval, of having to live against the stream of all the life around them in seemingly endless, hopeless isolation. But they carried on. Carl Hofer was the first painter to be thrown out of his teaching post at an academy and he was strictly prohibited from painting. There is the story that Gestapo agents came to his house and felt his brushes to see if they were wet. Nevertheless, he continued to paint, and to sell.

Karl Schmidt-Rottluff, one of the founders and leading masters of expressionism, was singled out for incessant persecution. He had a friendly doorman, who warned him every time the agents presented themselves downstairs, and sometimes he managed to hide in a closet the canvas he was working on. He had to dodge stool-pigeons who posed as customers for a portrait to tempt him into a commitment. He, too, never ceased to work.

The abstract sculptor Karl Hartung was able to carry on behind locked doors. It was a lonely life, the doorbell rang seldom—"isolated as though one were living in the catacombs."

Occasionally, a courageous dealer would bring a handful of people together. Once the Nierendorf Gallery staged a night lecture about the "degenerate" sculptor Gerhard Marcks. The affair was crowded and a repeat performance was scheduled, but word got out and the second lecture had to be canceled.

Willi Baumeister, Germany's most widely recognized abstract painter, also managed to carry on. During my visit to his home in Stuttgart on 18 November 1950, he dictated to me spontaneously an account of his existence during the years of persecution.

I was a Professor at the Frankfurt art school. In 1932, as a result of the activities of the well-known architect and architectural theoretician Schultze-Naumburg, who fought mightily against everything modern, I was attacked in the newspapers. Something characteristic happened to me. The Stuttgart art gallery offered to buy one of my paintings. This was around Christmas 1932. I sent them something, one might call it semi-abstract. Six weeks or so later the Director wrote back and asked if he could not exchange the picture for something a little more representational. I complied with his wish but soon another letter arrived, asking for a picture still less abstract. Thereupon I took from my parents' home one of my very early works, of 1912 perhaps, a landscape I had painted at the age of 18, strongly influenced by Cézanne. This picture was accepted, but hung not in the gallery itself but in one of the offices of the State Library.

After Hitler's election, news of the dismissals was passed along by word of mouth. My name was at the top of the faculty list. Our Frankfurt chief, Professor Wiechert, was pensioned off and the new man sent me a rude letter of dismissal on 31 March 1933. Next day there were mysterious chalk marks at my door, the day after that the lock had been tampered with so that I lost control over my belongings there: My wife was expecting a baby and I arranged to move to the house of my parents-in-law in Stuttgart.

At once there was a cooling off among friends and acquaintances against the man who had been singled out for dismissal. The dismissal was bad, but the social ostracism that followed was worse.

I now earned my living as a typographic designer, but cautiously, so as not to get too well known and not to be too active. I continued to paint behind closed doors. Hitler's speeches had the effect of renewing dangerous aggressions against modern painting. My pictures were removed from the state and municipal galleries of Germany. The ostracism increased step by step until 1937–8. An especially dangerous man was Count Baudissin, appointed by Hitler to the directorship of the magnificent Folkwang Museum in Essen. He demanded that "degenerate" paintings be removed from the private collections as well. That was about the worst that could happen to the painters and it was most depressing. Soon after that Ernst Kirchner shot himself in Davos. Oskar Schlemmer told me that Kirchner's suicide was directly connected with the appearance of Baudissin's article.

The constant utterances of Hitler, Goebbels, and the others sapped our energies and paralyzed us. This general paralysis and the results of increasing pressure were the reason for Oskar Schlemmer's illness, and also the cause of his death.

After the war started, things became especially uncomfortable because one had to show that one was working. In 1938 my friend Heinz Resch, the architect, had recommended me to a paint and varnish factory in Wuppertal, for whom I took on some jobs. They had a research institute for painting technique and now I worked for them on a monthly salary.

I had no public. No one knew that I continued to paint, in a second-story room in utter isolation. Not even the children and the servants must know what I was doing there. I carried the key always with me.

My friends in Wuppertal, Oskar Schlemmer among them, sent me humorous letters and postcards from time to time, with paste-up pictures and surrealist texts. I sent them, rather naïvely, a cartoon, cut from a U.S. newspaper, of an electric chair with Hitler on it. Suddenly I was summoned to Gestapo Headquarters. I was confronted by the Gestapo censor with my entire correspondence for the last year and a half. Thank God, Hitler in the electric chair was not among the intercepted letters. I extricated myself by writing a long report to the Gestapo, explaining that these were plans for a book dealing with color modulation and patina, in connection with an especially resistant paint for the camouflaging of tanks and pill boxes.

It was not until after the beginning of the war that I had my first visitors. We opened the boxes in the basement and I showed my pictures.

Terrible was the idea that one would never again be able to show such pictures in public. In 1943 I had to stop painting altogether, because my next-door neighbor was an SS general. A captain of the SS was billeted in my own room. All the pictures had disappeared, but if one happened to turn up by chance, I told the captain that it was a camouflage experiment. I still had a studio, which I did not dare to enter. It was then that I began to make illustrations, *Gilgamesch* and *Salome*, as a little personal revenge against this anti-Semitic business; finally Shakespeare's *Tempest*. They all were made in 1943, but published much later, after the war.

Yes, there was an uncorruptible core of creative integrity. The story of Willi Baumeister's life, typical of a group that has never been counted or listed, proves it. Nothing so strongly documents the sincerity and seriousness of these expressionist and abstract painters and sculptors as their urgent desire and their need to carry on against overwhelming odds. Above all this is a testimony not only to their character but to the validity of their art.

Oskar Schlemmer was a gifted painter, sculptor, choreographer, and teacher who taught at the Bauhaus in Weimar. In 1930 he saw his paintings and reliefs made for that school destroyed by the Nazis. In 1933 the Nazis removed him from his teaching post at Breslau and in 1937 exhibited his work as "degenerate art."

OSKAR SCHLEMMER *Letter to Minister Goebbels (1933)**

Berlin
April 25, 1933

Deeply shaken by what I hear from numerous cities in the Reich, including Dessau, Mannheim, and Dresden, where the museums' collections of modern art are to be placed in "chambers of artistic horrors," each picture labelled with the sum paid for it, exposed to the mockery and indignation of the public, I take the liberty of appealing to you with an urgent plea that you call a halt to these measures.

Please allow me to direct your attention to the period before the war, to the years between 1910 and 1914, when simultaneously all the artistically vital countries, like Germany, Russia, and France, experienced a spontaneous revolution of consciousness in the arts; the works which grew out of this revolution could not possibly have anything to do with Russian Communism or with Marxism, because these concepts did not yet exist!

It was a period in which the windows of the

*From Tut Schlemmer, ed., *The Letters and Diaries of Oscar Schlemmer* (Middletown, Conn.: Wesleyan Univ. Press, 1972), pp. 310–311. Copyright © 1972 by Tut Schlemmer. Reprinted by permission.

musty chambers of art were opened wide, when the doors suddenly stood ajar, and the artists were caught up in a delirium of enthusiasm for the new spirit they sensed being born.

It was in this enraptured mood that we young academy students were surprised by the war. We marched off to battle filled with genuine enthusiasm for a noble cause, for the ideals of art! In the name of my fallen comrades I protest against the defamation of their goals and their works, for those which found their way into museums are today being desecrated.

That was not what they died for! After the war, the survivors, now in their forties, continued their interrupted work in the pre-war spirit,

largely oblivious to and uninterested in the political occurrences around them.

These days pictures by both living and deceased modern painters are being systematically defamed! They have been branded alien, un-German, unworthy, and unnatural. The political motives ascribed to them are in most cases totally inappropriate. Artists are fundamentally unpolitical and must be so, for their kingdom is not of this world. It is always humanity with which they are concerned, always the totality of human existence to which they must pay allegiance.

Oskar Schlemmer

CARL R. BALDWIN *Haacke: Refusé in Cologne**

Last spring several of the museums of Cologne— genial hosts to and purchasers of contemporary European and American art in recent years— invited artists to suggest projects that could be realized and displayed in one or another of the participating museums under the banner of "Projekt '74." Among other things, the event was designed to commemorate the 150th anniversary of the founding of that dean of Cologne art institutions, the Wallraf-Richartz Museum.

Hans Haacke submitted the following project on April 20:

Manet's *Bunch of Asparagus* of 1880, coll. Wallraf-Richartz Museum, is on a studio easel in an approximately 6 x 8 meter room of "Projekt '74." Panels on the wall present the social and economic position of the persons who have owned the painting over the years and the prices that were paid for it.

In these soberly designed panels, placed behind glass within thin black frames like diplomas in doctors' offices, the visitor was to learn, among other things, that Charles Euphrassi, a Parisian banker and serious amateur of art, bought it for a thousand francs the year it was painted—200 francs more than the artist was asking for it. In gratitude, Manet dashed off another small painting, this one with only one asparagus stalk, and sent it to Euphrassi with a note: "This stalk was missing from your bunch." Subsequent owners of

the whole *Bunch* were Alexandre Rosenberg, father of the art dealer Paul Rosenberg; Paul Cassirer, art collector, editor of the satirical publication *Simplicissimus* and a member of the avant-garde "Berlin Secession" group before World War I; Max Liebermann, a celebrated artist and collector of Impressionist works; Käthe Riezler, his daughter; and Maria White, his granddaughter. In 1968, the Kuratorium of the Wallraf-Richartz Museum (a sort of "Association of Friends of the Museum"), presided over by the financier Hermann J. Abs, teamed up with the city of Cologne to raise the funds needed ($340,000) to acquire the picture for the museum. On April 18, 1968, Abs, on behalf of the Kuratorium, presented the work to the museum in commemoration of the first anniversary of the death of Konrad Adenauer.

At first glance, Haacke's examination of the pedigree of *Bunch of Asparagus* seems benign enough, and one can imagine circumstances in which such an adumbration of information would cause an institutional bosom to swell with pride. However, Haacke's proposal was rejected, and there ensued a lengthy correspondence between the artist and various museum officials. This has only partially clarified the reasons for the rejection. Apparently, the sticking point was Haacke's interest in the career of Hermann J. Abs, the museum's benefactor; in addition to providing carefully drawn profiles of the family backgrounds, professional careers and social and economic cir-

---

*From Carl Baldwin, "Haacke: Refusé in Cologne," *Art in America*, November–December, 1974, pp. 36–37. Copyright © 1974 by Art in America, Inc. Reprinted by permission.

Das Spargel-Stilleben
erworben durch die Initiative des
Vorsitzenden des Wallraf-Richartz-Kuratoriums

Hermann J. Abs

Geboren 1901 in Bonn. – Entstammt wohlhabender katholischer Familie. Vater Dr. Josef Abs, Rechtsanwalt und Justizrat, Mitinhaber der Hubertus Braunkohlen AG. Brüggen, Erft. Mutter Katharina Lückerath.

Abitur 1919 Realgymnasium Bonn. – Ein Sem. Jurastudium Universität Bonn. – Banklehre im Kölner Bankhaus Delbrück von der Heydt & Co. Erwirbt internationale Bankerfahrung in Amsterdam, London, Paris, USA.

Heiratet 1928 Inez Schnitzler. Ihr Vater mit Georg von Schnitzler vom Vorstand des IG. Farben-Konzerns verwandt. Tante verheiratet mit Baron Alfred Neven du Mont. Schwester verheiratet mit Georg Graf von der Goltz. – Geburt der Kinder Thomas und Marion Abs.

Mitglied der Zentrumspartei. – 1929 Prokura im Bankhaus Delbrück, Schickler & Co., Berlin. 1935-37 einer der 5 Teilhaber der Bank.

1937 im Vorstand und Aufsichtsrat der Deutschen Bank, Berlin. Leiter der Auslandsabteilung. – 1939 von Reichswirtschaftsminister Funk in den Beirat der Deutschen Reichsbank berufen. – Mitglied in Ausschüssen der Reichsbank, Reichsgruppe Industrie, Reichsgruppe Banken, Reichswirtschafts-kammer und einem Arbeitskreis im Reichswirtschaftsministerium. – 1944 in über 50 Aufsichts- und Verwaltungsräten großer Unternehmen. Mitgliedschaft in Gesellschaften zur Wahrnehmung deutscher Wirtschaftsinteressen im Ausland.

1946 für 6 Wochen in britischer Haft. – Von der Alliierten Entnazifizierungsbehörde als entlastet (5) eingestuft.

1948 bei der Gründung der Kreditanstalt für Wiederaufbau. Maßgeblich an der Wirtschafts-planung der Bundesregierung beteiligt. Wirtschaftsberater Konrad Adenauers. – Leiter der deutschen Delegation bei der Londoner Schuldenkonferenz 1951-53. Berater bei den Wiedergutmachungsver-handlungen mit Israel in Den Haag. 1954 Mitglied der CDU.

1952 im Aufsichtsrat der Süddeutschen Bank AG. – 1957-67 Vorstandssprecher der Deutschen Bank AG. Seit 1967 Vorsitzender des Aufsichtsrats.

Ehrenvorsitzender des Aufsichtsrats:
Deutsche Überseeische Bank, Hamburg – Pittler Maschinenfabrik AG, Langen (Hessen)
Vorsitzender des Aufsichtsrats:
Dahlbusch Verwaltungs-AG, Gelsenkirchen – Daimler Benz AG, Stuttgart-Untertürkheim – Deutsche Bank AG, Frankfurt – Deutsche Lufthansa AG, Köln – Philipp Holzmann AG, Frankfurt – Phoenix Gummiwerke AG, Hamburg-Harburg – RWE Elektrizitätswerk AG, Essen – Vereinigte Glanzstoff AG, Wuppertal-Elberfeld – Zellstoff-Fabrik Waldhof AG, Mannheim

Ehrenvorsitzender:
Salamander AG, Kornwestheim – Gebr. Stumm GmbH, Brambauer (Westf.) – Süddeutsche Zucker-AG, Mannheim
Stellvertr. Vors. des Aufsichtsrats:
Badische Anilin- und Sodafabrik AG, Ludwigshafen – Siemens AG, Berlin-Munchen
Mitglied des Aufsichtsrats:
Metallgesellschaft AG, Frankfurt
Präsident des Verwaltungsrats:
Kreditanstalt für Wiederaufbau – Deutsche Bundesbahn

Großes Bundesverdienstkreuz mit Stern, Päpstl. Stern zum Komturkreuz, Großkreuz Isabella die Katholische von Spanien, Cruzeiro do Sul von Brasilien. – Ritter des Ordens vom Heiligen Grabe. – Dr. h.c. der Univ. Göttingen, Sofia, Tokio und der Wirtschaftshochschule Mannheim.

Lebt in Kronberg (Taunus) und auf dem Bentgerhof bei Remagen.

Photo aus Current Biography Yearbook 1970 New York

Hans Haacke. Excerpt from "Manet Projekt '74". (Reproduced by courtesy of the artist.)

cumstances of the artist and past owners of the work, Haacke included the same kind of information about Abs, noting his position as an officer of the Reichsbank during the Nazi era and his continuing importance during the post-war period of political and economic reconstruction.

Carl Andre, Robert Filliou and Sol LeWitt withdrew from "Projekt '74" in protest against what they took to be the censorship of Haacke's work, and the artist arranged to show the work in the Paul Maenz Gallery in Cologne, substituting a full-scale color reproduction for the original Manet still-life (but taking pains to include the frame, which bears a label referring to the Kuratorium's dedication of its gift to Adenauer, architect of that remarkable post-war reconstruction). Daniel Buren obtained a small-scale xerox copy of the panels of information and attached it to his own work in the show with the comment: "Art remains Politics"—a pointed rebuke of the official watchword of "Projekt '74." "*Kunst bleibt Kunst*" ("Art remains art"). Before Buren's work could be seen in its revised form, however, the order was given to cover the offending modification with sheets of paper, effectively obliterating a second artist's acerbic reflection upon "Projekt '74." Buren's work, as modified by the museum, remained in place; Frank Gillette and Newton Harrison removed their works in protest.

In the course of his correspondence with Haacke, Dr. Horst Keller, director of the Wallraf-Richartz Museum, gave the following reasons for rejecting the work:

First, that it was unacceptable because it contained an error: by devoting an entire panel to Abs, as one of a sequence of panels which described the artist and the owners and as part of a project which purported to "present the social and economic position of the persons who have owned the painting," Haacke gave the impression that Abs had been one of the owners of the work; the museum, under an obligation to the public only to transmit or allow transmission of accurate information, could not countenance this inaccuracy. In rejoinder, Haacke pointed out that he had nowhere asserted or even suggested that Abs had been an owner, and he pointed to the bold-type caption for the panel on Abs which stated: "*Bunch of Asparagus* acquired through the initiative of Hermann J. Abs, Chairman of the Wallraf-Richartz Kuratorium."

Second, that the work was unacceptable because it seemed to call into question Abs's idealistic motives in implementing the acquisition of

the work by the Kuratorium: "It would mean giving an absolutely inadequate evaluation of the intellectual and spiritual initiative of a man if one were to relate in any way the host of offices he holds in totally different walks of life with such an idealistic engagement." This aspersion, by implication, could adversely affect the museum's ability to attract devoted support from the private sector: "A grateful museum, however, and a grateful city or one ready to be moved to gratefulness must protect initiatives of such an extraordinary character from any other interpretation which might later throw even the slightest shadow on them. . . ."

Third, by overemphasizing the connection of the museum with the world of finance, Haacke's work calls into question the very purpose and function of the museum itself, and implies that it is not wholly devoted to the embodiment and dissemination of intellectual and spiritual values:

A museum knows nothing about economic power; it does indeed, however, know something about intellectual and spiritual power. (*Von einer wirtschaftlichen Macht weiss auch ein Museum nichts, wohl aber et was von de geistigen Macht.*)

In a letter to the author dated Sept. 25, 1974, Dr. Keller elaborated upon this point:

"A museum knows nothing about economic power . . . ," etc., was intended to underline the difference between the constantly moving world of economics and the point of rest and finality embodied by a museum. I have been active in museum work for over 25 years . . . and have dispensed large sums of money for exhibitions, by and large with excellent results both in terms of their effect on the public, and in terms of keeping the books in balance. My remark, therefore, applies only to those areas in which a museum plays an intellectual and spiritual role. . . . Of course a public collection needs money to be vital and alive—and from as many different donors and benefactors as possible. . . . However, my experience over the years indicates that one should discuss the price of a work to be acquired only up to the point of its acquisition, and I believe that Haacke should have let this aspect of a museum's life alone. . . .

In addition to these reasons, it seems probable to me that the directors of "Projekt '74" were not eager to allow exhibition of a work in which the specter of Nazism is shown to brush against Manet's still-life at several points. The museum visitor would have discovered, for example, that Max Liebermann was stripped of all his official positions in 1933 and saw his own work banned from exhibition and removed from public collections. He saved the Manet from possible confiscation by sending it to Switzerland, for deposit in the Kunsthaus in Zurich. Liebermann died in 1935, and his daughter took the Manet with her to America in 1938, where it remained in the family's hands until its recent sale to the Kuratorium. Liebermann's wife Marthe committed suicide in 1943, "to avoid impending arrest" by the Nazis, according to Haacke's text. And Haacke's deadpan listing of positions occupied by Hermann J. Abs from the 1930s to the present would have reminded museum-goers that the chairman of the Kuratorium was one of the chief custodians of the financial interests of the Third Reich. (The source for much of Haacke's information was a standard *Who's Who* of West German finance.) Haacke notes that Abs served a brief term of imprisonment after the war, was exonerated in the de-Nazification process and then went on to become a leader of the phenomenal growth of the West German economy during the 1950s and '60s. Finally, observers of Haacke's work might have pondered that this chain of events led to the return, with a good deal of publicity and institutional self-satisfaction, of the Manet to Germany under the aegis—or so it might appear—of some of the same financial interests that had helped to make Nazism a going concern in the first place.

All things considered, one can understand why the Wallraf-Richartz was made extremely uneasy by Haacke's matter-of-fact presentation of this information. Art institutions regard themselves as temples of culture, quiet places for the enjoyment, even veneration, of splendid objects that had been hallowed by the years and by the beneficent actions of donors, past and present. To question the ways and means by which such objects are acquired and to scrutinize the actions of benefactors in domains that lie outside the sanctuary of Art is rather like questioning a medieval bishop about his goods and chattels at the very moment when he is elevating a sacred vessel at the altar. Haacke's recent work has demonstrated that the offering of "matter-of-fact" information can constitute sacrilege.

The letter from Dr. Keller also contained the following answers to questions posed by the author (the two letters are compressed and excerpted into question-and-answer form here for convenience's sake):

Q: By using the expression, "Art remains art" (*"Kunst bleibt Kunst"*), did the Wallraf-Richartz Museum intend to imply that art is, or should be, a manifestation of "pure" thought and feeling, and that it does not, or should not, interest itself in social, economic, or political facts and ideas?

A: You will not surprised if I answer with a simple "No."

Q: In a communication with Haacke, you objected to his listing of the various positions occupied by Abs in the world of business and finance. Do you have any reason to believe that Abs would have himself objected to Haacke's straightforward presentation of facts concerning Abs' professional associations?

A: I must answer with a decided "Yes," for reasons which I explained clearly enough in my letter to Hans Haacke.

Q: According to Haacke, Daniel Buren's work, which incorporates a small-scale reproduction of Haacke's project, was "vandalized" by Prof. von der Osten [director of all Cologne municipal museums and codirector of the Wallraf-Richartz Museum], who directed that the Haacke reproductions which Buren had attached to his work, together with a statement that "Art remains Politics," be covered up with sheets of white paper. Did this occur? If it did, can you explain this most unusual action of a museum in willfully altering an artist's work?

A: A clarification is in order here: Daniel Buren agreed to the pasting-over of his work—a work which he had altered as an afterthought, without giving us any notice or obtaining our consent—and from that point on until the close of the exhibition there was no further alteration of the work, either on Buren's part or on the museum's part. In any event, it is not uncommon practice for a museum to paste over an artist's work, when an artist has expressly disregarded an agreement previously reached with a museum—a point which Buren was quick to acknowledge in a conversation with us.

COMMENTS

1. Here is a case when the artist, in making his definition of art, is being challenged by the museum director. Is Keller, in rejecting Haacke's project, being a censor of art?

2. Did Keller make a convincing case for his suppression of the Haacke exhibit? In

principle, should museums withhold from the public the sources from which they obtained their art?

3. Are there any differences between Haacke's project and what was done by the Nazis in the 1937 exhibit of "degenerate art" when the prices paid by the museums were shown next to the paintings? (In both cases there were no explanations printed.) What happens to the work of art itself when subjected to these practices? Suppose that the David Caspar Friedrich landscape painting bought by the Nazis for Hitler's Linz Museum today had next to it the facts of its purchase from funds raised by the confiscating of "degenerate art." How would this affect the public's response to the art of a great nineteenth-century painter? Is there an argument for museum "neutrality" in suppressing the histories of ownership of works of art?

THE McCARTHY ERA

WILLIAM HAUPTMAN *Suppression of Art in the McCarthy Decade**

In recent years there has been a serious reevaluation by art historians of the significant American contributions in the 1940s and 1950s to 20th-century art. The grim facts remain that an almost pathological fear of communist infiltration in the first decade after World War II resulted in one of this country's most shameful endeavors to deny artists their basic freedom of expression.

The late Senator Joseph McCarthy never centered his attacks on either art or artists. But his colleagues in Congress often equated all seemingly radical activities—especially artistic ones—with political extremism. Nowhere is this view more evident than in the bitter attacks of George A. Dondero, the Republican representative from Michigan. Trained as a lawyer, with no background in art or art criticism, Dondero launched a one-man campaign to purge American art of what seemed to him to be a second communist front. His assaults were principally political, though he claimed on esthetic grounds all modern art was communist inspired because of the "depraved" and "destructive" nature of its forms. In a congressional speech on August 16, 1949, he explained the use of the major 20th-century styles as vehicles for destruction.

Cubism aims to destroy by designed disorder.
Futurism aims to destroy by the machine myth.
. . .
Dadaism aims to destroy by ridicule.
Expressionism aims to destroy by aping the primitive and insane.
Abstractionism aims to destroy by the creation of brainstorms. . . .

Surrealism aims to destroy by the denial of reason. . . .

Dondero asserted that these styles or "isms" were un-American since they originated in Europe. That some American artists utilized these styles seemed ample proof to him that American advanced art was rapidly becoming a communist-inspired menace. In an interview with Emily Genauer, then a critic for the *New York World Telegram* but subsequently released by the newspaper because of Dondero's vague charges of her sympathies with left-wing organizations, Dondero summed up his views:

Modern art is Communistic because it is distorted and ugly, because it does not glorify our beautiful country, our cheerful and smiling people, and our material progress. Art which does not glorify our beautiful country in plain, simple terms that everyone can understand breeds dissatisfaction. It is therefore opposed to our government, and those who create and promote it are our enemies.

Dondero severely criticized American artists who refused to acknowledge the above principle. In various speeches, he described them as "human termites," "germ-carrying vermin," and "international art thugs." He also concluded that modern artists who advocate freedom to experiment in a nontraditional style were charlatans because (1) they really could not draw; (2) they were insane; (3) they were involved in a plot to make the bourgeoisie nervous; and (4) they were committed to degrade their art for the purpose of communist propaganda. As examples of

*Originally published as William Hauptman, "The Suppression of Art in the McCarthy Decade," *Artforum* vol. 12, no. 2 (October 1973), pp. 48ff. Copyright © 1973 by California Artforum, Inc. Reprinted by permission of *Artforum* and William Hauptman.

European artists who had imposed their anti-American ideas on American artists, he named, among many others, Picasso, who had publicly acknowledged his communist leanings, Braque, Léger, Duchamp, Ernst, Matta, Miró, Dali, Chagall—all of whom, he claimed, were active weapons of the Kremlin.

Art museums and professional art associations also became favorite targets for Dondero's assaults. The Metropolitan Museum of Art, the Museum of Modern Art, the Art Institute of Chicago, the Fogg Museum, the Corcoran Museum, and the Virginia Museum were bitterly denounced for supporting exhibitions of modern art. The Artists' Equity Association and the American Federation of Arts, both artistically liberal organizations, were accused of communist leanings. Of the former, Dondero claimed to have discovered that "of the 77 officers, directors, and governors . . . 69 have left-wing connections—and more significant, 42 members [of the Communist Party]."

It was apparent that Dondero had no concept of artistic activity under any form of dictatorial government. In Genauer's interview with Dondero, it was pointed out to him how coincidental his speeches were to those of Lenin and Stalin. Similarly, Alfred Barr, Jr., himself the target of right-wing attacks, devoted a long article to proving that modern art and communism or fascism were in direct opposition. Dondero's charges furthermore disregarded a United States Court ruling of 1946 (*Hannegan v. Esquire,* 327 U.S. 46) that "A requirement that literature or art should conform to a norm smacks of an ideology foreign to our system."

In Congress, Dondero's fellow representatives rarely rebuked his charges openly; indeed only a small handful of congressional individuals privately admitted their disagreement. Of the few whose opposition is a matter of public record, the criticism of Senator Jacob Javits is particularly noteworthy:

Criticism of the record of individuals as citizens or residents of the United States and discussion of their political backgrounds and present beliefs is one thing, but an effort to discredit all modern art forms is quite another and one of which note should be taken and which should be deprecated, for my colleague's personal opinion of modern art is his privilege, but my colleague's suggestion that it should all be lumped together and discredited—perhaps suppressed—because he believes it is being used by some—even many—

artists to infiltrate Communist ideas is a very dangerous use of the word "communism." The very point which distinguishes our form of free expression from communism is the fact that modern art can live and flourish here without state authority or censorship and be accepted by Americans who think well of it.

Similarly, many enlightened art editors and museum directors published objections to Dondero's attacks. Alfred Frankfurter of *Art News* summed up these counter protests with a typical rationale:

Only a great, generous, muddling democracy like ours could afford the simultaneous paradox of a congressman who tries to attack Communism by demanding the very rules which Communists enforce wherever they are in power, and a handful of artists who enroll idealistically in movements sympathetic to Soviet Russia while they go on painting pictures that would land them in jail under a Communist government.

Many artists attacked by Dondero were vocal in their opposition. Perhaps Ben Shahn's comments were the most eloquent. He pointed out that what right-wing congressmen were trying to suppress, namely freedom of thought, was in essence the heart of artistic creation; to deny the artist the right to paint or sculpt whatever themes and in whatever style he chooses was to deny his entire freedom.

Dondero's influence was greatest in two spheres of artistic activity between 1946 and 1956: first, in the condemnation and suppression of art exhibitions which displayed modern art or art by suspected communists; second, the censorship and attempted destruction of large-scale mural decoration in prominent buildings. The targets were particularly government-sponsored work.

The first major show ridiculed by Dondero's direct instigation was a State Department-sponsored exhibition, organized in 1946 as a goodwill gesture to the governments of Europe and Latin America. This exhibition, called "Advancing American Art," fully accorded with the standard practice of exhibiting American art abroad, a program originated under State Department auspices in 1938 as part of the Cultural Cooperation Program. The general purpose of this kind of sponsorship was defined by former Secretary of State William Benton before hearings of an appropriations subcommittee in 1948:

[It is to demonstrate that Americans who] are accused throughout the world of being a materialistic, money-mad race, without interest in art and without appreciation of artists and music . . . have a side in our own personality as a race other than materialism and other than science and technology.

For "Advancing American Art," the State Department allotted about $49,000, and instructed Leroy Davidson to purchase paintings he considered outstanding and of lasting value. Within this narrow budget, Davidson purchased 79 works by 45 well-known artists of the period. Included in the purchase were works by John Marin, Marsden Hartley, Georgia O'Keeffe, Philip Guston, Milton Avery, Loren MacIver, William Gropper, Abraham Rattner, Hugo Weber, Reginald Marsh, Stuart Davis, Jack Levine, Yasuo Kuniyoshi, Adolph Gottlieb, Shahn, and others. From this collection, "Advancing American Art" was divided into two traveling exhibits, 40 paintings for Europe, the remainder for Latin America, each exhibition to tour for a five-year period.

Soon after the announcement of Davidson's purchases, various groups protested the selection. The *Baltimore American,* a right-wing newspaper, was probably the first to print a formal protest in an editorial in October, 1946, on the basis that

The State Department, which officially is refusing to compromise with international Communism, is currently sponsoring an art exhibition which features the work of left-wing painters who are members of Red fascist organizations.

Thereafter the influential American Artists Professional League (mostly illustrators and commercial artists) sent a letter of complaint to the *Art Digest.* Dated November 6, 1946, the letter claimed that the show was overwhelmingly one-sided toward modern art, thus precluding a fair representation of the contemporary art scene. Albert Reid, the national vice-president of the organization, also protested Davidson's choices because they did not in any sense represent styles "indigenous to our soil." This protest was the beginning of what has been described as "the cold war in the art world."

Other organizations began to publicly voice their antagonism to the show. Disapprovals were published by such professional societies as the Society of Illustrators, Allied Artists, and the Salmagundi (Watercolor) Club—all of which were composed primarily of commercial artists. The basis of protest was that the selection of modern examples of art seemed to reflect communist leanings, and that many of the painters involved were themselves associated with communist efforts.

Groups not directly associated with the art world also bitterly attacked the exhibition. Particularly vehement and abusive rebukes came from newspapers and magazines owned by William Randolph Hearst. Like Dondero, Hearst equated any form of artist radicalism with communism, and assumed that all of the work produced in a nontraditionalist manner was a disguised means of communist propaganda. His newspapers continually illustrated examples of the show, particularly those by Davis, Marin, and Shahn, often using vilifying captions to distort their content and value—an action not unlike that taken by the Nazi government for their exhibition of "degenerate" art in 1937.

Prominent members of the federal government joined in the controversy. In March, 1947, President Truman denounced a painting of a circus scene by Kuniyoshi, which, in Truman's opinion, represented "a fat, semi-nude circus girl." Truman added that "the artist must have stood off from the canvas and thrown paint at it . . . if that's art, I'm a Hottentot." Less than a month later, *Time* magazine reported that Secretary of State George C. Marshall (the target of a McCarthy attack later in 1951) was incensed by the show's radicalism. Marshall, under whose aegis the show was originally organized, finally ordered "no more taxpayers' money for modern art."

Shortly thereafter the State Department, caught in the middle of a politically embarrassing situation, ordered a halt to "Advancing American Art." This unprecedented action unfortunately established a precedent for dealing with exhibitions in which accused painters and sculptors were involved. It demonstrated the power and influence of Dondero's views.

The termination of the show while it was still in Europe and Latin America aroused an enormous number of protests from intellectual circles. All were shocked that the State Department, who created and financially supported the exhibit in the first place, would go to such extremes to appease a small group politically on the right. Various art journals protested the cancellation, and in June and July respectively, the American Federation of Arts and many American museum directors voiced their opinions lamenting the State Department decision.

In 1948 the State Department decided rather

than keep the paintings it would sell them at a public auction. Preference in the bidding went to educational institutions and to World War II veterans. The results of the auction yielded a 95% loss on the original $49,000 investment. The final irony, it seems, came when the Hearst organization, whom the *Art Digest* blamed for exerting the most pressure on the federal agency, bought five of the auctioned pictures for the Los Angeles County Museum, a museum heavily endowed by Hearst's publications.

In 1951 and 1952 the condemnation of exhibitions dealing with modern art became intense. Two major shows were under intense pressure to be canceled or, at the very least, to withdraw works by artists suspected of associating with left-wing causes.

The Los Angeles City Council sponsored a major exhibit in Griffith Park of the current trends in American art. By its very intention, the undertaking was at that time a courageous act. Almost immediately, protests were lodged by some commercial artists and illustrators, hardly represented in the show, claiming that the political background of some of the participants was questionable. As a result, a committee within the City Council was appointed to investigate these charges. After considerable debate, three members of the Building and Safety Committee headed by Harold Harby introduced a resolution stating that it was the official opinion of the committee that "ultramodern artists are unconsciously used as tools of the Kremlin . . ." and that in some cases, abstract paintings were actually secret maps of strategic United States fortifications. As evidence of the claim of communist infiltration, Harby singled out two works in the show. Rex Brandt, a local artist, was severely criticized for incorporating "propaganda" in his second-prize painting *First Lift of the Sea* because he had included what appeared to be a hammer and sickle in the sail of a ship. Brandt, who for many years had been a boating enthusiast and the head designer for a major boating firm, explained that the section in question was nothing more than a traditional craft insignia used to designate the Island Clipper. Nevertheless, Harby pressured Brandt into eliminating the objectionable symbol. Significant criticism was also directed against a sculpture by Bernard Rosenthal, *Crucifixion*. The Harby committee selected this work to demonstrate how communist-inspired art distorts traditional themes and subjects them to sacrilegious mockery. Harby

described the work as a "travesty on religion because it made Jesus look like a frog," and lamented that he could not buy it to insure its destruction.

Liberal factions of the art world protested these actions vigorously. Eastern museum officials jointly sent an official protest to the Los Angeles City Council pointing out again that the same type of repression, under the guise of patriotic duty, was common in Nazi Germany, and, indeed, a reality in present-day Soviet Russia.

However, the issue of whether modern art was communist-inspired and whether avant-garde artists were hired by the Soviet government to propagandize American secrets raged intensely in Los Angeles until January, 1952. Amid hearings, arguments, demonstrations, protests, and counter-protests, the City Council ruled by an 11−3 vote that there was no substantial evidence in support of a vast communist plot within the framework of modern art.

While these questions were being debated, a similar situation occurred in New York in connection with "American Sculpture 1951," a large retrospective of recent sculpture organized by the Metropolitan Museum of Art. The show was attacked by some unauthorized members of the conservative National Sculpture Society, who claimed, as before, that modern art was definitely linked to totalitarianism, and that it "endanger(s) the fundamental freedom of our work and national life." Furthermore, Don de Lue, the head of the society, firmly asserted that because the Metropolitan was guilty of supporting "aesthetic leftism," it was, therefore, advocating political leftism. Lloyd Goodrich, for a long time an outspoken foe of these charges, answered these accusations:

In a day when freedom of thought and expression are threatened by reactionary elements more than ever in our recent history, this injection of false political issues into artistic controversy and broadcasting them to an uninformed public is a despicable act.

The federal government itself contributed to some extent to the strong anti-modern-art feelings. Although it did not actively support any private group's views, the U.S. Government sympathized with the idea of communist influence in the art world, and indeed maintained an official policy of censorship. In 1953, at the height of McCarthy's power, A. H. Berding, then a chief spokesman for the United States Information Agency, delivered a speech before the American Federation of Arts stating that "our government should not sponsor examples of our creative energy which are non-representational." This statement was followed by an explanation of the types of works which the USIA officially banned from circulating shows; examples included

works of avowed Communists, persons convicted of crimes involving a threat to the security of the United States or persons who publicly refuse to answer questions of Congressional committees regarding connection with the Communist movement.

Despite these feelings, the USIA felt secure enough to lend support to an exhibition in connection with the Olympic Games of 1956. The exhibit, entitled, "Sport in Art," was organized by the American Federation of Arts with partial funding from *Sports Illustrated* magazine. The plans for the show called for an extensive tour of major American cities, including Washington, D.C., Louisville, Denver, Dallas, Los Angeles, and San Francisco, before the final showing in the National Gallery of Victoria in Melbourne, the host city for the Olympics. The heavily publicized tour was well attended and met virtually no resistance to the inclusion of examples of modern art until the show reached Dallas.

Up to that time, Dallas citizen groups had had a long history of attempting to suppress the showing of advanced art in local museums. The traditional reason behind these acts was the supposed connection of modernism in the arts with communism, though in one case the reason was blatant anti-Semitism. Earlier examples of protests in Dallas included the "In Memoriam" show, where it was charged that six of the 12 artists represented in the exhibit had communist affiliations. Also severely criticized was "Sculpture in Silver," another American Federation of Arts exhibit, because of the inclusion of a small work by William Zorach, believed to be a communist.

A good deal of protest was also directed toward the Dallas Museum, where "Sport in Art" was to be housed. On March 15, 1955, just a few months before the installation of the show, the Public Affairs Luncheon Club, a group of 400 women headed by Mrs. Florence Rodgers, a former member of the Dallas Art Association, drafted a resolution declaring that the museum was placing too much emphasis on "all phases of futuristic, modernistic and non-objective" work,

while neglecting many traditionalists "whose patriotism . . . has never been questioned." Specifically, the group demanded the removal of works by Hirsch, Gross, Davidson, Grosz, Picasso, Rivera, and Weber. In a release, the members of the club explained that the underlying principle behind these demands was that modern artists were used by the Kremlin as "instruments of destruction." As proof of this assumption the club quoted verbatim from Dondero's 1949 speech (though not acknowledged) of how modern art "aims to destroy." In April, the trustees of the Dallas Museum issued a reply:

that it was not Museum policy to knowingly acquire or exhibit work of a person known by them to be a Communist or of Communist-front affiliations; that they had obtained the Attorney-General's list (of known Communists) and would be glad to be guided by it, . . . that they were reluctant to destroy work by artists accused of subversion.

By the time "Sport in Art" was scheduled to open, the Dallas patriotic groups were at fever pitch to stop the public showing of suspected artists. The main group to declare its opposition to the exhibit was the Dallas County Patriotic Council, an organization composed of the American Legion, the Daughters of the American Revolution, the Veterans of Foreign Wars, and several other conservative groups. Under the directorship of Colonel Owsley, the Council demanded the removal of works by Zorach, Kuniyoshi, Kroll, and Shahn, as well as a public declaration by the Dallas Museum of a firm policy not to exhibit works by avowed communist supporters. A spokesman for the Council clarified these demands:

We are not interested in esthetics or in traditional versus modern art. We are not interested in the excellence of the art or the story the art portrays. We are not even interested in the nationality, morals, education, religion, or good looks of the artist. We are interested only in seeing that the Dallas Art Association refrains from showing works by Communists or Communist-front artists whose records of Communist-front affiliations are public information obtained by Congressional committees.

The Council had not checked their charges; none of the artists denounced by Owsley was in fact listed as a subversive or a communist by the Subversive Activities Control Board. Zorach, Kuniyoshi, Kroll, and Shahn had been intensely investigated, though each of their files in Un-

American Activities Committee records was prefaced by the following statement: "This report should not be construed as representing the results of an investigation by or findings of this Committee. It should be noted that the individual is not necessarily a Communist sympathizer. . . ."

On February 11, 1956, the Dallas Art Association announced that the Museum would ban no pictures, that it would stand firmly on the belief that there was no evidence to suggest communist infiltration. Despite this proclamation, the USIA felt that the charges against the show were significant. Apparently fearing the fate of the 1946 State Department show, "Sport in Art" was canceled after its Dallas preview. Government officials attempted to hide the fact that the protest by the Council was the sole reason for their decision.

Less than a month later, the USIA found itself in the midst of a similar controversy. Under its direction the American Federation of Arts was again called upon to organize a major retrospective of American art. Entitled "100 American Artists of the Twentieth Century," and scheduled for a tour abroad, it was claimed that among the artists involved ten were politically "unacceptable" and "pro-Communist." The 42 trustees of the Federation unanimously voted not to participate in the show if any of the artists were barred from exhibiting. Again yielding to outside pressure, the USIA withdrew its support and canceled the tour—an action officially condemned on the Senate floor.

These controversies, still present despite McCarthy's censure in Congress two years earlier, resulted in an even tighter and more restrictive control on traveling exhibitions. The USIA announced shortly after the termination of "100 American Artists" that it would ban from such exhibits "American oil paintings dated after 1917" —the year of the Russian Revolution—because the artist might arouse suspicions of communist sympathies. In contrast to this policy, the American Federation of Arts pointed out a speech made by President Eisenhower on the occasion of the 25th anniversary of the Museum of Modern Art in New York:

Freedom of the Arts is a basic freedom, one of the pillars of liberty in our land. . . . As long as artists are at liberty to feel with high personal intensity, as long as our artists are free to create with sincerity and conviction, there will be healthy controversy and progress in art.

Just as attempts were made to condemn art exhibitions, so were there efforts to censor and destroy single works of art, particularly large mural commissions in public buildings, often because it was believed that the artist in question was using the public buildings as a forum for communist propaganda. At the New School for Social Research, four murals had been painted in 1930 by the well-known and much accused Mexican painter, Jose Clemente Orozco, with the commissioned subject to be "social revolutions astir in the world." The panels depicted the Mexican Revolution, then in full bloom, the nonviolent movement in India, the Chinese Revolution led by Sun Yat-sen, and the Russian Revolution, which included large portraits of Lenin and Stalin. In 1951, teachers and students alike began to harass school authorities over the Russian portion of the work, alleging the portraits and theme were offensive. The school responded by placing a plaque below the panel asserting that the view expressed did not reflect that of the school, but by the summer of 1953, protests called for the destruction of the entire work. Dr. Hans Simons, president of the school, compromised these demands by covering the offensive section of the work with a large curtain. This measure was explained as being only temporary while there was a "period of great unease about Russia." The drape was subsequently altered and removed.

At approximately the same time, a controversy flared up over the work of Orozco's countryman, Diego Rivera. In 1922 he had been commissioned by Edsel Ford to paint a mural in Detroit called *The Age of Steel*. In 1952, Eugene I. van Antwerp, the former mayor of the City, argued that the work contained a good deal of blatant communist propaganda and represented the city's work force as "ugly and decadent." The Detroit Art Commission, however, refused to yield to the immense pressure exerted by him and his followers, and permitted the large mural to stand.

Although these examples of threatened murals were significant instances of the imposition of current political ideology on art, no case was more celebrated or controversial than the commission awarded to Anton Refregier for the Rincon Annex Post Office in San Francisco. This instance serves as an apt and sometimes terrifying summary of the issues and fears so clearly present during the first postwar decade.

Born in Moscow in 1905, Refregier left Russia for Paris in 1920 to further his art studies. By 1923 he immigrated to the United States, and in 1933 became a naturalized citizen. In America he, along with other writers and artists, became associated with left-wing causes, especially during the Depression years. Along with his Russian heritage these alliances caused various groups to label him a communist supporter. Refregier was reputed to be one of the country's best mural painters. In 1941 he entered a national competition for a mural to depict the history of California in the Rincon Annex Post Office. Sponsored by the Federal Section of Fine Arts, 82 leading artists competed, with the final prize of $26,000 being awarded to Refregier. The commission required that the artist must

relate to the people in contemporary idiom the history of their own experience, not as a pageant, but as the growth of the city, a struggle of men against nature, and later on, the development of various inner tensions.

Refregier began work on the 240-foot mural late in 1941, but was interrupted by the war; the work was not completed until 1949. During this time there were 91 official conferences and inspections by officers of the Public Building Administration, a stipulation of the contract. In final form, the work consisted of 27 panels showing aspects of California history; the titles are as follows: *A California Indian Creates; Indians by the Golden Gate; Sir Francis Drake; Conquistadores Discover the Pacific; Monks Building the Missions; Preaching and Farming at Mission Dolores; Fort Ross—Russian Trade Post; Hardships of the Emigrant Trail; An Early Newspaper Office; Raising the Bear Flag; Finding Gold at Sutter's Mill; Miners Panning Gold; Arrival by Ship; Torchlight Parade; Pioneers Receiving Mail; Building the Railroad; Vigilante Days; Civil War Issues; Chinese Riots; San Francisco as a Cultural Center; Earthquake and Fire of 1906; Reconstruction After the Fire; The Mooney Case; the Waterfront—1934; Building the Golden Gate Bridge; Shipyards During the War; War and Peace.*

The panels were criticized for a variety of reasons. The last panel, showing the birth of the United Nations, for example, included the founding fathers signing the declaration and establishing the peace-keeping organization. When submitted for approval, the government disapproved of the sketch because of the "undignified way" in which Roosevelt had been drawn. Refregier explained that he purposely selected a portrait of Roosevelt after the Yalta meetings, already aged and ill. The government saw this as a slanderous portrait and censored it.

The Veterans of Foreign Wars lodged protests over the section showing the waterfront strike of 1934. Refregier had painted the scene vividly, re-

lying on accounts of the strike as well as on newspaper accuracy. The V.F.W. and the Hearst newspapers objected to one figure in the scene who quite obviously wore a hat belonging to the V.F.W. organization. The V.F.W. insisted no member of their organization was involved in the strike, and that the artist's inclusion of the hat implied that the organization supported the strike. The newspaper pictures Refregier relied upon, when presented to the V.F.W., clearly showed a member of their organization present in at least one photograph. But the federal authorities, under strong pressure, demanded the removal of the hat, which was painted out. Refregier was again forced to alter his designs in the section *Torchlight Parade,* depicting the winning of the 8-hour workday. In celebration of the event, Refregier included a figure holding up a sign which read "Ship Caulkers Union Won an 8-hour Day in 1865." The American Legion and the Sailors' Union protested vigorously, and verbally abused the artist while working on the section. Pickets were organized around this section in an attempt to physically prevent its completion. Refregier was forced to overpaint the sign.

Other arguments developed over the mural. In the panel depicting the establishment of the Spanish missions, protests arose about priests who, it was claimed, were represented as too fat and undignified. Refregier was forced to slenderize these figures. Objections were also raised about the portrayal of Francis Drake in armor. It was alleged that the painting, as a result of this detail, implied that war and aggressiveness played a large part in the history of the state. The inclusion of a child in a newspaper office was interpreted as signifying the use of child labor. Disapproval was voiced over the use of a British flag in the Four Freedoms painting, a hammer and sickle in the United Nations panel, and even the inclusion of a red tie on one of the figures in the same section.

Finally, groups such as the American Legion, the V.F.W., the D.A.R., Associated Farmers, the Young Democrats of San Francisco, the Sailors' Union, and the society of Western Artists called for the destruction of the entire work. The American Legion and the V.F.W. declared the work "subversive and definitely designed to spread Communistic propaganda." Others claimed in addition to the communist associations, that the work depicted California history in a distorted and abhorrent style.

Some prestigious members of Congress joined in the criticism. Richard Nixon, then a representative from California, wrote a letter concerning not only the Refregier murals, but the subject of "questionable" art in general. Dated July 18, 1949, the letter was addressed to C. E. Plant, a past commissioner of an American Legion Post in California:

I wish to thank you for your letter as to whether anything can be done about the removal of Communist art in your Federal Building [the Rincon Annex Post Office], . . . I realize that some objectionable art, of a subversive nature, has been allowed to go into federal buildings in many parts of the country. . . . At such a time as we may have a change in the Administration and in the majority of Congress, I believe a committee should make a thorough investigation of this type of art in government buildings with the view to obtaining removal of all that is found to be inconsistent with American ideals and principles.

The most outspoken critic was Representative Hubert Scudder of California, who emphatically supported destruction of the murals. He claimed that the artist was known to be associated with 23 well-known communists, and condemned the mural because it was "artistically offensive and historically inaccurate . . . and cast a derogatory and improper reflection on the character of the pioneers and history of the great state of California." He also mentioned that the figures were "cadaverous, soulless pioneers," involved in "sadistic scenes of riots, earthquakes, and strikes."

On March 5, 1933, Scudder introduced into Congress a joint resolution (JR 211) directing "the Adminstrator of General Services to remove the mural paintings from the lobby of the Rincon Annex Post Office Building in San Francisco." As was pointed out to Scudder even before submitting the resolution, the removal of the murals would have insured their destruction.

Support for Scudder's bill came from a number of local and national conservative groups, as well as right-wing newspapers. Particularly emphatic in their desire to have the works destroyed were editorials in the *San Francisco Argonaut*, a newspaper Scudder later admitted was influential in his campaign.

An extraordinary number of responses—perhaps the most conclusive and unified of the decade—originated from private groups and so-cieties to defeat the measure. One list of citizens opposing the resolution consisted of over 300 artists, historians, and representatives from museums, universities, and cultural groups. Among professional institutions opposing the resolution were the three major San Francisco museums. The Museum of Modern Art in New York, the American Federation of Arts, and Artists' Equity. Foreign art journals and the *London Times* published protests; one German art journal said that "In a country which on paper—has the best constitution in the world, today it is becoming difficult to live, to think, and to act according to that constitution." The noted scientist Julian Huxley wrote to the artist:

I am much distressed about the Bill introduced by Congressman Scudder to authorize the removal of your murals in the Rincon Annex Post Office. This seems to me a highly injurious proposal. It is injurious because it would mean the destruction of what, to judge from my recollection of your sketches and from reproductions of the finished murals, is a remarkable work of art, and an outstanding example of the growing tendency in your country to try to exert political control over freedom of thought and expression, and to impair the liberty of the creative artist. . . . The lamentable state of biology and philosophy in the U.S.S.R. shows what happens when creative thought and expression is subjected to control on political or ideological grounds. It is most unfortunate that, just when the free world is protesting against this form of tyranny in the Iron Curtain countries, actions like that of Republican Scudder are trying to introduce a similar tyranny in your great country.

Scudder's resolution was given to the Committee on Public Works, chaired by Dondero, for hearings. On May 1, 1953, the entire history of the mural was reviewed by Scudder before a subcommittee; each major point of criticism, along with documents an witnesses, was presented. The decision on whether there was enough evidence to warrant the murals' destruction could not be reached, and the resolution was shelved. The saving of Refregier's murals represented the most important defeat of the attempt by certain government individuals to control public artistic endeavors.

COMMENTS

1. Comparison between Dondero's attitude toward contemporary art and the attitudes of the Soviet authorities, on one side, and the Nazis, on the other, is tempting. Did they have

similar objectives? Did they employ or propose similar methods? On what did Dondero and Lenin agree?

2. Is the distinction between criticism and censorship always clear? How would you state the difference? Are the crucial differences those of motive, of interest, or of action, some combination of them, or "none of the above"?

3. Much of the greatest art was produced under authoritarian governments at times when artists were subject to strict censorship. Why then should we be concerned about censorship of the arts? Has something changed to make the problem more significant today?

4. Suppose a statute were offered that would permit suppression of bad art—art that is offensive because of poor quality from an aesthetic or art-historical point of view. Would you support it or oppose it?

ARTISTIC SPEECH AND THE FIRST AMENDMENT

With the now accepted and increasingly important place of philosophy and "ideas" in all modern art, including literature, it should be no surprise that expression in the visual arts falls within the intellectual freedom protected by the first amendment to the U.S. Constitution. After all, we speak of artists making their "statements," and we debate passionately over the intricate meanings that artists attempt to communicate to us. In a long line of "symbolic speech" cases, beginning with the 1931 decision in *Stromberg v. California,* 283 U.S. 359, that a law prohibiting display of a red flag as a symbol of protest was unconstitutional, the U.S. Supreme Court has recognized that speech may be nonverbal. Yet the mandate of the first amendment is absolute in its terms: "Congress shall make *no law* abridging the freedom of speech" (emphasis added). Thus, once nonverbal expression like visual art is recognized to be within the province of the first amendment, the very nature of law necessitates some distinction between protected expression and nonprotected expression. Much of the Supreme Court's first-amendment litigation has centered on trying to draw those lines.

The values underlying free speech apply with special force to art and artists. The paramount value is the significance of individual self-expression as an aspect of liberty. Thus, in *Whitney v. California,* 274 U.S. 357 (1927), Justice Brandeis wrote: "Those who won our independence believed that the final end of the State was to make men free to develop their faculties." Second is the value of artistic freedom in the search for "truth." Art is frequently the vehicle for the artist's ideas, and even if the ideas are unorthodox and judged to be false by the majority of society, we still recognize that truth emerges from the free play of ideas. Philosophers and writers like John Stuart Mill (*On Liberty,* 1859) and John Milton (*Areopagitica,* 1644) have shown that even false ideas have value, in that truth is known by the encounter with falsity.

Alexander Meiklejohn, in *Free Speech and Its Relation to Self-Government* (1948), argued that the need for individual choice and decision-making in a system of self-government meant that "public speech" (relevant to the processes of self-government) should be absolutely protected, although "private speech" may be regulated or suppressed. Originally, Meiklejohn included artistic expression within the category of "private speech" entitled to less protection but, reflecting on criticism of his theory, he later drastically expanded the "public speech" category to include artistic expression (Alexander Meiklejohn, "The First Amendment Is an Absolute," 1961 Sup. Ct. Rev. 245). This modification seems appropriate; art is necessarily public speech.

Reminiscent of Meiklejohn's theory is an approach of designating "political" speech as closest to the core of the first amendment and thus worthy of special protection. There is language to this effect in several opinions, notably that of Justice Brennan in *New York Times v. Sullivan,* 376 U.S. 254 (1964). Brennan wrote that the "criticism of government and public officials" was the "central meaning" of the first amendment. Yet when this idea became the basis for a "two-tier" theory of speech in *Young v. American Mini-Theatres,* 427 U.S. 50 (1976), and in *F.C.C. v. Pacifica Foundation,* 438 U.S. 726 (1978), Justice Brennan found himself in dissent. In *American Mini-Theatres,* the Court upheld a Detroit zoning ordinance that dispersed "adult" movie theaters and prohibited them within 500 feet of residential areas. Distinguishing between "political debate" and "material that is on the border line between pornography and artistic expression," Stevens wrote that less protection was to be awarded the latter. This was true even if "erotic materials" had "some arguably artistic value."

While the two-tier theory of speech has not captured a majority of the Court for most forms of speech, it is rigidly adhered to in the area of commercial speech. Speech merely proposing an economic transaction was originally categorically excluded from the first amendment. It was then brought within the first amendment at a lesser level of protection in *Virginia Pharmacy Board v. Virginia Consumer Council,* 425 U.S. 748 (1976).

In addition to commercial speech, other "well defined and narrowly limited classes of speech" were once thought to be wholly outside the first amendment.

> These include the lewd and obscene, the profane, the libelous, and the insulting or "fighting" words—those which by their very utterance inflict injury or tend to incite an immediate breach of the peace. It has been well observed that such utterances are no essential part of any exposition of ideas, and are of such slight social value as a step to truth that any benefit that may be derived from them is clearly outweighted by the social interest in order and immorality. [*Chaplinsky v. New Hampshire,* 315 U.S. 568 (1942).]

Several state interests—such as avoiding "offensive" art, "obscene" art, or provocative art that "incites" to violence—have been put forward as justifications for restricting artistic speech.

The "offensiveness" state interest is often invoked against art, perhaps because the value of art sometimes consists in the degree to which its original conception is "shocking" or "new." The flaws in invoking offensiveness are its subjectivity (what is "offensive" to one person is not to another) and generality. Anything is potentially offensive, and so the risk of a sensitive audience's veto over art they do not like is present whenever this interest is accepted. Nevertheless, the Supreme Court has shown special solicitude for "captive audiences," especially when speech is aural. If speech is written or visual, as in the case of visual art, the rebuttal that the audience may "avert its eyes" is possible, as Justice Harlan noted in *Cohen v. California,* 403 U.S. 15 (1971). Still, consider the case of *Close v. Lederle,* set forth later in this chapter. "Obscenity" may be an extension of the "offensiveness" justification for curtailing speech and is discussed also later in this chapter.

The final significant justification for suppressing speech is the "incitement to violence or lawless action" standard. For example, it is certainly conceivable that painting a swastika on the sidewalk in a Jewish neighborhood could produce violence or disorder of a kind that the law should be interested in preventing. A work of art with a politically subversive message could be attacked as endangering a similar (if broader) interest in national security. The famous test first urged by Justice Holmes in *Schenck v. United States,* 249 U.S. 47 (1919), was the basis of the later incitement test.

> The most stringent protection of free speech would not protect a man in falsely shouting fire in a theatre and causing a panic. . . . [T]he question in every case is whether the words used are used in such circumstances and are of such a nature as to create a clear and present danger that they will bring about the substantive evils that Congress has a right to prevent.

The test took on new meaning in later years and eventually fed into the "incitement" standard that governs today:

> The constitutional guarantees of free speech and free press do not permit a State to forbid or proscribe advocacy of the use of force or of law violation except where such advocacy is directed to inciting or producing imminent lawless action and is likely to incite or produce such action. [*Brandenburg v. Ohio*, 395 U.S. 444 (1969).]

One might also mention that the categorical exclusion of "fighting words" (provoking *immediate* violence) from constitutional protection, noted in *Chaplinsky*, still applies in theory but is a very narrow exception indeed (but see *People v. Radich*, later in this chapter).

As opposed to total suppression, "reasonable" regulation of the time, place, and manner of expression in public places is a real threat to art. The traditional first-amendment bias against regulation of the content of speech allows regulation of the form or manner of speech. In the case of art, however, form is often at least as important as content.

Thus, art is again particularly vulnerable to this diluted version of censorship. Take the large projects of an artist like Christo, for example. The legal issue in assessing the validity of a time-place-manner regulation would be the seriousness of the harm to state interests (such as boat traffic, if he were wrapping an island in plastic) as weighed against his claim of access to a public place in order to present his artistic statement. In such cases the Supreme Court has vacillated between a broad "guaranteed access" view, which is now accepted as governing *traditional* public places such as streets and parks (*Lehman v. Shaker Heights*, 418 U.S. 298 (1974)), and a narrow "equal access" perspective, which merely stresses the need to avoid discrimination in providing access to *novel* public forums. It is not clear how the Court would handle a claim that a particular underrepresented (perhaps "shockingly new") artistic school is being denied access to, for example, a federal courthouse.

MORAL CENSORSHIP: LIBEL

As indicated in *Chaplinsky v. New Hampshire*, 315 U.S. 568 (1942), libel and obscenity were traditionally viewed as categorically outside first-amendment protection. Yet libel was brought within the protection of the first amendment by *New York Times v. Sullivan* (1964). In that case, in which respondent Sullivan sued the *New York Times* for publishing a full-page ad depicting his official conduct as police commissioner as contributing to an "unprecedented wave of terror" against blacks, Justice Brennan wrote: "Respondent [and] the Alabama courts [stress] statements of this Court to the effect that the Constitution does not protect libelous publications. Those statements do not foreclose our inquiry here." The *New York Times* case constitutionalized libel law by prohibiting "a public official from recovering damages by a defamatory falsehood relating to his official conduct unless he proves that the statement was made with 'actual malice'—that is, with knowledge that it was false or with reckless disregard of whether it was false or not."

In subsequent cases, the *New York Times* case limit on liability has been extended to *public figures* as well as to public officials. In *Curtis Publishing Co. v. Butts*, 388 U.S. 130 (1967), the Court recognized that "our citizenry has a legitimate and substantial interest in the conduct of such persons, and the freedom of the press to engage in uninhibited debate about their involvement in public issues and events is as crucial as it is in the case of 'public officials.'" The decision in *Gertz v. Robert Welch, Inc.*, stated that "as long as they do not impose liability without fault, the State may define for themselves the appropriate standard of liability for a publisher or broadcaster of defamatory falsehoods injurious to a private individual." Public figures continued to be governed by the *New York Times* case actual malice standard.

Silberman v. Georges is the only case known to your authors in which an artist was sued for "libel by painting." At the trial the judge permitted the case to go to the jury, which awarded plaintiffs Silberman and Siani $30,000 each. Here is the decision of the Appellate Division reversing the trial court.

Silberman v. Georges
91 A.D. 29 520, 456 N.Y.S.2d 395 (1982)

MEMORANDUM DECISION

Judgment, Supreme Court, New York County, entered January 29, 1982, unanimously reversed, on the law, and the complaint dismissed, with costs (one bill). This defamation case should not have gone to the jury, the "statement" made by defendant in his obviously allegorical and symbolic painting being one of critical opinion only at most and constituting no accusation of criminal or antisocial conduct. Further, the fair meaning of the picture does not exceed appropriate comment, nor was there any showing of malice whatever. In addition, plaintiffs were not damaged in any way by defendant's expression. It is to be noted that the trial justice himself had grave doubt, as demonstrated by his expressions on a motion to set aside the jury's verdict for plaintiffs, that a case had been made out. The difficulty was that, though appropriate respect was accorded the jury's function in deciding issues of fact, the court should have decided the question of law of whether plaintiffs had, at a minimum, presented sufficient evidence to raise a question of fact to go to a jury. . . .

The instrument by which plaintiffs-respondents claim to have been libeled is a painting called "The Mugging of the Muse," exhibited [for which read "published"] before the Alliance of Figurative Artists prior to the commencement of this action. The plaintiffs and defendant, all three of them artists known in the world of painting, had been friends for sometime. They had come to a parting of the ways as the culmination of a dispute over refinements of their respective views of aspects of their art. Against the background of this prologue, defendant painted the offending picture, and presented it at one or more showings, and also permitted its magazine publication, to—it is claimed—the injury of plaintiffs.

The picture shows an apparent attempt at assassination on a city street by three males, armed with knives, upon a barefoot woman, scantily draped in a red cloth, the appearance of which suggest that it might be a bath towel. This scene is observed by a blue-winged cherub, standing between a hydrant, from which is spewing forth a fluid of the same color as the towel, and a brick wall, the lower aspect of which is covered by a yellowish overlay. The only other details are a collared brown, otherwise nondescript dog confronting the attackers, and a bent stanchion bearing a "no standing" sign. A crepuscular background of purplish hue contrasts with nearer overhead lighting, suggesting a street corner lamp. The only clue found within the picture, which might suggest identity of any of the actors, is supplied by masks on the faces of the two "downstage" assassins, claimed by plaintiffs to depict them. Quite obviously the trial jury found by its verdict that this was so intended by defendant. Indeed, part of the evidence at trial had been that, at a slide presentation of the subject picture, the audience had reacted with a gasp of recognition when that slide flashed upon the screen. There is no serious question of fact that the resemblance between the masks and the plaintiffs was more than coincidental and that they were the persons depicted. Defendant avers that, in any event, the portrayal was allegorical only and constituted no more than an expression of opinion. Plaintiffs claim that, to the contrary, the depiction held them up to ridicule and scorn, that they had been equated with muggers and robbers and accused of criminal conduct, that their reputations had been impaired, and that they had been cast in a derogatory and socially unacceptable light. This does not comport with any reasonable interpretation of the evidence in the case. The picture, viewed as though written words, may be described as "no more than rhetorical hyperbole." . . . And the very presence of the cherub and the bloody hydrant underscores the fanciful nature of the presentation.

For the purpose of this disposition there is no necessity to consider the question of whether libel may be committed through a picture as it might be via a writing. We assume that one may

Paul Georges. The Mugging of the Muse, *1983, oil. (Photo by Ken Showell. Reproduced by courtesy of the artist.)*

be deemed the equivalent of the other. The picture could not be intended, viewed by any reasonable person, as an accusation by defendant that either plaintiff had actually participated in an assault or related crime such as attempted homicide, or had any intention of so doing. It is undoubtedly an allegory in that it uses persons and symbols to convey a hidden meaning which must be extracted by a ratiocinative process, possibly entirely speculative. In its worst possible aspect, it accuses plaintiffs of engaging in destruction of something symbolized by the lady in red. In the context provided by the factual background and the use of the word "Muse," that figure could be representative only of the arts; therefore, the painting states that plaintiffs' artistic beliefs and activities are destructive of the arts. It says nothing more. Far worse commentary is written almost daily by newspaper and magazine critics of every aspect of the arts and is deemed to be no more than an expression of opinion.

Further, there was no proof of injury to plaintiffs. The picture's effect might well have been extreme embarrassment, the probable result of any well-aimed critical shaft, but that is not cognizable injury. . . . Nor is a showing of intent on defendant's part to assure that plaintiffs would be recognized as his targets indicative of malice; neither gross irresponsibility nor reckless disregard can be inferred from the fact that defendant, while at work on his picture, gave no attention to warnings that its characters portrayed plaintiffs. . . . The painting, viewed as though it were a writing, did not "expose a person to hatred, contempt or aversion, or to induce an evil or unsavory opinion of him in the minds of a substantial number of the community. . . ." No such inference was demonstrated. Indeed, special damages were neither pleaded nor proven in this case, nor was there a claim of libel *per se,* and, on this basis alone, it should not have gone to the jury.

COMMENTS

1. Libel must be susceptible to proof that it is "false," and the lawyers for Georges made that argument: the intention of the painting was to present an allegory, a metaphor that did not purport to represent reality and could not be falsified. The New York Civil Liberties Union submitted an amicus brief to the Appellate Division underscoring this point: the painting cannot be libelous because it is based on the artist's imagination and not on objective truth or falsehood. Would you buy such an argument? Suppose an artist paints an allegory showing you beating your wife and exhibits it on the sidewalk in front of your home. Okay? Even if you don't beat your wife?

2. On appeal, Georges emphasized that no defamatory statement of *fact* was involved, but merely the artist's *opinion* of a certain school of art. Although it is difficult to draw the line between fact and opinion, first-amendment law does make the distinction: false statements of fact are not protected by the first amendment, yet opinions are protected even if "false." As the U.S. Supreme Court stated in *Gertz v. Robert Welch, Inc.,* 418 U.S. 323, 329–340 (1974), "Under the First Amendment, there is no such thing as a false idea. However pernicious an opinion may seem, we depend for its correction not on the conscience of judges or juries but on the competition of other ideas." Note the analogy to the principle of "robust debate" discussed by Justice Brennan in *New York Times v. Sullivan,* 376 U.S. 254 (1964).

3. If we think of the Georges painting as criticism, that is, as an opinion about the artistic quality of Silberman's and Siani's works, the undesirable consequences of the trial decision become painfully clear. Criticism is an important category of protected speech, and pictorial criticism (e.g., cartoons) is as important to a free society as criticism in the form of words.

MORAL CENSORSHIP: OBSCENITY

Although a case involving government suppression of sexual obscenity in the United States was reported as early as 1815, it was not until the 1957 decision in *Roth v. United States,* 354 U.S.476, discussed later in this chapter, that the U.S. Supreme Court directly confronted the question of whether the first-amendment guarantee of freedom of speech and press extended to and protected obscenity. A brief description of the development of the law of obscenity in the United States provides a historical background against which to consider the pre-*Roth* cases and materials that follow.

In Colonial America, obscenity laws were directed against the Puritan-derived crimes of blasphemy and profanity. Then, as now, the definition of obscenity reflected the cultural and philosophical development of society. In the early nineteenth century, "obscene" generally referred to something depicting violence or the supernatural. For example, in *Knowles v. State,* 3 Day 103 (Conn. 1808), the defendant was convicted of showing an indecent representation of a "horrid and unnatural monster" that had no eyes, whose ears were misplaced, and whose skin was copper-colored.

The early sexual obscenity cases arose prior to the enactment of statutes purporting to deal with such matters. Instead, the courts held that obscene expressions of sexual content were acts of public indecency and as such legal offenses indictable at common law.

However, it was the legislatures rather than the courts that spearheaded the drive against obscenity (henceforth referring to sexually obscene material). During the first half of the nineteenth century, various states enacted statutes banning the importation and distribution of obscene materials within the state. Such enactments typically emphasized the intention to protect the morals of youth.

The first federal antiobscenity statute, Section 28 of the Customs Law, 5 Stat. 566 (1842), was enacted primarily in response to a specific problem. The law was directed only toward pictorial art; printed words were not thought to be dangerous. Under it, all "indecent and obscene prints, paintings, lithographs, engravings, and transparencies" were to be seized and destroyed. It related only to material sought to be imported and did not regulate commerce between the states. There is general agreement that the statute was aimed primarily at the French postcard trade. For almost a century after its passage, the customs law was not enforced in court by suits against travelers, although customs officers undoubtedly relied on it as authority to confiscate works entering the country.

Similarly, there were few prosecutions for obscenity under the state statutes. In the 1870s, however, in response to the undeviating persistence and lobbying of one Anthony Comstock, a grocery clerk by profession, Congress put some teeth into legal controls against obscenity. In adopting legislation in 1873 and amending it in 1876, Congress proscribed the sending of obscene material through the mails, thereby allowing the post office to inspect and censor mail. The basic structure of the Comstock Act has not been altered since 1876. Thus, the federal antiobscenity power has been derived through its controls over the customs and postal services.

As mentioned above, only recently have seizures of allegedly obscene pieces by the Customs Bureau when collectors try to import them become a commonly used method of censoring art. The following case illustrates the pre-*Roth* standard for obscenity which justified this form of governmental censorship.

United States v. 113 Prints
128 F. Supp. 280 (D.C.D. Md., 1955)

The government's libel in this case seeks (1) the forfeiture and confiscation under 19 U.S.C.A. §1305(a) of one unbound volume of a portfolio of 113 prints entitled "Die Erotik der Antike in Kleinkunst und Keramik" by Gaston Vorberg, imported from Germany, and alleged to be obscene, and (2) delivery of the same to the Library of Congress pursuant to 22 U.S.C.A. §614(d).

The prints, in sepia, are mounted on cards, 11 in. by 14 in. Most of them depict Greek, Roman, Etruscan or Egyptian statues, vases, lamps or other artifacts, which are decorated with, or otherwise display, erotic activities, features or symbols. Many of them show acts of sodomy and other forms of perverted practice. The portfolio is accompanied by a 24-page folio text, printed in German, which relates the subjects shown on the plates to the life of the period as expressed in its literature, with numerous quotations from and translations into German of erotic passages from classic authors.

19 U.S.C.A. §1305 provides:

All persons are prohibited from importing into the United States from any foreign country . . . any obscene book, . . . picture . . . : Provided further, That the Secretary of the Treasury may, in his discretion, admit the so-called classics or books of recognized and established literary or scientific merit, but may, in his discretion, admit such classics or books only when imported for noncommercial purposes.

The proviso was added by the Tariff Act of 1930.

The word "obscene" is not a technical term of the law and is not susceptible of exact definition since the intangible moral concepts it connotes vary in meaning from one period to another. . . . The standards to be applied are not those of pagan Greece or Rome, nor those of the Victorian era, but the court must try to find "the present critical point in the compromise between candor and shame at which the community may have arrived here and now." Judge Learned Hand, in *U.S. v. Kennerley.*

The test applied in the leading case of *Regina v. Hicklin,* . . . whether the tendency of the matter charged as obscenity is to deprave and corrupt those whose minds are open to such immoral influences, and into whose hands a publication of this sort may fall," was substantially followed in *U.S. v. Bennett,* and other early cases, and was often applied to those portions of a book charged to be obscene rather than to the book as a whole. This standard "has now been generally repudiated and for it has been substituted the test that a book must be considered as a whole, in its effect, not upon any particular class, but upon all those whom it is likely to reach."

Claimant contends that the portfolio is a scientific or scholarly work in the field of archeology, and is therefore not within the statute under the rule applied by the majority of the court in the Parmelee case, supra, quoting from *U.S. v. One Book Entitled Ulysses,*

. . . "It is settled," says the court in the Ulysses case, "that works of physiology, medicine, sci-ence, and sex instruction are not within the statute, though to some extent and among some persons they may tend to promote lustful thoughts." It should be equally true of works of sociology, as of physiology, medicine and other sciences—to say nothing of general literature and the arts—that "where the presentation, when viewed objectively, is sincere, and the erotic matter is not introduced to promote lust and does not furnish the dominant note of the publication," the same immunity should apply.

Erotica in ancient times may well be a recognized segment of the field of archeology, although it may be doubted whether an interest in archeology is the dominant motive of all those who work that corner of the field. Claimant is a microchemist, who describes himself as an amateur in archeology, and has taken some courses in that subject. He is not a member of any learned society and has not produced any work in that field, but is gathering background materials. He has offered in evidence a number of books, one or two printed in the United States and the others printed abroad, which deal with the same or similar subjects, and which have been sold in or imported into this country. One of the books, a study of red figured Greek vases, shows that the decorations on such vases covered the whole field of Greek life and thought, and among the illustrations are a number depicting erotic activity. Such a book is clearly within the rule of the *Ulysses* and *Parmelee* cases, and even of the *Besig* case. In some of the other books offered in evidence, which deal with erotica in ancient times, almost all of the illustrations depict erotic features or activity, including what most normal people in the United States today would consider perverted activity. I doubt whether such books would come under the rule announced in the passages quoted above from the *Ulysses* and *Parmelee* cases, especially in view of the fact noted by Judge (late Chief Justice) Vinson in his dissent in the Parmelee case, "that when the governing provision was last re-enacted in 1930, Congress inserted for the first time a proviso indicating that it did not regard the 'so-called classics or books of recognized and established literary or scientific merit' as ipso facto without the prohibition against the importation of obscene books." 113 F.2d at page 741. This does not mean, of course, that the character of a publication does not enter into a determination of whether it is obscene.

This case involves a portfolio of prints, most of which, in my opinion, would be regarded as obscene by a majority of normal men and women in the United States today. Claimant says that he has seen all of the activities depicted in Vorberg publicly exhibited in European museums, and many but not all exhibited in United States museums. What is done in Europe is not determinative here. And although a vase depicting an erotic scene may be included in a group of vases on exhibition in a museum in this country, I do not believe the present state of the taste and morals of the community would approve the public exhibition of a collection of objects similar to those shown on the prints, nor the public exhibition or sale of the prints themselves, although in my opinion most normal men and women in this country would approve the ownership of such a publication by a museum, library, college or other educational institution, where its use could be controlled.

These prints are not illustrations in a bound book, but are mounted on cards for display apart from the text. I cannot extend the exemption applied in the *Ulysses* and *Parmelee* cases to this portfolio.

The government agrees that the review of this portfolio by the Treasury Department after its seizure by the Collector of Customs, dealt only with the question of obscenity, and not with the exercise of the discretion of the Secretary of the Treasury under the proviso quoted above. The pertinent Customs Regulation, 19 C.F.R. sec. 12.40(g), reads as follows:

In any case when a book is seized as being obscene and the importer declines to execute an assent to forfeiture on the ground that the book is a classic, or of recognized and established literary or scientific merit, a petition addressed to the Secretary of the Treasury with evidence to support the claim may be filed by the importer for release of the book. Mere unsupported statements or allegations will not be considered. If this ruling is favorable, release of such books shall be made only to the ultimate consignee.

I find the portfolio is obscene within the meaning of 19 U.S.C.A. §1305(a), but will withhold the entry of any order herein for a period of thirty days, to give the claimant an opportunity to file a petition with the Secretary of the Treasury under the regulation quoted above; and if such a petition is filed. I will withhold the entry of an order until after the Secretary has acted on the petition.

General obscenity statutes seek to interfere with the right of adults to read or see material of their own choice. In contrast with general laws prohibiting sales to adults, state legislatures have greater latitude in restricting certain types of distribution, such as the thrusting of explicit sexual materials on unwilling recipients through unsolicited mail and public display and the distribution of such materials to minors. These *specific* statutes are considered here.

In *United States v. Thirty-One Photographs*, 156 F.Supp. 350 (S.D. N.Y., 1957), Dr. Alfred Kinsey, on behalf of the Institute for Sex Research, attempted to import all kinds of hard-core pornography for his social-science research. New York Customs officials pounced on the importation. By no stretch of the imagination could the seized materials be characterized as "classics" or works of "scientific merit." But the Institute urged admission of the material on the grounds of its own scientific purpose, based on the special qualifications of Kinsey to receive them, rather than on the merit of the materials themselves.

The Supreme Court directed release of the impounded works in an opinion that had potentially startling implications:

I fail to see why it should be more difficult to determine the appeal of [confiscated] matter to a known group of persons than it is to determine its appeal to a hypothetical average man. . . . The question is solely whether, as to those persons who will see the . . . material, there is a reasonable probability that it will appeal to their prurient interest.

The government did not appeal the decision. Wouldn't the above rationale be broad enough to require release of any confiscated pornography to any scholar whose motives for importing were not prurient but intellectual? In fact, need one even be a scholar?

The enemies of pornography at the Customs Bureau have not always seen fit to censor only the hard-core. In the 1930s an assistant collector of customs began a letter as follows:

Sirs:

There is being detained . . . two packages addressed to you, containing obscene photo books, "Ceiling Sistine Chapel," Filles-Michael Angelo, the importation of which is held to be prohibited under the provisions of the Tariff Act. [Quoted in Ann Lyon Haight, *Banned Books: Informal Notes on Some Books Banned for Various Reasons at Various Times and in Various Places* (New York: R.R. Bowker, 1955), pp. 12–13.]

Within the federal domain itself there is the added difficulty imposed by different standards of censorial discretion: once Customs has cleared material for importation, the post office may still refuse to allow it through the mails based on its definition of obscene.

Promoters of the movie *Naked Maja* tried to send postcards portraying on one side a color photograph reproduction of Goya's painting and on the other a plug for the film ("the most breathtaking canvas that ever came to life"). . . . The [Post Office] General Counsel found . . . them non-mailable—the Goya reproduction was too prurient when used for these advertising purposes. A hearing followed, enlivened by the distributor's persistent attempts to have a psychologist swear that the cards, in his opinion, would have no harmful effect "on average persons." The Hearing Examiner refused to hear such claims, and, "applying all the yardsticks," he "found as a fact" that these Goya reproductions were "obscene." The Judicial Officer concurred. When the case was appealed to the courts, the Department of Justice, having taken over the defense of the censorship action, withdrew its defense and, in effect, reversed the Post Office by abandoning any effort to sustain its order in court contest. James C. Paul and Murray L. Schwartz, *Federal Censorship: Obscenity in the Mail* (New York: Free Press of Glencoe, 1961), pp. 182–183.

The United States is a party to the Agreement for the Suppression of the Circulation of Obscene Publications, 37 Stat. 511 (1911), T.S. No. 590. The agreement was signed at Paris in 1910, ratified by the United States, and put in force a year later. It was subsequently amended by a Protocol signed in 1949 which became effective in 1950 (1 U.S.T. 849, T.I.A.S. No. 2164, 30 U.N.T.S. 3).

Under Article 1 of the agreement, which has the force of a treaty, each contracting party agreed to take measures to facilitate the suppression of "obscene writing, designs, pictures or objects" where such materials constituted the subject matter of an offense against international legislation of the country. Each country was to define obscenity according to its own standards. Although the *Roth* court (see below, p. 286), paid lip service to the existence of this international obligation, the Supreme Court has ignored its implicit requirement for a national standard by which the question of obscenity can be judged.

As one might expect, the criminal laws of obscenity applying to adults in foreign countries differ widely, running from virtually total freedom of expression to strict and repressive censorship by official government boards. Most countries also restrict unsolicited mailings of offensive materials and regulate public displays of such matter. Distributions or sales to children are likewise banned in almost all foreign jurisdictions. In recent years, however, a trend toward substantial reevaluation and revision of obscenity legislation has appeared. A summary of the obscenity laws in other countries is presented in *The Report of the Commission on Obscenity and Pornography* (Washington, D.C.: U.S. Government Printing Office, 1970), pp. 339–352. Comparative perspectives are reported in greater detail in *Technical Report of the Commission on Obscenity and Pornography,* vol. 2: *Legal Analysis* (Washington, D.C.: U.S. Government Printing Office, 1970), pp. 91–241.

Many states exempt from criminal liability people who distribute obscene materials in the course of scientific or artistic pursuits. This type of statutory exemption usually reads substantially as follows:

> This Act shall not apply to persons who may possess or distribute obscene matter or participate in conduct otherwise prescribed by this Act, when such possession, distribution, or conduct occurs in the course of law enforcement activities, or in the course of bona fide scientific educational or comprehensive research or study, or bona fide objects of art or artistic pursuits, or like circumstances or justification, where the possession, distribution or conduct is not related to the subject matter's appeal to prurient interest. [Okla. Stat. Ann. tit. 21, §1021.1]

The Commission on Obscenity and Pornography, appointed by President Lyndon B. Johnson in 1968, recommended model legislation for the states reflecting this exception. Because the commission recommended repeal of all existing state laws prohibiting the distribution of obscene material to adults, the exception for art was recognized in the prohibitions of Section 2, controlling the "Sale and Display of Explicit Sexual Material to Young Persons," and Section 3, regulating "Public Displays of Explicit Sexual Materials." For example:

> Explicit sexual material means any pictorial or three-dimensional material depicting human sexual intercourse, masturbation, sodomy (i.e., bestiality or oral or anal intercourse), direct physical stimulation of unclothed genitals, flagellation or torture in the context of a sexual relationship, or emphasizing the depiction of adult human genitals, *providing, however,* that works of art or of anthropological significance shall not be deemed to be within the foregoing definition. [§3(d)(ii) of Recommended State Legislation of *Report of the Commission on Obscenity and Pornography,* 67.]

The arguments before the Supreme Court in *Roth v. United States* (and in *Alberts v. California,* its companion case), 354 U.S. 476 (1957), were at such a high level of abstraction that the factual backgrounds of the cases were irrelevant. At issue was whether the federal and California obscenity standards violated the expression guarantees of the first amendment. Accordingly, the Court did not even pass on the merits of the materials alleged to be obscene. In the 5–4 decision, the *Roth* Court, in an opinion by Justice Brennan, held that "obscenity is not within the area of constitutionally protected speech or press." In arriving at this conclusion, the Court relied on numerous dicta to that effect, as well as on historical evidence that suggested to the majority that the first amendment was never intended to protect obscenity. At page 484, the Court said:

> All ideas having even the slightest redeeming social importance—unorthodox ideas, controversial ideas, even ideas hateful to the prevailing climate of opinion—have the full protection of the guaranties, unless excludable because they encroach upon the limited area of more important interests. But implicit in the history of the First Amendment is the rejection of obscenity as utterly without redeeming social importance.

The *Roth* Court went on to define "obscene material" as "material that deals with sex in a manner appealing to prurient interest" and "prurient interest" as "lustful thoughts . . . itching, morbid or lascivious longings . . . a shameful or morbid interest in nudity, sex or excretion." The Court's test for determining whether material was obscene, and therefore not within the protection of the first amendment, was "whether [to] the average person, applying contemporary community standards, the dominant theme of the material taken as a whole appeals to prurient interest." The test so enunciated was the only one with which a majority of the Court agreed until the 1973 *Miller* decision (excerpted below).

The *Roth* Court further noted that "sex and obscenity are not synonymous" and that the "portrayal of sex, e.g., in art, literature and scientific works [is entitled to] the constitutional protection of freedom of speech and press" so long as it did not fall into the category of obscenity.

In *Jacobellis v. Ohio,* 378 U.S. 184 (1964), Justice Brennan wrote for the Court that "obscenity is excluded from the constitutional protection only because it is 'utterly without redeeming social importance'" (p. 191). The majority then stated that artistic creation was protected, since "material dealing with sex in a manner that advocated ideas, or that has . . . *artistic* value . . . may not be branded as obscenity and denied the constitutional protection" (emphasis added).

Shortly after *Jacobellis,* the Court undertook to crystallize the essences of *Roth* and subsequent decisions. In *Memoirs v. Massachusetts,* 383 U.S. 413 (1966), a three-part test of obscenity was articulated in a plurality opinion:

> Three elements must coalesce: it must be established that (a) the dominant theme of the material taken as a whole appeals to a prurient interest in sex; (b) the material is patently offensive because it affronts contemporary community standards relating to the description or representation of sexual matters; and (c) the material is utterly without redeeming social value (p. 418).

This plurality test represented only one of seven approaches taken by the different justices in their various opinions in *Memoirs.* However, its viewpoint became in effect the decisive one because it was enunciated in the lead opinion. In *Memoirs,* the Court reversed a holding by the Massachusetts Supreme Judicial Court that the book *Fanny Hill* was obscene, stating that the Massachusetts court had misapplied the constitutional obscenity standard.

Because of the multiplicity of viewpoints in *Memoirs* and the necessarily engendered confusion, the Court decided subsequent cases in an approach first resorted to in *Redrup v. New York,* 386 U.S. 767 (1967). In reversing several state convictions, the Court explained, in a *per curiam* opinion, that the materials in question were constitutionally protected regardless of which of the prevailing views was to be applied. The Court then disposed of thirty-one obscenity cases in similar fashion, frequently offering no rationale other than a citation to *Redrup.*

In 1973, for the first time since *Roth,* in deciding *Miller v. California,* 413 U.S. 15, the court agreed on a test for distinguishing constitutionally protected material from unprotected obscenity. Although the *Miller* court unanimously rejected the *Memoirs* formulation, only a bare majority of the justices—of whom only one was a member of the Court when *Memoirs* was decided—were in agreement with the enunciated constitutional standards.

Miller v. California
413 U.S. 15 (1973)

Mr. Chief Justice Burger delivered the opinion of the Court.

This is one of a group of "obscenity-pornography" cases being reviewed by the Court in a re-examination of standards enunciated in earlier cases involving what Mr. Justice Harlan called "the intractable obscenity problem."

Appellant conducted a mass mailing campaign to advertise the sale of illustrated books, euphemistically called "adult" material. After a jury trial, he was convicted of violating California Penal Code §311.2 (a), a misdemeanor, by knowingly distributing obscene matter, and the Appellate Department, Superior Court of California, County of Orange, summarily affirmed the judg-

ment without opinion. Appellant's conviction was specifically based on his conduct in causing five unsolicited advertising brochures to be sent through the mail in an envelope addressed to a restaurant in Newport Beach, California. The envelope was opened by the manager of the restaurant and his mother. They had not requested the brochures; they complained to the police.

The brochures advertise four books entitled "Intercourse," "Man-Woman," "Sex Orgies Illustrated," and "An Illustrated History of Pornography," and a film entitled "Marital Intercourse." While the brochures contain some descriptive printed material, primarily they consist of pictures and drawings very explicitly depicting men and women in groups of two or more engaging in a variety of sexual activities, with genitals often prominently displayed.

Apart from the initial formulation in the *Roth* case, no majority of the Court has at any given time been able to agree on a standard to determine what constitutes obscene, pornographic material subject to regulation under the States' police power. See, e.g., *Redrup v. New York,* 386 U.S., at 770–771. We have seen "a variety of views among the members of the Court unmatched in any other course of constitutional adjudication."

This is not remarkable, for in the area of freedom of speech and press the courts must always remain sensitive to any infringement on genuinely serious literary, artistic, political, or scientific expression. This is an area in which there are few eternal verities.

The case we now review was tried on the theory that the California Penal Code §311 approximately incorporates the three-stage *Memoirs* test, supra. But now the *Memoirs* test has been abandoned as unworkable by its author, and no Member of the Court today supports the *Memoirs* formulation. . . .

[W]e now confine the permissible scope of State regulation to works which depict or describe sexual conduct. That conduct must be specifically defined by the applicable State law as written or authoritatively construed. . . .

A state offense must also be limited to works which, taken as a whole, appeal to the prurient interest in sex, which portray sexual conduct in a patently offensive way, and which, taken as a whole, do not have serious literary, artistic, political, or scientific value.

The basic guidelines for the trier of fact must be: (a) whether "the average person, applying contemporary community standards" would find that the work, taken as a whole, appeals to the prurient interest; (b) whether the work depicts or describes, in a patently offensive way, sexual conduct specifically defined by the applicable state law; and (c) whether the work, taken as a whole, lacks serious literary, artistic, political, or scientific value. We do not adopt as a constitutional standard the *"utterly* without redeeming social value" test of *Memoirs v. Massachusetts;* that concept has never commanded the adherence of more than three Justices at one time. If a state law that regulates obscene material is thus limited, as written or construed, the Fifth Amendment values applicable to the States through the Four-teenth Amendment are adequately protected by the ultimate power of appellate courts to conduct an independent review of constitutional claims when necessary. . . .

We emphasize that it is not our function to propose regulatory schemes for the States. That must await their concrete legislative efforts. It is possible, however, to give a few plain examples of what a state statute could define for regulation under part (b) of the standard announced in this opinion:

(a) Patently offensive representations or descriptions of ultimate sexual acts, normal or perverted, actual or simulated.

(b) Patently offensive representations or descriptions of masturbation, excretory functions, and lewd exhibition of the genitals.

Sex and nudity may not be exploited without limit by films or pictures exhibited or sold in places of public accommodation any more than live sex and nudity can be exhibited or sold without limit in such public places. At a minimum, prurient patently offensive depiction or description of sexual conduct must have serious literary, artistic, political, or scientific value to merit First Amendment protection.

For example, medical books for the education of physicians and related personnel necessarily use graphic illustrations and descriptions of human anatomy. In resolving the inevitably sensitive questions of fact and law, we must continue to rely on the jury system, accompanied by the safeguards that judges, rules of evidence, presumption of innocence, and other protective features provide, as we do with rape, murder, and a host of other offenses against society and its individual members. . . .

Under the holdings announced today, no one will be subject to prosecution for the sale or exposure of obscene materials unless these materials depict or describe patently offensive "hard core" sexual conduct specifically defined by the regulating state law. . . .

[T]oday, for the first time since *Roth* was decided in 1957, a majority of this Court has agreed on concrete guidelines to isolate "hard core" pornography from expression protected by the First Amendment. . . .

Under a national Constitution, fundamental First Amendment limitations on the powers of the States do not vary from community to community, but this does not mean that there are, or should or can be, fixed uniform national standards of precisely what appeals to the "prurient interest" or is "patently offensive." These are essentially questions of fact, and our nation is simply too big and too diverse for this Court to reasonably expect that such standards could be articulated for all 50 States in a single formulation, even assuming the prerequisite consensus exists. Then triers of fact are asked to decide whether "the average person, applying contemporary community standards" would consider certain materials "prurient," it would be unrealistic to require that the answer be based on some abstract formulation. The adversary system, with lay jurors as the usual ultimate factfinders in criminal prosecutions, has historically permitted triers of fact to draw on the standards of their community, guided always by limiting instructions on the law. To require a State to structure obscenity proceedings around evidence of a *national* "community standard" would be an exercise in futility. . . .

People in different States vary in their tastes and attitudes, and this diversity is not to be strangled by the absolutism of imposed uniformity. As the Court made clear in *Mishkin v. New York*, 383 U.S., at 508–509, the primary concern with requiring a jury to apply the standard of "the average person, applying contemporary community standards" is to be certain that, so far as material is not aimed at a deviant group, it will be judged by its impact on an average person, rather than a particularly susceptible or sensitive person—or indeed a totally insensitive one.

We hold that the requirement that the jury evaluate the materials with reference to "contemporary standards of the State of California" serves this protective purpose and is constitutionally adequate.

The dissenting Justices sound the alarm of repression. But, in our view, to equate the free and robust exchange of ideas and political debate with commercial exploitation of obscene material demeans the grand conception of the First Amendment and its high purposes in the historic struggle for freedom. It is a "misuse of the great guarantees of free speech and free press. . . ." *Breard v. Alexandria*, 341 U.S. at 645. The First Amendment protects works which, taken as a whole, have serious literary, artistic, political, or scientific value, regardless of whether the government or a majority of the people approve of the ideas these works represent. "The protection given speech and press was fashioned to assure unfettered interchange of *ideas* for the bringing about of political and social changes desired by the people," *Roth v. United States*. But the public portrayal of hard-core sexual conduct for its own sake, and for the ensuing commercial gain, is a different matter.

There is no evidence, empirical or historical, that the stern 19th century American censorship of public distribution and display of material relating to sex in any way limited or affected expression of serious literary, artistic, political, or scientific ideas. On the contrary, it is beyond any question that the era following Thomas Jefferson to Theodore Roosevelt was an "extraordinarily vigorous period," not just in economics and politics, but in *belles lettres* and in "the outlying fields of social and political philosophies." We do not see the harsh hand of censorship of ideas—good or bad, sound or unsound—and "repression" of political liberty lurking in every state regulation of commercial exploitation of human interest in sex.

MR. JUSTICE BRENNAN finds "it is hard to see how state-ordered regimentation of our minds can ever be forestalled." These doleful anticipations assume that courts cannot distinguish commerce in ideas, protected by the First Amendment, from commercial exploitation of obscene material. Moreover, state regulation of hard-core pornography so as to make it unavailable to nonadults, a regulation which Mr. Justice Brennan finds constitutionally permissible, has all the elements of "censorship" for adults; indeed even more rigid enforcement techniques may be called for with such dichotomy of regulation. One can concede that the "sexual revolution" of recent years may have had useful byproducts in striking layers of prudery from a subject long irrationally kept from needed ventilation. But it does not follow that no regulation of patently offensive "hard core" materials is needed or permissible; civilized people do not allow unregulated access to heroin because it is a derivative of medicinal morphine.

In sum, we (a) reaffirm the *Roth* holding that obscene material is not protected by the First Amendment; (b) hold that such material can be regulated by the States, subject to the specific safeguards enunciated above, without a showing that the material is "*utterly* without redeeming social value"; and (c) hold that obscenity is to be determined by applying "contemporary community standards," not "national standards."

COMMENTS

1. "Contemporary community standards." What is the relevant "community" for application of the "contemporary community standards" criterion of the *Miller* test? With regard to prosecutions under *federal* obscenity statutes, the Supreme Court held that the relevant community is local (*Hamling v. United States*, 418 U.S. 87 (1974), reh. den. 419 U.S. 885 (1974)). The result is

> to permit a juror sitting in obscenity cases to draw on knowledge of the community or vicinage from which he comes in deciding what conclusion "the average person, applying contemporary community standards" would reach in a given case. . . . But this is not to say that a District Court would not be at liberty to admit evidence of standards existing in some places outside of this particular district if he felt such evidence would assist the jury in the resolution of the issues which they were to decide.

In *Jenkins v. Georgia*, 418 U.S. 153 (1974), the Court unanimously reversed a Georgia obscenity conviction for exhibiting the film *Carnal Knowledge*. As in *Hamling*, the Court paid little heed to concerns over the harmful effect of "local" community standards on those who published and produced or distributed for a national market. In construing a *state* statute, the Court held that "the Constitution does not require that juries be instructed in state obscenity cases to apply the standards of a hypothetical statewide community." The Court approved the trial court's instructions "directing jurors to apply 'community standards' without specifying what 'community.' . . . States have considerable latitude in framing statutes under this element of the *Miller* decision."

Does the use of "contemporary community standards" mean, in effect, that works of art that happen to be unacceptable to a majority of the given population at a time may be suppressed? If the course of art and literature waited on the contemporary tastes of a numerical majority, would cultural development be effectively stymied?

2. "Patently offensive sexual conduct." In *Jenkins*, after viewing the film, the Court ruled that it was not obscene because it was not "patently offensive," stating (at page 160):

> Even though questions of appeal to the "prurient interest" or of patent offensiveness are "essentially questions of fact," it would be a serious misreading of *Miller* to conclude that juries have unbridled discretion in determining what is "patently offensive." . . . [W]e made it plain under that holding "no one will be subject to prosecution for the sale or exposure of obscene materials unless these materials depict or describe patently offensive 'hardcore' sexual conduct."

3. After *Miller* and *Jenkins*, is all creative artwork protected? If, to be proscribed, a work of art must be shown to be only a public portrayal of hard-core sexual conduct for its own sake or for commercial gain, is the law of obscenity no more than a matter of academic concern to artists? Are courts competent to distinguish the constitutionally protected exchange of ideas from hard-core pornography?

4. "Serious artistic value" (and values, themselves). What does it mean for a work to have "serious artistic value"? What is the distinction between serious literary value and serious artistic value, and how is each proved? Is this criterion to be decided according to local community standards? In the defense of an allegedly obscene work of art, the testimony of an expert, most frequently a professor or a critic, is a practical necessity. Under the rules of evidence in most jurisdictions, once a person is qualified as an expert witness, he may give "opinion" testimony, which normally is disallowed if offered by nonexperts.

Clearly, protection for such work(s) stems from belief in the free development of the arts. In response to *Jacobellis* one commentator wrote:

> The rationale of a free development of the arts contemplates freedom not only from the compulsion of a moral judgment, but from the compulsion of a taste judgment as well. It is not only established morality, but also established taste, which compels allegiance to traditional forms. By subjecting critically neglected works, whether they be avant-garde or commercially oriented, to the risk of prosecution under the definitional standards, and privileging those works acknowledged as meritorious by the panjandrums of criticism, we may unwittingly be furthering a stultification of art by permitting the proscription of those vital and challenging expressions that vivify the creative process. Any prior determination of the first amendment right on the basis of merit obviously defeats its historic

rationale: that the survival of the best depends upon the unfettered conflict between individual forms. ["Obscenity Prosecution: Artistic Value and the Concept of Immunity," *New York University Law Review,* vol. 39 (1964), pp. 1063, 1084–1085.]

Does the *Miller* formulation overcome this criticism, or at least minimize the adverse ramifications of the "taste" or "quality" problem? Consider Judge Learned Hand's opinion in *United States v. Levine,* 83 F.2d 156, 157 (2d Cir. 1936), that common principles which will ensure the vindication of artistic works can never be formulated under obscenity statutes. If "quality" is the criterion for "serious artistic value," then does the artist have the burden of proving his innocence by proving the value of the work? Would this present additional constitutional problems? This problem has been raised in a related context:

> [The censorious] have managed to get laws enacted which require the rest of us to prove that the books they want to suppress have "literary value" or "redeeming social importance" or some similar pretentiousness. Those of us who can take our books or leave them alone are compelled to defend our choices. The burden of proof has moved mysteriously to us. [John Henry Merryman, "The Fear of Books," *Stanford Today,* Autumn 1966, p. 14.]

Under *Miller,* is there any reason a work cannot be both of serious artistic value and obscene? Has the Court recognized that artistic merit does not magically dispel lascivious effect? For the proposition that both the erotic and the shocking may be *necessary* and intentional elements of artistic appeal, see Abraham Kaplan, "Obscenity as an Aesthetic Category," *Law and Contemporary Problems,* vol. 20 (1955), p. 544.

Japan has recognized and dealt with this dichotomy. There expert testimony is allowable for the purpose of determining artistic merit, but then artistic merit itself is held to be irrelevant for the purpose of deciding whether the work is statutorily obscene. The Japanese Supreme Court fully recognized the artistic quality of *Lady Chatterley's Lover,* yet concluded in finding it obscene:

> Art and obscenity are concepts which belong to two separate, distinct dimensions; and it cannot be said that they cannot exist side by side. . . . [T]he obscene nature of the work cannot be denied solely for the reason that the work in question is artistic literature. . . . No matter how supreme the quality of art may be, it does not necessarily wipe out the stigma of obscenity. Art, even art, does not have the special privilege of presenting obscene matters to the public. Be he an artist or a literary man, he may not violate the duty imposed upon the general public, the duty of respecting the feeling of shame and humility and the law predicated upon morality. [*Koyama v. State,* 11 J.Sup.Ct.Crim. 997 (1957), discussed in Yasuo Takikuni, "Obscenity and the Japanese Constitution," *Kentucky Law Journal,* vol. 51 (1963), p. 703.]

The related "captive audience" and "offensiveness" state interests raise issues that are particularly difficult when they are invoked to suppress art. Not only are the visual arts more public and graphic than other forms of speech, but the social aspect of art appreciation (as opposed to the more private experience of reading, for example) makes art uniquely vulnerable to the claim of offensiveness. Jody Newmyer has elaborated:

> The social pressure of being part of a group of people one knows well, who may judge what one says about an art exhibition as indicative of one's own moral or life-style preferences, may increase timidity and orthodoxy. The kind of embarrassment felt by one who thinks he should be offended—or perhaps is actually offended—by a work of art, the feeling that one has been made a fool of in public or forced into an unwilling self-revelation, creates a corresponding anger and outrage toward the artist or exhibitor who has subjected one to such an experience. What may be considered minor departures from orthodoxy in printed form acquire heightened significance when they appear in forms which by their very nature must be open to a larger public view. [Jody Newmyer, "Art, Libraries, and the Censor," *Library Quarterly,* vol. 46, no. 1 (1976), p. 46.]

The special risks of these rationales to works of art are illustrated by the following case, *Close v. Lederle.* Consider whether the result would have been different if the court had had the benefit of the *Miller* decision, keeping in mind the fact that here no obscenity prosecution is involved.

Close v. Lederle
424 F.2d 988 (1st Cir. 1970), cert. denied 400 U.S. 903 (1970)

ALDRICH, Chief Judge.

Plaintiff, an art instructor at the University of Massachusetts, was asked by a superior if he would care to have an exhibition of his paintings on the walls of a corridor used from time to time for such purposes in the Student Union, a university building. He said that he would. The exhibition, which had been arranged for but not seen by the superior in charge, proved to be controversial. Several administrative meetings were held, attended by the university president, the provost, and other officials, and after it had been up for five of the twenty-four days scheduled, the exhibition was removed. Claiming that it was an invasion of his constitutional rights, plaintiff sued for a mandatory injunction ordering the officials to make the space available for the equivalent of the unexpired period. The district court, after trial, granted the relief and defendants' appeal.

Basically, the district court held that "embarrassment" and "annoyance," causing defendants to conclude that the exhibition was "inappropriate" to the corridor, was insufficient to warrant interference with plaintiff's right of free speech. This holding was not grounded upon a finding that defendants were unreasonable in their opinion. The court refused autoptic profference of the exhibition, apparently taking the position that, at least in the absence of express regulations as to what was impermissible, defendants had no right to censor simply on the basis of offensiveness which fell short of unlawful obscenity.

We disagree. We first consider the nature and quality of plaintiff's interest. Plaintiff makes the bald pronouncement, "Art is as fully protected by the Constitution as political or social speech." It is true that in the course of holding a motion picture entitled to First Amendment protection, the Court said in *Joseph Burstyn, Inc. v. Wilson,* that moving pictures affect public attitudes in ways "ranging from direct espousal of a political or social doctrine to the subtle shaping of thought which characterizes all artistic expression." However, this statement in itself recognizes that there are degrees of speech.

There is no suggestion, unless in its cheap titles, that plaintiff's art was seeking to express political or social thought. Cases dealing with students' rights to hear possibly unpopular speakers involve a medium and subject matter entitled to greater protection than plaintiff's art. Even as to verbal communication the extent of the protection may depend upon the subject matter. We consider plaintiff's constitutional interest minimal.

In this posture we turn to the question whether defendants have demonstrated a sufficient counterinterest to justify their action. The corridor was a passageway, regularly used by the public, including children. Several of the paintings were nudes, male or female, displaying the genitalia in what was described as "clinical detail." A skeleton was fleshed out only in this particular. One painting bore the title, "I'm only 12 and already my mother's lover wants me." Another, "I am the only virgin in my school."

The defendants were entitled to consider the primary use to which the corridor was put. See C. A. Wright, The Constitution on the Campus. 22 Vand. L. Rev. 1027, 1040–43 (1969). On the basis of the complaints received, and even without such, defendants were warranted in finding the exhibit inappropriate to that use. Where there was, in effect, a captive audience, defendants had a right to afford protection against "assault upon individual privacy," short of legal obscenity. Cf. Emerson, Toward a General Theory of the First Amendment, 72 Yale L.J. 877, 938 (1963). To quote from Professor Wright, supra at 1058,

There are words that are not regarded as obscene, in the constitutional sense, that nevertheless need not be permitted in every context. Words that might properly be employed in a term paper about Lady Chatterley's Lover or in a novel submitted in a creative writing course take on a very different coloration if they are bellowed over a loudspeaker at a campus rally or appear prominently on a sign posted on a campus tree.

Freedom of speech must recognize, at least within limits, freedom not to listen.

In hyperconcern with his personal rights plaintiff would not only regard his interest in self-expression as more important than the interests of his unwilling audience, but asks us to add nearly three weeks of such exposure to the five days he has already received. With all respect to the distinct court, this is a case that should never have been brought.

Judgment reversed. Complaint dismissed.

COMMENTS

1. Observe that this was a state university. As such, its action in removing the painting was "state action" and therefore subject to first amendment and state constitutional protections (see Gerald Gunther, *Constitutional Law,* 11th ed. [Mineola, N.Y.: New York Foundation Press, 1985], pp. 860ff.). Suppose the university had been private (e.g., Harvard University). Close would then have had no constitutional claim, although he might have had other legal bases for opposing removal of the paintings—breach of contract, for example.

2. For another case of offense to a captive audience by works of art—allegedly obscene stained glass windows—see *Piarowsky v. Illinois Community College,* District 515, 759 F.2d 625 (7th Cir. 1985).

3. Like many other concepts that have emerged in the judicial and scholarly development of the first-amendment free speech clause, that of offensiveness to a captive audience is troublesome. It is difficult to apply in a principled way and vulnerable to repressive application. See the discussion in Gunther, *Constitutional Law,* pp. 1211ff.

4. The brief season of "body art" in the 1970s produced a variety of bizarre artistic activities (i.e., by artists) that brought up a number of questions about censorship and the legal consequences of failure to exercise it. For an excellent discussion, see Bruce E. Mitchell, "Body Art: A Legal Policy Analysis" (student paper in the authors' files, January 1977), reproduced in John Henry Merryman and Albert E. Elien, *Law, Ethics and the Visual Arts.* © 1979. New York: Matthew-Bender, pp. 3-162ff. Here, to give the flavor, are two examples.

   A. Suppose a "body art" performer were to set himself up in a "live" electrified chair in an art gallery. On the wall is a switch that if flipped would activate the current, killing the artist. A sign by the switch alerts the gallery visitor to this consequence.

   B. Consider an exhibit at the Quay Gallery in San Francisco, "Still Life," by Ed Kienholz, which included a chair in which members of the audience could sit. Aimed at the chair was a gun set to go off randomly (a card informed the reader) sometime during the next one hundred years. The work was banned in Berlin but was shown in San Francisco without serious controversy.

What would be the legal consequences for the gallery visitor who threw the switch and killed the artist in the first example? What of the legal liability of the artist in the second example? Of the gallery owner in either example?

5. Chris Burden's often masochistic body art is controversial and may also be educational, in much the same way that the famous Milgram experiments revealed to us certain truths about ourselves. When Burden lies in a Soho art gallery near a sign asking people to push pins into his body, what is he asking us about ourselves? In "The Art-Martyr," *New York Magazine,* May 24, 1976, Dorothy Seiberling stated:

> By making a "performance" of horrifying experiences, Burden spotlights the barbarities we have come to take for granted. . . . By his provocative and often poetic confrontations with death, pain, isolation and fear, he confronts us with our own anxieties and vulnerability. . . . Burden's pieces [stimulate] a flood of questions, responses, interpretations.

Can coherent limits that distinguish between permissible and impermissible body art be framed without threatening the most valuable aspects of artistic freedom?

6. In the later 1970s, "artist" Kim Jones poured kerosene over three live rats and set them ablaze at the California State Fullerton Student Union Art Gallery. The Art Gallery director was fired. Was this appropriate?

POLITICAL AND SOCIAL CENSORSHIP OF ART

In December 1966, Stephen Radich, the proprietor of an art gallery on Madison Avenue in New York City, displayed in his gallery certain "constructions," comparable to sculptures, which had been created by an artist named Marc Morrel. These constructions were composed partly of United States flags or portions thereof and partly of other objects, including a Vietcong flag, a Russian flag, a Nazi swastika, and a gas mask. A patrolman noticed "what appeared to be the American flag in the form of a body, hanging from a yellow noose," in

Radich's second-floor gallery and issued a summons to Radich for having "publicly displayed the American flag that was defiled and mutilated." Radich was found guilty of "casting contempt" on the flag by the Criminal Court of the City of New York on May 5, 1967. His conviction was upheld by the New York State Court of Appeals on February 18, 1970. Then, on November 9, 1974, the federal district court reversed the decision. The Court of Appeals and the district court opinions follow.

People v. Radich
26 N.Y.2d 114, 257 N.E.2d 30 (1970)

GIBSON, Judge.

The issue is whether defendant's conviction of a violation of New York's flag desecration statute was in contravention of his right of free speech under the First Amendment to the Constitution of the United States. The particular penal provision found to have been violated provides, in substance, that any person who shall publicly mutilate, deface, defile, or defy, trample upon, or cast contempt upon the flag of the United States of America, either by words or act, shall be guilty of a misdemeanor (former Penal Law, §1425, subd. 16, par. d, now General Business Law, §136, subd. d). The constitutional question in respect of the proscribed defilement by an "act," rather than by "words," was expressly left open in *Street v. New York*, . . . which reversed our affirmance of a conviction under this same statute. . . . We have concluded that the conviction in the case now before us infringed no constitutional guarantee.

The defendant, the proprietor of an art gallery in the City of New York, publicly displayed and exposed for sale, certain "constructions," comparable to sculptures, which had been fashioned by an artist as expressive of protest against the Vietnam war and which, in each case, prominently incorporated the American flag.

The complaint, upon which defendant was charged and convicted, alleged, among other violations of the statute, that defendant publicly displayed the flag of the United States of America in the form of the male sexual organ, erect and protruding from the upright member of a cross; also, in the form of a human body, hanging from a yellow noose; and, again, wrapped around a bundle resting upon a two-wheeled vehicle, shown by photographs in evidence to resemble a gun caisson.

For the purposes of this opinion it seems necessary to discuss only the first of the constructions complained of. Testifying in his own behalf, the defendant said that this was protest art; and that during the exhibition of the constructions, background music, consisting of war protest songs, was played from a tape. Asked, on cross-examination, as to the use of the flag for the purpose of protest, he said that the object extending from the vertical member of the cross and wrapped in a small flag was representative of a human penis; that tassels at the base of this protrusion represented "probably . . . decorative or pubic hair, depending on what one decides it looks like to him." Asked as to the particular expression and protest intended to be conveyed, the witness said that perhaps the penis represents the sexual act, which by some standards is considered an aggressive act; that organized religion is also symbolized by the figure, which seems to suggest that organized religion is supporting the aggressive acts suggested.

Only recently this court had occasion to give extended consideration to section 1425 of the former Penal Law and specifically to paragraph d of subdivision 16 thereof. With regard specifically to the flag desecration statute it was squarely held that it was a valid statute in that, regardless of the major motivating factor behind its enactment, there was a clear legislative purpose to prevent a breach of the peace; that the Supreme Court long ago in *Halter v. Nebraska* stated: "[I]nsults to a flag have been the cause of war, and indignities put upon it, in the presence of those who revere it, have often been resented and sometimes punished on the spot." This court said that our statute was designed to prevent the outbreak of such violence by discouraging contemptuous and insulting treatment of the flag in public. . . . With regard to Street's purpose—to express indignation and protest—the parallel to the case before us is clear. Here, the expression, if less dramatic, was given far wider public circulation and, in consequence, perhaps, a measurable enhancement of the likelihood of incitement to disorder, by the placement of one of the constructions in a street display window of defendant's gallery on Madison Avenue in the City of New York, and the exhibition and exposure for sale of the companion pieces in the public gallery and mercantile establishment within. Implicit in the invitation to view was the opportunity thereby afforded to join in the protest, or in counterprotest, with the consequent potential of public disorder; or so the trier of the facts could properly find. . . .

While it seems well established that a clear violation of a valid statute may not be saved on First Amendment grounds, it is necessary in this case eventually to reach a somewhat different question, which is, whether or not the act said to constitute the violation is tempered by the application of the First Amendment. In other words, while burning, spitting upon and stomping upon the flag are clearly and inherently disrespectful, do we reach a point where other acts may be performed with regard to the flag which do not so easily admit of the requisite contemptuousness; where the intent behind the act may be of the purest sort, but where the results of the act may nevertheless have the effect which, as Chief Judge Fuld found in *Street*, the statute was validly designed to prevent—the arousement of passions likely to lead to disorder? . . . It becomes clear, upon considering Chief Judge Fuld's statement in *Street*, along with the authorities there cited, and the more recent cases discussed just above, . . . that a person with the purest of intentions may freely proceed to disseminate the ideas in which he profoundly believes, but he may not break a valid law to do it. The flag statute has been repeatedly held valid from the *Halter* case, on down, even through *Hoffman v. United States* and *People v. Cowgill*, where the flag was not, in either case, burned, spit or trampled upon, but was used, in each case, to further political or ideological viewpoints by employment as an article of clothing. There appears no significant difference between those situations and the one we are here considering. The defendant may have a sincere ideological viewpoint, but he must find other ways to express it. Whether defendant thinks so or not, a reasonable man would consider the wrapping of a phallic symbol with the flag an act of dishonor; he would consider the hanging effigy a dishonor; and to a lesser and more debatable extent it might found that wrapping the flag in chains, attaching it to a gas meter, and fashioning the other representations involved, were acts dishonoring the flag. The exhibitor who, as in this case, engages to join the artist in the commercial exploitation of the supposed expression of protest stands in no better position. . . .

Another argument is addressed to the factor of intent; but even if we assume that defendant had an honest political intent in exhibiting these constructions, or that he had no intent at all, that element is not essential to a conviction of violating a statute which is *malum prohibitum.*

No less tenuous is appellant's claim of denial of equal protection, predicated on the provision exempting from the operation of the statute "a certificate, diploma, warrant, or commission of appointment to office, *ornamental picture,* article of jewelry, stationery . . . or newspaper or periodical, on any of which shall be printed . . . said flag . . . disconnected and apart from any advertisement" (former Penal Law, §1425, subd. 16; emphasis supplied); and equally insubstantial is his contention based on the grammatical imperfection apparent in paragraph d of subdivision 16, it being clear beyond dispute that "flag" is the intended object, as it is the explicit object of every other act inhibited by the statute.

The judgment should be affirmed.

FULD, Chief Judge (dissenting).

I cannot agree with the majority that sufficient legitimate public interest is served by preventing the sale and exhibition of works of art—such as those which formed the predicate for the conviction of the defendant Radich—to justify interference with his right to free expression.

The defendant was the proprietor of a second-floor art gallery on Madison Avenue in New York City. He exhibited for sale seven sculptures, termed "constructions," by an artist named Marc Morrel, in which the latter made use of American flags, or what appeared to be parts of such flags, in various provocative shapes and forms to express protest, particularly against the Vietnam War. (See *Life* magazine, March 31, 1967, p. 22.) The defendant was charged with defiling and casting contempt upon the flag of the United States, in violation of section 1425 (subd. 16) of the former Penal Law.

At the trial, the Art News Editor of the *New York Times* testified that he considered the sculptures or constructions to be works of art, more specifically, a form of "protest art" which (he added) was in line with established artistic tradition. The defendant also testified; observing that this "protest art" was exemplified by the works of such artists as Michelangelo, Goya and Picasso, he went on to say that, although the works express a political viewpoint, neither he, nor the artist intended to defile or cast contempt upon the flag. It was his belief, he asserted, that the artist far from intending to do so, was seeking, rather, to convey the idea that others were condemning the flag by committing aggressive acts in its name.

The court, in affirming the conviction, places primary reliance upon *People v. Street,* in which we held that the State may legitimately circumscribe certain acts which are contemptuous of the flag. However, there is nothing in our opinion in that case which suggests that the mere fact that a person chooses to express himself by other than verbal means removes him entirely from the protections of the First Amendment. On the contrary, we wrote as follows:

It is the teaching of the cases that the constitutional guarantee of free speech covers the substance rather than the form of communication and that the right to employ a particular mode of expression will be vindicated only if it has been outlawed, not because of any legitimate State interest, but solely for the purpose of censoring the underlying idea or thought.

In other words, in the absence of a showing that the public health, safety or the well being of the community is threatened, the State may not act to suppress symbolic speech or conduct having a clearly communicative aspect, no matter how obnoxious it may be to the prevailing views of the majority.

Quite obviously, the act which was prosecuted in the *Street* case—the public burning of a flag on a street corner in a section of Brooklyn at a time when feelings undoubtedly ran high following the shooting of James Meredith—posed a threat to public order which the State could legitimately act to prevent. Indeed, in *Street,* we likened the public mutilation of the flag to "shouting epithets at passing pedestrians," a situation patently fraught with danger to the public peace. The same may not, however, be said of the art forms which the defendant before us displayed in the quiet surroundings of his upstairs art gallery on Madison Avenue in midtown Manhattan. In our modern age, the medium is very often the message, and the State may not legitimately punish that which would be constitutionally protected if spoken or drawn, simply because the idea has

been expressed, instead, through the medium of sculpture.

Unlike the situation in the recent case of *Cowgill v. California,* the artist in the present case unquestionably made use of the flag for the purpose of expressing his political philosophy or views, his dissatisfaction with, and opposition to, the Vietnam War and other activities carried on by the Government. The challenged "constructions" were, in effect, but three-dimensional political cartoons. It is quite true that one's political motives may not be relied upon to justify participation in an activity which is otherwise illegal. But it is equally true that an activity which is otherwise innocent may not be treated as criminal solely because of its political content.

Subdivision 16 expressly exempts from prosecution the display of the flag in or on an "ornamental picture," and, presumably, this exemption would apply to other forms of art as well. It is evident that the only reason why these works of Morrel were singled out for prosecution was not because the flag was used in the sculptures but solely because of the particular political message which those sculptures were intended to convey. In a very real sense, therefore, it was not the artist's *act* of making use of the flag which is being punished but solely the *protest* or the political views he was seeking thereby to express.

I have spoken principally of the artist who made the constructions in question. There is even less justification for proceeding against the owner of the gallery in which the works were being exhibited for sale, particularly in view of the absence of any proof that he himself actually intended to defile or cast the flag in contempt. Although it is true that intent need not be an element of a crime—provided it be considered *malum prohibitum*—this is not the case where the challenged conduct involves the expression of political views. The First Amendment is designed not merely to prevent prosecutions but to actively encourage and foster the free dissemination of ideas. Thus, even activity which is not, in itself, subject to the protection of the First Amendment may not be prosecuted in a manner which will have a chilling effect upon the free dissemination of ideas.

In sum, I do not understand how it may reasonably be said that the mere display of Morell's constructions in an art gallery, distasteful though they may be, poses the type of threat to public order necessary to render such an act criminal.

This prosecution, in my view, is nothing more than political censorship falling far outside our holding in *People v. Street.* It should not be constitutionally sustained.

The judgment appealed from should be reversed.

SCILEPPI, BERGAN, BREITEL and JASEN, JJ., concur with GIBSON, J.

FULD, C. J., dissents and votes to reverse in a separate opinion in which BURKE, J., concurs.

Judgment affirmed.

United States ex rel. Radich v. Criminal Court of New York
385 F.Supp. 165 (D.C., S.D.N.Y., 1974)

CANNELLA, District Judge.

. . . On the instant petition, Radich challenges his state conviction upon First and Fourteenth Amendment grounds, specifically, that: (a) the involved statute violates the First Amendment in that casting contempt on the American flag may not constitutionally be made a criminal offense; (b) the statute is unconstitutionally overbroad and vague; and (c) the statute violates the equal protection clause of the Fourteenth Amendment in that it arbitrarily bars sculpture which casts contempt on the flag while permitting other forms of expression, such as pictures, photographs and cartoons which cast contempt on the flag. As the Court finds the recent decision of the Supreme Court in *Spence v. Washington,* to provide a workable framework within which petitioner's First Amendment challenges can be analyzed, it is content in the conclusion that the New York statute is unconstitutional "as applied" to Radich, reserving to later courts the resolution of the broader constitutional questions which have been presented.

In recent years, numerous courts, both state and federal, have been called upon to determine the relationship between statutes prohibiting acts of flag desecration and the First Amendment's guarantee of freedom of speech. Such consideration has produced diverse results, as both the state and federal judiciary have been unable to either agree upon the standard to be applied, or uniformly determine which conduct is to be protected and which is to be proscribed. The commentators, on the other hand, while similarly unable to agree upon a uniform standard for balancing the guarantees of the First Amendment against the interests of the state in prohibiting acts of flag desecration, have almost uniformly opposed the imposition of criminal sanctions for conduct such as that engaged in by Radich. Although the Supreme Court has had several opportunities in years past to consider and define the limits of the protection afforded by the First Amendment to acts of flag desecration, including the direct appeal of petitioner's conviction, it was not until the term just passed that the Court provided direction for lower courts in resolving these controversies.

In the first flag related decision of the 1973 Term, *Smith v. Goguen,* the Court affirmed a First Circuit decision which had granted habeas corpus relief to a state prisoner who had been convicted of violating a Massachusetts statute making it a crime to "treat contemptuously" the flag of the United States. The district court and the court of appeals had concluded that the contempt provision of the Massachusetts flag misuse statute was both unconstitutionally vague and impermissibly overbroad. The Supreme Court affirmed on vagueness grounds alone, finding that the statute failed to draw reasonably clear lines between the kinds of nonceremonial treatment of the flag which are criminal and those which are not. Justice Powell, writing for the Court, specifically declined an invitation to address the substantive First Amendment arguments advanced. Mr. Justice White concurred in the result; the Chief Justice and Justices Blackmun and Rehnquist dissented.

In June of this year, subsequent to its decision in *Smith,* the Supreme Court, in *Spence v. Washington,* reversed the state court conviction of an individual who had been found guilty of violating a Washington statute proscribing improper uses of the flag. Spence, a college student, had hung a United States flag from his apartment house window. The flag was in an upside down position and had attached upon both of its sides a peace symbol fashioned of removable black tape. At trial, Spence testified that he had put the symbol on the flag in protest against the then recent invasion of Cambodia by United States forces and the killings at Kent State University. It was conceded by the state that the sole reason for the arrest was his placing of the peace symbol on the flag and exposing it to public view in that condition. The Supreme Court, in a *per curiam* opinion (three Justices dissenting), reversed the conviction. The Court found that Spence's use of the flag constituted the expression of an idea through activity, and that his conduct was sufficiently imbued with communicative elements as to bring it within the ambit of speech protected by the First Amendment. The Court then held that no state interest which arguably supported the prosecution had been sufficiently impaired by Spence's activity as to warrant the imposition of criminal sanctions. Hence, the Court in *Spence* may be said to have adopted a two-step analysis. First, a determination of whether flag related conduct is within the protections of the First Amendment, and, second, whether, upon the record of the given case, the interests advanced by the state are so substantial as to justify infringement of constitutional rights. Mr. Justice Blackmun concurred in the result and Mr. Justice Douglas separately concurred for reasons advanced by the Supreme Court of Iowa in *State v. Kool.*

In addition to the decisions in *Smith* and *Spence,* the Supreme Court, during the 1973 Term, summarily disposed of five other appeals involving the flag and its relationship with the First Amendment. Several of these summary decisions involved convictions pursuant to statutes similar to that at bar and the action of the Supreme Court with respect to these cases, when read together with the decision in *Spence,* well illuminates the path upon which this Court will now travel. . . .

THE INTERESTS OF THE STATE OF NEW YORK

Having thus concluded that petitioner's exhibition of the sculptures constituted speech and communicative expression coming within the purview of the First Amendment, the Court next turns to consider those state interests which might be advanced to support his conviction and the resulting suppression of expression. In *Spence,* the Court, drawing upon its earlier opinion in *Street v. New York,* addressed itself to three principal interests which conceivably could be called upon to justify state action against flag desecra-

tion: (1) prevention of breach of the peace; (2) protection of the sensibilities of passersby; and (3) preservation of the American flag as an unalloyed symbol of our country. In addition to these three primary interests, the Supreme Court noted certain additional factors which are as pertinent to the instant case as they were to the case then before the Court.

First, this was a privately-owned flag. In a technical property sense it was not the property of any government. . . . Second, appellant displayed his flag on private property. He engaged in no trespass or disorderly conduct. Nor is this a case that might be analyzed in terms of reasonable time, place or manner restraints on access to a public area.

Similarly, there is no evidence in the state court record which would demonstrate that the flags employed in the Morrel constructions were other than privately-owned flags and, it is clear, that the constructions were displayed in Radich's own art gallery; upon private property.

PRESERVATION OF THE FLAG AS AN UNALLOYED SYMBOL

In *Spence,* the Court discussed the state's interest in preserving the flag "as an unalloyed symbol of our country" in the following terms:

Presumably, this interest might be seen as an effort to prevent the appropriation of a revered national symbol by an individual, interest group, or enterprise where there was a risk that association of the symbol with a particular product or viewpoint might be taken erroneously as evidence of governmental endorsement. Alternatively, it might be argued that the interest asserted by the state court is based on the uniquely universal character of the national flag as a symbol. For the great majority of us, the flag is a symbol of patriotism, of pride in the history of our country, and of the service and valor of the millions of Americans who in peace and war have joined together to build and to defend a Nation in which self-government and personal liberty endure. It evidences both the unity and diversity which are America. For others the flag carries in varying degrees a different message. "A person gets from a symbol the meaning he puts into it, and what is one man's comfort and inspiration is another's jest and scorn" [citation omitted]. It might be said that we all draw something from our national symbol, for it is capable of conveying simultaneously a spectrum of meanings. If it may be destroyed or permanently disfigured, it could be argued that it will lose its capability of mirroring the sentiments of all who view it.

But we need not decide in this case whether the interest advanced by the court below is valid. We assume *arguendo* that it is. The statute is nonetheless unconstitutional as applied to appellant's activity. There was no risk that appellant's acts would mislead viewers into assuming that the government endorsed his viewpoint. To the contrary, he was plainly and peacefully protesting the fact that it did not. Appellant was not charged under the desecration statute . . . nor did he permanently disfigure the flag or destroy it. He displayed it as a flag of his country in a way closely analogous to the manner in which flags have always been used to convey ideas. In so assuming *arguendo* the Court stated:

If this interest is valid, we note that it is directly related to expression in the context of activity like that undertaken by appellant. For that reason and because no other governmental interest unrelated to expression has been advanced or can be supported on this record, the four-step analysis of *United States v. O'Brien*, . . . is inapplicable.

Notwithstanding the fact that petitioner has been convicted under the New York desecration statute of casting contempt upon the flag, it can not be said that his display of the Morrel constructions exhibited the flag in a fashion from which "it could be argued that it will lose its capability of mirroring the sentiments of all who view it." The construction and their display would have been valueless as communication and meaningless as protest were the flag not invoked by the artist in the fashion and form in which it was. Unlike the flag which is burned, destroyed or otherwise substantially and permanently disfigured, thereby divesting it of its "capability or mirroring the sentiments of all who view it," Morrel's use of the flag simply transferred the symbol from traditional surroundings to the realm of protest and dissent. This shifting of context did not rape the flag of its universal symbolism. Those who are accustomed to emotions of pride when viewing the flag atop this courthouse, might well have been moved to revulsion when confronted with Morrel's works in the gallery. Others, perhaps, were deeply moved and made proud of our "constitutionally guaranteed 'freedom to be intellectually . . . diverse or even contrary'" when viewing the constructions; persons in whom the flag would otherwise stir no emotion. "A person gets from a symbol the meaning he puts into it, and what is one man's comfort and inspiration is another's jest and scorn." The quality of the flag as a symbol embraced within Morrel's sculptures was the expression intended by their exhibition. Unlike the consumption of the flag when it is burned as the *vehicle* for expression of an idea, the flag as displayed by petitioner in his gallery was itself the idea, the *sine qua non* for the artist's endeavors. The symbol was not consumed by the sculptures, but rather, flourished in all of its communicative majesty, unalloyed and undiminished. "It is the character, not the cloth, of the flag which" the State of New York has interest in preserving and, here, the symbolic character of the flag was neither trammeled upon nor dimmed.

PROTECTION OF THE SENSIBILITIES OF PASSERSBY

The second factor which was stated, analyzed and rejected by the Court in *Spence*, "that the State may have desired to protect the sensibilities of passersby," is similarly unavailing to the State of New York in the instant case.

It is firmly settled that under our Constitution the public expression of ideas may not be prohibited merely because the ideas are themselves offensive to some of their hearers" [citation omitted]. Moreover, appellant did not impose his ideas upon a captive audience. Anyone who might have been offended could easily have avoided the display.

Similarly, in the matter at bar, petitioner did not thrust his ideas upon a captive audience, but rather displayed the constructions in the privacy of his second floor art gallery. Nor can it be said that the construction which was desplayed in the gallery window and visible to persons located on the street below was so unavoidable as to require its suppression.

PRESERVATION OF THE PUBLIC PEACE

In affirming the lower court's conviction of the petitioner, Judge Gibson, speaking for the New York Court of Appeals, stated, "the prime reason for the statute [based upon the legislative history] was not to insure suppression of . . . ideas, but rather to insure preservation of the public peace." The Judge concluded that "a reasonable man would consider the wrapping of a phallic symbol with the flag an act of dishonor; he would consider the hanging effigy a dishonor; and to a lesser and more debatable extent it might be found that wrapping the flag in chains, attaching it to a gas meter, and fashioning the other representations involved, were acts dishonoring the flag," acts which would arouse passions in the average man likely to lead to disorder, thereby warranting abridgement of petitioner's First Amendment rights. This Court finds that such a standard which views the act of display as solely sufficient to allow for the imposition of criminal sanctions, apparently upon the premise that the act creates a possible or hypothetical danger to the public peace, is insufficient predicate upon which the exercise of constitutional rights may be chilled.

This Court has read and reviewed the transcript of petitioner's trial in the New York City Criminal Court and is unable to find in it any objective evidence whatever which would sustain the conclusion that a breach of the peace was either likely to occur, or an imminent result of petitioner's exhibition of the Morrel constructions. There is no evidence that any crowd had gathered outside of the gallery nor is there proof that any disturbance or altercation had occurred within the premises. The display of the Morrel pieces had been in progress for approximately two weeks prior to the time that the state acted, and, aside from an expression of outrage by one group which resulted in a civil law suit, there is absolutely no proof of any reaction whatsoever by any individual who viewed the sculptures. Thus, as in *Spence*, the notion that the state acted in preservation of the public peace "is totally without support in the record."

There is no question but that preservation of the public peace is a valid interest which the state may invoke in order to justify prosecutions for flag desecration. *Spence* and the earlier Supreme Court case of *Street v. New York* so state. Those other cases which have considered the validity of this interest have so concluded. The commentators do not disagree. Rather, the question at bar is to what extent must the state demonstrate the factual existence of this interest, i.e., how imminent must a breach of the peace be, before it can validly act to punish an individual for exercising his First Amendment rights.

Numerous courts have concluded, as did the New York Court of Appeals in *Radich*, that acts of flag desecration are, of themselves, always so inherently inflammatory as to pose so great a danger to the public peace as warrants the state to

act. Other courts have adopted the view that an act of flag desecration standing alone is insufficient provocation to justify the imposition of criminal sanctions or abridge First Amendment rights; other objective evidence which demonstrates the imminence of public unrest or a clear and present danger that a breach of the peace is likely must be adduced before a state may constitutionally act in a given case. A fair reading of *Spence*, and those other cases which have delimited the bounds of First Amendment freedoms, results in the conclusion that the latter view is the only one which is constitutionally sanctioned; the state's interest in preventing a breach of the peace cannot be said to arise merely in its assertion.

As Mr. Justice Holmes long ago stated, "[e]very idea is an incitement." So, too, every act of flag desecration and every employment of the flag in other than ordinary context must be viewed as a provocation, a calling out to others to react and counteract, to express support or disdain. As every expression of ideas may not be trammeled upon in derogation of the First Amendment, so, too, conduct regarding the flag, which is "sufficiently imbued with elements of communication to fall within the scope of the First and Fourteenth Amendments" may not be suppressed solely because it is done or because someone might find the act so reprehensible as to become violent. As has been stated:

a function of free speech under our system of government is to invite dispute. It may indeed best serve its high purpose when it induces a condition of unrest, creates dissatisfaction with conditions as they are, or even stirs people to anger. Speech is often provocative and challenging. It may strike at prejudices and preconceptions and have profound unsettling effects as it presses for acceptance of an idea. That is why freedom of speech, though not absolute, . . . is nevertheless protected against censorship or punishment, unless shown likely to produce a clear and present danger of a serious substantive evil that rises far above public inconvenience, annoyance, or unrest. [Citations omitted.] There is no room under our Constitution for a more restrictive view. For the alternative would lead to standardization of ideas either by legislatures, courts, or dominant political or community groups.

So too New York's undifferentiated fear that the display of the Morrel construction in Radich's gallery might provoke a reasonable person to commit unlawful and disruptive acts is insufficient under the Constitution.

While it is not the duty of this Court in the present case to determine the extent of the objective evidence which must be shown before a state may constitutionally suppress an act of flag desecration, whether the anticipated disorder be imminent or probable or whether such potential disorder present a clear and present danger to the public peace, the Court can unhesitatingly state that New York's unsupported assertion that a breach of peace might have resulted from the exhibition of the Morrel constructions, is not a permissible basis for imposition of criminal sanctions. When the constitutionally guaranteed right to freedom of speech and the free dissemination of ideas, be they popular or unpopular, is to be chilled or abridged, the state must demonstrate more than a mere speculative or hypothetical possibility of disorder; it must present to the trier of facts objective evidence which would lead to the conclusion that, at the very least, a disorder was in fact likely and imminent.

[O]ur task in a given case, and in this case, is to weigh the likelihood of violence against the right of free expression. The danger is that we will overuse "likelihood of violence" in order to be on the safe side. But the framers of the constitutional guarantees must have known they were taking some risk when they inserted the free speech clauses, for many utterances of unpopular ideas are fraught with the possibility of retaliatory action. . . . We must not water down the guarantees by undifferentiated fear or apprehension. *For our part, we will uphold incursions upon symbolic expression on the basis of probable violence only when we are convinced that violence is really probable.*

Our Constitution and the guarantees which are embodied in it are the supreme symbol and law of our nation. Its values and meaning surpass all other symbols and law. In seeking to afford our citizenry the right to speak freely, to assert views which may be unpopular to the majority, and, even, to deprecate those symbols which others hold dear, the framers consciously chose to construct a society and a nation in which the free dissemination of ideas, the thoughts of all free-thinking men, even the smallest dissenting voice, might be heard without fear of prosecution. This is our birthright as Americans. The "freedom to differ is not limited to things that do not matter much. That would be a mere shadow of freedom. The test of its substance is the right to differ as to things that touch the heart of the existing order." Although such freedom is not absolute, it may not lightly be abrogated.

The flag and that which it symbolizes is dear to us, but not so cherished as those high moral, legal and ethical precepts which our Constitution teaches. When our interests in preserving the integrity of the flag conflict with the higher interest of preserving, protecting and defending the Constitution, the latter must prevail, even when it results in the expression of ideas about our flag and nation which are defiant, contemptuous or unacceptable to most Americans.

For its own part, this Court does not subscribe to the views espoused by the petitioner by means of his display of the Morrel constructions, but his right to express his mind is guaranteed by our Constitution and, on the state of this record, the Court finds no cause for the state's abridgement of that right.

CONCLUSION

It is the opinion and decision of this Court that the conviction of petitioner, Stephen Radich, in the Criminal Court of the City of New York, as affirmed by the Appellate Courts of the State of New York, served to deprive him of his rights under the First and Fourteenth Amendments to the Constitution of the United States and that §1425(16)(d) of the New York Penal Law, now §136(d) of the New York General Business Law, is unconstitutional as applied to him.

Let the writ of habeas corpus issue forthwith upon the submission of an appropriate order.

COMMENTS

1. Observe that the defendant in the *Radich* case was the dealer not the artist. Suppose Radich had bargained for a lesser charge, pleaded guilty, and closed the exhibition? What remedy, if any, would Morrell have had? In general, what are the artist's remedies against actual or threatened censorship?

2. Judge Gibson of the New York Court of Appeals refers in his opinion to potential breaches of the peace (by outraged viewers) as a justification for the statute. Was there evi-

dence of such a breach here? Suppose there had been—would that affect your view of the case?

3. As a matter of social policy, do you prefer the result of the New York court case or that of the federal court? Why?

4. Should it make any difference whether the offending display is a work of art or not? Notice that Judge Fuld refers in his dissent to the testimony of the art news editor of the *New York Times*. What was the purpose of such testimony?

5. Do you see any similarity between the *Veronese* and the *Radich* cases?

Graffiti are a problem that can be complicated. Consider the case of Harald Naegeli.

JAMES GRAFF *Art in Jail: The Sprayer of Zurich**

Mainz, West Germany

After five years in West Germany as a celebrated artist, the so-called "sprayer of Zurich" was extradited to Switzerland from here and has recently begun a nine-month prison stint.

Harald Naegeli was found guilty by a Swiss court in 1979 of damaging property in the Zurich area by spraying it with graffiti. In March, West Germany's highest court refused to review a lower-court ruling approving Mr. Naegeli's extradition, marking a turning point in a controversy that has been simmering since the late '70s.

A weighty collection of artists, critics and West German politicians are up in arms over the prison term because they consider Mr. Naegeli's graffiti artistically significant. They view the case not as property damage but as artistic repression, committed in the name of a peculiarly Swiss passion for public cleanliness. Former West German Chancellor Willy Brandt declared his solidarity with Mr. Naegeli, Joseph Beuys and other artists filed a complaint against the Swiss with the European Commission on Human Rights, and German cabinet member Juergen Moellemann even tried to negotiate with the Swiss for an alternative to incarceration. The Swiss were unmoved.

"Switzerland is such a petty bourgeois, money-loving nation that culture is viewed as a threat there," Mr. Naegeli says.

Zurich state prosecutor Marcel Bertschi says culture has nothing to do with it. "Even if Rembrandt or Picasso were to paint on somebody's wall without permission, it would be property damage," he says.

Mr. Naegeli, age 44, with a rumpled academic air and a passion for chess, is by his own reckon-

ing not the kind of man one would expect to be a graffitist. The son of a prominent and wealthy Zurich psychiatrist, he studied art briefly in Paris and made collages before turning to "public art."

In the late '60s, Mr. Naegeli sold one of his works to the Zurich Kunsthaus, which has since removed several of his later efforts from its outer walls. Mr. Naegeli acknowledges his debt to such modern masters as Pablo Picasso, Paul Klee and Joan Miro, but considers his formal education insignificant.

Mr. Naegeli first reached for the spray can in 1977 as an act of protest against what he saw as the increasing depersonalization of Zurich through large, concrete buildings. "I was very irritated and wounded by the destruction of the city," he says. "I wanted to attack the architecture."

Mr. Naegeli began with more or less typical slogans on public buildings. On banks, for instance, he wrote: "Help me, Jesus. I love only money."

But such run-of-the-mill graffiti left Mr. Naegeli unsatisfied. "I found that people could read it quickly and then say, 'Yea, OK,' or 'Oh, no' and that was that. Since I had always drawn, I suddenly realized that I should use figures."

Mr. Naegeli roamed the streets of Zurich after midnight with a single spray can in a plastic bag. The idea of protest was still central, but Mr. Naegeli decided he wanted to create art as well. His figures of women, long-limbed and elastic jesters, fish and other-worldly beings were drawn within seconds with a minimum of lines and a maximum of movement.

"The running, chasing, dancing lines," critic

Manfred Schneckenburger wrote, "put their snakelike fingers to the wounds we have hacked in our cities, diagnosing the agony of unimaginative concrete."

The "sprayer of Zurich" soon gained a local notoriety. A group of businessmen established a bounty of 3,000 Swiss francs (about $1,300) for information leading to his arrest, while police patrolled the streets with dogs in an effort to catch the graffitist red-handed.

Mr. Naegeli avoided capture with a combination of luck and camouflage. For example, in Zurich he often posed as a man walking his dog; in the southern Swiss town of Tessin he pretended to be a conventional watercolorist.

In June 1979 the police finally caught Mr. Naegeli in the act. He fled the country and was sentenced in absentia to nine months in prison and restitution of $45,000 in cleaning costs. "With unprecedented consistency and ruthlessness," the court's official judgement read, Mr. Naegeli had "made the inhabitants of Zurich insecure for years and shaken their legally justified belief in the inviolability of property." Mr. Naegeli says that's a compliment.

Altogether, Mr. Naegeli says he has sprayed about 8,000 figures in 30 European cities. Most have been removed. The city of Cologne found the most effective method to be a combination of boiling water applied at very high pressure, and considerable elbow grease. The city of Stuttgart fined Mr. Naegeli $1,110 for property damage, while Frankfurt's cultural adviser had Mr. Naegeli's work put under city protection.

The German art world seemed to jump at the chance Mr. Naegeli provided to show that it was open-minded and not shackled by such bourgeois notions as property damage. The sprayer's expressed intention to "make art that doesn't fit into museums or the rest of the art business"

didn't deter his supporters. The Higher School of Art in Wiesbaden invited him to apply for a guest professorship, the mayor of Osnabruck encouraged him to spray in his city, bar and cafe owners offered to pay for original Naegelis sprayed in their establishments, and museums and galleries sent proposals for exhibitions.

But Mr. Naegeli has refused all offers of payment, "in defense of my own autonomy." Nor has he sprayed his work in galleries or museums: "That's no longer graffiti, those are pictures."

In 1982 the Cologne Art Union displayed photographs of Mr. Naegeli's graffiti in a joint exhibition with a New York graffitist named Fred, who sprays on canvas and sells his work in several European galleries. "These people simply have no political idea," Mr. Naegeli says of his colleagues from the New York subways. "They are striving for a career in society and are satisfied if they make it into the art market." At the same time, Mr. Naegeli acknowledges that his own independence rests largely on the inheritance he received when his mother died in 1973.

The West German government conveniently ignored the Swiss request for Mr. Naegeli's extradition because of all the support he received. But when he returned from a trip to Norway in August 1983, a computer check at the Danish border uncovered Interpol's warrant for his arrest.

With his legal appeals exhausted, Mr. Naegeli has gone to jail confident that his fate has destroyed "the false image the Swiss uphold as the world's freest country." The only Swiss concession in the case has been the suggestion that it would look kindly on a request for mercy. Mr. Naegeli will not consider making such a request. "I'd rather go to prison than acknowledge the state's authority by begging it for mercy," he says. "In the future I will put all my hope on the utopia of art."

COMMENT

In the case of Harald Naegeli, is censorship involved? Suppose his art consisted of burning offensive buildings or breaking windows, always with the utmost care to prevent injury to human life. Would putting him in jail be a repressive act?

CENSORSHIP AND ART MUSEUMS

The Los Angeles County Museum, which is supported in part from public funds, came under attack by the county board of supervisors because of an exhibition the museum was soon to open. A story in the *Los Angeles Times* on March 23, 1966 by Harry Trimborn, and one on

March 24 by Peter Bart, described the objections of members of the board, who urged that the museum remove certain works and parts of works from what was labeled a revolting and pornographic exhibition. Although the county counsel believed that the board had the authority to order the works removed and that their statement was "tantamount to an order," the museum officials treated it as a request.

The exhibition of paintings and three-dimensional tableaux by Edward Kienholz was defended by the executive committee of the museum in a statement that said in part: "Mr. Kienholz, in developing new art forms, has achieved international recognition as a commentator on important and real, if not pleasant, aspects of society." The committee said that it was the responsibility of the museum's professional staff to decide on the artistic worthiness of exhibitions. The request of the board of supervisors was seen as a restriction on the museum's obligation to present works "that represent an honest statement by a serious artist." The museum officials declared that the proposal for the show had received approval of, first, the modern art staff, then the staff as a whole, and finally the Contemporary Art Council, which includes important local collectors.

One of the supervisors had suggested that the exhibition was designed as a retaliatory parting shot by Dr. Richard F. Brown, the former director of the museum, whom the supervisor said had been fired. Brown denied he had been fired and said the proposal for the exhibition had come not from him but from another member of the staff. Brown remarked that the museum decided on the exhibition "in spite of its controversial nature of content . . . in all sincerity because the professionals at the museum—with the help of others in the art world—decided that Kienholz was one of the most vital and important artists working in Southern California today."

Kienholz himself commented that he was unhappy about the controversy. "I am not interested in that kind of publicity. It can only hurt, not help. People may now come to see my work for the wrong reasons." He stated that the works represent the human condition without sham and hypocrisy, and, he added, "I want to take [the viewers] up to the point of seeing them and let them go on from there."

The two works in the exhibition in particular that had been called pornographic were "Roxy's," which represents a room in a house of prostitution, and "Back Seat Dodge," depicting a couple, the female clothed, the male made of chicken wire with no clothing, reclining in an amorous embrace, and while the legs of the female figure are apart the male figure is not *in situ*. The present director commented that the museum intended to show "Back Seat Dodge" with the door closed, although docents conducting tours might open it if they wished, that a one-dollar fee was being charged to enter, and that no one under eighteen would be allowed to see the exhibition.

Warren M. Dorn, the supervisor who initiated the board's action with a letter to the museum's board of trustees and who was seeking the Republican nomination for governor, also objected to the reclining female figure in "Roxy's." That tableaux shows, among other things, the jacket of an Army sergeant and a portrait of General Douglas MacArthur hanging on the wall. Dorn said the presence of these objects was "unpatriotic." "I am most vehemently opposed to having this kind of expression shown by a public institution to the public at large," Dorn stated. "While certain of the objects or creations are quite meaningless, others are most revolting and, I feel, pornographic in nature. . . . This kind of expression is not art in any sense as far as I am personally concerned and I feel it would be most unfortunate if, under the guise of art, this type of thing is shown to the public." While he said that the supervisors should not "in any way" restrict the museum in its choice of works of art, he added, "Certainly some of these so-called works of art . . . go way beyond the limits of public decency."

Supervisor Frank G. Bonnelli called the exhibition "a dastardly thing." Another, Kenneth Hahn, who was considering running for the nomination of lieutenant governor, said he would move to reduce the salaries of the museum staff if the exhibition were not canceled. There was speculation that the supervisors might attempt to cut off county funds for the museum. In the end, however, the exhibition opened, and funds were not cut off.

THE HANS HAACKE CASE

The following series of letters and editorials explores the disagreement between artists and museums over the function of art in society.

Correspondence Between Haacke and the Guggenheim Museum*

From: Hans Haacke

To: All interested parties

Re: Cancellation of Haacke one-man exhibition at Guggenheim Museum

Date: New York, April 3, 1971

On April 1, 1971, I was informed by Thomas Messer, Director of the Solomon R. Guggenheim Museum, that he had cancelled the exhibition of my work scheduled to open on April 30, 1971, because three major works for the show dealt with specific social situations. In his opinion, such subjects do not belong in museums unless they come in a generalized or symbolic form.

Despite my offer to modify two of the works in ways that would not affect their integrity, but which eliminated all grounds for Mr. Messer's charge of "muckracking," he persisted in his position.

Mr. Messer is wrong on two counts: First, in his confusion of the political stand which an artist's work may assert with a political stand taken by the museum that shows this work; secondly, in his assumption that my pieces advocate any political cause. They do not.

Two of the three works are presentations of large Manhattan real estate holdings (photographs of the facades of the properties and documentary information collected from the public records of the County Clerk's office). The works contain no evaluative comment. One set of holdings are mainly slum-located properties owned by a group of people related by family and busi-

ness ties. The other system is the extensive real estate interests, largely in commercial properties, held by two partners.

On March 25, I met Mr. Messer's objections of possible libel and "muckracking" by substituting fictitious names for the principals and generalizing their addresses.

The third work is a poll of the Guggenheim Museum's visitors, consisting of ten demographic questions (age, sex, education, etc.) and ten opinion questions on current socio-political issues ranging from "Do you sympathize with Women's Lib?" to "In your opinion, should the general orientation of the country be more conservative or less conservative?" The answers to the questions are to be tabulated and posted daily as part of the piece. Following standard polling practices, I tried to frame the questions so that they do not assert a political stance, are not inflammatory and do not prejudge the answers. I have conducted polls of the art public previously at the Howard Wise Gallery, at the Museum of Modern Art and at the Jewish Museum.

The three pieces in question are examples of the "real-time systems" which have constituted my work for many years. A brief explanatory statement about my work was contained in the announcement for my last New York show at the Howard Wise Gallery in 1969:

The working premise is to think in terms of systems; the production of systems, the interference with and the exposure of existing systems. Such an approach is concerned with the operational

---

*Letters reprinted by permission of writers. See also "The Guggenheim Cancels Haacke's Show," *New York Times,* April 7, 1971; *Village Voice,* April 15, 1971.

structure of organizations, in which transfer of information, energy and/or material occurs. Systems can be physical, biological or social, they can be man-made, naturally existing or a combination of any of the above. In all cases verifiable processes are referred to.

Since the Guggenheim invitation resulted from that show, Mr. Messer could have had no doubts about the nature of my work. In turn, I had no reason to suspect that any of my work was unacceptable to the Museum. Reference to our social and political environment by many different artists and in many different forms are a frequent feature at exhibitions in New York Museums.

It was only during this past January that I learned, for the first time and after working on the show for more than 6 months, that Mr. Messer had any qualms about my work with social systems, and it was not until mid-March, that he told me specifically that the Guggenheim Museum had a strict policy of barring work that referred to the social environment in other than symbolic, indirect or generalized ways.

After accepting the Guggenheim invitation a year ago, I deferred invitations to three other museum shows in Paris, Krefeld and Buenos Aires, so that I could concentrate my energies upon this project.

If I wanted to remain true to my philosophical premises, I could not comply with Mr. Messer's insistent demands to essentially modify or eliminate the three works. Verifiability is a major ingredient of the social, biological and physical systems which I consider as mutually complementary parts of the encompassing whole.

Whatever one's esthetic opinion may be, it would seem to be obvious that the Museum has no right to ban or censor the work of an invited artist just because it may deal with political or social issues. By doing so, Mr. Messer is guilty of censorship and infringes on the artist's right to free expression within the walls of the Guggenheim Museum.

Mr. Messer has taken a stand which puts him completely at variance with the professed attitudes of all the world's major museums except for those located in countries under totalitarian domination and must put him in potential conflict with every artist who accepts an invitation to show his work at the Guggenheim Museum.

*   *   *

The Solomon R. Guggenheim Museum, 1071 Fifth Avenue, New York City 10028

March 19, 1971

Mr. Hans Haacke
95 East Houston Street
New York, New York

Dear Hans Haacke:

You asked me to write to you about my misgivings concerning your implementation of the planned Haacke show at the Guggenheim Museum. Let me therefore review the whole matter:

When we began our joint exhibition project, you outlined a threefold investigation and proposed to devote separate exhibits to physical, biological, and social systems. From subsequent detailed outlines, it appeared that the social category would include a real-estate survey pointing through word and picture to alleged social malpractices. You would name, and thereby publicly expose, individuals and companies whom you consider to be at fault. After consultation with the Foundation's president and with advice from our legal counsel, I must inform you that we cannot go along with such an exhibition outline.

From a legal point of view it appears very doubtful that your findings could be so verified as to be unassailable if a libel suit were directed against The Solomon R. Guggenheim Foundation. Verification of your charge would be beyond our capacity while, on the other hand, unchecked acceptance of your allegations could have consequences that we are not prepared to risk.

Considered from the vantage point of the Museum's purpose and function, a muckraking venture under the auspices of The Solomon R. Guggenheim Foundation also raises serious questions. We have held consistently that under our Charter we are pursuing esthetic and educational objectives that are self-sufficient and without ulterior motive. On those grounds, the trustees have established policies that exclude active engagement toward social and political ends. It is well understood, in this connection, that art may have social and political *consequences,* but these, we believe, are furthered by indirection and by the generalized, exemplary force that works of art may exert upon the environment, not, as you propose, by using political means to achieve political ends, no matter how desirable these may appear in themselves. We maintain, in other words, that while art cannot be arbitrarily con-

214 E 3 St.
Block 385 Lot 11
5 story walk-up old law tenement

Owned by Harpsel Realty Inc., 608 E 11 St., NYC
Contracts signed by Harry J. Shapolsky, President('65)
                    Martin Shapolsky, President('64)
Principal Harry J. Shapolsky(according to Real Estate
Directory of Manhattan)

Acquired 8-21-1963 from John the Baptist Foundation,
c/o The Bank of New York, 48 Wall St., NYC,
for $237 600.- (also 7 other bldgs.)

$150 000.- mortgage at 6% interest, 8-19-1963, due
8-19-1968, held by The Ministers and Missionaries
Benefit Board of the American Baptist Convention,
475 Riverside Drive, NYC (also on 7 other bldgs.)

Assessed land value $25 000.- , total $75 000.- (including 212 and 216 E 3 St.) (1971)

216 E 3 St.
Block 385 Lot 11
5 story walk-up old law tenement

Owned by Harpsel Realty Inc., 608 E 11 St., NYC
Contracts signed by Harry J. Shapolsky, President('63)
                    Martin Shapolsky, President('64)
Principal Harry J. Shapolsky(according to Real Estate
Directory of Manhattan)

Acquired 8-21-1963 from John the Baptist Foundation,
c/o The Bank of New York, 48 Wall St., NYC
for $237 600.-(also 7 other bldgs.)

$150 000.- mortgage at 6% interest, 8-19-1963, due
8-19-1968, held by The Ministers and Missionaries
Benefit Board of the American Baptist Convention,
475 Riverside Drive, NYC (also on 7 other bldgs.)

Assessed land value $25 000.-, total $75 000.- (including 212-14 E 3 St.) (1971)

228
Bl
24

Ow
Con

Ac
c/
fo

$1
in
he
The

Ass

Hans Haacke. Excerpt from "Shapolsky et al. Manhattan Real Estate Holdings, a Real Time Social System, as of May 1, 1971." (Reproduced by courtesy of the artist.)

fined, our institutional role is limited. Consequently, we function within such limits, leaving to others areas which we consider outside of our professional competence.

From earlier conversations we had on this subject, it was my understanding that our premise would be acceptable to you and I still hope it is. In itself, the presentation of systems, whether physical, biological, or social, poses no problem and your capacity as an artist to imbue such orders with symbolic significance renders each of them esthetically susceptible and thereby a fit subject matter for a museum. By contrast, the implied charge that you propose to inject would render the same displays inappropriate for presentation in this museum though not necessarily elsewhere since it would hopelessly confuse assumptions under which we now function.

Please let me know as soon as possible what your intentions are. I hope very much that we can proceed with the Haacke show without diluting your creative intentions but also without prejudice to our institutional code.

> Yours very sincerely,
>
> *Thomas M. Messer*
> Director

JOSEPH JAMES AKSTON AND THOMAS M. MESSER *Editorials on the Haacke Case**

The issues underlying the cancellation of the Hans Haacke exhibition at the Guggenheim Museum go far deeper than a simple misunderstanding between an artist and a museum director. There is, in fact, a general disagreement between artists and the cultural institutions in regard to what is the function of art in society. Because of the importance of the Haacke case, we are devoting our editorial page to a guest statement by Thomas Messer, Director of the Guggenheim Museum.

Much of the contemporary art has gone beyond traditional aesthetic boundaries in order to deal with reality and life. Hans Haacke's systems are real, rather than symbolic, systems; therefore they can be "offensive" enough to change something in society, although their intent is less political than Picasso's *Guernica* or Rauschenberg's series of anti-war prints. Theoretically, an artist is now allowed to do anything he wants, as long as the work is clearly distinct from reality and contained within the set limits of painting and sculpture. Thus, cultural boundaries have actually replaced censorship by taking away some of the effective power of art. In a similar way, almost anything can be shown today in a movie, written in a book, or presented on stage because there is a general agreement that whatever is said or shown is not true but "artistic." Evidently, this is one of the reasons why artists are now trying to make their works more real—so as to become effective again. . . .

> *Joseph James Akston*
> President and Editor

Guest Editorial by Thomas Messer:

It would be tempting to use this page for a refutation of various allegations made in connection with the cancellation of the Hans Haacke exhibition by the Guggenheim Museum. But the issues that have developed around this incident are too important and too full of implications for the future relationship between museums and artists to be reduced to the mere airing of grievances. It seems preferable therefore to focus upon the area of doubt and uncertainty that this and similar occurrences at other museums have recently brought out.

Haacke proposed to show photographs of slum scenes as a pictorial commentary upon malpractices in local real estate ownership. As a part of Manhattan's landscape these subjects, with their social implications, would not ordinarily have caused a problem. What did raise questions and what in our minds introduced a highly dubious dimension was the artist's decision to label each photograph with a card giving the owners' names, addresses, and other particulars. No evaluative comment was proposed, it is true, but none was needed. The photographs of

---

*From "Editorial," *Arts*, vol. 45, no. 8 (Summer 1971), p. 4. Copyright © 1971 by Arts Magazine. Reprinted by permission.

the slum properties spoke for themselves. The property owners, individuals and companies, were to be held up to public scrutiny and embarrassment without warning and without an available forum for rebuttal. The required information culled from public records was to be awakened from archival slumber through the power of art in an implicit accusation staged under the auspices of an art museum. The trustees of the Solomon R. Guggenheim Foundation and I feared the possibility of legal action and we foresaw procedural complications of many kinds if the museum were to be propelled into extra-artistic situations beyond its natural scope. After unsuccessful efforts at a mutually satisfactory compromise, the Haacke show was cancelled. The simplest and most compelling reason for such a painful decision rests on our belief that Haacke's intentions and his proposed action were incompatible with the purpose of an art museum for which, on different levels, the trustees and the director bear responsibility.

Should social malpractices be exposed if the evidence is dependable and verifiable? Certainly, but not through the auspices of an art museum. It is freely admitted that this conclusion is self-protective, that is, protective of the museum's functions as we currently understand it. Individuals and companies who would have suddenly found themselves the unsuspecting targets of a work of art could be expected to react against the artist as well as his museum sponsor. The possibility of a libel suit resulting from such a situation is therefore not farfetched. But the museum's sponsorship would hardly seem defensible even if the legal effects proved to be containable through the presumably unassailable nature of the assembled documentation—a rather large assumption on the part of the artist.

A precedent would, in any case, have been set for innumerable analogous presentations with predictably damaging effects upon the museum's central function. What would, for instance, prevent another artist from launching, again via a work of art, a pictorial documentation of police corruption in a particular precinct? What would stand in the way of a museum-sponsored artist attack upon a particular cigarette brand which the documentation assembled for this purpose would show to be a national health risk?

Where would such involvements lead the museum if in all such instances the party singled out for public scrutiny responded through lawsuits,

counter propaganda, and other means at their disposal. The answer is clear: the museum would be reduced to a forum for causes which are not within its domain. The attempt to remedy social ills through direct action on the socio-political level is beyond the museum's present capacity, and it is highly questionable whether an art institution should equip itself for such an undertaking. The consequences of such a course could only be the destruction of an established art purpose as commonly understood. The Haacke proposal relating to his "social system" display as he conceived of it thus posed a direct threat to the museum's functioning within its stated and accepted premises.

The issue has other, more deeply situated levels which are related, though not identical, to the preceding discussion. I am referring to the blurred and ever-elusive limits of art. Historic hindsight invites particular caution for anyone who contemplates an *off-limits* declaration for man-made material conceived as a work of art. It would be a contradiction of past experience to suggest that a particular medium (say photographs accompanied by standard filing cards), or a particular subject matter (say the Manhattan real estate (scene), were for these reasons alone aesthetically ineligible. After the incorporation of Schwitters' collages, Duchamp's readymades, Rauschenberg's combines, or the communicational subject matter of Pop art into the mainstreams of art, Haacke's real estate-cum-filing cards subject-medium might be joining an already venerable tradition.

Where do we draw the line? With the revealed identities of private individuals and the clear intention to call their actions into question, and by a concomitant reduction of the work of art from its potential metaphoric level to a form of photo journalism concerned with topical statements rather than with symbolic expression.

It has been suggested that I had no business admitting Haacke into a museum situation if I doubted his artistry. On the basis of work that I had seen prior to any museum initiative, I had no reason to doubt his *capacity* to be an artist when he chose to function as one. To the degree to which an artist deliberately pursues aims that lie beyond art, his very concentration upon ulterior ends stands in conflict with the intrinsic nature of the work as an end in itself. The conclusion is inescapable that the sense of inappropriateness that was felt from the start toward Haacke's "social system" exhibit was due to an aesthetic weakness which interacted with a forcing of art boundaries. The tensions within this contradiction in the work itself transferred itself from it onto the museum environment and beyond it into society at large. Eventually, the choice was between the acceptance of or the rejection of an alien substance that had entered the art museum organism. Of these two, the latter course, on balance, seemed preferable.

A related consideration has to do with consequences alone: Haacke's work implicates certain individuals from the safety of its museum sanctuary. Protected by the armor of art, the work reaches out into the socio-political environment where it affects not the large conscience of humanity, but the mundane interest of particular parties. Upon the predictable reaction of society the work, turned weapon, would recede into its immune "art-self" to seek shelter within the museum's temporary custody. Ad absurdum: If anything an artist proposes may be art and as such immune from the judgments and the criteria of life, what is there to prevent an artist-sponsored murder and subsequent insistence upon the irrelevance of ordinary justice?

The incident at the Guggenheim Museum is, perhaps, the most dramatic among similar conflicts but by no means an isolated one. Parallel developments have occurred in other museums and more of the same may be predicted unless there is a change of both procedure and attitude among artists as well as among museums. Haacke's show would not have reached a crisis resulting in the action taken if the traditional system of selection from completed objects had not rather abruptly given way to one predicated upon an improvisational working mode. This, in turn, came about through the evolution of a significant art current from object to concept, with a resultant blurring of formerly clear dividing lines between art and idea. The Haacke-Guggenheim confrontation, despite its painful aspects, may therefore have contributed to an urgently needed clarification. The sense of mutual offense somehow must be overcome so that a new community and interest between artists and art institutions may be developed. The mutual dependence which exists among contemporary artists and the modern art museum demands resolution of overaccentuated contradictions.

Thomas M. Messer, Director
The Solomon R. Guggenheim Museum

Editorial: Artists vs. Museums*

Several recent conflicts between artists and museums have focused attention on a new set of emerging problems. Relations between artists and museums are not likely to get easier, as basic premises for new kinds of art become more explicitly social or political, and as much new art continues to merge is themes, methods and mediums, if not its content, with life.

The most striking example of this kind of conflict is the cancellation by the Guggenheim Museum of Hans Haacke's exhibition, just a month before it was scheduled to open in late April. There was another sudden cancellation, earlier—less conspicuous because it happened in Canada—that of Carl Andre's traveling exhibition, to have been seen at the National Gallery of Canada, Ottawa, and subsequently in Vancouver. Also this spring a large exhibition of Sol LeWitt's was called off after it was well underway, due to a series of terminal misunderstandings between the artist and the New York Cultural Center.

Each of these episodes has its own particular circumstances; simply to become indignant is not much help in understanding complicated issues, and to generalize leads only to confused conclusions. In fact, each of these matters developed along very different lines. Nevertheless, taken together, they seem to form the beginning of a pattern (there have been other similar incidents too), symptomatic of a failure of communication between museums and artists (and art is about communication); it would be very unfortunate if this eventually were to jeopardize the involvement of museums with new art.

The Haacke affair is complex, with its implied mix of politics and esthetics with potential legal problems; the museum stated that certain of his new pieces, specifically two which identified

---

*From "Editorial: Artists vs. Museums," *ARTnews*, vol. 70, no. 3, May 1971, p. 25. Copyright © 1971 by ARTnews Associates. Reprinted by permission.

owners of large chunks of New York real estate, were possibly libelous, and in any case inappropriate to an art museum. Andre's case, on the other hand, involved straightforward radical politics: it was rumored that he might declaim the inflammatory manifesto of the Front for the Liberation of Quebec at his poetry reading which was to open the Ottawa show; when his poetry reading was canceled, Andre declined to show in Ottawa at all. Then Vancouver pulled out for obscurely related reasons. (Surely a better way could have been found to handle a problem which, after all, was merely anticipated—such as invoking the local laws, should the eventuality take place.) Again quite distinct was the situation which led LeWitt to call off his New York Cultural Center show: foremost was the fact that the time required for him to complete a group of wall drawings *in situ* had not been provided for in preliminary scheduling, that director Karshan would not reschedule, and that this time would have had to come out of the period allotted to the show. This clearly indicated a fundamental incomprehension by the museum of the nature of LeWitt's work.

Many artists today share a need to reach beyond traditional forms of art, and in doing so, they more often than not implicitly reject the art establishment and its institutions. It is important to recognize this, although it is difficult to say to what extent it may apply to each of the artists involved in these recent episodes. Many of these same artists have a greater need of these institutions than ever before, to validate and define their work as art, since the works' own boundaries are, in many cases, dematerialized or nearly dissolved. Perhaps it is this basic (and in some cases possibly debilitating) dependency on museums which created the irresistible desire on the part of so many artists to pass judgment on them, implicate them and engage them in challenges, often with a curious combination of self-righteousness and unrealistic avenging zeal. Assuming that some kind of constructive artist-museum cooperation is desirable and should continue, there are obviously responsibilities to be clarified on both sides.

An examination of some of the implications of the Haacke-Guggenheim affair is instructive: Haacke's show, covering the last years, was to culminate in three major new works of an informational nature, part of his continuing investigation of what he refers to as "physical, biological and social systems." These pieces took conclusive form only this January, although plans for the show had been under way for nearly a year. The museum objected to two of the new pieces, dealing with New York real-estate, ranging from commercial to luxury to slum. The information was culled from public records on file with the County Clerk. Two large holdings were selected by the artist, a pattern of ownership identified, and the data photographed and mapped. Several hundred photos with captions would have been the main elements of the pieces. According to Haacke, no "evaluative comment" was included. Whether such comment was either intended or implied is subject to dispute. Curator Edward Fry, who originated and was organizing the show, considers the pieces neutral and indeed, in rather traditional terms he calls them "part of the New York landscape." Haacke says that he envisioned the works as "revealing an existing system," and as a logical extension of his earlier technologically based pieces, as well as his more recent work.

On the other hand, the Guggenheim's director, Thomas M. Messer, interpreted the works as a "muckraking venture" which the museum could not encompass because of its policy to avoid "active engagement toward social and political ends." Both Messer and several trustees also feared libel suits. Messer's concern with institutional responsibility was an unavoidable factor in the case, as any publisher, theater owner, gallery owner or other responsible party who has ever been busted for sponsoring a controversial presentation can attest.

A further complication was that, after the museum's initial objection to the pieces, Haacke had agreed to partially veil the identities of the principal owners, and not specify exact addresses. However the changes which he made were, in the museum's view, so slight as to be even more provocative. At this point, there was some intransigence on both sides, time was short, and the whole thing was called off.

Artist and museum each immediately issued statements of their positions, and their somewhat differing versions of what had happened. There was apparently some ambiguity as to what the artist and the museum thought the other had agreed to, and was committed to. There was also the pressure of deadlines. Altogether, things could have hardly come out worse for all concerned. The artist lost his show, and lost a great deal of time—his protest that he was badly treated is not unfounded. At the same time, the resultant publicity casts the museum as a villain despite its many recent excellent efforts in showing new work (such as the last Guggenheim International) and gives it a black eye. The museum also lost much time and money. It is obvious that, whatever the details of the case, and there is much more than alluded to here, the fragile web of understanding between artist, curator and director broke. Cries of "censorship" immediately arose on all sides—not without basis—but the situation is more complex, and goes well beyond this issue alone.

Haacke's real estate pieces raise delicate questions as to whether it is legal—or fair—to appropriate identifiable private individuals for a work of art. Where is the line between public and private material? What if the artist even inadvertently distorts public material? What is invasion of privacy in this context? And where do such works stand ethically, aside from legally? Can public business records be damning, when no conclusions are drawn? Is the mere focusing of attention grounds for libel? Do the facts alone condemn? Are very large property holders still private individuals? Haacke's pieces differ from more familiar, outrightly political works dealing with public figures; he lifts individuals out of obscurity for public scrutiny, if not for public judgment, indeed, unlike the investigative reporter he likens himself to ("Museums should be like newspapers," he says), in these pieces he seems to strike at random, like a bolt from the blue.

Intimately connected with whatever difficulties Haacke's real-estate works may hold is the straightforwardness of his presentation of the material which, according to Messer, is a direct transposition from life, sacrificing the "immunity" of the work of art in treating specific material, as well as its power of transcendence through metaphor. This "immunity" is, of course, precisely what the artist wants to discard. Paradoxically, in the outcome of the confrontation which Haacke's work provoked, perhaps because it touched upon a peculiarly American sensitiveness to those nerve-ends labeled "privacy" and "property," the work was in fact both powerful (in the sense of efficacious) and metaphorical beyond anything Haacke might have envisioned in the way of public effect; it is perhaps stronger canceled than it would have been exhibited. Yet one wonders at this mysteriously potent quality of aggravation, for the works, seen in themselves, appear close to what Haacke calls them—neutral

disclosure of existing situations. Indeed, partly because of their visual dullness (hundreds of nearly identical building facades), partly because of the difficulty of really digesting written material in a museum situation, and partly because of the apparently very real absence of "social realist" comment or any other kind, the pieces seem, in fact, as innocuous as can be.

By contrast, Rauschenberg or, more blatantly, Fahlstrom or Peter Saul, present in framed "pictures" subject matter which is far more inflammatory in a specific sense than anything Haacke has proposed—even including his piece in last summer's Museum of Modern Art "Information Show," which was a poll of visitors' attitudes about Gov. Rockefeller's position on Vietnam (on the basis of which frankly provocative item one might have thought the Guggenheim would have been forewarned, long before its own Haacke show blew this spring). In the cases of Fahlstrom or Saul, who are often openly insulting and purposefully obscene, one may conjecture that the boundaries of a traditional art work can, at present, effectively neutralize subject matter. Thus questions about the Haacke pieces are partly about what happens when art extends itself to an unfamiliar degree into real life. To this extent, regardless of opposing opinions, the work *does* and means to become political.

In view of the directions many artists are now taking, it is clear that museums must develop more satisfactory ways of working with them— new flexibility, as well as new alertness to problems which may arise. Museums may have to resign themselves to some unforeseen shocks, and at times may find it preferable to stand by their choices despite qualms, running certain risks in the interest of broader ends. At the same time, artists must realize that they cannot have *carte blanche*, that there are certain inherent contradictions to the aims of artists and museums, that at present the very existence of museums depends on the voluntary support and good will of often conservative individuals—this is the reality of the museum structure in the U.S., since it is not state supported to any significant degree. Now that artists are frequently approaching museums as either forums or sites, pieces are often tailored to an occasion or place, and made just before the show. Some sort of specific knowledge of artists' intentions obviously must be grasped long in advance, and a curator-turned-impresario must keep in close touch with developments. This is only fair to both sides, since it is obvious that this is a problematic as well as fruitful symbiosis, given the inherent conservatism of museums, and the inherent radicalism of many artists. Aware of this, many artists should, and doubtless will, seek alternatives to formal museum presentations. But as they continue to work together, continued *contretemps* will pose a threat to museum involvement with the avant garde, which should not be lightly cast away by either side, in view of the difficulties with which it was attained, and the benefits to be had all around, not least of all for the public.—E.C.B.

Artists vs. Museums, continued*

ARTnews' May *Editorial* examined recent clashes between artists and specifically focused on the cancellation of Hans Haacke's exhibition at the Guggenheim, which was to have taken place last spring.

The following is a response from Hans Haacke:

In your editorial on the Guggenheim Museum's cancellation of my exhibition I found several inaccuracies in reporting, deplorable omissions and an unfortunate confusion of the real issues. The net result is that an uninformed reader, in spite of your expressions of sympathy for my situation, must come to the conclusions that the Guggenheim might have had a point.

You repeatedly and unquestioningly adopt the Museum's argument that my works were potentially libelous and plead for understanding of Thomas Messer's "institutional responsibility" as the Museum's director.

The Guggenheim's legal counsel in this affair was Mr. Chauncey Newlin, a member of its Board of trustees, who has intimated, in conversations with me and journalists, that he personally disapproves of the kind of work I do. No unbiased outside lawyer was consulted by the Museum nor would Mr. Messer accept my attorney's offer to meet with Mr. Newlin, because as he said at the time, the legal aspects of the affair were only a side issue.

Even before I replaced the individual names in the two real-estate works with fictitious names as a gesture of good will, there had never been any grounds for libel. This is the consensus of several lawyers familiar with the material in question. The display of information retrieved from public records of the County Clerk's office, without evaluative comment, is legally unassailable. In a recent letter to a New York museum official, my attorney, Jerald Ordover, wrote: "It is my opinion that Hans Haacke's two 'real estate' pieces are not defamatory or libelous and could not result in any legal action taken against the Museum or Gallery which exhibited them."

Your statement, "there was some intransigence on both sides, time was short, and the whole thing was called off, is incorrect, except for Mr. Messer's intransigence. At his request I submitted samples of the real-estate pieces, with fictitious names in place of the individual names, together with the questionnaire for my poll of the Museum's visitors. Both Edward Fry, the curator of the exhibition, and I were expressly excluded from the examination of the material, which Mr. Messer conducted privately with Mr. Newlin. The same evening Mr. Messer told Edward Fry that the show was cancelled, without giving me a chance to respond to whatever new objections he had. There was no "pressure of deadlines," as you say. I had suggested postponing the opening for one or two weeks because the complete freeze on all preparations by the Museum as of mid-March had invalidated my working schedule. At some point even Mr. Messer proposed postponing the show to the fall (provided I scrap the three works he objected to). The haste with which Mr. Messer cancelled the show leads one to suspect that he was determined to kill it.

You report the Museum's policy to "avoid active engagement toward social and political ends," however, you fail to present my position on this as outlined in a statement of April 3: "Mr. Messer is wrong on two counts: First, in his confusion of the political stand which an artist's work may assert with a political stand taken by the museum that shows that work; secondly, in his assumption that my pieces advocate any political cause. They do not."

You contend, "there was apparently some ambiguity as to what the artist and the museum thought the other had agreed to, and was committed to." This is not true. There could not have been any ambiguity because until the arrival of Mr. Messer's letter of March 19, 1971 (one year after the invitation), giving his reasons for censoring the three works, I had not received any written communication from the Museum. Neither Edward Fry, who was fired because he pub-

*From "Editorial: Artists vs. Museums, Continued," *ARTnews*, vol. 70, no. 5, September 1971, p. 21. Copyright © 1971, by ARTnews Associates. Reprinted by permission.

licly defended freedom of art at the Guggenheim Museum, nor myself had received any oral guidelines. We therefore worked upon the assumption that aside from budgetary and technical limitations, I was free to show what I chose. The three works under discussion took conclusive form in the fall, not, as you report, in January.

You totally ignore the third work in dispute. This was a poll of the Museum's visitors, consisting of 10 demographic questions and 10 questions referring to current socio-political issues. Mr. Messer prudently avoided mentioning this work in writing because it was impossible to generate a legal smoke-screen for its rejection; in a meeting with the curator and my lawyer Mr. Messer demanded the elimination of all directly political questions, a demand with which I, naturally, could not comply.

The facts allow only one conclusion: Thomas Messer is guilty of censorship and has deliberately infringed on the artists' right to free expression within the walls of the Guggenheim Museum. This is the real issue!!! You unfortunately allude to it in your 1,800 word editorial only in one sentence. In this context Mr. Messer's remark on CBS Radio deserves wider publication: "Obviously Mr. Haacke is free to take the aspect of the exhibition that we objected to to any other place. He is even free to show it under his own auspices. We have neither the power nor the wish to suppress this. I don't think we have censored anything. We have judged that Mr. Haacke's exhibition, or the part that we are referring to, is inappropriate for presentation at the Guggenheim Museum." Presenting the Museum's legal gibberish at length without thoroughly checking the facts and learning of its weak underpinnings, you become, unwittingly, an accomplice of the censor.

The Museum's policy of banning works that make direct reference to the socio-political environment, conveniently announced 6 weeks before the opening, remains without a clear comment from you, as if it were an esthetically, morally and legally unassailable position. This is another of the main issues of this case and would deserve a separate article.

Repeatedly you refer to the responsibilities artists have to museums. In your concluding paragraph you spell out that these responsibilities go beyond those covered by existing laws. You imply artists should exert self-censorship by showing only those works in museums that will not alienate conservative supporters of these institutions. In effect you seem to be saying that an important quality of works in museums is their potential for fund-raising drives, and that artists act irresponsibly if they do not follow the rules of this game.

It is most alarming if an editor of an important art magazine appears to publicly condone such a perverted state of affairs. I hope I have misinterpreted you and would appreciate a public clarification because this transcends my dispute with the Guggenheim Museum.

ARTnews is pleased to have Mr. Haacke's reiteration of his position. Many of the points in his letter have been discussed in exhaustive detail in other journals since our May issue went to press.

At the outset, when the Guggenheim's cancellation of Haacke's show was made public, statements from all parties appeared repeatedly in the *N.Y. Times,* the *N.Y. Post,* the *Village Voice, Newsday,* on CBS-TV, etc. The "inaccuracies" and "omissions" to which Mr. Haacke alludes involve material which we considered superfluous to repeat. Any interested observer—indeed, any uninterested observer—could hardly have helped being *au courant.*

Subsequent events have emphasized the peculiar complexities of the case, and weakened the ideological positions, such as they were, of both sides. It should be obvious by now that statements by all parties made at different times encompass numerous contradictions. Chronologies, compromises, shifts of positions, relative degrees of intransigence, etc., are of small interest now, especially in the absence of any significant news facts.

Therefore to some of Mr. Haacke's more substantial points:

The Guggenheim Museum's *implied* ban on art works directly engaging the real socio-political environment is indeed a major issue, and is indeed deserving of a separate article. However, our *Editorial* dealt with the present particular and specific case.

ARTnews neither "repeatedly" nor "unquestioningly" "adopts" the museum's position that the Haacke real-estate pieces as projected were potentially libelous, nor does ARTnews "plead" for understanding of the museum's position. (Mr. Haacke is surprisingly free with innuendo.) Indeed, we questioned the likelihood of such a dramatic eventuality as a lawsuit ever being provoked by works which we characterized as "seemingly innocuous."

Nevertheless, despite the opinion of Mr. Haacke's lawyers (hardly a more objective authority than the Guggenheim's lawyers), it would be naïve to ignore the possible consequences of the selective lifting of information about private individuals from the public record for public exhibition.

The moral as well as the legal issues raised by Mr. Haacke's projected works are so irresistibly provocative, especially in the light of the furor they have already created, that it is absurd for Mr. Haacke to suggest that our speculations reflect the museum's "legal gibberish" (a curious remark from the artist who himself had recourse to legal advice); it is even more absurd to imply that recognition of real-life complexities, which his real-estate works set out deliberately to engage, casts ARTnews as the museum's "accomplice." In fact, while Mr. Haacke claimed that the two disputed real-estate pieces were "non-evaluative," he was clearly aware of their political and judgmental implications. (Interestingly, however, it was the museum's director, Thomas Messer, who specifically politicalized the works, at least in print, in statements to the press.)

Mr. Haacke either misread or twisted our conclusions concerning the problems of museum-artist relationships, and the responsibilities for both sides which are engendered by recent trends in art.

Far from suggesting that artists exert "self-censorship" to comply with institutional limitations, we emphasized that it is the nature of art to be ahead of institutions. Institutional acceptance for new ideas is never to be counted upon; the history of old and new art makes this only too clear. It is inevitable that politically radical art should evoke strong institutional reactions and resistance. Such art would be worth little if it did not. Politically provocative ideas escalate an already-existing incompatibility.

However, one basic and often ironical fact is obvious: once an artist undertakes to work with a museum, he is in effect already in a situation of compromise. It is naïve to expect that a museum must always be "good," or that it can or will ignore what it sees as its own self-interest. The artist accepts a known situation when he undertakes to work with a museum. A politically active artist of course places himself in a particularly touchy position, which can become almost unbearably self-contradictory in certain circumstances, even when both parties set out to operate in good faith. But a clear and deliberate choice—whether the artist should or should not work in and with a museum—is available from the start.

The alternative of showing outside an official art context, which faces many artists today, is in certain ways unattractive. The nonautonomous nature of art-works such as Haacke's (wheat field, bean plants, myna-birds, documentary photos, etc.) demands an art-context to allow them to function as art; this is what makes the present case so painful. For by denying the artist his show, the museum did in effect "destroy" the work. The cancellation of the exhibition, and especially, the manner in which it took place, was thus particularly damaging to Mr. Haacke and by extension to artists at large—as witness the long list of artists who publicly protested, and some of whom also took part in demonstrations during two weekends in May. It is probably for this reason that the whole situation appears to artists as such a threat; it has become almost second nature for many avant-garde artists to work with a museum context in mind. In this respect the museum's actions can be seen as extremely self-destructive to its position in the art community.

Museums have remained until recently more or less unaffected by the drastic changes in publishing, theater, film and other branches of communications and the arts. The tendency toward greater daring and flexibility is strong; one wonders whether museums will change with the artists, or specialize their functions to deal only with conventional mediums of art.

Some Haacke non-exhibition spin-offs: the socio-political poll (which was not discussed in our *Editorial* because it was not a stated reason for cancelling the show—whether it might have become one remains conjectural) is currently included in a group show at the Milwaukee Art Center. Fragments of the real-estate pieces have been widely published by now. So far nobody has been sued. Perhaps during the coming year, the disputed pieces will be exhibited in a museum context, and we will have the opportunity to see the works as originally intended—and to observe the consequences, if any.—E.C.B.

COMMENTS

1. Some months after the Guggenheim rejection, Haacke did exhibit his project in another New York art museum. There was little press comment, and no legal action was taken against the institution.

2. Between March 12 and April 13, 1974, at the Stefanotty Gallery in New York City, Haacke exhibited information about the members of the Solomon R. Guggenheim Museum board of trustees. This information indicated who were family members and the corporate affiliations of the trustees. Among the latter were three officials of the Kennecott Copper Corporation, and Haacke cited Chile's then President Salvador Allende's views on Kennecott delivered in a speech to the United Nations on December 4, 1972.

THE MANZONI CASE

In considering Manzoni's case, below, which of the three—the artist, the museum director, or the magistrate—has the right to define what is art? Apparently both Manzoni and Bucarelli considered the "Merda d'artista" to be art. If that is so, was the magistrate acting as a censor of art?

*ARTnews Column, October 1974**

But is it art? In the '50s, protesting against the commodity status of the saleable art object, the late Italian-born artist, Manzoni, saved his own excrement. Every day he had it canned in little tins duly signed, numbered, dated and labeled. *"Merda d'artista."* These he then offered for sale at the current price of gold, on an ounce for ounce basis. Manzoni achieved a certain success, perhaps by appealing so directly to the "anal-retentive" component in all collecting. At the full-scale retrospective of his work held last March at the Tate Gallery in London, though, the majority of British critics did no more than turn up their noses at such passé gesturalism.

It does, however, seem that Manzoni has created something of a posthumous stench in his native Italy. Palma Bucarelli, director of the National Museum of Modern Art in Rome, was recently harangued before a local magistrate for exhibiting the little pots. Although Bucarelli was acquitted of the charges laid against her, the magistrate delivered an astonishing judgment aimed at preventing similar occurrences in the future. Praising the laudable sense of public duty of those who had preferred charges, he found that "*Merda d'artista* has nothing at all in common with any of the established conceptual definitions of art,

and contrasts with the goals which the administration of the state inclines towards." The magistrate argued that if the work had been bought with public money (which it had) it constituted the most serious misuse of funds. Bucarelli's defense that *Merda d'artista* was a significant manifestation of Manzoni's polemical stance against the treatment of art as merchandise was summarily dismissed, "it being evident that the weaknesses, the mistakes and the degrading moments, which every artist goes through, like ordinary mortals, should not necessarily be put under the eyes of the public under the auspices of institutions of the state, particularly when they take the most vulgar, gratuitous and useless of forms."

The sheer absurdity of the proceedings would undoubtedly have delighted Manzoni, but the issues at stake were serious enough. They concerned both censorship of artists and the freedom of museum directors to act independently of the "goals of the state." The judgment was so ambiguous that many Italian commentators saw it as a potentially alarming precedent. Although a protest has been lodged by the International Association of Art Critics, Bucarelli was technically acquitted, and an official reversal of the statements made in court thus seems improbable.

*From "Collage," *ARTnews,* October 1974, pp. 68–69. Copyright © 1974 by ARTnews Associates. Reprinted by permission.

IS IT ART?

The Haacke and Manzoni cases, among others, raise a basic question: Is it art? This is a question that courts are reluctant to decide, for reasons like those stated by Justice Holmes in *Bleistein v. Donaldson Lithographing Co.*, 188 U.S. 239, 251 (1903):

> It would be a dangerous undertaking for persons trained only to the law to constitute themselves final judges of the worth of pictorial illustrations, outside of the narrowest and most obvious limits. At the one extreme some works of genius would be sure to miss appreciation. Their very novelty would make them repulsive until the public had learned the new language in which their author spoke. It may be more than doubted, for instance, whether the etchings of Goya or the paintings of Manet would have been sure of protection when seen for the first time.

Still, if the law is to treat works of art differently from other objects (for example, giving First Amendment protection to expressions that have artistic value; protecting works of fine art "of recognized quality" against damage or destruction; and so on), the question has to be faced. It has most often been faced in customs cases, where an imported object is duty free if it is a work of art, but may otherwise be subject to duty. Here is the way the law developed.

In *United States v. Perry*, 146 U.S. 71 (1892), the United States Supreme Court held that not all art would be admitted into the United States duty free, but only fine art would be. The Court defined the fine arts as those "intended solely for ornamental purposes, and including paintings in oil and water, upon canvas, plaster, or other material, and original statuary of marble, stone or bronze."

In *United States v. Olivotti & Co.*, T.D. 363309, 7 Ct. Cust. App. 46 (1916), the Customs Court established the "representational test" of art:

> Sculpture as an art is that branch of the free fine arts which chisels or carves out of stone or other solid material or models in clay or other plastic substance for subsequent reproduction by carving or casting, imitations of natural objects, chiefly the human form, and represents such objects in their true proportions of length, breadth, and thickness, or of length and breadth only. (7 Ct. Cust. App. at 48.)

The Court concluded that Congress never intended to include all artistic objects within the duty-free category of "works of art," which included

> only those productions of the artist which are something more than ornamental or decorative and which may be properly ranked as examples of the free fine arts, natural objects as the artist sees them, and appealing to the emotions through the eye alone. (7 Ct. Cust. App. at 48.)

In 1928 the Customs Court recognized that the representational test was an inappropriate standard. The case concerned the classification of Brancusi's bronze sculpture "Bird in Flight." As art, the sculpture would be admitted duty free. As a "manufacture of metal" the piece would be taxed at 40 percent ad valorem, its value determined by declaration of the importer, who was valuing it, as a work of art, at $600,000. In *Brancusi v. United States*, T.D. 43063, 54 Treas. Dec. 428 (1928) the Customs Court overruled customs officers and held that "Bird in Flight" was a work of art. The Court explained the development of art since the *Olivotti* decision.

> This decision was handed down in 1916. In the meanwhile there has been developing a so-called new school of art whose exponents attempt to portray abstract ideas rather than to imitate natural objects. Whether or not we are in sympathy with these newer ideas and

the schools which represent them, we think the fact of their existence and their influence upon the art world as recognized by the courts must be considered.

The Court heard expert testimony from both sides. On cross-examination by the government, the sculptor Jacob Epstein was asked:

Q. Do you mean to tell us that [sic] Exhibit 1 if formed up, that a mechanic, that is a first class mechanic, with a file and polishing tools could not polish that article up?
A. He can polish it up, but he cannot conceive of the object. That is the whole point. He cannot conceive those particular lines which give it its individual beauty. That is the difference between a mechanic and an artist, he cannot conceive as an artist.

Judge Waite also questioned witnesses. He pointed to "Bird in Flight" and asked William Henry Fox, the director of the Brooklyn Museum of Art:

Q. Before you would have selected a Barye or a known painting or piece of sculpture you would have selected this?
A. I would select that as the work of an artist I esteem as an artist.
Q. You would have selected it more as a curiosity?
A. No, sir, I would not, I would select it because of its appeal to me as an object of art, as a beautiful piece, because of its beauty, its symmetry, its quality that gives me pleasurable emotion.
Q. Do you think the rank and file of people who visit your museum would be educated by that form?
A. I hope they will be, sir. I think they will appreciate its beauty.

The Court noted the artistic value of the sculpture and then reached a significant holding that was, unfortunately, distinguished and minimized for almost thirty years:

The object now under consideration is shown to be for purely ornamental purposes, its use being the same as that of any piece of sculpture of the old masters. It is beautiful and symmetrical in outline, and while some difficulty might be encountered in associating it with a bird, it is nevertheless pleasing to look at and highly ornamental, and as we hold under the evidence that it is the original production of a professional sculptor and is in fact a piece of sculpture and a work of art according to the authorities above referred to, we sustain the protest and hold that it is entitled to free entry under Paragraph 1704. . . . 54 Treas. Dec. at 430-31.

COMMENTS

1. Observe that in such cases the court relies on expert testimony—by artists, art historians, dealers, critics, and museum professionals—to guide its decision whether the object is art. The California Art Preservation Act, (supra, p. 163) expressly directs the use of expert testimony on the question whether a work is "fine art" "of recognized quality." When such an expert testifies that, in his opinion, a work is not art, or fine art, or of recognized quality, is he acting as a censor?

2. How about the following rule: "If it is made by an artist it is art."? But who decides whether the maker is an artist? If we answer that an artist is one who makes art, we are running in a circle.

3. In 1959 the following statute (PL 86-262, 73STAT. 549 (1959)) defining works of art free of duty was enacted:

(a) Original paintings in oil, mineral, water, vitreous enamel, or other colors, pastels, original mosaics, original drawings and sketches in pen, ink, pencil, or watercolors, or works of the free fine arts in any other media including applied paper and other materials, manufactured or otherwise, such as are used in collages, artists' proof etchings unbound, and engravings and woodcuts unbound, lithographs or prints made by other hand transfer

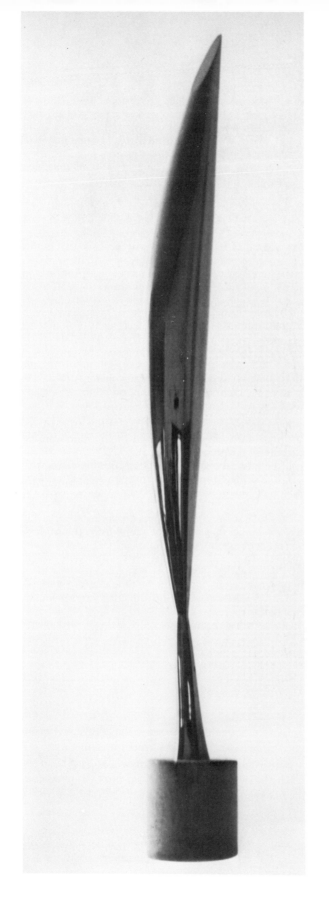

Constantin Brancusi, Bird in Flight, *1926, 53¼", polished bronze. (Photo courtesy Sidney Geist.)*

processes unbound, original sculptures or statuary; but the terms 'sculpture' and 'statuary' as used in this paragraph shall be understood to include professional productions of sculptors only, whether in round or in relief, in bronze, marble, stone, terra cotta, ivory, wood, metal, or other materials, or whether cut, carved, or otherwise wrought by hand from the solid block or mass of marble, stone, alabaster, or from metal, or other material, or cast in bronze or other metal or substance, or from wax or plaster, or constructed from any material or made in any form as the professional productions of sculptors only, and the term 'original' as used in this paragraph to modify the words 'sculptures' and 'statuary', shall be understood to include the original work or model and not more than ten castings, replicas, or reproductions made from the sculptor's original work or model, with or without a change in the scale and regardless of whether or not the sculptor is alive at the time castings, replicas, or reproductions are completed. The terms 'painting', mosaic', 'drawing', 'work of the free fine arts', 'sketch', 'sculpture', and 'statuary', as used in this paragraph, shall not be understood to include any articles of utility or for industrial use, nor such as are made wholly or in part by stenciling or any other mechanical process; and the terms 'etchings', 'engravings', and 'woodcuts', 'lithographs', or 'prints made by other hand transfer process', as used in this paragraph, shall be understood to include only such as are printed by hand from plates, stones, or blocks etched, drawn, or engraved with hand tools and not such as are printed from plates, stones, or blocks etched, drawn, or engraved by photochemical or other mechanical processes.

"(b) Original works of the free fine arts, not provided for in subparagraph (a), subject to such regulations as the Secretary of the Treasury may prescribe as to proof that the article imported represents some school, kind, or medium of the free fine arts. The term 'original works of the free fine arts' as used herein shall not be understood to include any article of utility or for industrial use."

The statute reflected a ten year study by the American Association of Museums Committee on Customs and was supported by the American Federation of Arts, the American Association of Museums, American Institute of Architects, United States Committee of the International Association of Plastic Arts, the International Council at the Museum of Modern Art, College Art Association of America, and the National Art Education Assciation (Derenberg and Baum, "Congress Rehabilitates Modern Art," *New York University Law Review*, 34[1959], p. 1228).

4. Does this statute resolve the "Is it Art?" question for customs purposes? Clearly not. Experts will still have to guide the decision maker on a variety of questions: Is the painting "original"? Are the objects in question "professional productions" of "sculptors"? And so on.

5. More generally, the ingenuity of artists and the value society places on creativity in art both work against definitions. Definitions may be out of date by the time they are adopted. They can impede or distort the work of artists and become the instruments of censorship by definition: if it doesn't meet the definition, it isn't art.

6. In the following case, is Toche acting as artist? Is the result of his action a work of art?

THE TOCHE CASE

Jean Toche, an artist whose previous history showed that he considered political activism the subject and purpose of his art, protested against the arrest of the artist Tony Shafrazi by the New York City Police Department for spray-painting Picasso's "Guernica," which was on exhibit in the Museum of Modern Art. The following handbill was sent through the mail to C. Douglas Dillon, president of the board of trustees of the Metropolitan Museum of Art.

Handbill
Ad Hoc Artists' Movement for Freedom

AD HOC ARTISTS' MOVEMENT FOR FREEDOM
February 23, 1974

Artist Tony Shafrazi has freed GUERNICA from the chains of property, and returned it to its true revolutionary nature.

ARTIST TONY SHAFRAZI MUST BE RELEASED IMMEDIATELY.

His arrest is a crime against FREE SPEECH.

The erasure of this angry and justified SHAFRAZI/ PICASSO political conceptual art work denouncing all genocides is a crime against Freedom of Expression and Artistic Freedom.

The Museum of Modern Art of New York, the City of New York, the State of New York and the Government of the United States must drop, at once and forever, all charges against him and his art.

THOSE GUILTY OF THESE CRIMES AGAINST TONY SHAFRAZI AND HIS ART MUST NOW PAY:

Because property is the antithesis of art,

Because, in the name of property, museums arrest art and artists, instead of addressing themselves to the life-and-death issues of people and people's needs.

Because art is not to be thought as the exclusive privilege of a ruling class to be used, possessed or manipulated as that ruling class wishes,

Because of the cultural crimes committed against all people and artists by trustees, directors, administrators, curators of museums and so-called art benefactors— murderers of people and perpetrators of racism, sexism, oppression and repression—who are still in positions of power and control of the present cultural institutions, and who stole legally or illegally the culture of all people,

WE NOW CALL FOR THE *KIDNAPPING* OF:
    museum's trustees,
    museum's directors,
    museum's curators,
    museum's benefactors,

To be held as WAR HOSTAGES until a People's Court is convened, to deal specifically with the cultural crimes of the ruling class, and with decision of sanctions, reparation and restitution, in whatever form decided by the People and the Artists.

Jean Toche, Artist & Coordinator,
AD HOC ARTISTS' MOVEMENT FOR FREEDOM,
New York, New York.

COMMENT

The response of Dillon was to call in the FBI, and Jean Toche was arrested. (It should be pointed out that in the winter of 1974 the Metropolitan Museum of Art had recently experienced attempts to disrupt its activities and along with other art museums in New York felt threatened by activities of anti-Vietnam war protesters, the Shafrazi incident being the most publicized.) Do you consider Dillon's response appropriate? Further, a U.S. District Court judge ordered that Toche be given a psychiatric examination, which along with the defendant's arrest roused the ire of many in the art world. Was this an appropriate action by the judge? In the absence of any precedent, should Toche have welcomed the opportunity to be the first artist in history declared legally sane?

The Arrest of Jean Toche*

We protest the arrest by agents of the Federal Bureau of Investigation of Jean Toche and we demand that all legal charges against him be dropped. We state the following:

When Tony Shafrazi defaced Picasso's *Guernica* at the Museum of Modern Art, he committed a deplorable act against artistic freedom, no matter what romantic motives may have inspired it. When the Guerilla Art Action Group on February 28, 1974, hailed that act, it committed a grave injustice against freedom in art.

No one has the right to unilaterally and arrogantly "join" another artist's work. Tony Shafrazi has not "joined Picasso in a collaboration work," as defined by the Guerilla Action Group; rather, he has attempted to suppress the artistic freedom of Picasso by infringing on the artist's inviolate right to make a statement without censorship, alerting, annexing or parasitic "joining."

On the same February 28, 1974, Jean Toche issued a statement in the name of the Ad Hoc Artists Movement for Freedom, extolling the Shafrazi act. In a document full of pseudo-revolutionary bombast the group hailed the "freeing" of *Guernica.* The document even protested the cleaning of *Guernica* as an erasure of "the joint Shafrazi-Picasso political conceptual art work" and a "crime against Freedom of Expression and Artistic Freedom." The letter also called for the kidnapping of museum trustees, directors, administrators, curators and benefactors.

On March 27, 1974, Jean Toche was arrested in his home by the FBI acting on a complaint of Douglas Dillon, President of the Metropolitan Museum of Art.

Though we condemn the senseless act of Shafrazi and the totalitarian logic of his defenders, we nevertheless demand that Jean Toche be freed of all legal charges.

The Director of the Metropolitan Museum of Art must have known, as did the art world as a whole, that the call for kidnapping could not have been anything but symbolic in essence. It was made in a public letter, against an unspecified number of people of various categories. We believe that Mr. Dillon acted not against a real threat, but against a statement he must have understood to be metaphoric, in an act of vengeance against an artist who for years played a role in the antiwar movement and the movement for artists' rights vis-à-vis the establishment and the museum hierarchies.

The arrest of Jean Toche was essentially a political act. It is in this sense we come to his defense as artists and the art-workers in a common bond against a power structure which is acting as an enemy of freedom in art.

Joyce Kozloff	Rudolf Baranik
Yvonne Rainer	Arnold Belkin
Corinne Robins	Louise Bourgeois
Salvatore Romano	Allan D'Arcangelo
Larry Rosing	Hans Haacke
Tom Wesselmann	Phoebe Helman
Robert Wiegand	Joan Semmel
	Jack Sonenberg
	May Stevens

COMMENTS

1. Is every question about the content and display of an exhibition a "censorship" question? If not, how might questions of selection and display be separated from questions of artistic freedom?

2. What should be the principal elements of a museum policy for dealing with problems of the kind raised or suggested by these cases?

3. The case against Toche is dormant. Tony Shafrazi now runs a successful art gallery in Soho, featuring graffiti art.

4. What is your opinion of various devices used by museums (such as "fair notice" warnings or notices prohibiting children from viewing certain shows) to forestall outside censorship? Are these "preventive devices" themselves a form of censorship? What do you think of the way the Kienholz problem was resolved at the Los Angeles County Museum of Art?

5. Do the Haacke, Manzoni, and/or Toche cases raise the same old questions in different form, or are the questions themselves new? Conceptual art, process art, and other "media" that have left aside the creation of objects—paintings, drawings, sculpture, prints—have im-

*Originally published as "On the Arrest of Jean Toche," *Artforum,* vol. 8, November 1974. Copyright © 1974 by California Artforum, Inc. Reprinted by permission.

portance for some artists. Do they create different social problems? Real social dangers? Do you agree with the writers of the letter to *Artforum* about Toche?

6. In her editorial on the Haacke affair at the Guggenheim, Elizabeth Baker raised important questions worth answering: Is it legal—or fair—to appropriate identifiable private individuals for a work of art? Where is the line between public material and private material? What if the artist even inadvertently distorts public material? What is invasion of privacy in this context? And where do such works stand ethically, aside from legally? Can public business records be damning when no conclusions are drawn? Is the mere focusing of attention grounds for libel? Do the facts alone condemn?

7. Should museums have the right to censor the art of artists they have agreed in principle to show? Is the question one of repression or of simple breach of contract?

CONTROVERSIAL PUBLIC ART

One of the best essays on controversial public art served as the introduction to the catalog *Controversial Public Art* written by Gerald Nordland for his exhibition sponsored by the Milwaukee Art Museum in October 1983.

GERALD NORDLAND *Introduction to* Controversial Public Art, *October 1983**

In the years following the Civil War the United States knew what to do about public art. Every concerned state and many cities and villages of whatever size felt a need to memorialize those who had served or died in that conflict. Generals on horseback, soldiers in uniform, individuals and groups were commissioned and rendered in bronze or marble for placement in city squares, parks and in niches at the courthouses. There was no question about the meaning of these monuments. They were public in the sense that they reflected a state of mind and a sympathy for the sacrifice that was being memorialized. Though the dates of the conflict were not distant, the facts of the experience and the shared quality made these memorials as real and as meaningful as the heroic portrait figures of Washington, Jefferson and Lincoln which had become the standards of American public art.

In the great "official" celebrations such as the World's Columbian Exposition in Chicago in 1893 we were less certain about our art symbols and more tentative in our search for public icons. It was good enough in our palaces of justice to produce painted or sculptural allegories of law, com-

merce, science, agriculture, music and equity. But now Daniel Chester French's 65-foot-tall *The Republic,* done for the Exposition, was a Greek draped female figure holding a staff in one hand and a globe surmounted by an eagle in the other upraised hand. It was not an image that captured the American mind. *The Republic* was exposed to the public but it was not a symbol shared and understood.

The problem of public sharing of the iconography of contemporary art is not a uniquely American problem. It is present in those areas of the world where advanced ideas of culture vie with traditional ideas in the visual arts, literature, music, theater, architecture and city planning. The unique and personal researches of a painter or sculptor in his studio, of a poet or novelist in his study, or of the musician or the designer may gradually find their way into the common awareness and affect the look and the style of the times. However, the work of the public sculptor or painter, the architect and the city planner, does present itself to the great public audience in an often abrupt and immediate fashion. The audience may be engaged by the idea or by the tech-

*From Gerald Nordland, Introduction to *Controversial Public Art: From Rodin to de Suvero* (Milwaukee: Milwaukee Art Museum, 1983). Copyright © 1983 by the Milwaukee Art Museum. Reprinted by permission.

nology. Oftentimes the audience is predisposed against new forms because they are new, and therefore surprising and unexpected.

With the triumph of Modernism there has been a progressive codification of the artist's intentions through the evolution of visual vocabularies beginning with Impressionism and succeeded by Symbolism and Post-Impressionism, Fauvism, Expressionism, Cubism and the related developments—Futurism, Constructivism, Neo-Plasticism—and followed by Surrealism and the post-war developments Abstract Expressionism, Pop Art, Minimalism, Earthworks and Photorealism. The very private specialization of interest on the part of the artist at each point in his evolution calls upon the observer to familiarize himself with the intentions of the artist and to evaluate his degree of success in achieving his goals. Since the community that is willing and able to devote the energy and effort required to understand the artist's motivations is not large, there is an important but limited audience for new forms in those galleries and museums specializing in the presentation of a visual art but not in the public at large.

When a modern artist is called upon to create work for public placement in or on government buildings, in city plazas or parks, in airports and corporate urban spaces, he is challenged with the question of how the work will be apprehended by the casual passerby. The work he produces has to grow out of the ideas, materials, and techniques which he has been mastering throughout his career. Since his forms, his esthetic responses, and his sensibility have been shaped in his independent effort to achieve individuality and recognition, he cannot be expected to revert to a popular idiom or to a mass audience iconography. . . .

One likes to believe that public servants no longer conceive of themselves as being above the law or capable of destroying public property which had been commissioned through due process and brought into existence under administrative safeguards. Even today, however, social leadership, moneyed taste, and economic power exercise influence in high places where academic achievement and professional competence may prove less strong.

The high visibility of public art works tends to dramatize the importance of any discussion or controversy that may develop around the origination, symbolism and social meaning of such works. While we are no longer a monolithic society in which a single social, religious or political view can suffice for all, we may crave that now dis-

tant and simplistic mode. As a pluralistic society we will inevitably cultivate diversity, simultaneous co-existence of differing if not polar social and political views. Traditional monumental forms— portraits of statesmen, images of mounted horsemen, memorial fountains or flagpoles—have become less meaningful with the passing of time. In search for fresh and significant forms to serve symbolic or memorial purposes, these forms have become progressively abstract, as in the sunken stone structure of the Vietnam Memorial in Washington, D.C., which although much discussed, seems on the way to ever-widening approval.

There have been notable setbacks in the success of public art in the recent past, just as there have been outstanding successes. These setbacks have occurred for the most part in experimental endeavors intended to broaden awareness of contemporary esthetic concerns. These projects have been defeated through extra-legal violence and by legal subterfuge. Misunderstanding has been the most common factor in these unfortunate incidents. The artist's effort to engage the thoughts and feelings of the viewer through a new visual language has not been received as the merit of the offering. The success of public art must be related to the power of the work to generate public response and a dialogue of meaning. The public must be invited to experience, discuss and grow with a given project and to tolerate freshness and unexpected possibilities not previously associated with monumental civic art.

Artists, architects, city planners, civic leaders and responsible citizens must not focus on the unfamiliar but recognize that fresh and original forms in public art can be a force for education, for raising the spirits of a community (as in the Oldenburg example), establishing a hub for a new civic activity (as in the Calder case in Grand Rapids), and for a new and prideful self-respect (as in Chicago's Picasso and most all of the early examples herein discussed).

One of the obstacles to clear thinking about public art is connected with "immutable verities"—unchanging and invariable standards for the appreciation of works of art. What is familiar is comfortable and the shock of the new often makes clear perception impossible. In reality, the viewer's appreciation of works of art is always changing, growing, deepening, expanding, and sometimes narrowing and contracting. The satisfaction sensed in a bland work of public art may subside into boredom, indifference, and contempt on closer scrutiny and continued contact.

In contrast the work which is initially perceived as radical or shocking, will tend to become less shocking on repeated viewing and its dissonances or surprises will become new expectations for viewing other works of public and private art. Finally, the "shocking" work will be perceived rather abstractly as a product of its generic type and it will be seen for its purposeful design. The sculpture will not change but its perception will pass through many stages of understanding, affection and pride. The public satisfaction we recognize in *La Grande Vitesse* and in St. Louis' Saarinen Arch is powerful evidence that America is continuing to find great and meaningful solutions to these monuments to public vision. It is hoped that we can continue to make the effort with idealism and imagination, with intelligence and humor.

GERALD NORDLAND *The Moscone Memorial Controversy**

Mayor George Moscone and Supervisor Harvey Milk of San Francisco, California, were assassinated in November, 1978, by gunfire from a Smith & Wesson revolver in the hands of an elective member of the Board of Supervisors, Dan White. That infamous crime was much discussed in the national newspress for a number of months because of White's unusual defense in which he claimed that his junk food diet, which included Twinkies, had reduced his capacity to tell right from wrong.

San Francisco's new downtown convention center was in the process of being planned and civic leaders chose to name the new facility in honor of the slain Mayor. Subsequently a competition was held for one artist to make a memorial portrait of the late Mayor for that site. Robert Arneson was chosen from 20 candidates by an appointed committee of art experts—the Moscone Convention Center Joint Committee of the San Francisco Art Commission. All of the nationally known artists who competed were asked to submit a sketch "sufficiently detailed so that judgment can be made." Arneson's sketch, submitted April 23, 1981, shows a broadly smiling head mounted on an unadorned pedestal above a three-tiered base. The final work proved to be a larger than life sized ceramic bust atop a ceramic pedestal measuring close to 8 feet overall. The artist embellished the pedestal with biographical notes, sketches and additions, including "California State Senate Majority Leader," "liberal Democrat," a number of favorite sayings: "Trust me on this one," "Duck Soup," and listings of his schools and his children's names. Perhaps most controversial was the imprinting of a Smith & Wesson revolver, the suggestion of bullet holes in the pedestal, and the bloodlike splatters of red glaze. The inclusion of the words "Bang, Bang, Bang" and the inscription "Twinkie" blazoned on a yellow patch brought the whole assassination forward into the community consciousness once again.

When the $126.5 million Moscone Convention Center was dedicated in San Francisco on December 2, 1981, the portrait of the slain mayor was shown on a draped pedestal, at the specific urging of Mayor Diane Fienstein, the Chief Administrative Officer Roger Boas, and Mayor Moscone's widow. There was uniform approval of the design and execution of the portrait likeness but strong criticism regarding the references to the murder weapon, the murderer and his defense. The bust was officially rejected on December 8, 1981, by a vote of seven to three with two absent. The Art Commission received a letter well before time for the vote from Mayor Diane Feinstein, urging rejection of Arneson's work as "inappropriate for the hallmark of a great convention center." The Mayor was said to have noted that memorials to Abraham Lincoln, the Kennedys and Martin Luther King contain no references to their killers. There was general agreement among a special committee composed of three Art Commission members, three outside art experts and a Redevelopment Agency commissioner—that "the work was extraordinarily distinguished . . . and it would be a crime for the city of San Francisco to lose it." Robert Johnson, the curator of prints at the California Palace of the Legion of Honor and a member of the committee spoke strongly in

*From Gerald Nordland, "The Moscone Memorial Controversy," in *Controversial Public Art: From Rodin to di Suvero* (Milwaukee: Milwaukee Art Museum, 1983), pp. 51–52. Copyright © 1983 by the Milwaukee Art Museum. Reprinted by permission.

favor of the work: "It's obviously struck a nerve and that's exactly what art is all about," he said. Again, he argued that the Commission's vote was "not an aesthetic one, but a political one."

The disappointed ceramic sculptor, upon advice of counsel, returned $18,500, half-payment for the work, which he had delivered on time. Mayor Feinstein's letter claimed that Arneson's pedestal did not reflect the "spirit of non-violence to which the City committed itself when it claimed for itself the name of St. Francis." She also added sternly that "an artist must be held accountable to his or her maquette" and that there be "assurance that guidelines will not be spurned and standards disregarded."

The April 23, 1982, issue of the *San Francisco Examiner* carried the item that Grant Avenue gallery owner Foster Goldstrom had just paid $50,000 for the controversial Robert Arneson bust of the late Mayor George R. Moscone and said, "I bought it for the statement of the art. It is unquestionably his [Arneson's] greatest work. There's no question," he added. Goldstrom took possession of the work following its exhibition at the San Francisco Museum of Modern Art, June 27, 1982, and has exhibited it elsewhere in Northern California in public circumstances.

COMMENTS

1. Controversial modern public sculpture has come about even when private groups and businessmen seek to upgrade the image of their city. In 1983 the city of Denver experienced a heated controversy that involved not just the artist and his commissioners but also groups in the community such as students, feminists, and Native Americans, who are not customarily involved. The artist was the sculptor Red Grooms, famous for his "zany tableaux" of subjects often found only in paintings, such as a rodeo, the storming of a Japanese castle, and, in the humorous "Ruckus Manhattan," an image of the big city. His 20-foot-long, 3,000-pound painted steel sculpture called "Shoot-Out," which depicts a crouching Indian firing at a cowboy, was installed at the entrance of the University of Colorado's Denver campus in August 1983. The work was commissioned by a Denver oilman, Donald F. Todd, and some partners, who had hoped to inspire other businessmen to support public art. "We were trying to bring a little bit of art, a little bit of public culture, to Denver. We were trying to do something good, and it backfired."* What "backfired" was the reaction of those who passed through and looked at the plaza of an office and condominium complex where the work was first installed in Denver. Protests about the sculpture's size, not its content, reportedly forced relocation of the sculpture. It was moved to a traffic island owned by the University of Colorado at Denver, located near the entrance, which was relandscaped just for this purpose. Many university students, faculty members, and others who first saw the work in this second setting were upset either by its "ugliness" or by its caricaturizing of the American Indian. Feminists and Native Americans saw Grooms's piece as trivializing violence. A Native American representative, Vivian Locust, found it "a bit insensitive. . . . The Indians are still suffering yet, and they can't find any humor in it." The Colorado spokesman for the American Indian Movement, Frank Black Elk, told Peterson: "They're still showing this demeaning idea of what the Indians were. It was not the Indians shooting at the cowboys; native people were peaceful, harmonious people. It was the cavalry shooting at the Indians, committing atrocities against the native people."

The Colorado University board of regents reversed the university administration's position on the resiting of Grooms's work and asked that it be removed. The board denied having bowed to pressure exerted by Native Americans and having engaged in censorship. A board spokesman said: "We believed that the placing of that statue at that particular place was an inappropriate combination of structure and location. We didn't think it was an appropriate piece to be placed at the entrance to our university."

The final location of "Shoot-Out" is in a small garden alongside the Denver Art Museum, separated from the street by a wall that prevents outsiders from seeing it in its entirety. Don-

*All quotations are from Iver Peterson's "Sculpture of a Shoot-Out Stirs Protest in Denver," *New York Times,* October 6, 1983.

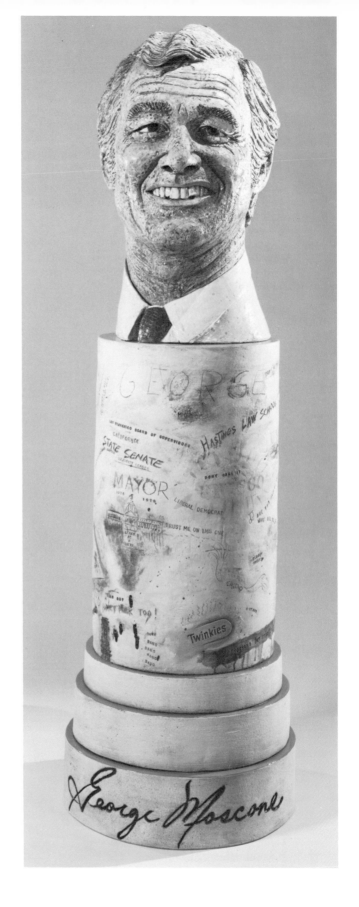

Robert Arneson. Portrait of George *(memorial bust of Mayor George Moscone), 1981, 94" high, ceramic. (Collection Foster Goldstrom. Reproduced by courtesy of the artist.)*

ald Todd commented, "I know my partners feel they've been burned by this, and they don't want to hear about public art again."

2. The files of the San Francisco Art Commission contain the letters sent to the Moscone Joint Committee. Most are adamantly either for or against the sculpture. Numerically, the letters are evenly split: 20 pro, 20 con. On December 10, 1981, the *San Francisco Chronicle* published the results of a phone-in poll that it had conducted on the question "Do you like the Moscone statue?" The results were: Yes 8,678 (39%)—No 13,636 (61%).

From October 21, 1983 to January 15, 1984, the exhibition "Controversial Art" produced by Gerald Nordland was shown in the art gallery of the San Francisco Art Commission (!) across from City Hall. Included in the exhibition was the Moscone bust by Arneson. The work was thus shown across the street from where Mayor Moscone was shot and where Mayor Feinstein, who had rejected it for Moscone Center, has her office. Recall that it was the San Francisco Art Commission that formally turned down Arneson's sculpture. The exhibition caused considerable interest in the city, but there was no movement to have Mayor Feinstein and the Art Commission change their views and place the bust in the Moscone Center. If one regards the rejection of the Arneson portrait as censorship, then historically its exhibition, sponsored by the agency that would not accept it for a permanent public location, is without precedent.

3. Arneson had a long history of animating the pedestals of his sculptures with commentary, and this should not have been unknown to the Art Commission. In the instance of the Moscone bust, Arneson was in effect supplying his own graffiti. The pedestal significantly enhanced the meaning and artistic value of the Moscone bust while simultaneously rendering the work offensive to the former mayor's heirs. Which side should have prevailed? Could anything have been done to prevent this dispute?

4. What should have been the answer to Mayor Feinstein's complaint that memorials to the Kennedys and others did not contain references to their killers? Was Mayor Feinstein using her influence as mayor to act as an art censor? (The members of the Art Commission serve at her pleasure.)

5. What if San Francisco had accepted the work and then locked it in storage? Would that have constituted censorship?

6. Suppose the city received a credible threat to destroy the ceramic sculpture if it was installed in the Moscone Center (there were such threats, but we know little about their credibility). What should be the city's response?

7. Suppose the work were installed despite such threats and then reduced to rubble by an enraged iconoclast while a guard's back was turned. Review the materials on the California Art Preservation Act in Chapter 3. If it had been in force at the time, would the Art Commission be legally liable under it?

8. Re Grooms's "Shoot-Out" and its relocation, if a public work of art is patently offensive to a minority group in the community, should it be removed from a public place? (After protests by Native American students, Stanford University removed the Indian as a school symbol.)

9. Notice that in controversies over public art, especially in some of the cases that follow, people will often defend the work of art but disregard its public location. Until recent years, modern artists made art on their own terms, assuming it would go to private collectors or museums. It was antimodern to make any concession to others in order to sell a work of art. Today artists are divided about whether to take into account the public that must live and work with their art.

CHRISTO'S PUBLIC ART

In the authors' judgment there is no more imaginative, ambitious, and daring artist working on public art than Christo. His many projects, such as "Valley Curtain," "Running Fence," "Surrounded Islands," and "Wrapped Pont Neuf" have been well documented. To our knowledge there has been only one instance when Christo "cheated" on his excellent reputation for complying with all environmental and legal restrictions imposed on his projects (that one instance is summarized in a footnote to the quoted material that follows). None of

Red Grooms. Shoot-Out (Wagon Piece), *1980, painted bronze. (Photo courtesy Marlborough Gallery.)*

Christo. The Gates, *Project for Central Park, New York, 1984. Drawing in 2 parts, pencil, charcoal, pastel, crayon and map. (Photo by Wolfgang Volz. Reproduced by courtesy of the artist.)*

Christo's works has been easy, and it is part of his art to involve the legal system. As much as the finished, though temporary, conception, Christo considers everything that leads up to it as part of the work of art. What follows is Christo's proposal for "The Gates: Project for Central Park" in New York City, and its rejection in a report issued in February 1981, prepared by Gordon J. Davis, then commissioner of parks and recreation for the city of New York.

CHRISTO *Proposal for "THE GATES: PROJECT FOR CENTRAL PARK" (1980)*

When I arrived in New York City in 1964, I was fascinated by the skyline. However, throughout the 1970s I became more aware of the truly important elements of this City: its people and the way in which the City's space is used.

Central Park was chosen as the site for my Project because of the unique way it is walked by so many people. *The Gates: Project for Central Park* creates a direct relationship between human height, the time it takes to walk through the Project, and the intimacy experienced in touching the work of art.

The Gates will be 15 feet high with a width varying from 9 to 28 feet, according to the width of the walkways, creating a series of portals crossing perpendicular to the selected footpaths of Central Park. Attached to the horizontal crosspiece at the top of each steel gate, the fabric will come down to 5 feet 6 inches from the ground when there is no wind at all. *The Gates* will be spaced generally at 9-foot intervals allowing the golden apricot color woven panels to wave horizontally and touch the next gate when there is a light breeze.

The Gates are planned to remain in place for 14 days about the last two weeks of October 1984 or 1985, after which the approximately 25-mile-long work of art shall be removed and the ground left in its original condition.

The Gates will be entirely financed by me. Neither the City nor the Park shall bear any of the expenses for *The Gates*, and no grants or foundation money shall be used. As has been done for the previous projects, my preparatory drawings, sketches, and other works are sold in advance by my wife and dealer Jeanne-Claude Christo to museums, dealers, and private collectors throughout the world.

A written contract shall be drafted between the Department of Parks and our organization. Legal services for *The Gates* are provided by Theodore W. Kheel and Scott B. Hodes. The contract will be based upon the agreements made in California with all relevant governmental agencies at the time of the construction of the *Running Fence* project. This brought complete satisfaction to the authorities and international attention to the area.

The contract shall require us to provide:

1. Personal and Property Liability Insurance holding the Department of Parks harmless.

2. Environmental Impact Statement that is being prepared.

3. Removal Bond providing funds to the complete satisfaction of the Parks Department.

4. Full co-operation with the Community Boards, the Department of Parks, the New York City Arts Commission, and the Landmarks Commission.

5. Employment of local Manhattan residents.

6. Clearance for the usual activities in the Park and access of Rangers, maintenance, clean-up, Police and Emergency Service vehicles.

7. Direct cost of the Park's Supervision shall be charged to us.

8. The configuration of the path of *The Gates* shall be selected together with the Department of Parks.

9. No vegetation or rock formations shall be disturbed.

10. Only vehicles of small size will be used and will be confined to the perimeter of existing walkways during installation and removal.

11. Great precaution will be taken in the scheduling of *The Gates* so as not to interfere with any of the wildlife patterns.

12. All holes shall be professionally backfilled with natural material, leaving the ground in good condition and it shall be inspected by the Department of Parks which will be holding the Removal Bond.

13. Financial help shall be given to the Department of Parks in order to cover any possible additional clean-up task, secretarial work, or any expenses that might occur in direct relation to *The Gates*.

Full-size prototype tests have been conducted by our Engineers on the steel frames, their bottom support systems, and the fabric panel connections.

By involving the entire topography of Central Park, *The Gates* will be uniquely and equally shared by many different groups, thereby becoming a true Public Work of Art, revealing the rich variety of the people of New York City. Walking through *The Gates*, following the walkways, *The Gates* will be a golden ceiling creating warm shad-ows. When seen from the buildings surrounding Central Park, *The Gates* will seem a golden river appearing and disappearing through the foliage of the trees and highlighting the footpaths.

By up-lifting and framing the unnoticed space above the walkways, the luminous fabric of *The Gates* will underline the organic design in contrast to the geometric grid pattern of Manhattan and will harmonize with the beauty of Central Park.

GORDON J. DAVIS, COMMISSIONER, DEPARTMENT OF PARKS AND RECREATION *Report and Determination in the Matter of Christo: "The Gates"*

SUMMARY AND DETERMINATIONS

SUMMARY

Public art in the conventional sense is sculpture, painting or ornament which decorates, adorns, enlivens and often humanizes architectural space. Broaden the definition, and public architecture and landscape architecture are themselves forms of public art. The Brooklyn Bridge, Grand Central Station and Central Park are such works of public art.

The proposed exhibition of Christo's 11,000 to 15,000 gates arching over 25 miles of Central Park's pathways is also public art on a public works scale. Whether in the context of Central Park, or imagined in another—the entire shore rimming Manhattan Island, say—the multitude of banner-hung gates appeals in almost the same way that a convocation of tall ships appeals to us: as a festive, celebratory, not-to-be-forgotten event. But what does a Christo happening, however magical and transitory, mean to Central Park?

Inspired by England's landscaped gardens and Olmsted's urbanized Jeffersonian philosophy, Central Park is an expression of America's artistic, engineering and political genius. It is, to the surprise of some people, completely man-made. For many years politicians and a Parks Department that were indifferent to park preservation allowed its grand naturalistic design to be severely mutilated in a number of areas. Not until the historic preservation and conservation movements gained respectability and political strength in the 1970's was Central Park's status as public art of the highest order recognized. It became a designated scenic landmark, and the task of restoring its former beauty and improving its social utility was begun.

The restoration of Central Park as the great urban garden it was meant to be is a major goal of the current Parks administration. We are not just rebuilding a fountain here, a cast-iron bridge there, and elsewhere a meadow. Systematically, over the next ten years, we will rebuild Central Park. In the language of the historic preservationists we are restoring much of its original nineteenth century appearance for "adaptive reuse" in the late twentieth and twenty-first centuries.

This preservation effort is not simply a matter of physical restoration. It also entails developing new ways of involving the public in the Park's rehabilitation and new procedures for managing the Park's day-to-day use. New programs designed to complement the Park's physical master plan include creation of new park information centers, an Urban Park Ranger Corps, publishing new regulations governing large events and new rules on use of park lawns for athletics and team sports.

We have tried to think with Christo that The Gates would promote public consciousness of these efforts, that it would be a comment on the Park itself in the same manner as Christo's Running Fence commented so mysteriously and splendidly on the California hills and Western sky. Finally, however, because of The Gates' impact we are led to conclude that this would not be the case.

The Gates' "impact" on Central Park will not be simply or even principally a matter of the physical consequences that might result from its installation. Rather, it is the less tangible "impact" of The Gates which may well have the more lasting and widespread consequences: because of the project's systematic and complete alteration of a landmark space and the essentially political process by which it would achieve official approval; because of its immense costs and the peculiar moment in the Park's history when it would gain government sanction; because it would have been deemed appropriate or reasonable notwithstanding its obvious distance from the design and artistic vision that shaped the Park's creation and the restoration now underway; and because of the precedent all of this creates both legally and in terms of future Parks Department policies. For all of these reasons one must be concerned about the impact of Christo's project on how Central Park is understood, appreciated and perceived, on how the Park is used or should be used, on the manner in which it is or is not preserved as a unique historic landscape and the priority given to such efforts.

The search for answers to these questions required this Report's extensive consideration of Central Park's early and contemporary history, its design and restoration, and how it has been and will be managed and used in the past, the present and the future. These are subjects which Christo has treated minimally or not at all. As the artist in this instance he was free to do so without being cast out as subversive. For the Parks Department to follow suit, surrounded as it is with the terrible consequences of such past failures of vision and comprehension, would be tragic.

DETERMINATIONS

We have concluded that The Gates must be declined; the project is, after all, in the wrong place at the wrong time[1] and in the wrong scale.

In all these respects the defects of the physical project mirror the defects in the artist's grasp and understanding of Central Park.

Because of what The Gates offers as public art, our decision is one made more in sorrow than in anger. But, weighing the many considerations in this Report, and being mindful of the substantial

unknown risks inevitable in such a venture[2] one comes to understand that The Gates simply cannot and should not be forced to fit into New York's greatest public space.

2. The risks would be considerable even assuming strict compliance with necessary conditions upon installation and removal of the project. But Christo's self-confessed willingness to break the law, if all else fails, in order to achieve his artistic ends may well pose far more sweeping risks than the risks of physical impact associated with the project. While Christo has typically fulfilled his commitments regarding physical damage and site restoration matters, his record of compliance with applicable environmental laws and government regulations is quite another matter. In order to complete his 18 foot high, 24.5 mile nylon Running Fence, Christo proceeded with that section which ran into the Pacific Ocean at Bodega Bay, Marin County, with full knowledge that he did not have the requisite legal permits to do so. The episode is discussed in an article by Calvin Tomkins that appeared first in the New Yorker and then in a revised form in the 694 page volume Christo published in 1978 documenting Running Fence:

"Christo was hiding out because of a report (which later proved false) that he was about to be served with an injunction by the California Attorney General. After three years of legal maneuvering with state and county officials, after seventeen public hearings and two court decisions, Christo had defied the law. He had gone ahead and taken his eighteen-foot-high nylon fence into the Pacific Ocean at Bodega Bay, in Marin County, without a permit from the California Coastal Zone Conservation Commission, which has jurisdiction over everything constructed within a thousand yards of the ocean along the entire 1,072 miles of the California coastline. The night before, Christo and a specifically trained group of his workers had unfurled eleven white nylon fence panels and run them down a steep cliff to the last steel fence post on shore; this morning, starting at dawn, Christo's marine and land engineers had collaborated successfully on the trickiest part of the whole Running Fence operation, which involved pulling a tapered nylon panel out along a heavy cable to a raft that had been towed into position and anchored some six hundred feet offshore the day before. . . .

"Christo was determined to finish the coastal portion of the fence before the injunction came. That way, he figured, he could comply with the law by agreeing to remove it, whereas if he received the injunction and went on to build the fence in spite of it he would be in contempt of court. The one certainty at this point was that Christo was going to build his Running Fence, complete, and take whatever legal consequences there might be. . . .

"'It's funny,' he said when I joined him. 'If I go to jail and people ask why I am there, I will say, 'For building my fence.'

"'What about your good name?' I asked him. In the public hearings, Christo's lawyers had said repeatedly that his only capital was his good name and that he would keep his word and obey the law. 'Do you lose your good name now by going to the ocean?' 'Ah, my

1. In addition to the matters covered in the referenced pages it is important to note at this point that Christo's proposed exhibit period during the last two weeks in October would occur, in part, during the same time as the preparation for and the running of the New York City Marathon, which is held each year on the next to last weekend in October. The Marathon is, of course, one of the Park's largest events.

Accordingly, Christo's April 9, 1980, permit application requesting permission to erect The Gates for a two week period in the fall of one of the four years between 1982 and 1985 is denied pursuant to Article IV, Section 16(d)(1)–(4) of the Parks Department's Rules and Regulations, consistent with the policies discussed previously in this Report in Section IV(b), inasmuch as:

1. Installation of The Gates involves alteration of 25 miles of Central Park's pedestrian path system, at a cost in excess of $5 million; in these

---

good name.' Christo smiled. 'But what about my good name as an artist?' he said after a moment, his voice rising. 'It is more important I cheat the law than I cheat my art.'"
It may well be that any serious discussion of Christo's Gates should end on this point. That certainly would be a rational response of a public agency which is requested to issue a detailed legal permit for a mammoth construction project on public land by an individual who has, in effect, boasted of his past willingness not to be bound by the laws which it is the function of such permits to implement. However, the matter of Christo's apparent willingness to violate the legal constraints which might be imposed upon his work is relegated to a footnote here because more significant considerations lead inevitably to the conclusion that the project as a whole must be rejected regardless of any controls that might be imposed upon its execution.

respects, creation of The Gates requires the largest, most comprehensive physical and visual alteration of Central Park since completion of its construction in 1873.

2. Relatedly, The Gates is likely to generate crowds throughout the Park of unprecedented size on individual days and during the entire course of its two week exhibit period as well as for periods prior to and after the formal exhibit time.

3. Installation and display of The Gates, involving the entire Park, will occur during a four to five month period prior to mid-October when Central Park is already heavily used by the public and extensively scheduled for events of various sizes and duration.

4. Approval of The Gates as proposed would be inconsistent with present Parks Department permit policies applicable to Central Park and, as a result, such action may establish a precedent, both in terms of those policies as well as possible future judicial proceedings, requiring approval to be given to other events of similar scale and magnitude.

5. For these reasons The Gates will (i) substantially interfere with the ordinary use and enjoyment of the Park by the public and (ii) be of such a nature and duration that it cannot reasonably be accommodated in the park location selected for its exhibition.

COMMENTS

1. In the first reason given for denying Christo's application, observe the reference to the great physical scope and the $5 million cost of the project. As for scope, Christo's record is excellent; he has brought off other big projects (wrapping miles of Australian coast; building the 22.5-mile "Running Fence") and left the sites in perfect condition. As for cost, Christo would pay it all, as he has in prior projects. How is cost relevant to Commissioner Davis's decision?

2. Given the various uses to which Central Park has been put in its long history, how credible is the report's rejection of "The Gates" on the grounds of inappropriateness to the site?

3. At this writing, Christo still has not been given permission to build "The Gates," but he persists in trying. He has given the city of New York the most detailed, complete, and accurate survey of Central Park ever made, and at no cost to the city.

4. Christo was born and brought up in a communist society where as a young man he worked with thousands of others on such projects as cleaning snow away from railroad tracks so that tourists passing through Bulgaria would have a good impression of that country. In his projects, Christo combines his communist experience with capitalism, which allows him to finance his projects as an entrepreneur as well as a creator. Christo's living and working in noncommunist societies has unlocked his imagination and encouraged him to take on "impossible" feats year after year. His purpose is to create something beautiful and memorable, to give everyone the experience of art outside the museum and gallery. No artist's work is as public as Christo's—and, most dramatic of all, he pays for it himself.

5. Commissioner Davis's footnote 2 in the excerpt above deals with Christo's extension of "Running Fence" into the Coastal Zone without the required permit from the Coastal Commission. This damaging (to his reputation and his plans for subsequent projects, as here)

contravention of both the law and his own artistic principles, which call for meticulous compliance with applicable laws, is the only such lapse by Christo known to the authors. In all other cases he has treated the process of acquiring permissions and public cooperation and participation as an essential aspect of the work of art.

6. Suppose it could be argued plausibly that a public official blocks a Christo project by refusing to grant a permit merely because he does not like the project, even though all the statutory conditions for the permit have been fully met? That appears to have been the situation with extension of the "Running Fence" into the Coastal Zone. What should the artist do?

7. Is Commissioner Davis's decision lawful? What is its legal basis? According to pages 84ff. of his "Report and Determination," the commissioner's discretion is broad, but it must be applied in a rational (i.e., related to applicable principles governing park use) and nondiscriminatory way. Does his reasoning convince you, or is this another case of censorship by denial of a permit?

GOVERNMENT PATRONAGE AND THE LIMITS OF ARTISTIC FREEDOM IN PUBLIC ART

A basic problem of modern patronage has been how much control the patron has over the artist. So axiomatic is the modern concept of art's dependence on freedom of thought and inquiry that it was written into the Declaration of Purpose of the National Foundation on the Arts and the Humanities Act of 1965 and passed by the U.S. Congress. Even a casual acquaintance with art history causes one to reflect, however, on the seeming paradox of the U.S. government's present and increasing commitment to support of the arts. Historically it was freedom from institutional and government patronage that early modern artists fought for because of what they felt was the long history of the artist's submission to the self-interest of his sponsors. The artist as a valued political and cultural rebel is very recent in human history. Before the nineteenth century, freedom as we think of it today was not essential to the creation of great art, as the varied and often authoritarian patronage shows. From antiquity, and with rare exceptions, the artist unquestionably served the needs of church, court, and commune. He was image-maker for cults, cities, and kingdoms, and always on terms set by the sponsor.

With the appearance of the cult of genius in the sixteenth century, and in 17th century Protestant Holland, artists began to create works of art for an open market. Great artists such as Dürer, Raphael, Michelangelo, and Titian knew that anything they made would find eager and willing buyers, yet these great figures also submitted to the personal demands of powerful patrons. Rubens worked for kings and lords even after personal wealth would have permitted him to paint exclusively for his own pleasure. Rembrandt knew the vicissitudes of the free market, and like many other Dutch artists he often had to resort to other means to supplement his income. It is with Dutch artists of the seventeenth century that we encounter the now familiar phenomenon of artists who cannot support themselves entirely by their profession but must teach or engage in some form of business. Even when free of government or church patronage, Dutch artists learned as others who followed that in the open market freedom could be curtailed if success meant conforming to the tastes of the public in order to survive by sales. Accordingly, Dutch artists often specialized in portraits, landscapes, or still lifes.

As a profession, art-dealing begins in the sixteenth century. By the mid-nineteenth century, the art dealer became crucial to the independence of venturesome artists such as the Impressionists. Without the much maligned profession of the art merchant, with his financial and moral support, modern art as we know it would not have come about. It is also to art dealers that we owe much of our private, corporate, and public collections of art. Prophetic of our own time, in the last century when art schools turned out more artists than the government could support, it was the art dealer who made contact with and encouraged middle-class collectors.

Why, then, if modern art evolved independently of government support, should our government fund the arts? Are not the authoritarian art policies of Nazi Germany and Communist Russia eloquent warnings of how the most creative art can be destroyed as well as prohibited when government actively intervenes in the world of art? Did not Picasso fight Franco most of his life? Matisse had no fellowships from the French, and the government did not give him a retrospective until many years after his death. Rouault was not a monk in a religious order. Hundreds of American artists steeled themselves to poverty, as well as public apathy and critical neglect, while working in a free enterprise system. Nevertheless, a surprising number of our most well known artists who helped to bring American art to international prominence after World War II, such as Pollock, Gorky, DeKooning, Rothko, and Newman, accepted government support during the Depression in order to keep active as artists. The Works Progress Administration (WPA) allowed many of the best American artists to continue in their profession at crucial moments in their careers. The Declaration of Purpose of the National Foundation on the Arts and Humanities Act of 1965 reads: "The practice of art and the study of the humanities require constant dedication. . . . It is necessary and appropriate for the Federal government to help create and sustain not only a climate encouraging freedom of thought, imagination and inquiry, but also the material conditions facilitating the release of this creative talent."

What is historically important about present U.S. government funding of the arts is that lessons have been learned from authoritarian sponsorship. These have been combined with the need to sustain the traditional decentralized, pluralistic support system for art from the private šector. Unlike Egyptian pyramid-building, Depression-era U.S. programs of sponsorship were predicated on "human economic relief" rather than the self-interest of a ruler. For the first time the government recognized that artists were citizens and poor.

Because so much that Americans take for granted in their present patronage system is new and hard won, it is worth recalling the seemingly irreconcilable interests and attitudes that had to be brought together. How, for example, could there be a public art whose origins were centered on the artist's self?

During the WPA times many artists on the government payroll found a new social consciousness that they could express in their art and thus satisfied sponsors and public by seemingly giving approval to the system. Today, a giant Calder stabile standing in Grand Rapids converted President Gerald Ford to government support of urban art, and an elegant Rosati abstract sculpture is the pride of Wichita, Kansas. Neither artist had to compromise his art to gain public acceptance, and neither sculpture speaks directly to the American political system or life-style. Crucial to phenomena such as this has been not necessarily greater public comprehension of art, but increased tolerance and a sense of civic pride in having fine art on display. The American public has accepted the fact that the best U.S. artists believe in art that is monumental in scale, but it has rejected monuments to individuals and political abstractions. As Charlotte Devree points out, post–World War II government-sponsored military cemetery art was predicated on clichés that its conservative artists and backers believed would appeal to the lowest common denominator of intelligence and taste. Such an attitude is less acceptable to a more sophisticated public in much of the United States.

In the last decade, leading American artists overcame their distrust of the government and corporations. The broad spectrum of interests, styles, and ideas in the art world that have received relatively evenhanded sponsorship from these two powerful sources have done much to change artists' attitudes. Many artists seem convinced that even with the backing of the government or business they can continue to create art essentially on their own terms. Conversely, lawmakers and executives have begun to change their stereotypical image of the artist as an impractical dreamer, rebel, or subversive. The international prestige and monetary value of the best art have helped in this regard, as has the experience of corporate leaders in seeing that artists like money and respect craft, budgets, and deadlines.

One of the most interesting and enlightening developments in current patronage is the change from the insistence of taxpayers that they should always get some tangible goods or services in return for their dollars. There are National Endowment for the Arts (NEA) grants, which allow the artist to work for himself and even to keep the work created. In the past, when artists were supported by living in a monastery, court, or household of the sponsor, it was customary for the patron to receive both the art and the services. It has taken several thousand years for patrons to recognize that the personal possession of art they paid for may not be more important than its benefits to society as a whole even when retained by the artist.

In the 1980 census, more than 400,000 Americans classified themselves as professional artists in all fields. Their unprecedented numbers are also accompanied by a support system unparalleled in variety if not adequacy. No previous culture has had as extensive government and business patronage, combined with an academic system that puts hundreds of artists on salary and tenure. Art dealers are more numerous than ever, but they cannot represent all the artists, and there seem to be too many galleries for the market to support. Even with the addition to the patronage system of architectural commissions, regional art competitions, and the purchasing power of museums, it has been estimated that only a very small percentage of American artists are able to work full-time at their professions or to support themselves entirely from their income as artists. Thousands of artists are still classifiable as poor. Why, then, do young people enter such a high-risk profession, in economic terms? One answer may still be that which impelled nineteenth-century artists to take their chances with the double-edged character of freedom of art, namely, that material insecurity is worth the spiritual satisfaction of contributing to culture through a unique form of self-fulfillment. Art alone allows an individual to conceive, execute, and possess, if he chooses, an object of value to himself and to humanity.

Perhaps younger artists are also very much aware, through legislation and public expressions of support, of an increasingly sophisticated attitude that the United States is taking toward art. It took eighty-seven years for proponents of federal recognition of a national arts policy to succeed, but they did. Of course, present optimism about government support of the arts may change when we have greater opportunity to assess whether, despite good intentions, we are exerting some kind of subtle pressure on artists, steering them away from courses they might have pursued on their own. A haunting question is whether the beneficial attitudes and actions of government and business are another way of co-opting the rebellious spirit that was so vital to modern art. Balanced against this concern voiced by older artists who saw themselves as alienated from society is the legacy of the 1960s. Artists have encouraged the making of art that was more socially integrated as a result of closing the gaps between the artist and public, art and life.

COMMENTS

1. For a review of the various government programs supporting art and artists during the Depression, see Francis V. O'Connor, ed., *Federal Support for the Visual Arts: The New Deal and Now,* 2d ed. (New York: New York Graphic Society, 1971); Francis V. O'Connor, ed., *The New Deal Art Projects: An Anthology of Memoirs* (Washington, D.C.: Smithsonian Institution, 1972);

Kenneth Evett, "Back to WPA," *New Republic,* November 24, 1973, pp. 21–22; and Milton W. Brown, "New Deal Art Projects: Boondoggle or Bargain?" *ARTnews,* April 1982, pp. 82–87.

2. For background on the genesis of the National Endowment of the Arts, see Richard Eels, *The Corporation and the Arts* (New York: Macmillan, 1967), pp. 60–68, 195–212.

THE ACT OF 1965

National Foundation on the Arts and Humanities Act
20 U.S.C. §§951ff.

This Act may be cited as the "National Foundation on the Arts and the Humanities Act of 1965."

DECLARATION OF PURPOSE

Sec. 2. The Congress hereby finds and declares—

(1) that the encouragement and support of national progress and scholarship in the humanities and the arts, while primarily a matter for private and local initiative, is also an appropriate matter of concern to the Federal Government;

(2) that a high civilization must not limit its efforts to science and technology alone but must give full value and support to the other great branches of man's scholarly and cultural activity;

(3) that democracy demands wisdom and vision in its citizens and that it must therefore foster and support a form of education designed to make men masters of their technology and not its unthinking servant;

(4) that it is necessary and appropriate for the Federal Government to complement, assist, and add to programs for the advancement of the humanities and the arts by local, State, regional, and private agencies and their organizations;

(5) that the practice of art and the study of the humanities requires constant dedication and devotion and that, while no government can call a great artist or scholar into existence, it is necessary and appropriate for the Federal Government to help create and sustain not only a climate encouraging freedom of thought, imagination, and inquiry but also the material conditions facilitating the release of this creative talent;

(6) that the world leadership which has come to the United States cannot rest solely upon superior power, wealth, and technology, but must be solidly founded upon worldwide respect and admiration for the Nation's high qualities as a leader in the realm of ideas and of the spirit; and

(7) that, in order to implement these findings,

it is desirable to establish a National Foundation on the Arts and the Humanities and to strengthen the responsibilities of the Office of Education with respect to education in the arts and the humanities.

DEFINITIONS

Sec. 3. As used in this Act—

(a) The term "humanities" includes, but is not limited to, the study of the following: language, both modern and classic; linguistics; literature; history; jurisprudence; philosophy; archaeology; the history, criticism, theory, and practice of the arts; and those aspects of the social sciences which have humanistic content and employ humanistic methods.

(b) The term "the arts" includes, but is not limited to, music (instrumental and vocal), dance, drama, folk art, creative writing, architecture and allied fields, painting, sculpture, photography, graphic and craft arts, industrial design, costume and fashion design, motion pictures, television, radio, tape and sound recording, and the arts related to the presentation, performance, execution, and exhibition of such major art forms. . . .

ESTABLISHMENT OF A NATIONAL FOUNDATION ON THE ARTS AND THE HUMANITIES

Sec. 4. (a) There is established a National Foundation on the Arts and the Humanities (hereinafter referred to as the "Foundation,") which shall be composed of a National Endowment for the Arts, a National Endowment for the Humanities, and a Federal Council on the Arts and the Humanities (hereinafter established).

(b) The purpose of the Foundation shall be to develop and promote a broadly conceived national policy of support for the humanities and the arts in the United States pursuant to this Act.

(c) In the administration of this Act no department, agency, officer, or employee of the United States shall exercise any direction, supervision, or control over the policy determination, personnel, or curriculum, or the administration or operation of any school or other non-Federal agency, institution, organization, or association.

ESTABLISHMENT OF THE NATIONAL ENDOWMENT FOR THE ARTS

Sec. 5. (a) There is established within the Foundation a National Endowment for the Arts.

(b) The Endowment shall be headed by a Chairman, to be known as the Chairman of the National Endowment for the Arts.

(c) The Chairman, with the advice of the Federal Council on the Arts and the Humanities and the National Council on the Arts, is authorized to establish and carry out a program of grants-in-aid to groups, or, in appropriate cases, to individuals engaged in or concerned with the arts, for the purpose of enabling them to provide or support in the United States—

(1) productions which have substantial artistic and cultural significance, giving emphasis to American creativity and the maintenance and encouragement of professional excellence;

(2) productions, meeting professional standards or standards of authenticity, irrespective of origin which are of significant merit and which, without such assistance, would otherwise be unavailable to our citizens in many areas of the country;

(3) projects that will encourage and assist artists and enable them to achieve standards of professional excellence;

(4) workshops that will encourage and develop the appreciation and enjoyment of the arts by our citizens;

(5) other relevant projects, including surveys, research, and planning in the arts. . . .

(f) The total amount of any grant to any group pursuant to subsection (c) of this section shall not exceed 50 per centum of the total cost of such project or production, except that not more than 20 per centum of the funds allotted by the National Endowment for the Arts for this purpose for any fiscal year may be available for such grants

in that fiscal year without regard to such limitation in the case of any group which submits evidence to the Endowment that it has attempted unsuccessfully to secure an amount of funds equal to the grant applied for by such group, together with a statement of the proportion which any funds it has secured represent of the funds applied for by such group.

(g) Any group shall be eligible for financial assistance pursuant to this section only if (1) no part of its net earnings inures to the benefit of any private stockholder or stockholders, or individual or individuals, and (2) donations to such group are allowable as a charitable contribution under the standards of subsection (c) of section 170 of the Internal Revenue Code of 1954.

(h) (1) The Chairman, with the advice of the Federal Council on the Arts and the Humanities and the National Council on the Arts, is authorized to establish and carry out a program of grants-in-aid to assist the several States in supporting existing projects and productions which meet the standards enumerated in section 5(c) of this Act, and in developing projects and productions in the arts in such a manner as will furnish adequate programs, facilities, and services in the arts to all the people and communities in each of the several States. . . .

(i) Whenever the Chairman, after reasonable notice and opportunity for hearing, finds that—

(1) a group is not complying substantially with the provisions of this section;

(2) a State agency is not complying substantially with the terms and conditions of its State plan approved under this section; or

(3) any funds granted to a group or State agency under this section have been diverted from the purposes for which they were allotted or paid,

the Chairman shall immediately notify the Secretary of the Treasury and the group or State agency with respect to which such finding was made that no further grants will be made under this section to such group or agency until there is no longer any default or failure to comply or the diversion has been corrected, or, if compliance or correction is impossible, until such group or agency repays or arranges the repayment of the Federal funds which have been improperly diverted or expended. . . .

(l) The Chairman shall correlate the programs of the National Endowment for the Arts insofar as practicable, with existing Federal programs and with those undertaken by other public agencies or private groups, and shall develop the programs of the Endowment with due regard to the contri-bution to the objectives of this Act which can be made by other Federal agencies under existing programs. . . .

THE LEGISLATIVE HISTORY

House Report (Education and Labor Committee) 618, 89th Cong. (1965)

SUMMARY OF BILL

The bill (H.R. 9460) incorporates the proposals of President Lyndon B. Johnson as embodied in H.R. 6050, together with amendments reflecting suggestions made by witnesses. The bill contains important provisions and objectives found in related bills in this and earlier Congresses designed to authorize Federal programs for the arts and the humanities.

The bill establishes a National Foundation on the Arts and the Humanities, whose purpose is to develop and promote a broadly conceived national policy of support for the humanities and the arts in the United States. Its organization is shown in the accompanying chart:

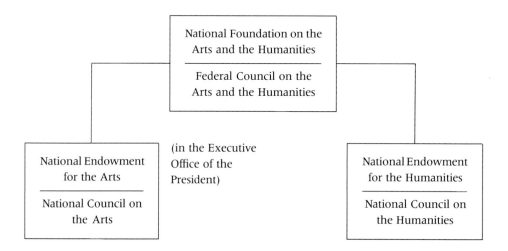

Such sums as may be necessary are authorized for administration of the Foundation. It is not possible at this time to determine the volume of grant applications in each category. The grant review and processing staff depends largely on the volume of applications. Administrative expenses of the National Science Foundation were about 19 percent of program costs in 1952, and by 1956 they had dropped to 3 percent.

Based upon the actual authorization of $5 million for each endowment, it is expected that administrative costs will be about 15 percent. Depending upon the volume of applications, the success of the effort to obtain private gifts, and the additional funding authorized under this activity, it is anticipated that the administrative cost ratio of the Foundation eventually will parallel that of the National Science Foundation.

BACKGROUND

This legislation has evolved as the result of many studies by this committee and by privately financed organizations. Proposals for programs of Government assistance in this area date back to the early days of this Nation.

In recent Congresses, this committee has conducted many hearings, in and out of Washington, relating to the need for Federal support for the arts and the humanities. Outside the Government private groups of citizens have also conducted similar studies. The most recent of these were those conducted by the Commission on the Humanities and the Special Studies Project on the Performing Arts conducted by the Rockefeller Brothers Fund.

Testimony on the present legislation, as well as testimony given in previous Congresses, and the reports of private commissions and panels clearly indicates:

1. There is a financial crisis facing the arts in the United States, which stems primarily from the inadequacy of private sources to support artistic excellence at an appropriate level and to foster and develop an environment which would fully stimulate the resources of American creative expression. . . .

PURPOSE OF LEGISLATION

President Lyndon B. Johnson, in transmitting the administration's specific legislative proposals on March 10, said:

This Congress will consider many programs which will leave an enduring mark on American life. But it may well be that passage of this legislation, modest as it is, will help secure for this Congress a sure and honored place in the story of the advance of our civilization.

In the same vein, former President Eisenhower's Commission on National Goals in its 1960 report said:

In the eyes of posterity, the success of the United States as a civilized society will be largely judged by the creative activities of its citizens in art, architecture, literature, music, and the sciences.

The function of the proposed Foundation—giving key recognition to the values of the humanities and the arts—is to correct the imbalance between science and the arts. It will thus assure that the United States will increase its contribution to the advance of civilization, as suggested by President Johnson, and thus achieve a goal suggested by President Eisenhower.

The arts and humanities are closely allied partners. The programs of the two endowments would be mutually beneficial; each would serve to strengthen the other. Knowledge in the hu-

manities is fundamental both to the practice and appreciation of art. The arts flourish best in a climate in which they are fully understood and appreciated; and the arts translate into tangible, creative and abiding form, the scope of human knowledge.

The Foundation would serve to decentralize the arts in the United States, so that artistic excellence could be enjoyed and appreciated by far greater numbers of our citizens, in each State of the Union.

The Humanities Endowment, emphasizing quality rather than quantity, and research at the highest levels of education, would serve to strengthen teaching, to improve university curriculums, and to attract the best teaching talents to humanistic studies. Witnesses pointed to the growing scarcity of talented teachers in the humanities, and to the increasing difficulties with regard to their recruitment.

The Foundation would have a profound impact on the burgeoning desire on the part of our citizens for greater exposure to cultural excellence. This desire is manifestly related to the increasing availability of leisure time in an era of growing prosperity. The committee believes that leisure can bring to our Nation great new opportunities for self-improvement and fulfillment and that the activities of the Foundation would be significantly in accord with this concept.

Almost alone among the major governments of the world, the U.S. Government until recently has displayed relatively little concern for the development and encouragement of the artistic and cultural resources of its citizens. The National Council on the Arts, established in 1964, was an important first step taken to correct this situation. A comprehensive and well-coordinated program, however, is urgently needed to implement this partial beginning and make it fully meaningful. The Foundation would serve this purpose.

The broad-based programs envisaged by the Foundation would serve not only to deepen our understanding of our friends and allies throughout the world, but would strengthen the projection of our Nation's cultural life abroad and enable us better to overcome the increasing "cultural offensive" being waged by Communist ideologies.

The partnership between the arts and humanities implicit in the Foundation would lead to a better comprehension of man in relation to his environment, in such areas as the proper growth of our cities, the better evaluation of behavioral problems and their solutions, the better adaptation of our modern technology to the exchange of information.

The Foundation would serve to coordinate the activities of private citizens, distinguished in the arts and humanities and concerned with their full development: Our Nation's leading artists and scholars, and cultural leaders in the States and local communities.

MINORITY VIEWS

We oppose enactment of R.H. 9460, and urge that it be rejected by the House of Representatives.

Lack of Adequate Study

Aside from the merit, or lack of merit, in this legislation, the House at the very least, should recommit this bill to the Committee on Education and Labor with instructions that it be given the careful and detailed committee study which legislation of such significance deserves.

This far-reaching bill, creating Federal czars over the arts and humanities, was "railroaded" through the committee on June 24, 1965, after about 15 minutes of consideration. Even a motion from the minority side that the bill be read was summarily rejected by the majority. Such procedure is particularly disturbing in light of the fact that when the committee met on June 24, the members were presented for the first time with a new committee print, dated the same day, containing a number of significant amendments which the minority members, at least, had never seen before.

Thereafter, several additional amendments, which we had never seen, were quickly adopted in committee with a minimum of discussion, and the bill was hurriedly reported with a haste that

was positively breathtaking. The result, H.R. 9460, is a measure so full of ambiguities as to puzzle the mind, paralyze the faculties, and numb the imagination. One who now ventures to read carefully the reported bill will soon find himself lost in a maze of bureaucratic organizational structure with a minimum of light to comprehend what the provisions actually mean or are intended to achieve. . . .

Danger of Encouraging Mediocrity

The bill should also be rejected on the merits. We believe the Congress should proceed very cautiously before authorizing any expansion of the Federal role in, and control over, the arts and humanities. In particular, we caution against a Federal program of direct subsidies to the arts which may well result in a lowering, rather than an elevation, of the cultural level of our Nation.

Russell Lynes, one of the editors of *Harper's* magazine, has said:

I am not worried about creeping socialism in the arts, but about creeping mediocrity. The less the arts have to do with our political processes, I believe, the healthier they will be.

Mr. Lynes argues that, at best, a program of Federal subsidies will create an arts bureaucracy in Government which will make decisions by committee vote and contribute to a spirit of compromise and conservatism in art. At worst, such a program could lead to attempts at political control of culture. He goes on to say, "The arts are a sitting duck for any politician who feels the need of making headlines."

The *Washington Post,* on May 6, 1965, reported an interview with Thornton Wilder, one of our greatest living writers, as follows:

[Wilder] rejected as unnecessary a program of Government subsidy for the creative artist.

COMMENTS

1. For an assessment of the NEA in operation, see two articles by Malcolm Carter: "The NEA: Will Success Spoil Our Biggest Patron?" *ARTnews,* May 1977, pp. 33–47; and "The National Endowment for the Arts Grows Up," *ARTnews,* September 1979, pp. 59–63. See also John Beardsley, *Art in Public Places: A Survey of Community Sponsored Projects Supported by the National Endowment for the Arts* (Washington, D.C.: Partners for Livable Places, 1981). Beardsley's work, in addition to reproducing the works that were commissioned, also contains a helpful bibliography on the subject. The text, though uncritical, provides background for the many commissions carried out during the previous fifteen years.

2. What is your estimate of the declarations of purpose behind the government support systems? If you agree with these purposes, can it be said that the role of the government as defined in the NEA act is sufficient? Consider the following:

> Congresswoman Bella Abzug has introduced a bill (H.R. 8563) to establish an emergency program of federally-financed employment of unemployed artists. Under the bill when unemployment exceeds 6.5% nationally, the National Endowment for the Arts must undertake a program of employment for artists to be administered by the states under federal grants-in-aid as well as by the NEA directly (partly for purposes of the Bicentennial). The bill would thus establish formally the efforts on the federal and state levels to use the Comprehensive Employment and Training program to employ artists in artistic work for public-works programs. [*Art & the Law,* Fall 1975, p. 4.]

Would you have supported Abzug's bill? Why or why not?

3. Have the objections stated in the minority views on the National Endowments bill, above, been justified by experience?

4. From the artist's standpoint, why should he seek and receive government support? What has changed since 1948 and the following statement by Russian-born, naturalized American sculptor Naum Gabo?

> I want to issue a warning to all those who hold the chains of power over the world today: to the self-appointed dictators as well as the properly elected statesmen; to the ordained commissioners as well as to the chosen heads of political departments; to the man on the street as well as to the self-appointed representatives of public opinion—the artist, the pushed and battered artist of today, warn them all that they will do better and will get more out of me if they leave me alone to do my work. They will never succeed, no matter how hard they will try, to enslave my mind without extinguishing it. I will never enlist in the suite of heralds and trumpeters of their petty glories and bestial quarrels. They may vilify my ideas, they may slander my work, they may chase me from one country to another, they may eventually succeed in starving me, but I shall never, never, conform to their ignorance, to their prejudices. We artists may dispute and argue amongst ourselves about ideologies and ideals—but nothing will more potentially bind us together than the revolt against the blind forces trying to make us do what we don't believe is worth doing." [The Trowbridge lecture of 1948 at Yale University, in Herbert Read and Leslie Martin, *Gabo: Constructions, Sculpture, Painting, Drawings, and Engravings* (London: Lund Humphries, 1957), p. 179.] (This material was originally copyrighted and published in *Gabo* by Read and Martin (1957) p. 179, and is reprinted herewith by permission of Lund Humphries Publishers, Ltd., London, England.)

THE CALDER CONTROVERSY

One of the pioneering modern public sculptures in the United States, a work that encouraged many other cities to reject traditional figural art for modern and abstract work, was Calder's "Grande Vitesse." This was the first sculpture made possible by the NEA "Art in Public Places" program. Its story follows.

GERALD NORDLAND *The Grand Rapids Calder Controversy**

In 1967 the City of Grand Rapids applied for a National Endowment for the Arts Art in Public Places grant for a sculpture for Vandenberg Plaza, the center of its urban renewal program. The first city to receive such a grant, whose purpose was to honor American sculptors with commissions

*From Gerald Nordland, "The Grand Rapids Calder Controversy," in *Controversial Public Art: From Rodin to di Suvero* (Milwaukee: Milwaukee Art Museum, 1983), pp. 48–49. Copyright © 1983 by the Milwaukee Art Museum. Reprinted by permission.

for major works to be displayed in public places, Grand Rapids was selected largely on the basis of its proposed site, to (as stated in 1966) "test the practicability of Art in Public Places." The grant of $45,000 required that the community raise matching funds for the purchase of a work by an American artist who was to be selected by four NEA appointed professionals and three representatives of the recipient community. Matching funds were raised primarily from local private foundations by the Mayor's Sculpture Committee chaired by Mrs. Nancy Mulnix, but additional funds were contributed by the community at large to the $127,900 needed for the entire project.

Calder, distinguished for his imposing stabiles in other public places, was selected by the panel, accepted the commission, and armed with drawings and photographs of the site for which his work was destined, had by the spring of 1968 produced a maquette which was approved by Mrs. Mulnix and other members of the Sculpture Committee.

Meanwhile, "Public Will Have No Sculpture Say" was a headline in the *Grand Rapids Press* (August 28, 1967), quoting panelist painter Adolph Gottlieb, who doubted the possibility of choosing public art by popular vote: "Artists and public are seldom in rapport. What is important is that an artist make a creative statement which, if it is worth anything at all, will become accepted in time."

Soon letters were appearing in the *Grand Rapids Press* complaining that the committee's selection of Calder, with his French affiliations and modern style, was unpatriotic, undemocratic, and above all unrepresentative of the taste of a midwestern majority and their culture. The money might be better spent on a music hall, a skating rink, or shoes for needy children, critics continued. If a sculpture was necessary it should at least be heroic, like the Lincoln Memorial, and portray Senator Arthur Vandenberg, for whom the new civic center was named.

The controversy intensified when it was learned that plans for the pool and fountain originally intended for the site were being jeopardized. Supervisor Robert Blandford, a member of the county's finance committee, headed the faction favoring the pool, but was defeated by the Kent County Board of Supervisors, with the result that $1,800 of piping and foundation had to be removed by the city. Finally a "very bad" sketch of the stabile was (regrettably, according to Mrs. Mulnix) published in the *Grand Rapids Inter-preter* on April 9, 1968, at last giving the public an idea of the anticipated sculpture. "The abstract character was derided in letters to the editor, and a song ridiculing the project was aired on a local radio station." Meanwhile requests for a tax levy to cover shipping costs and construction of supports for the sculpture were turned down.

In defense of the proposed sculpture, its potential for psychological, cultural, and economic renewal as a focal point of Grand Rapids' downtown center, which like the Piazza San Marco or Lincoln Center, would become a hub of cultural activity, was cited. Calder's biographer, James Johnson Sweeney, also helped to prepare the city for the stabile, minimizing the criticism it had (as yet unseen) received, prophesying that Grand Rapids would some day refer to it affectionately as "our Calder . . . Art becomes a daily habit. You have to live with it to have an appetite for it. . . . [The piece] will set the pattern for civic life, make people think harmoniously and keep them always inquisitive."

But both before and after the gala dedication of *La Grande Vitesse* (a characteristically witty pun on the city's name) on June 14, 1969, the negative reactions of the public seemed to outweigh the positive. The people resented their lack of participation in the selection process, did not understand the work ("what does it symbolize?"), thought it an ugly piece of junk, or felt the money should have been spent on improving ghetto conditions or to commission a local artist.

In 1975 an anti-Calder faction opposed Mrs. Mulnix's reappointment to the Michigan Council for the Arts, and disgruntled letters still appeared in the *Grand Rapids Press* during the spring arts festival. However, by 1973 "the public reaction was so favorable that the city adopted [*La Grande Vitesse*] as an official symbol, emblazoned on everything from the mayor's stationery to the municipal sanitation trucks." Vandenberg Plaza, which came to be known as Calder Plaza, has, since 1970, attracted thousands to its yearly arts festival and was central to the nationally acclaimed *Sculpture Off the Pedestal* exhibition (1973) which was widely supported by local business and industry. This exhibition, inspired by *La Grande Vitesse*, caused a burgeoning of community interest in and support for contemporary art, resulting in the city's acquisition of an earthwork by Robert Morris, an environmental sculpture by Joseph Kinnebrew, and sculptures by Mark di Suvero and Robert Watson. The former's *Moto Viget* (1977) engendered an "extraordinary level of public support" throughout a controversy "as lively as the one that surrounded the Calder." GSA Commissioner of Public Buildings N.A. Panuzio's decision to reject the sculpture (because it differed from di Suvero's original maquette) was only reversed after months of ardent petitioning by the people of Grand Rapids. In this instance only a very small minority objected to the sculpture, while the majority were willing to fight the U.S. Government to keep their di Suvero. Apparently Calder's defenders were correct in their predictions, and Grand Rapids is still undergoing the cultural growth sparked by *La Grande Vitesse*.

COMMENTS

1. Can government-financed art programs be apolitical? Should they be? See the discussions by Hilton Kramer in "The Threat of Politicization of the Federal Arts Program," *New York Times,* October 16, 1977, p. 1, and by Robert Brustein, "Whither the National Arts and Humanities Endowments," *New York Times,* December 18, 1977. Arts and Leisure Section, p. 1. Brustein concludes his long article as follows:

> When the twin Endowments were first created, many of us had hopes that America had come of age culturally, that it could support the minority of talent, that the imperatives of artistic and intellectual excellence would no longer be overshadowed by the democratic demands of political necessity. For 12 years, those hopes have been more or less sustained. Whether this condition will continue to prevail is an issue now shrouded in serious doubt and considerable uncertainty.

If a choice is to be made between funding educators and popularizers on the one hand, and artists and scholars on the other, between a government adult-education program or supporting creativity in the arts and scholarship, where do you stand?

2. Is government support inevitably a form of censorship? In commissioning works of art and supporting certain artists, is the government presenting an official standard of taste? Consider the following.

GOVERNMENT COMMISSION OF WORKS OF ART: THE COMMISSION OF FINE ARTS

The federal government supports the arts by commissioning artists to decorate its public buildings and to design public monuments and memorials. It also employs artists to produce postage stamps, coins, medals, and insignia. The process by which the government decides which artists will receive federal commissions is interesting and raises significant questions about government and the arts.

The Commission of Fine Arts was established in 1910 to "advise upon the location of statues, fountains, and monuments in the public squares, streets, and parks in the District of Columbia, and upon the selection of models for statues, fountains, and monuments, erected under the authority of the United States and upon the selection of artists for the excecution of the same" (40 U.S.C. §104 [1910]). The commission also advises generally "upon questions of art when required to do so by the President, or by any committee of either House of Congress" (40 U.S.C. §104 (1910)).

Since the commission was first established, its duties have been enlarged from time to time by executive order. For example, according to the executive order of November 28, 1913, questions of art with regard to new structures for the District of Columbia must be submitted to the commission for comment and advice. Also, Congress has sometimes stipulated that plans for certain buildings or monuments must be submitted to the commission and approved by it.

The commission consists of seven "well-qualified judges of the fine arts," who are appointed by the President for a period of four years each. It meets two days a month. The members do not receive any compensation other than travel expenses. The commission's budget ($420,000 proposed for 1987) is used for the travel expenses, salaries of supporting staff, and costs of the commission's publications.

The commission has stated that it prefers to retain its advisory capacity. It has opposed efforts to transform it into an administrative body, along the lines of government-supported arts councils and ministries of fine arts in other countries, with the responsibility for spending large sums of money as government subsidies for public art projects (*Art and Government*, Report to the President by the Commission of Fine Arts [1953], p. 11). One might surmise from this attitude that the commission does not wield much power. The commission's enabling legislation states that it is to *advise* on the selection of artists for federal projects and to *advise* on models produced by those artists. Only a few congressional enactments call specifically for the commission's approval of certain works of art before they can be accepted by the government. However, in actual practice, federal agencies and Congress, because they do not have artistic expertise, defer to the opinion of the commission. Below are examples of how influential the Commission of Fine Arts can be where "government art" is concerned.

The Commission of Fine Arts has played a central role in the selection of artists and designs for sculpture to decorate war memorials. The following article criticizes this role and the commission's preference for traditional sculpture, until recently.

CHARLOTTE DEVREE *Is This Statuary Worth More Than a Million of Your Money?**

There is almost no hint in official government sculpture that truly creative sculptors exist in the United States today. In thirteen World War II Battle Monuments newly completed or under construction in Europe, North Africa and the Philippines, for which commissions totaling $299,540 have already been given, and in new Federal buildings in this country, the sculpture is if anything a series of monuments to official esthetic numbness, and to the vacuum that exists between the creative sculptor's studio and the official Washington desk.

In a world of change, Federal sculpture is changeless. It is the same old, over-familiar dilution of the Neo-Greek, the last pitifully weak showing of a once great force. That a flabby modern rendering of this overworked mode might now be meaningless to vacuity, and that slippery streamlined nudes and chastely draped marble maidens to commemorate the dead of the last war might constitute an artistic and emotional affront, never seems to occur to those responsible. Officials assume that they choose the best. In the realm of esthetic sensibility, they know not what damage they do.

Officials who give out government commissions are happy that sculptors are well paid. For *Buddies,* and reliefs at Anzio, Paul Manship netted $45,000. For two horse-groups by James Earle Fraser and Leo Friedlander, respectively, at Arlington Memorial Bridge Plaza in Washington, D.C., each sculptor made $107,000. And for *Iwo Jima,* Felix deWeldon is said to have obtained clear, from a fund raised by the Marine Corps League, a sum probably in excess of $350,000. Though these sculptors worked on the final piece of furnished full-scale plasters, usually the sculptor for his fee furnishes only a half-size plaster.

Artistically appalling as deWeldon's enormous bronze triumph in Washington is in its stylistic resemblance to sculptural monuments of the Nazis and the Soviets, Donald DeLue's figure commemorating 9,385 Americans who fell in the Normandy invasion and just after, is drearier in its funeral implications. At the St. Laurent cemetery, on a stunning bluff overlooking Omaha Beach where Americans landed in June 1944, there now towers DeLue's 22-foot bronze male nude, its arms flung gracefully in the air, the figure upward-flying from a watery-surfaced fish or wavelike form—symbolizing the English Channel. The figure is sleek, wind-tossed, Milles-like. It represents, DeLue says, nothing so banal as victory but rather the spirit of young American manhood triumphing over the pain and death of battle. At its base bronze letters read: "For mine eyes have seen the glory of the coming of the Lord." . . .

Between sculptors (mostly members of the tightly governed and mainly academic group of sculptors who have formed the National Sculpture Society) who regularly *get* government commissions, and sculptors who do *not*, there is a complex mechanism of suave Washington officialdom, with the Commission of Fine Arts its central cog. This is the machinery by which so many monumental sculptural errors are achieved; agencies that choose the architects—who usually serve the Neo-Classic tradition and who chose the sculptors—submit all plans to the Commission of Fine Arts for approval. In effect the Commission, headed by David Finley, Director of the National Gallery, has life-or-death jurisdiction over the design of all Federal buildings and their decoration in this country, except those of the Treasury and the Armed Services; over all monuments in Washington parks and all local government buildings in Washington; over private buildings on conspicuous Washington streets; over acceptance of works of art offered as gifts to the government; over Federal battle monuments, and over anything erected in Georgetown. Though the capital architect is technically a free man, he frequently seeks Commission guidance. Since its establishment by Congress in 1910, the Commission has passed upon more than a thousand items, from the Lincoln Memorial to the installation of a marker at a Spanish-American War memorial in Tampa. With members appointed by the President representing architecture, sculpture, painting and landscaping, its powers are loose but vast.

The Commission is theoretically not responsible for the initial choice of architect on which hangs the choice of sculptor. Yet for World War II Battle Monuments, by far the largest recent Federal artistic project, the Fine Arts Commission suggested to the Battle Monuments Commission (which does not pretend to know about art) that it retain as consulting architects a firm that is successor to a firm headed by a former Commission member, Paul Philippe Cret. Thus the matter was kept in the family. A Mr. Harbeson—of Harbeson, Hough, Livingston and Larson of Philadelphia—

suggested architects for the battle monuments, and he and the architects and Lee Lawrie (also a former Commission member) as sculpture consultant, chose the sculptors. Mr. Harbeson and Mr. Lawrie have overseen their work. And the Fine Arts Commission has duly approved it.

Approval is usually given to a one-third-size maquette, after which the sculptor furnishes a half-size plaster model. Full-size casting and carving in stone are customarily done by workmen abroad. Where carving is involved, photographs are taken when workmen are almost finished and shown to the American sculptors that they may make corrections on eight-by-ten glossies and so guide the carvers in finishing up.

Thus nameless British workmen carved the four stuffed-doll-like effigies of servicemen by Wheeler Williams which stand against a wall in the Cambridge cemetery commemorating the missing dead. For the half-size plasters, Williams' fee was $20,540. Three symbolic reliefs cut by one Jean Juge amply decorate the facade of the memorial at Epinal near the Rhine—Mr. Juge worked from models by Malvina Hoffman for which (plus a figure) she received $35,150. At Suresnes near Paris, a gracious marble lady wearing billowy drapery, by Lewis Iselin, is kept company by two reliefs by the same sculptor, for which he got $13,800. A companion figure there, a more austerely draped marble lady, is by John Gregory ($7,000). . . .

That amazing statuary, paid for by public funds, publicly appears only when finished, and that none but insiders have known it was in process is not, officials feel, their fault. They point to the democratic nature of their method of selection, and most seem unaware that it is open to criticism. They explain patiently that the Congress passes an appropriation bill for each battle monument and each Federal building and that these bills are reported in the *Congressional Record.* Open committee hearings may be held and anyone may appear and speak up. Any sculptor is free to send photographs of his work to any official and ask to be considered. Actually the only sculptor-lobbyist to appear on Capitol Hill in a long time is Wheeler Williams, who recently tried, without success, to persuade congressmen to appropriate more money for the decoration of buildings.

The Public Buildings Service works smoothly with the Commission of Fine Arts. Public Buildings architects frequently design Federal buildings and always submit plans by whatever architects—

including choice of sculptor and his preliminary small-scale models—to the Commission for approval. Sculptors (all must have security clearance to get Federal work) who made plasters for assorted door panels, entrance figures and small and large statuary for the six Federal buildings started by this office since the end of World War II, are National Sculpture Society members Sidney Waugh, Joseph Kiselewski, Heinz Warneke, Edmond Amateis, Leo Friedlander, Paul Jennewein and Edwin Rust. Jennewein's trylon has a spectacular location on the plaza before the new U.S. District Court House in Washington. A Public Buildings architect conceived the trylon, made accurate drawings of its shape and rough sketches of its figures from which Jennewein made plaster models. The trylon is a three-sided marble shaft with pinched corners; figures symbolizing constitutional freedoms, carved on its sides by a workman, look like appliquéd animal crackers. The effect is about as interesting as canned soup.

The other main agency through which sculpture is erected in Washington is the National Capital Parks division of the Department of the Interior. Its most dramatic recent acquisitions are those two horses at Arlington Bridge, and *Iwo Jima*. Before *Iwo Jima*, the horses broke records for size.

Iwo Jima also happened within the family as its sculptor, Felix deWeldon, is the sculptor member of the Commission of Fine Arts. DeWeldon was a successful society-portrait sculptor in England and came to this country with an impressive social backing which eased his entrée into top Washington circles. Truman sat for him in the White House and appointed him to the Commission. While serving in the Navy, deWeldon saw the Iwo Jima photograph and, inspired, advanced the idea that it ought to be made into a big bronze monument—by Felix deWeldon. He was at work on a full-scale plaster when the matter came before the Fine Arts Commission, which

had the decency to protest strongly at first but later approved. The Marine Corps League raised money from Marines and friends. It reportedly paid deWeldon $554,000, out of which he is said to have paid $150,000 for casting, plus costs of transportation. *Iwo Jima*'s total cost, including preparation of site, reached $850,000.

David Finley, chairman of the Fine Arts Commission, is the acknowledged head of the congenial Federal-arts family. . . .

If Mr. Finley, admiring the work of a modern sculptor, desired a sculpture by him to be placed, for example, where the Jennewein trylon stands now, could he have brought this about? No, not really. You see, in each case the architect should be free to choose that sculptor who would carry out the spirit of the building. Mr. Finley might make a suggestion but to force a choice on the architect would be, on Mr. Finley's part, to go beyond his proper role. He was, in theory, in favor of open competition for Federal sculpture but thought that, in practice, it worked rather a hardship on the sculptors. So many would work so hard and spend so much time on their entries, and only one could win. This would cause hard feelings. Other officials, asked the same question, made the same answer in about the same words.

There is of course no guarantee that open competition would result in meaningful Federal sculpture. Just what might take its place brings up questions. To what extent must public taste be taken into account, since public funds are involved? What is public taste, anyhow, and how far has it been corrupted by ineffectual government sculpture? Isn't there some suitable mean point in style between pseudo-Greek statuary and the avant-garde? Wouldn't there be a public howl if abstract sculpture were to appear on Washington's sedate streets or in a battle monument? The questions are thorny but, at the moment, largely academic. . . .

THE VIETNAM VETERANS MEMORIAL

Twenty-five years after Devree wrote "Wouldn't there be a public howl if abstract sculpture were to appear on Washington's sedate streets or in a battle monument?" she was absolutely correct. It took that long for the United States to fight a war that was one of its rare military defeats and to finally decide to hold an open competition for a monument to those who had fought and died in it. Many years had to pass before David Findley and his views were replaced on the Fine Arts Commission. It also took that long for modern artists to reconsider their disinclination to make government-commissioned memorials and to focus on the dead.

Modern sculpture, for example, celebrates life and living and came into being in opposition to art that celebrated death and the dead.

By the end of the 1970s, it was clear that the traditional sculptural public monument, such as those Devree described, had outlived its credibility and therefore its usefulness. There seemed to be no alternative by which an artistic monument could be a dignified, socially unifying, and compassionate remembrance of the dead. A century ago, Rodin's "Monument to the Burghers of Calais" celebrated not only fourteenth-century civic martyrs but also heroism in defeat, such as France had experienced before the guns of the Prussians in 1870. One of Rodin's radical innovations in humanizing the monument was to make all six burghers the same height, which for him meant that they were equal in courage.

An equivalent gesture can be found in the Vietnam Veterans Memorial in Washington, D.C., designed by Maya Ling Lin. The names on that monument are not accompanied by rank, and every letter is capitalized the way it appeared on the computer printout given to the artist by the Pentagon.

MAYA LING LIN *Statement on Her Winning Design for the Vietnam Veterans Memorial in Washington, D.C.*

Walking through this park—the memorial appears as a rift in the earth, a long, polished black stone wall, emerging from and receding into the earth. Approaching the memorial, the ground slopes gently downward and the low walls emerging on either side, growing out of the earth, extend and converge at a point below and ahead. Walking into the grassy site contained by the walls of the memorial, we can barely make out the carved names upon the memorial walls. These names, seemingly infinite in number, convey the sense of overwhelming numbers, while unifying those individuals as a whole. For this memorial is meant not as a monument to the individual, but rather as a memorial to the men and women who died during the war as a whole.

Brought to a sharp awareness of such a loss, it is up to each individual to resolve or come to terms with this loss. For death is for each a personal and private matter, and the area contained within this memorial is a quiet place, meant for personal reflection and private reckoning. The thick granite walls, each 200 feet long and 10 feet below the ground at their lowest point (gradually ascending toward ground level), effectively act as a sound barrier, yet they are of such height and length so as not to appear threatening or enclosing. The actual area is wide and shallow, allowing for a sense of privacy, and the sunlight from the memorial's southern exposure, along with the grassy park surrounding and within its wall, contribute to the serenity of the area. Thus this memorial is for those who have died, and for us to remember them.

The memorial is composed not as an unchanging monument, but as a moving composition, to be understood as we move into and out of it; the passage itself is gradual, the descent to the origin slow, but it is at the origin that the meaning of this memorial is to be fully understood. At the intersection of these walls, on the right side, at the wall's top, is carved the date of the first death. It is followed by the names of those who have died in chronological order. These names continue on this wall, appearing to recede into the earth at the wall's end. The names resume on the left wall, as the wall emerges from the earth, back to the origin, where the date of the last death is carved, at the bottom of this wall. Thus the war's beginning and end meet; the war is "complete," coming full circle, yet broken by the earth that bounds the angle's open side, and contained within the earth itself. As we turn to leave, we see these walls stretching into the distance, directing us to the Washington Monument, to the left, and the Lincoln Memorial, to the right, thus bringing the Vietnam memorial into a historical context. We the living are brought to a concrete realization of these deaths.

ALLAN TEMKO *The Vietnam Veterans' Memorial: Environmental Design**

The path turns, and the ground opens in a downward sweep of grass to the V of polished black granite: two outflung, tapering walls, 493 feet long overall, inscribed with the names of 57,939 victims, dead or unaccounted for, listed in the order they perished. That's all. Except for flowers, ribbons, and other modest remembrances placed at the base of the walls or tucked in crevices between the granite slabs, there is for the time being no other adornment—although an unfortunate flagpole and military statuary group are to be added at the insistence of veterans groups and conservative politicians—in this sunken park within a park.

The planned additions will only harm the purity of this design. No U.S. flag is needed to tell us that this is one of the most profound statements of national reconciliation—of suffering compassion and ultimate sorrow—in all of American art. It is an abstract parable of war and peace, death and life, past and present, whose patriotic strength doesn't count on military force but moral truth. . . .

It had taken 10 years for the veterans to convince opponents of the war, inside and outside government, that their dead comrades should be remembered. They obtained one of the finest remaining open sites in Washington and started raising $7 million from corporations and from individuals such as the Texas superpatriot H. Ross Perot. It's not hard to understand the preference of Perot and his friends for gung-ho figurative sculpture that tells a story of American heroism, perhaps on the order of the Iwo Jima memorial. What is baffling is the unrelenting hatred aimed at the winning design.

That the winner was Maya Ling Lin of Athens, Ohio, a soft-spoken Chinese-American who was then a 21-year-old senior at Yale, only infuriated conservatives, by no means limited to unlettered former grunts of working-class background. Yale-

man William F. Buckley's *National Review* dismissed her design as "Orwellian glop." It was called "Jane Fonda's Wall."

Yet Lin's design met every requirement of the competition.

Under terrific pressure, the Fine Arts Commission has accepted the demand for a conventional sculptural group of three GIs by Frederick Hart, a third-place finalist in the competition who has been pitched into the winner's seat with Lin. These young figures could have come from Hollywood central casting for a war film.

Because we ostensibly could not otherwise tell that they are Americans, an oversized flag—big enough for an aircraft carrier . . .—will be displayed on a 50-foot pole. The base of the flagstaff will be emblazoned with the insignia of the services. There will be a hortatory inscription. . . . Originally the Perot group wanted the flagstaff at the vertex of the angle and the statuary facing it on the opposite rise of ground. Happily, the Fine Arts Commission—strengthened by the American Institute of Architects . . .—refused to approve these locations, or others that would have interfered with the view of the Lincoln Memorial, and instead placed statuary and flagstaff tactfully at a distance from the memorial itself. While some claim it's "hidden in the trees," it is actually in a gracious setting when one approaches from the Lincoln Memorial, which most people do.

Perhaps they will compare the sculpture with Daniel Chester French's figure of the Emancipator, and remember the healing words of the Second Inaugural Address. Perhaps, too, they will one day realize that the black walls, going silvery gray in bright sunlight and darkening in shade, are all that this monument needs to make us feel the complex lessons of what was the longest, least successful, and in some ways the cruelest of America's wars.

FREDERICK HART

I have from the start conceived the work of sculpture with three goals in mind: first, to preserve and enhance the elegant simplicity and austerity

of the existing design by Maya Ling Lin; second, to create a work which interacts with the wall to form a unified totality; and finally, to create a

*From Allan Temko, "Environmental Design / 57,939 Names on Polished Black Granite," *San Francisco Chronicle,* April 11, 1983, p. 6. Copyright © 1983 by Chronicle Publishing Company. Reprinted by permission.

sculpture which is in itself a moving evocation of the experience and service of the Vietnam Veteran.

I have attempted to do this by means of understatement. The sculpture is removed from the area of the wall; it does not intrude or obstruct. Compared to the sale of the wall, that of the sculpture (8') is quite small; it does not attempt to compete or to dominate.

The gesture and expression of the figures are directed to the wall, effecting an interplay between image and metaphor. The tension between the two elements creates a resonance that echoes from one to the other.

The figures are treated in the realist manner. They are close to life-size and stand on a low base which is incorporated into the landscape. One senses the figures as passing by the treeline and caught by the presence of the wall, turning to

gaze upon it almost as a vision. The portrayal of the figures is consistent with history. They wear the uniform and carry the equipment of war; they are young. The contrast between the innocence of their youth and the weapons of war underscores the poignancy of their sacrifice. There is about them the physical contact and sense of unity that bespeaks the bonds of love and sacrifice that is the nature of men at war. And yet they are each alone. Their strength and their vulnerability are both evident. Their true heroism lies in these bonds of loyalty in the face of their aloneness and their vulnerability.

I see the wall as a kind of ocean, a sea of sacrifice that is overwhelming and nearly incomprehensible in its sweep of names. I place these figures upon the shore of that sea gazing upon it, standing vigil before it, reflecting the human face of it, the human heart.

COMMENTS

1. There is an excellent discussion of the controversial aspects of the Vietnam Memorial in Joan Pachner, "Whose Memorial Is It Anyway?" (paper in the authors' files, 1982).

2. In the case of Maya Lin's design, which was commissioned, the artist did everything possible to protect the integrity of her concept despite extreme pressures, arguably amounting to censorship, as recounted in brief by Temko. In the following case, *Silvette v. Art Commission of Virginia,* the artist has volunteered his work and is in an entirely different position. What is the fundamental difference? Why is it legally significant?

Silvette v. Art Commission of Commonwealth of Virginia
413 F.Supp. 1342 (D.C., E.D.Va., 1976)

OREN R. LEWIS, Senior District Judge.

This controversy between David Silvette, a portrait painter, and the Virginia Art Commission . . . has been brewing for many years—It reached the boiling point in 1972 when the Art Commission suggested that Mr. Silvette modify a portrait he had submitted for acceptance by the Commonwealth.

After appealing to the Governor without success, Mr. Silvette filed a pro se petition for a declaratory judgment in the Circuit Court of the City of Richmond. . . .

By letter opinion dated January 16, 1974, the state trial court declared that the Art Commission's Rule 4(c) puts the artist in the position of coerced submission to avoid ultimate rejection and is a direct restraint on his freedom of expres-

sion—By order entered February 1, 1974, the Art Commission was prohibited from applying its Rule 4(c) as a condition to considering portraits as gifts to the Commission.

On February 8, 1974, Mr. Silvette had a messenger deliver the finished portrait of Dr. Morton to the Art Commission for approval as a gift to the State—The Art Commission called a special meeting for February 9, 1974, to review the portrait, and recommended to the Governor that the portrait not be accepted upon the following grounds:

Members of the Commission reviewed the painting carefully and thoroughly. All members felt that the head was well-painted, but that the remainder of the painting was not up to standard of the painting done on the head. It was felt that the figure was painted in such a manner that the subject appears not to be seated on the chair. The left hand appears to be poorly painted.

The lower end of the subject's necktie is so prominent as to be a disturbing factor so much so as to lead the viewer's eye "out of the picture."

The several books at the right shoulder of the subject are so placed in the composition, and are of such vivid color that, again, the viewer's eye is taken away from the center of interest.

The shadows on the coat are all of the same value, where some shading would have given the figure a better three-dimensional quality, which has been so skillfully executed in the head of this painting.

In view of these comments, the Commission recommends to the Governor that the portrait not be accepted.

The Governor rejected the portrait of Dr. Morton on February 25, 1974.

The plaintiff claims that the action of the Art Commission in rejecting Dr. Morton's portrait constituted an unlawful censorship of free artistic expression through the use of a subterfuge form of censorship and represents an unequal enforcement of the law—He further contends that the granting of the power of approval to the Governor and the Art Commission is an unconstitutional delegation of legislative powers and that the statutes in question . . . are unconstitutional because of vagueness and because there is no provision for review.

The Supreme Court of Virginia reversed the state trial court on March 11, 1975.

Of course an artist has the right to paint as he chooses. It does not follow, however, that he has the right to compel the Commonwealth to accept and display any or all of his paintings tendered as gifts.

A somewhat similar situation was presented, and determined by the Third Circuit, in *Avins v. Rutgers, the State University of New Jersey,* 3 Cir., 385 F.2d 151 (1967), wherein the author of a rejected article he had submitted to the Rutgers

Law Review asserted that the rejection of his work by the Editorial Board of the Law Review violated his constitutional right of freedom of speech. The Court of Appeals, after noting that the right of freedom of speech does not open every avenue to one who desires to use a particular outlet for expression, concluded—

. . . [H]e does not have the right, constitutional or otherwise, to commandeer the press and columns of the Rutgers Law Review for publication of his article, at the expense of the subscribers to the Review and the New Jersey taxpayers, to the exclusion of other articles deemed by the editors to be more suitable for publication. . . ."

An artist is in a somewhat analogous situation—He cannot compel the acceptance of his painting any more than an author can force the publication of his article.

Further, the adversary function of the Art Commission in this case is quite similar to that of the Editorial Board of the Law Review in Rutgers—They both involve an assessment of judgment. In this case, an artistic judgment—a conclusion which delights the chosen and offends the rejected.

Someone or some group must ultimately determine whether a work of art has substantial artistic and cultural significance in order to advise and counsel the Governor in re its acceptance. This duty to advise and counsel includes the right to state the reasons therefor—and suggesting changes in a portrait intended as a gift to the States, as was done here, does not violate the artistic First Amendment right of free artistic oppression.

The artist may or may not choose to make the suggested changes—However, neither the artist nor the donor has the right to compel acceptance of the tendered painting in an unaltered or altered form. The authority to accept for the Commonwealth rests with the Governor under the statute.

Therefore this suit should be dismissed at the cost of the plaintiff.

COMMENTS

1. Would the fact that the Virginia Art Commission was composed either of art experts or of laymen inexperienced in art criticism affect your view of this case?

2. How would you evaluate the Art Commission's criticism of Silvette's portrait on the basis of inconsistency of style? Are there any good historical precedents in art for what Silvette did?

3. Suppose that approval of the Art Commission was mandatory rather than advisory. Would their rejection of a proposed gift by an artist be an abridgment of his right of free speech?

4. If there is a difference between selection and censorship, what is it? Is the action of the Art Commission classifiable as one or the other?

THE GENERAL SERVICES ADMINISTRATION

The General Services Administration (GSA) is responsible for the construction of buildings for the use of the federal government. These buildings include government structures in Washington, D.C., as well as federal buildings (post offices, courthouses, etc.) throughout the nation. In January 1963 the administrator of general services issued a direct policy order that established a fine arts allowance of one-half of 1 percent of the estimated construction cost of each new federal building. Fine arts, including murals, sculpture, and artistic work in other media "shall reflect the national cultural heritage and shall emphasize the work of living American artists" ("Design Administration," GSA Handbook, June 19, 1968). Within these guidelines, the project architect is responsible for determining the size, location, and nature of the proposed art work. Having made this determination, the architect then requests the chairman of the Arts Council, for the National Endowment for the Arts, to recommend three to five qualified artists. Depending on the significance of the proposed work and on availability, artists of local, regional, or national reputation are considered for recommendation. For the purpose of developing this recommendation the chairman forms an appropriate panel of qualified individuals. The makeup of the panel varies from project to project due to the art work required and the geographic area involved; however, the panel always includes the project architect.

The National Endowment submits the list of recommended artists to the GSA Fine Arts Design Review Panel, which consists of the commissioner of the Public Buildings Service, the director of the Office of Fine Arts and Historic Preservation, and the assistant commissioner for Construction Management. The panel makes final recommendations to the administrator of general services. The administrator makes the final selection of the artist for the building. The artist who is selected must submit a model of his work to the Commission of Fine Arts for comment and advice. The commission's evaluation of the design is very important to its final approval by the administrator. For an account of GSA commissions, see Jo Ann Lewis, "A Modern Medici for Public Art," *ARTnews*, April 1977, p. 37.

Even after a decision is made and the proposal approved and the artist selected, there can be problems if the people who live and work in the public building object to the art. They are a captive audience, compelled by their employment to inhabit the place where the work is publicly shown. An example of this kind of problem is described in *Art Workers News* of June–July 1976, p. 6. The project architect for a new federal building and courthouse in the city of Baltimore made the required proposal for incorporating fine art in the project. A nominating committee of "distinguished art experts" appointed by the National Endowment for the Arts invited submissions from artists and made its nominations to the GSA's Fine Arts Review Panel. That panel made its recommendations to the GSA administrator, who made the selection. Observe that this procedure makes no provision for participation by the building's occupants.

The artist selected was George Sugarman, and his maquette for the large sculpture for the building was publicly shown. Several federal judges objected to it on safety and aesthetic grounds. An account of Sugarman's experience with the judges follows.

MARCIA B. NELSON *The GSA Art-in-Architecture Program and Baltimore Federal**

... When Sugarman visited the site in December, 1974, he was asked, though the request was unusual, if he would mind meeting with the judges to review his proposal. Sugarman innocently and graciously agreed, but added that a meeting would be fruitless until he had prepared the model of his work. Later, the sculptor told a reporter: "I didn't know the judges and I didn't expect them to know anything about art, but if I was going to really say the sculpture was a community thing, I couldn't isolate the judges. After all, they're part of the community." As it turned out the judges thought they were a bit more than merely "part of the community."

In August 1975 Sugarman presented a cardboard maquette to the GSA Design Review Panel. Present at the meeting were several Baltimoreans, including representatives of the Mayor's Office, the architect, Charles Lamb, citizens interested in the city's Inner Harbor development project (some from the office of the Commissioner of Housing and Community Development), and local art experts. The design was enthusiastically approved and George Sugarman received one-third of the commission price, as agreed.

The maquette was not displayed at RTKL's offices until mid-September, when it was arranged within a model of the building and its plaza. The judges reviewed the work on or about September 18, 1975, and drafted a letter of protest to GSA Administrator Sampson, with copies to Maryland's congressional delegation and former Rep. Edward A. Garmatz, for whom the building was to be named. The protest was primarily esthetic, with one brief comment on the safety factor that was emphasized increasingly as time went on. Judge Northrop wrote that the judges "vigorously protested" the placement of Sugarman's sculpture in the plaza:

The proposed sculpture is inappropriate for the [building] and is not in keeping with either the design or purpose of the building. The contours of the structure itself present a danger both as to possible injury to individuals moving around it as well as a potential shelter for persons bent on mischief or assault on the public.

To support his contention, Judge Northrop also misconstrued Sugarman's explanation of the significant role of color in his work, which "has a tremendous emotional impact, and the experience of the spectator, in seeing the color allied to a three-dimensional form, is something that is quite novel at first, in fact, quite shocking." Northrop called this concept "anachronistic" (?) to the court's function and claimed that there was no need to artificially generate emotional impact outside the courthouse.

The letter's tone indicated that the judge was perturbed that his committee was not consulted earlier, per their requests, since they felt it their "duty to see that whatever artwork is displayed either within or without this building is appropriate and reflects the history and dignity of this Court." This clearly indicated that the judges had a mistaken notion of the purposes for which the Art-in-Architecture program was instituted. There is no hint that the program intended to hold art accountable to the courts. Perhaps the judges felt that art is just another piece of furniture and that their committee was within its rights in passing judgment. In the same letter, Judge Northrop implied that the GSA and the architect had gone along with several other requests regarding building facilities and accoutrements.

A series of meetings and exchanges of correspondence followed this initial, fairly mild, protest. Sugarman himself was asked to meet with the judges on three separate occasions, to hear their objections and discuss the concept of his sculpture. At the first meeting, Sugarman recalls trying to explain his attempt to express the ideals of an open and accessible government to Judges Northrop, Kaufman and Blair: "I tried very hard to meet the challenge of some symbolic idea, of openness and access—this is a democratic government. I know the courts are imperfect, etc., but still, you are here to serve the people." But the judges felt that a spirit of freedom and openness was not appropriate for a building where some people go out the back door with handcuffs on. They wanted a sculpture that reflected the "gravity of the law."

Meanwhile, there was a changing of the guard at the GSA. On November 21, 1975, Jack Eckerd took over as Ford's new GSA Administrator. Sugarman soon became aware that the new administration was less supportive of the arts. The new

*From Marcia B. Nelson, "Public Art and Politics: The GSA Art in Architecture Program and Baltimore Federal" (student paper in the authors' files, 1982). Footnotes omitted.

George Sugarman. People's Sculpture. *1976, polychromed steel. (Baltimore Federal Center. Photo courtesy of the artist.)*

Administrator became familiar with Sugarman and his sculpture when letters from Congressmen, particularly Senator J. Glenn Beall, Jr. (R-Md.), asked that the sculpture project be halted and that the GSA "initiate a new selection process for a sculpture which is more acceptable to the judges." Kenneth Duberstein, GSA's Director of Congressional Affairs, committed a catastrophic error in a letter to Senator Beall, dated (Friday) January 13, 1976. A very misinformed Duberstein assured Beall that meetings with the judges had gone well and that "the judges have been assured that the final work will *not* be executed without their concurrence" (emphasis added). To make matters worse, Duberstein added that "only an artwork *satisfactory to the judges* will be placed at the Courthouse" (emphasis added).

At this point Sugarman was perfectly entitled to keep the one-third payment for his commission and junk the whole project. But he began to sense the important principles at stake and decided to fight. Thalacker was behind him all the way. At the suggestion of Thomas Freudenheim, Baltimore Art Museum Director, Sugarman tried reaching the judges with a more sophisticated aluminum maquette, containing slight revisions to counter the asserted security concerns. Before the second meeting took place, Jack Eckerd had already called a halt to new GSA commissions. His lack of commitment was obvious. Sugarman's $4000 painted aluminum maquette did not impress the judges. Their protests grew stronger and Duberstein's letter was used as ammunition to kill the project.

After a second batch of mail had arrived from Senator Beall and his congressional colleagues, Eckerd sent PBS Commissioner Nicholas Panuzio to meet with the judges. A few days later, in April 1976, the Sugarman commission was suspended. GSA Program Director Donald Thalacker remembers telling Panuzio that the citizens of Baltimore would be outraged, as would the national art community. Panuzio was a disbeliever.

The suspension sparked an angry response from many citizens and art lovers, led by Artists Equity Association President John Blair Mitchell. Letters were written to the GSA and to the editor of the Baltimore Sun, questioning the insertion of a veto step in the selection process. An account of the whole ordeal, quite rationally explaining the judges' reactions and beliefs, appeared in the local paper. There was also another show of weakness on the part of the GSA when a spokes-

man neglected to defend the integrity of the selection process since it did not allow tenants to voice their concerns. It did not look as though the program, weakened from within, could withstand the attack.

But there was hope. A third meeting was planned with George Sugarman, GSA officials, and the judges. Before it could take place, however, Judge Northrop, who was quite miffed by the negative press he had been getting, sent another inhospitable letter to Eckerd, reminding him of GSA's potential liability for injuries, under the Federal Tort Claims Act. The public safety issue was supplanting the esthetic objections originally voiced. At the end of June the third meeting took place, this time with all nine judges instead of the committee of three. To allay security concerns the architect, Charles Lamb, and Sugarman proposed three revisions: recessed lighting would be installed, parts of the sculpture would be opened up, and television monitors would sweep the area where the sculpture would stand. In short, every concession short of scrapping the project was made.

Still dissatisfied, Northrop wasted no time in calling out the troops. He solicited security reports from the U.S. Marshal, who enlisted reinforcements from the Secret Service, the FBI, and a bomb squad of the Baltimore Police Department. Using the results of the various reports as authority, Judge Northrop again demanded that Eckerd prevent Sugarman from installing his sculpture. The judge listed a whole plethora of potential dangers:

It was specifically pointed out that: the artwork could be utilized as a platform for speaking or hurling objects by dissident groups demonstrating in front of the building; . . . the configuration lent itself to all types of molestation of the unsuspecting drawn to the artwork; its contours would provide an attractive hazard for youngsters naturally drawn to it; and, most importantly, that the areas of concealment produced by the contours of the structure could well be used to secrete bombs or other explosive objects. . . .

If explosives were detonated from within . . . a further effect would be the conversion of the aluminum strips or segments of the sculpture to flying shrapnel throughout the general area.

This new and imaginative "bomb scare" rationalization was the last straw. AEA marshaled its forces. Various stinging rebuttals of the judges views appeared in the press. A petition was circulated and support for Sugarman and the GSA commission grew. Art critics and community members praised the "people sculpture" for its esthetic value and expressed concern over the threat of censorship of art. New allies appeared, two of whom were from Maryland's congressional delegation. One of them, Representative Parren J. Mitchell wrote GSA officials that he found the judges asserted veto power amazing and called their objections "downright silly." The GSA was deluged with similar letters of support from concerned citizens and art critics who realized the enormity of the issue. New York Times critic John Russell summed up the fears: "The case matters to all of us on several counts. If it turns out that the "Art-in-Architecture" program of the G.S.A. can be negated by a minority of those who will make use of a new building, that program could soon be brought to a standstill." In Sugarman's own words, "It's about the whole idea of what public sculpture is, the whole principle of not letting a few people decide on art."

On August 13, 1976, a GSA News Release announced that a public hearing, a totally unprecedented event, was scheduled for September 8, 1976, 10:00 a.m., to help determine what should be done. Two days later Sugarman finally broke his silence in a Baltimore Sun interview. Summing up the ridiculous but frightening controversy, he said, "The whole thing is ironic. I tried to make a sort of peacable kingdom and they [the judges] are making it into a battleground."

To shorten a very long story, the two-hour hearing, chaired by Commissioner Panuzio, attracted over 150 interested parties and generated 74 pages of transcript. Of the 22 witnesses who testified, Edward A. Garmatz was the sole objector. None of the judges, nor their congressional supporters, nor the various members of the law enforcement agencies testified or submitted written statements. Sugarman spoke last and expressed his gratitude. He was so overwhelmed with the show of support that he began to weep.

Donald Thalacker described the hearing as the turning point. The strong show of support by the public, artists and non-artists alike, scared the Congressmen off. The judges were nine very powerful men, but 150-plus voters held some political clout as well. On October 13, 1976, Panuzio announced GSA's decision to go ahead with the sculpture.

But the judges' actions did have an adverse effect on the GSA Program. Those who attended the hearing were informed by Panuzio that Administrator Eckerd had issued a new policy decision, reducing the alotted budget for art in federal buildings by 25% (from ½% to ⅜% of the construction cost), and requiring at least one community member on the panel.

Judge Northrop was quite predictably upset about the decision. In a letter to Eckerd, dated October 19, 1976, he implied threatened court action to prevent the installation. The irrational and emotional tone of the letter reveals that the judge had harbored bad feelings about the project from the start, partly because of his distorted, and unfortunately unremedied, understanding of the GSA commissioning process.

If Mr. Sugarman had not *ignored* our request to meet with us *before he completed the design* of the sculpture, he might well have avoided all security hazards. We understand that this is the first instance in which an artist commissioned by the GSA has not consulted with the tenant in advance. [Emphasis added.]

This time the judge threatened to summon the court's "power" to block the installation of Sugarman's sculpture. He asserted the power to issue orders for the safety of employees and visitors, which extended "to areas adjacent to the courthouse and would include the power to prevent the erection of or require the removal of structures which would create security problems." For a reason that still remains a mystery, the threatened action never materialized and the GSA stood firm on this *final* final decision. . . .

COMMENTS

1. What is your reaction to the role of the judges in the Sugarman commission? Did they properly use their official positions? The Richard Serra case, below, was also instigated by a judge (Judge Edward Re of the U.S. Court of International Trade).

2. During the Sugarman affair, the captive-audience issue did not arise, but the issue of security did. In the case that follows, you will see echoes of the Baltimore commission.

RICHARD SERRA'S "TILTED ARC"

No work of public art paid for by the taxpayers has created as much controversy and attracted as much international attention as the 1981 installation of Richard Serra's "Tilted Arc" in New York City. No other work has brought the purpose of government support of public art into question as much as that work. For the best single account, see Calvin Tomkins, "Tilted Arc," the *New Yorker,* May 20, 1985, pp. 95–101. For a clear statement of the issues, see Alvin Lane, "Public Art vs. Public Sentiment," *New York Times,* July 13, 1985, p. 21. And for an interesting commentary on those involved in the debate, see Robert Storr, "'Tilted Arc': Enemy of the People?" *Art in America,* September 1985.

In 1979 the General Services Administration, as part of its Art-in-Architecture program, commissioned internationally recognized American sculptor Richard Serra to create a sculpture called "Tilted Arc" for the Federal Plaza located in Lower Manhattan. The commissioning process, which took two years, started with the GSA project architect establishing a budget of one-half of 1 percent of the estimated cost of the new Jacob Javits Federal Building in Foley Square. The GSA then asked the National Endowment for the Arts to appoint art professionals, primarily from the region of the project, who met with the design architect for the purpose of nominating three to five artists for the proposed work of art. Three well-known members of the art world—two museum people and a critic—were the experts. This artist-nominating panel met at the project site and reviewed the visual material submitted by artists who had been proposed by the GSA, the NEA panelists, and the project architect. Richard Serra was their choice, and he was approved by the GSA administrator. A fixed price contract of $175,000 was negotiated. A key clause of the contract read as follows:

> *Article 6: Ownership.* All designs, sketches, models, and the work produced under this Agreement . . . shall be the property of the United States of America. All such items may be conveyed by the Contracting Officer to the National Collection of Fine Arts—Smithsonian Institution for exhibiting purposes and permanent safekeeping.

Richard Serra and his lawyer, Gustave Harrow, contend that the artist was given "unequivocal commitments" that the proposed work would remain permanently installed because it was to be made specifically for the location ("site-specific") and because its removal would result in conceptual "destruction" of the work of art. The artist's understanding was that removal for "safekeeping" referred to perilous times when the physical safety of the art was in jeopardy.

Between 1979 and 1981, Serra studied the site, a decoratively paved square and inoperative fountain flanked on two contiguous sides by federal buildings. The study included observing the flow of pedestrian traffic to and from the federal buildings. Serra made many drawings and a model, which was approved. Fabricated of Cor-ten steel that has a permanently rusted surface, and weighing 73 tons, the final curved sculpture is 12 feet high, 120 feet long, and 3 inches thick. It tilts one foot off its vertical axis and is securely anchored to the steel and concrete plaza. Serra's avowed intent was to create a work of art that was confrontational with respect to the viewer and the setting, as he sought to "alter and dislocate the decorative effect of the plaza." In an interview he added, "I find the idea of populism in art defeating. It is the needs of art, not the public, that come first."

Describing his own work, and specifically "Tilted Arc," at a public hearing in March 1981, Serra said:

> I don't make portable objects. . . . My sculptures are not objects meant for a viewer to stop, look and stare at. . . . I am interested in a behavioral space in which the viewer interacts with the sculpture in its context. . . . "Tilted Arc" was built for the people who walk

Richard Serra. Tilted Arc, 1981, *3 plates (2-1/2" thick) 12' × 120', corten steel. (Federal Plaza, New York City. Photo courtesy Blum Hellman Gallery.)*

and cross the plaza, for the moving observer . . . to engage the public in a dialogue that would enhance, both perceptually and conceptually, its relation to the entire plaza. . . . The viewer can learn something about a sculptural orientation to space and place. . . . The viewer becomes aware of himself and of his movement through the plaza. As he moves, the sculpture changes. Contraction and expansion of the sculpture result from the viewer's movement . . . the perception of . . . the sculpture . . . [and] the entire environment changes. . . . I laid the curve out on the ground with paint and chalk and observed people walking in and out of the buildings. . . . The placement of the sculpture did not interfere with access to the main entrances. . . . On the concave side the sweep of the Arc creates an amphitheater-like condition . . . a silent amplitude which magnifies your awareness of yourself and the sculptured field of the space. The concavity of the topological curve allows one to understand the sweep of the entire plaza. . . . At the ends the curve appears to be infinite.

At the time "Tilted Arc" was commissioned, the GSA selection procedure did not include input from the local community, which was represented otherwise by only a single official. Thus the sculpture's installation came as a complete surprise, or shock, to the local inhabitants. From the moment of installation in 1981 to the present, there have been protests from many of the 8,500 workers in the two federal buildings. The first petition calling for the sculpture's removal was initiated by one of the federal judges, Judge Re, and it was signed by 1,500 who pass daily by the work.

The objections range from the complaint that the sculpture is ugly and inappropriate to the site, through arguments that it destroys the coherence and utility of the plaza, to allegations that it is a public danger (criminals can lurk behind it; it would amplify the damage caused by bombs). Its opponents also argue that the confrontational nature of the work invites graffiti and other forms of physical abuse to the work, compounding its unsightliness.

Four years after the installation and beginning of the protests, goaded by Judge Re, the GSA's regional administrator for the New York area, William Diamond, made the decision to hold public hearings on the question of relocating "Tilted Arc." (The transcript of the hearings ["In the Matter Of: A Public Hearing on the Relocating of the 'Tilted Arc' at 26 Federal Plaza, March 7–9, 1985"], on which this section is based, was produced by the GSA.) Even before the hearings began, Diamond made it clear to the media that he thought the GSA had "made a mistake" and that the work should be relocated. He appointed a panel comprised of a dealer in Impressionist paintings, a lawyer who had experience with art litigation, two GSA officials, and himself to hear three days of testimony from more than 180 people. Diamond made it clear at the outset that the issue was not the aesthetic merits of "Tilted Arc," and that the hearing was not intended to be precedent-setting or an attack on the GSA program. "What we are deeply concerned about is the fact that this piece, for three and one-half years, has made it impossible for the public and the federal community to use the plaza." The panel's recommendations were to be forwarded to Washington, D.C., and the acting administrator of the GSA, Dwight Ink.

Richard Serra, his attorney, and many who testified protested against the hearings on the grounds that Diamond had set himself up as "prosecutor and chief judge" while on public record as biased against the sculpture's remaining. Harrow, echoed in different ways by many others at the hearings, put the question: "Whether a rational decision, processed through procedures designed to insure impartiality and excellence in selecting an artist and his concept, can be reversed after the fact through an ad hoc process, in order to rescind the government's commitments."

In three days of hearings, fifty-six people spoke for removal of "Tilted Arc," and more than 120 spoke for its retention.

Arguments for Removal Opposed to the sculpture were individual federal employees, residents of the community, federal judges, a few lawyers, heads of federal agencies housed in the two buildings, representatives of environmental protection groups, urban planners, and a few artists and art historians. From more than six hundred pages of testimony, the arguments for removal could be summarized as follows.

Legal Argument. The government has full title to the work and can move it. Public art must include the public viewpoint, and "Tilted Arc" has impaired the use and enjoyment of a public space. The artist can have a voice, but not a veto, in the decision. The government has an obligation to remove the work, since a mistake was made by the three nominators: in a display of the "arrogance of power" there had been no community input before "Tilted Arc" was installed. Hence, the GSA had committed a wrong against the public, which must now be corrected. The New York State law on artists' authorship rights does not prevent removal and/or destruction of the work, but Serra can withdraw his name from the work if it is relocated without his consent somewhere in the state. With two hundred public works installed, it was argued that the Art-in-Architecture program, like modern sculpture itself, was established and no longer in danger and that hence there was no concern about a dangerous precedent.

Artistic Deficiencies. A few laymen argued that the work is not art, and many others argued that it is ugly, brutal, and intimidating. "Tilted Arc" has no "idea" or humor. It has unpleasant associations—with a "fortress," all types of "barriers," "iron curtains" and totalitarianism, subway or building construction, and "antiterrorist barricades," "the business end of a cleaver."

Quality-of-Life Argument. By its size, location bisecting the plaza, and grim character, "Tilted Arc" has made useless for people one of the few precious open pedestrian areas in crowded Lower Manhattan. "It is a piece of steel dominating a place where people should meet." People missed the previous ceremonies, such as the swearing in of thousands of new citizens, and other public gatherings in the plaza and pointed out that at noon there are more people assembling now in the streets behind the federal buildings. The previous "openness" and free access of the plaza had been destroyed, and views of Foley Square and its historic buildings were blocked. People are embarrassed by and avoid the plaza. The "quality of life" in the square has been reduced, which in turn violates a GSA directive of December 1, 1978, as to the program's purpose.

Violation of the Architects' Moral Right. The architects of the federal buildings and plaza were not consulted during the selection process, and if they had been they would have protested against "Tilted Arc" and its placement. Serra has violated the moral rights of the architects with respect to their "site-specific" plaza. By his own admission, Serra set out to confront what the architects had done and to destroy the decorative character of their plaza. In the architects' view, Serra ignored the existing three-dimensional elements of the square and with his sculpture cut across a handsome decorative stone pavement. "It is an unsightly piece of work," and they call for removal of "this piece of unnecessary embellishment from out previously simple and artistic forecourt." In the words of Judge Dominick Dicarlo, "This may top the usual example of chutzpa: the person who kills his mother and father and then asks for mercy on the grounds that he is an orphan."

Safety Argument. "Tilted Arc's" "design faults" include constant maintenance problems in removing often obnoxious graffiti that include ethnic insults and traces of urine. It has made the plaza's space indefensible and is a hazard to security, an incitement to "nuisance behavior," and a haven for muggers. A security officer for the two federal buildings protested that it was impossible to surveil the plaza for such activities as drug-dealing and that the concave side of the sculpture would have a "blast wall effect" for a terrorist bomb planted in front of it.

Challenges to Serra. A former Works Progress Administration artist, Harold Lehman, who had himself seen one of his big public murals destroyed, made the point that Serra has not always been consistent toward his site-specific works and their immovability. In Paris, when his piece "Clara-Clara" was made specifically to go inside the Pompidou Center and did not fit, Serra, who was then in Canada, agreed to its relocation in the Tuileries Gardens. It was pointed out that art museums are full of what were once site-specific altarpieces and ceiling paintings. Others reminded the panel that six blocks from Foley Square was another Serra public sculpture near the exit of the Holland Tunnel, so that he was well represented in New York City and the city had indeed recognized his importance. Serra deliberately set up a confrontation between his sculpture on the one hand, and the public and the plaza on the other hand. He won in his intention, but his art lost in terms of public response and damage to the site.

Summary of Arguments for Removal. In the words of Judge deCarlo:

> What the proponents of removal are requesting is a restoration of the architects' artistic concept of a very site-specific plaza destroyed by the iron wall. They wish to undo the alteration and dislocation of the decorative function of the plaza. They wish to reclaim the open space of what was once one of the largest pedestrian areas of Manhattan. They wish to experience again the cultural activities and take part in the public events that ended when the plaza was fractured. The proponents of removal are not attacking art. They only wish to exercise the critical choice that is a necessary prerequisite of art. The advocates of the wall would deprive us of the right to distinguish between the beautiful and the ugly, between true art and the willful defacement of a beautiful architectural space. To deny this right is to make art impossible. It is those who would do so who are the enemies of art and the ambassadors of barbarism.

Arguments for Retention Through his own efforts and those of friends here and abroad, Serra mobilized a large and impressive cross-section of the international art world, and many public figures wrote letters or testified on his behalf. In addition he secured more than four thousand signatures on petitions calling for retention of his sculpture. Many who testified on Serra's behalf did not necessarily like his art, or the particular sculpture involved. Some artists who testified for him thought "Tilted Arc" gave public sculpture a bad name, others believed that the artist had a moral obligation to make a more viewer-friendly public art, and many sympathized with the federal workers. But these same artists spoke for Serra because they had gone through or might encounter similar experiences, or in the belief that principles or larger issues were involved. All this caused Diamond and others to observe: "The further away you are, the more you want it to stay."

Legal Argument. In good faith, Serra and the GSA had made a legally binding contract after going through the required processes of selection. The government cannot renege on its contract. That would be a breach of contract, an act of censorship, a suppression of the artist's right to freedom of expression, and a bad precedent for government-sponsored public art. It could lead to eventual loss of the Art-in-Architecture program, Fascist-like control, or nothing but bland art in the future. Its chilling effect could cause artists to not participate in the Art-in-Architecture program. Until now, the GSA had stood behind two hundred artists and their works. The public hearings were likened to vigilantism, and the outcome would lead domino-like to challenges to many of the two hundred previously installed GSA public sculptures. There must be no recall of public art once it has been installed. The site-specific nature of "Tilted Arc" had been clearly understood by the GSA, as had the fact that its removal would destroy the piece. Hence Section 6 in the contract was invalid. Calling public hearings was improper. Art was not democratic, and its selection for public sites should be not by popular consensus or referendum but by experts, as in this case.

Artistic Argument. Many art professionals testified to the beauty and power of "Tilted Arc" and how it may be Serra's best work in a very distinguished career. (Rare was the testimony about "Arc" as a public sculpture.) Serra was reckoned perhaps the leading post–World War II modern sculptor with respect to public art, and a figure of considerable international influence. New York City's reputation as the most important art center in the world was at stake. Frank Stella credited Serra with bringing "visual culture into public space." Many had pleasant associations with the curved steel form, seeing it as very American in its rough textures and confrontational stance, likening it to speed and ships, or comparing its experience with those of the pyramids and Gothic cathedrals. Many applauded what it did to the previous space of the square by making it into a "sculptural space."

Time Argument. Historians and curators pointed to the history of modern art and how so often controversial art in public required time to be understood and appreciated. William Rubin, of the Museum of Modern Art, suggested that a ten-year period before reassessment would be appropriate.

Site and Quality-of-Life Argument. Serra had indeed carefully studied the site. The two federal buildings were architecturally undistinguished, the plaza fountain had not worked for some time, and community events were few and infrequent even before the work's installation. (Some quipped that the hearings should be about the removal of the federal buildings.) The sculpture did not impede access to building entrances or exits. Many from the world of the performing arts pointed out that "Tilted Arc" was a natural or acoustically wonderful "bandshell" and that they would willingly perform before it in a series of public concerts. The GSA had not only failed to conduct a public-education program before the work was installed, it had also failed to make imaginative and systematic use of the sculpture and the square since 1981.

Serra adopted a defiant attitude throughout the proceedings, threatening to fight the sculpture's removal in court as a breach of contract and, if he failed, to leave United States. His stance toward public art was: "Placing pieces in an urban context is not synonymous with an interest in a large audience, even though the work will be seen by many people who wouldn't otherwise look at art. The work I make does not allow for experience outside the conventions of sculpture as sculpture. My audience is necessarily very limited." Serra and his many defenders cited President Reagan's commendation of the Art-in-Architecture program and his statement at the award of National Medals of Arts: "In an atmosphere of liberty, artists and patrons are free to think the unthinkable and create the audacious; they are free to make both horrendous mistakes and glorious celebrations. Where there is liberty, art succeeds."

At this writing, the result of the above is that, following the hearings and report from Diamond's panel, Dwight Ink, the acting administrator of the GSA ordered the setting up of a panel of experts who represent the present and possible future location of "Tilted Arc" to determine the sculpture's fate. Declaring that this was not the equivalent of ordering immediate removal, Ink would not comment on what he would do should the new panel recommend that "Tilted Arc" remain where it is.

COMMENTS

1. Would relocation of "Tilted Arc" to another public site, with or without Serra's consent, constitute censorship and suppression of the artist's right of free speech? One of your authors (Merryman) thought so and wrote the panel opposing removal. Another (Elsen) did not and supported its relocation.

2. Is this a case of a captive audience having the right not to look at a work of art that for four years has deeply disturbed so many people? Is there an analogy to *Close v. Lederle?* How do you apply the "captive audience" concept in such a case: the sculpture in place offends many, if not most of the people who use the buildings and plaza, but its removal will offend some others. Which "captive audience" should prevail, or is the concept simply inapplicable in such a case?

3. What is the function, social or otherwise, of public art? (Was the answer to this question given or clarified by the hearings?) For whose benefit is public art? Is it for the artist, and the public be damned, or the reverse? Does the fact that two hundred GSA-sponsored works remain in place suggest that public art should be to the mutual benefit of the artists and their audiences?

4. In an August 8, 1985, *New York Times* article, Douglas C. McGill reported: "The City of St. Louis is considering calling a referendum on whether to remove a major sculpture in the downtown area by Richard Serra. . . . A bill filed . . . by one of the 28 alderman . . . proposes that St. Louis voters decide next August whether to remove the sculpture entitled "Twain," which covers nearly an entire city block." According to the president of the board of aldermen, "It's been a controversial fixture since the day it was installed. I think a number of aldermen have somewhat silently said, 'I don't like it, but who am I to judge what is art?' Now some are saying that these pieces of iron are not art, it's just causing maintenance problems, and it's a valuable piece of property that should be developed." McGill reports that Serra's lawyer, Gustave Harrow, believed the St. Louis bill "was a reaction to the outcome of public hearings in New York in March on 'Tilted Arc.'" Harrow went on to say:

> This is a sort of chain effect. It's a scapegoating reaction that might have been anticipated from the manner in which the hearings were conducted here. It vindicates our position that this kind of approach to art can have enormously destructive effects beyond itself. . . . It's one thing to have some complaining and negative reaction, and it's another thing to reach the level of a city-legislated resolution to put it to the voters. That is precisely the thing that would force art to be judged by a common denominator, which art cannot be.

Keeping in mind that Harrow is Serra's hired legal gun, are his comments nevertheless justified? Would the removal of one or two Serra sculptures lead to such a referendum on all public art? Are public referendums on public art—either before or after a work is installed—a bad thing?

5. In the past few years more artists are showing an interest in what might charitably be called viewer-friendly public art, resulting from a collaboration with architects, landscape designers, and civic and neighborhood groups. The GSA itself has moved away from its 1979 procedures, and before a work is commissioned there is a more extensive exploration within the community of what is needed and wanted, and appropriate people are sought out for the design-review panel. When artists are selected, they are encouraged to meet with community groups where there can be a give and take. Is this a desirable development?

6. Almost simultaneously with the Serra hearings, an article by Charlotte Curtis appeared in the February 12, 1985, *New York Times* ("A Budding Clamor"), which summarized the results of the first use of a 1 percent law to commission a major public sculpture by the Airport Commission of Columbus, Ohio.

In conjunction with a new international air terminal built by the city of Columbus, $150,000 was appropriated from the "percent of construction for art" by that city. A commission was given to Roy Lichtenstein, who made a tall, painted sculpture using his famous brushstroke motif. Red, yellow, blue, and black were used for the vertically stacked strokes that resembled those Lichtenstein had used in his paintings. Lichtenstein called the work "Brushstrokes in Flight." The work was dedicated in May 1984 and received a quiet reception. The anticipated public controversy and excitement was not forthcoming. Because of its placement, it was difficult for people to see the sculpture in its entirety from the arrival and departure ramps and lounges inside the airport. One had to go on foot to the sculpture's courtyard to see the whole work.

According to Charlotte Curtis, "The powerful businessmen of the Central Ohio Marketing Council really liked 'Brushstrokes.' They decided it projected just the 'dynamic, modern' image they wanted for their 'Discover Columbus' development campaign. Now, they plan to print a drawing of the brightly colored sculpture on each and every mailing piece, and use it as their logo." Lichtenstein approved this use of his sculpture by the city. The sculpture has become so popular that it is being moved to a better site, where it can be more easily seen. In Curtis's words: "The community has discovered that there's more to life than Ohio State football."

7. "Percent of construction for art" commissions do not always enjoy the fate of Lichtenstein's work. In January 1985 an established artist named Irene Siegel began work on a fresco commissioned for $10,000 by the city of Chicago for the new Conrad Sulzer Regional Library. The fresco, which covers four walls, has as its subject Virgil's *Aeneid*. One wall that

Roy Lichtenstein. Brushstrokes in Flight, *1984, 26' high, painted aluminum. (Commissioned for Port Columbus, Columbus, Ohio.)*

depicts the Trojan horse and Troy's burning is painted in bright reds, oranges, and pinks. Two other pastel-colored walls show Aeneas and Dido, who as queen of Carthage fell in love with Aeneas. A black wall interprets Aeneas's voyage to Hades. Throughout, Siegel has liberally used quotations from Virgil, Goethe and Kazantzakis.

The *Aeneid* murals have roused the displeasure of some in the community, who object to the inscriptions on the grounds that they are frightening and look like graffiti. The imagery, except for the Trojan horse, is faulted for its indecipherability. A group calling itself "Uprave" has actually filed suit to have the paintings removed on the technical grounds that the artist did not live up to the commission, which specified fresco. According to an August 31, 1985, article in the *New York Times*, an Uprave representative charges that Siegel just hosed down a wall with plaster and applied paint to it. Siegel responded that she did apply her paint to the wet plaster in a true fresco technique. The suit accuses city officials of failing to ask the artist for a full and complete description of the proposed work and of paying her too soon. The city official who is coordinator of special projects for Chicago's Office of Fine Arts, which commissioned the fresco said, "The city has an obligation to protect the fresco. And we will."

Other citizens have complained to city officials that they want more of a say in the public art of their neighborhoods, citing the "Tilted Arc" example in New York City. The alderman who represents the district where the Siegel mural is located has proposed a new law that requires the expression of public opinion in the placement and choice of public art. Siegel comments: "I can see my struggle with the community in my fresco. But that's a tradition with artists. When Michelangelo's 'David' went into the square, the public stoned it. An artist is not a computer. You can't paint with restrictions. If you try to please everyone in art, art would become advertising." For the last portion of her painting, Siegel saved the following line: "Who put this thing up?"

Suppose that Uprave prevails in the suit, and the city is obliged by the court to remove the fresco. Illinois does not as yet have a moral right law that would protect the murals from intentional destruction and allow the artist to retrieve them at her own expense. Fresco is a medium in which the paint is bonded to the plaster, and the plaster is attached to the wall surface behind it. Removing a fresco is complex, difficult, and might cost more than the original commission. It might be easier to remove the four walls, if the structure permitted.

8. Many state and local governments have enacted laws requiring that a certain percentage of the budget for new public buildings be reserved for acquiring fine art for those buildings. Crucial to the operation of "percent of construction for art" laws, as seen in the Siegel case, are such matters as what kind of art is eligible for the expenditure and who selects it. Section 15813 of the California Code, enacted in 1976, amends the original bill and changes "fine art" to "works of art." This term is defined to include "crafts" as well as fine arts. Selection and placement is in the state architect rather than the Arts Council. There are no specific provisions for community input. But the California statute does include some interesting provisions: (A) The artist retains the right to claim authorship of the work. (B) Unless the contract provides otherwise, the artist retains the right to reproduce the work," including all rights to which the work of art may be subject under copyright laws." (C) If the contract so provides, the right to a percentage of the proceeds if the work is sold (other than as part of the sale of the building). (D) The right to purchase the work at the highest bid price, if it is sold by the state. To these rights must now be added those of the California Art Preservation Act.

In 1954 the city of Tacoma, Washington repealed its one-percent for art law. The story is told in the following excerpt.

ERIC SCIGLIANO *Tacoma Repeals One-Percent Law**

Maybe it's just an angry gesture by the citizens of a troubled mill town, who feel they have better things to spend their tax dollars on than art in their public places. Or maybe it's a harbinger of challenges to come in all kinds of cities. While New York continues to argue over Richard

Serra's *Tilted Arc*, Tacoma, Washington, has become the first local government in the country to overturn, by popular initiative, a one-percent-for-art ordinance.

Tacoma, an old industrial town of 150,000, is the butt in the Northwest of the sort of jokes that are reserved for New Jersey back east. But it joined the public-arts vanguard in 1975, when it passed a law reserving one percent of its construction budget for art—just two years after Seattle, its more glamorous big-sister city, passed a similar pioneering ordinance. Seattle has since spent $1.75 million on more than 1,000 artworks. Tacoma's one-percent ordinance lay fallow until 1980, due both to a dearth of public construction and to lack of enforcement. It has so far generated just ten commissions, worth $375,000.

Tacoma's one-percent program was emblematic of its new, aggressive civic dynamism in the late '70s and early '80s. One by one, the city's old industries—wood products, fishing, copper smelting—were hit by hard times. A new breed of Tacoma leaders responded with every trick they could find to put a brighter face on the town. They lured away the Port of Seattle's biggest shipping company, restored Tacoma's grand old movie palace as a performing-arts center and launched a major redevelopment of the dilapidated waterfront.

Tacoma's proudest project was the construction of a $44 million sports dome to compete with Seattle's Kingdome. The trouble began when the much-ballyhooed Tacoma Dome met the little-noticed one-percent ordinance.

The city decided to spend the dome's art budget to the greatest visible effect: on a single large work for its roof, which is visible to the thousands of drivers on the nearby interstate highway. After a full selection process (members of the final jury were Diane Vanderlip, curator of contemporary art at the Denver Art Museum, architect Michael Graves and Ira Licht, former head of the NEA's Art in Public Places program), the New York light sculptor Stephen Antonakos won the bid with a plan to ring the dome with neon. The cost was $272,000.

Then city engineers were told by the dome's contractors that the brackets necessary to attach the lights could make the dome's roof leak.

The city requested and approved a new proposal from Antonakos for an interior neon piece at the same price. The result, two 12-by-96-foot walls of exuberant pink, red, blue and green lines, squiggles and crosses, was installed in August 1984. Meanwhile, a group called the No Neon Committee organized to try to block its purchase. Shock at the notion of neon as art was a main motive for the outcry, even though the plan for the sculpture was widely exhibited in Tacoma before the work was installed; some Tacomans complained that Antonakos' sculpture looked like the town's tawdry Pacific Avenue strip. But one No Neon leader, painter and greeting-card designer Carolyn Bondy, insists she's not another know-nothing blindly opposed to the new and the abstract. She labels the Antonakos "unexciting. If they wanted something in neon, they should have gone to one of the creative neon artists in this area." Mayor Doug Sutherland says that more than 150 bid invitations were sent to "all the local artists we had had any contact with. Most said the size was beyond their capabilities." Bondy also points to the extravagance of a city with sagging industry and 9.2 percent unemployment making such a purchase.

In June 1984 a suit brought by the No Neon Committee to block the contract on the grounds that it was not competitively bid was dismissed in Pierce County Superior Court.

Bondy and others joined to pass a non-binding ballot measure to ban the scupture by a nearly 75 percent majority in Tacoma's 1984 primary. The city did not heed this urging. Sutherland sees Antonakos' piece not only as "a major statement, quite fitting for the dome," but as an attention getter for the sort of corporations Tacoma is trying desperately to attract. He adds that the hubbub over it, let alone any scrapping, "sends out a terrible signal" to those targets.

The city conducted a hearing and a poll at the dome on whether to show, cover or remove the neon wall. The choice of selling it was not formally proposed, but Seattle's mayor and arts commission fueled the flames by declaring they'd be glad to take it. In the end, the sculpture remains, and promoters renting the dome have the option of turning the lights on or off. Most reportedly opt to turn them on.

Sutherland appointed a task force to review Tacoma's one-percent program and suggest reforms. The No Neonites didn't wait for the results. Determined to block further commissions, they gathered enough signatures to put a measure, this time binding, to repeal one-percent on last November's ballot. And they supported the candidacy of Carolyn Bondy, who had entered public life through the neon fight, for mayor.

On the task force's recommendation, the Tacoma city council offered a ballot countermeasure rewriting the one-percent ordinance, setting a $50,000 limit on city commissions and exempting public utilities from the ordinance. (Otherwise, upcoming sewer projects might have generated over $1 million in commissions, a nightmarish prospect to opponents of big arts spending.)

Bondy, arguing that the neon issue typified "a pattern of not listening" and "misplaced financial priorities" in Tacoma government, came in second to Sutherland in the nonpartisan primary. She lost in the general election but proposes to run for city council next time.

The repeal of one-percent passed—narrowly—so Tacoma is barred from spending its construction moneys on art for at least two years. The effect on actual expenditures may not be great: according to Zia Gipson, the Tacoma Arts Commission's executive director, with sewage projects excluded one-percent commissions would have amounted to only a fifth of the city's upcoming arts budget.

Bondy now wants to see in place of the one-percent ordinance a privately funded program to buy public art. The Tacoma Arts Commission is considering how to mend its community ties through what Gipson calls "programs with a broad public appeal." The Antonakos commission and ensuing controversy "could have been handled better," she acknowledges. But time may heal the wounds. One drugstore owner who had petitioned against the light sculpture recently confided that it was growing on him. "If they took it away now," he said, "I'd miss it."

In the early 1980s, after many years of general support in the press for the use of taxpayers' money to fund public sculpture, critical reactions stemming from conservative sources began to appear. See Ernest Van Den Haag, "The Government Should Stay Away," and Michael Joyce, "Government: Patron of Last Resort," both in *Journal of Arts Management and Law*, vol. 13, no. 1 (Spring 1983). Even the NEA challenge grant program came in for criticism (Joan K. Davidson, "Is the NEA Challenge Grant a Trojan Horse?" *Art in America* [May–June 1979], pp. 10–11, 13). The most extreme attack on government-supported public art came in the following article.

DOUGLAS STALKER AND CLARK GLYMOUR *The Malignant Object: Thoughts on Public Sculpture**

Millions of dollars are spent in this country on public sculpture—on sculpture that is created for the explicit purpose of public viewing, placed in public settings, and constructed generally by contemporary artists without any intention of commemorating or representing people or events associated with the site. The objects in question may be clothespins, boulders, or tortuous steel shapes. The money may sometimes come from private sources, but much of it comes from public treasuries.

One of the clearest and most general attempts to provide a justification for financing and placing these objects in public spaces is given by Janet Kardon, who is the Director of Philadelphia's Institute of Contemporary Art. "Public art," Ms. Kardon writes, "is not a style or a movement, but a compound social service based on the premise that public well-being is enhanced by the presence of large scale art works in public spaces." Large scale art works executed, to be sure, not to public taste but to the taste of the avant-garde art community. Elsewhere, she writes: "Public art is not a style, art movement or public service, but a compound event, based on the premise that our lives are enhanced by good art and that good art means work by advanced artists thrust into the public domain." The justification here is moral rather than aesthetic, phrased in terms of well-being rather than those of beauty. Public art is good for us. Her thesis is put simply and with clarity; it is perhaps the same thesis as that put forward by many writers who claim that public art "enhances the quality of life" or "humanizes the urban environment," even "speaks to the spirit."

Our view is that much public sculpture, and public art generally as it is created nowadays in the United States, provides at best trivial benefits to the public, but does provide substantial and identifiable harm. This is so for a variety of reasons having to do with the character of contemporary artistic enterprises and with prevalent features of our society as well. We will discuss these issues in due course, but for now we want to make our view as clear as we can.

There is abundant evidence, albeit circumstantial, pointing directly to the conclusion that many pieces of contemporary public sculpture, perhaps the majority, are not much enjoyed by the public at large—even though the public firmly believes in a general way that art is a very good thing. In short, the outright aesthetic benefits are few and thin. Perhaps the public is wrong in its distaste or indifference, perhaps members of the public *ought* to take (in some moral sense, if you like) more pleasure in these objects thrust upon them, but these questions are wholly beside the point. Government, at whatever level, only has a legitimate interest in publicly displaying contemporary art in so far as that display provides *aesthetic* benefits to the citizenry. Many artists, critics and art administrators think otherwise, and claim for contemporary public sculpture, and for contemporary art more generally, various intellectual, pedagogical, or economic virtues which are appropriate for the state to foster. By and large the objects in question have no such virtues, so even if governments did wish to foster them, they could not properly or efficiently do so by placing contemporary sculpture in public environs. Further, there are identifiable harms caused by public contemporary art. These harms are akin in structure, though perhaps not in degree, to the harms often said to be caused by the public display of pornography. After considering the arguments developed subsequently, we hope the reader will conclude that this last contention is not so outrageous as it may seem to be at the outset. Thus, our argument runs, public contemporary sculpture does little or nothing to enhance the quality of life generally, and governments have no intrinsic interest in promoting it. Whatever legitimacy there is to government support of such displays derives from the tradition of serving the special interests of a very limited group of citizens—those served, for example, by museums of contemporary art. But this justification is overwhelmed by the fact that publicly displayed contemporary sculpture causes significant offense and harm, and does so in a way that intrudes repeatedly into people's normal living routines.

Doubtless some people will misread our argument and take it to be an attack on contemporary art *per se.* Our reasoning in no way depends on whether contemporary art is in general good or bad, or on whether particular pieces are or are not good art. It depends only on the facts (or what we claim to be facts) that much of the public derives minimal aesthetic pleasure from such contemporary art as is publicly displayed, that a significant segment of the public is offended and harmed by such displays, and that governments have, in these circumstances, no legitimate interest in furthering *public* art. Accordingly, this view is in no way a denigration of contemporary art; it is, however, a denigration of certain accounts of the value of that art, specifically those which find in the works of various artists, or schools of artists, vital lessons which the public desperately needs to learn.

PUBLIC OPINION OF PUBLIC SCULPTURE

Contemporary public art is public *contemporary* art, and there is considerable evidence that the communities into which it is "thrust" do not revere it, like it, or (sometimes) even tolerate it. Examples abound, and we offer only a few that are representative.

In October 1980 a piece of public statuary was unveiled in Wilmington, Delaware. The piece was executed by Richard Stankiewicz, known for his "junk" art of the 1950's. The unveiling was received with cat-calls and denunciations from much of the public audience. In Pittsburgh, there has been popular, organized resistance to a proposal to build a piece of modern cement sculpture on a vacant lot on the North Side of the city. The people of the North Side, a middle-class working community, want a fountain not a piece of modern sculpture. (It may or may not be relevant that the sculptor is not a resident of the community, but lives in the Squirrel Hill district of Pittsburgh, a predominantly affluent and academic neighborhood.)

Alexander Calder and Claes Oldenburg have each left a work in the city of Chicago. One rarely hears anything good said of them by Chicagoans who dwell outside of the Art Institute of Chicago. Away from the shadows and in the sunshine of the Letter-to-the-Editor columns, there is dismay at Calder's "Flamingo" and Oldenburg's "Batcolumn." But the public dislike for these works hardly compares with the crescendo of distaste for a recent exercise in "Rag Art" at Chicago's Federal Building. A typical response to the exhibition bears quoting:

Q. Please tell me how to complain about those unsightly canvas rags that have been wrapped around the pillars of the John C. Luzinski Federal Building. Those rags are a disgrace. While you're at it, what's all that scrap metal doing strewn around? Many blind people go in and out of the building, and it's a wonder no one trips over this garbage.

F. G., Franklin Park

The *Chicago Sun-Times* kindly informed the resident of Franklin Park that "the rags and scrap metal are objects d'art," which would have to be tolerated through December of 1978. And so into the winter of that year pedestrians in the Second City had to suffer the assaults of both the elements and the artistes.

In 1977, Carl Andre, the well-known "minimal" artist, executed a public sculpture for the city of Hartford, Connecticut for $87,000. Andre's "Stone Field Sculpture" consists of 36 boulders deposited in rows on a lawn. Mr. Andre has assured us privately that "Stone Field Sculpture" seems to have settled rather nicely into Hartford, and that there is no real public outrage directed at it. His assurance notwithstanding, the *Hartford Courant* was filled with articles like these in the summer and fall of 1977: "Criticism of Park Art Doesn't Rock Sculptor"; "Sculpture Foes Shaping Plans"; "Rock Opponents Tighten Stand." Taking note of this public indignation and even joining it, the city fathers considered refusing payment but were advised by attorneys that the contract with Andre was valid and binding. Works by Sugarman, Ginnever, di Suvero, and other sculptors have created even more intense controversy in other cities, not simply because the public objected to paying for the works, but because significant segments did not want the objects publicly displayed in the settings into which they had been, or were to be, thrust. (These cases, and many more, are recorded apologetically in Donald W. Thalacker's book, *The Place of Art in the World of Architecture*.)

The public distaste for today's public sculpture often goes well beyond mere words. The common responses include petitions, assemblies, litigation, and, occasionally, direct action. Enraged by what is thrust at them, the public often takes up a kind of vigilantism against contemporary public sculpture, and in community after community spontaneous bands of Aesthetic Avengers form, armed with hammers, chisels, and spray-paint cans. Jody Pinto's "Heart Chambers for Gertrude and Angelo," erected on the University of Pennsylvania campus for Ms. Kardon's own Institute of Contemporary Art, was turned into rubble overnight. Barnett Newman's "Broken Obelisk" was rapidly defaced when it was put on display in 1967. Removed to Houston, Texas, it is now placed in a pool away from errant paint. Claes Oldenburg's "Lipstick" was so thoroughly defaced at Yale that the sculptor retrieved it. Of course, for any object there is some thug or madman willing or eager to destroy what he can of it, but the defacement of some pieces of public sculpture seems to enjoy a measure of community support or at least tolerance.

The examples could be continued into tedium. On the whole, the public does not like today's public art. Of course, some people do actually take pleasure in "Batcolumn" or in the twisted, painted tubes and rusted shards that can be found in almost every large American city. But the vast majority, convinced that art is a good thing, still takes no pleasure in the actual pieces of public art themselves. An expensive piece of contemporary sculpture has a life cycle of a predictable kind, a cycle frequently noted by others. Received with joy by a small coterie of aesthetes and with indignation by a sizable element of the community, the sculpture soon becomes an indifferent object, noticed chiefly by visitors. If it is very elaborate or very expensive, the local citizenry may try to take whatever minimal aesthetic pleasure they can from the thing; typically, after all, they paid a bundle for it. In time the aesthetes move on, no longer interested in a piece that is derrière-garde. But the public must remain.

It is sometimes urged, rather opaquely, that there are significant economic benefits to be derived from public art. The case is seldom developed in any detailed fashion, and there is good reason to doubt that public support of permanent or quasi-permanent public art structures can lean very much on such considerations. These are some of the reasons.

First, the presence of public sculpture in booming areas is not evidence that the art itself makes significant contributions to the economies of

Winston-Salem, or Charlotte, or Seattle. The effect is most likely in the other direction. (The same holds, of course, for the performing arts. As Dick Netzer remarks, "It is hard to believe that the presence of the Charlotte Symphony has much, if anything, to do with that area's booming economy.")

Second, while art may provide economic benefits for a few centers where the variety, or quality, or number of objects and events is markedly better than in surrounding areas, it cannot have much economic effect when more widely and, from the point of view of public patronage, more justly distributed. People may very well go to St. Louis to view its arch, but how many now go to Oberlin, Ohio, to see Tacha's "Streams" or to Chicago to see "Batcolumn"?

Third, those who point to the alleged economic benefits of public art almost always neglect to consider opportunity costs: Would the money spent on public art have produced greater economic benefits if it had been invested in capital equipment or in subsidies for business or for public transit or in amusement parks? And, finally, even in those circumstances where the availability of cultural amenities provides or would provide significant economic benefits, there is no evidence that public sculpture of the sort bedecking our cities and towns contributes very significantly to that benefit. The forms of artistic culture which attract people and their money may very well be, as it seems to us, chiefly those of museums, music, and theatre.

Ms. Kardon's claims for the benefits of public art are unjustified and unjustifiable, and they can only result from a failure to be candid about the social conditions of contemporary art. Contemporary art has a small audience composed of some of the very rich who can afford to buy it and some of the not-so-very rich who go to galleries and museums to see it. The audience for this art takes pleasure in it for any of several not very complex reasons: because of the aesthetic appeal of a particular object, because of an interest in a segment of cultural history, because of the notoriety of its creator, because they find it an amusing joke (on other people), or perhaps, simply because they have been led to believe that they *ought* to enjoy it.

The aesthetic pleasures of contemporary art are not shared generally or widely, and the citizenry who must pay for and daily observe a public sculpture can take no pleasure in a joke played on others; for if Mr. Andre's "Stone Field Sculpture" is a joke, it is a joke played on the citizens of Hartford themselves. Some people, attending to the histories of past art that has proved to be great art, might be more tolerant about the untoward reactions to "Stone Field Sculpture" and its equivalents. Monet and Renoir caused quite a stir in their time, and the public did not take much pleasure in their works. Yet many of these same paintings have proved in time to be good, even great, art. Indeed, believing that this is a recurring and prevalent course of events with novel art in any form and time, it might seem prudent to take a different view of adverse reactions to our revolutionary and experimental works of public sculpture. This would be a mistake, for the appeal to art history wholly misses the point at issue: It is not for government to promote new conceptions or realizations of art. In short, the ultimate aesthetic quality of the works is not in question; their public display is.

THE PROPRIETY OF GOVERNMENT SUPPORT

If today's public sculpture is not much enjoyed for its aesthetic qualities, and if it carries no effective and important message which will enlighten the public, how does it improve the quality of life? How are citizens made better off by its presence? Advocates may dig in their heels and claim that those exposed to such pieces just *are* better off, whether they know it or not, for seeing and living with the things. But an inarticulable and unidentifiable benefit is no benefit at all, only special pleading.

Government at various levels may be legitimately concerned to promote the public welfare, but it cannot be legitimately concerned to promote activities with no demonstrable or even very plausible connection with the well-being of the citizenry. The argument for public art fails entirely if it is based on considerations of direct general welfare. What remains to be said in defense of public sculpture is only a kind of analogy. Governments at various levels support museums, even museums wholly or partly given over to contemporary art, and such support is ordinarily thought to be entirely proper. The public at large is thought to benefit by having art collections available, and a small segment of the public does benefit from active and repeated use of such collections. Why, it might reasonably be asked, is public sculpture any different? Granted that only a small segment of the population actively enjoys the things, why should not the government support that interest while providing to others the availability in case they change their minds or their tastes? The answer brings us to another conclusion: The objects of contemporary public sculpture are not benign or indifferent.

Public sculpture presents *moral* issues which outstrip related questions, such as those associated with the social justice or injustice of public funding of the arts, exactly because the works of public art are indeed thrust upon the public. They are unavoidable; if one goes about one's normal routine in Pittsburgh or Denver or New York or Grand Rapids one *will* see public sculpture, willy-nilly, like it or not. The moral questions associated with the public display of large pieces of contemporary art are rather like the moral issues surrounding the public display of public pornography. The analogy between public contemporary art and public pornography is revealing, and we will pursue it, not because we believe that the harms caused by public contemporary art are the same harms as those caused by public pornography, but because the different harms in the two cases arise in similar ways, and belong to similar categories.

PUBLIC SCULPTURE, PUBLIC PORNOGRAPHY

The public display of pornography is widely claimed to cause several kinds of harm in several ways. In the first place, merely seeing pornographic depictions of events offends many people who do the seeing. The offensiveness of these displays to such people is at least partly aesthetic—it involves their immediate repugnance at what they perceive. (It is in that way different from the repugnance which is expressed by evangelical prudes at anyone, anywhere, gazing upon pornographic displays, no matter how much pleasure the gazer may find.) There are philosophers, such as Joel Feinberg, who treat offenses of this kind as something other than harms, but we see no real basis for sustaining such a distinction. An offense given is a harm done, however minor and relatively unimportant a harm it may be.

Second, the public display of pornography is claimed to have a kind of reflective effect on some people. On reflection, if one is a woman, one is *humiliated* by the depiction of women as simply and rightfully objects of lust who are nothing more than sexual slaves. Third, the public display of pornography is claimed to have indirect effects which do substantial harm: It is alleged to promote sex crimes, for example, and to cause or to

sustain the repression of women and discrimination against them. More clearly, the public display of pornography violates the interests of those who value modesty, who are offended by pornographic displays, and who wish society not to develop in such a way that immodesty and pornography are ubiquitous. The public display of pornography can be reasonably expected to contribute to the further erosion of taboos against immodesty and public sexuality in various forms, and thus to cause the evolution of society in such a way that is inimical to the interests of those who prefer a society whose members confine their eroticism to private circumstances. These are rather familiar objections to public pornography, and anyone who has thought or talked much of the subject has met versions of them. Most have a valid analogue in public art.

A good deal of today's public sculpture offends the public eye. It offends twice: once because it is simply unsightly, as with garbage, auto salvage yards, and scrap heaps; and again because it is unsightly *art*. It is offensive to be presented with rags and scrap metal, but perhaps equally offensive to be told that an unsightly mess must be respected as art. What the gentleman from Franklin Park felt in downtown Chicago may perhaps not be fairly characterized as revulsion, but he was surely offended by the art objects, quite as genuinely as are those who must pass by drive-in theaters exhibiting pornographic films.

There is a related harm of the second kind, a reflective harm which is a kind of insult or humiliation. Viewing public sculpture and finding it ugly or silly or simply commonplace, the common person brings his own eye and mind into direct conflict with the judgment of the aesthetic and political authorities. He can only draw one of three conclusions. Either his own judgment is hopelessly flawed, so that he is a complete aesthetic incompetent; or else that of the authorities is flawed in like fashion; or, finally, he and his fellow citizens have been made the butt of a joke by the artist, his associates, and his admirers. The second conclusion is not widely held, though it is a logical possibility, and is doubtless sometimes true. In the first case, the citizen can only be humiliated by an object which, try as he will, he cannot find the beauty of; in the third case, he can only be insulted and righteously indignant at those who have erected an object which is an expression of contempt for the public. Both to the timid and to the self-confident, the object acts with malice. We are not sure that the harm associated with the humiliation and insult given by public sculpture is altogether less intense than the humiliation some people feel at public pornography. And the harm is repeated and repeated and repeated. The citizen can only escape by moving his domicile or work or normal activities, or by cultivating indifference.

In a third way, as well, the erection of public sculpture of the contemporary kind harms the interests of citizens who find it offensive: It begets more of the same. It does so directly by means of artistic influence, through mechanisms familiar to everyone. It does so indirectly by influencing the sense of beauty in the youthful, and thus causing them to welcome more of the same. Everyone has an interest in society developing in such a way that his own aesthetic sensibilities are not everywhere outraged; for much of the citizenry, most works of today's public sculpture act against that interest.

THE ICONOCLAST AT LARGE

The harm done by public sculpture to the interests of the public is real harm, less vivid and perhaps less important than some other social harms, but real enough. To those harms we have noted, we must add the general harm, in the case of publicly financed public sculpture, of having to finance an object from which no benefit is derived, and the special exquisiteness of having to finance one's own humiliation. We should also note that the forms of resistance to public sculpture are rather like the forms of resistance to public pornography: People write letters, hold rallies, circulate petitions, sue, and deface. In short, the analogy between public contemporary art and public pornography should not be lightly dismissed, for it is sound. This is not to say that there are no occasions when a public sculpture, even a contemporary public sculpture, is by intent or by chance so executed that it catches the public taste, pleases many, and offends few. Undoubtedly, there are such happy events, but the impressionistic evidence we find, at any rate, is that they are extremely rare.

THE PLACE OF REASON

By and large, the art community has addressed the issues we have raised only obliquely and disingenuously—as problems of salesmanship. This stance often shows up in articles that appear in art magazines whose audience is primarily the artistic community. In content if not in style, these discussions of public distaste for contemporary public sculpture are very much akin to discussions of "market resistance" in industrial trade magazines. An unmistakable instance of this focus on salesmanship is a recent suggestion that the friends of public sculpture should try to develop a tradition of contemporary public pieces in a community by introducing first one, then another, and then yet another and even more contemporary works. In brief order, this sort of sculpture will, by its very numbers, come to dominate public areas and perhaps seem to the public familiar, expected, and appropriate. This seems nothing more than the standard corporate strategy of market proliferation to secure increased sales, indeed to dominate the marketplace for a certain type of product, be it cigarettes or breakfast cereals.

Big time art is an industry that has moved out of the cottage, an industry that has an articulate and influential lobby at many levels of government. That industry has captured a piece of the public purse, quite as surely as have the tobacco farmers and dairymen, and thereby has obtained a substantial and diverse subsidy. Like some purloined letter, the most hidden part of that subsidy lies out in the open: It is the cost to those who must regularly view contemporary public sculpture and endure whatever harm it occasions them. If large scale sculptures were required to be housed behind walls, or away from the course of daily routine, the real costs of these pieces would be more evident. Instead, public display transforms internal costs into external ones which are diffused, subjective, and not easily measured.

Artists, critics, and art administrators may find this argument to be simply an endorsement of philistinism, but that is a grievous confusion. Philistines are people too, and, whether or not one shares their tastes, the moral point of view requires that their interests be considered. If art is serious then aesthetic values must interact with moral values and aesthetic reactions must also help determine moral obligations. The artistic community generally is constitutionally allergic to close argument and clear statement, preferring allusion and non-sequitur. But any serious discussion about art and social obligation cannot be so self-indulgent, and that is why we have found Ms. Kardon's statements so welcome. If there is a serious defense of the view that today's public art enhances public well-being, it is not enough to presuppose it, allude to it, imply it, or suggest it. Give it.

COMMENTS

1. Stalker and Glymour criticize supporters of tax-supported public art for not developing a case with hard facts and figures. "The artistic community generally is constitutionally allergic to close argument and clear statements, preferring allusion and non-sequiturs." What do you think of the authors' rhetoric and methodology? On what kind of evidence is their argument based?

2. Given the fact that Stalker is a philosopher and Glymour is a historian, what do you make of their failure to criticize "aesthetic avengers," who vandalize public sculpture? How convincing is their argument, which equates the harm of public art with the public display of pornography? Do they understand *Roth* and *Miller?*

3. Stalker and Glymour write: "It is not for government to promote new conceptions or realizations of art" and "The argument for public art fails entirely if it is based on considerations of direct general welfare." Do you think they are aware of the rationale behind the establishment of the NEA?

4. "The Malignant Object" was published in 1982 during a severe American economic depression. Note the authors' allegation that those behind public sculpture neglect to consider "opportunity costs," that the money might be better spent elsewhere. Is there a true choice between art and playgrounds, skating rinks, or shoes for needy children?

5. What public sculptures discussed in this chapter give credence to or contradict Stalker and Glymour's arguments?

6. Stalker and Glymour's objections to government subsidy of public art have been echoed in Edward Banfield, *The Democratic Muse: Visual Arts and the Public Interest* (Cambridge, Mass.: Harvard University Press, 1984). See also Kate Linker, "Public Sculpture: The Pursuit of the Pleasurable and Profitable Paradise," *Artforum,* Summer 1981, pp. 37–42; John Beardsley, "Personal Sensibilities in Public Places," *Artforum,* Summer 1981, pp. 43–45; and Don Hawthorne, "Does the Public Want Public Sculpture?" *ARTnews,* May 1982, pp. 56–63. Albert E. Elsen's *Rodin's Thinker and the Dilemmas of Modern Public Sculpture* (New Haven: Yale University Press, 1985) gives a case history of the basic problems caused by placing modern sculpture in public places early in this century.

7. Stalker and Glymour are scornful of the idea that public art can bring economic benefits to the community. For an impressive response, see Lois Friedland, Agnes Zimmerman, and Anthony J. Radich, *Art Spaces and Economics* (Denver, Co.: 1983), a publication produced for the Arts, Tourism, and Cultural Resource Committee of the National Conference of State Legislatures.

BIG QUESTIONS

1. What do we mean by "public art" (as opposed to art in public)?
2. How should public art be selected? Who should decide, and by what criteria?